CORAL SNAKES OF THE AMERICAS:
Biology, Identification, and Venoms

CORAL SNAKES OF THE AMERICAS:
Biology, Identification, and Venoms

Janis A. Roze

Department of Biology
City College and Graduate School of the City University of New York
and
American Museum of Natural History, New York

KRIEGER PUBLISHING COMPANY
MALABAR, FLORIDA
1996

Original Edition 1996

Printed and Published by
KRIEGER PUBLISHING COMPANY
KRIEGER DRIVE
MALABAR, FLORIDA 32950

Copyright © 1996 by Krieger Publishing Company

FROM A DECLARATION OF PRINCIPLES JOINTLY ADOPTED BY A COMMITTEE OF THE AMERICAN BAR ASSOCIATION AND A COMMITTEE OF PUBLISHERS:

This publication is designed to provide accurate and authoritative information in regard to the subject matter covered. It is sold with the understanding that the publisher is not engaged in rendering legal, accounting, or other professional service. If legal advice or other expert assistance is required, the services of a competent professional person should be sought.

All rights reserved. No part of this book may be reproduced in any form or by any means, electronic or mechanical, including information storage and retrieval systems without permission in writing from the publisher.
No liability is assumed with respect to the use of the information contained herein.
Printed in the United States of America.

Library of Congress Cataloging-in-Publication Data

Roze, Janis A., 1926–
    Coral snakes of the Americas : biology, identification, and venoms / Janis A. Roze.
      p. cm.
    Includes bibliographical references and index.
    ISBN 0-89464-847-0 (acid-free)
    1. Micrurus. 2. Leptomicrurus. 3. Micruroides. 4. Coral snakes. I. Title.
QL666.O64R69 1996
597.96—dc20   93-1912
                                                                CIP
                                                                 Rev.

10 9 8 7 6 5 4 3 2

Contents

List of Tables — vii
Preface — ix
Introduction — xi

PART I GENERAL INFORMATION

Chapter 1 Overview — 3
  Old World Relatives — 3
  Red Snakes: A New World Phenomenon — 3
  History of Coral Snake Studies — 3
  Names and Folklore — 5
  Coral Snakes as Endangered Animals — 9

PART II FORM AND DISTINGUISHING FEATURES

Chapter 2 External Features — 13
  Body Covering: The Skin and Scales — 13
  Differences Between Males and Females — 19
  Reproductive Organs — 20
  Coloration and Diversity of Color Patterns — 25
  Size and Growth — 29

Chapter 3 Internal Features — 35
  Skull and Skeleton — 35
  General Internal Anatomy — 43
  Genetic Blueprint: Karyotypes — 45

PART III BIOLOGY AND EVOLUTION

Chapter 4 Ecology — 51
  Ecological Distribution and Habitats — 51
  Human Influence on Distribution and Ecology — 53
  Activity Periods and Seasonal Incidence — 54
  Sharing of Life Needs — 55

Chapter 5 Feeding and Food — 57
  Searching for Prey — 57
  Overpowering and Swallowing the Prey — 58
  Food — 59
  Cannibalism — 61

Chapter 6 Reproduction — 63
  Reproductive Cycle — 63
  Internal Reproductive Cycle and System of Males — 64
  Internal Reproductive Cycle and System of Females — 64
  Courtship and Mating — 65
  Egg Laying and Incubation — 65
  Laboratory Incubation of Eggs — 67
  Embryonic Development — 67
  Shape, Size, and Number of Eggs — 67
  Hatching and Hatchlings — 69
  A Reproductive Success Story: The Uruguayan Coral Snake — 69

Chapter 7 Enemies and Defense — 71
  Predators and Parasites — 71
  Defense Against Enemies — 73

Chapter 8 Mimicry: Imitation Fellowships — 77
  History of Mimicry Studies in Coral Snakes — 77
  Diversity of Coral Snake Mimicry — 78
  Mimicry Related to Size and Growth — 81
  Mimicry Between Venomous Coral Snakes — 81
  Errors in Human Perception That Confirm Mimicry — 82
  Coral Snake Mimicry by Other Animals — 82
  Objections and Alternative Suggestions for Mimicry — 82

Chapter 9 Biogeography, Origin, and Evolution — 85
  Biogeographical Distribution — 85
  Origin and Evolution — 87
  How Fast Do Species Evolve? — 90

PART IV VENOMS AND SNAKEBITE

Chapter 10 Venoms in Biology — 93
  Biological Significance of Snake Venom — 93
  Evolution of Coral Snake Venom — 93
  History of Coral Snake Venom Research — 94
  The Value of Coral Snake Venom and Its Use in Medicine — 96
  Is the Coral Snake Venomous to Itself? — 96

Chapter 11 Studies of Coral Snake Venom — 99
  Biting Mechanism and Venom Apparatus — 99
  Venom Extraction and Venom Yield — 100
  Venom Toxicity — 101

Keeping Coral Snakes in Zoos and Colonies for Research ... 102

Chapter 12 Chemical and Biological Characteristics of Venom ... 105
Venom Composition and Its Action ... 105
Effects of Venom on Organisms ... 106

Chapter 13 Coral Snakebite Accidents ... 109
Statistics on Human Accidents with Coral Snakes ... 109
Nature and Way of Coral Snakebites ... 110
Symptoms of Coral Snake Envenomation and Case Reports ... 111
First Aid and Summary of Professional Treatment ... 116
Coral Snake Antivenins and Other Remedies ... 117

PART V IDENTIFICATION, DESCRIPTION, AND DISTRIBUTION BY COUNTRIES

Chapter 14 Identification ... 123
Distinction Between Venomous and Nonvenomous Coral Snakes ... 123
Key for Identification of Genera and Species ... 124

Chapter 15 Description of Species and Subspecies, with Keys to the Subspecies ... 131
Genus *Leptomicrurus*, the Black-backed Coral Snakes ... 132
    L. collaris and subspecies ... 132
    L. narduccii and subspecies ... 134
    L. scutiventris ... 135
Genus *Micruroides*, the Western Coral Snakes ... 136
    M. euryxanthus and subspecies ... 136
Genus *Micrurus*, the American Coral Snakes ... 138
    M. albicinctus ... 138
    M. alleni ... 139
    M. ancoralis and subspecies ... 140
    M. annellatus and subspecies ... 142
    M. averyi ... 144
    M. bernadi ... 144
    M. bocourti ... 145
    M. bogerti ... 146
    M. browni and subspecies ... 146
    M. catamayensis ... 148
    M. circinalis ... 149
    M. clarki ... 149
    M. corallinus ... 150
    M. decoratus ... 151
    M. diana ... 152
    M. diastema and subspecies ... 152
    M. dissoleucus and subspecies ... 158
    M. distans and subspecies ... 161
    M. dumerilii and subspecies ... 163
    M. elegans and subspecies ... 167
    M. ephippifer and subspecies ... 169
    M. filiformis ... 170
    M. frontalis and subspecies ... 171
    M. frontifasciatus ... 175
    M. fulvius and subspecies ... 176
    M. hemprichii and subspecies ... 180
    M. hippocrepis ... 182
    M. ibiboboca ... 183
    M. isozonus ... 184
    M. langsdorffi ... 185
    M. laticollaris and subspecies ... 186
    M. latifasciatus ... 187
    M. lemniscatus and subspecies ... 188
    M. limbatus and subspecies ... 192
    M. margaritiferus ... 193
    M. medemi ... 194
    M. meridensis ... 194
    M. mertensi ... 195
    M. mipartitus and subspecies ... 195
    M. multifasciatus and subspecies ... 199
    M. multiscutatus ... 200
    M. nebularis ... 201
    M. nigrocinctus and subspecies ... 201
    M. ornatissimus ... 206
    M. paraensis ... 207
    M. peruvianus ... 208
    M. petersi ... 208
    M. proximans ... 209
    M. psyches ... 210
    M. putumayensis ... 210
    M. pyrrhocryptus and subspecies ... 211
    M. remotus ... 213
    M. ruatanus ... 213
    M. sangilensis ... 214
    M. spixii and subspecies ... 215
    M. spurrelli ... 218
    M. steindachneri and subspecies ... 219
    M. stewarti ... 220
    M. stuarti ... 221
    M. surinamensis and subspecies ... 221
    M. tschudii and subspecies ... 223

Chapter 16 Distribution by Countries ... 225
Maps ... 231
Color Section ... 245
Pattern Section ... 263
Appendix A Scientific and Common Names of Coral Snakes ... 273
Appendix B Summary of the Composition of Coral Snake Venom ... 277
References ... 279
Acknowledgments ... 301
List of Museums ... 305
Name Index ... 309
Subject Index ... 313
Scientific Name Index ... 319
Venom and Snakebite Index ... 325

List of Tables

1. Longest known specimens for the species and subspecies of coral snakes. 30
2. Range of the tail length/total length ratio 33
3. Variation in number of teeth and remarks on grooved condition, where observed 40
4. Karyotypes of coral snakes 46
5. Distribution of coral snakes in three Amazonian localities 52
6. Dimensions of two clutches of eggs of *Micrurus fulvius tenere* 68
7. Maximum and average venom yield for several species of coral snakes, compared to the estimated lethal dose of dry venom in mg for an adult human 102
8. Selective characteristics for distinguishing true (venomous) from false (non-venomous) coral snakes 124

Dedicated to Karl P. Schmidt who knew the most about coral snakes
and to all herpetologists and snake enthusiasts
who will study and care for them in the future.

Preface

Years have elapsed since the conception of this book. Its history illustrates one person's "journey with the coral snakes." It has been a long and rewarding journey. On the way, I learned to appreciate the remarkable features of coral snakes and their unique ways. I became a student of coral snakes and they became my teachers.

While living in Caracas and teaching at the Universidad Central de Venezuela, I first became interested in this unusual group of snakes. In the 1950s and 1960s, I published several papers dealing with South American reptiles, including coral snakes. During that time, I had active correspondence with Karl Patterson Schmidt, the authority on coral snakes at the Field Museum of Natural History in Chicago.

In 1958, I planned a research trip to different North American museums to study Venezuelan reptiles and looked forward to finally meeting Dr. Schmidt and exchanging ideas and information about coral snakes. It was an exciting opportunity because every herpetologist I had met had only praise and appreciation for KP (as herpetologists fondly referred to him), the biologist we all hoped would eventually publish a monograph on coral snakes. Before going to Chicago, I stopped at the American Museum of Natural History and then continued to Washington. From the National Museum of Natural History (then the United States National Museum) I telephoned KP that I would be coming the following week. And then tragedy struck. Two days before our meeting, the sad message came from Chicago: Dr. Karl Patterson Schmidt had died from complications following a snakebite suffered while he was examining a live specimen of the African boomslang.

Later, Robert F. Inger, who took over responsibilities as chairman of the Department of Herpetology at the Field Museum, invited me to look over the papers and manuscripts left by KP. Bob Inger himself subsequently published several posthumous papers by KP and handed over to me whatever coral snake data was left. We realized that KP kept most of his information in the file cabinet of the mind, and that he wrote his papers by integrating the written data with the memory data. Both Bob Inger and Hymen Marx, a trustworthy herpetology hand at the museum, urged me to take over what KP had started and prepare an overall publication on coral snakes. I was also greatly encouraged by Ernest E. Williams, now Curator Emeritus of the Museum of Comparative Zoology, Harvard University, where part of the material KP had studied was deposited. Especially warm support was received from the late Charles M. Bogert (then chairman of the Herpetology Department of the American Museum), Richard G. Zweifel, and Charles Myers who opened the doors and snake shelves of the American Museum to me as a home base for my coral snake research. In 1959, the museum named me research associate, starting a long and rewarding association with the museum where most of my herpetology research has been carried out.

The 1950s and 1960s were "post-sputnik" years when the United States was pouring billions of dollars into scientific activities in order to stimulate research in all disciplines of science. At that time, any recognized scientific institution could get almost any reasonable grant for scientific research. The American Museum of

Natural History, and particularly Richard Zweifel, promptly arranged a grant from the U.S. Public Health Service that covered my 2 years of research, with travels to museums in Europe and North, Central, and South America. After having published a checklist and some papers, I continued working on coral snakes at a slower pace with several interruptions when I was a visiting professor at the College of Mount Saint Vincent and Manhattan College and later at the City College of the City University of New York. Two years were also spent as a visiting scholar at the United Nations Institute of Training and Research and at the International Center for Integrative Studies in New York. My colleagues, friends, and associates have been waiting for the appearance of a book on coral snakes for a long time—since 1965. Finally, time and opportunity have converged to help me to put together a major publication on coral snakes. Thank you for your patience!

Today, in retrospect, it seems that an initial curiosity about coral snakes and a fatal snakebite to an admired and highly regarded herpetologist, combined with a successful Russian space shot, significantly changed my way of life by bringing me to the United States and focusing my interest on this unusual group of snakes.

Introduction

New World venomous coral snakes are a most unusual group of land animals because they are conspicuously beautiful and highly venomous. Coral snakes are also one of the most successful major snake groups in the Americas. The 124 species and subspecies of coral snakes are distributed from the United States to Argentina and on several continental islands (Map 1). Canada and Chile are the only continental countries in the Western Hemisphere that do not have coral snakes. Paradoxically, even though they are present in almost every country of the Americas, they are very difficult to find. Their success rests upon the interplay between such factors as powerful venom, unusual defensive behavior, and skillful use of brilliant coloration. This coloration advertises their highly venomous nature, serves as a device of concealment, and scares, surprises, and confuses possible enemies.

Coral snake success is also based on their remarkable ability to adapt to a wide variety of environments. They are found in the dry and unyielding deserts of Peru, Ecuador, northern Mexico, and the southwestern United States; in the rich tropical rainforests of eastern Central America and the Amazon basin; in the flat lowland cerrado savannas of Brazil; in the llanos of Venezuela and Colombia; in the mountain environments of the Andes; and as far north as the temperate regions of the eastern United States. Even the Amazon and Orinoco basins are the preferred habitat of the swamp and river-dwelling *M. surinamensis*.

The largest coral snake genus, *Micrurus*, is one of the two most widely distributed snake genera in the New World, an honor it shares with the rattlesnake genus, *Crotalus*. Each has adapted to environments that the other has found inhospitable. The largest and most dangerous coral snakes are abundant in the vast Amazonian rain forest where rattlesnakes are practically unknown. On the other hand, rattlesnakes are found as far north as Canada, where no coral snake is found.

Although coral snakes are docile, secretive creatures that will not bite unless provoked, one of the odd facts about them is that for some unknown reason, on occasion, they are cannibalistic. In spite of their docility and fascinating coloration, coral snakes more than once have demonstrated their dangerous nature. One such deadly proof is woven into the early history of the United States. The first fatality of the American Civil War was caused not by an exchange of bullets, but by a bite of the eastern coral snake, *Micrurus f. fulvius*. The culprit is said still to be preserved in the Augusta, Georgia Museum.

A different kind of recognition of the potential danger of coral snakes was provided by the elders of Florida's Pinellas County, who from 1935 to 1938 paid a $2 bounty (equivalent to about $35 today) for each eastern coral snake delivered to the courthouse. The coral snake and the eastern diamondback rattlesnake, *Crotalus adamanteus*, were considered the most dangerous snakes of the county. As a result, about 2,000 coral snakes fell victim to the snake hunters (and 7,500 rattlesnakes), and endangered the solvency of Pinellas County's treasury. In response, the bounty was reduced to $1 per snake and finally, in October 1938, the offer was suspended. Incidentally, many specimens of the non-venomous false coral snake *Lampropeltis triangulum* were mistaken for *M. f. fulvius*, adding numbers to Pinellas County's snake massacre.

This example of mistaken identity in Pinellas County illustrates that many nonvenomous or mildly venomous snakes imitate the coloration and behavior of the venomous coral snakes. A later chapter discusses mimicry of the venomous coral snakes by their imitators, the false coral snakes. The true or venomous coral snakes of the family Elapidae are the main topic of this book.

For ease of reference, the numerous illustrations in this text have been arranged in the following order: Figure, Map, Color, Pattern. The figures—drawings and diagrams—appear throughout the text in appropriate locations, while the map, color, and pattern sections are collected in the back of the book, following the text. The map section shows this distribution of all species and subspecies. The color section contains detailed full-color photographs of more than 50 species and subspecies. Finally, for use in identification, color patterns are illustrated in the pattern section.

Part I
GENERAL INFORMATION

Chapter 1
Overview

Old World Relatives

New World coral snakes belong to a family of deadly venomous snakes, Elapidae, that is found in all major regions of the world, except Europe. Due to their highly toxic venom and specialized venom apparatus with fixed front fangs, the elapids are very dangerous to humans and higher vertebrates. Old World elapids include such well known species as cobras (*Naja*), the king cobra (*Ophiophagus hannah*), mambas (*Dendroaspis*), kraits (*Bungarus*), the black snake (*Notechis atra*), the death adder (*Acanthophis antarcticus*), many dangerous Australian elapids, and several lesser known Asian species. All of them have a predominantly neurotoxic venom that acts on the nervous system and finally paralyzes the respiratory system of the victim. This is a feature that coral snakes share by "family tradition" with their larger and more powerful cousins of the Old World.

Somewhat more distant coral snake relatives are the venomous sea snakes of the family Hydrophiidae found particularly in the Pacific world, around Australia, Oceania and the Indian Ocean from Asia to Africa. Only one species of sea snake, *Pelamis platurus*, is known to reach the Pacific side of the Americas. Thus far, the Atlantic Ocean has been free from venomous sea snakes. Sea snake venom is also predominantly neurotoxic.

Red Snakes: A New World Phenomenon

The extraordinary beauty of the coral snakes so enchanted the remarkable German traveler and explorer Prince Maximillian zu Wied-Neuwied that, as early as 1820 (p. 107), he dedicated a publication exclusively to the Brazilian coral snakes. In this review, handsomely illustrated with hand-painted color plates, he exclaimed:

> "Nowhere on our earth can one find such delightful and beautifully colored snakes as these (coral snakes). They have a pattern of alternating black and intensively red rings that are enhanced by narrower whitish or greenish white ones."

Maximillian recognized that this bright red coloration of snakes is indeed restricted to the New World. More than 120 different forms of venomous coral snakes have a variety of color patterns that feature red, black, and white or yellow bands and the false coral snakes display at least as great a variety of color patterns with red bands and spots.

In addition to coral snakes and their imitators, there are other snakes in the New World that have red coloration, some only during early juvenile stages, such as the emerald tree boa, *Corallus caninus*, which turns green in its adult stage, and the uniformly red snakes, *Pseudoboa*, which become greyish black in adult life. Actually, nearly 20% of all snakes in the New World have some red coloration at least some time in their lives.

In the Old World, no snake has the brilliant red intensity of coral snakes. The closest any Old World snake comes to the coloration of coral snakes is *Calliophis macclellandi*, the red ringed snake or Taiwan coral snake, an elapid of eastern China and adjacent areas, including Taiwan. It has brownish-red and black crossbands. Some specimens of *Cylindrophis rufus*, the pipe snake, also are red and black. Another elapid, *Calliophis sauteri*, the striped Asian red snake, has black and reddish longitudinal stripes. The family Elapidae seems to have an inherent potential to produce red-colored species, but only the American coral snakes have managed to specialize in red coloration.

Why is this red snake phenomenon restricted to the New World? Earlier naturalists referred to the "genius loci" of the Americas, a "local phenomenon" that favors red coloration in snakes. The same was also suggested for the prehensile tails found in quite a few American mammals other than monkeys but practically absent in the Old World.

History of Coral Snake Studies

Naca-naca, *chumbé-pé*, and *ibiboboca* are some of the indigenous names given to coral snakes long before Europeans arrived in the New World. While they are widely distributed, coral snakes did not play as prominent a part in the ancient Mesoamerican civilizations as the rattlesnake did. Crotalids figure grandly in Mexican and Central American pyramids and temples, especially as the Mesoamerican god Quetzalcoátl, or feathered serpent. Indeed, the rattlesnake's presence in high Mesoamerican religions is unsurpassed by any other species of snakes in the ancient histories of humankind. Even cobras and the king cobra of the Old World never received the adulation and adoration given the rattlesnake in the Aztec-Toltec-Maya-Zapotec system of cultures.

The only place where coral snakes have a magical significance is among Indian groups in Humahuaca, a magical valley in northern Argentina. During their carnival festivities, a complex cage featuring a precisely sculpted and painted coral snake, *Micrurus corallinus*, is paraded in the streets. Thus, the coral snake is part of a ceremony of invoking the deeper spirits of the earth.

The earliest European mention of South American coral snake appears to have been made by the early explorer of the New World, Joseph de Anchieta (1560). In his descriptions of the New World he notes ibiboboca, the Indian name for the Brazilian coral snake. Its common name was later established as its scientific name, *Micrurus ibiboboca*. In 1648, the magnificent treatise, *Historiae Rerum Naturalium Brasiliae* by Georgius Marcgravius de Liebstadt appeared. Herein the author, Jorge Markgrave (as the Brazilians call him), described the ibiboboca coral snake and its highly venomous nature. As an accomplished scholar, scientist, artist, and astronomer, Marcgravius traveled around Brazil and thoroughly described the astronomy of the southern skies, as well as local geology and other natural sciences. Very soon after he finished his work on South America, Marcgravius rushed to Africa to survey that continent as well. In Africa, an untimely death overtook him at the incredible age of 34 and his Brazilian volumes were published posthumously. Thus, most of the Brazilian treatises probably were written before Markgraf (as the Germans call him) was 30 years old. In 1820, Prince Maximillian zu Wied-Neuwied, another New World explorer, named ibiboboca *Elaps marcgravii*— a just tribute to Marcgravius' brilliant and integrative mind. Unfortunately, the name turned out to be technically invalid and the older name, *Micrurus ibiboboca*, is now the valid scientific name for this coral snake.

Early Christian missionaries in Latin America accumulated enormous amounts of information on the geography, history, and natural history of the newly discovered world. Among the earliest writers describing the coral snakes of South America was Padre Joseph Gumilla. The fruits of his long voyages in the early 18th century appeared in his book, *El Orinoco Ilustrado* (*The Illustrated Orinoco*) in 1741. His copious observations span the geography, history, folklore, and natural history of the people, animals, and plants around Orinoco, mainly in Venezuela and Colombia. He is also one of the earliest authors to recognize the highly venomous nature of coral snakes:

> "... They are called coral snakes because of the predominant red coloration, interspaced with black, grey, yellow and white ..., however, they vary in coloration in accordance with the variety to which they belong; ... but even though they vary in color, their mood does not: so much so that from the snakes that are known from there, none approaches the violence of venom of coral snakes ..."

Padre Gumilla also described an interesting antivenin remedy and belief from the region around Caracas: the belief that a caiman tooth offers effective protection against all kinds of venoms and poisons. Apparently, the belief originated in western Africa and was brought to Venezuela by black slaves. Padre Gumilla (1741, p. 428) wrote:

> "... the discovery of the virtue of such tooth is a modern one, and it happened as follows: a slave in the haciendas of Caracas wanted to kill another slave and gave him secretly as many poisons and herbs as he knew; but seeing that he exhausted himself in vain because his enemy was as healthy as ever, ... one day the malevolent black said to the other: comrade, and if a mal cristiano (evil Christian) would want to give us venom, what remedy do you know? The other extended his arm, rolled up the sleeve, and showing him a tooth of caiman tied to the flesh, explained ingeniously: 'friend, having this tooth no poison would harm you!' The rumor spread and, with the experience, also the appreciation ..."

The first species of the coral snake, *M. lemniscatus*, was scientifically described in 1758 by Carolus Linnaeus, the Swedish naturalist and father of modern taxonomy.

The works of Linnaeus spurred an epoch of exploration of natural history and descriptions of new species of animals and plants. Among the most significant works from this time that relate to coral snakes are those by F. M. Daudin (1801, *Histoire Naturelle Générale et Particuliere des Reptiles*, eight volumes), other publications of Prince Maximillian zu Wied-Neuwied (1820, 1824, 1825–1833), as well as those of J. Wagler (1824, 1830), and J. B. Spix and Martius (1823–1831). Several of these featured individually handpainted color plates.

An interesting early scientific "christening" is that of *Elaps surinamensis*. This species was first described by Cuvier in *Le Regne Animal* (1817), one of the most significant systematic works of that time. Yet, rather than describing an actual specimen, Cuvier's original description consists merely of a reference to a figure in a much older publication by Seba, *Locupletissimi ...* in 1735 (see Fig. 61, p. 221).

These early publications were followed by major works that included a growing number of new species of coral snakes by scholars such as H. Schlegel (1837) at the Leyden Museum and the formidable team of A. M. C. Duméril, G. Bibron, and A. Duméril with their *Erpétologie Générale* (1834–1854) active at the Paris Museum. As Vanzolini (1977–1978) noted:

> "the senior author, Constant Duméril, the disciple of Cuvier, an autocratic soul, planned the work according to the old tradition ... The authority of masters is revered ... the criteria of authorship are extremely subjective ... [He] was the Professor of un-limited power over collections and ideas. Thus, all materials from the French long maritime voyages and terrestrial explorations ... were cannibalized into the Erpétologie ..."

Marie-Firmin Bocourt, another French naturalist, incorporated descriptions of several coral snakes in the *Mission Scientifique* to Mexico and Central America (1885–1902).

In the United States, Holbrook (1838–1840 and 1842, second edition) described the North American coral snakes in his remarkable work on North American herpetology.

The most complete treatise on coral snakes is found in the volumes of *Iconographie Générale des Ophidiens* by Giorgio Jan of the Milan Museum, handsomely illustrated by Ferdinand Sordelli and published between 1860 and 1881. Jan's understanding of the importance of coloration in the classification of coral snakes was extraordinary (see Jan, 1858, 1859a, 1859b, 1859c, 1863a, 1863b). George A. Boulenger of the British Museum described several coral snakes, and his prolific herpetological research culminated in the publication of his famous catalogues, including *Catalogue of the Snakes in the British Museum (Natural History)* (1893–1896). Until very recently, Boulenger's book was a fundamental reference for any significant research in herpetology of Latin America and still is an invaluable resource, bearing witness to his herpetological genius. Boulenger was preceded in herpetology at the British Museum by J. E. Gray (1849) and A. Günther (1858, 1868). Günther also wrote the first review of coral snakes in 1859 and the herpetology part of the well-known *Biologia Centrali-Americana* (1895).

No less prolific than Boulenger was the remarkable American herpetologist, Edward D. Cope, whose publications on the herpetology of tropical America (1859, 1860a, 1860b, 1862, 1868, 1869, 1870, 1886, and many more) cover many aspects of the systematics and morphology of coral snakes as well as several voluminous catalogues and checklists of American amphibians and reptiles (1875, 1887, 1900).

Working in the Berlin Museum, Wilhelm Peters, its "kustos," described new species of coral snakes in several publications (1862, 1869, 1871, 1881). F. Steindachner (1867), herpetologist at the Vienna Museum, reported on the reptiles collected on the circumnavigating voyage of the Austrian ship *Novarra* (1857–1859). He was followed by a prolific herpetologist, Franz Werner, who described several new species of coral snakes (1896, 1897, 1900, 1901a, 1901b, 1903, 1904, and 1927). F. Müller (1878b, 1880, 1882, 1883), active at the Basel Museum, described specimens from Central and South America.

After the initial scientific research on coral snakes in the 18th and 19th centuries by European scholars, New World biologists took the lead. Among these early workers, Cope was the most prolific. S. E. Baird and C. Girard (1853) described the Texas coral snake, *Micrurus fulvius tenere*. E. Hallowell (1855, 1860) and R. Kennicott (1860) also described several new species and subspecies of coral snakes. The Brazilian biologists were no less active. In addition to identifying their snake fauna, their focus was directed to the snake bite calamities that annually claimed the lives of 8,000 to 12,000 Brazilians in the last century.

A large part of current herpetological research in the New World is done by the U.S. biologists, but significant groups of Latin American herpetologists are active in Argentina, Brazil, Colombia, Costa Rica, Mexico, Uruguay, and Venezuela. Most recently, research has been done in Nicaragua, Honduras, Peru, Ecuador, Guatemala, and Panama, with occasional but valuable contributions in Paraguay and Bolivia. These publications are mentioned under the species descriptions, including the contributions of the late Karl P. Schmidt, the greatest authority on New World coral snakes.

Herpetologists and biologists who have contributed to the knowledge of herpetology, including coral snakes, are mentioned in *Contributions to the History of Herpetology*, edited by Kraig Adler (1989) and published by the Society for Study of Amphibians and Reptiles.

Names and Folklore

The common English name of coral snake alludes to the obvious and beautiful coral-red bands present in a variety of patterns in the different species of *Micrurus*. The term "coral-red" refers to the red Pacific marine coral, *Corallia rubra*, much used in the manufacture of precious jewelry and artistic figures in the Far East. This is not one of the reef-building corals (Madreporaria) but one of the stinging corals, several species of which are found in tropical seas.

Many different kinds of snakes have a coral-red color and thus are called coral snakes (or corales) by the natives of the regions in which they are found. Some of these are nonvenomous or mildly venomous snakes that belong to the families Colubridae and Aniliidae.

Thanks to U.S. herpetologists, every species and subspecies of coral snake in the United States has been given a distinctive common (or vernacular) name. Thus, the North American coral snake (*Micrurus fulvius*) has several subspecies: *M. fulvius fulvius*, found from North Carolina to Mississippi, is the eastern coral snake; *M. fulvius tenere*, of Louisiana and Texas and northern Mexico, is the Texas coral snake, sometimes popularly called the harlequin coral snake or simply harlequin snake. The mimics of these snakes, with which they are often confused, include the scarlet snake, several forms of milk snake, shovelnose snake, some king snakes, and others. Similarly, the beautifully colored desert species *Micruroides euryxanthus* is called the western coral snake. It has a northern subspecies, *M. euryxanthus euryxanthus*, the Arizona coral snake, and the southern subspecies, found south of the border in the Sonoran Desert, *M. euryxanthus australis*, called the Sonora coral snake or *Coralillo de Sonora*.

Unfortunately, in Latin America, where most of the species are found, very few distinctive common names exist. There are, nevertheless, some interesting names applied to coral snakes in various Spanish- and Portuguese-speaking countries to the south. The most common of these, of course, is the name *coral* (pronounced with the accent on the "a"), which is applied to almost any snake that has red bands on the body. In some cases, such as with *M. psyches* in Venezuela where the snake can appear purplish by the invasion of blackish overtones over the red bands, the snake is called *Coral Morada* (purple coral snake).

In Brazil, where Portuguese is spoken, coral snakes are called *Cobra Coral*. *Cobra* in Portuguese simply means snake, and not the true cobras of Asia and Africa, which belong to the genus *Naja*. Occasionally, they also refer to the coral snake only as *Coral*, or *Cobra Coral Verdadeira* (true coral snake), to distinguish the real (venomous) coral snake.

Another widely used Spanish name, particularly in Mexico, is *Coralillo* or *Coralilla*, a kind of diminutive for coral. In order to distinguish the venomous coral snakes from the inoffensive ones, the name *Coral Ponzoñosa* or *Coral Venenosa* is used in all parts of Latin America where people recognize there is a difference between the venomous and nonvenomous or mildly venomous coral snakes.

A related common name in Spanish, applied to several species of nonvenomous colubrid coral snakes that have uniformly red coloration on the entire body without black bands or markings, is *Madre de Coral* (mother of the coral snake). The name apparently has its origin in the belief that uniformly red-colored species, as found in the colubrid genera *Pseudoboa* and *Clelia*, give birth to the banded venomous coral snakes.

Some salamanders with some red coloration in Latin America are also called *Madre de Coral* for the same reason. A Venezuelan name given to snakes with uniform red body coloration is *Coral Macho* (the male coral) in the belief that they actually are males of the red, white, and black-banded venomous coral snakes (*Micrurus*). In Venezuela the *Coral Macho* includes such colubrid snakes as *Pseudoboa coronata* and juveniles of *Pseudoboa neuwiedii*.

In Colombia, several other names are used for the venomous species in addition to coral. Several names are applied to the subspecies of *Micrurus mipartitus* (Color 43). This species has a unique coloration among the coral snakes: it has only one red band on the head and a few on the tail only; the rest of the body is covered by red and white (or yellow) bands. A well-known name for this coral snake is *Rabo de Ají* (*rabo* is tail and *ají* is hot red pepper). This may have two meanings. *Ají*, the hot pepper (*Capsicum annuum*), is intensely red and quite similar to the red coloration found on the tail of the *Rabo de Ají*. Second, the fruit of the red hot pepper is slender and pointed at one end, not dissimilar to the tail of the coral snake. This is related to the belief in Colombia and also in Venezuela that the *Rabo de Ají* stings with its tail and the sting is deadly. Other names applied to this species in Colombia are *Rabo de Candela* (fire or flame tail), *Matagatos* (cat killer), *Gargantilla* (necklace or choker) and *Cabeza de Chocho*. The Central American *Micrurus multifasciatus* is also called *Gargantilla* or *Coral Gargantilla*, particularly in Costa Rica, but also in Panama and Nicaragua. It is a large species with a color pattern of red and black bands. Usually, the red band on the head is particularly intense as are the long red tail bands. Campbell and Lamar (1989) collected quite a few interesting names applied to coral snakes where they are found.

In an earlier treatise of venomous snakes of Colombia, García (1896) reported a folkloric name, *Coral Cabeza de Chocho*, for *M. mipartitus decussatus* in the Cordillera Occidental of Colombia. *Chocho* has two meanings: an old man, thus, coral snake with a head like that of an old man; or a plant, called *jequiriquí* (*Abrus precatorius*) with a colorful fruit that reminds one of the red coloration of the head of *M. mipartitus decussatus*. The allusion to the old man is particularly charming. In the Andes, many old people are bald; their head skin is reddish and thus similar to the red head of the coral snake. Another coral snake, *Coral de Ponzoña de Mocoa* is mentioned by García as *Elaps markgravii* but judging from the color picture in his book, it is apparently a *M. hemprichii ortoni*.

The belief that coral snakes or snakes in general sting with their tail spine is found practically throughout Latin America. García (1896, p. 64) gives an account by the prefecto of Mocoa that relates to the potency of the venom of coral snakes and to this phenomenon of stinging with the tail. The story, offered in free translation, is a mixture of fact and fiction and includes references to several coral snakes:

> "The Indians tell me that the venom of the small snake [probably refers to *M. dumerilii transandinus*] kills very quickly. A person stung by the tail would not manage to live even an hour. Sometimes it bites with the mouth but its bite does not produce any ill effect. My father, while performing the duties of prefecto in 1860, walking on a path in the Istmo de Bermeja, found a Coral de Ponzoña [probably, *M. hemprichii ortoni*]. He wanted to grab it but one of the Indians, in spite of the respect that they had for my father, made him fall back, warning him that this snake had venom. They proved their assertion by putting a rotten log near the restrained snake. The snake at once introduced its sting into the log. When the blade of a knife was put near the snake, one could hear the vibration that the sting produced. In accordance to the information that I have been able to obtain, the Coral de Ponzoña stings with its tail sting with the speed of a sewing machine needle."

The vibration of the tail described by the prefecto de Mocoa probably relates to coral snake mimics rather than the real coral snake. Coral snakes do not vibrate their tails, but species of the colubrid genera *Oxyrhopus* and *Erythrolamprus* are known to vibrate their tails when restrained; they occur in the area of Mocoa.

The tiniest coral snake from the Caribbean coast of Colombia, *Micrurus dissoleucus*, is called *Coralilla* or *Candelilla*. *Candela* is flame or fire, and locally also is used to signify the flame of the candle. Thus, the name is a diminutive that means the little flame-like one or flamy one. *Coral Rey* (king coral snake) is applied to the *M. ancoralis jani* (Color 7), a very beautiful triad-type coral snake from the Choco region of Colombia. A local name for coral snakes in Peru is *naca-naca*, used particularly for *Micrurus t. tschudii* (Color 59) and *M. spixii obscurus* but also for other species. In Argentina the name *Boicora* is applied to *M. corallinus* (Color 13), a single-banded coral snake found also in southeastern Brazil and Paraguay. *Ibiboboca*, sometimes also *Ibiboca*, is a common Indian name of several coral snakes in Brazil. It was immortalized by the German herpetologist Merrem in 1820 when he gave the species the scientific name of *Elaps ibiboboca*, but *M. corallinus* is also called *Ibiboboca* by the Indians.

In Suriname, where Dutch is spoken, the names applied to most coral snakes are *kraalslang* and *krarsneke*, while in the few places where French is spoken the names most used are *corail* or *serpent-corail* (coral snake).

A widely held belief in Costa Rica is that coral snake bites before 6 AM or before sunrise are usually fatal, but bites inflicted after 6 AM are not fatal. As explained by the noted Costa Rican herpetologist Picado (1931), the observation might be correct but the explanation is not. It seems that the venomous coral snakes are predominantly nocturnal in Costa Rica and cease their activities at sunrise. Sunrise occurs shortly after 6 AM in Costa Rica. Several inoffensive coral snake mimics are more diurnal and begin their activities or are still active after sunrise and might be confused with the venomous coral snakes. Thus, the nonvenomous bite might be produced by the false coral snakes.

I have heard a similar belief in the coastal area of Venezuela, except that the hour is sunset. Before 6 PM the coral snake bites are not dangerous, whereas after 6 PM they can be fatal and must be treated by a doctor or by a "curandero" (medicine man). Again, sunset in Venezuela is shortly after 6 PM when, especially in drier areas in northern Venezuela, venomous coral snakes become active. Some false coral snakes are active earlier in the day but not even they are active during the hottest midday period.

In the llanos of Colombia and Venezuela, the local llaneros suggest that to kill a snake one should take a handful of hair from a mare, cut it into small pieces, and put the pieces into milk. During the night the snake will come and drink the milk and die. Lactating women—and there are many of them in the llanos—must be careful during the night because snakes, including coral snakes, like to sneak up while they are asleep and suck their breasts dry, leaving little milk for the babies. This belief may be used as an excuse by some women who do not succeed in rearing babies well. Chances are that some diseases or parasites may be preventing the normal lactation or growth of children, with the snakes taking the blame.

European colonizers and conquerors of the New World immediately became fascinated by the brilliant coloration of coral snakes. The name coral snake seemed to express its peculiar characteristic well. At the same time, it stifled the imagination and prevented recognition of the rich variety of species among coral snakes. All snakes that had some red coloration became coral, coral snake, or cobra coral. By contrast, the rich folkloric diversity of local Indian names found among the original dwellers of the New World, particularly among the tribes of South America, reveals their keen knowledge of snakes. Their common names usually do not allude to the red coloration but quite imaginatively include such features as habitat, role in nature, and color pattern in general.

In Guaraní, an Indian language recognized as the second official language in Paraguay and spoken in several other countries in South America where Guaraní live, there are several names for coral snakes. *Mbói-chumbé* is the Guaraní name of venomous coral snakes but also it is applied to other snakes with red-black-yellow coloration as well, whether venomous or not. *Mbói* means snake and *chumbé* means banded like a ribbon or belt. A more specific name for venomous coral snakes with a short, blunt tail such as *M. frontalis* (Color 27) in Paraguay is the ancient, now little-used name, *mbói-chumbépé* (pé = cut). *M. lemniscatus* is also called *mbói-chumbé guasú*. A still more ancient name in the Guaraní tongue that was used for coral snakes is *mbói-corá*. Several coral snakes, in addition to being called *mbói-chumbé*, are also called *mbói-yvyvóvó* (snake that cuts or penetrates into the earth). This name apparently alludes to the habit of some coral snakes of digging into debris or soft soil or into termite nests when pursued (Gatti, 1955).

Nahuátl, a language related to the language of the Aztecs, is still spoken in some areas in central Mexico and has several names applied to venomous coral snakes, or *coralillos*. One is *cuicuicoátl* meaning snake of diverse colors (*cuicuiltíc* means different colors and *coátl* means snake). *Tlapapalcoátl* is another name meaning colorful, multicolored snake (*tlapapalli* means several colors and *coátl* means snake). This name, according to Rafael Martín del Campo (1984), Mexican herpetologist and student of ancient cultures and their language, is applied to both true and false coral snakes. Much more popular and better known among Mexican people, past and present, is another *coátl*, *quetzalcoátl*, the rattlesnake. Most of the ancient temple pyramids of the Aztecs, Toltecs, Zapotecs, and Mayans offer homage to the god Quetzalcoátl, but only in one ruin in western Mexico is there found a serpent relief that appears to represent the color pattern of a coral snake.

Presently, Mexicans, including Mexican Indians, make a fairly good distinction between the bad or venomous coral snake, *Coralilla Mala* or *Coralillo Ponzoñoso*, and the good coral snake, *Coralilla Buena*. In the lowlands of Guerrero, for example, there is a belief that the bad coralillas live in the wild, while the ones found near or in the huts or other human dwellings are harmless and domesticated. These snakes would not harm a *cristiano*, or a good Christian. As a matter of fact, there is a popular belief, noted by Gadow (1911), that a harmless snake lives beneath the water container in every home. It is known that some species of false coral snakes are more likely to live near human settlements than the true coral snakes. In the Mexican plateau there is also a conviction about coral snakes that defies sober explanation. Here it is believed that venomous coral snakes have a little red light on their snout that shines when they move during the night.

A leading Mexican herpetologist, Miguel Alvarez del Toro (1983), tells of several interesting beliefs from the state of Chiapas. Chiapanecos believe that coral snakes are the masters of the leaf-cutter ants that form long columns carrying pieces of freshly cut green leaves. When a small, temporary stream impedes their advance or cuts their path to the source of juicy plants, these ants appeal to the coral snake who stretches its body across the rivulet or small stream and forms a bridge for the ants. Perhaps this belief rests on the fact that coral snakes are known to live in leaf litter where ants abound and some are associated with ant nests (see section on reproduction).

Chiapans believe that pregnant women are able to hypnotize any venomous snake with a fixed stare. Stories tell of people in danger of snakebite narrowly escaping by calling a pregnant woman who, looking firmly at the snake, hypnotized it. One wonders about the origin of such a belief. Is it possible that a pregnant woman feels special about herself and that a firm self-confidence and courage evoke respect from a snake? It is known that when a snake is handled gently but firmly it will bite only in extreme conditions. This is especially true when the person relating to the snake displays no significant fear or hate. Many sensitive herpetologists and other persons who handle snakes know of the importance of respectful but firm handling of them. Somehow, the snake seems to sense it and act in accordance with the behavior or attitude of fear or confidence by biting or not. A pregnant woman's firm trust in herself as a carrier of new life might calm the snake, thus making it immobile. This could be interpreted as a hypnotic state.

A delightful belief found in several states of Mexico is the following recipe for getting rid of venomous snakes. When a snake goes to drink water, in order not to poison itself, it leaves its venom on the nearest stone. The trick is to destroy the venom while the snake is busy drinking. On its return the snake discovers that its venom is gone, and in despair commits suicide by beating itself to death against the stone. Obviously, some other phenomenon might have given rise to such a romantic belief.

If these defense remedies fail, Chiapans suggest a more extreme, alternative method to survive the deadly coral snake bite. The bitten victim must capture the culprit and bite it all along its length. In this way the human will be cured fast without endangering his or her life.

The Akawai Indians from Guyana call *M. lemniscatus kumung* meaning "the one who lives in the ground;" another name used by the Guyana Indians is *maccouracourra*, while the Warao Indians in the Orinoco delta of Venezuela use the name *juba* (pronounced "hooba") even though it is frequently applied to all snakes. A similarly looking coral snake, *M. isozonus*, is called *Coral Norteña* by Venezuelans but the Guahibo, Acavai, and Cuiva Indians call it *huayamacaicha* (Campbell and Lamar, 1989). These names are actually used for most coral snakes.

The Yanomami, a major tribe living in a large area between Brazil and Venezuela, recognize different species of coral snakes. One species, *M. hemprichii*, is called *nanim uxirimake*, considered as male, while another name for the same species is *nanim-uxirimkyk*.

An interesting and imaginative name in a local Creole dialect for coral snakes in Great Corn Island (Isla del Maíz Grande), Nicaragua, is *Babaspul*. It is a local-modified phonetic pronunciation of "barber's pole." The name is applied to the coral snake because of its similarity to the old-time advertising sign for a barber shop (a pole, still found painted red, white, and blue; the black bands of coral snakes sometimes look iridescent blue). The barber's pole tradition apparently originated during the times when barbers' tasks included bloodletting. After this procedure, the bloody bandages were washed, and, still red, hung outside the barber's shop for drying. They served to advertise the shop. The Babaspul from the Great Corn Island, which is inhabited mostly by English-speaking descendants of runaway slaves and remnants of the Misquito Kingdom of the Caribbean, has red, white, and black bands. During a collecting trip to Nicaragua and these islands, with Edward Seligmann, Jr., Richard G. Zweifel, and Jaime Villa, we found this coral snake that turned out to be an undescribed subspecies. Upon learning its local name, I immortalized it by giving the snake the scientific name *Micrurus nigrocinctus babaspul* (Roze, 1967).

In the United States some popular verses offer clues for distinguishing the venomous coral snakes from their nonvenomous mimics. One such goes:

> Red on yellow kill a fellow;
> Red on black, poison lack.

Another:

> Red on black, friend of Jack
> Red on yellow, bite a fellow.

Thus, if the red bands touch the yellow bands, the snake is venomous; if the red bands touch black, it is not. This verse is correct for most species found in the United States, but could be fatally misleading farther south.

In order to provide common names to all coral snakes, I have tried to find local names wherever known. For other species, I have given common names by selecting some distinctive characteristics or geographic location associated with the coral snake (see Appendix A). This, I hope, will offer an easier way of dealing with coral snakes for people not comfortable with scientific names. The latter are sometimes jawbreakers even for scientists.

Coral Snakes as Endangered Animals

As we will see, the increase of degraded, altered, and partially denatured environments due to human activities in the New World has had a significant impact on the presence and abundance of many animals. Coral snakes are no exception.

Some coral snakes, such as *M. nigrocinctus babaspul* from the Little Corn Island of Nicaragua, have been disturbed and even eliminated from their environment. Some countries have made efforts to protect some of their animals, including coral snakes.

Official Protection of Coral Snakes in the United States

While no coral snake appears on endangered or protected lists nationally, some states have become concerned about the precarious presence of some species. In New Mexico, protective control of *Micruroides e. euryxanthus* is exercised by the State Game Commission Regulation No. 563, which regulates its collection and destruction. Herpetologists, however, recommend some protection for this species as well as monitoring the protection of its habitat. *Micruroides e. euryxanthus* is perhaps the most docile and nonaggressive species, easy to handle and mistreat. Left unprotected, in a few years it might reach endangered status. No protection or regulations of any sort for *Micruroides e. euryxanthus*, whose common name is the Arizona coral snake, have been declared by Arizona, however. It was abundant in Arizona many years ago and still is in some places.

No protection is afforded to *M. fulvius tenere*, the Texas coral snake, and *M. f. fulvius*, the eastern coral snake. North Carolina considers the eastern coral snake peripheral to the state, principally due to the destruction of its habitat. The eastern coral snake has become rare or very rare in some parts of Florida. One recalls the Pinellas County bounty offer that in the 1930s netted 2,000 dead eastern coral snakes for a bounty of $2 apiece. Today, in many parts of Florida a $100 bounty would not bring in 100 specimens, dead or alive.

Fortunately, a general societal concern for the natural environment is increasing not only in the United States but throughout the Latin American world as well. American herpetologists, naturally, are the most concerned about protection of many species of amphibians and reptiles as well as their natural habitats. One of the first concerns about the protection of amphibians and reptiles has been expressed by R. E. Ashton, Jr., S. R. Edwards, and G. R. Pisani from the Society for Study of Amphibians and Reptiles, who published "Endangered and Threatened Amphibians and Reptiles in the United States" (1976). This listing includes several coral snakes.

Latin American Concern and Protection of Fauna

Several countries of Latin America, such as Mexico, Colombia, Costa Rica, Brazil, Venezuela, and Ecuador, to name a few, have become concerned about the destruction of their flora and fauna, including some coral snakes. This concern has been translated into strict controls of collecting permits and many other limitations imposed on visiting foreign scientists.

With the increasing destruction of natural resources and environments and with the establishment of natural reserves and national forests as well as natural areas of protection for Indians, such as in Brazil and Venezuela, concern is growing and it is respected by all serious scientists, museums, institutes of learning, and governments throughout the world.

One difficulty, however, is that governments and politicians are frequently unaware of the universality of scientific knowledge and the importance of its open sharing and exchange, particularly in biology. The current political perception erroneously equates biological research with economic activities, such as foreign exploitation of resources for solely economic gains.

The study of natural history and biological systematics is quite different from this perception. Findings are not kept secret and sold as in commercial and industrial ventures, but published and available to any scientist in any country of the world. The collected specimens of coral snakes, for example, while deposited in the recognized museums or other established institutions of learning in Europe and North America, are considered the common patrimony of humankind. They are well cared for and are available for study by any qualified professional anywhere in the world. Any interested Mexican, Central, or South American scientist or student of biology has access to the coral snakes or other animals and plants deposited in these museums.

On many occasions, Latin American students in the United States, for example, have been able to obtain an appropriate training in biology, studying the specimens of their own country in any of the large U.S. museums. They have returned home with biological degrees to continue research of their natural environment. In addition, loans of specimens are frequently arranged by the museums to be sent to Latin American colleagues. They include specimens not only from their own country but from any other country as well. This fact is little known and used by the Latin American scientists.

When I was living and working at the Universidad Central de Venezuela in Caracas, I periodically borrowed coral snakes and other specimens for scientific research from museums in New York, Chicago, Washington, Cambridge (Massachusetts), Ann Arbor, San Francisco, London, Vienna, and several more. They had been originally collected in Venezuela and in other Latin American countries. I felt they were "our" specimens available to me as a biologist of Venezuela.

Instead of stringent, radical protection of natural flora and fauna, it would be more advantageous to establish rational protection and controls with arrangements for sharing the collections and the results of scientific research. One way of doing this would be to establish alliances between national and foreign biologists and recognized museums and institutes of learning for the cooperative exploration of nature and the fight against exploitation and destruction of national flora and fauna. One recent example in 1984–1985 is the cooperative effort between the Academia de Ciencias Físicas, Exactas y Naturales de Venezuela and several institutions in the United States, such as the National Museum of Natural History in Washington, U.S. Fish and Wildlife, the Smithsonian Institution, the American Museum of Natural History in New York, the Missouri Botanical Garden, the New York Botanical Garden, and several more. This expedition to Cerro Neblina, Venezuela, in which I had the privilege of participating, netted many new species of plants and animals including a new coral snake. This 18-month expedition, with the participation of more than 150 Venezuelan and U.S. scientists, demonstrated the usefulness of collaboration between the scientists of both countries in sharing knowledge and specimens.

It is quite important to acknowledge that no biological or ecological field research or collection performed by biologists has ever even remotely endangered or depleted any species in nature. On the contrary, it is the work of field biologists and ecologists that has provided the knowledge about animals and plants essential for better management and, where needed, protection of animal diversity and nature in general.

The most effective protection of animal and plant diversity can be accomplished by protecting the natural environments, particularly forests and unique ecosystems. The deforestation, degradation, and general destruction of many environments by humans are the main activities that endanger species of plants and animals.

Part II
FORM AND DISTINGUISHING FEATURES

Chapter 2
External Features

As dwellers in ground litter and in somewhat subterranean conditions, coral snakes have a cylindrical and quite slender body. The head is roundish and can barely be distinguished from the body. The eyes are round and quite small as compared to those of most other snakes, especially some of the false coral snakes. The pupil is round or slightly elliptical. The diameter of the body is almost unchanging from the neck to the anal region. Beyond the anus, the tail tapers off and can be short and blunt or somewhat longer. This varies from species to species (see section on size and growth).

Body Covering: The Skin and Scales

The slender coral snake body is covered in its entirety by scales, as is the case with all reptiles. The scales are the horny outer layer of the skin formed by dead cells filled with keratin. Beneath the outside cover is the live skin that secretes the outer layer. Although each individual scale can be clearly observed as a separate hardened segment of the skin, they are in fact connected to each other by a thinner fold or crease. These interconnecting creases are concealed beneath the scales, but they can be seen when the snake sheds its skin. The shed skin or molt is like a piece of fabric sewn together into a very long and narrow tube. On this long tube of shed skin, the different scales are like thicker shields held together by thinner, flexible creases.

In live snakes the creases between the scales allow for considerable flexibility and expansion of the body. This is particularly useful when a coral snake swallows a large prey. Its neck and body can expand considerably as the prey passes into the stomach, where, at times, it can be seen as a large elongated lump. This loose arrangement of scales also allows for flexibility in the sinuous snakelike movements, and it protects the body against external injuries.

The head as well as the body and the tail have quite specific arrangements of scales. The size, shape, and particularly the number of scales in the body are important for classification of individual species and even more so for subspecies. In snakes, the largest scales are called plates, scutes, or shields. We will call the scales covering the head "shields." For the sake of clarity, in describing the shape or measuring the size of a shield or scale, its length is considered to be in the direction along the length of the body, while the width is measured across or perpendicular to the body.

Head Shields

The coral snake head is typically covered by shields of a definite number and shape (Fig. 1). The point of the snout is covered by the rostral shield,

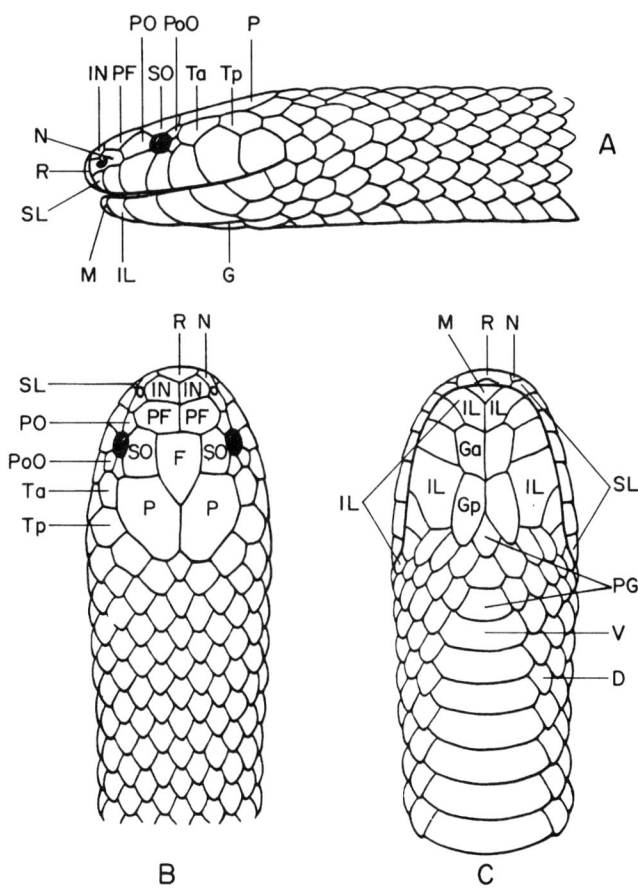

Figure 1. Head shields of *Micrurus isozonus*: A) Lateral view, B) Dorsal view, C) Ventral view.

usually simply called the rostral, that is visible from above. It is followed on each side by a nasal in the center of which is the nasal opening. Extending from the opening above and below are frequently found small grooves that partially or completely divide the nasal, and we can speak of a prenasal and postnasal shield. The postnasal is almost always larger than the prenasal. Dorsally, between the nasals and following the rostral, is a pair of internasals that are usually wider than they are long, followed by a pair of prefrontals. The latter are longer and wider than the internasals, but shorter than the single frontal shield that follows them. The frontal is usually longer than it is wide. It can be longer or shorter than the distance from the snout to its anterior border. The frontal is somewhat hexagonal or partially pentagonal in shape, always with a pointed end that extends between the parietals that follow it. On each side of the frontal is a supraocular that is narrower than the frontal. Only in *M. surinamensis* (Fig. 2A) and in *M. dissoleucus* is the frontal narrower than the supraoculars. The pair of parietals are the largest shields of the head, after which begins the region of the dorsal body scales. The orbit of the eye is surrounded by ocular shields. The pupil of the eye is roundish or slightly elliptical. Between the nasal and the eye is the preocular, approximately pentagonal in shape. Above the eye is the supraocular, already mentioned, and behind the eye is usually a pair of postoculars. Some coral snakes such as *M. annellatus balzani* have only one postocular. Behind the postocular is one anterior temporal followed by one or two posterior temporals. To simplify the description, a formula of 1+1 and 1+2 temporals is used. In some species this formula is quite uniform, while others show variation; some individuals have 1+1, others 1+2 temporals. One interesting exception is *L. collaris* in which almost all the individuals have 0+1 temporals. The space of the first temporal is occupied by the upward extension of the sixth supralabial that is in contact with the parietal (Fig. 3A). The upper lip is normally covered by seven supralabials, the third and fourth of which are in contact with the orbit of the eye. One exception, again, is *M. surinamensis* that has only the fourth supralabial in contact with the eye (Fig. 2B and Color 57).

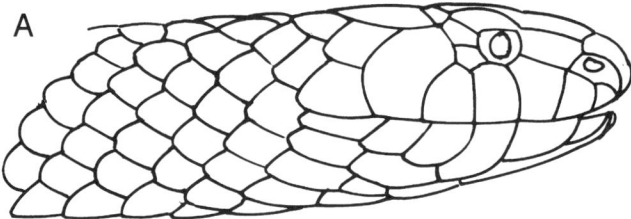

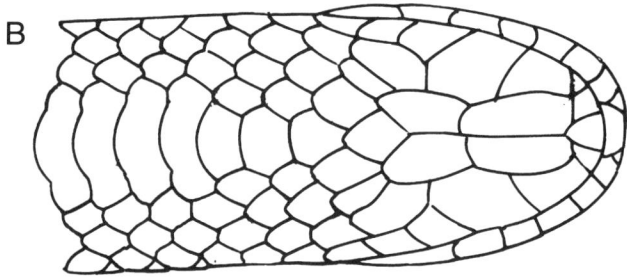

Figure 3. Head shields of *Leptomicrurus collaris*: A) Lateral view, showing the sixth supralabial in contact with the parietal, B) Ventral view, showing the mental in contact with the first pair of genials.

Below, opposite the rostral on the lower jaw, is a single mental shield (Fig. 1C). The lower lip is normally covered by seven infralabials, between which are two pairs of genials, also called chin shields. The first infralabial meets its opposite behind the mental. One exception is the species of *Leptomicrurus* (Fig. 3B) in which the first infralabials as a rule are separated due to the contact of the mental with the anterior pair of genials. However, occasional specimens of other species might have the same condition, especially in *M. mipartitus*. Of the two pairs of genials, the posterior pair is longer than the anterior. The one exception is *Micruroides*, which have only one pair of genials (Fig. 4), followed by two or three somewhat irregular postgenial shields, also called gulars. Following the genials are the preventrals; then the ventrals begin, which are considered body scales.

On occasion, some of the head shields show abnormalities by fusing or splitting. In earlier times, these abnormalities caused scientists to describe a new species to science without realizing that the single individual they were studying was merely an aberrant specimen of an already known species. This occurred particularly in the last century and earlier in this century. It was practiced in systematic biology before the realization that a population or a species is best described when several specimens have been examined and the variation of their characteristics properly understood. In coral snakes, common aberrations have caused mistaken descriptions of at least six species. The

 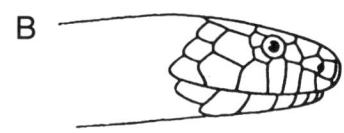

Figure 2. Head shields of *Micrurus surinamensis*: A) Dorsal view, showing the frontal narrower than the supraoculars, B) Lateral view, showing only one supralabial (fourth) in contact with the orbit.

External Features

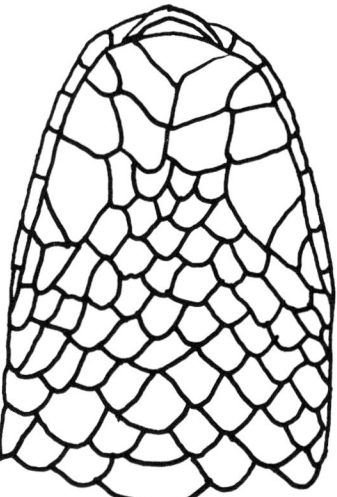

Figure 4. Ventral view of the head of *Micruroides euryxanthus*, showing only one pair of genials.

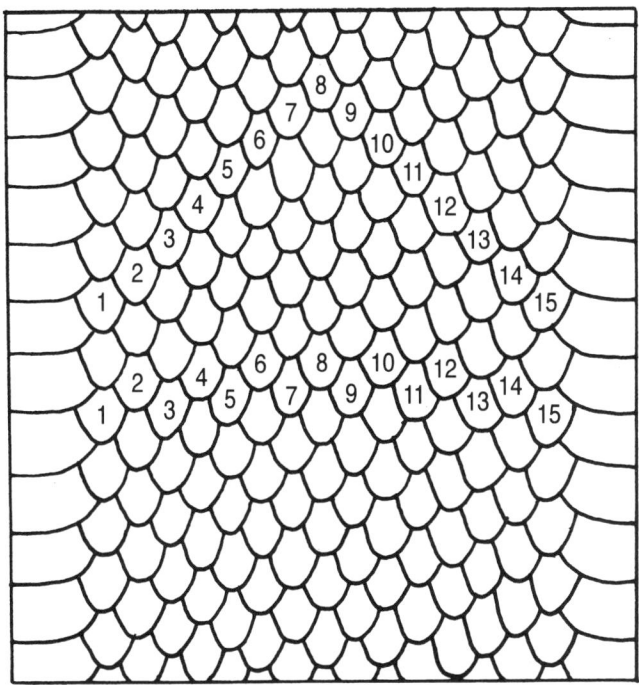

Figure 5. Two ways of counting dorsal scale.

British herpetologist George A. Boulenger described at least four new species to science of coral snake from single specimens with aberrant arrangement of head shields. In earlier days of his coral snake studies, Karl P. Schmidt (Schmidt and Schmidt, 1925) described a new species *M. helleri*, from Peru from an aberrant specimen. He later recognized his error and sank the name into the synonymy of *M. lemniscatus* to which it belonged. More recently, I was able to rescue this name. It turned out that *M. lemniscatus* is divided into several subspecies, one of which is represented by Schmidt's name and specimen. The current name of this subspecies, once again, is *M. lemniscatus helleri*.

Scales on the Body and Tail

The body of the coral snake is covered by two kinds of scales: smaller dorsal scales uniformly cover the dorsal and lateral parts while the belly is covered by larger ventral scales. Dorsal scales on the lateral parts of the body are similar to those on the back but are somewhat wider. Dorsals begin immediately behind the head shields, both dorsally and laterally. The dorsals can be counted in several ways across the body (Fig. 5), but the number of longitudinal rows of dorsals is surprisingly uniform: all three genera of coral snakes have 15 longitudinal rows of dorsals. The region immediately behind the head is somewhat less regular, and for three to four (occasionally up to eight) ventrals there can be 18, 17, or 16 dorsal rows. The shape of these dorsal neck scales might be more roundish, irregularly round, or square. This variation does not seem to be fixed for each species but varies from individual to individual.

Ventrals cover the belly and are sometimes two but most often three times or more wider than long. For the purpose of counting scale rows, the first ventral is defined as the first scale that is in contact with the first dorsal row (Fig. 1C) (Dowling, 1951). Usually, this excludes several scales between the first ventral and the posterior genials. These "no man's land" scales are referred to as preventrals or postgenials. In almost all snakes each ventral scale corresponds to one vertebra. As the vertebral column starts at the level of the first ventral scale, by counting ventrals we can know the number of body vertebrae.

The body and the ventral scales end at the anal scale or plate that covers the anal opening (Fig. 6). The posterior border of the anal opening is roundish and it is slightly smaller than the ventrals. In all species of coral snakes except *M. hemprichii* the anal opening is obliquely divided, while in the latter species the anal opening is entire. Beneath the anal scale is the cloacal opening. The tail starts beyond the cloacal scale and continues to its terminal point, which is rather pointed and covered by a single scale. In many species the tail tip is like a roundish spine, which may have given origin to the belief that the tails of coral snakes produce a mortal wound.

The scales beyond the anus are called subcaudals or caudals and are usually divided. In some species such as *M. diastema* several subcaudals are undivided, but a few undivided scales might be present in occasional specimens of other species as well. When they are present, the undivided scales are always restricted to the first few subcaudals behind the anus.

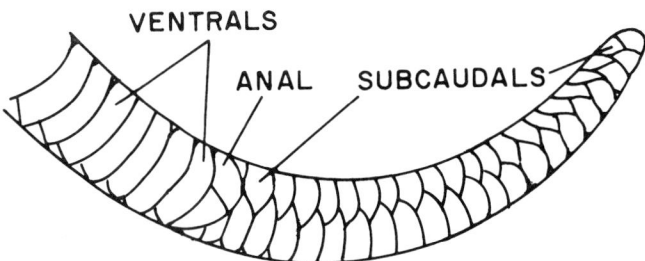

Figure 6. Position of the anal plate (divided), ventrals and subcaudals.

On the tail the number of dorsal rows decreases rapidly. In addition, the dorsals near the end of the tail may differ from midbody dorsals in size and shape.

Except for the large constrictors, coral snakes have the highest number of vertebrae among the snakes; concordantly, they have the most ventral scales. For example, a *L. narduccii melanotus* from Rio Itaya, Iquitos, Peru (AMNH 53657) has 374 ventrals and 35 subcaudals, giving a total of 409 vertebrae. Surprisingly, the smallest number for coral snake ventrals is registered for a specimen of one of the largest species, *M. surinamensis*, an individual from Manjuru, Brazil that has only 156 ventrals. Adding its 35 subcaudals, the specimen has a total of 191 vertebrae.

The range of variation and mean of the number of ventrals and subcaudals are important for distinguishing many species and subspecies. They are briefly reviewed in the section on classification and keys for distinguishing the species. The numbers of ventrals and subcaudals are also different between males and females (see section on differences between males and females).

Scale Organs

Some scales have tiny pits and tubercles that can be seen with a simple microscope, and several head shields have irregularly distributed minute tubercles that are well distinguishable on live or recently preserved specimens. These might be sensory receptors, probably tactile, but at present their function is unknown.

Some groups of coral snakes, such as the Central American *M. nigrocinctus* and some single-banded Mexican and South American species, have conspicuous tubercles on the first two to three rows of the dorsal scales above the cloaca (Fig. 7). Called supraanal tubercles, they are mostly found in males. If present in females, they are barely perceptible as small keels on some supraanal scales. One possible function of the supraanal tubercles or keels could be to help coordinate the alignment of male and female bodies during copulation.

Microscopic Ornaments of the Scales

The minute surface sculpture of coral snakes can be studied with the electron microscope, which reveals patterns of microornamentation or microdermato-

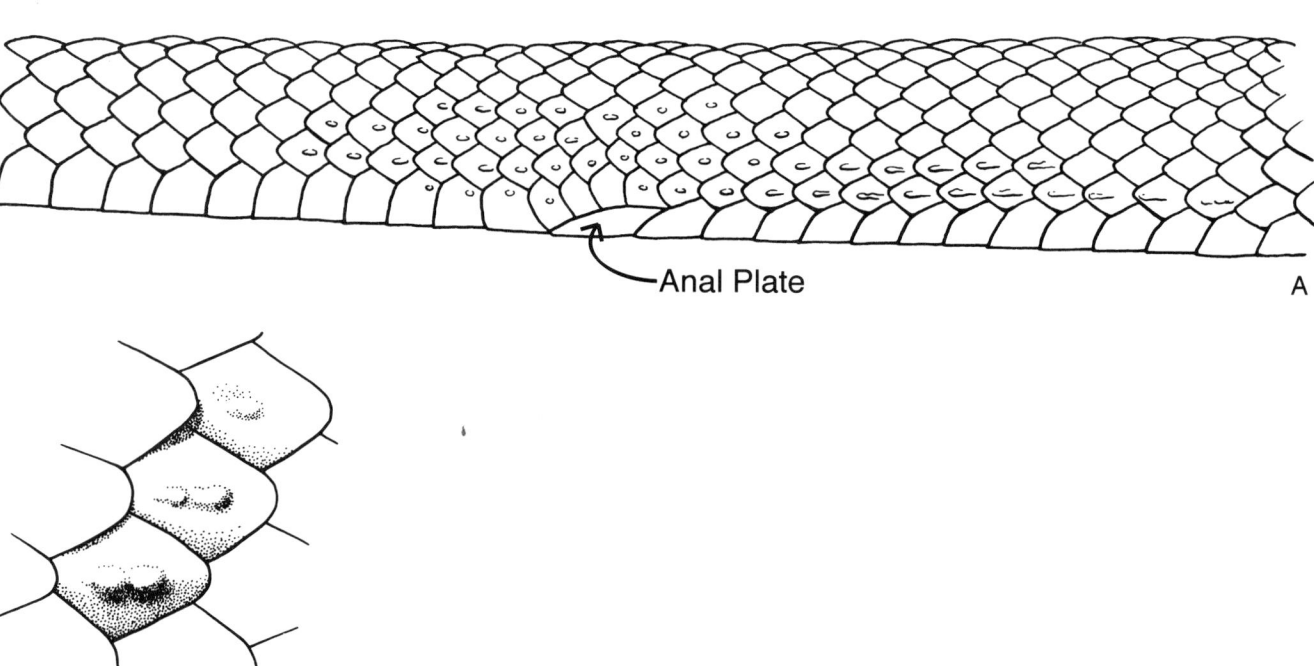

Figure 7. Position of supraanal tubercles or keels (in males of *Micrurus nigrocinctus divaricatus*): A) General view of the anal region, B) Detailed view. (Drawn by Samuel McDowell)

glyphs. With every significant increase in magnification the "scale landscape" changes and new patterns emerge.

For example, a scale of *M. e. australis* that looks perfectly smooth at an optical microscope magnification of 42 times its normal size (Fig. 8A) shows a pat-

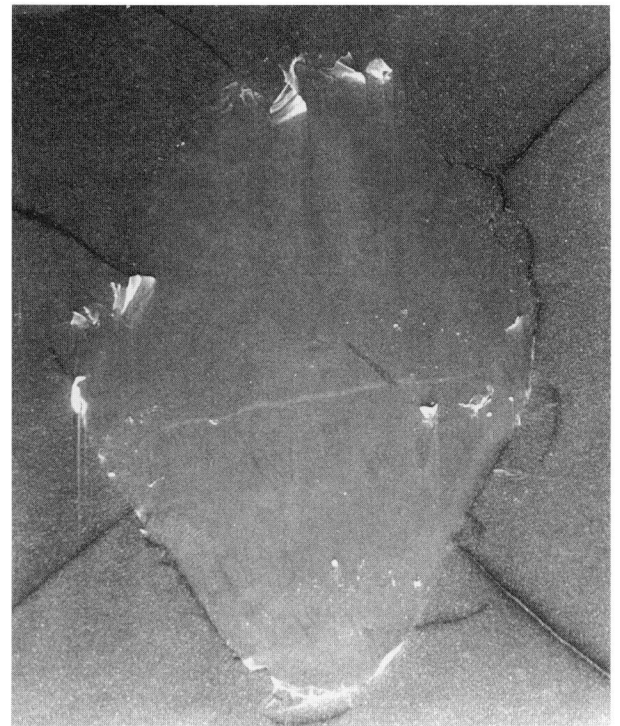
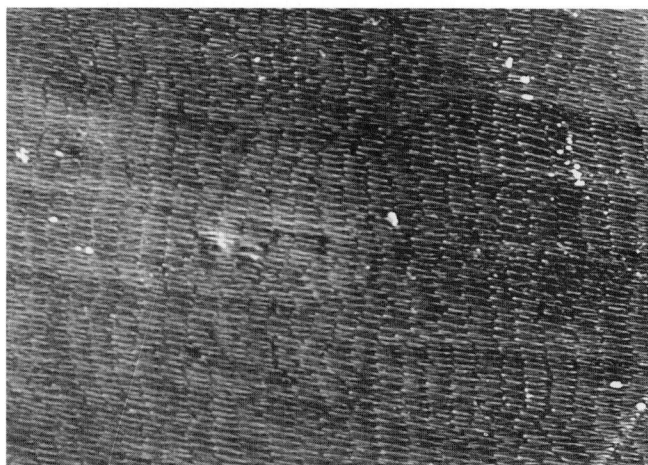
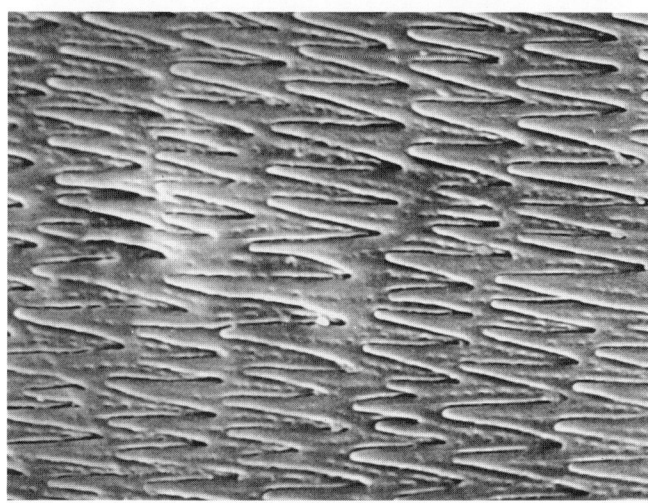

Figure 8. Microornamentation of dorsal scales of *Micruroides euryxanthus australis*, magnified: A) 33×, B) 1000×, C) 9500×.

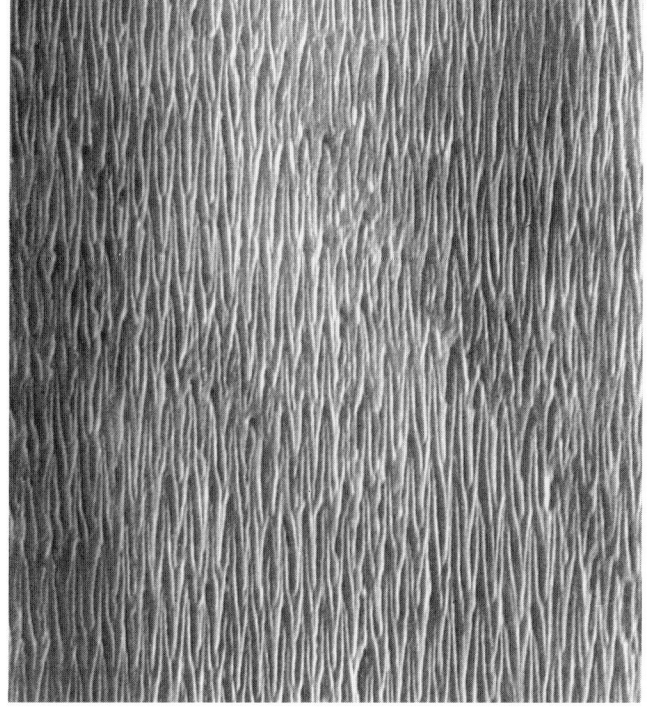

Figure 9. Microornamentation of dorsal scales of *Leptomicrurus scutiventris*, magnified: A) 1000×, B) 4750×.

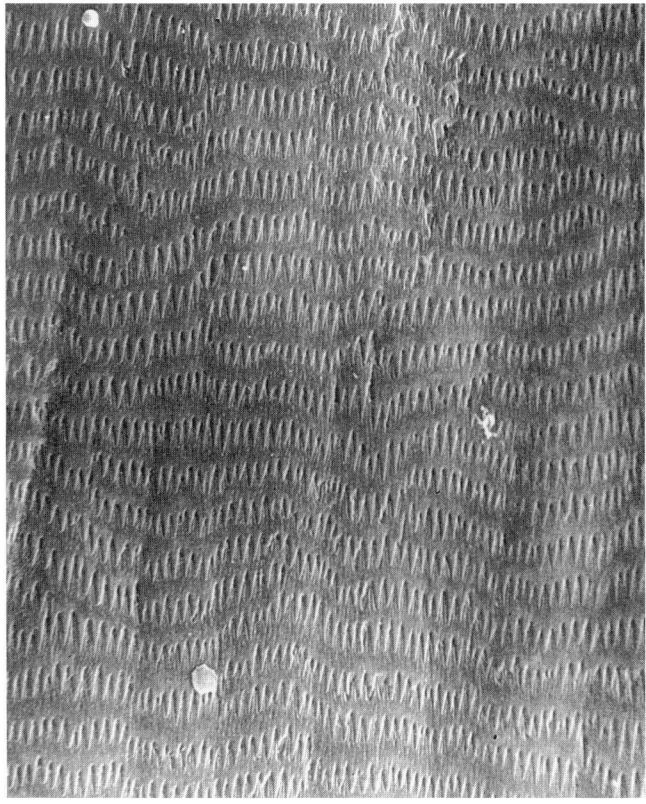

Figure 10. Microornamentation of dorsal scales of *Micrurus frontalis multicinctus*, magnified 2000×.

tern of irregular waves of small keels covering the entire scale in sinuous rows (Fig. 8B) when magnified 1000× by a scanning electron microscope. At 5000× a relief of regular continuous rows of spinelike structures appears with an irregular series of needle point dots between and on these spines (Fig. 8C). This echinate surface of flattened spinelike rows arranged in somewhat irregular waves is found in many species of snakes. In other coral snakes such as *L. scutiventris*, few structures are revealed at 1000× but the landscape changes at 4750× (Fig. 9B). Somewhat more developed but still partially smooth surface ornaments are found in *M. frontalis multicinctus* (Fig. 10). As magnification moves from 4,500× (Fig. 11A) to 10,000× (Fig. 11B), *M. distans zweifeli* shows the emergence of microornaments of ridges and valleys that partially conceal the echinate pattern seen at lower magnification. *M. browni taylori* has a similar microornamentation (Fig. 12) as does *M. m. semipartitus* (Fig. 13). *L. n. melanotus* has a somewhat more irregularly uniform microornamentation as revealed at a magnification of 1000× and 5000× times.

There are no detectable differences in the basic echinate pattern among the three genera of coral snakes, but some species show individual differences that could be used to tell them apart.

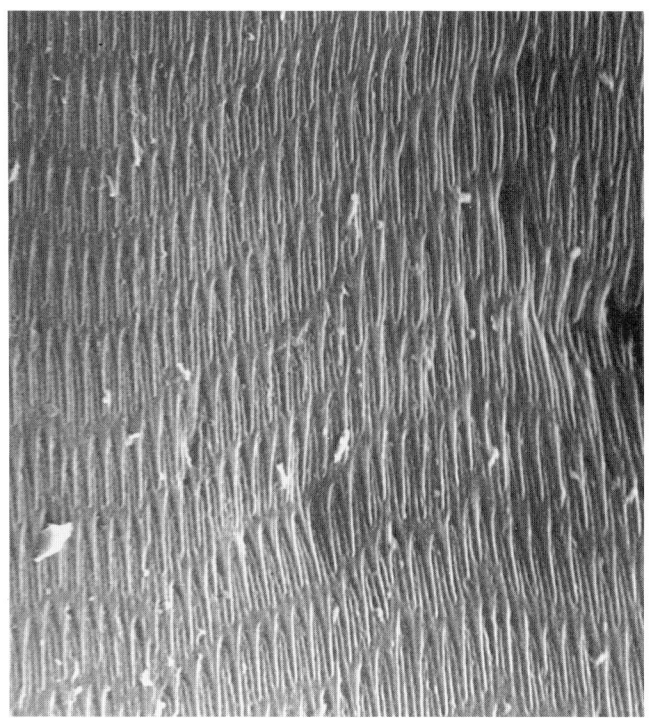
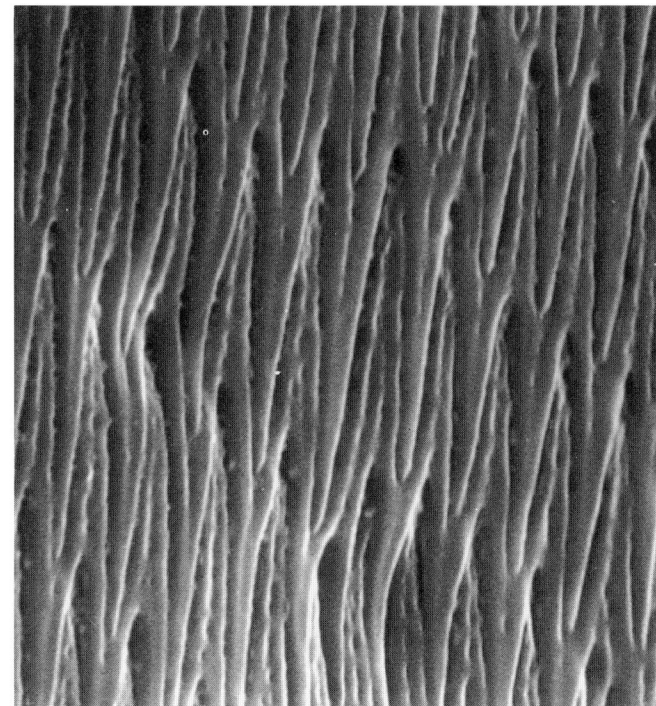

Figure 11. Microornamentation of dorsal scales of *Micrurus distans zweifeli*, magnified: A) 4500×, B) 10,000×.

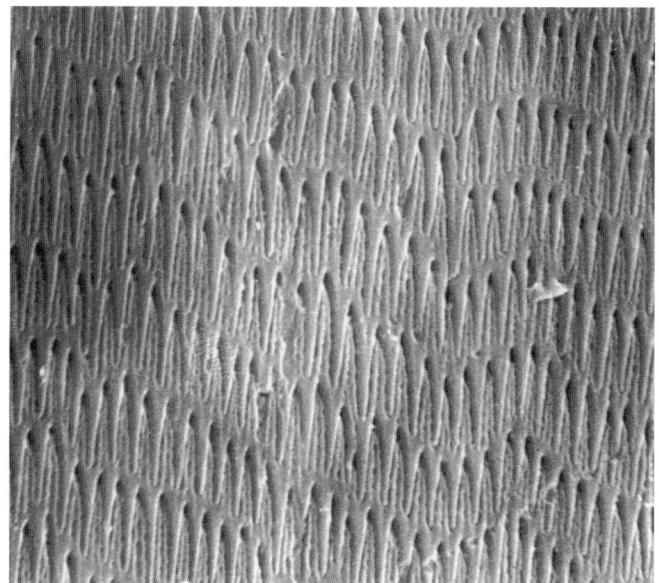

Figure 12. Microornamentation of dorsal scales of *Micrurus browni taylori*, magnified 5000×.

Shedding

As the snake grows, it periodically has to eliminate the old outside skin or outer epidermis (stratum corneum). The deeper skin layers secrete substances that help loosen and finally separate the dead outer layer. Shortly before shedding, the snake looks more opaque and has lost much of its coral snake brilliance. As snakes have no moving eyelids, before shedding their eyes appear to be covered with a bluish or grayish opaque lens. During shedding, the snake is partially blind, very nervous, and irritable. Humidity in the air helps to loosen the outer epidermis and when the time has come to shed the skin, the coral snake rubs its head, particularly the lips, against some hard and rough surface to break the bond of the old skin. Once this has been accomplished, the snake slides out as from a long tube, leaving the shed skin inside out. The whitish, semitransparent tube of epidermal skin comes off in one piece in which all the scales can be clearly identified. Sometimes (especially when living in poor conditions in captivity) the snake skin becomes torn and is shed in several pieces, especially when there is not enough humidity in the cage.

Coral snakes shed approximately 2 to 10 times a year depending on how fast they grow and how humid their environment is. During the first few years of life, actively growing coral snakes shed more frequently than adults do, and in captivity some coral snakes seem to shed more frequently than under natural conditions. In Venezuela, I observed a medium-size *M. isozonus* that shed twice in the course of 5 months of captivity. The same snake shed a third time 3 months later in its new quarters at the American Museum of Natural History in New York.

Differences Between Males and Females

From the outside it is practically impossible to distinguish a female coral snake from a male specimen. An experienced herpetologist might notice a difference in the thickness of the tail. Immediately behind the cloaca, the male has concealed a pair of internal sex organs, hemipenes. While it is not possible to see them from outside, they expand the tail a bit. By comparison, the tail of the female tapers off behind the anus somewhat faster than that of the male. Sex organs are described in the next section.

Sexual dimorphism is very clearly expressed in the numbers of ventrals and subcaudals. Comparing individuals of the same species or subspecies, males have a considerably lower number of ventrals but a higher number of subcaudals than do females. The difference is so pronounced than in many species the ranges of ventrals of the two sexes do not even overlap. For example, in *L. n. narduccii* the males have 261 to 278 and the females have 316 to 325 ventrals, while the subcaudals vary from 25 to 27 in males and from only 19 to 20 in the females. In males of *M. f. fulvius* the ventrals range from 197 to 217, while in the females from 219 to 233. The subcaudals in the males of the same coral snake range from 40 to 47, but only from 30 to 37 in the females. In quite a few species the sexual

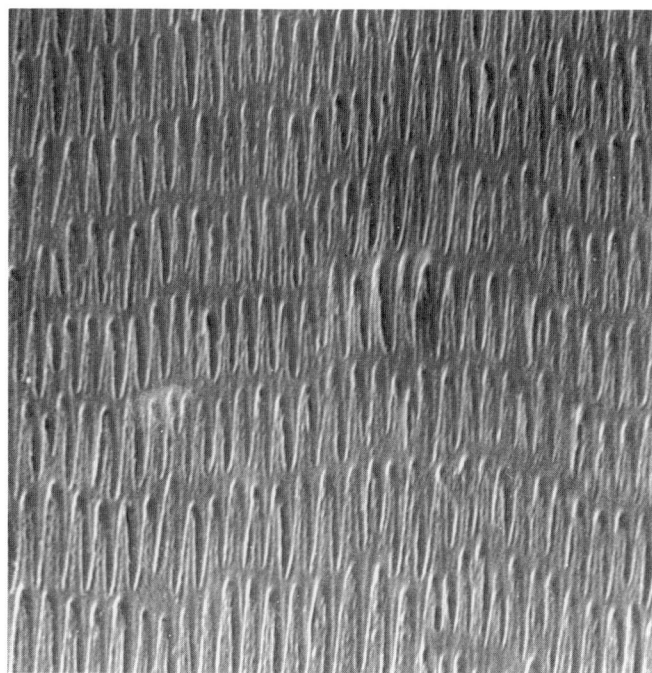

Figure 13. Microornamentation of dorsal scales of *Micrurus mipartitus semipartitus*, magnified 5000×.

dimorphism in scale counts is less pronounced and ranges overlap. For example, the males of *M. t. tschudii* have 188 to 213 ventrals while females have 206 to 224. A few species, particularly those with a short tail such as the subspecies of *M. frontalis*, have hardly any differences in the number of ventrals and subcaudals. For example, males of *M. frontalis brasiliensis* have 220 to 236 and females have 224 to 238 ventrals.

As the females have normally more ventrals but fewer subcaudals than the males, the sexual dimorphism in the number of ventrals and subcaudals becomes less pronounced when one counts together the ventrals and the subcaudals. For example, the males of *M. isozonus*, which have short tails, have 199 to 217 ventrals and 26 to 33 subcaudals, and the females have 215 to 225 ventrals and from 25 to 29 subcaudals. The variation of the combined ventrals plus subcaudals in the males is from 229 to 243 (averaging 233.2) and from 241 to 253 (248.7) in the females showing only a minimum of overlap. On the contrary, in *M. clarki*, which has a long tail, the counts become much more overlapping. The males of this species have from 191 to 197 ventrals and 53 to 58 subcaudals, with the sum of ventrals plus subcaudals varying from 243 to 255 (249.3). The females of this species have from 206 to 216 ventrals and 34 to 42 subcaudals, with the sum of ventrals plus subcaudals varying from 247 to 254 (250.8). This clearly approaches the male counts. Due to this sexual dimorphism in the number of ventrals and subcaudals, it is quite important to first determine the sex when identifying a coral snake.

In many occasions, the range of ventrals and subcaudals helps to distinguish subspecies. For example the aquatic coral snake *M. s. surinamensis* has from 156 to 174 ventrals in males and 170 to 187 in females as compared to its companion subspecies, *M. s. nattereri*, which has from 186 to 193 ventrals in males and 197 to 206 in females, showing a nonoverlapping difference.

In some species, the coloration shows some sexual dimorphism, even though it is less pronounced and somewhat overlapping. The males of *M. s. surinamensis* usually have the nuchal black band complete ventrally, while the females have it almost always interrupted or at least considerably narrowed ventrally. Some subspecies of *M. diastema* display the same phenomenon although it is less pronounced.

On the average, the males have fewer black body bands but more black tail bands than the females. For example, the males of *M. clarki* have from 13 to 17 (14.8) and the females have 14 to 19 (16.6) black body bands. The males of the same species have from 6 to 9 (7.4) and the females only 5 to 6 (5.7) black tail bands. *M. isozonus*, on the contrary, has practically the same number of triads—10 to 13 (11.2) in the males and 10 to 14 (11.8) in the females—yet the mean is higher for females than for males.

Reproductive Organs

One remarkable characteristic of coral snakes, shared with other snakes and lizards, is the presence of two male sex organs called hemipenes, meaning "half penis." Each hemipenis is actually a complete organ in itself. When not in use, the hemipenes are inverted hollow tubes inside the tail starting just behind the anus. During copulation, they are everted or turned inside out, like the fingers of a rubber glove that has been peeled off, and emerge from the cloaca. Each organ has a long retractor muscle that pulls it back again when copulation is over (see section on reproduction).

When not everted, the hemipenes are invisible from outside, except that in males the area behind the cloaca is slightly enlarged (see section on differences between males and females). The opening of each organ, or the hole through which it is everted, can be detected by lifting the anal plate. The hemipenes can be examined either in situ (i.e., when they are not everted) or in the everted position. By making a midsagittal incision behind the cloaca, the hemipenes can be seen as two whitish tubes that run along each side of the tail. The tubes can be cut open lengthwise and the characteristics of the organ observed in the inverted position. The hemipenes can also be everted in fresh specimens with an injection of alcohol or a similar fluid in the posterior part of the tail. This will force the organ out. When collecting snakes in the field, herpetologists normally determine the sex of each specimen and try to evert the hemipenes. This is more easily done in fresh specimens and allows for better observation of the hemipenis.

The length of the hemipenis can be measured in situ using the number of subcaudals as a measuring stick. The value of using the subcaudals as a unit of measurement is that the length of the hemipenis with respect to the number of subcaudals does not change or changes very little within a species. On the other hand, measuring in centimeters gives distorted values as a small specimen will have a short organ while a very large specimen of the same species will have a long one.

As the length, shape, and ornamentation of the hemipenis vary from species to species, they are useful in the identification of the species and species groups. The coral snake's hemipenis is typically a bilobed or bifurcated organ. It has a sperm-carrying groove, the sulcus spermaticus, that runs from the base to the apex of the organ. The sulcus is also bifurcated and each fork reaches the apex of each of the lobes of the organ.

The two principal types of hemipenes of coral snakes are short and bilobed (Fig. 14) and long and bifurcated (Fig. 15). There also are several interesting

External Features

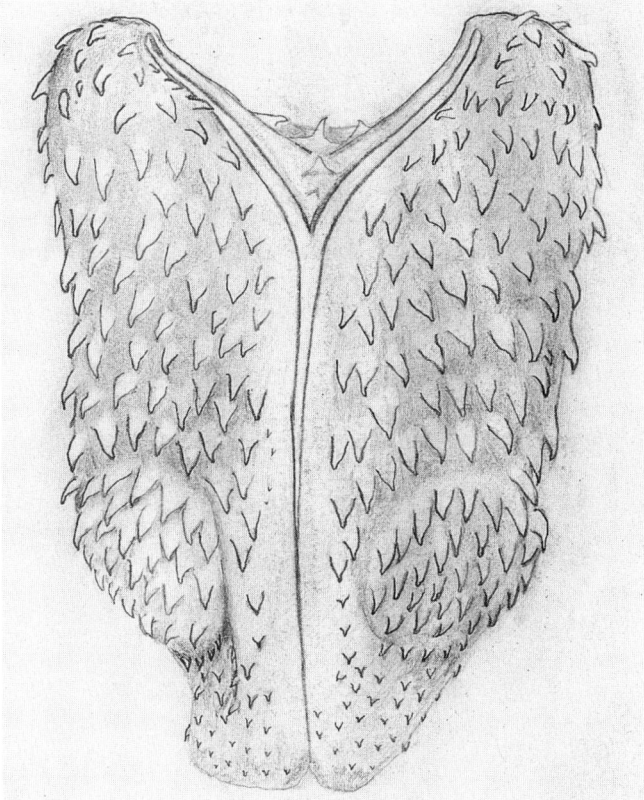

Figure 14. Short and bilobed hemipenis of *Micrurus lemniscatus diutius*. (Drawn by Samuel McDowell)

two lobes is almost naked, with only a few large spines. At the base of the organ on both sides of the sulcus starts a roundish elevated structure, outlined by a depressed line but covered by spines. The line is continuous around the hemipenis dividing the lower part, with somewhat smaller spines, from the upper part, with somewhat larger and less numerous spines. This dividing line and difference in the size of spines makes the organ partially capitated. In this area the large fleshy spines are arranged in alternating fashion somewhat reminiscent of calyculated arrangement. Several Old World elapids, such as *Oxyuranus*, have spines still arranged in groups of three as remnants of the calyces, not dissimilar to those found in *M. lemniscatus* and several other species of this group. At the base of the organ, opposite the sulcus, is a naked fold, without spines, that reaches up to the second subcaudal (not observable in Fig. 14). The ridge of the sulcus enfolding

variations corresponding to the genera *Micruroides* and *Leptomicrurus* and some species groups of *Micrurus*.

Short and Bilobed Hemipenis

The short and bilobed hemipenis is not more than 10 or 11 subcaudals long and it is covered in most of its length by conspicuous, somewhat fleshy spines. This type of hemipenis is found in all South American triad type species such as *M. lemniscatus*, *M. ancoralis*, *M. frontalis*, *M. filiformis*, *M. spixii*, *M. tschudii*, *M. ibiboboca*, *M. surinamensis*, *M. hemprichii*, *M. decoratus*, and *M. isozonus*.

In *M. lemniscatus diutius*, for example, the organ is about 8 subcaudals long (Fig. 14) with the lobation taking place at the seventh subcaudal. Each lobe is a roundish short extension of the organ. The sulcus divides at the end of the sixth subcaudal and reaches close to the apex of each lobe. The base of the organ is naked, but at the second subcaudal, small spines start. From the third subcaudal on, large, approximately uniform spines cover the entire organ. On the lobes, the spines are a little smaller, while those particularly near the apex of the organ have a broad fleshy base with a hard, slightly bent spiny apex. The region between the

Figure 15. Long and bifuracated hemipenis of *Micrurus fulvius tenere*. (Drawn by Samuel McDowell)

Figure 16. Hemipenis of *Micrurus frontalis brasiliensis*.

the groove is also naked. The sulcus itself ends shortly before reaching the apex of each lobe of the organ. *M. frontalis brasiliensis* (Fig. 16) and *M. ibiboboca* have the same partially capitate condition, while *M. spixii* (Fig. 17A) and the *M. surinamensis* (Fig. 17B) have no clear capitated condition. In the latter species the spines are fleshy.

In *M. tschudii* the hemipenis is also bilobed, about 8 or 9 subcaudals long with a bifurcated sulcus. The entire base of the organ is naked with horizontal folds up to the third subcaudal where small spines begin. The spines increase in size toward the apex, but decrease in size again, and are relatively small on the lobes of the organ where they are few and distributed around the calyces. Thus, the organ is partially calyculated without forming a clear capitate condition. The somewhat rhomboidal calyces have spines on each corner. The sulcus divides around the seventh subcaudal and reaches near to the apex of each lobe.

Long and Bifurcated Hemipenis

The long and bifurcated hemipenis is up to 19 subcaudals long, with a clearly bifurcated upper part that gradually tapers off and usually ends in a soft or hard terminal spine. It has a naked base and a long naked fold that reaches and penetrates into the area where large spines begin and where the sulcus divides. Large hard spines cover the middle part and each branch of the organ. This type of hemipenis is found in almost all single-banded coral snakes (genus *Micrurus*) of the United States, Mexico, Central America, and South America (see section on coloration); in accessory triad-type species in South America such as in several subspecies of *M. dumerilii*, *M. sangilensis*, and *M. bocourti*; as well as in species with triad-type color pattern such as *M. laticollaris* and *M. elegans* from Mexico and Guatemala.

M. fulvius tenere, as representative of this group, has a bifurcated hemipenis around 16 subcaudals long (Fig. 15). The bifurcation takes place around the 9th or 10th subcaudal. The sulcus divides around the 8th or 9th subcaudal and each fork continues to the apex of the organ. The base of the organ is naked. Spinules and a few small spines begin at the third subcaudal and gradually increase in size until one subcaudal below the point where the sulcus bifurcates. At that level, large calcified spines appear and continue on each fork of the hemipenis but gradually diminish in size again toward the apex. The largest spines are around the area of bifurcation of the organ. Both forks of the organ gradually taper off toward the apex and end in a hard terminal spine, larger than the spines just below the

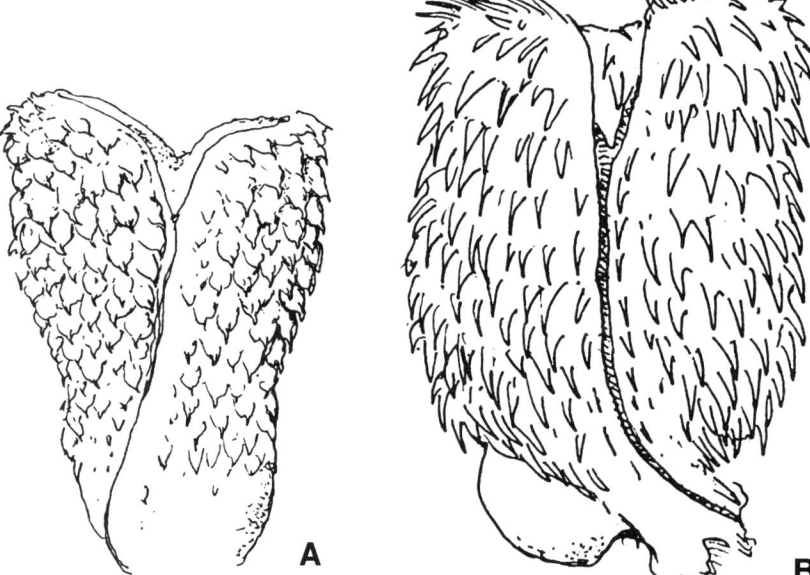

Figure 17. Comparison of spines of hemipenes: A) *Micrurus spixii obscurus* with fleshy spines, B) *Micrurus surinamensis surinamensis* with non-fleshy spines. (Drawn by Samuel McDowell.)

apex. A large naked fold runs from the base of the organ to the level where the sulcus bifurcates. The ridge of the sulcus is naked as is the area where the sulcus and the organ bifurcate.

The hemipenis of *M. diastema* is 14 to 16 subcaudals long, and the bifurcation starts at around the 10th subcaudal. The base of the organ is naked up to the level of the 4th subcaudal where tiny spines appear on the sulcus ridge. The largest spines are between the 8th and 11th subcaudal, and the naked fold extends from the base to about the 7th or 8th subcaudal. *M. distans* (Fig. 18A and B) has a similar hemipenis: it is only 13 subcaudals long, while the hemipenis of *M. bernadi* is 19 subcaudals long. The subspecies of *M. nigrocinctus* show some variation. *M. n. nigrocinctus* from Costa Rica has the upper part of the bifurcated extension tapering off to an almost whiplike structure (Fig. 20A) while the bifurcated portion of *M. n. divaricatus* is stouter and less whiplike (Fig. 20B), as is also the hemipenis of *M. n. mosquitensis* and that of *M. n. zunilensis*. *M. corallinus* also has a whiplike ending of the bifurcated organ.

A long and bifurcated hemipenis is also found in *M. latifasciatus*, but it is entirely naked up and beyond the level of bifurcation of the organ. The spines, small in size, appear near the apex of each fork. The hemipenis of this species (Fig. 19) was first described by Edward D. Cope (1895, 1900), the first herpetologist to use the characteristics of the hemipenis in the classification of snakes. Yet, he did not realize that the hemipenis was not completely opened (he studied it in situ by cutting open the inverted organ). Moreover, he used a different name for this species, *M. corallinus*, a species actually found in Brazil and not in Central America, where his specimen came from. *M. laticollaris* has a hemipenis 13 to 14 subcaudals long with bifurcation on the 8th subcaudal and with larger spines appearing about one subcaudal above the bifurcation of the organ. Near the apex are uniformly small spines that seem to form partially calyculated ornaments.

A long and bifurcated hemipenis is found also in such species as *M. alleni, M. browni, M. langsdorffi, M. putumayensis, M. proximans, M. steindachneri, M. peruvianus, M. mertensi, M. limbatus, M. ephippifer*, and several more.

Variations of Hemipenes

Several coral snakes have hemipenes that are different from the two types described above. A short but deeply bilobed hemipenis is found in genus *Micruroides*, while the hemipenis of *Leptomicrurus* is somewhat longer. The hemipenis of the *M. euryxanthus* (Fig. 21) is about 7 to 8 subcaudals long with short bifurcation (or bilobation) and a bifurcated sulcus that reaches to the apex of the organ. For about two subcaudals the base of the organ is naked followed by spines that continue to the tip of the bifurcation. However, on each side of the sulcus, as well as on the naked portion, a few scattered spinules extend downward to nearly the base of the hemipenis. At the level where the spines begin, the organ is slightly expanded and wider than the rest of the adjacent zones, suggesting a capitate condition. A longitudinal naked fold runs parallel to the sulcus

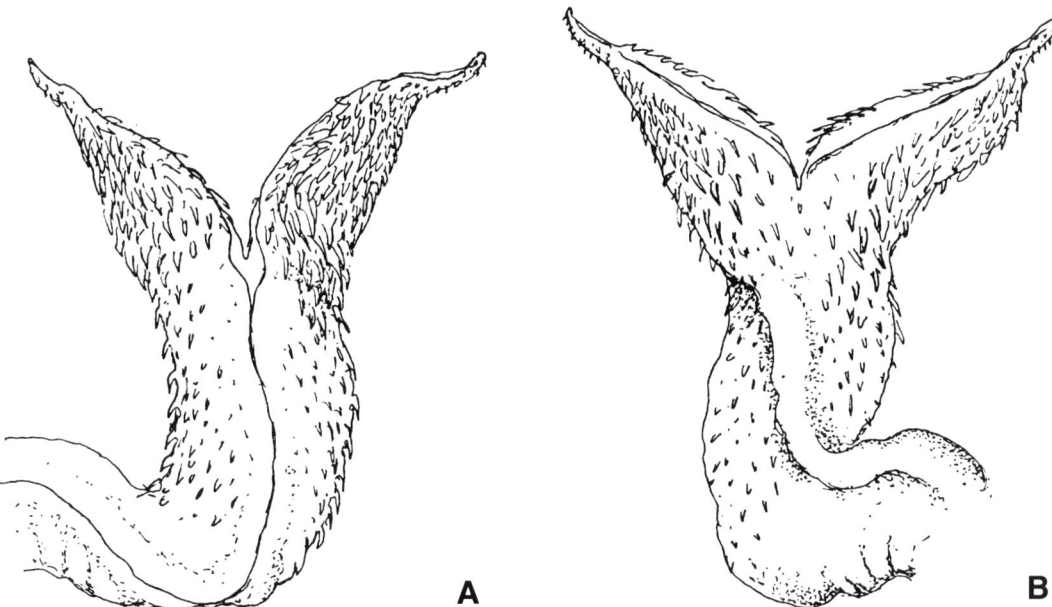

Figure 18. Hemipenis of *Micrurus distans distans* (MCZ 32013): A) Sulcate side, B) Asulcate side, showing smooth longitudinal fold opposite sulcus. (Drawn by Samuel McDowell.)

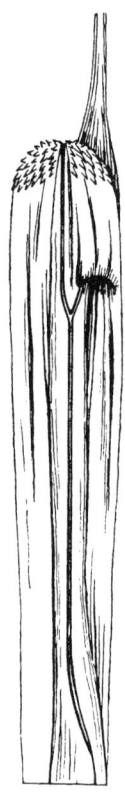

Figure 19. Outline of hemipenis of *Micrurus latifasciatus*, opened in situ. (From Cope, 1898 and 1900.)

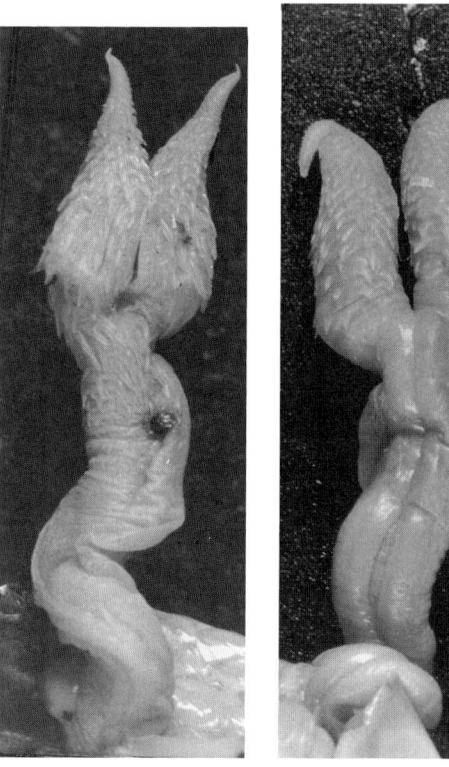

Figure 20. Hemipenis of *Micrurus nigrocinctus*: A) *M. n. nigrocinctus*, B) *M. n. divaricatus* (UM 69391).

Figure 21. Hemipenis of *Micruroides e. euryxanthus*. (Drawn by Frances Zweifel.)

from near the base to the area of the expansion of the organ. The area between the fold and the sulcus is covered by a few spinules. The spines are largest around the bifurcation of the organ but diminish in size toward the apex. Each fork of the organ ends in a small spinelike structure that is somewhat smaller than the surrounding apical spines.

L. scutiventris has a hemipenis 7 to 9, and occasionally up to 11, subcaudals long. The organ is bifurcated, with the sulcus also bifurcated (Fig. 22). Small spines start around the 2nd or 3rd subcaudal and gradually increase in size, but uniformly sized spines cover most of the organ. They diminish again in size toward the apex. The apex is slightly blunt with no terminal spine. A small naked fold runs from the base of the organ to about the area where larger spines begin. *L. n. melanotus* has a similar hemipenis but it is 13 to 15 subcaudals long. Hemipenes of *Micrurus meridensis* (Fig. 23A) and *Micrurus mipartitus* (Fig. 23B) show intermediate characteristics between the long-bifurcated and short-bilobed organs. In *M. mipartitus* the organ is about 11 subcaudals long and bifurcates around the 8th subcaudal. Small spines start from the third subcaudal and increase in size around the bifurcation but diminish again toward the apex. However, the small spines at the apex are distributed around poorly formed calyces. No naked fold, or at most a very small fold at the base can be distinguished.

Occasionally, interesting variation or abnormal development appears in the structure of the hemipenis. One such interesting specimen with a perhaps incompletely everted hemipenis is deposited in the National Museum of Natural History (USNM 193814) representing *M. annellatus* (Fig. 24) which normally has a hemi-

External Features

Figure 22. Hemipenis of *Leptomicrurus scutiventris*. (Drawn by Samuel McDowell.)

penis about 17 subcaudals long. In this specimen, the organ is reduced in size but apparently has spines of normal size that look enormous in comparison with the size of the hemipenis. Also, the bifurcated portion is reduced but the terminal spine is clearly present.

No easily distinguishable differences between the species are found in the reproductive organs of females. The spines and other structures of the hemipenis are apparently coordinated with structural extensions found in the oviduct that help to keep the organ in place during copulation.

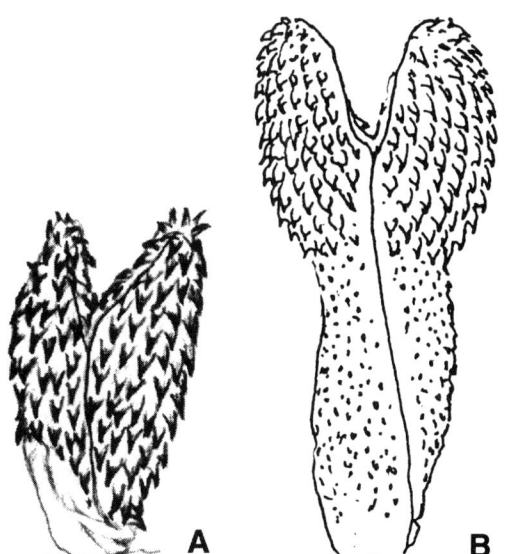

Figure 23. Hemipenis of two species with intermediate form of hemipenis: A) *Micrurus meridensis* (USNM 217256), B) *Micrurus mipartitus decussatus* (Renjifo collection 239). (Drawn by Samuel McDowell)

Figure 24. Hemipenis of *Micrurus annellatus annellatus* (USNM 193814).

Coloration and Diversity of Color Patterns

The brilliance of the red, black, and yellow color patterns of coral snakes has few rivals in the realm of snakes. The very name, coral snake, emphasizes its distinctive mark: the intensely red bands.

Within certain limitations, the coloration of each species and subspecies is surprisingly constant and is one of the best features for the identification of coral snakes. It also serves to establish relationships among the species and define groups of species with similar color patterns.

Several biologists have analyzed the rich diversity of color patterns of snakes, including coral snakes. The Swiss zoologist Adolf Portmann (1964), with his keen interest in colors and patterns in animal kingdom, and his associate Marianne von Harnack (1953) have studied animal color patterns of coral snakes within the total gestalt of a species. Based on his observations of color patterns and other features, Portmann suggested an interesting concept, *selbstdarstellung* (self-representation), a kind of primary characteristic of life forms in which the coloration is an integral part. Undoubtedly, color patterns of coral snakes are of considerable importance within the biogestalt of the species. The aposematic coloration serves to advertise the coral snake's venomous nature and its display is used for defense as well as concealment (see section on enemies and defense). These distinctive color patterns have also stimulated the appearance of many mimicry companions (see section on mimicry).

I follow the terminology of color patterns that has been developed by Schmidt (1936a) and Dunn (1954) with some additions and modifications and with a description of the special cases and aberrations in coral snakes that do not fit in any standard color pattern. Other authors who have contributed to the terminology of color patterns of coral snakes are Taylor and Smith (1943), Klauber (1943), Mertens (1956), Savage and Vial (1974), Savage (1980), and many more who have dealt with venomous or false coral snakes. More recently, Campbell and Lamar (1989) used a terminology distinguishing bicolored and tricolored coral snakes.

A useful terminology for the basic color patterns of coral snakes, venomous and nonvenomous, was also proposed by Savage and Slowinski (1990). They distinguished several basic color patterns: unicolor, consisting of uniform red dorsum (not known in elapids except as aberration); bicolor, alternating bands of black and light (red, yellow, or white; called bicolor in this book, as in *M. multifasciatus*); and tricolor, alternating black, red, and light bands. They divided the latter into five additional patterns: tricolor monads with red bands separated by light-black-light sequence (called single-banded in this book, as in *M. fulvius*); tricolor dyads (not known in elapids), with red bands separated by alternating black-light-black bands; tricolor triads with red bands separated by black-light-black-light-black (called triad-type or accessory black triads in this book, as in *M. frontalis* and *M. sangilensis*, respectively); tricolor tetrads with red bands separated by black-light-black-light-black (not known in elapids); and tricolor pentads with red bands separated by black-light-black-light-black-light-black-light-black (found in elapids only when abnormal fusion of two adjacent triads has occurred).

As red color bands in preserved specimens are indistinguishable from yellow or white bands, a terminology based on recognition of red bands as the principal reference would be useful only when the coloration of living specimens is known. Some coral snakes, such as *M. nigrocinctus zunilensis*, can have a bicolor pattern and tricolor monad pattern. Moreover, some exceptional color patterns of coral snakes do not fit into their terminology.

In describing color pattern, I used relatively few standard terms, albeit with a less rigorous terminology: single-banded coral snakes, triad-type coral snakes, accessory triad-type pattern, bicolor, and variations that do not fit in any (see below).

Body and Tail

The basic color pattern of coral snakes, with several interesting exceptions, consists of red, black, and yellow or white crossbands of different lengths and arrangements. The term *band* is used in preference to ring, because a ring can also be interpreted as a round ring figure on the back, as it is found in several boid snakes. The bands can be complete or incomplete and the length of each band is measured along the length of the body in number of dorsals and ventrals from its anterior to its posterior border. As the bands as a rule completely surround the body, they can also be seen on the belly. In addition to the body bands, the head and tail coloration also form an integral part of the banded color pattern.

The color appears particularly clean and intense immediately after the snake has shed its old skin. Shortly before shedding, all color bands become somewhat opaque and relatively drab because the external epidermal layer of the skin to be shed has grayish-whitish overtones that make the coloration beneath look dull.

Unfortunately, the beautiful red and yellow coloration of the coral snakes completely disappears in preservative. Thus, after a while museum specimens have only black and white bands. The red, yellow, and originally white bands or spots are uniformly white. It is for this reason that in species that are known only from preserved specimens, such as *M. spurrelli*, the original coloration in life is unknown.

Although reddish brown is found in occasional specimens, in life the red bands are usually intensely coral to dark red. In the light bands that can be yellow or white, the yellow is predominant in some species, such as *M. fulvius*, while in many other coral snakes the light bands can be either yellow or white, depending on the species. The yellow bands vary from intensely yellow, pale yellow, even yellowish green as in *M. spixii obscurus* (Color 56), to greenish white, creamy white or plain white. Some species, such as *M. lemniscatus* (Color 38), almost invariably have only white bands. In very large and old individuals the white bands occasionally have reddish or pinkish overtones. In South American species, white and creamy white bands are more frequent than yellow bands, while in North America yellow coloration predominates. As the white or yellow bands are usually very short, they serve to outline and enhance the stunning contrast of the much longer red and black bands.

The black bands are pitch black or, occasionally, bluish black. The anterior border of the black bands usually forms a straight line across the body, while its posterior border more or less follows and covers the entire scales (Pattern 1), forming a slightly roundish zigzag line due to the alternate disposition of the dorsal scales.

In many species, the red dorsal scales (sometimes the white as well) have black or brownish-black tips. The black tips on red scales vary from small black dots that are hardly perceptible to large spots occupying one half or more of the scale, as in *M. pyrrhocryptus* (Pattern 42). These black tips can be regular in size or irregular, making the red look spotted with black and less brilliant. In *M. f. fulvius*, for example, some specimens have abundant irregular black tips or spots, while others have very few or lack them altogether, as in some individuals from the southern tip of Florida (Pattern 23). In some species, such as *M. psyches* (Color 52), and *M. medemi*, the red can turn reddish-purple due to the invasion of blackish overtones. In several Amazonian coral snakes, such as *M. langsdorffi*, the red can be almost completely obliterated by black so that the red bands can be seen only on the belly. In the Amazon basin, there is a tendency toward reduction and obliteration of the red coloration, a kind of "Amazonian melanism phenomenon."

In larger and older individuals of all species of coral snakes, the intensity of red and yellow bands fades and the borders of the black bands become blurred. The black pigment tends to invade partially other bands resulting in a "progressive aging melanism."

The variety of coloration found in coral snakes can be reduced to four basic types of body color patterns: (1) single-banded, (2) triad-type coloration, (3) accessory triad-type color pattern, and (4) an array of others, usually bicolor patterns, that we will review briefly.

Single-banded Pattern

The most common is the single-banded color pattern that consists of single red and black bands separated by short yellow or white bands. In this pattern, the sequence of bands on the body is red-yellow-black-yellow-red and so on (Color 6). At least 27 species or 60 species and subspecies have the single-banded pattern. Several modifications have been derived from the single-banded pattern. Many individuals of *M. n. zunilensis* (Pattern 40) from Guatemala, for example, have lost the white bands resulting in a red-black-banded coral snake. In some subspecies of *M. diastema* and *M. nigrocinctus divaricatus* the white bands are sometimes reduced, almost nonexistent, and the red bands may have irregular black spots. The extreme of this pattern is found in some specimens of *M. e. ephippifer* in Tehuantepec, Mexico, in which the entire dorsal portion of the red band is black, while laterally and ventrally the red bands are clearly visible (Pattern 27). The Mexican coral snake, *M. bernadi*, has a red body on which the black bands are mostly reduced to black dorsal spots, sometimes without a yellow border (Pattern 7). A dramatic departure from the basic single-banded pattern is shown by such species as *M. stewarti* in which very large and irregular black bands or body spots are separated by irregular red bands. This pattern is probably produced by melanistic expansion of the many black tips on the red scales. It appears that these black tips have fused with the original black bands (Pattern 48).

Triad-type Coloration

The triad-type coloration consists of sets of three black bands separated by white, creamy-white, or yellow bands. Each triad, in turn, is separated from the next triad by a red band. The sequence of body bands in the triad-type color pattern is red-black-white (or yellow)-black-white-black-red, and so on (Color 14).

The black-white-black-white-black sequence constitutes one full triad. In *M. hemprichii* the triads (or fused triads as in *M. h. rondonianus* (Color 32) the latter) are separated not by red but by yellowish sepia bands. The total number and length of individual bands is important in distinguishing the 15 species, or 46 species and subspecies, that have the triad-type color pattern. All except two of the triad species are distributed in South America. In most species the triad pattern also continues on the tail. Interesting variations are found in the first triad situated immediately behind the head. In the majority of species the first triad is complete, i.e., consists of all three black bands before the first red body band (Color 27). In abbreviating the information on the number of complete triads, a specimen that has 12 body triads and two triads on the tail will be characterized as having 12+2 triads. In other species, such as *M. spixii obscurus* (Color 56), the first triad is not complete, consisting of only two black bands before the first red body band. In this case, we would say that the first black band of the first triad is absent. The triad formula of a specimen with this condition and five complete body bands, and with one complete tail band and two bands of the last triad on the tail is 2/3 5+1 2/3 triads. *M. dissoleucus* (Pattern 17) and *M. meridensis* have the first triad represented only by one black band. A specimen of this species with seven complete body triads would be characterized by a formula of 1/3 7+ 2/3. A somewhat different arrangement is found in *M. laticollaris* (Pattern 29) from Mexico and Guatemala. Its body is covered by triads, but the tail displays only single black-white bands. Moreover, the last triad on the body is also incomplete, consisting of only two black bands. In this case, the body triad formula might be, for example, 2/3 5 2/3 + (4), which would mean that this specimen has four single black tail bands. *M. elegans*, (Color 20) also from Mexico and Guatemala, has only one black band left from the last body triad. An example of its triad formula might be 2/3 10 1/3 + (8).

Accessory Triad-type Color Pattern

The accessory triad-type color pattern also consists of 3 black bands, forming a triad separated from the next triad by a red band. In accessory triads the central black band is several times longer than the outer bands. The outer black bands are quite irregular and vary in shape and size. These accessory triads apparently have been developed from single-banded patterns in which the black pigment on red scales has been concentrated along their border with the yellow bands, forming a short and quite irregular accessory black band. For example, *M. dumerilii* has four subspecies (*carinicauda, antioquiensis, transandinus* and *venezuelensis*) that are single-banded, but two (*dumerilii* and *colombianus*) (see Fig. 55, p. 164) with accessory-type color pattern. In some single-banded species such as *M. circinalis* (Pattern 11) there are some specimens in which the black tips on red scales tend to concentrate along the yellow borders, giving an impression of the beginning of an accessory black band.

Other Color Patterns

The rest of the species have interesting variations of alternating single bands of usually bicolor pattern. They can be red-black as in *M. nigrocinctus zunilensis* (Pattern 40) or *M. diastema apiatus*, apparently originated from the loss of yellow or white bands. In other bicolor species such as *M. limbatus spilosomus* (Color 41) and *M. bernadi* (Pattern 7), the regular black bands have been changed into irregular dorsal or ventral spots.

A special group of bicolor species is represented by *mipartitus-multifasciatus-multiscutatus-spurrelli*. They have either only black-red body bands as in *M. multifasciatus* (Color 45) or only black-white body bands as in *M. mipartitus* (Color 44). Yet, in both groups the head and tail are covered by intensely red bands.

In some Amazonian species the red bands have been completely replaced by black pigment, resulting in a black coral snake in which a series of pearly white spots form crossbands that separate the original black bands from the original red bands that have turned black, as in *M. albicinctus* (Color 5). In other species, such as *M. langsdorffi* (Colors 36 and 37), specimens exist with red and black bands clearly distinguishable, and others with only black bands always separated by scant white bands. In these specimens, the red bands that have turned partially or totally black can still be seen as red on the belly. Occasional specimens have only red and yellowish-grey bands with no black bands.

An extreme coloration is found in the species of *Leptomicrurus*. They have the dorsal part of the body uniformly black, and red or white spots are present only on the belly as, for example, in *L. scutiventris* or *L. narduccii* (Color 3). In the latter, some dorsal spots behind the head reach across the back and form short light crossbands.

Head Coloration

The head coloration shows some variation that is quite helpful in identifying many species and subspecies. As the head coloration is described in some detail under each species and subspecies, I will give here only a brief summary of the more important color patterns. The upper part of the head can be all black without a black nuchal band, as in the genus *Micruroides* (Color 4) and in *M. averyi* (Color 9). The head can be almost entirely black, including parietals, in which case we speak of a cephalic black cap or simply a black cap as in *M. dumerilii* (Pattern 20). In other species the snout is black, followed by one or more red and/or white yellow crossbands. If white and red crossbands are present, they are separated, usually by a black crossband, as in *M. lemniscatus* (Color 38). In some species such as *M. frontalis*, the head can be quite irregularly covered by black, red and white spots and bands. Below, the chin or neck is usually white or partially red. The mental and several of the first infralabials are usually black in many species. In such species as *M. clarki*, the chin is all white with the infracephalic shields weakly outlined in grey. Large spots are present on the chin shields in some species. Also of importance is the placement of the black nuchal band that might or might not reach and cover the tips of the parietal (Color 12). Some interesting head ornamentations are present in such species as *M. spurrelli* (Pattern 47) and, occasionally, also in *M. diastema aglaeope* (Color 15). The latter as well as others, such as *M. distans* (Color 18) and *M. diastema apiatus*, have a light snout or light spots on the snout and supralabials.

Color Aberrations

Once in a while these well-defined color patterns show interesting aberrations. They are presumably caused by genetic variations that are quite different from the regular color pattern of that species. These can be pigment aberrations, pattern aberrations, or a combination.

In pigment aberrations, also called chromatic displacement, one color is replaced by another. Melanism or all-black coloration found in otherwise banded species appears once in a while, such as in a uniformly black specimen of *M. fulvius tenere* reported by Gloyd (1938). Another example of pigment divergence from the usual is reported in *M. elegans veraepacis* by Schmidt (1936b) who observed live specimens in which the red bands were replaced by yellow or brownish yellow, while the original yellow bands were white (see also color photo in Campbell and Lamar, 1989). A milder version of color aberration is found in what has been called hyperxanthism, a condition of dark and very strong yellow bands as observed in *M. f. fulvius* (H. M. Smith and Ross, 1970) or occasionally in *M. e. euryxanthus*.

Color pattern aberrations are produced essentially by reduction, displacement, or fusion of the black bands. In normal single-banded coral snakes the black bands occasionally can be incomplete ventrally or reduced to irregular dorsal spots. This is occasionally found in *M. f. fulvius* (Meachen and Myers, 1961; Neill, 1963). In desert or dry regions, coral snakes show a tendency to reduce or even lose black bands. The holotype of *M. diastema alienus* is uniformly red above, with a black head and an incomplete nuchal band. The body in its entire length is uniformly red to the tail, where four long black bands are present. A very similar specimen of the same species was collected in 1973 by two herpetologists from the American Museum of Natural History, Grace Tilger and Carol Leavens, in Quintana Roo, near Puerto Juarez, Mexico. It is interesting to note that a false coral snake from Yucatán (*Lampropeltis triangulum blanchardi*) tends to exhibit the same reduction of black body bands or pigment, suggesting a faithful mimicry imitation. *M. diastema diastema*, however, living in a warm and humid environment, also occasionally exhibits the reduction of black bands to dorsal spots.

In triad-type coral snakes, the black bands tend to fuse and develop different color patterns. The most common fusion occurs between two triads in which the two outer black bands fuse, eliminating the red band between them. The result is a series of five consecutive black bands separated by yellow bands that is called quinquad. I have observed quinquads in all triad-type coral snakes (see also Azevedo, 1962a).

Occasionally, the black bands get split in half and displaced along the middorsal or midventral line, or they can form a diverse kind of aberrant black spots (see also Amaral, 1932a; Azevedo, 1962a). Some species do not display a well-defined color pattern but have many types of color patterns. One example of such polychromatism or polymorphism is found in *M. langsdorffi* as described by Soini (1974a).

Examples of aberrations that include both pigment and pattern modifications are albino coral snakes. The National Museum of Natural History in Washington D.C. has a preserved specimen of an albino *M. f. fulvius* in which the body is somewhat uniformly light without any black bands. (see also Hensley, 1959). Similar to albinism are examples of two amelanistic specimens of *M. corallinus* described by Hoge and Belluomini (1959) that had a total absence of black coloration. These two juveniles had only red and light rosy bands, the latter corresponding to the original black bands. Remarkably, both snakes were somewhat translucent with reddish eyes and rosy tongue, a coloration apparently produced by red blood cells in the peripheral blood vessels. In coral snakes, in spite of the red skin pigment, the occurrence of erythrism—the tendency to have all-red coloration—seems to be an albino-like condition and can also be called amelanism.

Size and Growth

One of the most frequently asked questions about coral snakes is, "How large are they?" This question does not have a simple answer because there are many species of coral snakes, each with its own size range.

Like most reptiles, coral snakes grow for their entire lives, but the rate of growth decreases as they "grow old." For each species, however, there is a genetically determined size range and we speak of small and large species as they are found in nature. To determine the genetic size potential of a species we need to measure many specimens. A large sample from a population will more likely include the smallest and the largest specimens than would a small sample. From a widely collected species, the "largest of the large" specimen will be found in some museum's collection, while the few known specimens from a less abundant and collected species might not represent the largest possible size. For example, *M. f. fulvius* is only a medium-large species, yet after several hundred years of active collecting, the longest known specimen is 1295 mm long, as reported by McCollough and Gennaro (1963b).

Longest and Shortest Coral Snake

The longest measured specimen for any species is that of *M. spixii princeps* from Santa Cruz de la Sierra, Bolivia, deposited in the Carnegie Museum, Pittsburgh (CM 126). Its overall length is 1,602 mm (5 ft, 3 in). As its tail seems to be incomplete, the actual length of the specimen was even greater. The second longest measured specimen with an overall length of 1520 mm represents a related subspecies, *M. spixii martiusi*, collected in 1915 in Campo Oriramba, Brazilian Guiana and currently in the Zoologisches Staatsmuseum, München, Germany (ZSBS 124/1915). As the other subspecies of *M. spixii* are also more than 1 meter long, this species can be considered the largest species of coral snake. The second largest species, *M. ancoralis*, is distributed in the Andes, as represented by a specimen of *M. a. ancoralis* with an overall length of 1486 mm, deposited in the British Museum (Natural History). The third largest species seems to be *M. lemniscatus*, because the length of all subspecies is more than 1 meter and a specimen of *M. l. helleri*, collected in Brazil and deposited in the Zoologisches Museum, Berlin, Germany, is 1390 mm long. In all, 14 species, coral snakes reach the length of more than 1 meter.

In measuring and reporting the overall length of specimens, some difficulties are encountered. Some specimens have been preserved for a long time or preserved in a liquid that has made them stiff, and hardened and twisted specimens are difficult to measure with precision. One way for partially overcoming the twisted specimen dilemma is to measure its length with a string running along the middorsal or midventral line. The length then can be obtained by measuring the string.

Another difficulty is created by comparing measurements from preserved specimens with freshly collected specimens. A recently collected specimen, re-

Table 1. Longest Measured Specimens for Species and Subspecies of Coral Snakes

Species	Sex	Museum & Number	Locality	Total length (mm)	Tail length (mm)
Leptomicrurus					
L. collaris collaris	M	AMNH	Brownsberg, Suriname	456	29
L. c. breviventris	M	FMNH 26658	Oko Mts, Guyana	388	28
L. narduccii narduccii	F	UM 69565	Buenavista, Santa Cruz, Bolivia	606	24
L. n. melanotus	F	USNM 232473	Río Corrientes, Pastaza, Ecuador	1,117	40
L. scutiventris	F	ANSP	Pebas, Peru	445	
Micruroides					
M. euryxanthus euryxanthus	F	FASC 9328	5 mi. N Wickenburg, Arizona, USA	551	
M. e. australis	M	ASDM 1212	10 mi. SE Alamos, Sonora, Mexico	440	39
M. e. neglectus	M	UMMZ 114637	16.3 mi. NW of Mazatlán, Sinaloa, Mexico	430	39
Micrurus					
M. albicinctus	M	Dresden	São Paulo de Olivenca, Brazil	600	
M. alleni	F	UFLA 31267	Río Frío, Heredia, Panama	1,165	105
M. ancoralis ancoralis	F	BM 1946.1.23.74	Paramba, Ecuador	1,486	84
M. a. jani	M	USNM 151718	Colombia ?	1,350	99
M. annellatus annellatus	F	FMNH 40199	Universidad de Arequipa, Peru	728	63
M. a. balzani	M	Genoa Mus. Type	Jungas, Bolivia	650	53
M. a. bolivianus	F	HM 2758	Jungas de Cochabamba, Bolivia	590	45
M. averyi	F	MZUSP	Reserva Ducke, Manaus Amazonas, Brazil	715	60
M. bernadi	M	UM 85967	Nexaca, Puebla, Mexico	504	66
M. bocourti	F	BM 1931 10.21.22	Ancón, SW Ecuador	820	73
M. bogerti	F	UIMNH 56835	N of Zanatepec, Sierra Madre, Oaxaca, Mexico	870	91
M. browni browni	F	MCZ 33666	Chilpancingo, Guerrero	830	90
M. b. importunus	M	BM 64.1.26.41A	Dueñas, Guatemala	836	120
M. b. taylori	M	FMNH 100051	Acapulco, Guerrero, Mexico	799	121
M. catamayensis	F	BM 1935 11.3.11	Loja, Ecuador	915	73
M. circinalis	F	FMNH 75953	Maraval, Trinidad	537	51
M. clarki	F	AMNH 119897	Cerro Azul, Panama	832	111
M. corallinus	F	MCZ 17861	São Paulo, Brazil	987	84
M. decoratus	F	NMB 2282	Brazil	638	43
M. diana	M	FMNH 195889	Serranía de Santiago, Pv.Chiquiticos, Boliva	998	54
M. diastema diastema	F	MHNB 689E	Mexico	895	84
M. d. affinis	F	AMNH 89632	San Lucas, Camotlán, Oaxaca, Mexico	735	80
M. d. aglaeope	M	ANSP 6858	Honduras	721	111
M. d. alienus	F	EWA 398	Mérida, Yucatán, Mexico	885	68
M. d. apiatus	F	AMNH 99977	Barillas, Huehuetenango, Guatemala	850	88
M. d. macdougalli	M	UIMNH 35632	La Gloria, Oaxaca, Mexico	633	98
M. d. sapperi	F	UMMZ 76126	Uxpermul, Campeche, Mexico	810	91
M. dissoleucus dissoleucus	F	NMB 2309	Maracaibo, Zulia, Venezuela	620	39
M. d. dunni	F	MCZ 38244	Panama City, Panama	376	29
M. d. melanogenys	M	CM 206	Bonda, Colombia	366	30
M. d. nigrirostris	M	NMB 14333	Colombia	384	30
M. distans distans	F	UCLA 2989	Guirocoba, Sonora, Mexico	1,075	103
M. d. michoacanensis	F	Dugès Museum	Tecpán de Galeana, Guerrero, Mexico	865	88
M. d. oliveri	F	AMNH 19837	East of Manzanillo, Colima, Mexico	950	110
M. d. zweifeli	F	USNM 37374	Magdalena, Jalisco, Mexico	810	80
M. dumerilii dumerilii	F	ANSP 6856	New Granada	922	83
M. d. antioquiensis	F	MLS 506	Segovia, Antioquia, Colombia	854	96
M. d. carinicauda	M	FMNH 2587	Orope, Táchira, Venezuela	775	122
M. d. colombianus	F	CM 197	Minca, Magdalena, Colombia	623	56

(*Continued*)

Table 1. (*Continued*)

Species	Sex	Museum & Number	Locality	Total length (mm)	Tail length (mm)
M. d. transandinus	F	FMNH 78109	Villa Arteaga, Antioquia, Colombia	948	inc
M. d. venezuelensis	F	NMW	San Esteban, Carabobo Venezuela	701	70
M. elegans elegans	F	AMNH 19720	Doubtful locality (D.F., Mexico)	555	48
M. e. veraepacis	F	BM 1946.1.21.39	Low forest, Verapaz, Guatemala	733	70
M. ephippifer ephippifer	F	AMNH 67960	Tehuatepec, Oaxaca, Mexico	926	75 inc
M. e. zapotecus	F	AMNH	Telixtlahuaca, Oaxaca, Mexico	758	75
M. filiformis		119232 MPEG	Cunha and Nascimento, 1978	960	
M. frontalis frontalis	M	UMMZ 63023	São Paulo, Brazil	1,190	56
M. f. altirostris	M	BM 1874 10.9.25	Departamento Soriano, Uruguay	878	41
M. f. baliocoryphus	M	CHINM 1823	Villa Federal Entre Ríos, Argentina	826	inc
M. f. brasiliensis	M	IB 33895	Brasilia, Territorio Federal, Brazil	1,122	
M. f. multicinctus	F	IB 7379	Tamarinde, Paraná, Brazil	687	
M. frontifasciatus	M	NMH Type	Bolivia	1,040	75
M. fulvius fulvius			McCollough and Genaro, 1963	1,295	
M. f. fitzingeri	F	USNM 10231	Guanajuato, Guanajuato, Mexico	850	74
M. f. maculatus	F	BM 1936 6.6.11	Tampico, Tamaulipas Mexico	722	65
M. f. microgalbineus	M	LSU 307	Xilitla, S.L.P., Mexico	736	71
M. f. tenere		EAL 2372	US 77, Kennedy County, Texas. Liner & Chaney, 1974	1,130	
M. hemprichii hemprichii	M	UPR R26(0-17)	Base Marahuaca, Amazonas, Venezuela	810	
M. h. ortoni	M	AMNH 28816	Luoula, río Upana, Ecuador	917	75
M. h. rondonianus	UCG	3145	Hydroelectric power plant Samuel, Rondônia, Brazil	819	59
M. hippocrepis	M	BM 1895 2.21.2	British Honduras, Belize	710	97
M. ibiboboca	M	SMF 9428a	Ilheus, Brazil	1,330	75
M. isozonus	F	AMNH 36066	Limão, Rio Caatinga Roraima, Brazil	885	63
M. langsdorffi	F	AMNH 52355	Iquitos, Peru	770	60
M. laticollaris laticollaris	M	KU 25928	12 mi S of Cuautla, Morelos, Mexico	728	82
M. l. maculirostris	M	KU 32546	Colima, Colima, Mexico	615	77
M. latifasciatus	F	AMNH 99975	Finca San Cristobal, Escuintla, Guatemala	1,140	123
M. lemniscatus lemniscatus	M	MNHN 4641	Guayane	1,060	87
M. l. carvalhoi	F	IB 16335	Pitanquiras, Brazil	1,310	90
M. l. diutius	M	MZUSP 4792	Oriximina, Pará, Brazil	1,173	106
M. l. helleri	M	ZMB 10846	Brazil	1,390	127
M. limbatus limbatus	F	UMMZ 123858	S slope, Volcán San Martín, Veracruz, Mexico	585	50
M. l. spilosomus	F	UNAM-LT 2733	Bastonal, Sierra de Sta. Marta, Veracruz, Mexico	550	50
M. margaritiferus	F	MVZ 163327	Vicinity of Huampami, río Cenepa, Peru	615	54
M. medemi	M	ILS 576	Villavicencio, Meta, Colombia	666	111
M. meridensis	M	USNM 217256	Lagunilla, Mérida, Venezuela	390	
M. mertensi	F	ANSP 11504	Valle de Jequetepeque, Peru	1,115	90
M. mipartitus mipartitus	M	AMNH 109783	Río Saija, Cauca, Colombia	522	inc
M. m. anomalus	F	NMW	Mérida, Venzuela	795	50
M. m. decussatus	F	AMNH 35526	Medellín, Colombia	1,005	47
M. m. semipartitus	F	CM 7290	Puerto La Cruz, D.F., Venezuela	840	60
M. multifasciatus multifasciatus	F	MCZ 26768	France Field, canal zone, Panama	878	46
M. m. hertwigi			Picado, 1931	1,130	
M. multiscutatus	F	NHMST (Holotype) 3131a	El Tambo, Cauca, Colombia	842	
M. nebularis	F	AMNH 91110	Rancho Teja, Ixtlán de Juárez, Oaxaca, Mexico	840	82
M. nigrocinctus nigrocinctus	F	KU 86261	San Antonio, Chinandega, Nicaragua	1,150	115

(*Continued*)

Table 1. (Continued)

Species	Sex	Museum & Number	Locality	Total length (mm)	Tail length (mm)
M. n. babaspul	M	AMNH 96996	Little Hill, Great Corn Island, Nicaragua	555	80
M. n. coibensis	M	BM 26.1.20.76	Isla La Coiba, Panama	476	60
M. n. divaricatus	F	MCZ 33342	Lancetilla, Honduras	1,080	111
M. n. mosquitensis	M	UF 10290	Tortuguero, Limón, Costa Rica	940	105
M. n. zunilensis	F	AMNH 99966	Puerto San José, Escuintla, Guatemala	970	101
M. ornatissimus	F	IPE	Chiguaza, P. Morona-Santiago, Ecuador	848	76
M. paraensis	F	MPEG	Cunha and Nascimento, 1978	530	
M. peruvianus	F	MCZ 13789	Perico, Cajamarca, Peru	433	39
M. petersi	F	USNM 158295	Plan de Milagro, Morona-Santiago, Ecuador	667	55
M. proximans	M	CAS 95767	2 mi E San Blas, Nayarit, Mexico	565	82
M. psyches	F	MBUCV n/n	Caripito, Monagas, Venezuela	910	79
M. p. pyrrhocryptus		Abalos and Nader, 1968	Pozuelos, Santiago del Estero, Argentina	1,240	70
M. p. tricolor	M	UCMNH 6988	Fortín Boquerón, Paraguay	885	57
M. putumayensis	F	TCWC 2193	Centro Unión, Loreto, Peru	805	77
M. remotus	F	USNM 83551	Salto Húa, Venezuela-Brazil boundary	567	47
M. ruatanus	F	USNM 83551	Isla Roatán, Honduras	567	47
M. sangilensis	F	FMNH 69550	San Gil, Santander, Colombia	600	60
M. spixii spixii	M	ZSBS	Manaos, Brazil	1,045	58
M. s. martiusi	M	ZSM 124/1915	Campos de Ariramba Brazil	1,520	75
M. s. obscurus	M	FMNH 59179	Marcapata, Peru	1417	57
M. s. princeps	M	CM 126	Santa Cruz de la Sierra, Bolivia	1,602 inc	65 inc
M. spurrelli	F	AMNH 89352	Condoto river, Colombia	633	42
M. steindachneri steindachneri	M	NMW 15750	Ecuador	770	110
M. s. orcesi	F	AMNH 88923	Baños, 1800 m. Ecuador	880	74
M. stewarti	F	FMNH 37220	Panama	883	78
M. stuarti	F	UMMZ 117187	Finca La Paz, San Marcos, Guatemala	745	85
M. surinamensis surinamensis	F	Silva (1994)	Amazonas, Colombia	1,350	—
M. s. nattereri	M	UPR 0-19	Puerto Ayacucho, Venezuela	904	109
M. tschudii tschudii	M	MHNL 270	Santa Rosa, Peru	550	48
M. t. olsoni	M	BM 1926 9.20.3	Desierto de Tumbes, Peru	730	60

laxed and killed by an anesthetic used in the field, is longer than the same specimen preserved over a period of time. This is illustrated by data obtained from two specimens of M. l. helleri from Bolivia deposited at the Field Museum of Natural History. One of them (FMNH 152316) was 1012 mm long when freshly killed but only 980 mm when measured preserved. Another specimen (FMNH 152317) from the same species and the same locality was 862 mm long when freshly killed and 835 mm when preserved. This represents about a 3% reduction in the overall length of preserved museum specimens.

As size is one measurement that allows many enthusiastic herpetologists, professional or not, to establish and improve records, Table 1 offers a list of the longest known specimen for every species and subspecies of coral snake. It includes specimens that I have measured in different museums and specimens reported by other authors.

Judging from these data, the females grow larger than the males; among the record-size specimens are 72 females but only 45 males. As a rule among snakes, the female reproductive organs and the necessity of carrying maturing eggs is related to a larger body size.

The two smallest coral snakes probably are M. dissoleucus melanogenys (366 mm long; CM 206) and M. dissoleucus dunni (384 mm). They are rivaled by Microides euryxanthus neglectus, M. e. australis, and L. scutiventris, with a record long specimen measuring 445 mm.

The smallest coral snake I have measured is a female specimen of L. scutiventris from São Paulo de Olivença, Brazil, deposited in the Naturhistorisches Museum, Vienna, Austria (NMW 9173). Its overall length is only 155 mm of which 6 mm represents its tail. No hatchlings are known from M. dissoleucus melanogenys, considered a rival in smallness to L. scutiventris. The second smallest specimen I have measured is a juvenile of M. a. annellatus with a total length of only 162 mm (LSU 26881), of which 14 mm corresponded to its tail length. The third smallest specimen is a male

Table 2. Range of the Tail Length/Total Length Ratio N = Number of specimens observed

Species	Males N	Ratio	Females N	Ratio	Species	Males N	Ratio	Females N	Ratio
Leptomicrurus					Micrurus (continued)				
L. collaris collaris	8	.062–.073	1	.062	M. d. aglaeope	1	.154	2	.102–.106
L. c. breviventris	2	.069–.072		—	M. d. alienus	48	.133–.163	30	.109–.121
L. narduccii narduccii	11	.055–.067	6	.037–.042	M. d. apiatus	22	.130–.168	18	.098–.109
L. n. melanotus	30	.055–.068	20	.040–.050	M. d. macdougalli	5	.130–.162	3	.111–.113
L. scutiventris	12	.057–.070	3	.039–.053	M. d. sapperi	32	.138–.168	21	.101–.118
Micruroides	83	.068–.086	61	.052–.073	M. dissoleucus dissoleucus	20	.085–.094	18	.062–.088
M. euryxanthus euryxanthus					M. d. dunni	13	.075–.088	6	.055–.065
M. e. australis	8	.085–.089	4	.060–.068	M. d. melanogenys	4	.072–.084	5	.049–.058
M. e. neglectus	2	.082–.091		—	M. d. nigrirostris	14	.071–.082	8	.051–.060
Micrurus					M. distans distans	13	.137–.151	10	.095–.113
M. albicinctus	15	.139–.157	5	.084–.090	M. d. michoacanensis	6	.133–.142	4	.101–.105
M. alleni	47	.125–.166	31	.084–.093	M. d. oliveri	3	.148–.159	3	.113–.118
M. ancoralis ancoralis	17	.069–.081	20	.050–.073	M. d. zweifeli	1	.140–.146	2	.098–.100
M. a. jani	18	.071–.083	14	.065–.072	M. dumerilii dumerilii	685	.121–.171	328	.089–.118
M. annellatus annellatus	31	.134–.156	19	.072–.097	M. d. antioquiensis	20	.137–.175	20	.090–.115
					M. d. carinicauda	8	.140–.175	11	.083–.114
M. a. balzani	7	.122–.127	7	.080–.089	M. d. colombianus	7	.146–.183	4	.089–.111
M. a. bolivianus		—	3	.076–.092	M. d. transandinus	32	.135–.185	34	.084–.123
M. averyi	3	.149–.181	4	.079–.095	M. d. venezuelensis	7	.148–.172	4	.087–.105
M. bernadi	2	.100–.131	4	.089–.103	M. elegans elegans	13	.132–.148	7	.085–.086
M. bocourti	21	.126–.157	19	.089–.096	M. e. veraepacis	10	.125–.155	12	.080–.095
M. bogerti	2	.143–.145	3	.104–.111	M. ephippifer ephippifer	21	.135–.147	18	.101–.113
M. browni browni	36	.125–.158	24	.099–.112					
M. b. importunus	3	.143–.160	1	.0993	M. e. zapotecus	2	.135–.144	2	.098–.104
M. b. taylori	12	.133–.160	12	.099–.124	M. filiformis	23	.066–.086	9	.061–.072
M. catamayensis	2	.113–.121	8	.077–.091	M. frontalis frontalis	143	.046–.069	131	.048–.057
M. circinalis	12	.123–.160	23	.083–.097	M. f. altirostris	14	.047–.062	11	.048–.058
M. clarki	7	.148–.163	6	.100–.109	M. f. baliocoryphus	12	.052–.063	9	.051–.059
M. corallinus	216	.127–.156	188	.076–.093	M. f. brasiliensis	38	.051–.068	36	.050–.062
M. decoratus	20	.061–.070	9	.056–.059	M. f. multicinctus	28	.059–.069	17	.050–.064
M. diana	4	.054–.067	1	.051	M. frontifasciatus	6	.072–.093	4	.073–.078
M. diastema diastema	35	.135–.157	30	.089–.107	M. fulvius fulvius	83	.106–.136	64	.078–.093
					M. f. fitzingeri	1	.136	6	.084–.092
M. d. affinis	2	.135–.151	3	.104–.106	M. f. maculatus	2	.137–.155	2	.090–.094

(Continued)

paratype of M. dumerilii venezuelensis (UIMNH ex. MCN 317) from Ocumare de la Costa, Venezuela, that measures 164 mm. A hatchling of the smallest M. fulvius tenere reported by Allen and Neill (1950) has the overall length of 178 mm. Yet, in this subspecies the size of hatchlings varies from 178 mm to about 210 mm, similar to the variation also known in M. f. fulvius.

Long-Tailed and Short-Tailed Coral Snakes

An interesting characteristic related to the size is the proportion of the overall or total length of the snake to its tail length. In other words, how long is the body as compared to the tail? In comparison to other snakes, the tail of the coral snake is quite short, reflecting the relatively low number of subcaudals. One way to express this characteristic is to divide the tail length by the total length of the snake, resulting in the tail length/total length ratio. The smaller the ratio is, the shorter the tail is. For example, for a specimen with a tail length/total length ratio of 0.15, the tail comprises 15% of its overall length, while a ratio of 0.08 tells us that the tail comprises only 8% of the total length of the snake. As there is a marked sexual dimorphism between the number of subcaudals in males and females, their tail length/total length ratio reflects this sexual dimorphism as well. The comparison must be made separately between the males and the females. In addition, the males have a greater range of variation of this ratio.

Comparing the range of variation for each species, coral snakes can be divided ito two well-defined groups: long-tailed and short-tailed species. As these groups also relate to the type of color pattern, we can draw some conclusions about their evolutionary relationships.

The long-tailed species comprise all single-banded coral snakes from Mexico, Central America, and South America; the accessory triad-type species of South

Table 2. (Continued)

Species	N	Males Ratio	N	Females Ratio	Species	N	Males Ratio	N	Females Ratio
Micrurus (continued)					Micrurus (continued)				
M. f. microgalbineus	8	.139–.145	5	.092–.096	M. nigrocinctus nigrocinctus	162	.128–.163	126	.093–.126
M. f. tenere	39	.118–.136	24	.072–.096					
M. hemprichii hemprichii	16	.089–.108	6	.078–.095	M. n. babaspul	1	.144	1	.112
					M. n. coibensis	3	.139–.151	4	.101–.118
M. h. ortoni	10	.089–.097	7	.082–.093	M. n. divaricatus	72	.112–.164	49	.095–.117
M. h. rondonianus	23	.079–.996	13	.073–.091	M. n. mosquitensis	61	.149–.166	43	.105–.124
M. hippocrepis	6	.133–.161	6	.096–.110	M. n. zunilensis	48	.133–.156	47	.098–.134
M. ibiboboca	35	.054–.072	25	.052–.072	M. ornatissimus	16	.134–.165	19	.080–.100
M. isozonus	41	.075–.089	24	.068–.078	M. paraensis	3	.128–.147	3	.088–.093
M. langsdorffi	26	.134–.162	26	.077–.098	M. peruvianus	3	.130–.146	4	.084–.098
M. laticollaris laticollaris	6	.111–.118	12	.101–.111	M. petersi	—		2	.082–.084
					M. proximans	7	.145–.157	5	.101–.116
M. l. maculirostris	8	.123–.134	1	.112	M. psyches	14	.148–.158	15	.089–.092
M. latisfasciatus	32	.146–.171	25	.104–.119	M. putumayensis	11	.151–.160	7	.087–.099
M. lemniscatus lemniscatus	20	.082–.089	15	.078–.084	M. pyrrhocryptus pyrrhocryptus	41	.065–.073	34	.057–.068
M. l. carvalhoi	92	.070–.083	51	.059–.077	M. p. tricolor	6	.064–.068	1	.062
M. l. diutius	28	.081–.106	21	.083–.088	M. remotus	3	.140–.143	4	.085–.086
M. l. helleri	112	.080–.093	73	.073–.095	M. ruatanus	10	.124–.141	5	.099–.105
M. limbatus limbatus	5	.132–.139	3	.085–.094	M. sangilensis	3	.155–.187	5	.092–.100
M. l. spilosomus	—		1	.090	M. spixii spixii	10	.049–.063	9	.050–.052
M. margaritiferus	—		2	.078–.095	M. s. martiusi	21	.049–.059	11	.053–.057
M. medemi	6	.152–.167	3	.087–.094	M. s. obscurus	74	.040–.062	37	.043–.055
M. meridensis	1	.102	—		M. s. princeps	26	.048–.062	17	.048–.057
M. mertensi	12	.120–.134	13	.080–.087	M. spurrelli	3	.086–.097	2	.067–.087
M. mipartitus mipartitus	8	.065–.076	6	.036–.061	M. steindachneri steindachneri	6	.086–.097	2	.067–.087
M. m. anomalus	5	.076–.086	11	.059–.074	M. s. orcesi	3	.144–.154	5	.080–.086
M. m. decussatus	56	.063–.070	51	.042–.060	M. stewarti	4	.136–.156	4	.093–.104
M. m. semipartitus	33	.083–.102	24	.066–.081	M. stuarti	1	.143	3	.094–.114
M. multifasciatus multifasciatus	16	.069–.080	13	.052–.060	M. surinamensis surinamensis	34	.112–.131	27	.091–.108
M. m. hertwigi	10	.072–.079	27	.050–.068	M. s. nattereri	7	.120–.123	3	.107–.110
M. multiscutatus	—		1	.054	M. tschudii tschudii	29	.075–.105	24	.071–.089
M. nebularis	2	.130–.136	4	.096–.102	M. t. olsoni	26	.080–.085	22	.076–.083

America; and the Central American species with triad-type color pattern (*M. elegans* and *M. laticollaris*). The only species with a triad-type coloration from South America that has a relatively long tail is the aquatic coral snake, *M. surinamensis*, with a range of variation for both subspecies between 0.11 and 0.13 in the males and 0.09 and 0.11 in the females. Apparently, swamp and aquatic living has favored the development of a longer tail.

Males of long-tailed species have a tail length/total length ratio of at least 0.11, usually more. The species with one of the longest tails in the males is *M. averyi* in which the tail length/total length ratio varies between 0.15 and 0.18 in males but only between 0.08 and 0.09 in females. *M. dumerilii venezuelensis* probably has the longest tail, with the tail length/total length ratio ranging between 0.15 and 0.20 in males and between 0.09 and 0.10 in females. The highest tail length/total length ratio in females is found in *M. dumerilii transandinus* with the range between 0.08 and 0.12.

The short-tailed coral snakes comprise all South American species with a triad-type coloration, except the *M. surinamensis*, *Leptomicrurus*, and the seemingly related group of bicolored coral snakes: *M. mipartitus*, *M. multifasciatus*, *M. multiscutatus*, and *M. spurrelli*. In this group, the range of the tail length/total length ratio is usually well below 0.10. *M. spixii obscurus*, with a tail length/total length ratio in males ranging between 0.04 and 0.06, has the shortest tail. The same ratio in females varies between 0.04 and 0.06. This reveals another observation regarding size, namely that in the short-tailed coral snakes there is hardly any difference between the tail length of males and females. Table 2 provides the range of variation of tail length/total length ratios for all species and subspecies of coral snakes. In many cases, this ratio can help to determining the sex of the specimen and in some cases it might help in the identification of the species.

Chapter 3
Internal Features

Skull and Skeleton

Skull and Dentition

The shape and proportions of individual bones of the skull of the different species of coral snakes vary, but the basic disposition is quite uniform. At the same time, some variation is also found from individual to individual of the same species. The skull of *M. frontalis* (Fig. 25) shows all the basic components of the skull of coral snakes and is quite similar to that of *M. isozonus* (Fig. 26), as well as to other species. The most recent and complete study of coral snake morphology is that by Alan Savitzky (1979), while a study of the skull was done by Scrocchi (1992), and head morphology by McDowell (1986).

Looking from above, the skull has a premaxilla followed by a pair of nasal bones, beneath which the septomaxilla is visible. The prefrontals are as a rule in contact in the genera *Micrurus* (Fig. 26) and *Leptomicrurus*, but separated in *Micruroides* (Fig. 27). The prefrontal connects to the maxilla below and its shape varies somewhat from species to species. The frontals that follow are somewhat triangular with slightly rounded angles and sides. Their anterior border can be almost straight as in *M. mipartitus* (Fig. 28) and *Leptomicrurus* or sinuous or invaginated as in several species of *Micrurus*. The large parietal region that follows is quite long and slender as in *M. mipartitus* (Fig. 28), with nearly parallel sides, or sinuously convex as in *M. dissoleucus* (Fig. 29) and *M. surinamensis* (Fig. 30). It can end in an almost pointed angle as in *M. dissoleucus*, *L. collaris*, and several others. The prootic bones border the supraoccipital on both sides, and the supraoccipital is followed by the exoccipital. A transverse ridge of the supraoccipital is present in larger species (cf. *M. spixii*) but reduced in smaller species (cf. *M. nigrocinctus*). The tabular that projects over the prootic and connects to the quadrate varies considerably in size and shape. It can be short as in *M. isozonus* (Fig. 26), or large and sinuous as in *M. mipartitus* (Fig. 28) and *M. nigrocinctus* (Fig. 31) and *M. tschudii* (Fig. 32A). The quadrate is loosely connected by a flexible ligament to the surangular of the mandible, between the postarticular and articular portions. The dentary bone of the mandible bears the mandibular teeth.

In addition to these structures observable from above, a series of additional bones of the skull can be identified in lateral and ventral views (Figs. 25B–C). The maxilla is a relatively short bone. It has little mobility except at the hinge with the ectopterygoid, a bone that is connected by a ligament to the quadrate. The maxilla-ectopterygoid articulation is broad in such species as *M. spixii* or narrow as in *M. surinamensis*, allowing for greater or lesser flexibility in rotation of the maxilla.

The fangs are relatively short and somewhat curved. The curvature is less pronounced in *Micruroides* (Fig. 33A), which has very short fangs that are directed more inward and backward than in *Micrurus* (Fig. 33B–E). The maxilla has one fixed fang with one or more replacement fangs (see section on biting mechanism and venom apparatus). The fangs are the only maxillary teeth in *Micrurus* (Fig. 33B–C) and *Leptomicrurus*, while *Micruroides* has one or two small teeth at the posterior end of the maxilla (Fig. 33A). The fangs are deeply grooved and frequently closed on the surface, forming a channel that is at least partially enclosed (shown in Fig. 33B). The maxilla bearing the fangs articulates with the prefrontal by two facets. In many species, such as *M. isozonus*, *M. lemniscatus* and several more triad-type species, the fangs are anterior to the prefrontal, while in single-banded species, such as the *M. corallinus*, the fangs are around the level of articulation between the prefrontal and the maxilla. In the former case, the chewing motion with maxillary rotation is more effective.

At its anterior end, the palatine bone is firmly connected, but a more flexible ligamentous connection between the palatine and the pterygoid allows for upward motion of the bone. This palatine-pterygoid articulation is reduced and the ends of the bones are thin. A short, lateral process, which can be curved or somewhat flattened (as in *M. lemniscatus*) is found at about the second palatine tooth. A second, conspicuously arched process extends from the center of the palatine to the posterior dorsal process of the vomer. The muscles that connect these structures enable the coral snake

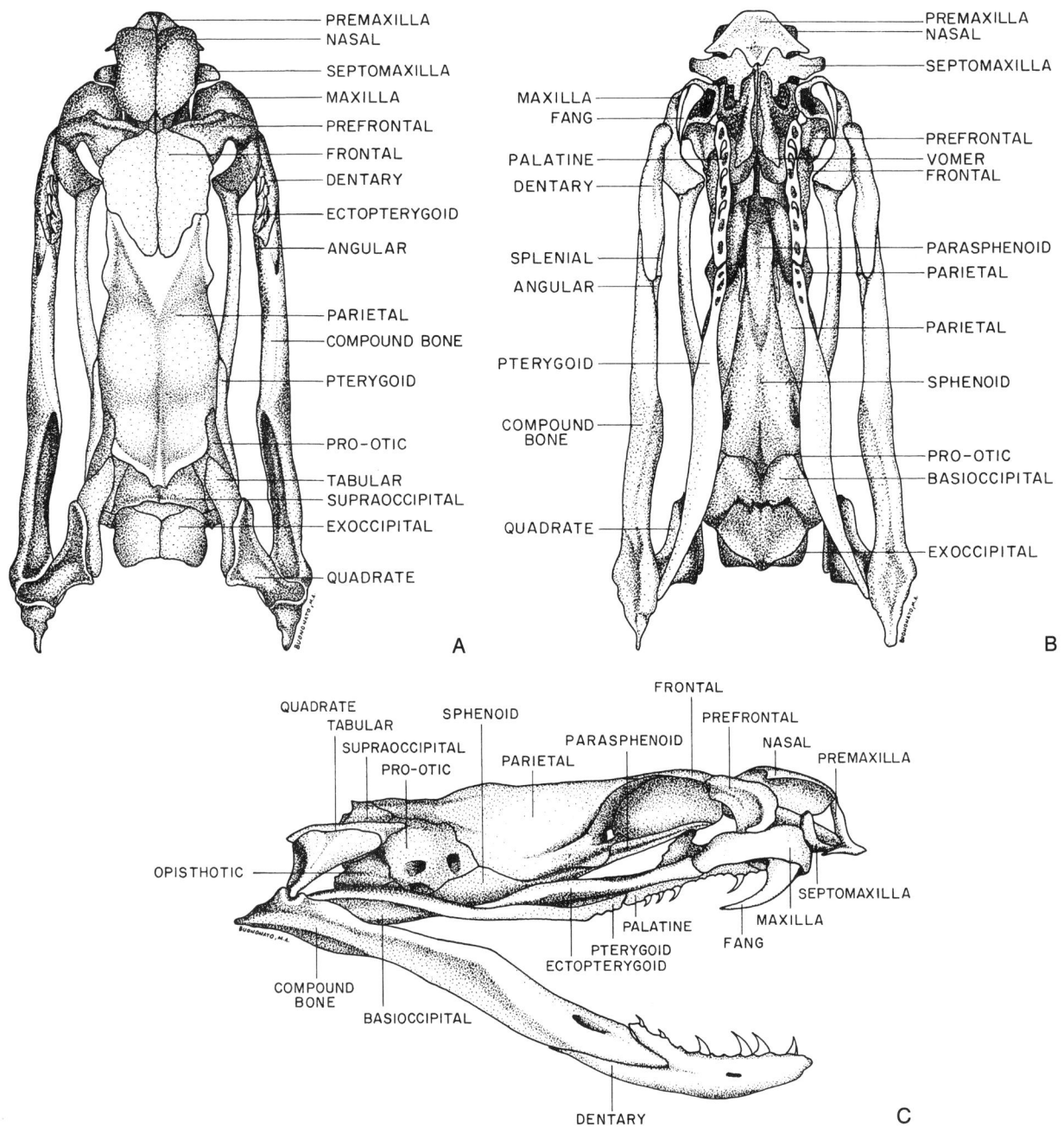

Figure 25. Skull of *Micrurus f. frontalis*: A) Dorsal view, B) Ventral view, C) Lateral view. Bones identified by name. Notes: Compound bone comprises fused surangular, articular and prearticular bones. Tubular bone is also called supratemporal by some authors. (Drawn from a specimen of Instituto Butantan from Aguas de Lindoya, São Paulo, Brazil by Marcus Buononato)

to erect the palatine, which includes the coral snakes in what McDowell (1970) described as "palatine erector" snakes. In *Leptomicrurus* the palatine is very long, reaching beyond the frontal-parietal suture (Fig. 34), while in the species of *Micrurus* examined and in *Micruroides* it is shorter and does not reach this suture.

The number of palatine teeth varies and the anterior teeth are larger and less bent than the posterior. *L. narduccii melanotus* and *M. multifasciatus* with long palatine bones have 10 to 11 teeth. In *M. lemniscatus*, the number of palatine teeth ranges from 8 to 11. In other species, the number of palatine teeth is less than 10. *M. spixii* and *M. isozonus* have 7 to 9, while the most frequent number of palatine teeth of *M. fulvius tenere* is 7 to 8. The lowest number of palatine teeth is found in *M. tschudii* (Fig. 32B), which has only 5 to 6 teeth, but, as we will see later, has a long row of pterygoid teeth. The palatine teeth can be long and sharp as in *M. surina-*

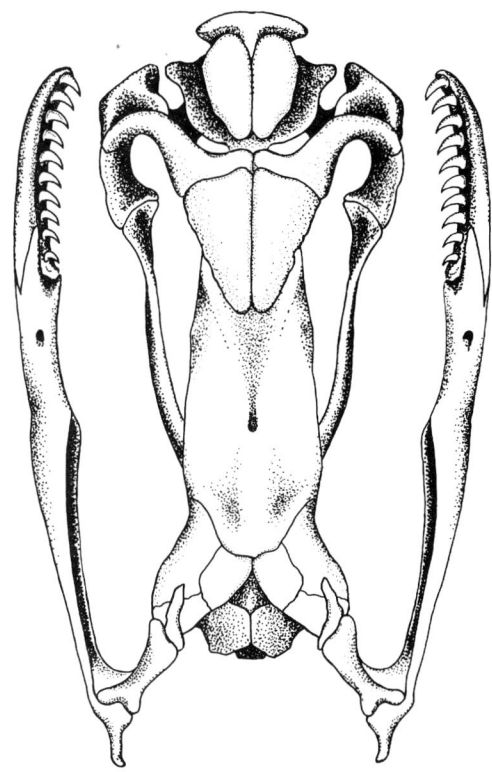

Figure 26. Skull of *Micrurus isozonus*, dorsal view (from Venezuela, drawn by Edgars Rutkis).

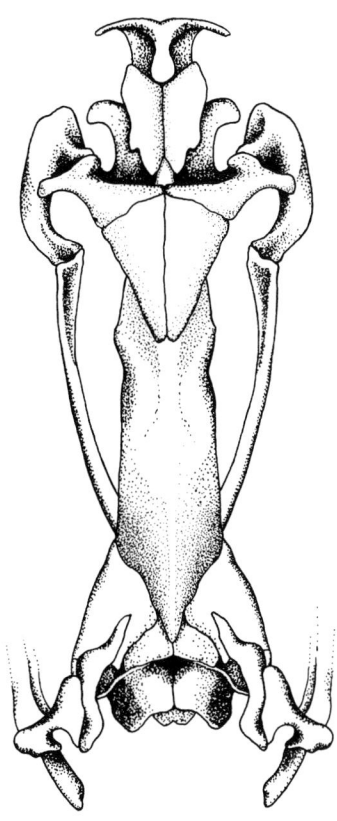

Figure 28. Skull of *Micrurus mipartitus semipartitus* (from Venezuela, drawn by Edgars Rutkis).

mensis or relatively small as in *M. frontalis*. Perhaps the most remarkable fact is that in most species the palatine teeth are somewhat grooved on the anterior inside surface. It is not known what function they have as there are no known glands around the palate in snakes separate from the main venom gland. The known numbers of palatine, pterygoid, and mandibulary teeth of the different species of coral snakes are shown in Table 3.

The pterygoid is a narrow bone that curves and expands posteriorly, in some species quite considerably, and bends so that its posterior, flattened portion

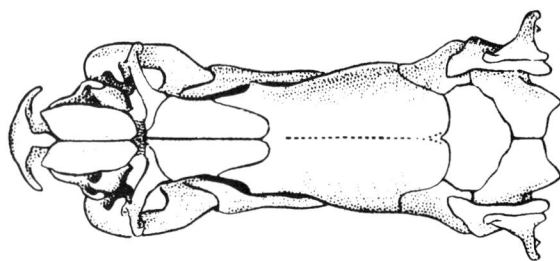

Figure 27. Skull of *Micruroides e. euryxanthus* (AMNH 74562, drawn by Frances Zweifel).

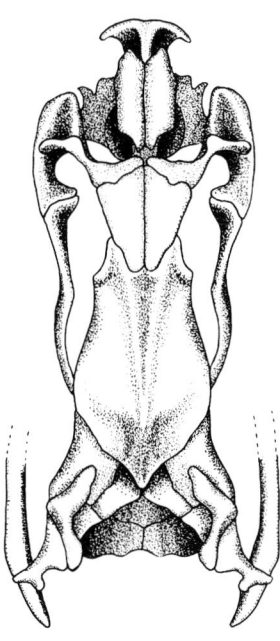

Figure 29. Skull of *Micrurus d. dissoleucus* (from Venezuela, drawn by Edgar Rutkis).

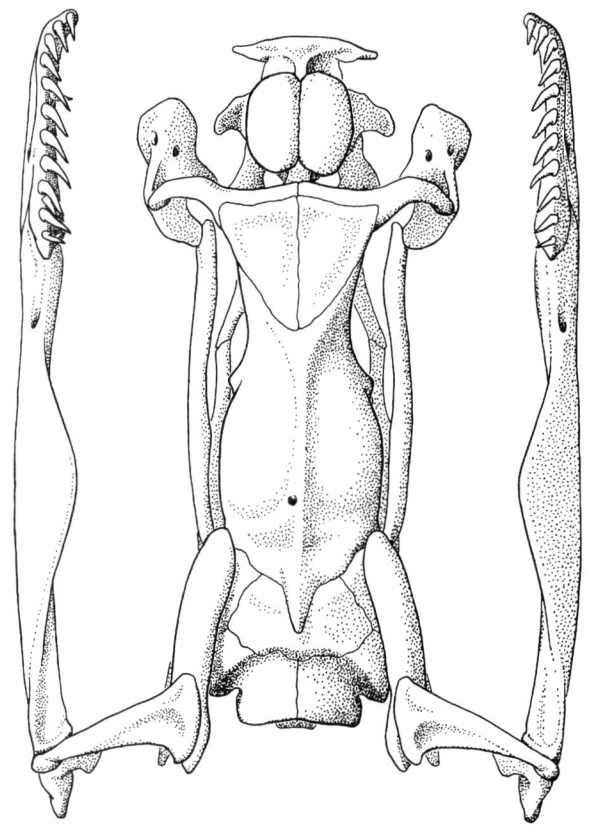

Figure 30. Skull of *Micrurus surinamensis* (AMNH 92980).

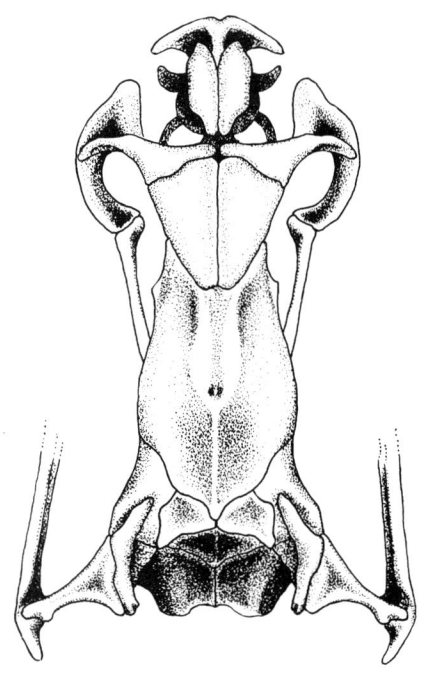

Figure 31. Skull of *Micrurus nigrocinctus zunilensis*. (Drawn by Samuel McDowell)

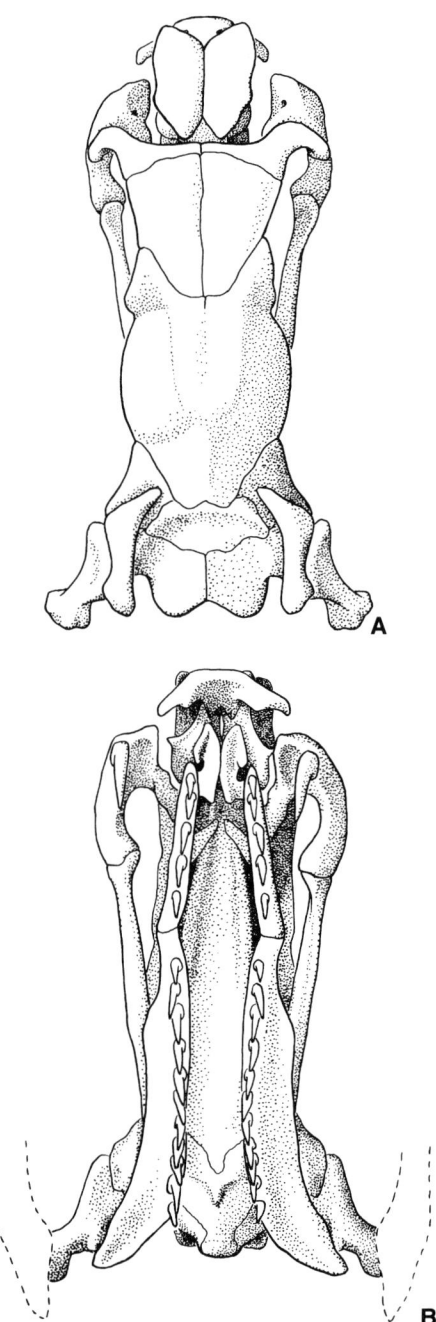

Figure 32. Skull of *Micrurus tschudii*: A) Dorsal view, B) Ventral view (MHNLP 270). (Drawn by Samuel McDowell)

lies obliquely at the posteriolateral wall of the skull. In some species, it extends beyond the end of the brain case but it is shorter in *Leptomicrurus*. The ectopterygoid that connects the maxilla and the pterygoid has a poorly defined articulation with the pterygoid. Pterygoid teeth decrease in size toward the posterior part of the mouth, and with two exceptions coral snakes have fewer pterygoid than palatine teeth. They range mostly between 3 and 5 teeth, but some species such as *M. fulvius* have 5 to 6 pterygoid teeth and *M. spixii obscurus*

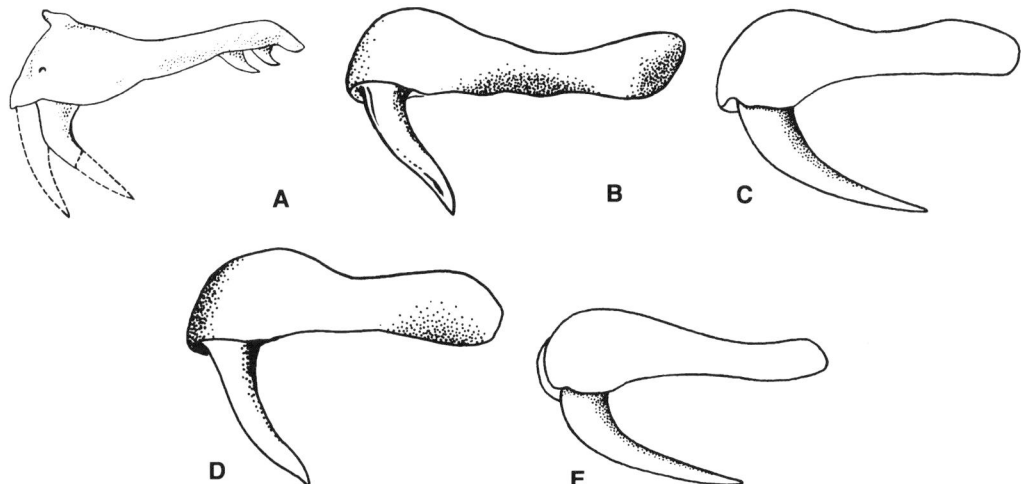

Figure 33. Maxilla and teeth of coral snakes: A) *Micruroides e. euryxanthus*, notice additional maxillary teeth, B) *Micrurus isozonus*, C) *Micrurus mipartitus semipartitus*, D) *Micrurus n. nigrocinctus*, E) *Micrurus d. dissoleucus*. (Drawn by Frances Zweifer and others)

has 4 to 7. *M. corallinus* and *M. coibensis* have only 3 to 4 pterygoid teeth. One specimen of *M. isozonus* had only 2 pterygoid teeth. The two exceptions in the number of pterygoid teeth are *M. surinamensis*, which was 16 to 18, and the two subspecies of *M. tschudii*: *M. t. tschudii* has 9 to 10, and *M. tschudii olssoni* has 11 to 13 pterygoid teeth. In *M. surinamensis* the previously mentioned long row of pterygoid teeth may be related to feeding habits. This species feeds predominantly on swamp eels and other fishes (see chapter on Feeding and Food), prey that might require an extra long row of teeth for managing the prey, dragging them into gullet, and swallowing them. The same might be true of *M. tschudii*, which feeds on powerful amphisbaenids and lizards.

The quadrate articulates with the mandible that features the only hinge (glenoid fossa) that connects the lower jaw to the skull. The quadrate is short in such species as *M. isozonus*, *M. ibiboboca* and *M. corallinus*, but long in *M. lemniscatus* and particularly long in *M. surinamensis*. The quadrate is connected to a blunt and small tabular. This bone is quite long in *M. surinamensis*.

The mandible, the lower jaw, is a compound bone that is long and compressed laterally. The postarticular process is short while the deep fossa (the primordial fossa) anterior to the jaw articulation is elongated but narrow. The mandible of *M. surinamensis* has a unique pseudocoronoid process not found in any other species. The dentary bone bears teeth that in many species are also grooved and decrease in size toward the posterior part of the mouth. The grooves are present on the external surface of the mandibular teeth as in *M. laticollaris* (Fig. 35B–D).

Head Muscles and Glands

The nomenclature of muscles in snakes is undergoing several changes, and I am following McDowell's (1986) proposed names and interpretation of snake head muscles (see also the section on biting mechanism and venom apparatus). As illustrated by *Leptomicrurus narduccii melanotus* (Fig. 36) the dominant muscle used to compress the venom gland is the *levator anguli oris*, which we will call the venom gland muscle (Fig. 36). It has also been called *adductor externus superficialis*. The venom gland muscle is divided into a dorsal portion (*pars dorsalis*) and a ventral portion (*pars ventralis*). The dorsal portion of the venom gland muscle originates as fibers (intrinsic fibers) on the lower postorbital region behind the orbit and on the parietal. In some species this dorsal portion begins with transparent connective tissue and as actual fibers over the *adductor externus medialis*.

The dorsal portion can be short or long depending

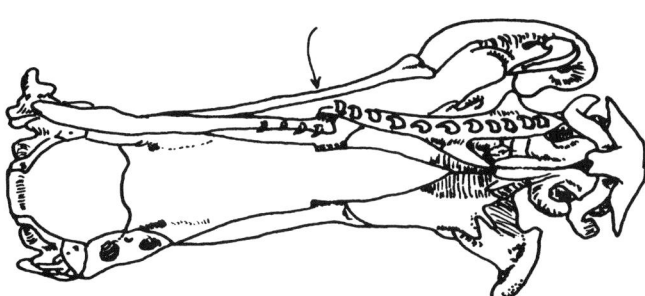

Figure 34. Ventral view of the skull of *Leptomicrurus narduccii melanotus*, showing the palatine reaching beyond frontal-parietal suture. (Drawn by Samuel McDowell.)

Table 3. Variation in Number of Teeth of Coral Snakes and Remarks on Grooved (gr) Condition, Where Observed

	Palatine	Pterygoid	Mandibulary
Leptomicrurus			
L. collaris breviventris	9	4	8–9
L. narduccii melanotus	10–11	4	9–10(grooved)
Micrurus			
M. ancoralis jani	12–13	7	11(gr)
M. a. annellatus	6–7	4–5	9–11
M. bernadi	7	5–6	8
M. b. browni	7	4	
M. corallinus	7	3–4	11–12(gr)
M. decoratus*	6	2	
M. diastema alienus	8	5	10–11(gr)
M. d. dumerilii*	7–8	6	10
M. e. ephippifer	7–8(gr)	3–4	10–11(gr)
M. filiformis	7–9	3–4	10–11 (gr)
M. frontalis altirostris*	8–9	3–4	10–11
M. f. fulvius	7–8	5–6(gr)	10–11
M. fulvius tenere	7–8(gr)	2–6	10–11(gr)
M. ibiboboca*	8	4	10
M. isozonus	8–9(gr)	(2)4–5(gr)	9–11 (gr)
M. laticollaris			11(gr)
M. lemniscatus carvalhoi*	6–7	6	10
M. mipartitus decussatus	9	3–4	9
M. m. multifasciatus	10–11(gr)	5	8
M. n. nigrocinctus	7(gr)	5	12(gr)
M. nigrocinctus coibensis	6(gr)	3–4	
M. nigrocincts divaricatus	7–8	4–5(gr)	11–12
M. peruvianus	6–8	4	9–10
M. putumayensis**	7–9	5	10–11
M. p. pyrrhocryptus*	7–9	2–4	10–11
M. spixii obscurus	7–9(gr)	4–7(gr)	12–13(gr)
M. spixii princeps	8(gr)	3–5	11(gr)
M. s. surinamensis	8–9	14–18	10–12
M. t. tschudii	5–7	11–13(gr)	9–10
M. t. olssoni	5–6	11–13(gr)	9–10

*Data from Scrocchi, 1993.
**Data from Lema, 1972.

on its extension on the head. It can be divided into the anterior portion (1a) and the posterior portion (1b). In such species as *M. corallinus* the venom gland muscle originates in the area behind the orbit on the parietal, anterior to the *adductor externus medialis*. In other species, such as *M. bernadi*, the posterior fibers of the 1b originate on the lateral surface of the *medialis* muscle, and in such species as *M. f. fulvius* (Fig. 37), *M. fulvius tenere*, and *M. nigrocinctus* the fibers arise farther back on the *medialis*. The venom gland muscle begins over the *medialis* as transparent fibers. In *M. ibiboboca, M. isozonus* and *M. frontalis*, the posterior fibers of the venom gland muscle cover the entire width of the *medialis*, and in *M. tschudii* (Fig. 38) the last posterior fibers of the venom gland muscle reach the level of the quadrate. *M. surinamensis* has the largest venom gland muscle, one that covers the entire upper surface of the skull and conceals the *medialis*. In *M. mipartitus* (Fig. 39), *L. multifaciatus*, and *L. narduccii* (Fig. 36) the last fibers are attached to the quadrate directly via some fascia. The venom gland muscle inserts on the lower posterior part and on the posterior part of the venom gland. The ventral portion of the venom gland muscle originates on the lateral surface of the mandible and inserts on the venom gland via a tendon. In *Micruroides* the muscle fibers insert directly on the gland sheath itself.

Other muscles present are the *adductor externus medialis, adductor externus superficialis* (called in earlier literature *adductor externus profundus*), *depressor mandibulae*, and *pterygoideus*. The last two are located at the end of the skull.

The hyoid extension of the tongue is relatively long in *Micrurus* (Fig. 40) but short in *Micruroides*.

Several major cephalic glands are found on the anterior part of the head (Fig. 36). The premaxillary gland and the nasal gland are situated in the snout,

Internal Features

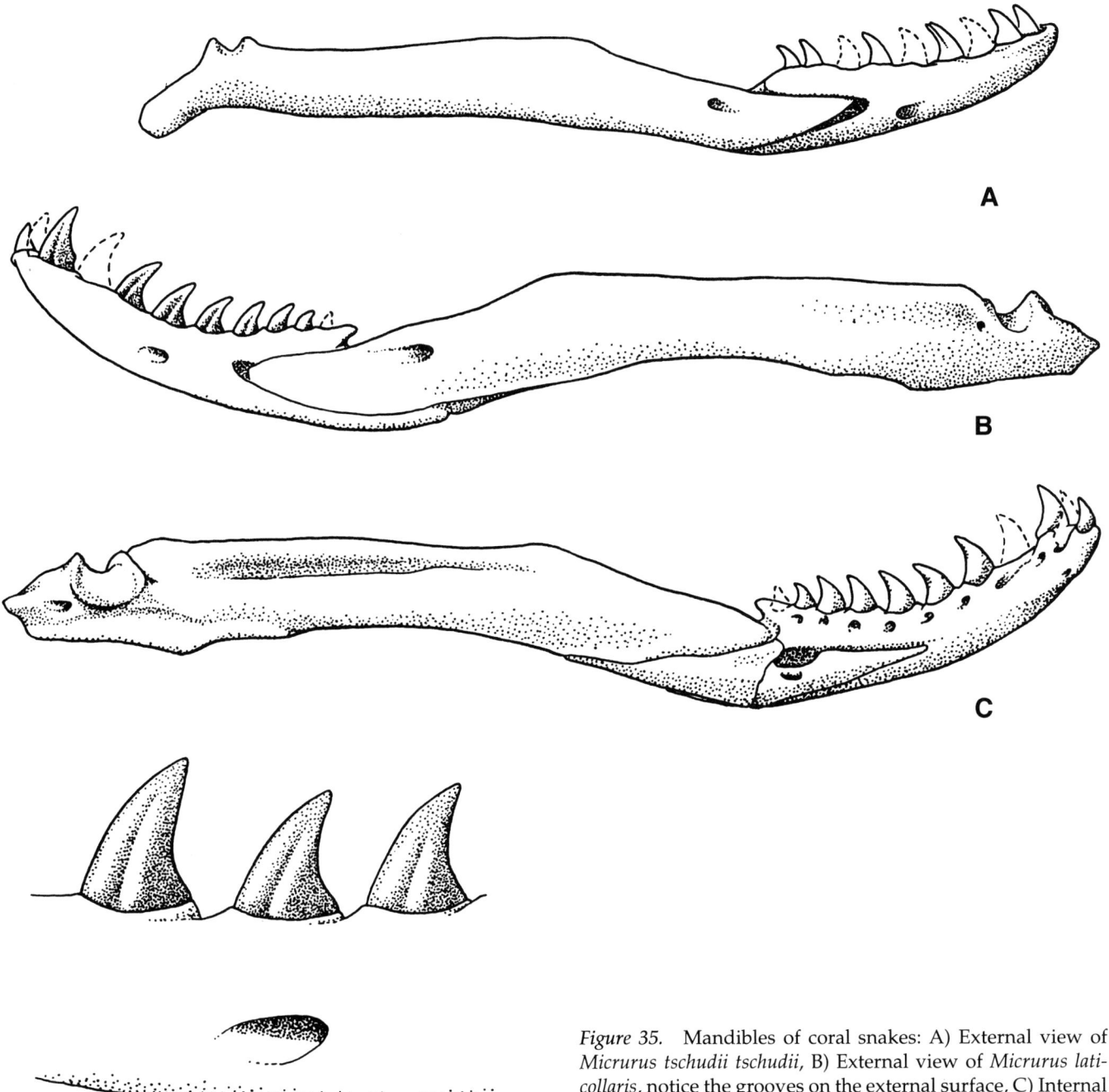

Figure 35. Mandibles of coral snakes: A) External view of *Micrurus tschudii tschudii*, B) External view of *Micrurus laticollaris*, notice the grooves on the external surface, C) Internal view of *M. laticollaris*, D) Detail of grooved mandibular teeth of *M. laticollaris*. (Drawn by Samuel McDowell.)

ventral and lateral to the nasal bone. The nasal glands of most coral snakes are quite large as compared to other snakes. They are particularly large in *Micruroides*, of moderate size in *M. f. fulvius*, and quite small in *M. lemniscatus* and *Leptomicrurus*. A mucus-producing supralabial gland runs along the upper jaw. The Harderian gland is located behind and deep to the eye (Fig. 36), and its function is not clear. The gland is fairly large, occupying a space between the eye and the dorsal portion of the venom gland muscle. It is large in *M. f. fulvius* (Fig. 37) and quite small in *M. surinamensis*. In *M. mipartitus* (Fig. 39) and in *L. narduccii* (Fig. 36) the Harderian gland is somewhat pointed posteriorly. The venom gland is an elongated and pea-shaped gland with a more-or-less bent posterior, lower portion. It consists of a posterior serous main venom gland, anterior mucous accessory gland, and a duct that leads to the upper portion of the fang. All are described in more detail in the section on biting mechanisms and venom apparatus.

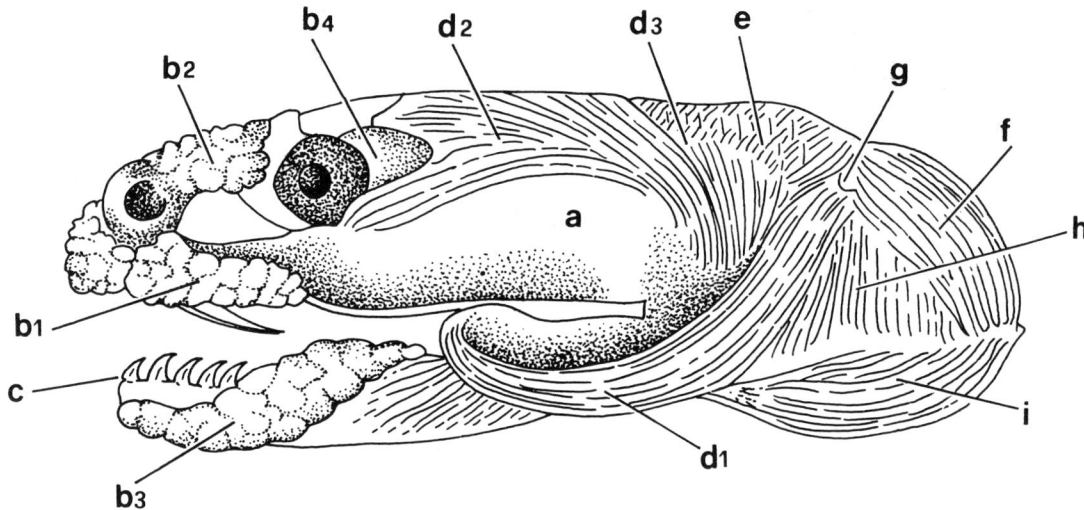

Figure 36. Head glands and muscles of *Leptomicrurus narduccii melanotus*. Glands: a—venom gland; b1—salivary gland, b2—nasal gland, b3—infralabial gland, b4—Harderian gland, notice absence of Druvernoy gland; c—mandibular teeth. Muscles: d1—levator anguli oris (adductor externus superficialis, auct.), ventral portion, d2—levator anguli oris, anterior dorsal portion, d3—lavator anguli oris, posterior dorsal portion, e—adductor externus medialis, f—depressor mandibulae, g—upper point of quadrate, h—adductor externus superficialis, i—pterygoideus superficialis. (From Roze and Bernal-Carlo, 1987; drawn by Samuel McDowell.)

The infralabial glands are situated on the lower jaw (Fig. 36) and some part of them is also involved in the secretion of venom. The grooved mandibular teeth may help to conduct venom from the infralabial venom glands into the bitten prey.

Vertebral Column

The skeleton consists of a long string of vertebrae that correspond in number to the external ventral and subcaudal scales. Except for the first vertebra (the atlas) and the tail vertebrae after the cloaca, all the vertebrae have long ribs attached to them. The ribs are movable and help in locomotion (Fig. 41).

The vertebrae look somewhat similar, but three regions can be distinguished: the vertebrae of the anterior region with strong hypophyses (Fig. 42,A1); the posterior region with reduced or absent hypophyses (Fig. 42,A3); and the tail or caudal region without ribs but with long hemal processes (Fig. 43,B4). The presence of large hypophyses on anterior vertebrae is a characteristic of the family Elapidae.

The main features of a coral snake's middorsal vertebrae are shown by *Micruroides e. euryxanthus* (Fig.

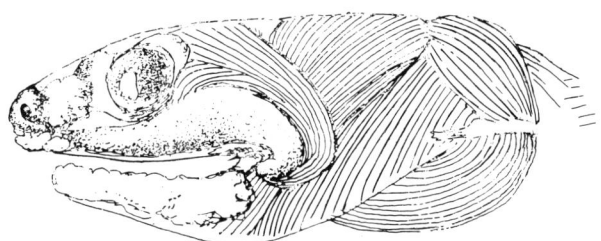

Figure 38. Head glands and muscles of *Micrurus tschudii*. (Drawn by Samuel McDowell.)

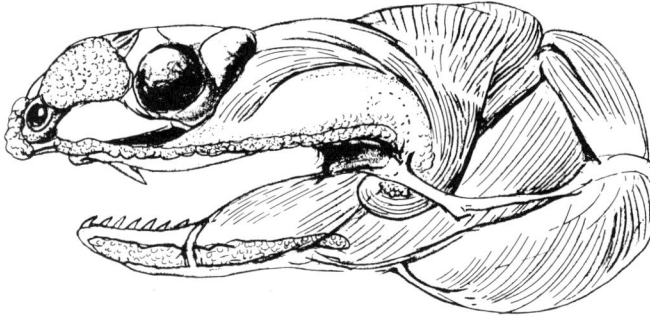

Figure 37. Head glands and head muscles of *Micrurus f. fulvius*. (Drawn by Samuel McDowell.)

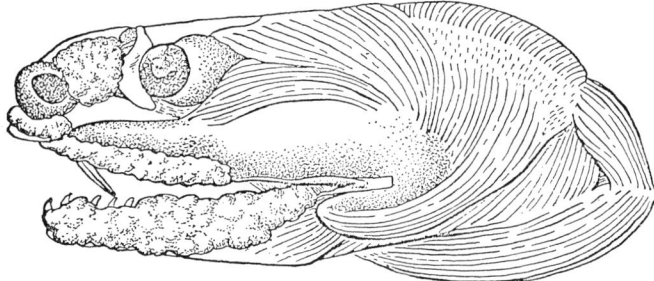

Figure 39. Head glands and muscles of *Micrurus mipartitus decussatus*. (Drawn by Samuel McDowell.)

Internal Features

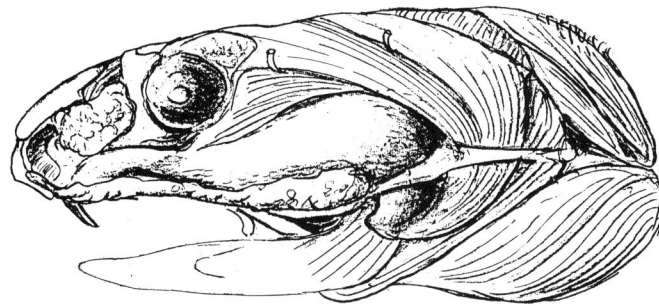

Figure 40. Head glands and muscles of *Micrurus spixii*. (Drawn from MNR 1533 by Samuel McDowell.)

42). A neural spine extends from the zygosphene almost to the rear edge of the neural arch. At the anterior end of the vertebra are the paired joints formed by the prezygapophysis of the vertebra and the postzygopophysis of the preceding vertebra. An additional joint is formed by zygosphenes that fit into the zygantra (paired cavities, one on each side on the back of the preceding vertebra). Beneath the neural arch is the cup on the front of the centrum that articulates with the condyle ball of the preceding vertebra. The hypapophysis is a somewhat curved projection of the posterior portion of the subcentral surface; it varies in size and length in different species.

The three genera have somewhat different vertebral features. In *Micruroides e. euryxanthus* (Fig. 42) the vertebrae are relatively high, even though their neural spines are low. The hypapophysis is curved even though it does not reach the posterior end of the condyle. In *Micrurus*, as represented by *M. frontalis* vertebrae (Figs. 43 and 44), the neural spine is high and not only is the hypapophysis curved, but it extends beyond the posterior end of the condyle. A similar configuration is also found in *M. spixii obscurus*. The neural spine is quite low in *M. surinamensis*. In *L. narduccii melanotus* (Fig. 45) representing *Leptomicrurus*, the vertebrae are comparatively much longer than in the other two genera, with a low neural spine that looks more like a ridge than a spine and does not reach the rear edge of the neural arch. The hypapophysis is convex and almost reaches the level of the posterior end of the condyle.

General Internal Anatomy

The internal anatomy of the coral snake is quite similar to the general features commonly found in snakes. The brief description of the internal anatomy is based on observations of a specimen of *M. surinamensis*. The digestive track starts at the mouth, which has teeth, salivary glands and a bifurcated tongue. The tongue is long and can be extended outside by an anterior opening without opening the mouth. The tongue flicking gathers information about the outside environment, including the presence of potential prey.

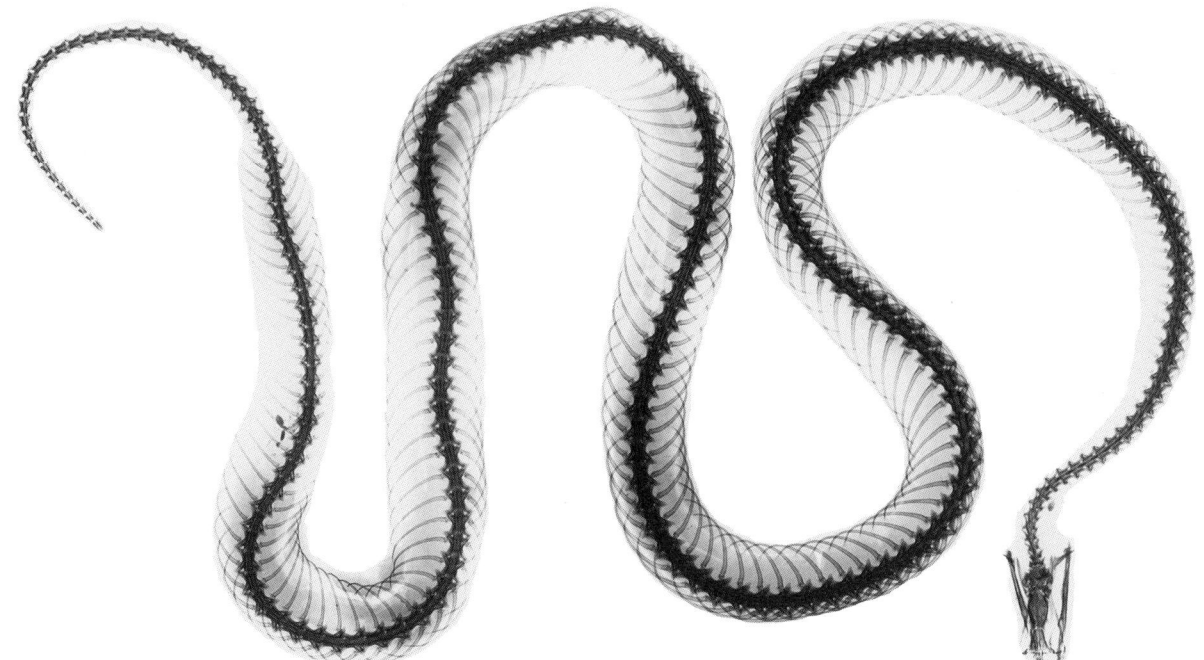

Figure 41. Skeleton of *Micrurus s. surinamensis*.

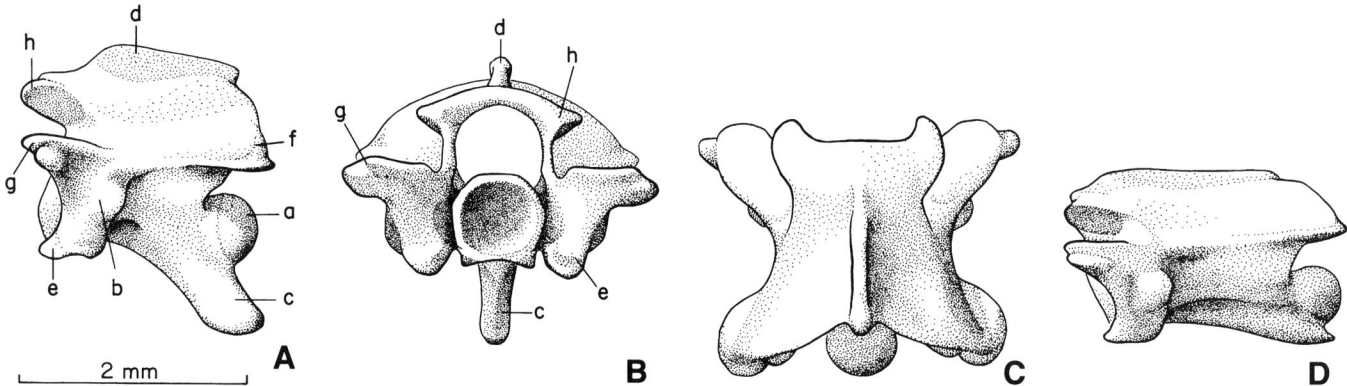

Figure 42. Vertebrae of *Micruroides e. euryxanthus*: A) Lateral view of anterior (17th) vertebra: a—condyle, b—diapophysis, c—hypapophysis, d—neural spine, e—parazygapophysis, f—postzygapophysis, g—prezygapophysis, h—zygosphene, B) Posterior view of anterior (17th) vertebra, C) Dorsal view of anterior (17th) vertebra, D) Lateral view of midbody (112th) vertebra. (Drawn from AMNH 72562 specimen by Frances Zweifel.)

The tongue can be retracted into a sheath in the floor of the mouth in front of the glottis. The digestive tract continues as a long alimentary canal (esophagus), and the stomach is a larger- and thicker-walled tube that gradually transforms into the small intestine, a corrugated pipe with bends that adhere to each other. The folded small intestine is enclosed in a peritoneal fold that externally appears to be a straight tube. Internally, the small intestine wall features villi and papillae. It terminates at the ileo-colic valve, where the digestive tract continues as a straight rectum of enlarged diameter and finally opens in the cloaca. The rectum has several perforated transversal septae.

In *M. surinamensis* the liver is long and narrow and begins at least 15 ventrals beyond the heart. Posterior to it is an isolated node of liver tissue and a network of hepatic ducts. About 10 ventrals behind the liver on the right side of the body is an elongated, oval gallbladder while a smaller irregularly shaped pancreas is on the left side. Just anterior to the pancreas lies the roundish spleen, about one third of the size of the pancreas. A duct from the gallbladder joins a common bile duct near the pancreas and the spleen. Fat bodies also begin about 8 ventrals behind the heart and a little anterior to the liver and continue as long, irregular strips beyond the small intestine.

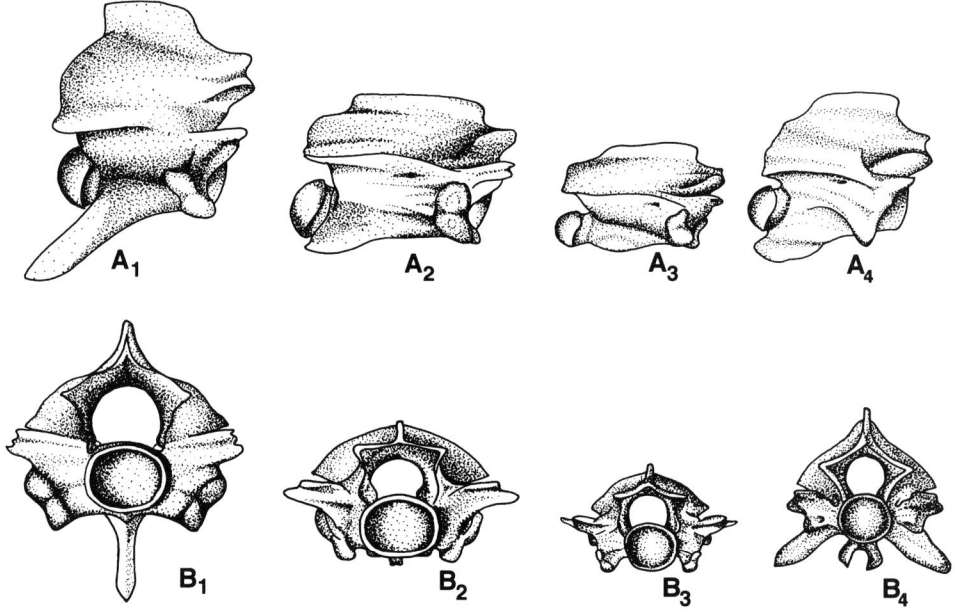

Figure 43. Sequence of lateral and anterior view of vertebrae of *Micrurus f. frontalis*: A) Lateral view of A1—anterior, A2—thoracic, A3—posterior, A4—caudal vertebrae; B) Anterior view of B1—anterior, B2—thoracic, B3—posterior, B4—caudal vertebrae. (Drawn from an Instituto Butantan specimen from Aguas de Lindoya, São Paulo, Brazil by Marcus Buononato.)

The respiratory system begins with the larynx and a long trachea reinforced with cartilaginous rings. The undivided windpipe continues to the only lung (the right lung) in the region of the heart. The lung extends posteriorly as a long structure, terminating in an air sac that extends almost to the posterior end of the liver. Only the anterior part of the lung has alveoli for active respiratory exchange. The lung is not entirely enclosed in a pleural compartment, but extends freely into the main body cavity. Like all snakes, coral snakes have no muscular diaphragm to separate the lungs and the heart from other abdominal organs. During inspiration they expand their ribs upward and forward. This enlarges the lung capacity in the pleural portion of the lung and pulls air from the outside through the open glottis. When the muscles relax, the ribs fall back and the body weight presses down on the lung, expelling the air. Some coral snakes can produce a slight hissing sound by actively expelling air, which probably involves some more active muscular participation and regulation of the opening of the glottis.

Coral snake circulation is accomplished by a three-chambered heart that has right and left atria and a single, partially divided ventricle. There is also a small sinus venosus that could be considered the fourth component of the coral snake heart. The sinus venosus receives blood from the anterior and posterior vena cava where it continues into the right atrium. The left atrium receives oxygenated blood from the lung via the pulmonary veins. As only one partially partitioned ventricle exists, the blood is only partially separated when it leaves via one of the arterial trunks to the body or to the lungs. Just anterior to the heart and on the surface of the trachea is a small, oval thyroid; two pairs of thymus glands are located anterior to the thyroid.

Figure 45. Vertebra of *Leptomicrurus narduccii melanotus*, lateral view.

Kidneys are long organs that have an asymmetrical arrangement. The left kidney begins several ventrals behind the small intestine, while the right kidney is displaced slightly more anteriorly and lies at the level of the small intestine. The adrenal glands are anterior to the kidneys and in males the testis and epididymis run along the kidneys parallel to the ureters. In males, the paired vas deferens connects epididymis and cloaca and conducts the sex products in the male into the cloaca where they enter the sulcus spermaticus of the hemipenis.

Genetic Blueprint: Karyotypes

The first study ever of the chromosomes of a coral snake, *M. lemniscatus carvalhoi*, was done by the Bra-

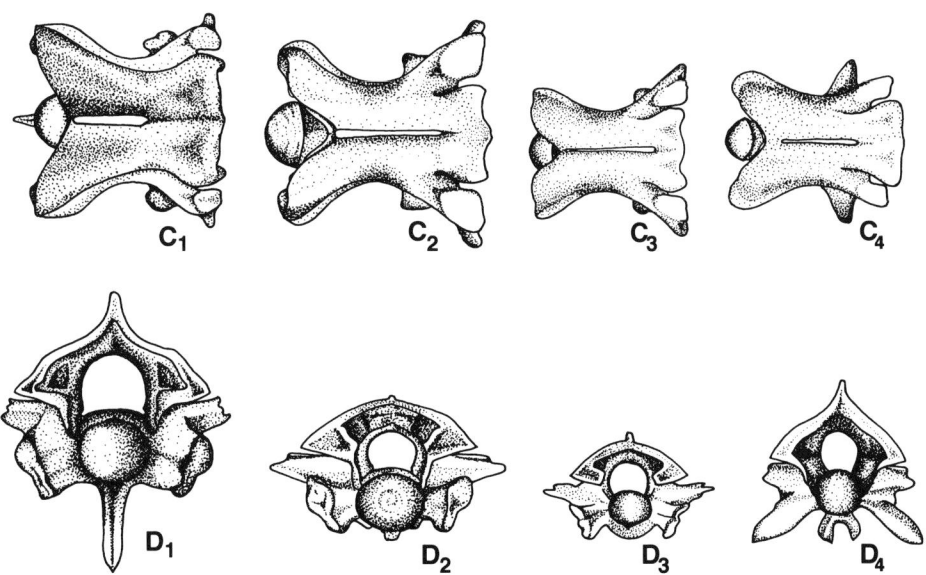

Figure 44. Sequence of upper and posterior view of vertebrae of *Micrurus f. frontalis*: C) Dorsal view of C_1—anterior, C_2—thoracic, C_3—posterior, C_4—caudal vertebrae; D) Posterior view of D_1—anterior, D_2—thoracic, D_3—posterior, D_4—caudal vertebrae. (Drawn from the same specimen as in Fig. 43 by Marcus Buononato.)

Table 4. Karyotypes of Coral Snakes

Species	Number of 2n (macro + micro chromosomes)	Secondary constriction	Reference
M. alleni	34 (14 + 20)	First pair	Gutiérrez and Bolaños (1979)
M. browni browni	26 (16 + 10)	First pair	Gutiérrez et al. (1988)
M. diastema apiatus	30 (14 + 16)	First pair	Gutiérrez et al. (1988)
M. diastema sapperi	30 (14 + 16)	First pair	Gutiérrez et al. (1988)
M. elegans veraepacis	30 (16 + 14)	First pair	Gutiérrez et al. (1988)
M. fulvius tenere	32 (16 + 16)	First pair	Graham (1977)
M. hippocrepis	30 (14 + 16)	First pair	Gutiérrez et al. (1988)
M. lemniscatus carvalhoi	42 (22 + 20)	First pair	Beçak and Beçak (1969)
M. multifasciatus hertwigi	34 (14 + 20)	Second pair	Gutiérrez and Bolaños (1979)
M. nigrocinctus nigrocinctus	26 (16 + 10)	First pair	Gutiérrez and Bolaños (1979)
M. nigrocinctus mosquitensis	30 (16 + 14)	First pair	Gutiérrez and Bolaños (1979)
M. ruatanus	26 (16 + 10)	First pair	Luykx et al. (1992)
M. surinamensis surinamensis	38 (18 + 20)	Second pair	Gutiérrez et al. (1988)

zilian geneticists Beçak and Beçak (1969). Graham (1977) investigated *M. fulvius tenere*, while Gutiérrez and Bolaños (1979, 1981) reported on karyotypes of the Costa Rican species and Gutiérrez et al. (1988) studied several more species and summarized the knowledge on coral snake karyotypes (Table 4). Luykx et al. (1992) added information about *M. ruatanus*.

The total number of chromosomes varies considerably from species to species and even between subspecies of a single species. *M. n. nigrocinctus*, *M. ruatanus*, and *M. browni* have the minimum of 26 chromosomes, while *M. lemniscatus carvalhoi* has the maximum of 42.

As an example of the variation in the number of chromosomes for subspecies belonging to the same species, *M. n. nigrocinctus* has 26, but *M. nigrocinctus*

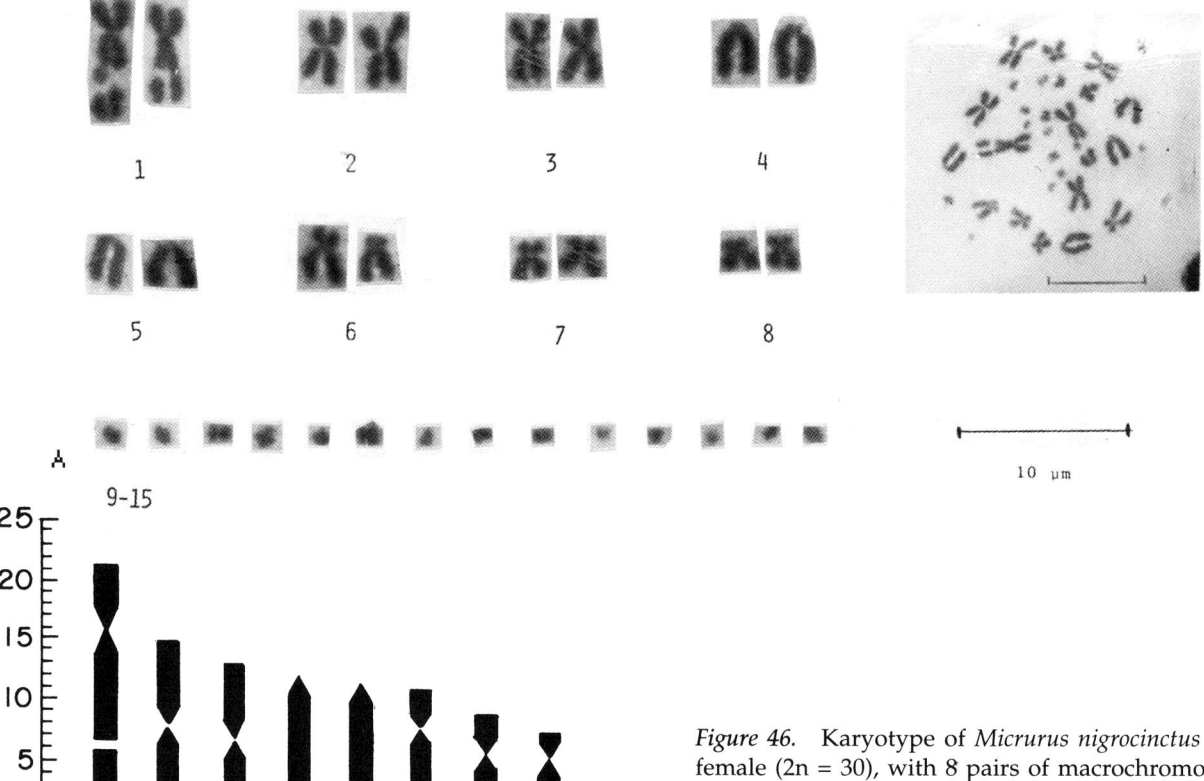

Figure 46. Karyotype of *Micrurus nigrocinctus mosquitensis*, female (2n = 30), with 8 pairs of macrochromosomes and 7 pairs of microchromosomes: A) Photograph, B) Schematic representation. (From Gutiérrez and Bolaños, 1979. Reprinted with the permission of the Revista de Biología Tropical.)

mosquitensis (Fig. 46) has 30 chromosomes. Actually, both subspecies have 16 macrochromosomes but *M. n. mosquitensis* has 14 microchromosomes, while *M. n. nigrocinctus* has only 10 microchromosomes. On the other hand, two subspecies of *M. diastema*, *M. d. apiatus* and *M. d. sapperi*, have identical karyotypes, with 14 macrochromosomes and 16 microchromosomes. Two quite unrelated coral snakes, *M. alleni* (Fig. 47) and *M. multifasciatus hertwigi*, have the same number of chromosomes (34). Yet, the first has 20 macrochromosomes while the second has only 14. Their karyotypes are quite different in spite of the similarity of chromosome number. *M. fulvius tenere* has 32 chromosomes, 16 of which are macrochromosomes and 16 of which are microchromosomes. *M. lemniscatus carvalhoi* has the highest number of microchromosomes, 22.

These numbers indicate the potential usefulness of chromosome studies for systematics and in definition of species, even down to the subspecies level. This is especially true when morphological characteristics do not provide a clear picture. But up to now, very few species have been studied karyotypically.

In coral snakes, as far as karyotypes have been studied, the male has a pair of equal sex chromosomes, ZZ, whereas the female has a heteromorphic pair, ZW, as observed in *M. fulvius tenere*, *M. diastema*, and the two subspecies of *M. nigrocinctus*. In other words, in coral snakes the female gamete will determine the sex of the descendant.

In all species of coral snakes the length of the Z sex chromosome represents a practically uniform 11% (10.9% to 11%) of he total length of the chromosome complement (Gutiérrez et al., 1988). This compares favorably with the whole family of Elapidae in which the relative length of the Z sex chromosome ranges between 10% and 12%.

Another uniform coral snake karyotypic feature is a secondary constriction in one pair of macroautosomes, a condition they share with several Old World elapids but not with cobras, *Naja* (Gutiérrez et al., 1988). All except two have a secondary constriction on the first pair of chromosomes. *M. multifasciatus hertwigi* and *M. surinamensis* have a secondary constriction on the second pair of chromosomes. This might indicate a significant phylogenetic difference from the other species. This possibility is supported by the distinctive color pattern of *M. multifasciatus* and by the long row of pterygoid teeth of *M. surinamensis*.

The two triad-type South American coral snakes, *M. lemniscatus carvalhoi* and *M. s. surinamensis*, have

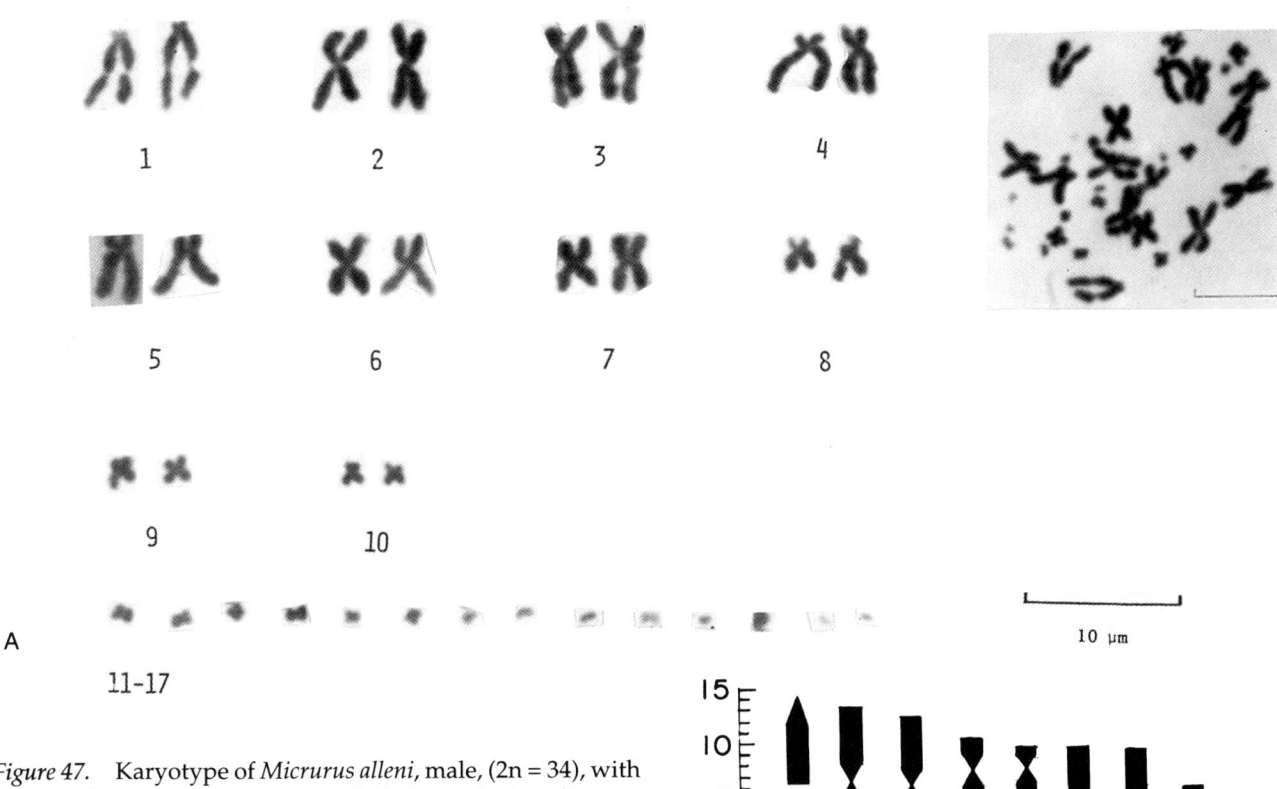

Figure 47. Karyotype of *Micrurus alleni*, male, (2n = 34), with 8 pairs of macrochromosomes and 10 pairs of microchromosomes: A) Photograph, B) Schematic representation. (From Gutiérrez and Bolaños, 1979. Reprinted with the permission of the Revista de Biología Tropical.)

several features different from the Central American species. They have the highest number of chromosomes (42 and 38 respectively) and a high number of acrocentric macrochromosomes. Gutiérrez and colleagues, to whom we owe most of what is known about coral snake karyotypes, suggest that the South American coral snake features are derived from a hypothetical primitive elapid, while the karyotype of *M. multifasciatus hertwigi*, reported under the name of *M. mipartitus* by Gutiérrez and Bolaños (1979), is close to a primitive elapid karyotype with its 14 macrochromosomes and 20 microchromosomes. This would concur with this species' undifferentiated bicolor color pattern, a hypothetical primitive feature of coral snakes.

M. alleni has metacentric chromosomes in pairs 2, 3, 6, 7, and 10 (Fig. 47), while pair 8 of the same species is submetacentric. *M. fulvius tenere* has pair 6 and the sex chromosome W subtelocentric (Graham, 1977). Acrocentric chromosomes are found in pairs 1, 4, and 5 of *M. alleni* and in all except pair 4 of *M. lemniscatus carvalhoi*. The Z sex chromosome is submetacentric in *M. fulvius tenere* and in *M. nigrocinctus*. The W chromosome of the latter species is acrocentric.

Part III
BIOLOGY AND EVOLUTION

Chapter 4
Ecology

Ecological Distribution and Habitats

Coral snakes occupy almost all of the major ecological regions of the New World, from sea level to 3,000 m high. In the unforgiving low- to median-altitude deserts of coastal Peru and Ecuador are found such desert-dwelling coral snakes as *M. mertensi* and *M. catamayensis*. In the rocky, cactus-filled deserts of northern Mexico and the southwestern United States live *Micruroides euryxanthus* and *M. distans*, while in the semidesertic Yucatan, Mexico, dwell *M. diastema alienus* and *M. e. ephippifer*. In the Brazilian semidry caatinga scrub formations is found *M. ibiboboca*. Several species such as *M. isozonus* and *M. d. dissoleucus* are found in the llanos savannas of Venezuela and Colombia where dry and rainy seasons alternate; and in the cerrado savannas of Brazil dwells *M. frontalis brasiliensis*.

Coral snakes have also invaded diverse ecological environments of several continental islands of Central and South America, from the desertic and semidesertic environments of Isla Tiburón, Mexico, and Isla Margarita, Venezuela, to the island rain forest in Great Corn Island, Nicaragua. This makes coral snakes an excellent group for studying and demonstrating adaptive radiation.

A great number of coral snakes live in the lowland rain forest, or tropical jungle, particularly in Amazonian Brazil, the Guianas, Venezuela, Colombia, Ecuador, Peru, and Bolivia. This area harbors the largest species of coral snakes, such as *M. spixii* and *M. lemniscatus*, as well as the "blackish" species from the genus *Leptomicrurus*, *M. margaritiferus* and *M. albicinctus*. It is also inhabited by the only species of coral snake closely associated with water environments, the aquatic coral snake, *M. surinamensis*. Found frequently in humid and swampy terrestrial habitats in addition to its watery world, this coral snake feeds exclusively on fish, confirming its predominantly aquatic habitat (Roze, 1983).

The largest number of species of coral snakes live sympatrically in the Amazon basin, a phenomenon that is quite interesting from the ecological standpoint. In the region of Iquitos in the Peruvian Amazon, only 90 m above sea level, at least 9 species coexist (Dixon and Soini, 1977, 1986); in the region of Santa Cecilia on the upper Amazon in Ecuador, 340 m high, 5 species of coral snakes are sympatric (Duellman, 1978); finally in Belém in eastern Brazil, a few meters above sea level, 6 species of coral snakes coexist (Cunha and Nascimento, 1973, 1978). Comparing the distribution of the Amazonian species of these three localities (Table 5), we find that Amazonia is not as uniform as it has been considered to be.

Only three species, *M. lemniscatus*, *M. surinamensis*, and *M. spixii* are found in all three places. The distribution of these species, even though represented by different subspecies, covers the entire Amazonian region. The only subspecies found in all three localities is *M. s. surinamensis*. Two other species, *M. filiformis* and *M. hemprichii*, are in both Belém and Iquitos, while five are common both to Iquitos and Santa Cecilia. Four coral snakes are present in only one locality; three of them are in the upper Amazon, while only one, *M. paraensis*, or perhaps two, are restricted to the lower Amazon. Villavicencio in Colombia, a biogeographically intriguing area, has 8 species of coral snakes.

Going further north from the Amazonian region, the tropical rain forests have only 2 to 3 sympatric species of coral snakes. In the Atlantic tropical rain forests in Nicaragua and Costa Rica *M. alleni*, *M. nigrocinctus mosquitensis*, and *M. multifasciatus hertwigi* coexist. The tropical rain forest on the Atlantic side of Mexico harbors *M. d. diastema* and *M. e. elegans*.

A simple general rule of distribution can be confirmed: the number of species of coral snakes decreases going from the equator to the temperate regions. This is particularly interesting in comparing the same major ecological region, or biome, such as the above example of the tropical rain forest (see the section on biogeographical distribution).

Many coral snakes are found in mountain environments and several are endemic or restricted to small areas. *M. multiscutatus* is found only in the Cauca region of Colombia; *M. nebularis* is endemic to a limited area of the Sierra de Juarez, Oaxaca, Mexico, and *M. limbatus* is only distributed in the tropical rain forest and wet montane forest around Los Tuxtlas, Veracruz, Mexico.

Table 5. Distribution of Coral Snakes in Three Amazonian Localities. Name in parenthesis is the subspecies of the species found in that region (Present +; absent −)

	Ecuador Napo: Sta. Cecilia 340 m	Peru Loreto: Iquitos 90 m	Brazil Pará: Belém 0–40 m
L. collaris	−	−	+ (collaris)
L. narduccii	+ (melanotus)	+	−
L. scutiventris	+	+	−
M. filiformis	−	+	+
M. hemprichi	−	+ (ortoni)	+ (hemprichii)
M. langsfdorffi	+	+	−
M. lemniscatus	+ (helleri)	+ (helleri)	+ (lemniscatus)
M. paraensis	−	−	+
M. putumayensis	−	+	−
M. spixii	+ (obscurus)	+ (obscurus)	+ (martiusi)
M. surinamensis	+ (surinamensis)	+ (surinamensis)	+ (surinamensis)

The highest-dwelling species seems to be *M. fulvius fitzingeri*, found on the Mexican plateau up to 3,000 m. *M. petersi* has been found to 2,800 m in the Andean forest in Ecuadorian Andes, and *M. mipartitus decussatus*, a cloud forest dweller, is known to reach an altitude of 2,700 m, also in Andean forest, in Cordillera Central of Colombia.

Some species of coral snakes live within restricted altitudinal and ecologically defined ranges, while others, such as *M. tschudii olsoni*, cover a very broad altitudinal range, being found between sea level and 1,500 m. The altitudinal distribution of a species can be modified by special ecological conditions, for instance, the extension of a semidesertic environment to what originally had been a humid low montane forest. In this case, the cloud forestlike vegetation remains only along the streams and humid gorges that project down from the cloud forest higher up. One interesting example of this downhill extended distribution is illustrated by *M. mipartitus semipartitus*, normally found in the cloud and wet montane forests above 800 m in northern Venezuela. In some places on the north side of the Cordillera de la Costa it penetrates downward along the wet corridors of vegetation around the creeks and gorges fed by the rain above. These cloud forestlike vegetation corridors are surrounded by dry mountain grassland and, lower, by semiarid vegetation of the coastal lowland, mostly created by deforestation. Along these valley gorges *M. mipartitus semipartitus* still maintains its distribution downward to such places as Camurí Chico, Macuto, an altitude of barely 100 m (Roze, 1953).

Within their general ecological environments, coral snakes are found in a variety of habitats that are usually quite specific for every species. In the tropical rain forest of the Amazon region of Iquitos, Henderson, Dixon, and Soini (1979) found coral snakes in the following habitats: primary rain forest (inhabited by *L. scutiventris*, *M. spixii*, and *M. hemprichii*), secondary rain forest (*M. putumayensis*, found also in the previous habitat), second growth forest (produced by the regrowth of a destroyed original rain forest), riparian environment (*M. surinamensis*), cultivated land and edificarian areas (*M. filiformis*), open vegetation (*M. lemniscatus*), and ubiquitous and edge vegetation (*M. langsdorffi*).

Some species, such as *M. fulvius tenere* and *M. f. fulvius*, are found in a variety of dry to humid habitats, natural as well as altered by humans. Some populations of *M. fulvius tenere* even live in habitats in northern Mexico that approach desert conditions.

Knowledge of coral snake distribution and habitats is important for biologists to find and study them or for other people to avoid them and prevent unexpected bite accidents. But, except for a few species, coral snakes are not abundant in nature (see section on feeding and food). A field biologist, even a herpetologist who has a good knowledge of their ecological distribution and behavior, can never count on finding coral snakes during a field trip of a limited duration. I have frequently collected for days without finding a single coral snake. In about 540 days spent in expeditions and shorter and longer field trips of general collecting in South America, I collected or observed only 63 coral snakes. This amounts to an average of one coral snake for 8.6 days of field work. However, I have observed and studied more than 200 live specimens in captivity and more than 2,000 preserved specimens in museum collections. Thus, the importance of museum collections becomes very obvious. The scarcity of specimens for many species of coral snakes is one reason why they are not well known, and their elusive habits are a key for their success in at least partially avoiding decimation by humans.

Human Influence on Distribution and Ecology

The example given above of the impact of human-created gradual aridification of the habitat on the distribution of *M. mipartitus semipartitus* is repeated in many different ways in all countries of the New World, where agriculture and urbanization have dramatically influenced, modified, and destroyed much of the original vegetation. Ever-increasing road networks, the death corridors for so many animals, are part of the "paving of the globe" process that has taken its toll on coral snakes. Roads have frequently reduced or fragmented the distributions of many species of coral snakes or entirely eliminated them in certain areas.

Many coral snakes have followed *M. mipartitus semipartitus* in becoming scarce or even completely unknown in many areas where humans have degraded most of the original vegetation. One story of the impact of human-generated changes on animals is told in "The ecological impact of man on the South Florida herpetofauna" by Larry Wilson and Louis Porras (1983), which includes *M. f. fulvius* and its severely reduced presence in some areas. In addition, Paul Müller (1970) wrote about human influence on Brazilian vertebrates.

Until now, human activity has not brought about total extinction of coral snakes on the continents. On one Atlantic island of Nicaragua, Isla del Maíz Grande or the Great Corn Island, the last few individuals of the beautiful *M. nigrocinctus babaspul* (Babaspul as the local people call it) struggle to survive the rapid growth of human population. The associated intensive growing of coconuts, bananas, and other agricultural products has modified the original environment and has nearly decimated the Babaspul. During one of our field trips in 1966 (see section on names and folklore), we discovered the Babaspul only on Little Hill, apparently the last refuge with intact original vegetation. Intensive searching elsewhere on the island did not yield any coral snakes. Interestingly, the younger inhabitants told us there are no coral snakes on the island, while the elderly people remembered the Babaspul as being relatively frequent 50 years ago. It is quite possible that in the next 10 or 20 years the last natural habitat of the Babaspul will be transformed, and this particular coral snake will cease to exist. Members of the oldest and largest family on Isla del Maíz Pequeña near Great Corn Island told us that the Babaspul once did exist on this smaller island, but no one has seen it for several decades. The American Museum of Natural History probably has the last known specimen believed to have come from the Little Corn Island, collected in 1922. When Jaime Villa (1972b, 1984) revisited the island he did not find a single Babaspul.

Coral snakes are similarly endangered or are near extinction on the Isla Roatán, Honduras (Wilson and Hahn, 1973), and on the Colombian island of San Andrés (Dunn, 1945), to mention a few.

On the mainland the human impact on ecology has begun to take its toll on coral snakes as well. The rate of destruction of nature in Latin America is much more accelerated and dramatic than most people realize. The llanos and pampas grasslands are gradually becoming semidesertic due to burning and overgrazing. The huge Amazonia is increasingly destroyed for agricultural development, industrial mining, and electrification developments, with loss of fragile tropical habitats. Foothills are eroded because of unwisely managed, usually small agricultural fields. Deserts are spreading in Mexico, as well as in Central and South America. This destruction is accompanied by a profound faunal change also affecting coral snakes.

A different example of destructive intervention by humans was mentioned in the introduction. Concerned with the danger of venomous snakes bites, Pinellas County of Florida, from 1935 to 1938, offered bounties for each coral snake killed. This helped to eliminate about 2,000 *M. f. fulvius*. However well-intentioned, the offer was based on fear and ignorance and probably will never be repeated again in the United States or in any other civilized country because of better knowledge of coral snakes, their behavior, and their current scarcity in the environment.

As is the case with other animals, some coral snakes have been able to adapt to human, urban, and suburban conditions, especially in Latin America. Spanish-speaking people use the delightful term *convivencia*, meaning "living together," to refer to this mutual adaptation, even though most people would prefer to avoid convivencia with coral snakes.

Some coral snakes successfully occupy whatever limited environments are available under city conditions in spite of human activities around them. They find enough food and are able to carry out their reproductive activities, thus becoming true suburbanites! This, of course, poses danger to children who love to play in abandoned lots and undisturbed bushy and grassy areas between houses.

In Caracas, Venezuela, one of the fastest-growing, modern Latin American cities, at least three species of coral snakes are found, but each occupies a somewhat different habitat. The most abundant species, *M. isozonus*, known principally in the llanos savannas, has become a comfortable suburban dweller. It is found in such open areas as abandoned grass and bush-covered lots, between major buildings, in urban gardens, and in not-yet-developed suburban areas. In addition, Stephan Gorzula, a Venezuelan herpetologist, has found this species in human houses also in the llanos at El Manteco, Venezuela. *M. mipartitus semipartitus*, normally found in cloud forests or in humid primary and secondary forests, is present in valleys descending from Cerro Avila into the northern fringes of the city. Unlike *M. isozonus*, which may be a relatively recent invader of the grassy openings in the Valle de Caracas, the earlier distribution of *M. mipartitus semipartitus* encompassed the entire valley before it became one of the central arteries of human activities in Venezuela. With the disappearance of the montane forests, the distribution of *M. mipartitus semipartitus* keeps shrinking. The third species, *M. d. dissoleucus*, usually found in dry lowlands of northern Venezuela and in the llanos, is found in dry, open areas of the city where almost all vegetation has been razed for urban development as well as in dry, temporary river beds on the fringes of the city, created by the destruction of the original vegetation. Each of these three species occupies a different ecological niche; thus they are able to coexist.

Another coral snake that seems to have adapted well to urban life is *M. n. nigrocinctus*, found in the suburbs, golf courses, and gardens, of San José, Costa Rica.

In the littoral around Santos, the recreational beaches of the large São Paula metropolitan population in Brazil, people periodically burn down all the grasss and bushes around beach homes and undeveloped or abandoned lots in order to kill or chase away venomous snakes including *M. corallinus*. This species also seems to thrive in a semiurban littoral environment.

On the other hand, newly created grasslands, secondary forests, and agricultural fields, particularly in the tropics, have provided opportunities for some snakes to adapt to the modified environment, especially where the prey animals have also been able to penetrate into the "organized nature" of cultivated fields, banana plantations, and other agriculturally changed environments. William Beebe (1946) describes gathering 17 specimens of *M. l. lemniscatus* during a 10-day period of nightly collecting in a rice field in the tropical rain forest of Kartabo, Guyana. In addition to the coral snake, the Akawai Indians helped him collect 5 species of colubrid snakes in the same rice field. Their presence was characterized by two remarkable things. First, all the snakes were feeding on swamp eels, also active in the wet environment of the rice field, and second, all species had at least some red coloration. Some are considered false coral snakes, such as the *Erythrolamprus aesculapii* and *Hydrops triangularis fasciatus*, while of the other ground-dwelling colubrids, *Liophis breviceps* and *Oxyrhopus petola* have red and black bands and *Pseudoboa coronata* is uniformly red dorsally with a black and white head.

Activity Periods and Seasonal Incidence

Coral snakes have adapted not only to the diverse ecological conditions but also to the different natural cycles within which the ecological and climatological features play a significant role.

Many, if not most, coral snakes are active during the day and night especially during the early morning or late evening hours. Not enough observations have been made of their activity periods, but enough data exists to safely conclude that the diurnal activity is predominant. Activity periods are associated with ecological conditions. In desertic or semidesertic environments, coral snakes such as *M. mertensi* and *Micruroides e. euryxanthus* tend to be nocturnal because heat and sunlight are too strong during the day. Where trees and other vegetation provide a shady and cooler environment, and in higher altitudes and latitudes, coral snakes tend to be more diurnal and crepuscular. Cloud forests and high altitude vegetation are particularly propitious for diurnal activity. Test, Sexton, and Heatwole (1966) studied the reptiles in Rancho Grande, Venezuela, and found *M. mipartitus semipartitus* active and foraging only in the daytime. Of 12 specimens I observed in the same area, only one was found at night (at 11:00 PM). The rest were active during the day, including crepuscular. Charles Bogert collected a coral snake in Tejocotes, Mexico, over 2,000 m high at 11:00 AM when it was busily devouring a ground-dwelling colubrid snake *Rhadinaea taeniata aemula*. The coral snake turned out to represent an undescribed subspecies, and Bogert's specimen served as holotype for the new species, *M. ephippifer zapotecus*. Occasionally nondesertic coral snakes are known to be nocturnal, such as *M. corallinus* (Mertens, 1966), found in the littoral regions of Brazil. In São Paulo and Minas Gerais, *M. lemniscatus* and *M. frontalis* have been observed active during the day and at night, even though mainly during the rainy season (Sazima and Abe, 1991).

The eye of the coral snake has a roundish pupil, and the retina (according to the dictum of Walls, a well-known "eye specialist" for animals) is well suited to "crepuscular if not nocturnal" activities.

I suspect that the dramatic change and destruction of original environments by humans have had an influence on the ways of coral snakes, including on their activity periods. It might be for this reason that *M. f. fulvius* and *M. fulvius tenere* are known to be diurnal and nocturnal.

An interesting adaptation to local conditions is known in *M. isozonus*. Its predominant environment is mainland Venezuela in the llanos and in the valleys of the Cordillera de la Costa, where I found this coral snake to be predominantly diurnal or crepuscular. However, during an expedition of the Sociedad de Ciencias Naturales La Salle of Venezuela to Margarita

Island, Venezuela, we collected and observed the same species only at night (Roze, 1964). Margarita Island for the most part is semidesertic and quite hot during the day and this coral snake has adapted to a more nocturnal way of life.

Larger cycles can be observed, for example, in the tropical lowland rain forest, where many coral snakes and probably about half of the reptiles of the tropics are found (Dixon, 1979). In many instances rainfall seems to be a determining factor in the incidence of terrestrial snakes, including coral snakes. While very little is known about coral snakes, the greatest visible abundance of snakes in the upper Amazon is found in February and August, when also the largest number of hatchlings appear and the rainfall is quite low. Yet, snakes are still active in March, April, and May, which are usually months of heavy rain. The months of lowest snake incidence are January and July, the two months preceding the high incidence months of February and August (Henderson et al., 1978).

Rainy seasons in other areas of the tropics such as the llanos of Colombia and Venezuela and in the rest of northern South America make a clearly marked wet weather season, locally called "invierno," meaning winter, which has nothing to do with the winter of the temperate regions. In the llanos, coral snakes are somewhat more active or more visible around April and May, the first months of rainy weather, as well as in a lesser rainy season in November and December. Quite a few coral snakes have been collected in the llanos in August, when conditions are relatively dry but still green in many parts in the "llanos bajos" (low llanos). A lesser rainy season occurs in October, November, and December, but this varies considerably from region to region and from year to year.

Bill Lamar, who has spent several active years in herpetological field research in Latin America, particularly in Colombia, commented about the cyclic activities of coral snakes:

> "One of the things that most impressed me about coral snakes (and some other species) was what seemed like cyclic occurrences. The trend was to see no specimens of a given species for perhaps two years, and suddenly, in a span of a few weeks, to encounter a number of them. This was true in Meta with *M. spixii*, and in Cundinamarca with *M. mipartitus*. In Cundinamarca we lived at 1,800 m in cloud forest along the western versant of the Cordillera Oriental. In February *M. mipartitus* began to appear everywhere, often in the act of feeding upon *Atractus werneri*. We even had them in the house! At such a time, they would invariably be found during the day." (Lamar, personal communication)

In the Estación Biológica Henry Pittier, Rancho Grande, Venezuela, I observed a similar situation over a period of 10 years with *M. mipartitus semipartitus*. For several years, no coral snake would be seen, and then several would appear in a relatively short time period. Shorter cycles also occur, and in this wet montane tropical forest or cloud forest two times more *M. mipartitus semipartitus* have been observed in August than in other months by Test, Sexton, and Heatwole (1966).

Sharing of Life Needs

When different species share the same environment they tend to have somewhat different niches. Ecological resources partitioning occurs among sympatric coral snakes and between coral snakes and other species of snakes that have similar, but not identical ways of life. They may occupy a different habitat or microhabitat within the same general environment (see the previous section on ecological distribution and habitats), may be active at different times of the day, or feed on preys different in kind or size. For example, of the three coral snake species living in the Valle de Caracas, mentioned before, *M. mipartitus semipartitus* lives in humid forests, *M. isozonus* is in the grassy, bushy places, and *M. d. dissoleucus* is usually present in semiarid areas with sparse vegetation (see section on human influence on distribution and ecology).

In the Santa Marta region of Colombia, *M. dumerilii colombianus* is a medium-sized snake that no doubt feeds on larger prey than the much smaller, but sympatric *M. dissoleucus melanogenys*. Another example of coral snakes occupying different microhabitats occurs along an altitudinal gradient in Michoacán, Mexico (Duellman, 1965b), where in the arid tropical scrub forest *M. distans michoacanensis* occupies a somewhat lower altitudes (up to 500 m) and is larger in size than *M. l. laticollaris*, which reaches altitudes of 1,000 m.

A particularly rich example of resource partitioning is described by Henderson, Dixon, and Soini (1979), who studied 8 species of coral snakes in the Iquitos region of Peru (see section on ecological distribution and habitats). Only one species, *M. surinamensis*, is semiaquatic. Of the 2 species that are found in open spaces, *M. filiformis* is predominantly present in or near human constructions and is quite slender and small, probably feeding on small snakes, while *M. lemniscatus helleri*, one of the largest coral snakes, feeds on a wide variety of prey including swamp eels, caecilians, amphisbaenids, lizards, and snakes, and is one of the few coral snakes that can be termed euryphagic. Of the three species found exclusively in the primary rain forest, *M. hemprichii ortoni* feeds almost exclusively on invertebrate onychophorans; *M. spixii obscurus*, one of the largest known species, feeds on snakes, lizards, and caecilians; and the tiny *L. scutiventris* feeds on small snakelike lizards. *M. putumayensis*, found in primary and in secondary rain forest, is a medium-sized snake that feeds on small colubrid snakes. And, finally *M. langsdorffi*, a ubiquitous (i.e., found in several environments), can switch from one set of living conditions to another.

Of all the coral snakes from the region, only the *M. putumayensis* and *M. langsdorffi* are not found to live together, in spite of the versatility of the latter species. As both are of similar size and similar requirements, they seem to avoid each other, especially in a single habitat. They have patchy distributions that do not overlap locally, even though *M. langsdorffi* feeds on blind snakes and worm snakes. Only colubrid prey are shared by these two species. The ecological picture becomes even more complex when other sympatric snakes are considered. Litter-dwelling, partially subterranean colubrids of the genus *Atractus*, several of which are known as coral snake mimics, apparently feed on invertebrate prey and are smaller than most of the coral snakes. Moreover, all *Atractus* are nocturnal, while coral snakes in Iquitos are predominantly diurnal. A widespread common pit viper, *Bothrops atrox*, is also sympatric with the coral snakes. Yet, it is able to live in many diverse habitats and feeds on a great variety of invertebrate and vertebrate prey. This variety of habitat and prey prevents active competition with the coral snakes, who are generally more restricted in both.

Chapter 5
Feeding and Food

Searching for Prey

Due to their limbless body form, their active, foraging habits, and their partially secretive ground living, coral snakes have developed special ways to procure food. Their powerful venom plays a large part in overpowering prey, yet hunting for prey is not as simple a task as it might appear. Coral snakes share their habitats not only with animals that can be eaten, but also animals that in turn can eat the coral snake. For this reason, when the coral snake goes on a foraging hunt, it is keenly alert and constantly employs sight, smell, and taste to evaluate any big or small moving or even stationary organisms. It must determine as quickly as possible whether the moving object is potential prey, a predator, or something neutral.

After leaving its safe shelter under a log, stone, or termite nest, the coral snake crawls slowly around on the litter, sand, or grass. It moves its head randomly right and left, examining the environment. Once in a while it will poke its head under objects on the ground or under leaves to explore beneath them. Where possible the coral snake will crawl under large objects in search of prey, or it will explore burrows made by other animals. A Florida herpetologist, Wilfred Neill (1957), observed that an occasional specimen of *M. f. fulvius* would thrash around its tail with a probing motion, perhaps intending to flush out prey animals living within the litter.

These random movements during hunting are accompanied by occasional tongue flicking. When something of interest appears before the snake, tongue flicking becomes more frequent. Tongue flicking acts as a sensor, perceiving chemical clues about an animal or object. When the forked tongue is brought back into its sheath, where it is normally kept, it brings back to a special "tasting" organ, called Jacobson's organ, whatever few molecules of chemical substances have been in the air. Actually, it is a smelling process, and we could say that snakes smell with their tongues or "taste" the air for what it contains. The coral snake's mouth is so arranged that it can flick its tongue through a small notch in its upper lip without having to open its mouth.

Any movement in the environment will stop the coral snake's random search. It will point its head in the direction of the movement and increase its tongue flicking. By smell and sight it will try to identify the source and nature of the moving object. The same behavior can be also observed in a caged coral snake when something is moving outside the cage but close to the glass wall. When the animal is not identified as prey, and especially when it is a larger animal, the coral snake will quickly withdraw, without flicking its tongue or pointing its head.

Another strategy for hunting is to "sit and wait" until prey passes by. This has been observed quite frequently in cages, but it is difficult to say if the snake uses the same method in a natural, unrestricted environment. In the cloud forest of Rancho Grande, Venezuela, I observed several *M. mipartitus semipartitus* during the day moving slowly through the jungle floor with the characteristic right and left random head movement as well as in "sit and wait" position. Immobile, one particular coral snake was apparently quite alert and remained still for some time. As I slowly approached, it reacted to my presence by moving quickly away when I was about 2 meters from it. It is possible that I disturbed a "sit and wait" hunter, but I did not observe this snake actually hunt for passing prey.

It seems that coral snakes are able to detect a trail of "odor footprints" left by a prey. As they move around, many animals, including reptiles, secrete small quantities of pheromones used as a means of communication and recognition between two individuals of the same species, particularly between males and females. With their poorly developed eyesight and restricted range of hearing, snakes largely depend on chemical cues of communication. However small the quantities produced, the pheromones can be detected, for example, not only by the males in search of a female of the same species, but also by other animals, including their predators. Thus, leaving a trail of pheromonal "footprints" on the path is a double-edged sword: they help coral snakes find their prey, but a predator can locate a coral snake as well by the "odor footprints" it leaves behind. Some interesting observations on the ability of coral snakes to follow a pheromonal trail left by a prey snake have been made by Gehlbach (1971) and Greene (1984).

When prey has been located and recognized, the coral snake points its head in that direction. As its sight is poor, the senses of smell and taste give clues and guide the snake toward the prey. Its tongue flicking increases considerably, and the lateral movement of its head is replaced by a focused attention in the direction of the prey until the snake is close enough to strike. If the prey begins to show agitation and starts moving away, the coral snake will speed up its approach. When the prey is immobile or slow, the coral snake will approach it more slowly and tentatively, still flicking its tongue and hesitating. But once the prey is within striking distance, the coral snake seizes it with a quick, striking motion. A coral snake's striking distance depends on the size of the body loop just behind the head. For an average-sized coral snake, this a short stretch of no more than 10 centimeters. Due to its limited vision, the first strike is not always successful. If the prey is not a quick-moving animal such as a lizard that can escape easily, the coral snake will strike again until the prey is secured.

Overpowering and Swallowing the Prey

The coral snake will bite the prey wherever it can. Contrary to most other venomous snakes, the coral snake will hang onto its prey and continuously chew the bitten place. This helps to introduce more venom into the bite and incapacitate the prey. The coral snake is able to regulate the amount of venom it uses and it is probable that more venom is used for larger and more active prey. As venom does not act instantaneously, a struggle with the bitten victim ensues with violent thrashing, pushing, and pulling. Even though the coral snake chooses an appropriate prey, its own life is not infrequently in danger because the prey can be a strong or somewhat venomous snake.

In 1885, the British Museum of Natural History proudly displayed a preserved *M. frontalis* that had partially swallowed an amphisbaenid lizard (*Leposternon polystegum*), a powerful limbless reptile. The amphisbaenid had its head protruding from the coral snake's side. Apparently, in its powerful struggle, the amphisbaenid had torn through the stomach and body wall of the coral snake but had eventually died from the venom. The wounded coral snake also died.

Whatever the efforts of its prey to get free, the coral snake maintains its biting grip, even when the prey bites or strangles the coral snake. As it relies mainly on its venom, the coral snake does not strangle its prey even though at times some body loops are made around the prey's body. Sometimes these loops are a response to struggling on the part of the prey snake. The coral snake might also use a body loop to get a firmer hold on a lizard or smaller snake. Furthermore, the body loop helps to press down and dominate the violently thrashing prey.

When the prey is a larger snake, the coral snake appears to try to avoid its bites by moving its own body out of danger while by holding onto the prey. To distract the prey from biting vital parts of their bodies and heads, some coral snakes such as *M. isozonus* and *M. frontalis* and many more display a curved tail tip and move it in an erratic, jerky fashion so it looks like an active snake's head. The prey snake or lizard is confused by this apparent imitation of a "head end" by the coral snake's tail, and this apparently distracts attention away from the coral snake's more vulnerable body parts.

Not infrequently, prey do bite coral snakes in spite of their efforts to prevent it. I observed a particularly violent struggle of wiggling, twisting, and strangling bodies between a *M. isozonus* and a Venezuelan racer (*Mastigodryas boddaerti*). While the coral snake was holding on to the bitten prey snake, it received about 10 bites, some even in the head, from the desperate victim before the racer succumbed to the effects of the venom and was swallowed by the coral snake.

Eric Phillips (1962), who collected many coral snakes during his 20 years in Paraguay, observed a fight in captivity between a *M. f. frontalis* and a rear-fanged false coral snake *Erythrolamprus aesculapii*. Both snakes bit each other and both died. The false coral snake died in a few minutes; *M. f. frontalis* died 19 hours later. However, during the struggle the coral snake bit itself as well, which may have caused, or contributed to, its demise.

As the venom takes effect, the struggle of the prey becomes less intense and feebler, with periods in which both adversaries remain immobile. This works to the advantage of the coral snake because with every passing moment, the venom incapacitates and finally kills the prey.

On occasions when the situation warrants, the coral snake drags or pulls the almost-overpowered and feebly resisting prey into a position that is better arranged for swallowing.

The struggle may last from a few minutes to 15 to 20 minutes, depending on the size and vigor of the prey, the place where it was first seized, and presumably the amount of venom used by the coral snake. When the first strike is near vital organs, the effect of the venom might be faster. On the other hand, a lizard seized by a leg can offer a long and painful struggle to the coral snake.

On occasions, as observed in captive specimens, the coral snake bites and then releases the prey, but then finds it again and continues the process of feeding.

In addition to *M. fulvius tenere*, this is known in *M. f. frontalis* and *M. lemniscatus* as reported by Lankes (1928, 1938) and Mertens (1956). This might not happen in nature where a lizard or snake, once bitten, could run away. It seems that the usual method of coral snake feeding features biting and holding on to the prey until it is overpowered.

The preswallowing maneuvers and even swallowing itself can occur when the prey is still alive and resisting the coral snake that is swallowing it. Sometimes, perhaps due to hunger, a coral snake seems to be so eager to swallow the prey that it disregards the active resistance of the prey.

As will be seen, one coral snake, *M. h. hemprichii*, feeds on a very curious group of invertebrate animals, onychophoran "walking worm" (*Peripatus*). These are softbodied animals about 5 centimeters long that defend by secreting a very sticky substance that repels most predators. No one has observed *M. h. hemprichii* feeding on these curious invertebrates, but the coral snake must have some special way to overcome the defensive shooting of the sticky substance.

Once the coral snake has overpowered the prey, it starts a series of preingestion maneuvers that arrange its prey for swallowing. These maneuvers frequently start even before the prey is limp and completely paralyzed. Without releasing its grip on the bitten place, the coral snake starts "jaw-walking" along the prey's body, moving towards its head. In jaw walking, the jaws are extended laterally while holding on to the body of the prey. Coral snakes that feed on reptiles are almost always able to identify the head end of the prey, apparently by the overlapping scales on the prey's body, as was discovered by Harry Greene (1976). If the coral snake starts "jaw walking" in the direction of the tail of the prey snake, it eventually recognizes its error and reverses direction, as I once observed in a *M. d. dissoleucus*. Once it reached the tip of the tail the coral snake "jaw walked" all the way back to the head, "traveling" all along the other side of the prey snake's body. In nature, however rarely, for one reason or other prey snakes are sometimes swallowed tail first. In a specimen of *M. b. browni* from Oaxaca, Mexico, deposited in the University of Colorado Museum (UCM 40082), I found four freshly swallowed specimens of a litter-dwelling colubrid snake (*Geophis sallei*). Three of the prey snakes, practically undigested, were swallowed head first, while the fourth had been swallowed tail first.

When the coral snake reaches the prey's head, it begins to swallow it using alternating jaw movements over the head. Swallowing sequences are interrupted by brief pauses until the prey's entire body has been engulfed. During swallowing, alternating lateral movements of the head allow the fangs and the lateral palatine teeth to be slightly shifted first on one side and then on the other, pushing the coral snake's head over the prey snake's body (McDowell, 1970). As the prey gradually disappears into the coral snake, some loops posterior to the coral snake's head help push the prey further inside, accompanied by stretching of the head and neck region over the prey. The tail of the prey disappears faster than the rest of the body. Some coral snakes try to speed up the swallowing of the tail by pushing and rubbing their heads against the ground or some other hard surface.

The entire process of swallowing prey can last from 2 minutes to almost an hour depending on the size and length of the prey. Several species of coral snake, after having finished the swallowing, raise their heads almost vertically from the ground as if giving a sign of completion of the swallowing process. Tongue flicking and adjusting the mouth and the jaws, including bending the head and yawning, follow. At the same time, the coral snake is quite alert and ready to seek additional prey.

Food

As coral snakes are ground and litter dwellers, their food consists of animals found in that same environment. Almost all species of coral snakes feed on snakes or snakelike animals such as snakelike lizards, "two-headed" amphisbaenids, and caecilians.

The diet of several coral snakes also includes swamp eels and knife fish (*Gymnotus carapo*), both snakelike fishes. In short, anything that is snakelike could be coral snake prey, even though prey preferences are found for most species.

Unfortunately, except for a few interesting studies such as by Greene (1973a, 1984), Vitt and Hulse (1973), Cunha and Nacimento (1973, 1978), and Dixon and Soini (1986), and a summary by Roze (1983) and a few earlier reports, little effort has been made to study the diet of coral snakes.

One way to study the diet is to open the stomachs of museum specimens. If the coral snake has been preserved soon after captured in the field, its stomach contents will be largely unchanged.

The swallowed prey has to travel through the coral snake's digestive track until the prey has been digested in its entire length. The digestion acts like a meat grinder at the level of pyloris where the digestive juices begin to act on the prey. Up to that level the prey remains completely undigested, even undamaged, because the coral snake does not chew or otherwise deform the prey. However, as the prey nearly always is swallowed head first, it is the head that gets digested first. This often makes the identification of the prey specimen more difficult.

The food known to be eaten or found in the stomachs of coral snakes is mentioned under the description of every species and subspecies (see description of species and subspecies). This does not include species that have been fed to coral snakes in captivity. In many instances they include the known prey animals, but also many other species that are exotic to coral snake distribution. In captive conditions coral snakes will occasionally accept even baby white mice, "the pink mice," and hatchling venomous pit vipers.

The major groups of animals eaten by coral snakes are snakes, lizards, amphisbaenids, caecilians, fishes, and other food animals. The summary of coral snake diet is based on a compilation of data that I have gathered by studying stomach contents of museum specimens and by observing and collecting coral snakes in the field; it is supplemented by reports from other herpetologists.

Of the 81 species and subspecies for which I have been able to determine the diet, 61 (or 75%) are ophiophagous, but only 29 coral snakes (36%) feed exclusively on snakes. Popular prey among the snakes are the blind snakes (*Leptotyphlopidae*) and the worm snakes (*Typhlopidae*). Both families are primitive, wormlike snakes. No less than 16 species (20%) of coral snakes studied feed on these peculiar litter-dwelling and burrowing snakes, but only 3 coral snakes (4%) feed exclusively on them. For example, the predominant prey of *Micruroides euryxanthus* is the *Leptotyphlops humilis*, but occasionally it will also feed on *Chilomeniscus cinctus*. The only known food of *M. e. ephippifer* is a Mexican blind snake (*Leptotyphlops phenops*). The three most frequently eaten snakes in Central America are the inoffensive and somewhat secretive colubrids of the genera *Ninia* and *Geophis*, while in South America the most frequently eaten snakes belong to *Atractus* and *Liophis*. Among the snakes consumed are also several species of false coral snakes (*Pliocercus, Erythrolamprus, Scaphiodontophis,* and *Hydrops*) and pit vipers; for example, the Peruvian desert pit viper (*Bothrops pictus*) is eaten by *M. mertensi* and copperheads (*Agkistrodon contortix*) are consumed by *M. fulvius tenere*.

A remarkable phenomenon among coral snakes is cannibalism, which is reviewed in the next chapter. No less than 7 species and subspecies (or about 9%) of coral snakes are known to eat their own kind.

Lizards are the second richest food source. Thirty-three species and subspecies of coral snakes (41%) feed on lizards, but only 11 coral snakes (14%) feed exclusively on lizards. *Leptomicrurus* are known to feed only on a snakelike teiid lizard, *Bachia*, which has legs that are considerably reduced. No less than 10 species of coral snakes feed on *Bachia*, while skinks and skinklike lizards of such genera as *Eumeces, Scincella, Gymnophthalmus,* and *Mabuya*, which have short legs and move in a somewhat snakelike manner, are also preferred prey of many coral snakes. The strong and fast-running diurnal teiid lizards, such as the whiptail lizards (*Cnemidophorous*) and the related teiid genera *Ameiva* and *Kentropyx*, form part of the the diet of 7 coral snakes. As far as is known, *M. ruatanus* feeds exclusively on the Roatán whiptail lizard (*Cnemidophorus lemniscatus ruatanus*) (Wilson and Hahn, 1973).

Appropriately, the snakelike prey of coral snakes includes the interesting reptilian group of amphisbaenids. Closely related to lizards, they have no limbs to speak of, a stout body, and a tail stump that is almost indistinguishable from the head "stump"; hence, the common name of "two-headed snakes" or "two-headed lizards." They can deliver a powerful and quite nasty bite. This, however, is no impediment to being on the menu of at least 13 species of coral snakes (16%). Several subspecies of *M. frontalis* feed predominantly on amphisbaenids (Sazima and Abe, 1991). Two coral snakes feed exclusively on amphisbaenids, including *M. t. tschudii*, which feeds on *Amphisbaena occidentalis*.

Particularly interesting coral snake prey are the limbless snakelike caecilians, which are actually amphibians. Superficially they are similar to the amphisbaenids. Caecilians live in a moist or swampy environment; like most amphibians, they would dessicate and dry to death in the absence of moisture. The diets of 9 species of coral snakes include caecilians, and 2 of them, *M. m. mipartitus* and *M. bocourti* are known to feed only on caecilians. *M. corallinus* in Brazil is known to be a great and exclusive consumer of caecilians and amphisbaenids.

One of the food items most widely consumed by coral snakes is not a reptile but a fish: the swamp eel (*Synbranchus marmoratus*). While only 7 species and subspecies of coral snakes feed on swamp eels, they are eaten in Central America as well as in South America. All subspecies of *M. lemniscatus* feed predominantly, though not exclusively, on this versatile eel that can traverse long distances in moist grassy fields outside water. Swamp eels constitute a substantial part of the diet of *M. surinamensis*. In addition to eating swamp eels and confirming its aquatic and semiaquatic habitats, this coral snake is known to feed on other fishes such as electric eels, knifefish (*Gymnotus carapo*), catfishes (*Callichthys callichthys*), and several more. *M. surinamensis* is the only species that feeds exclusively on fishes.

One interesting exception to the coral snake vertebrate diet is the onycophoran invertebrate of the genus *Peripatus*, considered an intermediate evolutionary group between the legless earthworms and legged arthropods. Both subspecies of *M. hemprichii* are specialists in feeding nearly exclusively on *Peripatus*. While occasionally they also consume snakes and amphisbaenids, more than 90% of their diet consists of several species of *Peripatus*. This diet has been confirmed in *M. h. hemprichii* in Pará, Brazil, and in *M. h. ortoni* in eastern Peru. It is possible that this coral snake normally feeds on *Peripatus* and that only during a shortage of this food will it resort to other prey. It would be most interesting to study the feeding behavior and regime of this coral snake.

Very occasionally, the stomach contents of a coral snake include such items as centipedes, remnants of scorpions, and other invertebrates that might have been in the stomach of the coral snake's prey lizards or prey snakes. Remnants of small rodents and mammalian hair have also been found in the stomachs of several species of coral snakes. These too might have been in the stomachs of the prey animals swallowed by the coral snake. In the stomach of a *M. n. zunilensis* I found a snake egg that might or might not have been swallowed directly by the coral snake. The stomach was otherwise empty, which leaves the egg-eating behavior of the coral snake an open question.

Very little can be said about the quantitative relationships of coral snake prey. Greene (1973a, 1984) made a survey of the two U.S. subspecies of *M. fulvius*, but this study combines the food of both subspecies. Thus far these are the best data we have. *M. f. fulvius* and *M. fulvius tenere* feed on a variety of snakes and lizards as well. Of the 149 items of snakes, the most abundant prey is the rough earth snake (*Virginia striatula*) (19 specimens), the ringneck snake (*Diadophis punctatus*) (11), and the brown snake (*Storeria decayi*) (11), making a total of 41 prey snakes or 27% of its total diet. The two preferred prey lizards are the ground skink (*Scincella laterale*) (21) and the glass lizard (*Ophisaurus*) (13), totaling 34 (or 54%) of the 62 lizard prey items found by Greene.

However, skinks have the ability to break off their own tails, leaving them in the predator's mouth while escaping. Thus a tail in the coral snake's stomach does not always mean a successful hunt of the entire specimen. Size, seasonal abundance, and distribution of prey influences prey selection by coral snakes. For example, in the United States skinks are more available in spring and fall and are eaten more frequently than at other seasons.

The length and weight of the prey also vary considerably. *M. fulvius* eats lizards that are not longer than 40 centimeters and weigh up to about 10 grams. These sizes are within easily manageable dimensions. Young coral snakes will eat smaller prey. Of the snake prey, coral snakes select either species of small secretive snakes or young and subadult individuals of the large and active ground-dwelling snakes such as the king snakes, milk snakes, garter snakes, and others.

During a hunting period, coral snakes quite frequently will consume more than one prey, presumably when the coral snake has not eaten for a while. Especially when it is not too large, the first prey will trigger what could be called a "feeding excitement" or "warm up" exercise for more food. A hormonal rearrangement and increased alertness occur and the coral snake becomes visibly more excited and more alert and responds more readily to movement in the environment. It increases tongue flicking, has more active head movements, and displays accelerated and more intensive patterns of search for new prey. In nature this translates into a greater success at locating and eating several prey items in a short time. The stomach contents of several museum specimens illustrate this phenomenon. For example, a 810 mm long specimen of *M. latifasciatus* (UMMZ 120437) from Guatemala had swallowed 4 specimens of secretive colubrid snakes: 1 *Geophis nasalis* and 3 specimens of *Adelphicos quadrivirgatus*. Except one, they were undigested, suggesting that at least 3 of them were swallowed during the same hunting period or very close to it. The prey snakes were 220 mm, 270 mm, and 250 mm long. The total combined weight of the prey was about 65% of the total weight of the *M. latifasciatus* that swallowed them. Coral snakes are able to consume prey specimens up to 130% of their body weight (Greene, 1984), not necessarily all at once. Larger coral snakes will eat larger prey, but too large a prey specimen can endanger the life of the coral snake or even be fatal when the coral snake misjudges the power of the adversary and the effort required for swallowing it; e.g., *M. f. frontalis* in the British Museum, torn apart by the amphisbaenid it swallowed. Neill (1968) also related a fatal "meal" case on the part of an *M. f. fulvius*.

As coral snakes eat animals that, in turn, eat other animals, they form part of complex food chains. From the ecological standpoint, coral snakes are mostly tertiary consumers, occasionally even quaternary or quinquenary consumers. For instance, an insect eats plant material (as primary consumer) and is eaten by a lizard or amphisbaenid (secondary consumer), which in turn is eaten by a coral snake (tertiary consumer). When a coral snake eats a snake that has eaten a lizard, it becomes a quaternary consumer. That is one reason why there are not too many coral snakes in nature. Due to the decrease of energy-food at every feeding level, the longer the food chain, the fewer individuals are present at the end part of this eat-and-be-eaten sequence. On the other hand, as coral snakes eat only a limited variety of food—they are stenophagous feeders—their abundance is also conditioned by the availability of their specific prey.

Cannibalism

By far the most intriguing phenomenon of the ways of coral snakes is their low-level but persistent cannibalism. Hoge and Federsoni (1981) described an interesting and dramatic case that took place in a cage in the Instituto Butantan.

"... When eight hatchlings of *Micrurus corallinus* were born, all alive, they were kept together overnight. In checking them next morning, only four specimens were found alive. Of the rest of the specimens, only the tails were protruding from the mouths of their cannibalistic brothers. The four surviving brothers also died due to ruptured digestive tract produced by the entrance of too large a food item". [sic]

This story confirms several interesting facts: first, that *Micrurus corallinus* is cannibalistic; second, that hatchlings can begin to feed the same day they are born if food is available; and third, they can overpower prey as big as themselves.

In addition to *Micrurus corallinus*, cannibalism is known in *M. ibiboboca* (Amaral, 1933), *M. circinalis*, and *M. lemniscatus diutius* (Wehekind, 1955), *M. p. pyrrhocryptus* has been observed to be cannibalistic in captivity (Abalos, Baez, and Nader, 1964).

When Loveridge (1938, 1944) described cannibalism in *M. f. fulvius* for the first time, this produced some interesting speculation as to the interpretation of why cannibalism exists in such relatively highly evolved vertebrates. One such speculation, as noted by Harry Greene (1973a), was offered by Ardrey, the popularizer of the idea of interpreting and extrapolating human social behavior from animal social behavior. In his book, *The Social Contract* (1970), Ardrey advanced the idea of human aggressivity as a biological-social imperative, derived from our animal past. As a proof of his assertion, he gave Loveridge's description of cannibalism in the eastern coral snake. This constitutes a misinterpretation, to say the least, of cannibalism. Cannibalism in coral snakes does not illustrate any uncontrollable aggressivity as Ardrey would see it, nor does it imply aggressivity *sensu humanum*. Cannibalism exists to some extent in several groups of vertebrates, even though this is an exception rather than the rule.

About 2% of the prey of *M. f. fulvius* are other *M. f. fulvius*. In Florida, however, about 4.5% of the total prey is made up of specimens of its own kind. Adult specimens can consume other adult individuals of similar size, but only up to a certain size. In the Museum of Comparative Zoology there is a specimen of *M. f. fulvius* (MCZ 4896) 620 mm long that swallowed and later disgorged another *M. f. fulvius* (MCZ 46897) 535 mm long. The prey coral snake constituted 86% of the length of the predator.

Less frequent cannibalism is known in *M. fulvius tenere*. Curtis (1952) found that a 479 mm long specimen of *M. fulvius tenere* in Anglina County, Texas, had swallowed a hatchling of its own kind, only 178 mm long. He offered a curious explanation of this evident case of cannibalism. As a brown snake (*Storeria decayi*) was also found in the stomach of *M. fulvius tenere*, Curtis suggested that both male coral snakes attempted to simultaneously swallow the same prey snake. The one started swallowing the brown snake from its head and the other from the tail tend. The larger *M. fulvius tenere* kept swallowing until it engulfed not only the brown snake but also the younger "brother" of its own kind. This is unlikely as coral snakes usually are able to find the head end of the prey by the scale overlap on the prey's body (Greene, 1976).

Cannibalism in coral snakes requires comments. The size of the snakes does not seem to play a major role apart from the general limitation of too large a prey, as in the example of *M. corallinus* hatchlings mentioned before. Cannibalism is not limited or restricted to one or another sex. Both males and females are involved in cannibalistic feeding. The only difference is that the males are cannibalistically homeovorous (cannibal on the same sex) and cannibalistically heterovorous (cannibal on the opposite sex) while the females thus far are known to be only cannibalistically homeovorous.

Coral snakes eat not only individuals of their own kind (intraspecific cannibalism), but also feed on other species of coral snake, which is interspecific cannibalism. Examples are *M. lemniscatus diutius* feeding on its own congenere, *M. circinalis* in the island nation of Trinidad, and *M. spixii obscurus* feeding on *M. a. annellatus*. H. M. Smith and Grant (1958) reported that the stomach of a *M. n. nigrocinctus* "contained [a] nearly equally large coral snake," but they did not mention whether it was the same or another species of coral snake.

Several factors could be involved in establishing and maintaining a low-level cannibalism among coral snakes:

1. A weakly developed pheromonal communication system within the species, even though coral snakes are able to follow the pheromonal trail of a potential prey (Greene, 1973a).
2. Hunger pressure, especially in the food excitement stage after having consumed the first prey, which, as has been mentioned earlier, produces a state of hormonal excitement or "feeding excitement" in which the response to the stimuli of a second prey may predominate over the response to the stimuli of intraspecific recognition.
3. Similarity between the predator's and the prey's snakelike shape, size, movement, and behavior. As coral snakes are predominantly herpetophagous, particularly ophiophagous, their own kin display movements that can be easily confused with those of their prey, especially considering that the coral snakes' eyes are not well developed.

Chapter 6
Reproduction

Coral snakes are egg layers with an incubation period that varies depending on local conditions. The females lay their eggs and abandon them, so the hatchlings start their new life alone.

Reproductive Cycle

Because coral snakes are found in all climatic regions north and south of the equator—temperate, subtropical, and tropical—their reproductive cycles vary with their wide geographical distribution. Different ecological conditions, altitude, and latitude have favored three basic patterns of reproductive cycles or life histories (Dunham et al., 1988).

1. In the tropical regions where the majority of coral snakes live, the reproductive cycle centers around the alternating dry and rainy seasons. Mating takes place during the dry season, and egg laying occurs a short time before the beginning of the rainy season. For example, I found a female *M. isozonus* laying eggs on April 27th (shortly before the rainy season) in the Cordillera de la Costa region of Venezuela (Cúa, Miranda). I have also found that coral snakes such as *M. dissoleucus* and *M. mipartitus* lay their eggs during the dry season in northern Colombia (January and February). Several females of the latter species were found to be carrying mature eggs in January.
2. At the extremes of coral snake distribution, in the temperate regions with four seasons, temperature is the conditioning factor. Mating takes place in late fall or spring (as late as May in warmer areas), with egg laying following in the summer and hatching in the fall.

    Because the seasons are inverted in the northern and southern hemispheres, the dates of reproductive activities are similarly inverted. In the United States, for example, egg laying may occur as early as April (but usually in June and July), with the eggs hatching in August and September for *M. fulvius*. In southern Brazil, Uruguay, and Argentina, on the other hand, subspecies of *M. frontalis* lay eggs between the summer months of November and January and hatchlings emerge during the autumn months of February and March.
3. In tropical rain forest with high temperatures and humidity during practically the whole year and with limited cyclic changes, coral snake reproduction is irregular or even noncyclic. For example, *M. psyches* had mature eggs in the oviducts on June 22nd at Kartabo, Guyana. This corresponds to the rainy season in Trinidad, where this same species is known to mate during the period of January to May, with eggs laid between July and September (Emsley, 1977). Other rain forest-dwelling coral snakes probably fall into this category as well. On the other hand, data from the Iquitos region of the Peruvian Amazon suggest a more regular pattern. Females of *M. lemniscatus* were found to carry oviductal eggs only in June and July, and *Leptomicrurus narduccii melanotus* and *M. langsdorffi* in Ecuadorian rain forest in May (Duellman, 1978), suggesting an egg laying time of June, July, and August. It may be that several rain forest species have more regular breeding habits than have been recognized. But the observation that *M. spixii obscurus* in the same Iquitos region mated on July 29 (Dixon and Soini, 1986) suggests at least a different cycle than in the other species.

Extreme or restricted ecological conditions and harsh environments such as high montane forest or hot tropical and subtropical deserts force coral snakes to adapt to these local conditions. For example, the desert-dwelling *Micruroides e. euryxanthus* in Sonora has oviductal eggs both in the second half of May and at the end of July, suggesting an egg-laying phase that stretches from the end of July to September. This would correspond with the breeding dates of *M. fulvius* in the United States.

Where rain forest areas have been destroyed or drastically altered by human activity, the normally noncyclic rain forest coral snakes appear to have adapted to a cyclic pattern. For example, *M. browni taylori* lives in a degraded area near the ocean in Acapulco, Mexico, where the original vegetation has been almost completely replaced by mango trees and coconut groves. These snakes have established their living and breeding quarters in compost piles (Casas-Andreu and López-Forment, 1978). March is the driest month in this coastal region of Guerrero, with the rains beginning in June and the heaviest precipitation in September, because of tropical cyclones. Mature eggs of this subspecies are found in the oviducts in the second half of April and the beginning of May, suggesting that mating takes place in March (the dry period) followed by egg laying in late May and June (the beginning of the rains). A somewhat similar Atlantic-side example is *M. bernadi* in Nexaca, Puebla, with oviductal eggs in February.

Most of the knowledge about the reproduction of coral snakes that I summarize here has been gathered on species in the United States. Reproduction of the Texas coral snake (*M. fulvius tenere*) has been discussed by John Werler (1951, 1970), Sabath and Worthington (1959), Hugh Quinn (1979), and J. A. Campbell (1973). Reproductive activities in the eastern coral snake (*M. f. fulvius*) have been reported by Allen and Neill (1950), Stickel (1952), Telford (1955), Neill (1957), and Zegel (1975), with a comprehensive report by Jackson and Franz (1981).

The reproduction of *M. mipartitus decussatus* was discussed by Ayerbe et al. (1990), while data on eggs and reproduction of *M. f. frontalis* were presented by Azevedo (1960, 1961, 1962a), Araujo (1978), and Paulo Vanzolini et al. (1980), and data on *M. frontalis altirostris* by Vaz-Ferreira et al. (1970).

Internal Reproductive Cycle and System of Males

As in most secretive animals, the information on sexual cycles in coral snakes is gained through the dissection of preserved specimens, and practically the only definitive way to determine sexual maturity in small males is to examine the epididymis for the presence of spermatozoa. Such studies suggest that in most coral snakes males attain sexual maturity in 1 or 2 years; 11 to 16 months in *M. f. fulvius* and 12 to 21 months in *M. f. tenere*. At this age, these snakes are about 400 mm long. This means that a hatchling of this species born in July might either become sexually active in the spring breeding season of the next year or perhaps not until the following year. In other species, males may mature at smaller sizes, although their ages are unknown. In the Darién region of Panama, Charles Myers found a sexually mature male of *M. m. mipartitus* that was only 300 mm long. In smaller species, such as *M. dissoleucus*, males probably reach sexual maturity when they are about 270 mm long.

Upon maturation, the male reproductive system begins producing sperm in an ongoing spermatogenetic cycle. Once produced, the sperm are conducted to the epididymis by special ducts, the ductuli efferentes. During copulation the ductus defferens transports the sperm from the epididymis to the cloaca, and along the sperm duct (sulcus spermaticus) of the everted and inserted hemipenis into the oviducts of the female. Fat reserves, centralized in the fat bodies, and probably fat in the liver, provide energy for sperm production, particularly during the intensive period of spermatogenesis.

In *M. f. fulvius*, sperm production continues throughout the year and sperm may be stored in the epididymis for as long as 10 months. The situation is similar in *M. f. tenere*, but spermatogenesis is reduced or absent during the breeding period (May to July). The month of July is the only time that sperm are not found in either the ductus defferens or in the epididymis. This coincides with the egg-laying period when mating is unlikely to occur.

The spermatozoa are similar in all of the species of coral snakes, as they are in most snakes. They consist of an elongated, slightly curved head, followed by a constriction and a short neck region; a locomotor tail serves to propel the spermatozoan. Beneath the outer vestment, the tail has a mitochondrial region that provides energy necessary for movement. Deeper within, the tail consists of a sheath, a central axial filament surrounded by coarse fibers, and a short distal region with an endpiece (Fig. 48).

Internal Reproductive Cycle and System of Females

Females reach sexual maturity in about 2 years and are probably sexually active throughout life. More specifically, the female reproductive system usually reaches sexual maturity at the age of 21 to 27 months. However, as short a time as 15 months has also been suggested for *M. f. tenere*. Females of *M. f. fulvius* and *M. f. tenere* lay their first clutches of eggs in the summer of their third year of life. In these species, size and accumulation of body fat seem to have a role in sexual readiness. The minimum length of a sexually mature female is around 500 mm but the first clutch of eggs is laid when the female reaches about 550 mm.

The female reproductive cycle starts in winter and early spring with growth of the follicles in the ovaries. From March through the beginning of June, increased growth of follicles occurs in both ovaries simultaneously until the maximum size of follicles is reached. In *M. f. fulvius*, the ovarian follicles reach a maximum size of 30 mm to 40 mm in mid-June. In May, however, the weight of the ovaries has already begun to decline, and it diminishes rapidly in June after the ovulation has occurred. After ovulation, the 5-mm to 7-mm long corpora lutea persist for a short time and disappear in a

Reproduction

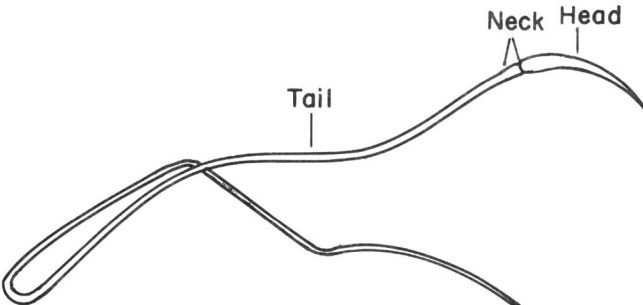

Figure 48. Schematic representation of coral snake spermatozoa. (Drawn by G. Fisher.)

few days. Minute ovarian follicles, representing the future eggs, remain until the next growth cycle early in the spring of the following year. At that time, several of them will begin development.

On the average, the right ovary apparently produces more eggs than the left. This is supported by the fact that the right oviduct, being larger than the left, usually contains more eggs. Studying females of *M. f. tenere*, Quinn (1971) found that the mean number of eggs in the right oviduct was 5.8 compared with only 4.8 in the left oviduct.

After ovulation, the eggs are fertilized in the oviduct by sperm that have been stored there since the last copulation. The female can keep viable sperm in the oviduct for 7 or more months and consequently sperm are often present in the oviduct from October through May or June. In *M. fulvius* the eggs reside in the oviduct somewhere between 30 and 40 days. These figures should be considered an extreme because in the northern range of coral snake distribution in North and South Carolina, hibernation tends to reduce the time available for mating. Thus, northern females must carry viable sperm for a longer period of time than would be usual for females of South American species.

M. browni taylori carries eggs in the oviduct from the second half of April to the middle of May (Casas-Andreu and López-Formet, 1978). Before that, females carry 7 to 11 maturing follicular eggs. Follicles, no larger than 0.9 mm, are found in females in May and June. This corresponds to the lasts days before egg laying and the post-egg laying period.

Courtship and Mating

Courtship and mating are complicated and difficult tasks for all snakes, but for coral snakes they are dangerous as well. First, in many areas coral snakes are not very abundant and finding a mate is a chore in itself. Second, as the food of coral snakes is largely other snakes, there is the danger of being mistakenly identified not as a potential mate but as a nutritional delicacy. The low-level but persistent cannibalism among coral snakes bears witness to this reality (see section on food). Active and clear chemical and/or behavioral communication between the mates and early arousal of the female are two necessary ingredients for a successful mating.

Very little is known of the courtship and copulation of most species. Judging from the mating behavior of coral snakes in the United States and observations of several other species, some common elements of courtship behavior can be recognized.

As observed in *M. f. tenere*, when a male finds a female, he flicks his tongue toward the place of first contact with her body. He then raises his head and neck and tilts his head down again, touching the female's back with his snout. Without flicking the tongue, he runs his nose along the dorsum of the female toward her head, he aligns his body with hers, and he arranges himself so that the vents of both are side by side. The bodies are crossed near the vents. Lifting his tail to about a 30° angle, the male exposes his vent and proceeds to evert the hemipenes. When sufficiently aroused, the female lifts her tail as well, exposing the gaping vent. With thrusting movements the male introduces one hemipenis into the female's cloacal opening. Only one hemipenis is used in copulation and there seems to be no preference.

When the male is not immediately successful in arousing the female, he may pursue her and repeatedly move his snout along her body until alignment is accomplished. If the male runs his snout toward her tail end instead of toward her head, he may pause and reverse direction when he reaches her vent area. A part of mating behavior that probably serves to arouse the female are successive strokes on her dorsum that the male makes using his body as well as his snout. Jerking motions and rubbing the chin over the female's dorsum have also been observed during the courtship of *M. f. fulvius*.

On one occasion Quinn (1979), observed a captive male who was introduced into a female's cage for mating purposes. The female bit the thrusting male and held him for about 2 seconds before releasing him. This may be an example of mistaken identification of a prey by the female, or it might be a part of courtship behavior. After the bite no courtship was performed, and the male apparently did not die from the bite.

Egg Laying and Incubation

Eggs are usually laid in rotten logs, in organic debris under stones, in subterranean shallow tunnels, and in other sheltered and concealed places. Termite nests and anthills are used as nesting sites by several southern species (see section "A reproductive success story: the Uruguayan coral snake" (*M. frontalis altirostris*)).

When the conditions for egg laying are not appropriate or the female is restricted or disturbed as, for example, in captivity, she can delay the egg laying for several days and probably several weeks. In nature this can happen due to bad weather conditions or scarcity of adequate environment and microhabitat. The proper site and materials must be available. It is probable that the female chooses and prepares the site where she will lay her eggs. On one occasion Santiago Ayerbe (Ayerbe et al., 1990) observed a captive female *M. mipartitus decussatus* lay one egg that was not viable. When she was given humid moss and rotting pieces of logs in abundance, she proceeded to build several tunnellike structures. Four days later, when the tunnels were finished, she laid 5 more eggs. In nature, the female would most probably either carefully select the site or make some adjustments to prepare or improve it.

Once her eggs are laid, the female abandons them. A report (J. A. Campbell, 1973) suggested that the female was possibly brooding the eggs by covering them with her body. Another suggestion of the association of a female with her eggs comes from Trinidad for *M. circinalis* (Mole, 1924). Brooding behavior is known in several genera of the Old World elapids, such as the king cobra (*Ophiophagus*), cobras (*Naja*), and kraits (*Bungarus*). In coral snakes, however, this does not seem to be the case. Observations of several species of coral snakes thus far indicate that the female does not relate to the eggs once they are laid.

The eggs are laid singly or in groups (Color 42). They can be adhered longitudinally or not.

As far as we know, coral snakes lay eggs only once a year, even though in the tropical rain forest where reproductive cycles are less conditioned by climate or environmental variations, more than one yearly clutch might be possible.

The incubation period varies from species to species. Even within the same species or subspecies the time for the development of the eggs can differ, depending on when the eggs have been actually fertilized and how long they are retained in the oviduct by the female. Once the eggs have been laid, temperature and humidity play significant roles in shortening or extending the incubation period. Fluctuating environmental temperature, dry spells, or occasional exposure of eggs can contribute to the irregularity of incubation time.

The only documented case of a complete sequence of mating, egg laying, and hatching for the same female is that of a *M. f. tenere*. Tryon and McCrystal (1982), observed a pair of coral snakes in captivity in the Houston Zoological Gardens. Copulation took place on May 12. Eight eggs were laid on June 18, 37 days after the mating. Removed from the cage, the eggs were incubated for 49 days. Eight healthy hatchlings emerged on August 6, suggesting that the time between fertilization and hatching is about 86 days. A remarkable fact is that the 8 eggs of this gravid female weighed 28.3 g, nearly as much as the female who weighed 32 g after the oviposition.

Another clutch of *M. f. tenere* eggs was incubated by the same biologists but at lower temperatures: 22 to 27°C, as compared to 25 to 32°C, maintained in the case described above. This clutch took 62 days to hatch.

The known incubation period for different subspecies of *M. fulvius* is between 45 and 92 days; the optimum time seems to be between 45 and 50 days. In extreme northern and southern areas of the western hemisphere or in higher altitudes with cooler climates, the development of eggs will take longer. The incubation period for *M. frontalis altirostris* in Uruguay is 70 to 80 days, while that of *M. mipartitus decussatus* in the Andes of Colombia extends between 84 and 90 days.

It is possible that in the tropical environment the incubation period for coral snakes outside the female's body is longer than in the temperate regions. One possible explanation is the relatively short time available for optimal development in the temperate region. Early frost and fluctuating cold weather restrict the time available for successful incubation. For these reasons, temperate region females retain eggs with developing embryos for a longer time in the oviduct than the tropical region. Prolonged retention of developing eggs in the oviduct would favor an evolutionary trend toward ovoviviparity in coral snakes.

Ayerbe et al. (1990) observed that after several weeks of incubation the eggs of *M. mipartitus decussatus* developed brownish sepia spots, giving them a mottled appearance. If this coloration is confirmed to be a general characteristic of this subspecies, the light coffee-brown mottled pattern might represent a cryptic adaptation to the environment in which the eggs of this subspecies are laid: organic debris, dry brownish leaves, decomposing bits of vegetation, and half-decayed tree trunks. As *M. mipartitus decussatus* is a somewhat more litter-bound snake, concealment of the eggs by an inconspicuous color pattern might prevent their discovery by sight-oriented predators.

Once laid, the eggs continue to grow in size and weight, mainly due to absorbed humidity and oxygen. Between egg laying and hatching, the eggs can increase from 20% to nearly 40% in size and almost double in weight.

Eggs of *M. mipartitus decussatus*, laid by a 700 mm long female, weighed 4.0 to 4.5 g 44 days after having been laid, or halfway through the incubation period. After 84 days of incubation, shortly before hatching, these same eggs weighed 6.4 to 6.5 g (Ayerbe et al., 1990). This amounts to a 62% increase in weight during the second half of incubation. Probably, the weight of the egg will double during the full incubation period of 87 days known for this subspecies.

Laboratory Incubation of Eggs

Usually, some of the eggs laid and/or incubated in captivity fail to hatch, either because of disturbance or trauma suffered by the female during capture, inadequate conditions of captivity, or inappropriate conditions for incubation. Some eggs, or even an entire clutch, might sometimes fail to be fertilized. Moreover, coral snake eggs seem to be delicate and require precise handling as well as correct conditions for a successful incubation.

After considerable experimentation and frustration, several relatively successful methods for incubating snake eggs under laboratory conditions have been developed. A general golden rule for the incubation of all reptilian eggs is to learn as much as possible about the natural conditions of the region in which the eggs are normally laid and try to re-create the basic conditions of temperature and humidity as closely as possible. Too much or too little of either factor can be decisive. Prevention of any outside contamination and disease must also be considered when preparing the containers and media for incubation. Organic material brought in from a natural environment might contain bacteria, fungi, or insects, some of which could be predators of or parasites on the incubating eggs. Eggs should be removed from the cage where they have been laid and incubated in a specially prepared container or plastic bag in such medium as vermiculite, moistened with equal volume of clean water.

Embryonic Development

No adequate studies have been made of the embryonic development of coral snakes. After the follicular eggs are released into the oviduct, fertilization takes place and the zygote is formed. Cell division begins some time thereafter, initiating embryonic development. The embryonic development is well underway while the eggs are still retained in the oviduct. The stage of embryonic development at the moment of egg laying depends on how long the female has retained the maturing eggs in her oviduct. Eggs can be laid at the gastrula stage (*M. frontalis altirostris*) (Vaz-Ferreira et al., 1970) or at the stage when the embryo has been already well formed and can be clearly recognized as a coral snake (*M. fulvius*) (Ditmars, 1907). *M. mipartitus decussats* reaches the stage of an unpigmented embryo with dark eye-spots and a heartbeat 20 days after the eggs are laid (Ayerbe et al., 1990). In this species, eggs take 85 days to hatch. *M. frontalis altirostris* embryos have full coloration and inverted hemipenes 7 days before hatching.

The developing embryo is protected by the shell and by several extra-embryonic membranes. The amnion, which allows absorption of oxygen and humidity for the embryo and, at the same time, prevents excessive desiccation. It is this membrane that in the evolutionary past enabled reptiles to lay their eggs on land and thus invade inland areas.

Shape, Size, and Number of Eggs

Coral snake eggs are elongated and semicylindrical, more regularly cylindrical than in most species of snakes (Color 42), apparently an evolutionary adaptation to the slender and very elongated bodies. Sometimes slightly bent or bulged eggs are produced. These have a more irregular shape, but they are always considerably elongated.

A soft, elastic, but quite tough and sturdy shell covers and protects the eggs from outside. In most species the shell is creamy white or yellowish white. Sometimes, the eggs can be slightly transparent, especially the whiter eggs, and careful observation can reveal aspects of embryonic development, especially once the body pigment has developed.

The size, weight, and number of eggs are determined by the general size of the species and by the relative size and age of the female. Also, the size and weight of the eggs are influenced by the number of eggs in the clutch. Coral snakes produce 1 to 13 eggs. There is one report of 23 eggs produced by *M. multifasciatus hertwigi* (Jaime Villa, in litt.). This is 10 more than the highest-known number for coral snakes and must be confirmed.

Examination of museum specimens, field observations, and the scant literature records suggest only a limited variation in number of eggs produced by the different species. A small species such as *M. d. dissoleucus* had 5 eggs, while a female of *M. dissoleucus dunni*, only 300 mm long, had 3. The large species, such as *M. lemniscatus helleri*, had 5 and 6 eggs, whereas a very large female of *M. s. surinamensis* (1,235 mm long) had 11 large oviductal eggs. Another large female of the same species at the Serpentarium of the National Institute of Health in Lima had 13 eggs. The data on coral snake eggs suggest that the maximum number of eggs laid by small species is between 5 and 8, for medium-sized species between 8 and 13, and for large species between 11 and 15.

Larger females usually lay larger and more numerous eggs even though the number is occasionally reduced, resulting in fewer but larger eggs. In their first year of breeding, females will produce 1 to 3 eggs. As they grow older, more eggs will be produced each season. However, the highest number of eggs might not necessarily be produced by the oldest and largest females. There is an optimum size and age of females for producing eggs, probably reached after 5 to 6 years. Beyond that, the number of eggs per clutch does not increase but fluctuates around the maximum, rarely reaching it.

M. f. fulvius produces 2 to 13 eggs, but the most common number is between 5 and 9, from females measuring between 650 mm and 900 mm total length (Telford, 1955). As large females sometimes have only a few eggs, the number of follicles that undergo growth at a given time might be influenced by metabolic and environmental factors. For example, a female about 570 mm long had 3 eggs, a 750 mm-long female had 7 eggs, and a 812 mm-long female had 5 eggs (Zegel, 1975).

A somewhat similar sequence is found in comparing female size and number of eggs in *M. f. tenere* (Sabbath and Worthington, 1959; Werler, 1970). This snake is known to produce 2 to 12 eggs, and typically 6 to 10 eggs are laid by fully grown females. An illustrative sampling shows that a 596 mm-long female had 3 eggs, a 610 mm-long female had 4 eggs, a 680 mm-long female had 3 eggs, a 710 mm-long female had 9 eggs, a 820 mm-long female had 7 eggs, and a 915 mm-long female had also 7 eggs.

The size and weight of eggs from the same clutch can vary considerably. In one clutch of 8 eggs of a *M. f. tenere*, the length of the eggs ranged from 33 mm to 44 mm, with an average of 36.3. The width or diameter ranged from 11 to 13 mm, averaging 11.6 mm. The same eggs ranged in weight from 2.9 g to 4.5 g, averaging 3.5 g. So, the average egg of this clutch measured 36.3 mm long and 11.6 mm wide and weighed 3.5 g. The hatchlings that emerged from the eggs measured between 196 mm and 210 mm, averaging 205.2 mm. Their weight ranged between 2.9 g and 3.3 g, averaging 3.1 g, which is slightly less than the average weight of the eggs when they were laid. In many instances, due to the humidity and oxygen absorbed during incubation, the hatchlings weigh more than the eggs from which they eventually emerge. The known range of length of hatchlings of *M. f. tenere* is between 173 mm and 210 mm.

The proportions of the dimensions of eggs can be expressed by the egg quotient, which is obtained by dividing the length of the egg by its width. The eggs grow allometrically, that is, as the volume increases the dimensions remain in about the same proportions, so that the egg quotient will not change very much.

As coral snake eggs are nearly cylindrical, a size index of the eggs is obtained by multiplying the length by the width. It allows comparison of the size of eggs of different clutches and species. For our average *M. f. tenere* egg with its dimensions of 36.3 × 11.6 mm, the size index is 421.1.

Comparing two clutches of *M. f. tenere*, one of 3 eggs laid by a female 710 mm long, the usefulness of measurements for their comparison becomes apparent (Table 6). The egg quotient of both clutches (not counting the infertile egg) is similar, averaging 2.68 and 2.35, respectively, but the size index is quite different: 225.3 for the first and 416.6 for the second clutch. For 26 freshly laid eggs of several clutches of *M. f. tenere*, the mean was 2.42. The smallest egg measured 23.6 × 9.0 mm and the largest 35.0 × 14.1 mm, giving size indices of 212.4 and 493.5, respectively.

M. f. fulvius eggs have similar sizes and dimensions. For a clutch of 7 eggs laid by a female 890 mm long, the average length was 38.8 mm and the average width was 13.7 mm, giving an egg quotient of 2.83 and a size index of 531.6. The egg quotient of *M. f. fulvius* ranges between 2.64 and 3.21, suggesting they are more slender than the eggs of *M. f. tenere*.

The Uruguayan *M. frontalis altirostris* lays somewhat larger eggs. The range of length and width is 35.8 mm to 48.2 mm and 12.1 mm to 14.2 mm respectively, averaging 41.8 mm in length and 13.4 mm in width. Their quotient ranges between 2.97 and 3.49, averaging 3.23. It means that the eggs of this coral snake are more elongated than those of *M. f. tenere* and a little more elongated than those of *M. f. fulvius*. The average size index is also somewhat higher: 560.1, indicating larger size and volume. Yet, two hatchlings of this set of clutches were 188 mm and 190 mm long, which is about the same length as average hatchlings of *M. f. tenere*.

Two eggs from *M. mipartitus decussatus* from Colombia measured shortly before hatching, with egg

Table 6. Dimensions of Two Clutches of Eggs of *Micrurus fulvius tenere*

	Length in mm		Width (diameter) in mm	Egg Quotient (EQ)	Size Index (SI)
	A) Laid by a 680 mm long female (3 eggs)				
	23.3	×	9.0	2.59	209.7
	25.0	×	9.2	2.72	230.0
	25.1	×	9.3	2.70	233.4
Mean	24.5		9.2	2.67	224.3
	B) Laid by a 710 mm long female (9 eggs)				
	28.7	×	13.0	2.21	373.1
	29.1	×	12.2	2.38	355.0
	29.1	×	13.2	2.20	384.1
	31.0	×	10.3 (infertile)	(3.01)	(319.3)
	31.0	×	13.2	2.35	409.2
	32.3	×	13.1	2.46	423.1
	32.6	×	13.6	2.40	443.3
	32.8	×	14.0	2.34	459.2
	35.0	×	14.1	2.48	493.5
Mean	31.3		13.3	2.35	417.6

EQ = Length/width.
SI = Length × width.

quotients of 2.37 and 2.50 and size index of 608 and 640, respectively, yielded two hatchlings, 200 mm and 220 mm in length.

A clutch of *M. circinalis* had an average egg size of 20 × 6 mm, with a quotient of 3.34 and a size index of 120, indicating a smaller and more elongated egg than in other species.

A clutch of 6 eggs of *M. isozonus* laid by a female approximately 680 mm long had average dimensions of 26.1 × 10.7 mm with an egg quotient of 2.44 and a size index of 279.3. This is close to the calculated average egg quotient (2.46) and average index (278.4) of this clutch. The range compares closely to several other coral snakes, particularly to those of *M. f. tenere*.

Hatching and Hatchlings

Once incubation is completed, the hatchlings or neonates begin to emerge from the egg through slits made from within the egg. The slit is usually longitudinal or oblique, 10 to 15 mm long, and typically the neonate protrudes its head through the slit. At times, several attempts at slitting the egg are made, producing two or more openings. The last slit is usually the one used to emerge from the egg. Initially, only the snout protrudes. The hatchling can remain in this position for from a few minutes to nearly half an hour. Once the full head is protruded, the hatchling takes its first peek at the world. Some embryonic fluid escapes from the egg, together with the head, apparently facilitating the emergence of the neonate. It can remain with its head outside the egg for from 15 minutes to more than 12 hours without any apparent movement, as if trying to get adjusted to the impressions of the world outside its egg. Not frequently, the head is protruded upside down or on one side and it takes quite a while for the hatchling to readjust its head upside up. One gets the impression that the hatchling cannot distinguish which side is up in this world until its senses become coordinated and the "right" picture of how things are organized outside the egg becomes clear. The position of the head upon emergence might also be influenced by the embryo's position within the egg.

Once its body begins to emerge, the neonate negotiates its complete exit from the egg in a relatively short time and proceeds to move around actively (Color 60A–D). From the first attempt at slitting the egg to complete emergence, the process of hatching can last from 3 to 26 hours.

The neonate has an umbilical scar on the last quarter of its body, marking the position of the umbilical cord through which it drew nourishment within the egg. The scar is clearly visible as a longitudinal midventral cut over 3 or 4 ventral scales. It remains as a visible scar for up to 1 year, but this seems to vary from species to species and also depends on the rate of growth.

The coloration of the neonates, especially the yellow and red bands, is paler than that of the adults. After the first molting (ecdysis), which can take place from a few days to 20 days after hatching, the coloration of the hatchlings becomes darker and more brilliant, approaching that of adults. A hatchling has the full complement of venom, moves actively around, and will start feeding in a day or two. Hatchlings of *M. s. surinamensis* start their aquatic life soon after hatching, which presumably occurs near the water: a lake, river, stream, or swamp. In the collection of the Museo de Historia Natural in Lima is a 266 mm-long hatchling, collected in Quistococha, Iquitos, Peru. For this very large species this is just about the neonate size. It has a clearly visible umbilical scar and fish vertebrae in its stomach. Feeding must have taken place about a week earlier in an aquatic or swampy environment. Judging from the size of the hatchling, the fish might have been its first catch very shortly after hatching. It also confirms that the hatchling is able to catch fish from the very beginning of its life.

The sex ratio of the neonates has not been established. Out of the total of 4 eggs of *M. f. tenere*, 2 of which hatched, both were males. In another case, from a clutch of 8 eggs, 5 were male and 3 were female. This would suggest that more males than females are produced, but the sample is totally inadequate and no conclusions can be drawn.

The sex of hatchlings can be determined by the ratio of tail length to total length, if one has the courage to handle the venomous, live hatchlings. In most species, the sexual dimorphism of the ratio of tail length to total length is quite marked (see section on differences between males and females), even though differences in proportion may be less pronounced among hatchlings than among adults. One way to safely measure live hatchlings is to place them into a glass tube of a diameter similar to that of the hatchling. Another is to wrap the snake into a sheet of transparent plastic, extend it, and measure its length. A more precise way to determine the sex of a hatchling is to take ventral and subcaudal counts. This, however, is quite difficult on live specimens and is not recommended to persons without adequate experience.

A Reproductive Success Story: The Uruguayan Coral Snake (*M. frontalis altirostris*)

The Uruguayan coral snake has found a particularly original way to insure protection and constant temperature for its eggs. It lays eggs in fungal chambers of the anthills of an agricultural ant, *Acromyrmex lobicornis*. Over a period of several years, three Uruguayan biologists, R. Vaz-Ferreira, L. Covelo de Zolesi, and F. Achaval (1970) made a thorough study of the anthills in which snakes and lizards lay their eggs. The eggs of the Uruguayan coral snake either occupy the nest alone or share with eggs of a colubrid snake, *Philodryas patagonensis*. The coral snakes penetrate into the central chamber of the ant nest through outside openings. The central fungal chamber is maintained by the ants as a major "agricultural" field for growing the fungus that provides nourishment for the colony. In this chamber the humidity and temperature vary only 2°C within a range of 25°C to 30°C, and it provides an excellent incubation place for coral snake eggs. Egg laying takes place in November and December and the hatchlings emerge some time in February or March. The coral snake usually lays 3 to 4 eggs (the range is 1 to 7) either separated or several adhered together along the longitudinal axis.

The ants that take care of the fungal fields also clean the eggs, preventing contamination by bacteria or molds as well as attack by predatory insects. In short, it seems that the ants take the eggs as an integral part of the "agricultural field" that they clean and protect against any outside agents. One benefit the coral snake in the anthill offers to the ants is protection from their natural predators, such as the "two-headed snake" (*Amphisbaena*) and blind snakes (*Leptotyphlops*) that feed on ants. In turn, both of these ant predators are eaten by coral snakes.

After 70 to 80 days of natural incubation in the central chamber, hatchlings just under 200 mm long emerge. Their emergence lasts several hours. Through one of the initial slits opened laboriously by the hatchling from within, the amniotic fluid escapes, partially protecting the emerging head of the hatchling. The head remains protruded and immobile for up to 4 hours. The ants avoid the ring of the amniotic fluid escaping from the egg, which becomes mixed with fungus and debris from the nest's environment. When an occasional larger ant attempts to bite the protruding head, the snake temporarily retracts it back into the egg. When the hatchling completely emerges from the egg, it travels quickly through the tunnels of the anthill until safety is reached. During the escape, only a few ants attempt to bite it. The total process of hatching may last up to 10 hours, and it usually seems to take place during the night.

Chapter 7
Enemies and Defense

Predators and Parasites

Just as coral snakes feed on a variety of animals, they in turn are preyed upon by an array of predators. In addition to natural predators, our human, mechanized world is the prime enemy of coral snakes. While a balance in nature is maintained by eating and being eaten, the added losses from direct killing as well as indirect means such as road kills and habitat destruction have influenced the distribution and abundance of many species of coral snakes.

Very little is known about coral snake predators in their natural environment. The most frequent predators seem to be birds (see Jackson and Franz, 1981) because several species have been observed feeding on coral snakes. In spite of its defensive behavior of flashy warning coloration, its dangerous bite, and its evasive techniques, birds are able to overcome the coral snake. Mimicry also plays some role in this ecological struggle (see section on mimicry).

In Panama and adjacent countries, puffbirds (*Malacoptila panamensis*) show a great ability to catch and feed on true as well as false coral snakes (N. G. Smith, 1969). The puffbird might sit quietly on a perch that is several meters high and observe the forest floor. Its relatively large eyes enable it to continue foraging in the dusk after most of the diurnal predatory birds have stopped their feeding activities.

When a coral snake passes, the bird dives and, without landing, snatches the snake with its heavy, slightly hooked bill, and returns to its perch. It will then beat the head of the snake against the branch until the snake no longer wriggles. On one occasion, N. G. Smith observed that after overcoming the snake, the puffbird placed the limp body across the branch and waited a short while before picking it up by the middle of the body and flying away. The puffbird eats the coral snake without the use of its short legs, negotiating the meal with a sequence of head snapping movements until the snake has been completely swallowed. Panamanian coral snakes such as *M. n. nigrocinctus* and *M. dissoleucus dunni* are known to be prey of the puffbird. Quite probably, jacamars (*Galbulidae*) and other species of puffbirds (*Bucconidae*) and South American trumpeters (*Psophia crepitans*) that hunt in a similar fashion are predators of coral snakes throughout Central and South America.

Some birds overcome a coral snake by pecking and destroying its head before the coral snake is able to deliver its dangerous bite. A laughing falcon (*Herpetotheres canchinnans*), collected in a second growth forest of Nicaragua by Howell (1957), contained several pieces of a recently eaten coral snake. The snake's head had apparently been severed and discarded before the falcon swallowed the rest of the body (see also Brattstrom, 1955). In Rio Verde, Goiás, Brazil, Sazima and Abe (1991) from the University of Campinas, Brazil, found remains of a *M. lemniscatus* together with remains of two species of false coral snakes, *Oxyrhopus* and *Apostolepis assimilis*, in the stomach of a laughing falcon. Laughing falcons have been observed eating false coral snakes also in Costa Rica (Pough, 1964). In this case, the falcon had fed on a *Pliocercus euryzonus*, a false coral snake that mimics *M. multifasciatus hertwigi*. Apparently, laughing falcons are one of the most common predators of coral snakes (Skutch, 1960, 1971) as they do not seem not to be easily confused or frightened by the conspicuous coloration of coral snakes. In the roost of a Brazilian roadside hawk, *Buteo magnirostris*, Sazima and Abe (1991) found remains of a false coral snake, *Erythrolamprus aesculapii*, that mimics *Micrurus frontalis* in Campinas.

Another report of the "decapitation technique" comes from Georgia, where a loggerhead shrike (*Lanius ludovicianus*) had apparently killed and decapitated a *M. f. fulvius* and impaled it on a barbed-wire fence (Stoddard, 1978). Shrikes seem to have the habit of impaling their prey birds, snakes, and other animals and returning several days later to eat the dessicated victim if no other food has been forthcoming. That shrikes feed on coral snakes has been confirmed by the observations of J. N. Layne in central Florida, as reported by Greene and McDiarmid (1981). Other known bird predators of *M. f. fulvius* are the red-shouldered hawk (*Buteo lineatus*) and American kestrel (*Falco sparverius*) (Jackson and Franz, 1981).

The strategy of decapitating the coral snake to avoid its dangerous bite does not always work. Kristin

Brugger (1989) from the University of Florida reported an interesting encounter between *M. f. fulvius* and a red-tailed hawk (*Buteo jamaicensis*). The hawk died from the coral snake bite with a partially eaten coral snake still in its talons. The bird showed symptoms of coral snake envenomation. Red-tailed hawks are known to feed on snakes by decapitating them first (Knight and Erickson, 1976) and apparently are not intimidated by the aposematic coloration of coral snakes.

Wild turkeys and peafowls in Mexico (Gadow, 1911) as well as chickens in Colombia (Ayerbe et al., 1990) are also known to feed on coral snakes by vigorously pecking the snake before swallowing it. Yet when Santiago Ayerbe in Popayan observed a chicken swallowing a *M. mipartitus decussatus*, he discovered a few hours later that the chicken had died. Upon dissecting it, he found that the coral snake had bitten its predator after being swallowed and had died still holding its bite in the wall of the chicken's stomach. This bite apparently produced a mortal wound "from within."

Several more species of birds, such as kiskadees, motmots, falcons, and other predatory birds known to include in their diet lizards and snakes, are possibly among the principal predators of coral snakes. In spite of the fact that naive birds of several of these predator species show innate avoidance of the conspicuously banded coral snake pattern and are frightened by it (S. M. Smith, 1975, 1976, 1977, 1978), the adults usually seem to be capable of overcoming at least smaller coral snakes.

Mexican biologist William López-Forment from the Universidad Nacional Autónoma de Mexico told me of an interesting type of predation on coral snakes he observed while doing field research with his colleague Gustavo Casas-Andreu in a dry coastal bushy area at La Poza, near Acapulco, Mexico. At certain times of the year, thousands, even millions, of army ants march in masses on the forest floor, scaring out and attacking the litter-dwelling animals. Hundreds of centipedes, crickets, earthworms, spiders, and scorpions try to escape the advancing front of the army ants and the ants kill and devour any animal that is not fast enough to escape. Among animals observed escaping were blind snakes, coffee snakes, and other litter-dwelling colubrids, as well as *M. browni taylori*.

Some clever birds follow the army ants' scare front from the air and feed on the escaping animals as well. As part of this carnage, López-Forment observed that a *M. browni taylori* was eaten by a groove-billed ani (*Crotophaga sulcirostris*).

In a mountain cloud forest near Rancho Grande, Venezuela, I came across an army ant marching front 100 meters wide with a spectacular diversity of desperately escaping litter-dwelling animals preceding it. These large army ant fronts can be heard from a fair distance away, up to 50 meters or even more, as an unfamiliar constant rustling sound, as if the wind were uninterruptedly passing over dryish leaves. The only coral snake observed in the "army ant attack," *M. mipartitus semipartitus*, escaped, but with some difficulty. Even though the coral snake's speed is much greater than that of the advancing ants, the snake did not flee directly from the ant frontline, but moved at an angle and tried to hide under the vegetation. A few minutes later the coral snake was chased out again by the advancing ants. This hide and seek was repeated several times until the snake crossed a small jungle brook and disappeared. A short time later, I saw a small colubrid snake, *Tantilla melanocephala*, attacked and killed by the ants, which converged by dozens on the victim and bit it to death. I could not observe whether the snake was actually eaten as I suddenly found myself part of the escaping litter animals before the advancing ant hordes, and I had to join in the hasty retreat.

It is possible that coral snakes are preyed upon by the army ants, especially in the Amazonian forest where the so-called marabunta ants attack in an all-devouring formation consisting of millions of large ants.

Much less is known about the mammalian predators of coral snakes. Probably peccaries (*Tayassu*) and coatis (*Nasua*) are predators of coral snakes, as well as the South American oppossum (*Didelphis*). Peccaries and coatis are somewhat frightened by the bright coral snake coloration and their tail display (Gehlbach, 1972). Yet, they are coral snake predators and can elicit their defensive display.

Not infrequently, domestic animals, particularly cats, attack and occasionally kill coral snakes, as they would also do with other snakes, lizards, and other wild animals. Encounters with a coral snake frequently end tragically for the cat predator as well as for the prey (Greene and McDiarmid, 1981). Apparently, the cat's hunting instinct is not stopped by the warning coloration of the coral snake. Inexperienced dogs pursuing coral snakes are occasionally victims as well.

Among snakes that prey on the coral snakes are other ophiophagous snakes, such as the false coral snakes (*Erythrolamprus aesculapii*) (Beebe, 1946), and the common pit viper (*Bothrops atrox*) (Greene, 1974), which is the most voracious and versatile "everything eater" of South America. Other species of coral snakes and even snakes of the same species will sometimes prey on coral snakes (see cannibalism in the section on food and feeding). Actually, all ophiophagous snakes are potential coral snake predators.

The smooth-fronted caiman (*Paleosuchus trigonatus*) has been found to eat *M. filiformis* (Dixon and Soini, 1977).

The most curious and unusual predator of small coral snakes is the bullfrog (*Rana catesbiana*), as reported by J. E. Minton (1949). One bullfrog, shot dur-

Enemies and Defense

ing a collecting trip in Texas, had eaten a 432 mm long *M. fulvius tenere*, which, in turn, had eaten a ground snake (*Virginia striatula*).

Very little is known about coral snake parasites (Lainson and Shaw, 1973). I have seen occasional specimens of *M. lemniscatus* and *M. isozonus* with ticks attached on the infracephalic scales, between the genials, and also between the temporals and the eye. In captivity, some species of coral snake submerge under water over prolonged periods of time, with only the head protruding. This behavior probably helps them to get rid of many external parasites such as ticks and mites.

Fungus infection and bacterial infection (*Clostridium*) of the mouth are found mostly in specimens in captivity.

The most abundant endoparasites are nematodes, which were studied by Harwood (1930, 1932) in *M. f. tenere*. I have found frequent nematode infection in the digestive tract and, surprisingly, in the shaft of the hemipenis of the aquatic species, *M. surinamensis*; nematodes have also been found in *Leptomicrurus narduccii melanotus* and *M. isozonus* and in subspecies of *M. lemniscatus*, *M. frontalis*, *M. diastema*, *M. nigrocinctus*, *M. mipartitus*, and several more. I found a particularly heavy infestation in a specimen of the Panamanian *M. m. multifasciatus* (MCZ 45395). It had the left hemipenis shaft so full of nematodes that it appeared they had damaged the organ.

Some species of coral snakes of *Micrurus* have blood parasites, the hepatozooic haemogregarines (Moreno y Bolaños, 1977); probably many more protozoan and larger nematode and trematode parasites will be found in many more species, such as those found in *M. spixii* (Lainson et al., 1991).

Defense Against Enemies

A coral snake journeying in its environment possesses a complex repertoire of behaviors with which to defend itself against predators, enemies, or competitors. One could say that a coral snake has a bag full of tricks for meeting any dangerous situation. These include behavior, color pattern, and form. Many biologists emphasize precision and details in their behavioral studies and tend to forget that all the defense features, active and passive, form a single, integrated dynamic defense gestalt of the snake that only makes sense in its natural environment. Thus, the advantages of the color pattern are combined with an array of behavior and morphological features that the coral snake will use as conditions demand. The defense and antipredator behavior of snakes with coral snake color pattern was reviewed by Greene (1988) and by Sazima and Abe (1991).

The brightly banded color pattern with appropriate behavior serves as a warning signal, advertising the coral snake's venomous nature to potential enemies. The efficacy of this signal has been the cause of mimicry fellowships (see mimicry) (Greene and Pyburn, 1973). Coloration also serves as a frightening mechanism, depending on the environment in which it is used. Most frequently, coral snakes use their bite as a last recourse, when all other defenses have failed.

The questions we must ask are: Can the predators be frightened into avoiding an attack by the coral snake's use of the color pattern and behavior? Can the same color pattern serve other purposes in nature? (Jackson et al., 1976).

Susan Smith (1975, 1976, 1977) performed several experiments and found that inexperienced motmots and kiskadees were frightened by coral snakelike artificial models. Frederick Gehlbach (1972 and 1973) experimented with rubber models that were made to "display" coral snakestyle self-mimicry, such as raising the tail as if it were the head and other behaviors. He found that this behavior was effective in scaring or confusing javelinas and coatis when combined with coloration.

Always remembering that in understanding coral snake defense coloration, behavior and environment go hand in hand (S. M. Smith and Mostron, 1985), let us follow a coral snake on its way, say, on the tropical rain forest floor. It slowly moves for some distance and then stops to explore the environment. While it is moving, the individual bands are not easily distinguishable, especially when the snake moves at a regular speed. The snake looks like an almost uniformly colored brownish-grey stripe that is moving—or even not moving—on the forest floor. It is not easy to detect a moving coral snake, and in certain conditions the snakes are nearly invisible. But when the coral snake stops, the brilliant bands suddenly become visible, perhaps surprising a predator if it is around. Amidst the dry leaves and jungle litter, the banded color can also have a concealing effect, especially when part of the coral snake's body is partially hidden beneath the litter and only "loose segments" of blotches or bands are visible. This effect is enhanced when there are sunshade patches on the jungle floor (Greene and Pyburn, 1973). In a second growth forest or edge vegetation, this is a particularly effective way of enhancing concealment.

Thus far, our coral snake has not encountered a predator but has continued on its own business. If a predator attacks and eventually tries to grab or press the coral snake against the ground, the snake will employ a series of rapid actions all "designed" to defend itself. Pressed against the ground, the coral snake will thrash around in seemingly erratic movements with very short pauses between the jerky motions. The erratic thrashings look quite random, but a more careful observation reveals that the coral snake tries to manipulate its body, particularly the head, into an optimum striking position. This can be observed when a coral snake, pressed against the ground during a collecting encounter, thrashes around as if aimlessly until it is in a good position and at a close enough range to the attacker to deliver its bite.

In most species of coral snakes, the erratic and thrashing behavior is accompanied by a defensive tail display. This consists of raising the tail and the end part of the body upright and holding, waving, and moving the uprised parts in a manner suggestive of a raised head (Color 27, 43). During this display, the tail end is curled up, which makes it look much stouter and blunter than it actually is (Greene and Seib, 1983). At the same time, the coral snake conceals its head beneath a body loop of the anterior part of the body. The effect is that the raised tail end appears to be the head, and the head remains fused among the body loops as an unimportant tail end.

Because several species of coral snakes (*M. mipartitus* (Color 43), *M. frontalis* (Color 27), *M. multifasciatus* (Color 45), species of *Leptomicrurus*, and several more) have red bands on the tip of the tail, the impression produced by the waving tail can be quite threatening: a head end with an intense red spot. This color-behavior defensive scheme apparently serves several purposes. First, it frightens the predator with a suddenly emerging, uplifted head; second, it distracts the predator's attention from the real head and also from the bitten or pressed down body part of the coral snake; third, when the coral snake is still free, the head and body can begin escaping in the opposite direction while the last-to-move "tail head" is still deceiving the attacker; and, fourth, the deception allows time for the coral snake to arm and deliver a bite. In short, it can be quite confusing to a predator.

Together with the defensive tail display, also called self-mimicry because it can be interpreted as imitation of one's own head (Gehlbach, 1972), many species of coral snakes flatten the posterior part or almost the entire body as does, for example, *M. surinamensis* (Color 58). This change in body size and shape is known as protean effect, because the coral snake looks larger than its actual size and somewhat deformed. The name is derived from the Greek god, Proteus, who escaped enemies by changing his form.

The defensive tail display is by no means an exclusive coral snake feature. Observed first in *M. f. fulvius* by Grijs and described in German in 1898, this phenomenon has attracted considerable attention from early naturalists to contemporary herpetologists (Mertens, 1956, 1957, 1960; Gehlbach, 1972; Greene, 1973b). In addition to the three genera of coral snakes, defensive tail display is found in the Old World elapids (*Calliophis*, *Bungarus*, *Maticora*) and in false coral snakes (*Pliocercus*, *Erythrolamprus*, *Lampropeltis*, *Simophis*) as well as in many boid, colubrid, and viperid snakes, and even amphisbaenids (Greene, 1973b).

Since coral snakes use the tail to imitate the "head end," it can be presumed that some predators will attempt to attack the false "head." On the average, males and females of *M. d. dumerilii* have about 2.9% of tail injuries, as found by Alberto Valdez (unpublished data) at City College of New York. Valdez examined 500 coral snakes, the largest coral snake population ever assembled from a single subspecies, currently deposited at the American Museum of Natural History, New York. About 4% of coral snakes have damaged or injured tails, as compared to almost 8% tail injuries among coral snake imitators that do not perform the defensive tail display. These percentages are not easy to interpret because some species may use the tail display to misdirect a predator's attack and suffer a tail injury, such as some boid snakes (*Eryx*), while others may use it more as a way to frighten and intimidate the attacker or as a device to confuse the predator. Coral snakes probably use tail display predominantly to intimidate the attacker but also to confuse it. It is interesting to note that captive coral snakes will display the defensive tail curling even when touched by potential prey released in the cage.

Thus far, I know of only two coral snakes (*M. corallinus* and *M. limbatus*) that do not use a defensive tail display. *M. corallinus*, when molested, only thrashes around and *M. limbatus* coils its tail from side to side without elevating it.

A very curious additional defensive display is known in *Micruroides euryxanthus*. When in full defensive tail display, this snake will enhance the display's effect by producing a popping sound with its cloacal lips (Bogert, 1960). The sound can be repeated several times while the threatening conditions persist. This would do no good against snake predators as they do not hear, but could be effective as a supplementary defensive feature against birds and mammals. I wonder if the popping sound is associated with emission of some repelling gases or other secretions. Many snakes emit defensive, unpleasant smelling secretions when attacked or handled roughly. Very occasionally, *M. fulvius* also produces the popping sound when molested persistently.

Some coral snakes, such as several subspecies of *M. frontalis* and some other species, will protrude one or the other hemipenis when handled violently or molested (Azevedo, 1960; Sazima and Abe, 1991). This could also be considered a surprise defense by which a spiny, threatening extension of the body suddenly emerges. This may also have produced the belief that coral snakes have a tail spine with which they can deliver a deadly sting.

M. frontalis brasiliensis is the only species, other

than occasional specimens of *M. fulvius* (Gehlbach, 1970), that I have known to show a death-feigning behavior. The only observation I made of this was during a photography session of coral snakes at the Instituto Butantan. Joaquin Caballero, a skilled Brazilian handler of venomous snakes, took several species of coral snakes out of the cages so I could take pictures. One of the *M. f. frontalis* specimens had to be restrained rather violently several times in the grassy backyard of the serpentarium. After several restraints, the snake suddenly rolled in an upside down position, with the body flattened almost over its entire length. It remained in this stiff and flattened pretend-death position for several minutes, even when Joaquin picked it up with the snake hook and put it down again (Color 23).

It seems that the bite is the last step of defense and is usually delivered when all the other defense measures have failed. As I observed in *M. f. brasiliensis*, the bite is frequently delivered simultaneously with lowering the tail lure, striking the attacker with the last seemingly erratic movement. After that, the coral snake maintains a bite grip if the strike has been successful, or repeats the strike when the attacker has been a collecting stick or other offender "incomprehensible" to the coral snake. Some species bite quite readily; others are difficult to induce to strike.

Some species are more defensively aggressive than others. *M. corallinus* is particularly known to be quite a treacherous biter. It does not display the defensive tail curling, but during the erratic thrashing it maneuvers its head into a position to strike, which it does when least expected. *M. n. nigrocinctus* is also known as a nervous and relatively aggressive coral snake, at least more aggressive than its cousin, *M. nigrocinctus mosquitensis*. Of the two U.S. coral snakes, *M. f. tenere* seems to be more nervous, erratic, and defensively more aggressive than *M. f. fulvius*, yet individual differences and local conditions may vary the striking behavior. The most vigorously biting coral snake I have observed was a *M. mipartitus semipartitus* in Rancho Grande, Venezuela. With the first contact of the butterfly net that I used to press it down, it at once began a series of thrashing, tail display, and biting attempts. When a bite was delivered to the iron ring or wooden handle of the net, the bite was released, but when the coral snake bit the net fabric, it hung on with the characteristic chewing motion. When I finally introduced it into the net, in the absence of any collecting bag, it even tried to bite through the butterfly net. Other individuals of the same species of coral snake in Rancho Grande were considerably less defensively aggressive. As a rule, coral snakes are not aggressive snakes unless disturbed, molested, or otherwise threatened. They apparently try to defend themselves with other than biting behavior, and a clear sequence of responses keyed to the degree of gravity of the attack can be identified. I have also observed *M. isozonus* to maintain a defense tail display while holding firmly onto a bitten prey snake, apparently in order to lure it away from the vital body parts of the coral snake that the prey snake was intending to bite (see Chapter 5, Feeding and Food).

Chapter 8
Mimicry: Imitation Fellowships

As we have noted, what in many countries are commonly called coral snakes include venomous, mildly venomous, and even nonvenomous species. This has produced considerable confusion because in many cases the dangerous elapid species are hard to distinguish from the more innocuous species. More careful observations reveal that the mildly venomous and nonvenomous species have colorations quite similar to those of the venomous snakes that exist in the same region, and as the coloration of the venomous coral snakes changes from region to region, the nonvenomous or mildly venomous species vary accordingly. In short, wherever the venomous and nonvenomous coral snakes live together, the latter look similar to their venomous counterparts.

This deceptive concordance of color patterns forms the basis for complex mimicry systems between venomous and nonvenomous species. Indeed, the complex and diversified array of coral snakes and their mimics is unique among vertebrate animals and has intrigued biologists for over a century. One puzzle, however, is that the phenomenon of coral snake mimicry is found only in the Americas. It does not occur in the Old World. There are only a few elapids with reddish bands in Asia and none of them approaches the brilliance and richness of coloration of the American coral snakes. These few Asian elapids have no known mimics. One interesting example, however, is an elapidlike snake, *Cylindrophis rufus*, which often is black-red or black-orange and has tail display much like the American coral snakes.

From a biological standpoint, mimicry systems are not fully interpreted as yet. Harry Greene and William Pyburn (1973) suggested, for example, that an important part of the mimicry maintenance is the innate avoidance of brightly banded snakes by potential coral snake predators. (See also section on enemies and defense; Gehlbach, 1972; S. M. Smith, 1975 and 1977.) They proposed that the tendency to attack colorful coral snakes varies from individual predator to individual predator, and it may be genetically determined. In other words, some individual predators would be more inclined to attack brightly colored snakes than others. Since attacks on coral snakes are frequently fatal, predators who innately tend to avoid them would have better chances to survive and reproduce. Their innate "avoidance wisdom" would be genetically transmitted to the next generation of predators, thus favoring mimicry systems with several species of brightly colored snakes.

Unquestionably, innate avoidance of conspicuous coloration also plays a significant role in predator's choice of a prey. Yet the great similarity of color patterns between venomous and nonvenomous coral snakes (Greene and McDiarmid, 1981; Roze, 1983; Pough, 1988; Smith et al., 1989) clearly indicates that more than a mere conspicuous coloration and its avoidance by predators is involved. The precision in imitation of the color patterns, as illustrated by a series of color photographs by Campbell and Lamar (1989), plays a central role in mimicry protection. Unless there is a selective advantage that favors the tendency toward almost indistinguishable concordance of color pattern between many pairs of mimicry companions, the mimics will not display the often stunning perfection in imitation. On the other hand, some powerful coral snake predators such as laughing falcons and puffbirds would probably pay little attention to the perfection of imitation, but might avoid conspicuous coloration as a natural precaution (see section on enemies and defense). In other cases, such as that described in the section on enemies, a red-tailed hawk died from a bite inflicted by its prey, a *M. f. fulvius* (Brugger, 1989). The hawk apparently did not avoid the conspicuous color pattern of the coral snake and paid with its life.

History of Mimicry Studies in Coral Snakes

One of the fathers of American herpetology, Edward D. Cope, while describing snakes found in the collection of the Academy of Natural Sciences of Philadelphia, noted in 1860 the curious fact that many venomous and nonvenomous coral snakes have quite similar patterns of red, black, and yellow bands (Cope, 1860b). Seven years later, Bates's travel companion in Brazil, Alfred R. Wallace, the famous British naturalist and codiscoverer with Charles Darwin of the process of evolution, correctly interpreted the similarities in coral snake color pattern as mimicry.

In this century, H. Gadow (1908, 1911) doubted mimicry as a valid explanation for similarities among coral snakes. After having observed many of them in Mexico, Gadow offered an unorthodox explanation of why there are so many red-colored snakes in America. He suggested that there is a "genius loci" for producing red snakes, a local American phenomenon that does not manifest itself in other parts of the world. R. Sternfeld (1913), an active herpetologist at the Senckenberg Museum, Frankfurt, Germany, rebutted several of Gadow's arguments, but many counterarguments against mimicry were raised. Robert Mertens (1956, 1957, 1966), active at the same museum as Sternfeld, produced several contributions on the mimicry of coral snakes and other animals based on his travels to Central and South America. His publications contain delightful color photos.

Several American herpetologists offered supplementary or alternative explanations to the coral snake mimicry phenomenon, notably Dunn (1954), Brattstrom (1955), Hecht and Marien (1956), Gehlbach (1972), Greene and Pyburn (1973), and Grobman (1978). Particularly interesting is the paper by Emmet R. Dunn, one of the "old guard" American herpetologists who studied a very large snake collection from Panama, gathered by the Clark census. This intensive snake-collecting effort yielded 13,912 snakes representing 108 species. No less than 1,175 of them had "coral snake" coloration. He noted that 726 (representing 6 species of *Micrurus*) were true coral snakes, 61.8% of the total number of individuals showing "coral snake coloration."

The German scholar of mimicry, W. Wickler (1968), in his book *Mimicry in Plants and Animals*, proposed an additional type of mimicry for coral snakes, called *Mertensian mimicry*. Wickler suggested that the mildly venomous coral snakes are actually models for the deadly venomous as well as for the nonvenomous coral snakes. This would provide a nonlethal learning experience to the predators. However, this type of mimicry has been considered just a version of Mullerian mimicry and not a different category of mimicry (Greene and McDiarmid, 1981).

In order to clarify mimicry in coral snakes, Harry Greene and Roy McDiarmid traveled extensively in Central and South America and gathered considerable field and museum information. In 1981, they published a comprehensive review and answered most of the objections raised by some biologists about mimicry in coral snakes that are summarized here. Pough (1988), another known mimicry scholar, reviewed mimicry and related phenomena in reptiles and Campbell and Lamar (1989) as well as Slowinski (1991) also offered a brief historical overview of mimicry studies and added information from their own field observations.

Diversity of Coral Snake Mimicry

Most species and subspecies of venomous coral snakes serve as models for one or more false coral snakes. Mimicry relationships among coral snakes represent a wide array from strict Batesian mimicry to extreme Mullerian mimicry and many gradations between these two. Mimics usually imitate not only the red, black, and yellow bands but also the correct sequence of bands, especially in snakes found south of the Rio Grande all the way to Argentina. The imitators belong mostly to the family Colubridae, the largest and the most diversified family of snakes, as well as to a small and primitive fossorial snake family, Aniliidae. As colubrid and aniliid snakes are the imitators, they are named false coral snakes, while elapid coral snakes are called true or venomous or simply coral snakes.

Some colubrid mimics are nonvenomous species from such genera as *Lampropeltis* that includes king snakes and milk snakes, and *Atractus*, a large South American group of burrowing and litter-dwelling snakes. They employ Batesian mimicry and their color patterns are 100% bluff; a truly dangerous model is imitated by a genuinely inoffensive mimic.

Mullerian mimicry is represented by such mildly venomous coral snakes as the colubrid genera *Oxyrhopus*, *Erythrolamprus*, and *Pliocercus*.

It is uncertain which mimics have a bit of venom and which are completely nonvenomous because the toxic nature of saliva and other oral glandular secretions has only recently been recognized. These mildly venomous secretions are associated with the rear fangs found at the end of the maxilla in some colubrids. Additional confusion is created because some species of false coral snakes (*Erythrolamprus*) from South America have both grooved and ungrooved rear fangs.

While studying snakes in Venezuela, I received several reports of bites by a false coral snake, *Erythrolamprus aesculapii*, that produced pain and local swelling and took several days to subside. R. L. Seib (1980) reported a rather severe local effect from a bite of the Guatemalan false coral snake, *Pliocercus elapoides*, which has small ungrooved rear fangs.

When a predator gets bitten by a mildly venomous colubrid mimic of a coral snake, the dangerous nature of the coral snake color pattern may be reinforced. Usually, the predator survives and in the future it will avoid both the model and mimic of this Mullerian mimicry system.

The most persistent mimicry companions of coral snakes are the small, litter-dwelling mimics of the genus *Pliocercus* (Greene and McDiarmid, 1981; Roze,

1983; Pérez-Higareda and Smith, 1986; Campbell and Lamar, 1989; Rand and Myers, 1990). The concordance reaches such perfection that by looking at the mimic it is actually possible to know the color pattern of the venomous model that lives there. The *Pliocercus* imitators have not only the same sequence of bands as the model, but the length of individual bands and the head coloration are astoundingly similar. For example, in its range in central Guatemala, *M. diastema apiatus* has short black bands and red bands sprinkled with black. *Pliocercus a. aequalis* from the same region has identical markings. In Yucatán, Mexico, *M. diastema alienus* has relatively long white and black bands and so does *Pliocercus elapoides schmidti* from Yucatán. This concordance also holds true in areas where the red bands are long. For example, in southern Oaxaca and Chiapas, Mexico, and in southern Guatemala, *M. latifasciatus* (Pattern 32) has very few black bands and long red bands, and so does the false coral snake, *Pliocercus elapoides diastemus*, from the same region. To make things even more perfect, *Pliocercus* has perfectly mimicked several coral snakes with unusual coloration. In *M. bernadi* (Pattern 7) the black bands are usually reduced to dorsal spots or incomplete bands. The same pattern is shown by sympatric *Pliocercus elapoides* ssp. In the Los Tuxtlas region of southern Veracruz, Mexico, the two species *Pliocercus elapoides salvinii* and *Pliocercus bicolor* imitate the unusually colored *M. limbatus* subspecies and *M. diastema sapperi* in the same region (Pérez-Higareda, 1980; Pérez-Higareda and Smith, 1986). Another atypically colored coral snake is *M. e. ephippifer* (Pattern 27) from Oaxaca. In this species the red middorsal bands are partially or completely covered by black spots. This coloration is repeated in *Pliocercus elapoides* spp., which lives in the same region. Perhaps the most interesting and convincing example of the perfect concordance of *Pliocercus* mimicry is found at the other end of the geographic distribution. In eastern Central America, two sympatric coral snakes, *M. multifasciatus* and *M. stewarti* are bicolored black and red snakes. *Pliocercus euryzonus* ssp (or subspecies of *P. aequalis*), which lives in the same area, has also lost the usual tricolor coral snake garb. It is bicolored with relatively long black bands that are similar to those of its venomous mimicry companions. This appears to be an example of three-way mimicry. Exceptional specimens of *M. multifasciatus* and *P. aequalis* can also be black-yellow (or cream).

In one or two cases *Pliocercus* combines the coloration of two sympatric models. For example, in southern Mexico and adjacent Guatemala it has black triads and long red bands. Additionally, the two white bands that separate the black bands of a triad have some irregular black spots. The models for this mimic are *M. e. elegans*, which has somewhat irregular black triads with black spotting on the white bands, and *M. diastema*, which has longer-than-usual red bands. Volumes could and probably will be written about the extraordinary capacity of *Pliocercus* to mimic different species of coral snakes. It is safe to say that *Pliocercus* specializes in mimicking *Micrurus* and is very adept at it. This genetic flexibility of mimicking coral snakes seems to set *Pliocercus* apart from its closely related genus, *Urotheca*. (See Savage and Crother, 1989, who synonymized both genera.)

Many examples of coral snake mimicry are known from South America. Every day the Instituto Butantan, the famous snake institute of São Paulo, receives dozens of snakes sent from many parts of Brazil. Among the cobras corais (coral snakes) the majority are false coral snakes, and several of these mimicry companions are remarkably similar. For example, the Brazilian false coral snake *Oxyrhopus trigeminus* (Color 24) is a mildly venomous colubrid mimic of *M. frontalis frontalis* from the same region. Both species have black triads and black head with white spots on the snout. Another even more perfect mimic imitating *M. lemniscatus carvalhoi* (Color 38) and apparently also *M. frontalis brasiliensis* (Color 27), is the false coral snake *Simophis rhinostoma* (Color 25) with perfectly developed triads and a red parietal band identical to that of its models.

In eastern Brazil, several groupings of venomous and nonvenomous coral snakes with concordant color patterns including *M. corallinus*, *M. frontalis*, and *M. lemniscatus* as well as *Erythrolamprus aesculapii*, *Oxyrhopus guibei*, and *Simophis rhynostoma* have been studied by the Brazilian herpetologists Octavio Marques and Guiseppe Puorto (1991) and Ivan Sazima and Augusto Abe (1991). Changing color patterns of *Erythrolamprus aesculapii* (Color 27), the false coral snake in eastern and southeastern Brazil, follow the color patterns of several coral snakes. Marques and Puorto (1991) observed that in the littoral region of eastern Brazil where the single-banded *M. corallinus* predominates, the false coral snake displays a single-banded or partially divided black band form (*E. a. monozona*) with while bands separating the black bands from the red bands as it is found in *M. corallinus*. In the areas where the triad-type coral snakes (*M. lemniscatus carvalhoi* and *M. frontalis* ssp.) are abundant, the false coral snake (*E. a. venustissimus*) displays a predominant color pattern of double black bands (diads) that are not separated from the red bands by white bands, similar to the one found in the venomous coral snakes.

Campbell and Lamar (1989) illustrated the extraordinary concordance of color patterns between the false coral snake *Erythrolamprus aesculapii* and *M. lemniscatus* in Suriname, but the same false coral snake looked like *M. hemprichii* in eastern Colombia and again like *M. spixii obscurus* where their distribution overlapped in Peru. Apparently, the identity of various subspecies or perhaps even species of this false coral snake must be interpreted in light of the distribution of coral snakes that the former imitate, similar to *Pliocercus* in Mexico and Central America.

A curious coral snake color pattern is found in snakes that in some regions are called *Gemela Confundida* (the confused twin snake) or *Culebra Añadida* (the added snake). This is the colubrid genus *Scaphiodontophis*, that ranges from Central America to western South America. Some subspecies such as *S. annulatus venustissimus* (H. M. Smith et al., 1986) have the entire body covered by a typical black-yellow-red band sequence and closely resemble coral snakes living in the same region, such as *M. nigrocinctus* in Central America. In other species of *Scaphiodontophis* the posterior part of the body is uniformly greyish or brownish with or without longitudinal dorsal rows of small dark spots that at times give an impression of longitudinal dark stripes, while the anterior part displays flashy red-yellow-black bands. Again, the band sequence is similar to that of local coral snakes. Such species as *S. a. annulatus* and *S. annulatus zeteki* have this "confused twin snake" appearance. Even more baffling is a Colombian species, *S. a. dugandi* (Roze, 1969), that has a coral snake pattern on the anterior part and on the tail, while the body between is greyish brown (Henderson, 1984). All the "confused coloration" species look as if two completely different snakes have been sewn together; one end is drab and inconspicuous and the other and is a brightly colored coral snake. When such a snake moves and stops in leaf litter, it is as if two different snakes are lying half concealed on the jungle floor. Apparently, the species of *Scaphiodonophis* combine cryptic coloration with flashy menacing display producing the impression of several individuals moving at once.

Many interesting examples of mimicry are found in the vast Amazon region. Two false coral snakes, *Erythrolamprus guentheri* and *Atractus elaps* show a remarkable versatility in the mimicry game. The first mimics two coral snakes, *M. langsdorffi* (Color 36) and *M. steindachneri* (Pattern 46), in southeastern Ecuador and northern Peru, where the mimicry companions display similar color pattern of red and black bands of approximately equal length separated by narrow white bands. Yet further south in central Peru, where an unusually colored coral snake, *M. margaritiferus* (Pattern 31), lives, *E. guentheri* has developed a different and quite uncoral snakelike color pattern, precisely like that of the venomous coral snake. This case of mimicry is particularly interesting because the color pattern of black with narrow speckled cross bands does not have any value as a flashy warning coloration. And yet, *E. guentheri* has taken the pain of changing its dress where a different venomous coral snake lives. Apparently, there is some advantage in its being associated with *M. margaritiferus*. To make things even more complicated, in the same region specimens of *E. guentheri* with red-black-white color pattern are also found. These specimens may mimic some other venomous coral snakes, possibly *M. petersi*, or perhaps a species of coral snake that has not yet been discovered.

E. guentheri is polymorphic; within one species individuals may have different color patterns or morphs and each imitates a venomous coral snake. The phenomenon of polymorphism is well known among butterflies, and it is particularly well developed in species that are engaged in mimicry. Polymorphism appears when a species does not have a clear mimicry choice, or where some individuals mimic one while others mimic another model species. Polymorphism can also appear in a population of an otherwise mimicking species when found in areas where no models are present.

Another example of polymorphic mimic is *Atractus elaps*. This nonvenomous colubrid from Amazonas has one form that mimics such Amazonian coral snakes as *M. lemniscatus helleri* and has triad-type coral snake coloration. Another form mimics *M. ornatissimus* and has single-banded black-yellow-red coloration. The same imitator also has a black-and-white morph that probably mimics *M. annellatus* and even *M. margaritiferus*.

The most complex assemblage of coral snake models and mimics has been found in the Iquitos region in Peru by a group of American herpetologists, including R. W. Henderson, J. R. Dixon, and P. Soini, who systematically collected amphibians and reptiles for more than 1 year. P. Soini actually collected in the region for 8 years. In the course of their work they found no less than 8 species of venomous coral snakes and 9 species of false coral snakes in the same region. While not all of the snakes can be identified as mimicry companions, the presence of 17 species of snakes with some kind of "coral snake" color pattern is an impressive assemblage. In addition, one venomous species, *M. langsdorfii*, is polymorphic. Its pattern varies from a single black-red-yellow or white pattern to a series of forms in which no black bands are present, or only light brown bands, or the body may be covered with yellow and red bands or irregular mottling on brown and red bands. The reason for such a variable polymorphism in a venomous species is unknown, but the many different variants suggest that mimicry may have an influence. It also increases the diversity of coral snake color pattern in the Iquitos region of Peru.

As reviewed by Pough (1988), Campbell and Lamar (1989), and Savage and Slowinski (1992), no less than 25 genera that have species of false coral snakes are found in Mexico and Central America: *Atractus**, *Chilomeniscus*, *Chionactis*, *Clelia**, *Dipsas**, *Elaphe*, *Erythrolamprus**, *Geophis*, *Gyalopion*, *Lampropeltis**, *Liophis**, *Ninia**, *Oxy-*

rhopus*, *Phyllorhynchus*, *Pliocercus**, *Pseudoboa**, *Rhinobothrium**, *Scaphiodontophis**, *Scolecophis*, *Sibon*, *Sonora*, *Stenorrhina**, *Symopholis*, *Tantilla**, and *Tripanurgos**. In South America there are 24 genera that have species of false coral snakes. In addition to the ones marked with an asterisk, South America has the following additional genera: *Anilius*, *Apostolepis*, *Drepanoides*, *Elapomorphus*, *Helicops*, *Hydrodynastes*, *Hydrops*, *Lystrophis*, *Phimophis*, and *Simophis*. Probably about 30% of all the snake species of the Americas have some coral snake color pattern (Slowinski, (1991, quoting Savage).

Mimicry Related to Size and Growth

With few exceptions, no large-sized colubrid snake imitates coral snakes. Yet, some cases are known in which a small juvenile of a large size colubrid mimics a coral snake. Apparently, proper size is an important component of deception as well as color pattern and behavior.

The Costa Rican king snake, found in highlands between Costa Rica and Panama, shows changes of coloration with age. Juvenile specimens have bright red-black-yellow bands and closely resemble the sympatric models, *M. alleni* and *M. n. nigrocinctus*. As *M. alleni* grows larger, its coloration becomes more melanistic, until in old age the red and white bands are heavily spotted by black. The same change in coloration is also found in *Lampropeltis triangulum gaigei*. As both mimicry companions grow larger, they become darker. When *Lampropeltis triangulum gaigei* finally outgrows its model coral snake, it becomes nearly uniformly black. This is apparently when the mimicry companionship ends. In high mountains of this region adult *M. n. nigrocinctus* are somewhat darker than the nearby lowland populations of the same subspecies. The concordance of blackness might have to do not only with mimicry but also with heat absorption in a colder climate.

Another example of "part time" mimicry is found in northern Venezuela. The banded hunter snake (La Cazadora Anillada), *Oxyrhopus p. petola*, is a mildly venomous snake that has only black and white bands in its juvenile stage. These look similar to those of *M. mipartitus semipartitus* (Color 44) from the same region. As *Oxyrhopus p. petola* grows, its white bands gradually turn red. This change further enhances its similarity to *M. mipartitus semipartitus*, which has red head and tail bands while the rest of the body is black-yellow or black-white banded. In the adult *Oxyrhopus p. petola*, the bands turn dark red until they are partially obscured by blackish overtones. At this stage its size is much larger than that of *M. mipartitus semipartitus*, the supposed model coral snake.

Mimicry Between Venomous Coral Snakes

More lessons about how mimicry works can be learned from studying mimicry partnerships between two or more elapid coral snakes. As both species are quite venomous, they represent an extreme case of Mullerian mimicry. In some cases there is apparent mimicry influence without producing strictly concordant color patterns. For instance, *Micruroides euryxanthus australis* (Pattern 1), found in the state of Sonora, Mexico, and *M. euryxanthus neglectus* (Pattern 2) found in the state of Sinaloa, have longer red bands where their distribution overlaps with *M. d. distans* (Color 18). The latter has brilliant red bands that are longer than the black bands. *M. e. euryxanthus*, found in Arizona and New Mexico where no *M. d. distans* is found, has shorter red bands that, moreover, sometimes have black spots.

Even though both mimicry partners are venomous, their color patterns do not converge to form something intermediate. Instead, one species adopts the color pattern of the other, thus acting like a true mimic. In eastern Brazil, the head coloration of *M. lemniscatus carvalhoi* resembles that of *M. frontalis brasiliensis* in areas where both live together. This coloration features irregular black body bands and the presence of black tips on the white scales, characteristics found in *M. f. brasiliensis*. In Venezuela, *M. isozonus* displays several features of *M. lemniscatus diutius* in areas where their distributions overlap, including such features as a defined white head band and neatly defined black triad bands. However, in areas of llanos where *M. isozonus* lives alone, the white head band can be quite irregular, with irregular black spots, and the triads are also somewhat less clearly defined.

In several instances where the distribution of a species with single black bands overlaps with a species of triad-type coloration, the first tends to mimic the second. All subspecies of *M. dumerilii* in northern South America are single banded except two in northern Colombia. *M. d. dumerilii* with accessory triad pattern is found in the lower Magdalena valley, where it lives together with a *M. dissoleucus nigrirostris*, a triad-type coral snake. The same is true with *M. dumerilii colombianus* which coexists with *M. dissoleucus melanogenys* in the Santa Marta region. Both species are approximately the same size. Occasional specimens of *M. dumerilii transandinus* will also feature black accessory bands.

M. mertensi (Pattern 36) is single banded in northwestern Peru. In the semidesertic mountains of southwestern Ecuador where it lives together with *M. bocourti* (Color 10), it has developed a weak but definite accessory triad color pattern and approaches the color pattern of *M. bocourti*.

In cases of strict Mullerian mimicry, the single-banded coral snake imitates the color pattern of the triad-type species and not vice versa. This has a bearing on the evolution of the color pattern of coral snakes (see section on origin and evolution of coral snakes). It also demonstrates that two quite venomous mimicry partners can derive a benefit from mimicry in spite of the fact that their bites can be fatal to predators.

A question that was raised earlier is: Can there be good mimicry without conspicuous or aposematic warning coloration? In the Amazon region, several single-banded coral snakes are nearly black or have a tendency toward melanism. *M. albicinctus, M. psyches, M. langsdorffi, M. putumayensis, M. steindachneri, M. margaritiferus, Leptomicrurus narduccii, L. scutiventris*, as well as quite a few of their mimics, are part of this complex. Their related subspecies living outside or on the fringes of Amazonia, such as *M. circinalis* in Trinidad and northern Venezuela and *M. ornatissimus* in eastern Ecuador, are brilliantly colored, single-banded coral snakes. At the same time, at least three large-sized triad-type coral snakes found in the Amazonian region, *M. surinamensis, M. spixii*, and *M. lemniscatus helleri*, are bright red and are mimicked by several species of equally brightly colored false coral snakes (*Erythrolamprus* and *Atractus*).

Errors in Human Perception that Confirm Mimicry

Even trained biologists have difficulty distinguishing between true and false coral snakes. More than one error has been made by knowledgeable naturalists and the culprit snakes have usually been the more perfect coral snake imitators from the genera *Erythrolamprus* and *Pliocercus*.

For instance, in 1758 Carolus Linnaeus, the father of modern ways of ordering and naming plants, described the first false coral snake, the mildly venomous *Erythrolamprus aesculapii*. In the types series of this species, however, he by error also included a venomous coral snake.

When the German naturalist Wagler described a mildly venomous Brazilian false coral snake *Erythrolamprus venustissimus*, he named it *Elaps venustissimus*, concluding that it must be a venomous elapid coral snake. A picture of his species appeared in the handsomely illustrated volume by Spix in 1824.

Even as recently as 1936, the German zoologist Ahl mistook a false coral snake of the genus *Pliocercus* for a venomous species and described it as *Elaps hertae*. *Elaps* was an earlier name used for all present-day venomous coral snakes.

During my studies of coral snakes, I periodically received specimens from most of world's largest museums. Three of them included false coral snakes with venomous coral snakes. To give justice to museums and herpetologists, such a mistake can easily occur when an unidentified collection is sent to a specialist for study. These collections frequently arrive at the museum before any detailed study has been made. The curator of a museum or a field collector makes a quick preliminary identification by a visual assessment and it is all too easy to confuse a model with a mimic. These errors illustrate the successful resemblance between the venomous and nonvenomous coral snakes, especially when they come from a region where the concordance between the model and the mimic is the best.

Coral Snake Mimicry by Other Animals

Over a century ago, A. R. Wallace observed the enormously large and conspicuously colored South American caterpillar of the sphinx moth (*Pseudosphinx tetrio*) and concluded that its coloration serves as warning to predators and advertises its unpalatability. This caterpillar reaches a length of about 15 cm and its color pattern of black, yellow, and orange-red resembles a small coral snake. It has a velvety black body interrupted by intensely yellow bands. The head, tail, and legs are orange-red. When this enormous caterpillar is molested or grabbed, it violently thrushes its tail in a way similar to the behavior of coral snakes. Its distasteful nature comes from eating toxic plants. Whether or not this caterpillar is a coral snake mimic is still in question. In Santa Rosa National Park, Costa Rica, where the caterpillars abound, D. H. Janzen (1980) observed a possible protective relationships between the caterpillars and birds such as great kiskadees and turquoise-browed motmots, which are known to be innately afraid of brightly colored snakes. Sphinx moth caterpillars live together in large numbers and tend to advertise their noxious nature with warning coloration similar to that of coral snakes (see also Vitt, 1992).

Another nonsnake example of possible mimicry of coral snakes are the young individuals of the Costa Rican turtles *Rhinoclemmys pulcherrima*. They have bright red-yellow-black rings on their carapace margin, a color pattern apparently used for flashy defense display, not necessarily for mimicry.

Objections and Alternative Suggestions for Mimicry

While most biologist have accepted the validity of the phenomenon of mimicry, there are some questions and alternative hypotheses (Gadow, 1908, 1911; Grobman, 1978) to explain why species from two quite different groups of snakes might look so similar. The United States has the worst examples of mimicry as compared to the astonishing perfection of imitation displayed by Latin American coral snakes. When observing true and false coral snakes in nature, one cannot help but be impressed by the extraordinary concordance of color patterns.

Greene and McDiarmid (1981) answered the most common objections to the concept of mimicry in coral snakes that I summarize in continuation (see also Campbell and Lamar, 1989).

First, how can a predator learn to avoid coral snakes? Their bite is mortal, and it is impossible to learn from a fatal experience. Mimicry can only be established and maintained when predators have the opportunity to learn about the dangerous nature of coral snakes.

There are many ways by which predators can learn or have innate fear reinforced without being killed. Some juvenile mammalian predators such as javelinas (*Tayassu*) and coatis (*Nasua*) (Gehlbach, 1973) and young bird predators such as motmots and kiskadees are known to have an innate fear of flashy coral snake color pattern (S. M. Smith, 1975, 1976, 1977). The more aggressive predators with less innate fear might be eliminated from the population. In addition, while smaller coral snakes might not deliver enough venom to kill a predator they might be able to make one sick. Apparently, larger coral snakes can control the amount of venom delivered in a bite and thus inject a sublethal dose. Also, predators that feed in social groups or in family units could learn of the dangerous nature of coral snakes by observing the calamities of a bitten, struggling fellow animal. Quite possibly natural selection would favor those predators who naturally avoid conspicuous color patterns, while many others will be genetically eliminated from the population (Greene and Pyburn, 1973). If a false coral snake is a mildly venomous species as in Mullerian mimicry, then its bite serves well to reinforce the dangerous nature of mimicry companions.

Second, how can a diurnal predator with color vision find and try to feed on a brightly colored coral snake that supposedly is active at night when colors are not highly visible?

In temperate regions, as in the United States or in the hot deserts, coral snakes are at least partially nocturnal. Many field observations have confirmed that further south coral snakes are quite active not only at night but also during the day. This is partially true even in the southern United States. Coral snakes are quite active in shady tropical and subtropical forests. Moreover, during the day foraging predators frequently uncover coral snakes as they hide in litter or beneath small objects. The surprising display of warning coloration, accompanied or not by a bite, would have the necessary effect to signal the venomous nature of a coral snake.

Third, the presence of too many false coral snakes in the same area where true coral snakes live gives predators a poor chance of encountering and learning about the dangerous nature of the venomous coral snakes.

It is quite difficult to know exactly how many models and mimics live in the same area. Large collections have been made in at least two regions: Brazil and Panama. They give some idea of the relative abundance of true versus false coral snakes. As I previously mentioned, in Panama models are more abundant than the mimics while in the São Paulo region in Brazil where the Instituto Butantan receives snakes, the number of mimics is higher than that of the corresponding models. However, research done with butterflies has shown that mimicry is still a valuable way to protect a given color pattern against predators, even when the mimics are more abundant than the noxious models.

Fourth, could it be that the model and mimic patterns look similar not because of mimicry but because of simple convergence (evolutionary convergence) of form and coloration as is known in other species of animals?

It is possible that in some cases convergence plays a role in making two color patterns similar in the same environment. Convergent evolution would even facilitate emergence of "utilitarian" mimicry resemblances. When one observes such mimics as *Pliocercus* and their perfect imitation of coral snakes, where not one but several coral snake species and patterns are involved in region after region, the conclusion is inescapable: convergence cannot account for such an extraordinary phenomenon. By one calculation I made, the chance that two genera of different "coral snakes" would look similar over an entire range of distribution is about 227 million to 1. There are not enough species of snakes in the entire world to make these odds remotely good.

Fifth, why don't the model and the mimic always live in exactly the same area? Why are adjacent but not overlapping distributions also found in some mimicry cases?

In an overwhelming majority of cases, the models and mimics are found in the same area. Some snakes with red color patterns might be present in areas of distribution of coral snakes without being necessarily engaged in mimicry imitations. As I mentioned in the section on enemies and defense, some young mammals and birds are frightened by bright color patterns, especially by red. This itself would protect flashy snakes and caterpillars from predators. On the other hand, there is one example, described by Paul Martin (1958) in Tamaulipas, Mexico, where the mimic (*Pliocercus*) occupies a different kind of habitat than that of the model coral snake, *M. fulvius tenere*. Both mimicry companions live in the same general region, but in different habitats. The mimic is found only in the cloud forest, while *M. fulvius tenere* is distributed in the tropical deciduous forest. Some predatory birds that feed on coral snakes are not normally restricted to the same habitats as are the terrestrial snakes. They hunt over the entire region and provide mimicry "decisions" about good and bad mimics.

Chapter 9
Biogeography, Origin, and Evolution

In spite of significant advances and multidisciplinary integration of knowledge from many disciplines (Vuilleumier, 1977), the biogeographical interpretation of the distribution patterns, as well as the origin and evolution of animals and plants and their biotas, are still characterized by uncertainties and partial evidences that remain open ended and subject to alternative interpretations. Coral snakes are no exception. Yet, this makes the subject interesting and creative and herein I offer one interpretation of the biogeography, origin, and evolution of coral snakes.

Biogeographical Distribution

Coral snakes alone are not a sufficiently large and diversified group to allow the definition of independent biogeographical units. On the other hand, an overview of the ranges of all the species of coral snakes shows that they conform to patterns and clusters of distribution described for major animal groups.

The contemporary geographical distribution of coral snakes is the result of several major geological, climatological, and ecological events and processes of the past, as briefly reviewed by Slowinski (1991). As a result of these historical events, it is possible to identify some patterns of distribution of this group of snakes. In reviewing the interpretation of biogeography of Central American herpetofauna that includes coral snakes, Savage (1982) suggested that some patterns of distribution are understood best by vicariance model (Nelson, 1973, 1975; Platnic and Nelson, 1978; Nelson and Platnic, 1981), others by dispersal hypothesis, and others by a combination of both.

Assessing the overall geographic distribution of coral snakes, several important features can be mentioned. First, there is an increase in the number of species (diversity) from north to south in the northern hemisphere, and from south to north in the southern hemisphere. For example, going southward, in Mexico and Central America the number of sympatric species of coral snakes is 1 (ex. *M. fulvius tenere* in Texas and northern Sonora, Mexico); 2 (ex. *M. d. distans* and *M. proximans* in Nayarit, Mexico), or at most 3 (ex. *M. alleni*, *M. nigrocinctus mosquitensis* and *M. multifasciatus hertwigi* in eastern Nicaragua). Going northward in the southern hemisphere, 1 species, (*M. p. pyrrhocryptus*), is present in central Argentina; 2 (*M. p. pyrrhocryptus* and *M. diana*) in southern Boliva, or 3 (*M. frontalis altirostris*, *M. decoratus*, and *M. corallinus*) in eastern Rio Grande do Sul, Brazil. Second, tropical South America, especially the Amazon region, is the region richest in number of species and subspecies. For example, in Iquitos region of Peru are found no less than 9 species (*Leptomicrurus narducci melanotus*, *L. scutiventris*, *Micrurus filiformis*, *M. hemprichii ortoni*, *M. langsdorffi*, *M. lemniscatus helleri*, *M. putumayensis*, *M. spixii obscurus*, and *M. s. surinamensis* (see Dixon and Soini, 1986; see also section on ecological distribution and habitats).

New World coral snakes may be grouped into three major biogeographical units or assemblages roughly comparable to Savage's (1982) historical source units that have contributed species of amphibians and reptiles:

1. North American-Mexican coral snakes (from the southern United States to Tehuantepec, Mexico)—comprising 2 genera, 12 species, and a total of 28 taxa (species + subspecies).
2. Central American coral snakes (from Tehuantepec to Panama)—comprising 1 genus, 13 species, and a total of 22 taxa.
3. South American coral snakes (South American continent)—comprising 2 genera, 45 species and a total of 75 taxa.

Micruroides is restricted to the North American-Mexican assemblage; *Leptomicrurus* is found only in the South American unit, while *Micrurus* is distributed over the entire area in the three biogeographical units (Map 1).

The increase in number of species from one region to the next is accompanied by an overall change in the taxonomic composition of each of these assemblages. This emphasizes the fact that each major assemblage has a unique combination of coral snakes with a degree of endemism and a very limited species overlap. When such overlap is present, it is restricted to the boundaries of two contiguous regions. In other words, no truly common elements or species for the three areas are present, except in the "biogeotone" areas where two major biogeographic units meet. For instance, only *M. n. nigrocinctus* penetrates even marginally into the northwestern tip of Colombia (*M. clarki*'s presence in Colombia still has to be confirmed); similarly, in the Darién area of Panama are found fringe populations of only four South American species: *M. m. mipartitus*, *M. dissoleucus dunni*, *M. ancoralis jani*, and probably *M. dumerilii transandinus*. These fringe penetrations between the two regions seem to be of a relatively recent occurrence, perhaps in the last 20,000 years.

Each one of the subcontinental assemblages can be subdivided into several smaller regions with unique areas of endemisms (Cracraft, 1985) and/or refugia (Haffer, 1969; Vanzolini and Williams, 1970), characterized by coral snakes associated with each one of them.

Finally, the degree of regional endemisms suggests that each biogeographical region corresponds to species clusters isolated from each other, with different degrees of differentiation and possibly independent evolutionary histories. This is considered in the next section on origin and evolution.

Most of the biogeographical subdivisions for coral snakes are concordant with those already defined for major groups of animals and plants. For herpetology these are faunal assemblages, physiographic regions, centers of endemisms or refugia as defined by Duellman (1966, 1979a, 1982a and 1982b), Vanzolini (1970 and 1981), and Vanzolini and Williams (1981), and partially by P. Müller's (1973) centers of dispersal (but see comments by Vuilleumier, 1977) or areas of regional endemisms for terrestrial vertebrates in Central and South America (see areas of endemisms as proposed for birds by Cracraft, 1985).

Tentatively, for coral snakes a distinction can be made between refugia and areas of endemism. While in several cases they overlap, such as the Chocó region of western Colombia-Darién, they represent the outcome of two different events (Cracraft, 1985).

The refugia model of speciation is based on a relatively recent discovery that during Pleistocene and even more recently, tropical forests of the world have undergone drastic and periodic changes of dry and wet periods. They have been caused by such events as elevations of mountains, alternate dry-wet climate, and glaciation that in South America took place around 250,000 and 130,000 years ago, the last being only about 14,000 years ago. These climatic fluctuations have deeply modified the vegetation of many seemingly immutable forest formations (Prance, 1973). During the dry periods, many species, including some coral snakes, have found refuge in remnants (refugia) of wet forests of relatively reduced dimensions. This enabled them to survive and adapt to the changing environment afterward as described by Haffer (1969) and Vuilleumier (1969, 1970, 1980) for South American birds. For South American herpetology, Vanzolini (1970, 1980, 1981, 1986), Vanzolini and Williams (1970), and Williams and Vanzolini (1980), and for amphibians Duellman (1972, 1982a, 1982b), Heyer (1973), and Lynch (1979) have defined and illustrated cases of forest refuges as a way of vicariant speciation, some with examples of coral snakes.

Some probable refuge examples for coral snakes are the eastern slopes of Ecuadorian Andes with *M. petersi* and *M. steindachneri*, and the Peruvian slopes of Andes (separated from the Ecuadorian Andes by the Huancabamba Depression in southern Ecuador) with *M. peruvianus* and *M. annellatus annellatus*. Usually, subspecies are not considered good indicators of the centers or refugia, especially in historical biogeography. However, in some cases it might be quite profitable to use subspecies as indicators, especially in defining or characterizing refugia, because of their relatively recent origin. Rondônia center might be another refuge, with *M. albicinctus* and *M. h. rondonianus* as examples, and llanos of Colombia and Venezuela another, with the endemic *M. isozonus*. It is possible that existence of some Pleistocene refuges have not provided a long enough time for speciation to occur (Cadle and Patton, 1988).

The areas of endemism are postulated patterns of distribution established to some extent by pre-Pleistocene events more than 2 million years ago, during which major dispersals and appearance of vicariance barriers facilitated the origin of new species. They might or might not coincide with refuges or might include them. One example is the Paria-Trinidad center of endemism, with *M. circinalis*.

One example of parapatric speciation by which two adjacent populations developed into different species is illustrated by *M. lemniscatus*, a widespread species divided into several subspecies, and *M. frontifasciatus*, found in the eastern slopes of the Bolivian Andes. During the last elevation of the Andes, a valley population of *M. lemniscatus* became isolated and underwent subsequent speciation, giving origin to *M. frontifasciatus*. In a later period, *M. frontifasciatus*, known to occur between about 500 and 2,600 m above sea level, expanded its distribution downward and became partially sympatric with the more lowland dwelling *M. lemniscatus helleri*.

To some extent, the units for coral snakes coincide with those suggested by Savage (1966, 1982) for the herpetofauna of Central America, by Duellman (1979, 1982a) and Lynch (1986) for the Andes of South America, by Dixon (1979) and Duellman (1982b) for tropical rain forest, and by Rivero-Blanco and Dixon (1979) for dry lowlands and savannas in northern South America. About 80% of the species of coral snakes have ranges related to these smaller biogeographical units.

The following is a representative list of physiographic units, slightly modified and adapted to coral snake distribution, that have representative species of coral snakes for each region:

I. North American-Mexico coral snakes
   1. Southern North America-Northern Mexico (*M. fulvius, Micruroides euryxanthus*)
   2. Mexican plateau (*M. browni*)
   3. Atlantic side-Veracruz (*M. bernadi, M. limbatus, M. elegans*)
   4. Oaxaca Sierra Madre (*M. nebularis*)
   5. Southern Mexico-Balsas (*M. laticollaris*)
   6. Tehuantepec (*M. bogerti, M. ephippifer*)
II. Central American coral snakes
   1. Pacific lowland Mexico-Costa Rica (*M. latifasciatus*)
   2. Atlantic lowland Yucatan-Guatemala (*M. hippocrepis*)
   3. Chiapas-Guatemala highlands (*M. stuarti*)
   4. Atlantic Panama region (*M. clarki, M. stewarti*)
III. South American coral snakes
   1. Chocoan, eastern Panama to northwestern Ecuador (*M. ancoralis, M. spurrelli*)
   2. Caribbean-llanos (*M. isozonus*)
   3. Guianas (*L. collaris*)
   4. North Amazon (*M. putumayensis, M. langsdorffi*)
   5. Amazonia (*M. surinamensis, M. spixii, M. hemprichi*)
   6. Rondonia-Mato Grosso (*M. albicinctus, M. h. rondonianus*)
   7. North Andean (*M. mipartitus, M. multiscutatus*)
   8. Central Andean (*M. peruvianus*)
   9. Pacific-Atacama desert (*M. mertensi, M. tschudii*)
   10. Upper Amazon (*L. narduccii, M. annellatus, M.steindachneri, M. margaritiferus*)
   11. Brazilian Caatinga (*M. ibiboboca*)
   12. Atlantic forest (*M. corallinus, M.decoratus*)

Origin and Evolution

Difficult biological detective work has to be performed when dealing with the origin and evolution of coral snakes. There are very limited data that can be used to establish the origin of this particular group of snakes, and the few known fossil records, represented mostly by vertebrae, give only limited information about the coral snakes and their ancestors of a far distant past.

Recent authors tend to agree that coral snakes are a natural group that forms part of the proteroglyphous elapids that include the African, Asian, and Australian species (McDowell, 1968; McCarthy, 1985). Elapids form part of the higher modern snakes, Caenophidia, but have evolved such unique characteristics as (1) proteroglyph venom-conducting fangs, i.e., canaliculate maxillary front fangs; (2) a levator anguli oris muscle (adductor externus superficialis auct.) divided into a ventral and dorsal portion around the venom gland and is the only muscle in charge of compressing the venom gland for delivery of venom; and (3) a Harderian gland restricted to the orbit. They have diverged from the colubrid snakes forming an independent lineage and are unrelated to viperids that also diverged from the same group (Haas, 1952; Anthony, 1955; Underwood, 1967; Kardong, 1980).

A significant new interpretation of elapid ancestry is that by Samuel McDowell (1986). After examining several morphological features related to the "corner of the mouth" of snakes, he concluded that proteroglyphous snakes that include elapids and sea snakes (hydrophiids) display features that in several ways make them more primitive than colubrids and viperids.

Here I attempt to present a tentative story of the origin and evolution (and "biogeographical journey") of coral snakes, as revealed in part by the available information, then an alternative hypothesis, and last a brief comment on a third hypothesis. The first hypothesis, a more plausible one, assumes a northern origin of coral snakes, while the second contemplates a South American origin. The third suggests coral snake origin from New World colubrid ("xenodontine") snakes.

Hypothesis of Northern Origin

The family Elapidae with fixed front fangs of proteroglyph type originated in the Old World. Coral snakes' ancestors separated from their eastern Asian elapid relatives, and about 25 to 30 million years ago, in the late Oligocene or early Miocene, entered the North American continent traveling across the migratory "highway" known as the Bering Land Bridge. At that time, a large faunal exchange across this land connection was favored because of the presence of subtropical to warm temperate climates and the occurrence of temperate rain forests and deciduous forests, as suggested by plant pollen (Wolf and Leopold, 1967). This land bridge is thought to have been the route taken by many New World snakes (Dowling, 1975; Holman, 1979) as well as by other animals coming from Asia.

Scant fossil remnants of *Micrurus* found in Nebraska in the upper Miocene strata going back about 12 to 15 million years ago (Holman, 1977) support the notion of the presence of coral snakes much farther north than the currently known distribution (see also Vanzolini and Heyer, 1985). The low neural spine of the vertebrae found in Nebraska suggests that the coral snakes' ancestors were most likely of secretive habits and somewhat fossorial. Once developed, coral snakes retained their successful secretive habits throughout their journey southward and eastward. This was also the time when the current species began to differentiate from each other (Cadle and Sarich, 1981).

A remarkable discovery of an elapid snake fossil from Miocene in Europe, said to be a coral snake and named *Micrurus gallicus* by Rage and Holman in 1984, poses several interesting questions and complicates considerably the explanation of the long evolutionary history of coral snakes. Related to this surprising find, the authors themselves raised the question: Is it due to dispersal or parallel evolution? While it points to the northern origin of coral snakes, the time frame of their evolution does not conform to other known data. On one hand, it is possible that the fossil species, described from France, is not a *Micrurus* but a burrowing or secretive elapid snake belonging to an Old World genus with vertebrae that appear quite similar to those of coral snakes due to burrowing habits. The variation of morphological features of vertebrae along the vertebral column of coral snakes is considerable. This could cause difficulties for a correct identification of the genus of fossil elapid snakes, even for seasoned paleontologists such as Rage and Holman. Max Hecht, a herpetological paleontologist and colleague at the American Museum of Natural History, is currently studying the identity of *M. gallicus* and I thank him for sharing his tentative ideas.

On the other hand, if the fossil snake in Europe is indeed a coral snake, it would confirm the origin of coral snakes in northern hemisphere or relate it to some post-Gondwana events. This would place their origin much farther back into history than the current evidence indicates.

An important indirect piece of evidence for our considerations in establishing hypotheses of the origin and evolution of coral snakes comes from biochemistry. Cadle (1983) suggested that Old World elapids and neotropical coral snakes evolved from a common ancestor that was initially present in the northern hemisphere. His interpretation is based on studying the biochemical evolution of serum albumin (Wilson et al., 1977). This approach has been actively developed only in the last 20 years and involves immunological comparison of serum albumins between different living species. This relationship between two species or groups can be measured in what is called AID units or albumin immunological distance units.

In addition, Mao et al. (1983), studying serum albumins of terrestrial elapids and sea snakes, concluded that *Micrurus* is related to and must be included in the Old World subfamily Elapinae, which also includes such genera as cobras (*Naja*) and kraits (*Bungarus*). They also concluded that the sea snake *Laticauda* is more closely related to other sea snakes, Hydrophiinae, than to Old World terrestrial elapids and coral snakes (for alternative view see McDowell, 1968).

Fossil records from the Pliocene and Pleistocene of Florida (Auffenberg, 1963; Meylan, 1982; also Holman 1958, 1959a, 1978) and Texas (Hill, 1971) tell of the presence of coral snakes in these areas at least 3 to 5 million years ago. The genus *Micruroides* in North America has additional teeth in the maxillae, apart from the fangs, a characteristic interpreted as more primitive than the advanced "toothless maxilla" of *Micrurus* and *Leptomicrurus*. On the other hand, their albumin-established age does not differentiate them significantly from other coral snakes (Cadle and Sarich, 1981).

After having occupied North America, coral snakes proceeded to Central America and, via the Panama connection, penetrated into South America where they have achieved the greatest diversity.

The Middle American fauna developed a unique assemblage of its own, composed of autochthonous species, in isolation from North and South America, probably during the late Miocene early Pliocene. When the Panamanian Portal connected North and South America again sometime in late Pliocene, the coral snakes had undergone vicariant differentiation in Central America, producing such species as *M. nigrocinctus*, *M. hippocrepis*, and *M. alleni*.

One remarkable phenomenon is the evolution of triad-type coral snakes, *M. elegans* and *M. laticollaris*, in the Atlantic and Pacific side of Mexico and western Central America. Both have apparently evolved the triad-type color patterns independently from the South American triad-type coral snakes. The Central American species have the hemipenis similar to that of the single-banded coral snakes, while the South American species (*M. frontalis*, *M. lemniscatus*, etc.) have their own unique bilobed design. It is a parallel evolution, or one could say that the triad-type color pattern in coral snakes has a polyphyletic origin.

In summary, the hypothesis of a northern and Old World origin of coral snakes and their migration into the New World by the end of the Oligocene and early Miocene or somewhat later is supported by the presence of Nebraska fossils and by the age of coral snakes as calculated from the biochemical evolution. Difficulty arises in explaining why there are so many species of coral snakes in South America.

Hypothesis of South American Origin

This hypothesis, less plausible than the first one, suggests the origin of coral snakes from their Old World relatives during the time of separation of the continents of Gondwanaland at the end of the Cretaceous, about 90 million years ago. This assumes the possibility that the age of coral snakes is actually greater than the Oligocene age estimated from the studies of biochemical evolution. Mao and his coworkers (1983) already noted that the age estimated from albumin evolution does not coincide with estimates derived from fossils. In accordance with this hypothesis, in part supported by Savage (1983) and Estes and Baez (1986), coral snakes originated in South America when Africa and South America began to drift apart. Elapids of the subfamily Elapinae, to which coral snakes are related, are present in Africa as well as in Asia.

It is principally in South America that coral snakes have achieved the greatest diversity, suggesting a long evolutionary time and different rates of vicariant or dispersal origin of species. During the Tertiary, they migrated into Central America and then continued into North America.

The great diversity of coral snakes in South America, as well as their wide distribution, strongly suggests that their ancestors were probably well adapted to the lowland tropical vegetation that was extensive throughout much of South America from the beginning of the Tertiary even before the uplift of the Andes, an event that took place around the Pliocene-Pleistocene boundary. As the upheaval of the Andes occurred, several populations became isolated and gave origin to different species of coral snakes, such as *M. catamayensis* and *M. bocourti*. In addition, some Andean passages such as the Huancabamba Depression, found in the Andes between Ecuador and Peru, allowed colonization of the Pacific lowlands west of the Andes by such species as *M. mertensi*.

Two difficulties arise in explaining this hypothesis. First is the appearance of the land connection between Central and South America during the Pliocene or 5.2 million years ago. During this period much of the faunal interchange between both continents took place (Simpson, 1980; Vanzolini and Heyer, 1985; Estes and Baez, 1985). Second is the presence of fossil coral snakes in Nebraska during the upper Miocene, which is earlier than the land connection.

However, Rosen (1976) proposed a vicariance model for interpreting the biogeography of the Caribbean region that could help us explain coral snake distribution in the New World. Rosen's idea is derived using the distribution pattern of the terrestrial fresh water fishes, amphibians, and reptiles. In accordance with this model, during the Late Cretaceous an early lower Central American archipelago (called the proto-antillean archipelago) connected Central and South America, allowing dispersal of organisms in both directions, from north to south and south to north.

This archipelago moved into the Caribbean at the early Tertiary, creating the Panamanian Portal and isolating North America from South America until the emergence of the Panamanian Isthmus in the Tertiary.

This hypothesis is congruent with data for fresh water fishes (Bussing, 1976, 1985), amphibians, and reptiles (Duellman, 1966, 1979), and Savage's (1982) data for Central American herpetofauna, and can be at least partially considered as explanation for the present distribution of coral snakes. Savage (1982) indicates that "Rosen's ideas of an ancient major dispersal event from South to Central America, followed by a major vicariance event (the development of the Panamanian Portal) are in complete agreement with herpetofaunal data." This model is congruent with the groups mentioned above as well as with angiosperms, but not with mammals (Simpson, 1969; Raven and Axelrod, 1974; Savage, 1982). This allows us to conclude that different groups of organisms present in the same areas may have different evolutionary histories.

After the dispersal into Central America, the ancestors of the coral snakes were able to reach northern Mexico, and from there North America, before or around the Miocene. Because of the appearance of the Panamanian Portal, North and Central American coral snakes became completely isolated from their South American relatives. Due to a combination of physiographic and climatic factors, there was fragmentation and isolation of the original populations, which underwent evolution in situ during much of the Tertiary, resulting in distinct species. These species constitute a group distinct and independent from the species of South America. Some of the known geological factors (vicariance events) that influenced the process were the uplift of the Sierra Madre in the Oligocene and the highlands of nuclear Central America in the Miocene, the closure of the Panamanian portal in the Pliocene, and the uplift of the Andes in the Pleistocene.

The common origin of the Central and South American coral snakes is still reflected in the primitive characteristics shared by a number of species in both regions, such as the single-banded color pattern with supraanal tubercles and the morphology of the hemipenis.

There are no known coral snake fossils in South America. The appearance of an older fossil record than the one found in North America for this particular group of snakes would corroborate this hypothesis.

Immunological comparison between African elapids and New World coral snakes could give another clue as to the possible relationship between these two groups. The comparative data between Australian and Asian elapids and coral snakes show divergence of these two groups around the Eocene, or about 47 million years ago by one estimate (Mao et al., 1983) and about 30 million years by another (Cadle and Sarich, 1981).

Hypothesis of Coral Snake "Xenodontine" Origin

This third hypothesis of the origin of coral snakes, deriving them from a group of South American colubrid (xenodontine) snakes, *Elapomorphus* and *Apostolepis*, was proposed by Savitzky (1978) and based on morphological studies of elapids and colubrids. Several authors (McCarthy, 1985; McDowell, 1986) have rejected this hypothesis and Cadle (1984) determined by albumin immunology that *Apostolepis* is closely related to colubrids. Allan Savitzki's work is a careful piece of research comparing many characters and is quite a valuable contribution to herpetology, but his hypothesis is not supported by the other findings as discussed above.

How Fast Do Species Evolve?

Almost nothing is known about the time it takes for a species or subspecies to evolve. In some cases, the geological history can provide some insights as to the duration of some of these events. A species in the Sierra Nevada de Santa Marta region of Colombia tells an interesting story of its evolutionary history. *M. d. dumerilii* is found in the northwestern lowlands around Santa Marta and Valle del Bajo Magdalena, while *M. dumerilii colombianus* is present higher up on Santa Marta mountain. As the main Santa Marta uplift occurred only 50,000 years ago (Gansser, 1973), it took about that much or less time of separation between the populations of *M. dumerilii* to allow for the evolutionary process (possibly vicariance) to originate two different taxa (subspecies). To some extent, the same process also explains the subspecific difference between *M. dissoleucus nigrirostris*, found in the lowlands of the Magdalena river valley, and *M. dissoleucus melanogenys*, present in the semidesertic formations at the base of the Santa Marta mountains.

Some species of coral snake might have originated thanks to some isolating events in Pleistocene, such as mountain uplifting and formation of refugia occurring during that epoch (see discussion in biogeography). Many species may have originated in pre-Pleistocene time (Cadle and Patton, 1988) more than 2.5 million years ago, and the formation of subspecies has followed at a later time.

The rate of speciation, most probably, is different for different species. The complex of species *M. nigrocinctus* that could also be called superspecies, which includes several island species and subspecies and mainland subspecies, offers an interesting case of isolative vicariance as well as adaptive radiation and migration.

The island coral snakes that belong to *M. nigrocinctus* complex are the Roatán Island coral snake, *M. ruatanus*, which has undergone accelerated speciation and has developed into full species, and two other island forms, the one found on Coiba Island (*M. n. coibensis*) and the other on Great Corn Island (*M. n. babaspul*). They have "reached" only a subspecies status. Other populations on several other islands, such as Taboga, San José, and San Miguel off the Pacific coast of Panama, can not be distinguished from the mainland populations of *M. n. nigrocinctus*. Island populations are known to have faster rates of speciation than mainland populations due to phenomena related to mechanisms of dispersal, selection pressure, and population genetics (MacArthur and Wilson, 1963, 1967). On the mainland, there is less chance of isolation and some of the genetic factors can not play a vigorous role in originating new species and subspecies. In addition, large zones of intergradation are found between some of the mainland subspecies of *M. nigrocinctus*.

Clines displayed by several subspecies of *M. diastema* offer evidence for different timetables and mechanisms of differentiation. This can be combined with special adaptation to different environments and extension of distribution over very gradually changing climatological and ecological conditions. This is illustrated by a combination of the presence of clinal changes and intergradation between *M. d. diastema* and *M. diastema sapperi* in eastern Veracruz, Mexico, or a large zone of cline graduation between *M. diastema sapperi* and *M. d. apiatus* in Chiapas and central Guatemala. *M. d. alienus* has a large zone of intergradation with *M. d. sapperi* (Blaney and Blaney, 1979) in eastern Campeche and Quintana Roo, Mexico.

Part IV
VENOMS AND SNAKEBITE

Chapter 10
Venoms in Biology

The study of the biochemical composition of coral snake venoms is closely related to their pharmacological effect. Toxinologists, a relatively new breed of scientists, are combining both of these fields as well as other studies related to toxins, venoms, and poisons wherever they occur in the living world, including how they affect animals and humans. Their studies are reported in the prestigious professional journal *Toxicon*, published by the International Society on Toxinology.

It is not the intent of this book to offer a complete survey of all the details of coral snake venoms and their action. First, the knowledge is as yet incomplete, and second, the main thrust of this book is to provide a summary of all aspects of coral snakes as a biological group.

Biological Significance of Snake Venom

Chemically and biologically coral snake venoms are made of natural organic compounds. The secret of their venomous nature is no secret because venoms consist of enzymes, other proteinlike substances, salts, and elements that are well known in living organisms. Venoms are extraordinary because their enzymes and toxins are built in such a way that their natural actions wreak havoc on several biological functions of other organisms and consequently destroy them. Used to overpower prey or in defense, venoms are critical to the coral snake's survival.

For snakes and many other animals, there are two ways of dealing with the prey or enemy. One is to overpower it by sheer strength or some special ability. Large snakes, for example, pythons, boas, and anacondas, rely on their considerable strength to subdue their prey; they have strength but no venom. The second strategy is to overcome the prey or defend against a predator using venom. This second strategy is particularly important when the enemy is much larger, stronger, and more dangerous than the defender. The defender's survival, to a large extent, depends on having a powerful and quick-acting venom as well as an effective means to introduce it into the prey or enemy. Coral snakes and other venomous snakes are usually smaller in size and weaker than their enemies, but they do have venom. With the appearance of venom, the absolute superiority of sheer strength in the animal kingdom was broken.

Before we proceed to deal with venoms, let us agree on a terminology. In biology, medicine, toxinology, and everyday life a diversity of definitions and concepts are used for distinguishing venoms, poisons, toxins, and other noxious substances. Terminology in frequent use in biology and medicine defines *venom* as a complex, noxious substance produced by a living organism that is introduced into another organism by means of biting, stinging, scratching, or similar means. Thus, snakes have venom, and in English we speak of venomous snakes. The term *poison* is used for all noxious substances, whether or not produced by living organisms, that in order to produce their effect must be eaten, drunk, or inhaled. By this definition, it is not appropriate to say "poisonous coral snakes," even though the expression is used quite frequently in common language. Toxins are any noxious substances produced by living organisms that affect and disrupt the functioning of another organism. Thus, venoms and poisons are toxins. One such toxin that forms part of coral snake venom is the coral snake neurotoxin (CNTX); a simple component of the venom can also be called a toxin.

Evolution of Coral Snake Venom

In a now-distant biological past, coral snakes developed their venom and their venom secretion system by the gradual modification of the biochemical content of the secretions of their oral glands (see biting mechanism and venom apparatus). These secretions increasingly facilitated the process of procuring, ingesting, and digesting food.

Coral snakes evolved and changed together with their venom and venom delivery system in accordance with the survival needs or evolutionary possibilities of their species (Kochva, 1987). From an ecological perspective, the way coral snakes used their venom always remained integrally incorporated in the overall performance of the species and its success. For each species and its venom there is at least a partially definable "venom niche," i.e., the functional role of venom for a snake. From the standpoint of evolution, the existence of the venom system increases the coral snake's efficiency in feeding and defending itself; the more successful the venom, the more feeding advantage the species has. An alert and "well fed" coral snake has better chances for survival and reproduction, thus ensuring the genetic transmission of an effective venom apparatus to the next generation.

Within the evolutionary context, the characteristics of venom can change under at least three conditions: (1) when a more successful adaptation of the species is achieved with respect to venom efficiency and prey specificity in the existing environment; (2) when there are ecological changes, usually slow, in the environment that require new adaptations and modifications, including those of the venom and venom delivery apparatus to meet the changing conditions; and (3) when a species gradually expands its distribution and adapts to new and different environmental conditions with new prey species.

At an early state in their evolution, probably some time in the Miocene, elapids, including coral snakes, began to specialize in the "neurotoxic approach," producing a venom that acts predominantly on the nervous system and that kills the prey or enemy by respiratory paralysis. As we will see, the complex coral snake venom is also cardiotoxic and hemotoxic and interferes in the function of several internal organs and physiological processes.

Different coral snake species have somewhat different venoms, but their main feature is the neurotoxic pattern. The venom might also show some changes ontogenetically, i.e., as an individual snake grows up, the characteristics of its venom change in order to adapt to different prey species. It is known that this is the case in rattlesnakes where the venom of adult snakes acts differently from that of juveniles. Correspondingly, we can expect that in coral snakes a change in diet from lizards to swamp eels, known to occur in *Micrurus lemniscatus*, might be accompanied by some changes in the constitution of its venom as it grows from juvenile to adult.

The same species and subspecies distributed in different geographical areas can develop different venom characteristics adapted more specifically to local conditions. These cases are examples of the way in which the venom might have undergone changes in the process of evolution.

History of Coral Snake Venom Research

The venomous nature of many snakes was known to the ancient cultures (Mayans, Hindus, Egyptians) long before Aristotle, Pliny, and Avicenne described the venomous snakes and noted symptoms of venomous bites for the Graeco-Roman world. But the mystery remained: What made snakebites so deadly?

Legends, beliefs, and stories of old maintained that the snake's bifurcated tongue actually inflicted the fatal wound. This uninformed and somewhat romantic belief in the snake "sting" has remained alive to present days and perhaps has its root in the two punctures caused by the pair of fangs, which could be interpreted as wounds from a sting of the bifurcated tongue or by a tail sting.

The tail sting is still a popular belief in many parts of Latin America. In a jar at the American Museum of Natural History where a specimen of *M. s. surinamensis* from Manjurú, Brazil, is kept is a note by its collector, Cooper, which laconically says, "Everybody convinced that it stings with tail." However cryptic, such field notes provide valuable information about the ways of the animals, as well as about local peoples' perceptions of the animals. García (1896) reported this belief about coral snakes from Cauca, Colombia, as told by the Indians (see section on names and folklore).

At the time the first brilliantly colored coral snakes were discovered, their venomous nature was only partially recognized by the early European naturalists who reported their discoveries. Such earlier scholars and naturalists as Prince Maximillian and others did not believe the Brazilian coral snakes were dangerous. In 1825, Maximillian Wied-Neuwied reported handling coral snakes and carrying them around in his pocket without being bitten. Of course, this proved their nonaggressive nature, but not the potential of their venom.

Another story of handling a coral snake that has a tragic outcome was related by the British writer and traveler, Rudyard Kipling, in 1891 in his short story *Reingelder and the German Flag*. In Uruguay, a seasoned German collector who had wandered all over the world collecting orchids met a compatriot, named Reingelder, who was collecting only coral snakes because they had the color of the German flag: black, red, and white (yellow). It was apparently the Uruguayan coral snake, *M. frontalis altirostris*. As written down by Kipling (1891, p. 7) in his rendition of German-accented English, the collector told him:
"I was hoontin' orchits and everyding else dot I could back in my kanasters... Dere was den mit me anoder man—Reingelder, dot was his name—and he was hoontin' also, but only coral-snakes—joost Uruguay coral-snakes, afery kind you could imagine... Dere is one snake, howefer, dot we who gollect know ash der Sherman Flag, pecause id is red and plack und white..." As the story continues, one day a native woman brought them the long sought-after coral snake, the "Sherman Flag". In spite of the warnings, Reingelder handled the coral snake by hand, until it finally bit him. He died that night. (I thank Bill Lamar for calling my attention to this story.)

The first monumental work on "North American Herpetology" in the United States was written in five copious volumes by Holbrook between 1836 and 1842. Holbrook was also of the opinion that coral snakes were inoffensive. However, he ascribed their inoffensive nature to their docility and not to the absence of venom fangs, or "instruments of destruction" as he called them, indirectly recognizing the venom-transmitting capacity of coral snakes.

It was Hermann von Ihering, a Brazilian scientist, who in 1881 was one of the first researchers to experimentally demonstrate the venomous nature of coral snakes in Brazil. He performed experiments letting a coral snake bite a pigeon. The bird died in about 5 minutes from respiratory paralysis, a characteristic of coral snake envenomation. He also observed that coral snake venom affects blood, producing hemolysis with changed shape of red and white blood cells. In his simple, yet scientifically correct manner, Ihering clarified another earlier misconception related to the mode of action of snake venoms. At that time, J. B. de Lacerda, a noted scientist from the Museu Nacional de Rio de Janeiro, Brazil, and other scientists in Europe were advancing the notion that the effect of the snake venom is due to poisonous molds and other pathological fungi found in the venom. This idea was similar to that of Buffon in ascribing the venomous effect not to the liquid itself but some organisms living in it. Ihering fed the dead pigeon to a fox without ill effect to the fox. If poisonous molds were to be blamed for the death of the pigeon, he argued, the fox would have showed the effects of the presence of poisonous fungi as well. Moreover, the venom acted much faster than any fungi could grow and poison the victim. To do justice to de Lacerda, his contributions to the understanding of diverse aspects of venoms and venomous snakes were considerable, earning him a place of distinction in the history of study of venomous animals and their venoms.

The first antivenin against snakebites in the New World was produced in Brazil by Vital Brazil at the turn of the century. At that time the number of deaths in Brazil by venomous animals was estimated to be about 12,000 a year, surpassed only by that of India. Recognizing the enormous need of the country to combat infectious diseases and venomous bites, and working under difficult conditions, Vital Brazil established the Institute of Serum-therapy in the State of São Paulo that later became Instituto Butantan. Vital Brazil was its first director. It was at this institute that world's first coral snake antivenin (soro anti-elapidico) was produced and continues to be produced to the present. Several illustrious Brazilian scientists are associated with the worldwide advance of knowledge in serum therapy and epidemiology around 1900. In addition to Ihering and Vital Brazil, these include Adolpho Lutz, de Lacerda, Oswaldo Cruz, and more recently Afranio do Amaral. Work on snake venom in Brazil was also carried out at the Instituto Oswaldo Cruz and the Instituto Vital Brazil, named after the distinguished scientists. Today, one of the sons of Vital Brazil, Oswaldo Vital Brazil, Jr., is following in the footsteps of his father, making considerable contributions to the study of coral snake venom.

Quite appropriately, in 1965 the Instituto Butantan commemorated the centennial of Vital Brazil's birth by organizing the First International Symposium of Venomous Animals. It gathered scientists from north and south, east and west. Currently, the institute is continuing the advance of knowledge in venomous animals under the direction of Willy Beçak, its current director, Iara Ferreira, head of the herpetology section, and Pedro Antonio Federsoni, in charge of the institute's museum.

In the 1980s, several new regional nuclei of snake venom production and research, including coral snakes, have been established in Brazil. The most active of them is Centro de Estudos de Animais Peçonhentos of the Universidade Catolica de Goiás under the leadership of Nelson Jorge da Silva. Others include Centro de Ofidismo at the Instituto de Medicina Tropical de Manaos with Paulo Buhrnheim and a team of scientists; in Belém, Pará, Oswaldo Rodrigues da Cunha and Francisco Paiva do Nascimento have formed a Centro at the Museo Paraense de Ciencias Naturais, and in Porto Alegre, Rio Grande do Sul, Thales de Lema is in charge of another snake venom research center.

Afranio do Amaral, an earlier director of the Instituto Butantan, came to the United States in the late 1920s and helped to establish the Antivenin Institute of America for which he served as Consulting Director. The Antivenin Institute of America was "an organization devoted to furthering the knowledge of venomous animals in general and to developing means of preventing death and relieving symptoms caused by their venoms." Thus, Amaral brought to the United States the knowledge, experience, and skill of Brazilian science in venoms and snakebite therapy. Some of the leading American herpetologists at that time gave their support to the institute, including Thomas Barbour, director of the Museum of Comparative Zoology, Harvard University; Raymond L. Ditmars, curator at the New York Zoological Park; and Lawrence M. Klauber, an engineer who loved to work in herpetology as curator at the San Diego Society of Natural History and who became the world's authority on rattlesnakes.

In recent decades, one of the most active venomous animal centers in the Americas is the Instituto Clodomiro Picado of the University of Costa Rica, where antisera against snakes are produced. The institute is producing an anticoral serum against North and Central American coral snake bites, and, more recently, a polyvalent anticoral serum that is effective against the venoms of most of the New World coral snakes.

Roger Bolaños, its earlier director, the late Luis Gonzalo Cerdas, José María Gutiérrez, and a team of scientists have developed a remarkable system of production of snake antisera and research activities that are worthy of the tradition of Clodomiro Picado, the father of herpetological and venom studies in Costa Rica. The antisera of the institute are among the best available coral snake antisera products offering the widest protection against coral snake bites. Another active researcher on snake venoms is Jesús Jiménez-Porras at the University of Costa Rica.

In the United States, except for some individual research, no concerted effort to study the nature of coral snake venoms was carried out until relatively recently. In the last three decades, however, more knowledge has been generated about coral snake venoms and their action by U.S. scientists than in the last 200 years. Scientists and their research on coral snake venom are mentioned in the chapters where their findings are incorporated.

The Value of Coral Snake Venom and Its Use in Medicine

Coral snake venom has remained one of the least-studied snake venoms. The reasons are diverse. Due to the relatively small size of coral snakes, venom extraction is difficult. Except for a few species, coral snakes are not at all abundant and, due to their predominantly inconspicuous habits, are difficult to find.

When Edward Seligmann, Jr. from the National Institutes of Health was establishing basic coral snake antivenin production and effectiveness standards for the U.S. government, he discovered that coral snakes, as well as their venom, are not as easily accessible as such abundant venomous snakes as rattlesnakes, water moccasins, and even the exotic cobras. He soon exhausted all the local resources and supplies and had to seek coral snakes and their venom from such distant places as Costa Rica and Colombia. While establishing biological standards for coral snake antivenin, Seligmann and his colleagues carried out a series of studies on coral snake venoms that are among the most comprehensive today.

As a result of the difficulties of obtaining coral snake venom, its price is unbelievably high. To say "it is worth its weight in gold" does not even approach its full value. Currently, the price of one gram of dry *M. f. fulvius* or *M. f. tenere* venom is about $1,200. One troy ounce of gold, on the other hand, is worth about $380. Now, as one ounce contains about 28 grams, the market value of one ounce of coral snake venom is about, yes, $33,000. It is more than 800 times more valuable than gold! Coral snake venom is the most expensive snake venom of U.S. venomous snakes and one of the most expensive in the world.

To extract coral snake venom looks as if it would be an excellent business, yet several difficulties make it not so appealing. Sherman and Madge Minton, well-known scholars of venomous snakes and their ways, warn against rushing into the venom production business in their book, *Venomous Reptiles* (1980). To obtain one gram of coral snake venom can take hundreds of extractions. To maintain purity of the venom is another problem, and finally, the market for snake venom is not large. Most scientists doing research on coral snake venoms usually try to collect or obtain snakes and to extract the venom they need. If they must purchase the venom, they will use well-established laboratories and snake farms.

Several snake venoms have been used for their specific properties in medicine. Preparations of diluted cobra venom, for example, were used in medicine, particularly as pain killers. As coral snake venom has a similar curare-type effect on the nervous system, a minute dose of it could be used as a simple nerve relaxant or analgesic.

Coral snake venom has ben used in homeopathic medicine where millionth and billionth parts of dilution are used to evoke symptoms at extremely low levels. Some illnesses have been found to respond well to treatment with such low-level dilutions. Whereas in the U.S. the practice of homeopathic medicine is very limited, its use is quite widespread in some Latin American countries.

Is the Coral Snake Venomous to Itself?

A frequent question asked not only about coral snakes but about venomous snakes in general is "Is the venom of coral snake toxic to itself?" Although no direct experiments have been performed, circumstantial evidence suggests that the venom of the coral snake is quite toxic to itself. In cases of cannibalism, the venom appears to be effective in overpowering the prey snake. For example, one of the earlier Costa Rican herpetologists, Picado (1931), observed a fight in captivity between a specimen of *M. multifasciatus hertwigi* and a *M. n. nigrocinctus* that resulted in the death of the former. While collecting in San Juan de Arama near the Serranía La Macarena, the late Colombian herpetologist Federico Medem observed a curious case of self-biting by *M. spixii obscurus*. In a defensive struggle against being captured, the coral snake bit itself and died the next day. Another specimen collected at the same time did not bite itself and survived for many days in the field station.

It is quite possible that a coral snake has some

natural resistance against small quantities of its own venom, but a large dose seems to be fatal. Secreted by special venom glands, the venom as a rule is kept separate until used and does not penetrate into the circulatory system of the owner of the venom. A coral snake can digest its own venom without any ill effect. Of course, a bitten and swallowed prey also contains some venom that does not harm the coral snake.

Chapter 11
Studies of Coral Snake Venom

Biting Mechanism and Venom Apparatus

As the main features that make a coral snake so dangerous are its venom and its way of biting, we will review in some detail the "instruments of destruction," i.e., the venom apparatus and how it functions. It comprises several venom-producing glands and their ducts, the fixed fangs that conduct venom into the bite, and muscles that squeeze the venom from the glands. The general layout of the coral snake's mouth, dentition, and muscles were discussed in the section on external features (Fig. 36).

On each side of the upper jaw behind the eye is the main venom gland. It is slightly elongated and somewhat asymmetrically peanut-shaped. Posteriorly, it usually bends around the angle of the mouth, but the angle varies from species to species. The bend is particularly sharp in *Leptomicrurus* and in *M. mipartitus* (Fig. 39). The bent part projects or extends below the angle of the mouth on the lower jaw, especially when the gland is full of venom. When the gland is empty, the posterior corner of the gland has been pushed upwards by the muscle and the bend is almost eliminated. Thus, in specimens of the same species, different shapes of the posterior-ventral part of the venom gland indicate the state of use of the venom. Moreover, a venom gland full of venom looks slightly granulated, while an exhausted gland with a minimum of posterior bend looks smooth from outside. The condition of the bent venom gland of coral snakes is similar to that found in several Asiatic elapids, such as the kraits (*Bungarus*) and *Calliophis*, but not in cobras (*Naja*).

The venom gland consists of a large posterior portion with serous venom-producing tissue and many tubules. The gland tapers off and forms a secretory duct at the level of the postorbital ridge, just behind and below the eye. It continues as a venom duct to the fangs. Surrounding the venom duct is a simple accessory mucus gland with many tiny tubules that also open into the duct (Fig. 49). The entire venom gland and duct system is covered by a tough connective tissue capsule that protects it from injury.

The venom is delivered by a pair of short fangs permanently fixed in an erected position. Except for *M.*

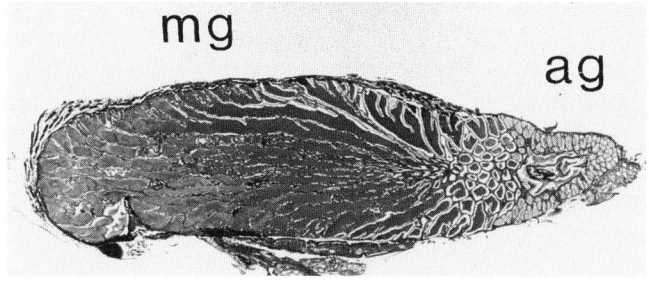

Figure 49. Cross section of venom gland (mg) and accessory gland (ag) of *Micrurus fulvius*. (Courtesy and photo by H. Rosenberg, 1967.)

euryxanthus, the fangs are the only maxillary teeth. Behind the fixed fangs a replacement fang as well as some reserve fangs are usually found. They are loosely clustered in a tissue fold behind the erect fangs. As the functional fang wears out or is lost, the replacement fang occupies the fang socket, becomes fixed in place, and begins to function as the venom delivery fang.

The only muscle in charge of expressing the venom gland is the M. levator anguli oris, frequently called in the literature M. adductor externus superficialis (McDowell, 1986). It surrounds the gland posteriorly and dorsally. The dorsal part of the muscle connects the gland to the skull or to the upper head muscle by fibers (faciae). The longest fibers of this muscle originate in the parietal area and terminate on the posteroventral bend of the venom gland. The ventral part of the muscle has its origin in the lower jaw near the venom gland and it inserts on the posterior part of the venom gland (Fig. 37). In addition to the muscle, a large ligament connects the postorbital-parietal region to the dorsal-anterior surface of the gland.

The emptying of the venom gland is a rather complicated procedure. The dorsal and ventral portions of the M. levator anguli oris interact by compressing the venom gland, forcing the venom secreted by the serous tissue through the tiny tubules and into the duct. In a way, the gland is pulled upward and medially by the combination of constrictions of the muscle, which ends up producing a posterior and lateral pressure on the gland. This forces the venom into the duct. As the muscle pressure is less at the duct level, the venom continues forward and mixes with the mucus secretion of the accessory gland.

Once mixed, the venom continues to flow anteriorly and arrives in the small pocket in the sheath that covers the fixed fangs. From here it is forced through the partially covered fang canal into the bitten victim.

The accessory gland consists of mucous epithelial cells and many short and narrow tubules that conduct the secretions into the venom duct. This secretion itself is not toxic or, perhaps, only slightly toxic. Even though no experimental evidence exists, it is possible that added to the venom, the secretion of the accessory gland "arms" the venom so that the maximum potency of the venom mix is achieved. Separated, the two venom components might not be as dangerous as the mixed and "armed" venom. In elapid snakes, the secretion of the accessory gland is always present in the venom duct, ready to be mixed whenever the venom is squeezed from the main venom gland.

The coral snake appears to be able to control the quantity of venom released. A bite can be delivered without using venom or with a considerable quantity of venom. James Fix (1980), working at the East Carolina University School of Medicine, made careful observations as to how and how much venom a coral snake delivers in each bite. In laboratory conditions, he induced a specimen of *M. fulvius* to bite a parafilm membrane covering a glass vial. In some cases the bite was delivered vigorously but no venom released, while on other occasions a full dose of venom was delivered. Usually the bite continued with chewing motion characteristic of the coral snake bite. He also observed that the bulk of venom frequently came from one fang only. On occasion, the coral snake would release a drop of venom actually before striking the parafilm membrane. As we will see later, it can be very confusing when, for example, the gravity of a coral snake's bite must be assessed as soon as possible.

In addition to the venom glands and biting mechanisms of the upper jaw, coral snakes have infralabial glands on the lower jaw that also secrete small quantities of venom, similar to that of the "real" venom produced by the main venom gland. These very small glands are found along the mandibles in the oral mucosa. They secrete venom and have tiny tubules that gather and release the venom into small ducts. The ducts of these infralabial glands open near the mandibulary teeth. In 1978, Michael W. Dix, working in Guatemala, was the first to report on these interesting additional venom glands in *M. nigrocinctus mosquitensis* and several more species from South America. It is possible that the use of the venom secreted from the lower jaw is related to the feebly grooved mandibulary teeth present in many coral snakes (Fig. 35D). The mandibular glands are only one twentieth the size of the main venom gland.

In some species, feeble grooves are also found in some upper jaw teeth other than fangs, but they are not associated with any known glands.

Venom Extraction and Venom Yield

Coral snakes have narrow cylindrical bodies and small heads and their fangs are short. As a result, the minute amount of venom they have is quite difficult to extract. The usual method of extracting venoms, used for rattlesnakes and pit vipers—letting them bite on a rim of a glass container covered by a rubber membrane—usually has limited success with coral snakes. Several additional methods have been devised for maximizing the venom extraction from coral snakes. One such method was devised by Federsoni (1979). It consists of a watchglass-type instrument with its rim made exactly the proper size to fit into the mouth of the snake. A modified Pasteur pipette inserted into the rubber stopper of a small flask has also been used (Di Tada et al., 1978). Each fang is inserted individually into the pipette to extract venom, which accumulates on the bottom of this pipette-container device. Nelson Jorge da Silva at the Universidade Católica de Goiás and Instituto Clodomiro Picado, Costa Rica have been successfully using simply a capillary-type glass micropipette for each fang (Fig. 50).

Regardless of which method of venom extraction is used, the snake is manipulated to make it bite the

Figure 50. Venom extraction from *Micrurus nigrocinctus nigrocinctus* using micropipette at the Instituto Clodomiro Picado, Costa Rica.

venom extraction device. One way of firmly holding the snake can be accomplished by using a large block of half-cut polyurethane foam, in which the snake is held gently so that only the head is free to bite the offered venom extracting vial (Fix and Minton, 1976). Another method of managing the snake during extraction is to put it in a freezer for 5 to 15 minutes. This makes the coral snake totally inactive for 5 to 10 minutes, during which time the venom can be extracted with micropipettes.

As a coral snake bites and hangs on to the bitten object, making slightly chewing motions, the release of venom is gradual and may take several seconds or even minutes. Spontaneous bite and release are the best ways to extract venom as it makes use of the snake's natural behavior.

The usually small and delicate coral snakes require a gentle but firm handling. Massaging the venom gland while the snake is biting has limited success in increasing venom yield. This procedure approaches closest to what frequently is called venom milking: squeezing of an organ to obtain its secretions, similar to milking a cow. Many biologists prefer not to speak of milking the venom as it is different from that of milking a cow.

Electric shock, applied to the muscle around the venom gland used in some larger snakes, is quite traumatic and does not seem to be useful for extracting venom from coral snakes.

In addition to avoid getting bitten while handling the snake during venom extraction, several precautions have to be taken. During the process of venom extraction, it is easy to damage the mouth and the membranes that cover the fangs and other mouth parts, making them bleed. The blood and secretions from other glands of the mouth, such as saliva, can get mixed into the venom making it impure. Infectious bacteria, such as *Clostridium*, might contaminate the venom. Unless it is processed at once, bacteria might produce some complications, especially if the venom remains or is used in liquid form. The usual way to handle the venom after extraction is either to dry it or to freeze-dry or lyophilize it, changing the venom into a powderlike substance. In captivity the venom can be extracted every 2 to 4 weeks.

The amount extracted varies considerably. The larger the snake the greater the quantity of venom, but some species secrete and store more venom than others. The first extraction after capture is the one that produces the largest amount of venom, unless the snake has bitten recently. The single largest quantity of venom ever recorded as extracted from a coral snake was 160 mg of dry weight from a 1350 mm long specimen of *M.s. surinamensis* of Colombia (Silva, 1994). The second largest quantity was 130 mg of dry weight, from a specimen of *Micrurus spixii obscurus*, slightly over one meter long, from Alto Marañón, Peru (Meneses, personal communication). Yet, the average yield from large specimens of the same subspecies is 41 mg. The average yield from *M. s. surinamensis* obtained by Silva (1994) is the remarkable 108 mg from specimens over 1 meter long, while other averages of the same species oscillate around 56 mg in other laboratories. The maximum yield from *M. p. pyrrhocryptus*, close to the same size as the previous ones and weighing 200 g, is 80 mg; that from *M. fulvius* is 28 mg. The average yield with good extraction method from *M. f. fulvius* is about 12 mg, but Fix (1980) managed to extract an average of about 20 mg from an adult of *M. fulvius*. Researchers at the Instituto Butantan, such as Wolfgang Bücherl (1963) and Helio Belluomini (1964), have from time to time reported on venomous snakes of importance to Brazilian epidemiology of snakebites and their venom yield. Of the two most common Brazilian coral snakes, *M. frontalis* has a maximum yield of 62 mg, while *M. corallinus* has a maximum of 65 mg. Their average yields are only 10 to 12 mg.

Findlay E. Russell in his laboratories has handled venom extraction of more than 1,500 venomous snakes. He determined that the maximum venom yield of *Micruroides e. euryxanthus* is 6 mg. It is probably the only coral snake that does not have enough venom to kill an adult person, especially due to the fact that its venom is considerably less toxic than that of *M. fulvius*. Russell's book, *Snake Venom Poisoning* (1980, 1983), is an invaluable source of information about snake venoms and snakebites.

The available data on the maximum and average yield of coral snakes is summarized in Table 7.

Venom Toxicity

One of the most difficult tasks in assessing the danger of a venom is to determine its toxicity to humans. The action of the venom is influenced by many unknown factors, such as the amount of the venom injected and the way it has been delivered. A bite near vital organs or body parts will be much more dangerous than a bite with the same amount of venom in a finger or toe. We will discuss the different factors determining the gravity of a coral snake bite in humans in the section dealing with human accidents.

A fairly precise measurement of the potency of coral snake venom is done in research laboratories by determining the LD50 lethal dose in experimental animals, usually white mice. While it does not tell how toxic the venom is for humans, it gives a good general idea of the potency of the venom.

As different animals have different sensitivities or resistances to coral snake venom, the toxicity for one animal might not give a clue to its effect on another

Table 7. Maximum and Average Venom Yield for Several Species of Coral Snakes, Compared to the Estimated Lethal Dose of Dry Venom in mg for an Adult Human (from various sources)

Species	Venom yield Maximum	Venom yield Average	Lethal human dose
M. e. euryxanthus	6	0.12	6–8
M. alleni	—	3	3–5
M. corallinus	65	10–12	6–8
M. d. dumerilii	—	5–7	4–6
M. frontalis (composite)	62	10–12	5–7
M. f. frontalis	—	10–12	5–7
M. f. altirostris	—	8–10	5–7
M. f. multicinctus	—	8–10	5–7
M. f. fulvius	38	10–12	4–6
M. f. tenere	—	10–12	5–7
M. isozonus	—	9	5–7
M. lemniscatus	27	8–10	5–7
M. mertensi	—	2	—
M. mipartitus decussatus	—	7	4–6
M. multifasciatus hertwigi	—	12	5–7
M. n. nigrocinctus	20	7	4–6
M. p. pyrrhocryptus	80	8	8–10
M. spixii obscurus	131	41	24–26
M. s. surinamensis	160	56	18–20

species. For example, cows are more resistant to coral snake venom than horses. Moreover, because of its greater body weight, a larger animal will be able to tolerate more venom than a smaller animal. The same is true in humans: a relatively small quantity of venom might kill a small child but not an adult. For this reason, the potency of a venom is calculated for kilograms (or grams) of body weight.

A team of Latin American scientists at the Instituto Clodomiro Picado in Costa Rica, working on coral snake antivenin production, established the LD50 for several species of coral snakes (Bolaños, Cerdas, and Abalos, 1978a, 1978b). They found that the most toxic venom for mice is that of M. lemniscatus (LD50 = 5 μg) and M. surinamensis (LD50 = 5 to 10 μg), while close rivals were the M. f. fulvius (LD50 = 9 μg), M. alleni (LD50 = 12 μg), and M. spixii (LD50 = 10–15 μg). Of the two most widely distributed Brazilian coral snakes, the venom of M. frontalis (LD50 = 15 to 20 μg) is somewhat more toxic than that of M. corallinus (LD50 = 25). The venom of M. d. dumerilii (LD50 = 17 μg) from northern Colombia is about as toxic as that of M. frontalis. On the other hand, Cohen, Berkeley, and Seligmann (1971) found that the most toxic venom for mice is that of M. multfasciatus hertwigi, which the Costa Rican team found to be only moderately toxic. Both teams established the high potency of the venom of M. n. nigrocinctus. Silva (1994) found that the most toxic venom is that of M. surinamensis (LD50 = 0.41 μg/gr).

An additional problem in the evaluation of the toxicity of venoms results from the fact that venoms of different species act in different ways because they contain different components. Very peculiar venoms are those of M. surinamensis, M. multifasciatus, and M. mipartitus.

Judging from research on mice and other animals, coral snake venom is one of the most potent of all venomous snakes of Central America, including all species of pit vipers, the bushmaster, and rattlesnakes; it is probably the most potent of South America as well. However, some rattlesnake venoms, such as the Mojave desert rattlesnake (Crotalus s. scutulatus) and the tiger rattlesnake (Crotalus tigris) might have a higher toxicity than most coral snakes. Sherman Minton kindly shared with me his unpublished research findings on the toxicity of the tiger rattlesnake, which has the lethal dose (LD50) of 0.056 mg/kg of mice, higher than for any coral snake.

Usually, but not always, the species of coral snakes that are larger in size, such as M. spixii and M. pyrrhocryptus, produce more venom, but these venoms are relatively less toxic. The same phenomenon occurs in other groups of snakes as well. Examples of this are the large species, king cobra in the Old World and bushmaster in the New World.

Taking into consideration data from human bite accidents and other information, the estimated lethal doses of coral snake venoms for adult humans vary considerably. Comparing them to the average yield, it is clear that all species, except M. e. euryxanthus, can kill one or more humans (Table 7).

Investigators comparing these estimated lethal doses for humans from species to species must remember that for some species this dose represents just about the maximum of production for a small specimen, while a large specimen of the same species can kill a human several times over.

Keeping Coral Snakes in Zoos and Colonies for Research

Zoos occasionally exhibit coral snakes because of their exceptional beauty and because they are little known to the public. In Europe in particular, a brilliantly red-colored snake is quite an attraction as there are no red snakes in Europe and Africa. Even in the United States, only a few people have actually seen live coral snakes except in nature books. M. e. euryxanthus in the Arizona-Sonora Desert Museum have always attracted interested spectators as have those in the United States where coral snakes live.

Controversy arose in 1985 when it was discovered that a coral snake exhibited in the Houston Zoo turned out to be a rubber model. The curator explained that the intent of the model was to give an opportunity to zoo-goers to observe closely what a coral snake looks like. The reason for this "white" deception was a good one: caged coral snakes tend to be very inactive and usually hide beneath any object in the cage so they are not easy to observe. I have seen many people in South American zoos in Venezuela, Brazil, and Argentina admiringly clustering around beautiful coral snakes.

For the purpose of research and extraction of venom, a number of scientists and professionals have maintained live colonies of coral snakes for shorter or longer periods of time. By far the largest colony of coral snakes in the United States was kept by William Haast at the Miami Serpentarium. For a period of several years he handled well over 1,000 specimens of *M. d. dumerilii* from the Barranquilla region in northern Colombia and more than 200 of *M. f. fulvius* and other species from the United States and Central America for the purpose of extracting venom. Bill Haast himself is an unusual "snake master" who has taken it upon himself to outwit and handle practically every species of venomous snakes of the world. In spite of having been bitten more than 200 times by quite a few of the most venomous snakes—and having almost died several times—he was never bitten by any of the many coral snakes he kept in the Serpentarium.

The Instituto Butantan in São Paulo, Brazil, is probably the largest snake institute in the world, receiving literally thousands of diverse species of snakes each year from many areas of Brazil. The institute has made an unusual arrangement with the local people trading live snakes for antivenin produced at the institute. The institute distributes specially constructed boxes and provides instructions for capturing and handling the snakes. The railroad system of Brazil transports them free of charge to the institute from wherever they are sent.

Afranio do Amaral (1930d), one of the Instituto Butantan directors for many years, described the steadily increasing stream of venomous snakes arriving at the institute. From its inception in 1901 through 1929, the institute received 2,400 coral snakes, the most abundant of which were *M. corallinus* with 1,967 specimens, followed by *M. frontalis* (327), and *M. lemniscatus* (100). This is valuable information because it can be reasonably assumed that the most frequent accidents with coral snakes occur with the most abundant species. By comparison, during the same period the institute received 47,000 South American rattlesnakes and 64,000 Jararacas, the Brazilian pit viper. However, it seems that one reason why considerably fewer coral snakes are sent to the institute is because some people in Brazil use them in voodoo ceremonies.

In Argentina, the 12,000 venomous snakes received at the Serpentarium of Santiago del Estero from 1960 to 1966 included 332 specimens of *M. p. pyrrhocryptus* used mostly for research of venoms (Abalos and Bucher, 1970). The most abundant venomous snake in that region is the South American rattlesnake which, by comparison, was represented by 6,300 individuals. The Center for Applied Zoology of the Universidad Nacional de Córdoba, where research on venom was carried out during 1974 and 1975, received 96 specimens of *M. p. pyrrhocryptus* out of a total of 3,150 venomous snakes.

A successful research colony of coral snakes was maintained over a period of several years by Joseph Gennaro at the University of Louisville School of Medicine. He used them in research on venom, anatomy, histology, and microstructures. One of his laboratory assistants accidentally injected herself with some venom while taking care of the snakes. This confirmed the fact that keeping coral snakes or any other snake in captivity is a delicate and serious task. Fortunately, the accident produced no serious consequences. Edward Seligmann at the National Institutes of Health maintained a small collection of live *M. e. euryxanthus*. In addition to venom extraction, he observed their feeding behavior and other activities that he generously shared with me when his venom studies were finished. The U.S. Army Medical Research Laboratory in Fort Knox, Kentucky, developed some of the best procedures for maintaining venomous snakes, including coral snakes that supplied venom to many snake venom research teams. B. D. Ashley and P. M. Burchfield (1968) summarized their experiences in an article that should be read by anybody who wants to keep colonies of venomous snakes. More recent recommendations are those by Pough (1991) and Weldon et al. (1992).

In captivity, the best food for coral snakes is their natural diet of snakes, lizards, or whatever they usually eat. Coral snakes are delicate feeders who frequently reject food and die. When their self-imposed starving is added to the stress of venom extraction, coral snakes might survive no more than a few months.

Chapter 12
Chemical and Biological Characteristics of Venom

Venom Composition and Its Action

As mentioned before, snake venom is an evolutionary modification of secretions by the oral glands. After several million years of evolutionary changes (Kochva, 1987), snake venom is the most complex biologically toxic substance known in higher animals.

The most-studied snake venom is that of *M. f. fulvius*, but recently research on several Brazilian coral snakes by Brazilian scientists has revealed interesting additional properties of coral snake venom. With growing interest in snake venoms, Mexican, Colombian, Argentinan, and Venezuelan biologists also have added to our knowledge of the composition and action of some coral snake venoms.

Coral snake venom is a yellowish viscous liquid varying from very pale to strong yellow from species to species and even from individual to individual. The venom of *M. surinamensis* is white or yellow, probably varying regionally (Aird and da Silva, 1991).

The venom can withstand high heat without loosing its inherent characteristics and toxicity. Thus, a heating up to 100°C for a brief period usually does not affect the toxic qualities of the venom. Boiling a dilute *M. f. fulvius* venom for 20 minutes in a water bath does not destroy its lethal properties (Cohen and Seligmann, 1966). The venom can also be frozen or subjected to low temperatures without affecting its toxicity. Lyophilization, frequently performed for preservation of the venom, does not seem to significantly influence or interfere with its toxic properties and antigenicity. Upon drying, the venom becomes a crystal-like substance that retains its toxicity and can be kept for a long period of time, especially at low temperatures. Some dried venoms have been kept more than 25 years without loss of potency.

The dry venom consists of about 70% to 80% proteins and their derivates. They represent an array of complex proteins, polypeptides of diverse molecular weight, and a variety of amino acids as building blocks. Using Lowry's method, Stevan and Seligmann (1969) determined that with one exception the protein content from species to species does not vary very much (from 0.8 mg to 1.20 mg). The one exception, surprisingly, is *M. fulvius tenere*, which has only half the amount of protein (0.49 mg) of *M. f. fulvius* (0.89 mg). If this is confirmed by additional research, it would add to the question of whether both coral snakes are subspecifically related. *M. e. euryxanthus* has the highest amount of protein (1.20 mg).

Most of the proteins are enzymes that act as catalysts by facilitating and accelerating biochemical reactions within the organism into which the venom has been introduced. In addition to the enzymes, several other proteins and polypeptides of relatively low molecular weight that do not catalyze anything exhibit some highly toxic properties either alone or in combination with other components of the venom. Some of these polypeptides are the lethal component of coral snake venom.

Coral snake venom also contains several glucoproteins, riboflavin, and other nonprotein substances. Riboflavin, in combination with one enzyme, L-amino oxidase, is responsible for the yellow coloration of the venom. The venom contains or probably contains some metallic salts from such elements as zinc, calcium, magnesium, and potassium. Their role in the venom is little known, but at least one metal, zinc, is associated with the activity of anticholinesterase (Kumar, Regent, and Elliot, 1973), an interesting enzyme that interferes with the function of the nervous system.

The most complete analysis of the venom of *M. f. fulvius* was accomplished by Ramsey et al. (1972) and Snyder et al. (1973) and of the venom of *M. fulvius microgalbineus* from northern Mexico by Possani et al (1979). Silva, Griffin, and Aird (1991) carried out comparative enzyme studies of 11 species and subspecies of Brazilian coral snakes, the most comprehensive to date. Earlier, Stevan and Seligmann (1970) made a comparative study of coral snake venoms using electrophoresis. The venoms show a considerable consistency in their electrophoretic patterns and, at the same time, some detectable differences between the species, such as between *Micruroides e. euryxanthus* and the species of *Micrurus*. These electrophoretic venom "fingerprints" of *M. nigrocinctus mosquitensis* and *M. nigrocinctus nigrocinctus* show a difference significant enough to question their subspecific relationships. *M. mipartitus de-*

cussatus has an electrophoretic pattern different from the other species of the genus *Micrurus*.

As much of the information about the composition of coral snake venom and its pharmacological action might be more technical than many readers would appreciate, Appendix B carries a summary of the substances found in coral snake venom and their main features.

Effects of Venom on Organisms

Research on different components of venom has helped to gain some valuable insights into the role and function of each individual fraction of the complex coral snake venom. But the observed clinical and biological effects of coral snake venom show there is a complex synergistic action of the venom as a whole on the bitten organism. In other words, the biochemical constitution and physiological effects as analyzed under laboratory conditions offer one picture, but the venom in its totality produces additional and enhanced effects that are achieved only by the combined action of all venom components.

Almost all coral snake venoms affect the nervous system, producing paralysis starting with the cranial nerves that control the face and other parts of the head and then the respiratory system. They also act on the heart; quite a few also act on the blood. Most coral snake venoms seem also to affect the lungs, kidneys, and several other internal organs. In addition, some coral snake venoms have been found to act on muscle tissue (myonecrotic). On the other hand, coral snake venoms do not destroy local tissues (proteolytic), cause bleeding (hemorrhagic), or produce significant edema.

Effects on the Nervous System

The most important property of the coral snake venom is its action as a neurotoxin, affecting the nervous system. It is accomplished by coral snake neurotoxins (CNTX), one of the lethal components of the venom. Oswaldo Vital Brazil (1980, 1987) reviewed the neurotoxic venoms, with many examples from coral snakes. By preventing the nerves from transmitting their messages to the muscles, the venom causes paralysis. When the muscles of the respiratory system are paralyzed, respiration stops and death occurs by suffocation.

Depending on the site of action of the venom, the neuromuscular blockade can occur at the nerve end of the bridge (presynaptic) or at the muscle end (postsynaptic).

The postsynaptic neurotoxins, known in most coral snakes as well as in many Old World elapids, occupy the receptor sites of the chemical messengers (acetylcholine, for example) on the muscle fibers. It is interesting that the coral snake neurotoxins do not affect the receptor "homes" of other chemical messengers, such as histamine, adrenaline, and noradrenaline (Moussatche and Melendez, 1979).

One type of action of the neurotoxic postsynaptic venom produced by *M. frontalis brasiliensis* and several other species is quite similar to the effect produced by curare, a famous plant poison in South America (Pellegrini and Vital Brazil, 1976; Vital Brazil and Barrios, 1950a, 1950b). These venoms are referred to as curare-type venoms, or curare-like envenomation. What seems to be of importance is that the action of these nondepolarizing postsynaptic neurotoxins can be reversed by such drugs as neostigmine. It was reported by Oswaldo Vital Brazil and colleagues (1977) of the venom of *M. frontalis brasiliensis* (see also Vital Brazil, 1980, 1987).

The presynaptic neurotoxin has been thus far discovered only in the venom of *M. corallinus* (Vital Brazil and Fontana, 1984). Thus far, it is known to be the only coral snake that has both the presynaptic and the postsynaptic neurotoxins.

Whereas not observed in human accidents, coral snake venom also indirectly affects the function of the brain. At a lethal dose, *M. f. fulvius* venom was found to decrease electric activity of the brain in experimental animals. At the early stage of envenomation, this effect reverses itself but becomes irreversible at the onset of the final respiratory paralysis (Vick, Cuichta, and Manthei, 1967).

For other animals, particularly invertebrates, in which other type of neuromuscular transmission mechanisms exist, the neurotoxic action of coral snake venom would not be effective. One wonders how the coral snake venom functions in such species as *M. hemprichii*, which feeds on *Peripatus*, an onychophoran invertebrate. It seems that in *Peripatus* the mode of nerve transmission is not cholinergic as in vertebrates, but glutaminergic. Some studies have been made on a related subspecies, *M. h. rondonianus* (Aird and da Silva, 1991).

Effects on the Heart and Circulation

Venom of several species of coral snakes interferes with the functioning of the heart and the cardiovascular system. This cardiotoxic effect has been observed in dogs. An experimentally lethal dose of *M. f. fulvius* venom produces shock in dogs with a marked effect on the cardiovascular system (Ramsey et al., 1972). As the venoms of several Old World elapids are known to produce a cardiotoxic effect, the presence of cardiotoxins in coral snake venom, which until recently were not considered an important toxic ingredient of the venom, is not surprising. A fatal human case of coral snakebite in Brazil, reported by Machado and Rosenfeld in 1971, gives strong support to the seriousness of the cardiotoxic effect of coral snake venom. The cause of death in the reported case was attributed to a chronic cardiac deficiency, but cardiotoxic complications aggravated by the venom can not be discounted.

Changes in blood pressure and a decrease in heart rate, observed in dogs, suggest that the cardiotoxins affect the heart muscles directly, independent from the neurotoxic effect on the central nervous system. Further circulatory complications involve retention and pooling of blood in the blood vessels of the lungs and viscera. This seems to be responsible for the fall of arterial blood pressure observed in coral snake envenomation.

Effects on the Blood

Whereas coral snake venom does not seem to produce hemorrhage, several species have hemolysins that interact with different blood components, particularly destroying the red blood cells. The most common effect is indirect hemolysis, probably caused by one of the most widespread venom enzymes, phospholipase A2 (PhA2). It acts on the red blood cells in the presence of blood serum, but does not affect human red blood cells separated from the serum. Some coral snake venoms such as *M. nigrocinctus* also have the direct lytic factor (DLF) that does destroy human red blood cells (Jiménez-Porras, 1967). Every species has different hemolytic action, direct or indirect. Cohen and Seligmann reported in 1966 that *M. fulvius* venom acts on red blood cells of dogs, mice, guinea pigs, and chickens, but does not affect human, sheep, rabbit, or monkey red blood cells. *M. frontalis* venom indirectly affects the blood of most animals, except oxen and humans. The venom of *M. laticollaris maculirostris*, on the other hand, does not have any direct effect on human red blood cells (Sosa et al., 1979).

Additional information on the effect of coral snake venom comes in a letter from Sherman Minton, a well-known herpetologist and venom specialist from the Indiana University School of Medicine: "Of the two coral snake venoms I have worked with (*M. fulvius* and *M. nigrocinctus*), the most striking effect on mice was production of dark red urine soon after injection of venom. I never checked to see if this was hemoglobin or myoglobin, but I have never seen it so dramatically with another snake venom." Apparently, the diversity of symptoms produced by coral snake venoms are far more complex than is known and only partially understood.

Local and Other Effects

As the pain in the local area of the bite suggests, several coral snake venoms act on local tissue, particularly on muscles. But this action is very limited and apparently does not produce significant impact on the body. As reported by Gutiérrez et al. (1983), no less than 5 coral snakes, *M. nigrocinctus mosquitensis*, *M. n. nigrocinctus*, *M. surinamensis*, *M. frontalis* (probably pyrrhocryptus), and *M. dumerilii*, show limited myonecrosis, the destruction of muscle tissue in the affected area. Some local effect is also known to be produced by the bite of *M. f. fulvius* (Weis and McIssac, 1971). The only venom thus far known not to produce local effect on muscles is that of *M. multifasciatus hertwigi*.

A bite accident with *M. m. mipartitus* reported in the section on human snakebite accidents suggests venom impact only on tissues. This is an interesting departure from the usual neurotoxic-cardiotoxic bite syndrome.

An indirect effect caused by coral snake venom is the reaction of the bitten victim's own body against the venom. It is an autopharmacological response of the bitten body produced by the release of several natural substances such as histamine, serotonin, and bradykinin. On occasions, the body produces them in sufficiently large quantities to considerably complicate the effect of the venom and make the accident more serious, especially when the person is sensitive to the venom. In a way, the autacoid substances have the effect of self-poisoning the bitten organism, triggered by the venom.

One remarkable component found in the venoms of most snakes, including most coral snakes, is the nerve growth factor, a component different in its action from the usual enzymes and toxins. It does not seem to be a toxic component, but an extremely powerful and target-specific protein that stimulates and controls the growth of sensorial and sympathetic nerve cells. Elapid as well as viperid and crotalid venoms contain this interesting factor, also found in salivary glands of mice and in the serum of humans and all mammals. Its presence in the venom gland, a modified salivary gland, is probably due to the excretory function of this gland in removing surplus nerve growth factor from the serum.

Chapter 13
Coral Snakebite Accidents

Statistics on Human Accidents with Coral Snakes

Coral snakebite accidents are not very frequent. In Brazil, for example, from June 1986 to December 1987, coral snakebites represented only 0.7%, or about 130 bite accidents out of 27,138 known snakebites reported by the Brazilian Ministry of Health. Actual numbers are, probably, twice that many (estimated 35,000 to 40,000 a year with no less than 250 by coral snakes). Yet in 1987 only 181 bites were fatal and it is not known if any of these were inflicted by coral snakebites (see Cartilha de Ofidismo-Cobral, 1988). In Brazil, an interesting rule of thumb says that all months with an "r" have a high incidence of snakebite accidents: January, February, March, April, September, October, November, and December.

The Hospital Vital Brazil in the Instituto Butantan, São Paulo, one of the important Brazilian hospitals that specializes in bites by venomous animals, has been accumulating statistics on treated snakebite accidents. For the period of 1902 to 1945, out of a total of 6,601 snakebites the hospital treated only 15 coral snakebites, all successfully (Fonseca, 1949). A more recent report by Rosenfeld (1971), covering the period between 1954 and 1965, reports 13 treated coral snake bites, two of which were fatal, or a 15% death rate. The offending species included *M. corallinus*, *M. frontalis*, and *M. lemniscatus*. This death rate is higher than the death rate by the neotropical rattlesnake (*Crotalus durissus*) (11.9%) and by the Brazilian pit-viper Jararaca (*Bothrops jararaca*) (0.325%), even though Jararaca produces most accidents; there were 625 treated accidents for the 12-year period. Combining all the known data from southeastern Brazil, including a report by Machado and Rosenfeld (1971) and one by Vital Brazil (1987) and several other isolated cases, the mortality rate of coral snakebite accidents from 1902 to 1971 is 7.2%. These are all treated bite accidents. The actual rate of death by untreated coral snakebites is much higher, estimated somewhere between 20% and 30%. About 66% of the bitten individuals are agricultural workers, persons around farmhouses, or persons walking in the woods or fields. Recently, João Luíz Cardoso (1985), director of the hospital, discussed 2,908 snakebite statistics. From 1966 to 1979 the hospital treated 19 coral snakebites, none fatal.

In Venezuela, about 250 deaths per annum are produced by snakebites (Roze, 1966). Judging from clinical symptoms, several deaths are attributable to coral snakebites. The estimated number of snakebites in Venezuela is about 2,500 to 3,000 yearly but most of them go unreported, as is the case with most Latin American countries. In Colombia, about double the number of snakebites occur, several of which are produced by coral snakes. In the Andes, the coral snake that causes most accidents is *M. mipartitus decussatus*; in the Colombian Amazon the snakes causing accidents are *M. spixii* and the aquatic *M. surinamensis*, as discussed in the section on symptoms of coral snake envenomation and case reports. In Argentina, *M. pyrrhocryptus*, in spite of its considerable size, seems to be a very docile snake. No accidents have been reported (Abalos and Pirosky, 1963; Abalos and Bucher, 1970). General accounts of snakebite in French Guiana are those by Chippaux et al. (1984) and Chippaux (1987).

In Central America, Costa Rica has taken a leading role in combatting ophidism, since Picado's (1931) pioneering work on venomous snakes. For example, in 1967 alone 7 patients were treated for coral snakebites as compared to 46 accidents produced by other venomous snakes. In Costa Rica, 37% of accidents by snakebites are caused by coral snakes. Around 10 coral snakebite accidents are treated yearly in the Hospital San Juan de Dios, San José, Costa Rica. (See the case of a bite by a coral snake from Costa Rica described in the next chapter.) De Franco Montalván et al. (1983a, 1983b) analyzed 160 snakebite cases in children in the Pacific coast of Costa Rica, several of which were caused by *M. n. nigrocinctus*. Cerdas et al. (1986) dealt with snakebites in the Atlantic region of Costa Rica. Since the availability of Costa Rican antivenin, "suero anti-coral," by Instituto Clodomiro Picado, no deaths have been reported by coral snakebites (see also Bolaños, 1982, 1884). In the Hospital of San Pablo, Bluefields, Nicaragua, 8 to 12 snakebite accidents are treated yearly; several end in death, including occasional coral snakebites. Most of them are during July through September when corn is harvested (see also Banton, 1930).

In the United States, about 8,000 to 9,000 snakebite accidents occur annually but only a small percentage of them are caused by coral snakes. In analyzing 460 fatalities from venomous animals in the United States that occurred from 1950 through 1959, Parrish (1963) reported 138 deaths (30%) by venomous snakes. Coral snakes were responsible for only two fatalities (0.4%). In another report, Parrish and Kahn (1967) discussed 11 snakebite accidents by coral snakes, only one of which was fatal. They further estimated that in the United States the mortality rate of coral snakebites is about 10%, and about 20 persons suffer bites by coral snakes annually.

Nearly all the published coral snakebite accident statistics and treatment records in the United States (see Shaw, 1971) deal with *M. f. fulvius* and *M. f. tenere*. As early as 1908, Willson discussed 8 coral snakebite cases, 6 of which proved to be fatal by respiratory failure. In a survey of 20 snakebite accidents, Neill (1957) reported 4 deaths, indicating 20% mortality by coral snakebites. Earlier estimates of coral snakebite mortality vary from 15% to 20%, given by Gloyd (1944) as well as by Pope (1955), to 20% to 75%, estimated by Stickel (1952).

In Florida, about 2% to 5% of all snakebites are inflicted by *M. f. fulvius* (McCollough and Gennaro, 1963a, 1970; Andrews et al., 1968), none of them fatal. About 2% of bites by the same species occur in Alabama with one fatality (Parrish and Donovan, 1964), and one coral snakebite in Louisiana from 1950 to 1959 was treated successfully (Parrish, 1964).

In a recent review, Kitchens and Van Mierop (1987) surveyed 39 bite accidents caused by *M. f. fulvius* in Florida, none of them fatal. Of these, 36 bites were inflicted on fingers and hands; 23 happened while voluntarily handling the snakes and 14 of the victims thought they were handling inoffensive king snakes. An additional danger signal is indicated by the fact that 8 victims were inebriated, mostly with alcohol. It is also revealing that from the 20 patients treated in the local hospital directly, 6 did not develop any symptoms while 10 showed local symptoms only. Most bites in the United States are on fingers, hands, or loose skin.

M. f. tenere seems to be less dangerous than its eastern counterpart. In Texas, they inflict about 1% of all snakebites (Parrish, 1964), and the degree of severity seems to be less serious than by other Texas venomous snakes, even though the coral snake is able to cause fatal bites (Stimson and Engelhardt, 1960). It seems that since the availability of the Wyeth coral snake antivenin, no bites in the United States have been fatal.

On the contrary, Waorani Indians, a small tribe in eastern Ecuador, probably have the highest snakebite incidence and mortality in the world. About 4.9% of all deaths in the population, as reported by Larrick et al. (1978, 1979), are caused by snakebites. As more than 20% of the population have also been bitten by coral snakes (Theakston et al., 1981), a good percentage of deaths could be attributed to Ecuadorian coral snakes. It is possible that several Indian tribes in the Amazon basin suffer considerably from snakebites.

Nature and Way of Coral Snakebites

Due to their relatively nonaggressive nature, coral snakes tend to avoid contact on exposure. When discovered, they move away or at least remain immobile. No coral snake, and no other snake for that matter, would attack humans unprovoked. The relatively small mouth makes it difficult to bite large surfaces, even though they are able to inflict a bite in any body part. For that reason, bites usually occur in anatomical parts with small, bitable surfaces.

While coral snake accidents are not common, several factors make them one of the most dangerous of all snakebites. First, coral snakes look harmless because of their beautiful coloration and essentially nonaggressive, evasive nature. Second, they are occasionally confused with their imitators, the false coral snakes. A bite from a nonvenomous false coral snake would produce no ill effect, thus "confirming" the mistaken belief that coral snakes are not venomous. Third, about half or even more of all coral snakebites produce no symptoms of envenomation (Parrish and Khan, 1967; Kitchens and Van Mierop, 1987), giving additional strength to the belief that coral snakes are not venomous.

Another complication is that the bite of most species of coral snakes produces very little if any local effect, except for occasional local pain and swelling that subside soon. The more serious symptoms may appear hours, even a day or longer after the bite, prolonging the false initial impression that no serious damage has been done.

On one occasion, Sherman Minton remarked that the "treatment of coral snake bites is a nightmare for the physician, however rare the bites may be." It is partially due to the appearance of expected as well as unexpected symptoms and complications. At times, the symptoms of a bite relate well with the known physiological and biochemical properties of the venom. Other times, the venom produces an effect that seems to be incongruent with what is known about a specific venom. Apparently, the bitten person's peculiar biological makeup and response to the venom produces a systemic response that varies from case to case.

Once the full impact of the venom becomes apparent, its effect on the different systems of the body can be varied, powerful, and confusing. Furthermore, as the main feature of the venom is its neurotoxic effect, in medical treatment most attention is given to combating its impact on the nervous system, particularly respiratory paralysis. The cardiotoxic symptoms might possibly be neglected or not considered serious. This is an oversight that can lead to a fatal outcome, especially in elderly people.

Findlay Russell (1980, 1983) clearly recognized this danger in seeking the correct treatment of snakebite. He suggests that any evaluation and treatment of a patient should not be guided by oversimplified definition of venoms as "neurotoxic," "cardiotoxic" or "hemotoxic" with a limited impact on one organ or tissue. Since venom consists of a complex set of fractions, acting synergistically, its impact can be quite different from patient to patient. Membrane permeability can cause many significant complications acting on several organs or systems simultaneously. Animal experimentation provides only limited information about the pharmacological impact of the venom. In order to optimize the treatment of a bite, he also suggests the need to carefully scrutinize pharmacological literature for a clearer understanding of venoms involved.

A venomous coral snakebite accident, regardless of severity, can be defined as a bite resulting in fang and/or tooth scratches and/or actual marks. As coral snakes have only one pair of short fixed fangs, usually a pair of punctures can be distinguished in the bitten site. Occasionally, additional scratch or puncture marks can be present, caused either by the ongoing chewing motion of the coral snake, by the short lower jaw teeth, or by the still shorter palatine or pterygoid teeth. As coral snakes have additional small venom-secreting glands on the lower jaw (see section on venom apparatus and biting mechanism), it is to their advantage to utilize the mandibulary teeth in biting as well.

Envenomation takes place when the venom is introduced into the bloodstream of the victim. A bite might turn out to be only a little more than a frightening experience with no or only limited effect when no venom is delivered. Or a bite accident might develop into a serious event that, unless appropriate medical treatment is obtained quickly, could lead to a fatal outcome.

Coral snakebites without any symptoms have been reported even with visible fang punctures, indicating that, in spite of the bite, no venom has actually been released. This can occur when the snake has exhausted its venom in recent previous bites or when it has used its ability to regulate the release of the venom. In nature, the coral snake does not use its entire supply of venom in one bite but rather uses it in accordance with the size of the prey or urgency of the situation. In Venezuela, I observed *M. isozonus* kill three prey snakes consecutively, with clear signs of death by venom. It is conceivable that coral snakes avoid using venom against a nonprey enemy such as humans, especially when the snake does not perceive the confrontation as a deadly threat. Or, in perceived extreme distress, the coral snake might use a large amount of its venom for defense. The result would be a fatal human accident. As we noted in the section on venom toxicity, almost all species of coral snakes have enough venom to kill an adult human.

The gravity of a bite accident depends on many factors such as the species and the size of the snake, the amount of venom delivered, the location of the bite, the body weight of the victim, and the victim's state of health and psychological state of fright and anxiety. Brief comments on each factor follow.

The venom toxicity varies from species to species. Although it is not always the case, frequently, the larger the species, the less toxic the venom. The toxicity of their venoms is also quite different.

As coral snakes can graduate the quantity of venom delivered in a given bite, the "mood" that determines the snake's venom delivery choice becomes very important in determining the degree of severity of an accident. The choice of nondelivery, for example, produces no envenomation and no symptoms beyond the simple pain of the punctured skin. A full dose of venom, on the other hand, might be very serious.

The bitten body part and the site of the bite determine the speed at which the venom can reach vital organs. Head and facial bites are much more serious than bites in feet or fingers. A bite that penetrates a vein, however, even in a hand, is equivalent to an intravenous injection of the venom that can produce a fatal outcome. Such an intravenous bite might lead to cardiovascular failure much faster than to respiratory stress; the cause of death might be heart failure.

The body weight of the victim also determines the outcome of the bite accident because the larger the bitten person, the more venom that person can withstand. Conversely, a child with less body weight will succumb much faster to the same quantity of venom.

A state of optimum health would help considerably in mobilizing the body's defenses to counteract and neutralize the venom impact. It is quite important but very difficult to keep calm when bitten by a snake. Fears, anxiety, and panic increase heart beat and accelerate circulation, leading to a faster distribution of the venom throughout the body. Confidence, balanced actions, and trust in one's own or the health care provider's ability to overcome the snakebite impact aid considerably in mobilizing the bodily defenses.

Symptoms of Coral Snake Envenomation and Case Reports

There is a variation in severity of coral snakebite accidents, but the basic symptoms for many species are similar. The following summary is based on cases of accidents with the North America coral snake (*M. fulvius*) and several Brazilian coral snakes, *M. frontalis* and

M. corallinus, as well as the Central American coral snake, *M. nigrocinctus*. Several authors such as McCollough and Gennaro (1963a, 1963b), Parrish and Khan (1967), Moseley (1966), Ramsey and Klickstein (1962), Rosenfeld (1971), Russell et al. (1975), Vital Brazil (1980), Russell (1980, 1982), and Kitchens and Van Mierop (1987) have reviewed current knowledge about coral snakebites. Useful summaries are also found in pamphlets produced by laboratories that produce antivenin: Wyeth Laboratories in the United States in English, Instituto Clodomiro Picado, Costa Rica, in Spanish, and Instituto Butantan, São Paulo, Brazil, in Portuguese. A well-illustrated Cartilha de Ofidismo (Cobral), published by the Ministry of Health of Brazil in 1988 and coordinated by Henrique Moises Canter, also offers a good summary on snakebite problems, including coral snakes.

When the coral snake bites, it hangs onto the bitten site with a biting and chewing motion. Usually, the snake must be forcibly removed from the bitten place. Initial local pain varies from insignificant to quite strong and is detectable several minutes after the bite occurs. In some cases, a painful burning sensation might travel along the bitten member (finger, arm). In most cases, the local pain subsides in a few minutes but can persist with the bite of *M. nigrocinctus* and *M. frontalis*. Numbness in the bitten area can also occur and persist. Following the initial local symptoms, if any, there is a period without any symptoms that may last from 1 to almost 32 hours. Usually, the next alarming symptoms are systemic in the form of apprehension, euphoria, giddiness, and dyspnea, as well as nausea and abundant salivation of sticky saliva. These are followed by vomiting, lethargy, and general weakness. Vision difficulties, problems focusing the eyes, and erratic and insecure movements can also appear. In more severe cases convulsions occur. Paralysis normally begins to appear from 4 to 16 hours after the bite and is of progressive bulbar type, involving several cranial nerves (Rosenfeld, 1971). In the human face, the flaccid paralysis associated with and characteristic of bites with neurotoxic effect begins to appear in muscles controlled by the third pair of cranial nerves as indicated by interference with upper eyelid movement. This partial external ophthalmoplegia and ptosis (difficulty of movement and paralysis of eyes and eyelids) can last through the whole process of envenomation. The next step in severity is paralysis of eyeballs, controlled by the fourth and sixth pair of cranial nerves. When disturbance of equilibrium occurs, at least the vestibular part of the eighth cranial nerve has also been affected. Difficulties in swallowing and speaking appear, combined with thick salivation when the fifth cranial nerve has been interfered with. As the severity of the venom impact advances, peripheral nerves can also become affected with gradual loss of most movement. Depression of blood pressure and general cardiovascular distress may or may not appear. Yet, sensory functions and conscious awareness remain unaffected. All these symptoms can be simultaneous with or followed by respiratory difficulties and the final respiratory paralysis that usually produces death in coral snakebite accidents. One indication of fatal outcome is the disturbance of reflexes followed by mydriasis, an excessive dilation of the pupil of the eye. Victims have died due to respiratory paralysis in as little as 4 hours after being bitten.

After having surveyed 11 coral snakebite cases and the existing knowledge of coral snakebites, Parrish and Khan (1967) proposed a classification of three grades of severity.

"Grade 0"—no venenation. Bite by a coral snake resulting in superficial scratch marks of fang punctures that results in minimal local swelling and no systemic signs and symptoms of venomation within the first 36 hours following the bite.

"Grade 1"—moderate venenation. Bite by a coral snake resulting in one or more scratch marks of fang punctures that results in minimal to moderate local swelling with one or more systemic signs and symptoms: euphoria, nausea, vomiting, excessive salivation, paresthesia in the bitten extremity, ptosis of the eyelids, weakness, abnormal reflexes, motor paralysis, depression, and dyspnea, but without complete respiratory paralysis in the first 36 hours following the bite.

"Grade 2"—severe venenation. Bite by a coral snake resulting in one or more fang punctures that results in minimal to moderate local swelling, with one or more of the systemic signs and symptoms listed in Grade 1 venenation and with complete respiratory paralysis within the first 36 hours following the bite.

An interesting side effect, that of periodically recurring pain in the bitten site, had been occasionally reported, even years after the bite accident. Muscle strength, lost during a severe envenomation, can take up to several months to return to normal, as reported by Kitchens and Van Mierop (1987).

A history of one interesting case was reported as early as 1883 by Frederick True on a coral snakebite received by Mr. Shindler, an employee of the U.S. National Museum (now National Museum of Natural History) in Washington D.C. Shindler was preparing a color sketch of a live eastern coral snake when it bit him in the left index finger. The coral snake held so firmly to the finger that it had to be removed by force, leaving one fang in the wound. Violent pain started at once in the finger and continued for about 2 hours, when symptoms of drowsiness appeared, which continued until the morning of the third day. In the evening of the first day Shindler called a physician. In the next 2 days the physician reported that the finger had swollen and that acute pain extended up the arm toward the region of the heart. The report on the symptoms as well as the description of the treatment give some flavor of the medical language used and the mode of treatment of that period, illustrating the limited medical knowledge of treatment of coral snakebites at that time (True, 1883, p. 27):

> June 1, 1882
> Symptoms—Partial delirium. Pulse at wrist of injured hand almost imperceptible; on the other side weak, irregular, compressible. Skin cold, clammy. Tongue tremulus, cool, white. Nervous, excitable, garrulous. Eyes dull, stupid in expression; pupils contracted. Jactation, nausea, persistent vomiting.
> Treatment—Saturated bandage with strong ammonia water, applied to wound.
> Prescription—Bicarbonate of soda ... 4 drachms
> Subnitrate of bismuth .. 1 drachm
> Water sufficient to dissolve soda. Teaspoonful every five minutes. Administered six doses.
> Symptoms—Nausea returned; vomiting ceased.
> Prescription—Aromatic spirits of ammonia 1 ounce
> French Brandy .... 3 ounces
> Teaspoonful every five minutes until six or eight doses had been given. Left patient comfortable. Tablespoonful every hour during the night.
> June 2, 8 a.m.
> Symptoms—Patient free from pain, pulse feeble, regular, still weak on injured side. General condition much improved, recovery certain. Continue use of recipe every two or three hours.

The onset of the neurotoxic facies is revealed by the phrase "eyes dull, stupid in expression; pupils contracted." The reported treatment probably contributed very little to overcoming the effect of the venom. The patient recovered completely in three days. Yet, about two months later, the pain recurred in the bitten finger extending to the knuckles. Several days later, an ulcer appeared on the bitten finger. The remarkable thing is that every year for about 10 years around the anniversary of the bite, the finger started hurting again, especially during the night, and continued for a period of about two weeks. In addition, a sore was formed that broke open with the loss of the nail.

This snakebite story was completed in 1895 by one of the great American herpetologists, Leonard Stejneger, a curator of herpetology at the same museum. In 1892, a friend of Shindler brought him from Brazil leaves and stems of a Brazilian vine (*Micania quacho*), a remedy against snakebite known and used in some parts of Brazil. An infusion of this remedy taken internally prevented the eruption and the sore but not the pain that recurred every year around the anniversary of the bite. Such recurring symptoms might be related to some chronobiological phenomena of biological rhythms of the bitten person that should not be overlooked in assessing snakebite accidents.

Since True's report, the first to cover coral snakebite accidents in the United States, authors offering case reports and other data have included Yarrow (1887), Coe (1891), Loennenberg (1894), and Barbour (1921). Stejneger (1895), already mentioned, offered a survey of coral snakes and their bites and Willson (1908) offered additional data. In 1938, Gloyd reported on an interesting bite accident by a black Texas coral snake, *M. fulvius tenere*, that did not have the normal colorful coral snake garb and was misidentified as a nonvenomous snake. While the bitten person survived the bite, she reported very intense pain, some local reaction, and some systemic symptoms.

More recent case reports with treatment of coral snakebites in the United States are those by Werler and Darling (1950), Schwartzwelder (1950), Allen and Neill (1950), Neill (1957), Andrews and Pollard (1963), and especially by Kitchens and Van Mierop (1987, p. 1617), who offered summaries of several illustrative cases, one of which was serious:

> "A 36-year-old man had been working on a horse farm for several years. He admitted to having been drinking beer with colleagues. While at the farm, the group observed a snake that they all agreed was a large coral snake. A wager was placed on which person would handle the reptile. The patient picked up the snake and was bitten on the right index finger. The snake held on and chewing motion was described. When the snake was pulled off by a friend several seconds later, the feeling of separating layers of Velcro was experienced. The patient came to the emergency department five hours later, when he was obviously inebriated. His blood alcohol level was 52 mmol/L (238 mg/dL). The only physical finding was minimal swelling of the finger. Fang marks were present from which small drops of blood could be expressed. He had no systemic symptoms. A skin test was negative; however, after receiving the first several drops of antivenin, the patient developed a frank anaphylactic reaction characterized by hives, wheezing, and intense shock that responded to fluids, epinephrine, dopamine, and the immediate discontinuation of the antivenin. Despite of the severity of the bite, it was decided that no additional antivenin should be administered. Within the next several hours, he developed diplopia, slurred speech, and intense generalized fasciculations. He was electively intubated endotracheally, but did not require mechanical ventilation. He developed total body weakness, being unable to move any muscle with the exception of his diaphragm and hands for the next six days. His serum creatine kinase level increased to a maximum of 18,000 U/L. After six days, the fasciculation abated and strength gradually returned. He was extubated. He did not have normal muscle strength until one month later."

In 1966, Moseley described a curious case of an eastern coral snake (*M. f. fulvius*) bite received by a laborer who was bitten in the thumb, index finger, and ring finger. He was treated with Instituto Butantan coral snake antivenin but required a tracheostomy to sustain respiration. When the patient's condition became worse, he received a 500 cc transfusion of whole blood donated by William Haast, a skillful snake handler, then director of the Miami Serpentarium. The generous donor had been bitten by almost 100 different venomous snakes of the world, many of them neurotoxic. He had been given cobra antivenin after his last bite accident. Remarkably, the patient bitten by the coral snake began to improve after receiving the Haast's blood. This combination of Haast's blood and antiserum-generated immunity helped the victim to overcome the coral snake venom, and in 10 days he was released from the hospital.

As Haast had not been bitten by coral snakes, his blood might have not contained any specific antibodies against coral snakebite, even though some cross-neutralization with other snake venoms might be possible. It does not seem to be possible to build and maintain antibodies against snakebites in humans. However, Theakston et al (1981), mentioned earlier, found that 21% of the Waorani Indians in eastern Ecuador he studied tested positively for coral snake antibodies (and 60% for pit viper antibodies). This shows not only that some antibody activity remains in the blood after the bite, but that Waorani Indians have a very high snakebite incidence.

Pettigrew and Glass (1984) reported a bite accident by *M. laticollaris* in southern Mexico. This case is interesting on several accounts. First, the offending snake was misidentified as nonvenomous, which somewhat delayed the initiation of the treatment. Second, it showed local effects, with swelling around the wound. Third, it illustrated the diverse neurological complications known in coral snakebites.

After 15 minutes the bitten American student felt nauseated and the right index finger, showing four fang punctures, felt numb. As the snake delivering the bite was thought to be a false coral snake (a king snake) no special precautions were taken. A serious treatment started only the next day when the patient began to lose his sense of taste and to have blurred vision and ptosis of the eyelids—symptoms associated with neurotoxic coral snake envenomation. He also had difficulties of speaking and chewing. The snake was then identified as *Micrurus laticollaris*, a coral snake from the Balsas river basin, and the bitten student was transported to the United States. In the next two days the patient had some loss of strength in limbs and a moderate respiratory stress but intubation was not performed. No snake antiserum was given, only steroids and antihistamines, but the patient was carefully monitored and repeatedly examined. The observed hematuria, and gastrointestinal bleeding were attributed to Coombs-negative hemolytic anemia and moderate coagulopathy. These symptoms disappeared spontaneously. The patient left the hospital 12 days later after all symptoms had disappeared.

The following case was kindly communicated to me by Carol Gracie and written down by Adrián Méndez, a young Costa Rican naturalist, whose father was bitten by *M. nigrocinctus*, 60 centimeters long, on the 4th of January, 1987:

"My older brother and my father tried to catch the snake. First, my brother stepped on it with his shoe and my father grabbed it two inches behind the head. The snake turned its head and bit him in his left index finger.

"My father started immediately a treatment that consisted of a tourniquet applied on the forearm. This was not effective because the arm swelled considerably and my father could not stand the pain so that after 5 minutes the tourniquet was removed. The following were the symptoms that developed after the bite:

"At the moment of bite, a strong pain in the bitten finger shooting toward the hand that felt like a fire; after 15 min.—visible swelling of one half of the hand; after 45 min.—pain in the arm that run from the arm to the heart (in the chest), together with strong nausea; after 2 hours—vomiting, followed by dizziness; after 4½ hours—loss of consciousness.

"The first medical assistance began in the Puntarenas Hospital two hours after the bite. The hospital did not have suero anticoral (anti-coral serum) and the only treatment consisted of an injection against pain until my father could reach the next hospital in San José. The only treatment in this hospital was injection of suero anticoral and rest. My father stayed in the hospital for 6 days, the first 3 of them were the most difficult due to his delicate state of health (caused by the bite).

"After the hospitalization, the physician suggested 4 months convalescence. During the first 3 months, part of the hand was insensitive, especially the first three fingers of the bitten hand. During the last month, while the hand was returning to normal again, the insensitive part became very sensitive to heat and hot objects (for example, touching a glass with hot water). Presently (May, 1987), my father has fully recovered from the bite and has no symptoms."

From a medical standpoint, the case lacks precise data, but it is a valuable summary of a snakebite accident produced by *M. n. nigrocinctus* in Costa Rica. The local pain and swelling were probably caused by the myotoxic action known of the venom of this coral snake, but they were apparently much stronger than in several other known cases of coral snakebite accidents.

Two reports of the bite of *M. corallinus* from Brazil, both fatal, illustrate the seriousness of that snakebite. One case, reported by the father-son professional team, Vital Brazil and Vital Brazil, Jr. in 1933, was summarized by the latter while discussing neurotoxic snake venoms in 1980.

> "19 years old, robust complexion, Brazilian ... On November 8 (1932) he arrived at the Instituto Vital Brazil requesting a specific treatment because he had been bitten by a venomous coral snake. Examination revealed numbness of the right arm, extending from the bitten to the axilar region. He complained of thoracic pain, blurred vision and muscular fatigue. He displayed a slight immobility of both eyelids and constant salivation. We examined him about 40 minutes after his arrival at the Institute. At that time, palpebral ptosis was conspicuous as well as difficulty of vision. The patient kept on his feet with a certain amount of difficulty, and his walk was swaying and uncertain like that of a drunk. There was abundant salivation. Shortly before, he had received 20 ml of soro antielapineo (antielapid serum) (obtained from animals immunized with the venom of *M. lemniscatus* and *M. frontalis*). After being hospitalized, the phenomena of envenomation progressed, the respiratory difficulty increased, the voice disappeared. The patient could hear, and demonstrated that he could understand but could not talk. Asphyxia became imminent requiring an urgent tracheotomy. Cyanosis, abundant sialorrhea and nasal hypersecretion was observed. Death occurred around six hours after the bite accident."

In the other case, reported by Machado and Rosenfeld (1971), a 50-year-old man died 6½ hours after being bitten by *M. corallinus* while being transported to the hospital of Instituto Butantan, São Paulo. The postmortem examination revealed pulmonary congestion, signs of cardiac insufficiency, and hemolysis as shown also in cylinders of hemoglobin in the kidneys. The patient seemed to have died from cardiac insufficiency.

A bite by the rare coral snake, *Micrurus a. annellatus* from Peru, was kindly communicated to me by Nelly Carillo de Espinoza from the Museo de Historia Natural of Lima, as told to her by the bitten person, Sr. Pedro Hocking. She commented:

> "The bite occurred in Iscocazin, Oxapampa province (Pasco) in 1985. He was bitten slightly in his right index finger and immediately felt intense pain that radiated up to the entire arm. At once he suck the blood from the bitten place with mouth. In few hours the pain disappeared from the arm, but the bitten place of the finger remained reddish and insensitive, but with a sharp stinging pain, similar to that produced by the bite of an ant (*Izula*). As he could not feel needle jab in the bitten place, he visited me ten days after the accident with his bitten finger still numb."

Apparently, there were no further complications from the bite.

A common way of getting bitten by coral snakes is by handling them. We already discussed the frequency of coral snakesbites associated with handling them, as summarized by Kitchens and Van Mierop (1987). On occasion, even herpetologists or people handling snakes in the field or for professional reasons get bitten in spite of precautions taken. Inquiring among herpetologists, I have received several reports of such accidents. One of these happened to Tom Stubbs, a herpetologist from Florida, who in 1964 was bitten by a coral snake in the Los Tuxtlas region in Mexico, probably by *M. diastema sapperi*. This bite produced no symptoms of envenomation. Ted Papenfus, a herpetologist from the Museum of Vertebrate Zoology, University of California, was bitten in June 1981 in Guatemala by *M. nigrocinctus zunilensis* through a plastic bag in which the snake was collected. It occurred while the herpetologist was checking the state of the snake and pinching its tail. One fang of the coral snake penetrated into the finger, but he pulled the hand away at once. A drop of blood was pressed out of the puncture wound and there were no local or other symptoms.

William Lamar (personal communication), while collecting a *M. filiformis* in Colombia, received two vigorous defensive bites. It occurred when the tiny specimen, less than 200 mm long, was swimming in a river and Lamar grabbed it by hand. The bite was symptomless, probably because it was delivered in a callous part of the hand where the fangs could not penetrate.

Contrasting with these symptomless bites is one carefully recorded bite case by the relatively little known *M. m. mipartitus*. It occurred in 1963 while William Duellman and Charles Myers, two seasoned herpetologists and field researchers, were on an expedition in a remote area near Tacarcuna, Darién, Panama. Charles Myers was bitten while he was examining the coral snake collected the night before. Perhaps it should be mentioned that during a field trip, the herpetological specimens, including snakes, are captured and kept alive in plastic or cloth bags until time is available to properly preserve them and take all the necessary field data. The following case history was kindly furnished to me by Dr. Myers, with additional notes related to the accident taken by Dr. Duellman. Both scientists fully realized the danger involved in being far away from any civilized area, in the midst of the Darién wilderness, where no medical help could be received. They probably also recognized that the small size of the specimen was a factor in Dr. Myers' favor and they decided to continue the expedition and observe the symptoms. This specimen, currently in the University of Kansas Museum of Natural History (KU 75763), is a young adult male, 385 mm long. Charles Myers summarized his bite experience as follows:

> "The bite occurred on July 7, 1963 in a Darién Camp. The following notes were a collaboration

between Bill Duellman and myself (as I remember, he wanted to do the cutting but finally settled for recording the event on paper).

8:47 AM—snake removed from bag and bit me on left ring finger, on middle of right side of proximal phalanx. The snake "chewed" for several seconds and left several fang marks. Local pain in less than 1 minute.

8:50—ligature tied around base of finger; some local swelling already evident.

8:52—fang perforations shallowly lanced and suction started with Cutter Kit.

9:15—swelling into proximal joint.

9:24—swelling completely obliterated knuckle and moving into adjacent knuckles.

9:26—little and middle finger cold to touch.

9:28—ligature removed from finger to wrist.

9:40—swelling and soreness in back of hand.

10:20—swelling has progressed to wrist.

10:25—faint soreness in lower arm.

10:43—swelling and numbness in adjacent fingers; pain in upper arm.

10:55—stopped suction and removed ligature (which had never been applied tightly). Pain felt in armpit.

1:00 PM—swelling has slightly subsided.

My hand was not back to normal use until the night of July 10, but numbness persisted in the hand for a week after that. Until the night of July 10, the bitten hand had remained swollen and sore, partly, perhaps because we took a 6-hour backpacking trip the day after the bite and I bumped it against trees a number of times, because I was feverish during this march in the midst of a tropical downpour and perhaps this was part of the aftereffects.

"The interesting aspects of this bite was [sic] the apparent lack of neurotoxic effects. The outward symptoms were more like one would expect from the bite of a small viper."

The symptoms produced by the venom of this species are indeed different from the neurotoxic facies observed in most coral snakebites. *M. m. mipartitus* belongs to quite a distinct species group of coral snakes that might have much more enzyme-related symptoms than the nonenzymatic toxins producing the neurotoxic effects. In addition, the venom of the *mipartitus-multifasciatus* group of coral snakes does not show any cross immunization with other species of coral snakes (Minton, 1967).

Santiago Ayerbe, a Colombian physician in Popayán and expert on snakebites, and colleagues (1979, 1980, 1981, 1990) reported several cases of bite accidents by a coral snake, locally called *Rabo de Ají* or *Cabeza de Chocho*, *M. mipartitus decussatus*. It is related to the species that bit Charles Myers in Panama. Two out of four cases were fatal. In one, Dr. Ayerbe described a bite accident by a 404 mm-long coral snake received by a schizophrenic male who died 6 hours after the bite, before reaching the hospital. The victim showed several of the neurotoxic symptoms including eyelid paralysis, sialorrhea, cyanosis, swallowing difficulties, and unstable walk. Later, difficulties talking appeared. No edema or local symptoms were observed. In the second fatal case, a 52-year-old female showed difficulties in kidney function, including hemoglobinuria, associated with hemolysis, but no neurotoxic symptoms. The patient had additional previous complications due to arterial hypertension and, later, cortical necrosis. A more recent report by Rodrigo Angel (1987) includes three more bites by the same species in Colombia, as well as other interesting notes on coral snakes.

Dr. Juan Silva Haad of Leticia, Colombia, another skillful Colombian physician knowledgeable in snakebite accidents, recently told me about a fatal snakebite case by *M. surinamensis*. The bite was inflicted in a foot while the victim was standing at the river.

The bites of the Arizona coral snake, *Micruroides e. euryxanthus*, produce some symptoms of envenomation but, due to their very small mouth and short fangs, bite accidents are very rare. Russell (1967) reported on four accidents, none fatal. None of the bitten persons experienced any respiratory or cardiovascular difficulties. However, some of the systemic symptoms were present. They were nausea, drowsiness, and neurotoxic facies including difficulties in vision and in focusing the eyes properly. An insecure and erratic walk appeared in several cases. The most carefully recorded case of a *M. e. euryxanthus* bite was written down by the late Frederick Shannon, a physician and a skillful herpetologist. It was reported by Russell in 1967. Dr. Shannon survived this bite to succumb several years later to a bite of a Mojave rattlesnake (*Crotalus scutulatus*), one of the most venomous U.S. rattlesnakes.

A significant fact is that all of these victims were voluntarily handling the Arizona coral snake. One of them was even trying to prove to a friend that it could not bite in large, exposed areas due to its small mouth.

Another "handling accident" with *M. e. euryxanthus* occurred to the late James Oliver, one-time director of the American Museum of Natural History, New York, and a well-known herpetologist. He was bitten while preparing the coral snake for photography. He was unaware of the biting attempt until a bystander called his attention to the chewing motion of the snake on his little finger. The fangs did not penetrate the skin and the bite was completely asymptomatic (Oliver, 1958).

First Aid and Summary of Professional Treatment

In spite of the fact that up to 60% of all coral snakebites are without symptoms, except for some local pain, by far the only reasonable attitude after a snakebit accident is to reach a hospital or professional medical help as soon as possible. If some bite marks are found, it should be assumed that the bitten person might be suffering envenomation. Yet, it might be up to several hours or even days, as in remote areas of South America, before a bitten person can reach medical help. For these cases some minimal first aid has been recommended. It includes keeping the victim at rest, comfortable and warm, immobilizing the bitten limb if necessary, and supporting and assuring the victim as much as possible. As some venom might be left on the skin near the puncture (see Fix, 1980, observations of some venom being "spilled" before the actual biting), the wound should be washed immediately with soap or some disinfectant. Beyond these general rules, authorities have different opinions as to the usefulness of other first aid procedures. A light tourniquet might be placed on a leg or hand, preventing the superficial circulation but allowing the deeper arterial circulation to continue. If applied, the tourniquet—rubber band, string, handkerchief or such—should not be tight and should be released every 10 to 15 minutes for 1 minute. Elastic bandage and splinting has been used against Australian elapid bites (Sutherland, 1982) and it might be useful against coral snakebites as well. Perhaps more than actually preventing the spread of the venom through the body, it is a psychological assurance to the victim. The value of cutting and suctioning the wound is not clear and should not normally be done unless the victim is far away from medical help and the bite looks quite serious. Dr. Russell suggests that the bitten person not eat or drink anything. Alcohol, in spite of earlier opinions, is not recommended as it accelerates the circulation and thus helps in distribution of the venom. What is definitely not recommended is cooling the bite area with ice. An important part of the first aid and subsequent treatment is to take the snake to the hospital for correct identification.

Ramsey and Klickstein (1962), Moseley (1966), Parrish and Khan (1967), McCollough and Gennaro (1970), Russell (1980), Arnold (1984), and Kitchens and Van Mierop (1987), offer summaries of the first aid and medical treatment for coral snakebites, while Hardy (1989) summarized the bibliography of snakebites in Latin America that includes coral snakes.

The most effective snakebite treatment is application of the specific coral snake antivenin, also called antivenom, described in the next section on antivenins. Inquiries about the availability of coral snake antivenin in the United States should be directed to National Communicable Disease Center, 1600 NE Clifton Road, Atlanta, Georgia 30307, or Oklahoma City Poison Control Center (telephone [405] 271-5454).

The physician will decide upon proper procedures to follow in accordance with the circumstances of each case. In addition to the antivenin, where required, the treatment usually includes antibiotics, tetanus prophylaxis, and other supportive measures. Narcotics and sedatives are not recommended. Even if no immediate systemic symptoms are observed initially, the patient should be left for observation for a day or two due to the frequent late onset of systemic symptoms. Means to maintain artificial respiration should be available and ready in case respiratory paralysis restricts or prevents breathing.

Coral Snake Antivenins and Other Remedies

Antivenins

Specific coral snake antivenin is produced by injecting gradually increasing nonlethal doses of snake venom into horses, goats, rabbits, or any other large mammal. Over time, the horse, the most commonly used animal in antivenin production, develops antibodies against the venom. The horse is bled and the red blood cells are separated and returned to the horse. The horse blood serum that is left is purified by eliminating unnecessary globulins and albumins and finally it is filtered in order to eliminate any possible bacteria or even remnants of their cell wall.

Antivenin is specific against the coral snake venom used in immunizing the horse. No coral snake antivenin is effective against all coral snakebites. But due to the similarities of venom among several species and their power of cross-neutralization, a combination of venoms can produce protection against several common coral snakes. Antivenins against other snakes, such as rattlesnakes and cobras, are not effective against coral snake venom, and, usually, vice versa. Therefore, only the specific antivenin is effective and, if applied sufficiently and on time, could save almost all the bitten individuals.

In the United States, Wyeth Laboratories (Marietta, Pennsylvania, 17547; telephone (717) 426-1941) produces and distributes the only coral snake antivenin available specifically against the North American coral snake, called "Antivenin (*Micrurus fulvius*), North American Coral Snake Antivenin." It is effective against North American coral snakes and partially effective against several other species of coral snakes in Central and South America. The instructions that accompany the product give a good summary of the antivenin and treatment modalities. Wyeth recommends that its antivenin be given intravenously. When applying antivenin, a skin test for sensitivity to horse serum is generally done, but see comments by Watt (1989) who cautions against it.

The first coral snake antivenin, called "soro antielapidico: genus *Micrurus*" was and still is produced by the Instituto Butantan (Caixa Postal 65, São Paulo, Brazil, telephone 813-7222) using the venoms of *M. frontalis* and *M. corallinus*. It is at least partially effective against several other coral snake venoms, including subspecies of *M. fulvius*, *M. spixii*, and several more.

Currently, one of the most active producers of coral snake antivenin is Instituto Clodomiro Picado (Universidad de Costa Rica, Coronado, Costa Rica, telephone 29-03-44). Its "suero antiofídico anti-coral" is effective against *M. nigrocinctus*, *M. fulvius fulvius*, *M. dumerilii*, *M. alleni*, and the venom of several other Central and South American coral snakes, but not against *M. multifasciatus* and probably *M. mipartitus*. They are also experimenting with an anticoral polyvalent serum, the "Panamerican serum" against nine species of coral snakes and probably many more from North, Central, and South America (Bolaños et al., 1978a, 1978b). Several researchers associated with the institute, such as Bolaños (1971), Bolaños, Cerdas, and Taylor (1973, 1975), and Cerdas (1978), have been exploring different aspects of immunization and production of antivenins.

In Colombia, a commercially available polyvalent coral snake antivenin, "suero anti-elapídico polivalente anti-micrúrico," is produced by the Laboratorios Probiol (Diagonal 183, No. 41-71, [or Apartado Aéreo 8001], Bogotá, Colombia; telephone 241-2666) under the scientific direction of César Gómez Villegas and with the collaboration of Juan Silva Haad. This antiserum is unique because it is effective not only against *M. mipartitus decussatus*, the coral snake producing frequent bite accidents in the Andes of Colombia and Ecuador, but also against *M. surinamensis* and *M. spixii* because their venoms, among others, are used in the production of the antivenin. At the National Institute of Health in Bogotá, active research in antivenins is also carried out by Juan Manuel Renjifo and his team.

Other workers in Latin America that have commented on antivenins include Kraus and Botelho (1923) and Barrio and Miranda (1966).

In the United States in the 1960s and 1970s, interest in antivenin production against snake venoms generated several studies focusing as well on the immunology, cross-neutralization, and antivenin effectiveness of coral snake venoms. Among the earlier researchers was Flowers (1966), working at the U.S. Army Mission in Costa Rica. Edward Seligmann and colleagues, working at the National Institutes of Health in Bethesda, Maryland, covered background information for production of standards for an antivenin against the venom of the North American coral snake. Their contributions include Cohen and Seligmann (1966); Cohen, Seligmann, and Berkeley (1967); Cohen, Dawson, and Seligmann (1968); and Cohen, Berkeley, and Seligmann (1971). Additional research has been carried out by Walter Kocholaty and colleagues at the U.S. Army Medical Research Laboratory, Fort Knox, Kentucky, including Kocholaty, Ashley, and Billings (1967) and Kocholaty et al. (1968, 1971a, 1971b). Other contributions include Russell and Lauritzen (1966), S. A. Minton (1967), and Munjal and Eliott (1971). A comprehensive and quite valuable summary of venoms and antivenins against venomous animals was published by the World Health Organization, entitled "Progress in the characterization of venoms and standardization of antivenoms" (1981). It also covers production of snake antivenins in the Americas including those of coral snakes. A recent list of where antivenins are produced is that of David Hardy (1989) that appeared in Campbell and Lamar's book, *The Venomous Reptiles in Latin America*.

Other Remedies

Over centuries, in several countries local remedies have been used against snakebites, including those of coral snakes. Most of them have not been investigated for possible beneficial effects and should not be discarded as superstition or as ineffective faith medicine. Even if they are faith remedies, their power of invoking faith in the bitten person for healing may be a useful tool in the treatment of snakebites where no other remedies are available.

One widely used oral remedy against snakebites in Brazil is "Especifico Pessoa," found in most general stores and small pharmacies in the interior of the country. It is a standard possession of every *garimpeiro* (gold prospector), *seringeiro* (rubber collector), and plantation worker. Until recently, health professionals have considered it an ineffective faith remedy. However, recent research on the properties of ethanol extract of the root of a Brazilian plant called Cabeça de Negra, contained in the "Especifico Pessoa," has yielded some active ingredients that might be effective against snake venoms (Ishiguro et al., 1982; Nakagawa et al. 1982. See also Vanzolini and Smith, 1983).

Among plant remedies, the infusion of the leaves and stem of the Brazilian vine (*Micania quacho*) was mentioned in relation to the treatment of a *M. f. fulvius* bite (see section on human accidents). The same vine is also used in Colombia. Carlos Pérez-Santos, a Colombian herpetologist, has been interested in plant remedies used against snakebites and kindly supplied the following list of plant remedies in Colombia:

Plant Remedies Used
Against Snakebites in Colombia

Common name	Scientific name
Cuartillito	*Peperomia nummulariefolia*
Guaco	*Micania*
Cuararina	*Aristolochia Klugii*
Ají picante	*Capsicum annuum*
Anturias	*Anthurim scandens*

Aristolochia and *Anthurium* are also used in some regions of Venezuela while in Panama *Quassia amara*, called locally guabito amargo, is used against some snakebites.

Several homeopathic healings of snake envenomation are used in countries of Latin America, such as Brazil and Peru, where homeopathic medicine is widely recognized, side by side with orthodox Western medicine. Acupuncture and acupressure healing systems suggest several pressure points to combat the snakebite effect. One such point is located on the inner side of the left leg, near the ankle bone. Acupressure practitioners do not claim to be able to heal the bitten person but to help in combatting the effect of the venom.

Recently, considerable interest has been generated by the use of electric shock in the treatment of snakebites. Initial results of such a treatment have been encouraging, so much so that *The New York Times* science section of August 5, 1986 (L. K. Altman) dedicated an article to advances in electric shock treatment of snakebites. A team of scientists at Michigan State University led by Jeffrey F. Williams are exploring this procedure. It was originally tried out by Ronald Guderian, a missionary physician in Ecuador, who successfully treated several snakebites (Guderian, MacKenzie, and Williams, 1986; see also Kroegel and Buschenfeld, 1986). However, because of too many unknown factors and uncertain usefulness, Russell and Wainschude (1973) urged caution concerning application of this therapy when it first became known quite a few years ago. Nothing substantial has been published to date.

Part V
IDENTIFICATION, DESCRIPTION, AND DISTRIBUTION BY COUNTRIES

Chapter 14
Identification

The three genera of coral snakes (*Leptomicrurus, Micruroides,* and *Micrurus*) found in the New World encompass 65 species or a total 122 species and subspecies. Yet, several more new species and subspecies are still waiting to be discovered.

The South American Andes and the Brazilian territory most likely harbor unknown coral snakes. On the other hand, the definition of some species and subspecies of coral snakes as proposed in this book will be modified once more coral snakes from crucial areas are collected and their variation and distribution better established. Several subspecies might turn out to be full species and vice versa.

The American coral snake genus *Micrurus* contains 54 species or 117 species and subspecies, distributed from eastern and southern United States to northern and central Argentina (Map 1). The genus *Leptomicrurus* with 3 species or 5 species and subspecies thus far known is found in northern South America, east of the Andes, from Colombia, Ecuador, Peru, and Bolivia to Venezuela, the Guianas, and northern Brazil. The smallest genus, *Micruroides* is restricted to the southwestern United States and northwestern Mexico. It contains only one species divided into three subspecies.

Studying the phylogenetic relationships of the New World coral snakes, Joseph Slowinksi (1991, 1995) recognized three natural groups within the genus *Micrurus* and proposed to divide the genus into three genera. All the South American triad-type species with bilobed hemipenis were retained in the genus *Micrurus* (for example, *Micrurus spixii*). Another genus was proposed for the group of single-banded species form North Central and South America with bifurcated hemipenis (for example, *Micrurus fulvius*). A third genus incorporated the bicolored body species with intermediate hemipenis (for example, *Micrurus mipartitus*.) For the group of single-banded species from North, Central, and South America with bifurcated hemipenis he proposed the name *Monadophis* (for example, [*Micrurus*] *Monadophis fulvius*). For the bicolored body species with intermediate hemipenis he proposed the name *Erythrokomophis* (for example, [*Micrurus*] *Erythrokomophis mipartitus*). His analysis of the relationships of coral snakes is a valuable contribution to understanding the natural groupings of New World coral snakes. However, I kept in this book the prevalent classification of coral snakes, even though the groups defined by Slowinski do represent natural units. They can be considered as subgenera of coral snakes (Roze, 1994). One reason for the choice of retaining the genus *Micrurus* as a single genus is that biochemical immunological evidence does not seem to show a significant difference between the species of coral snakes (Cadle and Sarich, 1981). A practical reason for keeping the genus undivided is that the coral snake venoms and antivenin systems in medical literature and reports use the name *Micrurus* as the accident-causing agent.

Distinction Between Venomous and Nonvenomous Coral Snakes

One of the most difficult tasks for a person not trained in herpetology is the distinction between the false coral snakes (Colubridae and Aniliidae) and the true coral snakes (Elapidae). That this is a complicated task was mentioned in the chapter on mimicry because even trained biologists have been deceived by the uncommon similarity between the false and true coral snakes, especially when they live in the same environment. The similarity, or more precisely the concordance, of color pattern and behavior of coral snakes is due to the imitation fellowship.

Only one feature is unique to the true coral snakes, namely the presence of short front fangs and, except for *Micruroides euryxanthus*, the absence of any other maxillary teeth. The false coral snakes have a maxilla with several to many maxillary teeth, but no front fangs (Table 8). Some false coral snake genera such as *Erythrolamprus* are rear-fang snakes, but they always have additional maxillary teeth. Unfortunately, to observe the teeth requires opening the snake's mouth. Even when the snake's mouth is opened, the fangs are not easy to detect because they are almost completely hidden by the fleshy fang fold, so the only visible structure in the anterior part of the upper jaw is a fleshy knot. Pressing it down, the small fangs can be seen protrud-

Table 8. Selective Characteristics for Distinguishing the True (Venomous) Coral Snakes from the False (Non-venomous) Coral Snakes

True coral snake (Elapidae)	False coral snake (Colubridae, Aniliidae)
Head morphology	
1. Front fangs present; no other maxillary teeth 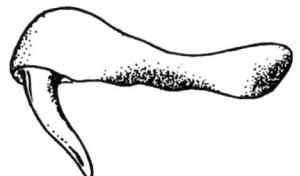	• No front fangs; several to many maxillary teeth 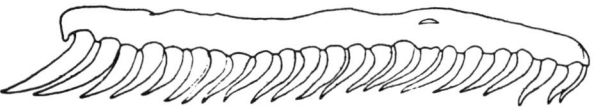
2. Loreal absent	• Loreal present or absent
3. Eyes quite small 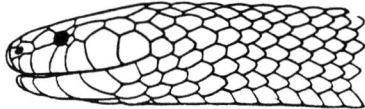	• Eyes usually large or small **Loreal** 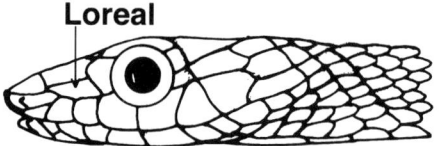
4. Head indistinct or hardly distinct from body	• Head distinct or a little distinct from the body
Coloration	
5. Usually black bands single or in sets of three (triads)	• Black bands single or double or in sets of three
6. Black bands usually complete ventrally	• Black bands complete or incomplete ventrally.

ing from their protective fold. This indeed is quite a complicated procedure, especially for an untrained person, when there is an urgent need to ascertain whether a coral snake is venomous or not.

No single external characteristic can be used to differentiate the true and false coral snakes, but a combination of several features might help to tell them apart. The loreal shield is invariably absent in the true coral snakes (Table 8). This shield is present in the most faithful coral snake imitators from the genus *Pliocercus* and in some others such as *Pseudoboa*, *Erythrolamprus*, and *Lampropeltis*.

The loreal might be absent or confused with the prefrontal shield found in some false coral snakes. If correctly determined, the absence of the loreal is a second useful feature to distinguish the coral snakes. In most true coral snakes, the head is almost indistinguishable from the body and the eye is small, smaller than the supralabials, while in many false coral snakes the head is larger, or at least wider than the body, and their eyes are large, larger than the supralabials. This does not apply to the false coral snakes of genus *Atractus* and several more.

Even less clues to separate coral snakes are found in the color pattern. The venomous coral snakes do not have black bands in pairs, as it is found in several species of false coral snakes of the genus *Erythrolamprus*. Incomplete black bands, i.e., interrupted ventrally or consisting of dorsal spots, are found in several false coral snakes, while the true coral snakes almost invariably have complete black bands. Very little else can be used to distinguish the true coral snakes from the false coral snakes. Table 8 offers some selective characteristics that can be used to separate the venomous coral snakes from the nonvenomous or mildly venomous species.

Key for Identification of Genera and Species

The three keys offered in continuation allow the identification of all the species of coral snakes. The first key allows differentiation of the genera. This key also separates the only species of *Micruroides*. The second key differentiates only the species of *Leptomicrurus*, while the third key is designed to identify not only the species of the genus *Micrurus* but all the New World coral snakes.

A particularly difficult key is the one covering the species of the genus *Micrurus*. It contains not only the largest number of species, but in several cases the poorly defined either-or characteristics make their identification quite difficult. One reason for this is the convergence of some characteristics of some species during the long evolutionary period of coral snakes. In other cases, a combination of several features is needed to separate the species. At times, the differences between subspecies of the same species are considerable. In order to accommodate all the subspecies for a given species, the species can appear in the key more than once. The identification of the species should be further

Identification

checked and confirmed, with a review of its characteristics and distribution offered under the description of species and subspecies.

Key to the Genera of Coral Snakes

1 Black above, without complete red or white bands except on head and behind it and on tail; genials in contact with the mental (Fig. 3B)
.... *Leptomicrurus* (p. 132)
1' Light bands or transversal rows of white spots alternate with black bands; genials separated from the mental by contact of the first infralabial (Fig. 1C) . . 2
2 Only one pair of genials (Fig. 4); entire head, including parietals, black; fangs followed by additional small tooth on maxilla (Fig. 33A)
.... *Micruroides* (p. 136)
2' Two pairs of genials (Fig. 1C); head almost never entirely black; fangs present only on maxilla (Fig. 33B)
.... *Micrurus* (p. 138)

Key to the Species of the Genus *Leptomicrurus*

1 Head black with a white nuchal band behind the parietals, 0+1 temporals (Fig. 3A)
.... *L. collaris* (p. 132)
1' Head with a red or white fronto-parietal band (Fig. 49), 1+1 temporals 2
2 More than 260 ventrals in males and more than 270 in females
.... *L. narduccii* (p. 134)
2' Less than 242 ventrals in males and less than 270 in females
.... *L. scutiventris* (p. 135)

Key to the Species of New World Coral Snakes, Subdivided in Two Subsets of Keys

x—Black bands in sets of three (triads) (Color 7)
.... KEY X
xx—Black bands not in sets of three .... KEY XX

KEY X—Black Bands in Triads

1 Anal plate undivided; black bands twice or more longer than red
.... *M. hemprichii* (p. 180)
1' Anal plate divided; black bands shorter or a little longer than red 2
2 Only fourth supralabial in contact with the eye; the central black band of a triad usually with slightly roundish borders dorsally (Color 57)
.... *M. surinamensis* (p. 221)
2' Third and fourth supralabials in contact with the eye; central black band usually with more or less straight borders 3
3 The first triad represented by only one black band (only one black band between the head and first red body band) (Color 17) 4
3' The first triad represented by two or three black bands 5
4 Maximum 11 triads
.... *M. dissoleucus* (p. 158)
4' Around 18 triads
.... *M. meridensis* (p. 194)
5 The first triad complete, consisting of three black bands (Color 27) 6
5' The first triad consisting of 2 black bands (2 black bands between the head and the first red body band) (Color 55) 16
6 The first two black bands combine in forming an anchor-shaped figure on the neck (Color 7)
.... *M. ancoralis* (p. 140)
6' The two first black bands do not form anchor-shaped figure 7
7 Head black with only one red frontal crossband (Color 59); the black nuchal band covers at least half of the parietals
.... *M. tschudii* (p. 223)
7' Black nuchal band does not cover the parietals or barely reaches the tips of the parietals; and/or head with a white and red crossband 8
8 Head with well marked white internasal and red parietal bands (Color 34) ....
8' Head without red and white crossbands or with irregular red parietal coloration; or all black with shields outlined with light or black with irregular white and red spots 13
9 Ventrals 270 to 316 in males and 275 to 333 in females
.... *M. filiformis* (p. 170)
9' Less than 270 ventrals in males and less than 275 in females 10
10 Subcaudals 20 to 28 in males and 19 to 27 in females
.... *M. ibiboboca* (p. 183)
10' More than 28 subcaudals in males and more than 27 in females 11
11 Ventrals 210 to 222 in males and 224 to 248 in females 12
11' More than 222 ventrals in males and usually more than 248 in females
.... *M. lemniscatus* (p. 188)
12 The central black band is less than twice as long as the outer; usually 1⅓ triad on tail; usually some black spots on the first red band
.... *M. frontifasciatus* (p. 175)
12' The central black band usually twice or more than twice as long as the outer band; usually 1⅔ or more triads on tail; the first red band usually immaculate
.... *M. lemniscatus* (p. 188)
13 Subcaudals 26 to 33 in males and 25 to 29 in females; with black frontal band and red parietal band
.... *M. isozonus* (p. 184)

C17 250

C27 253

C55 260

C7 248

C59 261

C34 255

C57 261

13' Subcaudals 17 to 27, usually less than 25, in males and 16 to 26, usually less than 23, in females; no distinct black and red bands; if parietals red, shields outlined by black or white 14
14 Triads 5 to 11 (rarely 12); when 12, first triad starts 5 or more dorsals behind the parietals 15
14' Triads 12 to 19; when 12, first triad less than 5 dorsals behind the parietals
.... *M. frontalis* (p. 171)
15 Black parietals fused or nearly fused with the first black body band
.... *M. diana* (p. 152)
15' Black parietals 5 or more dorsals separated from the first black dorsal band
.... *M. pyrrhocryptus* (p. 211)
16 Triads continue on tail 17
16' Only single bands on tail 18
17 14 to 19 complete body triads
.... *M. decoratus* (p. 151)
17' 4 to 9 complete body triads
.... *M. spixii* (p. 215)
18 The black nuchal band is 9 to 12 dorsals long
.... *M. laticollaris* (p. 186)
18' The black nuchal band is less than 5 dorsals long 19
19 White band and red band with a transverse series of black spots; black bands of a triad of approximately equal length (Pattern 22)
.... *M. elegans* (p. 167)
19' White bands without black spots or only black tips; central black band of a triad longer than the outer band (triads formed by accessory black bands) 20
20 Ventrals 210 to 216 in males and 227 to 237 in females
.... *M. catamayensis* (p. 148)
20' Less than 207 ventrals in males and less than 220 in females 21
21 7 to 13 complete triads in males and 9 to 14 in females
.... *M. dumerilii* (p. 163)
21' More than 14 complete triads in males and more than 14 in females 22
22 Ventrals 197 to 206 in males and 212 to 220 in females; subcaudals 43 to 50 in males and 32 to 35 in females; 5 to 8 black tail bands
.... *M. bocourti* (p. 145)
22' Ventrals 190 to 196 in males and 207 to 215 in females; subcaudals 47 to 53 in males and 35 to 37 in females; 7 to 10 black tail bands
.... *M. sangilensis* (p. 214)

Key XX—Black Bands Not in Triads

1 Body dorsally uniformly black, except for the first few very short complete red or white bands behind the head 2
1' Light body bands incomplete; may be represented by cross rows of white spots 4
2 Head all black, light collar behind parietals (Fig. 51); 0+1 temporals
.... *L. collaris* (p. 132)
2' Head with light crossband; 1+1 temporals 3
3 Ventrals 261 to 378 in males and 271 to 379 in females
.... *L. narduccii* (p. 134)
3' Ventrals 219 to 242 in males and 243 to 269 in females
.... *L. scutiventris* (p. 135)
4 Body bicolor (red-black or white-black) (Color 42) 5
4' Body with red-white-black bands 17
5 Black mostly reduced to dorsal spots, irregular dorsal and ventral spots, or a few black bands complete on red background 6
5' Two-color bands present or at least black with transversal rows of white crossbands 7
6 25 to 41 roundish black dorsal spots, a few of which might form complete black bands (Pattern 7); 4 black tail bands
.... *M. bernadi* (p. 144)
6' Angular, squarish, or irregular larger and smaller dorsal spots; irregular spots also on ventrals or black bands complete (Color 41); 6 to 12 black tail bands
.... *M. limbatus* (p. 192)
7 Sinuous butterfly-like black head band (Pattern 47)
.... *M. spurrelli* (p. 218)
7' Without butterfly-like head band 8
8 Body black with transversal "pearly" rows of white or red spots one scale long around the body .. 9
8' Light bands (white or red) usually 2 or more scales long alternate with black bands 12
9 Head with a light crossband on parietals; 17 to 61 black body bands in males and 18 to 75 in females (Color 8)
.... *M. annellatus* (p. 142)
9' No light crossband on parietals; usually more than 61 black bands in males and more than 75 in females (if less, original red bands can be seen ventrally and laterally) 9
10 110 to 141 black body bands, separated by "pearly" white crossbands; upper head all black (Pattern 15)
.... *M. margaritiferus* (p. 193)
10' Less than 110 black body bands; white spots on head shield present or absent 11
11 Ventrals 212 to 216 in females and 196 to 205 in males; only black bands on body, 70 to 90 in males and 85 to 90 in females (Color 15)
.... *M. albicinctus* (p. 138)
11' Ventrals 218 to 229 in females and 202 to 210 in males; 46 to 56 subcaudals in males; usually alternating black and dark red bands, 18 to 37 in males

Identification

and 29 to 47 in females; if only black bands are present, they are double the number of body bands (Color 36)
.... *M. langsdorffi* (p. 185)

12 Alternating long and short black body bands; 178 to 188 ventrals in males and 193 to 203 in females (Color 54)
.... *M. ruatanus* (p. 213)

12' Black bands of approximately equal length; usually more than 193 in males and more than 203 in females 12

13 8 to 15 black tail bands; 44 to 61 black body bands (Color 16)
.... *M. diastema* (p. 152)

13' Usually less than 8 tail bands; if 8, then less than 25 black body bands 14

14 Red bands two or more times longer than the black bands
.... *M. nigrocinctus* (p. 201)

14' Red or white bands shorter than the black bands 15

15 Only black/red on the body; ventrals around 295 in males and 325 to 329 in females
.... *M. multiscutatus* (p. 200)

15' Black/white or black/red bands present; ventrals less than 285 in males and 225 to 326 in females; almost always less than 325 16

16 Only black/white body bands; nuchal black band usually reaches parietal tips (Color 43); white bands usually 1 to 1½ dorsals long middorsally
.... *M. mipartitus* (p. 195)

16' Usually only black/red body bands; nuchal black usually does not reach parietal tips; white bands 2 or more dorsals long middorsally (Color 45)
.... *M. multifasciatus* (p. 199)

17 Head with at least one light (red or white) crossband (Color 18) 18

17' Head all black or almost all black (black cap) (Color 4) 46

18 Less than 10 black body bands 19
18' More than 9 black body bands 22

19 Black nuchal band does not reach parietals
.... *M. distans* (p. 161)

19' Black nuchal band reaches parietal tips 20

20 Black nuchal band covers 8 to 13 dorsals; black body bands 4 to 9 (usually more than 4) dorsals long,
.... *M. latifasciatus* (p. 187)

20' Black nuchal bands less than 8 dorsals; black body bands 5 or less dorsals long 21

21 Black nuchal band covers 2 to 3 dorsals; red scales immaculate or with small tips (Color 33)
.... *M. hippocrepis* (p. 182)

21' Black nuchal band covers 4 to 5 dorsals; red with large tips or irregular black spots
.... *M. diastema* (p. 152)

22 Black nuchal band does not reach parietals .. 23

22' Black nuchal band reaches parietals 28

23 Black tail bands 7 or more in males and 6 or more in females 24

23' Black tail band less than 7 in males and less than 6 in females 25

24 Males have supraanal tubercles; 32 to 39 subcaudals in females; 3 to 8 black tail bands in males, usually less than 7, and 3 to 7, usually less than 6, in females
.... *M. nigrocinctus* (p. 201)

24' Males without supraanal tubercles; around 42 subcaudals in females; 7–9 black tail bands in males and 6 in females
.... *M. diastema* (p. 152)

25 Ventrals 182 to 192 in males and 197 to 211 in females; at least some black dorsal bands 5 or more dorsals long, large regular black tips on red scales
.... *M. nigrocinctus* (p. 201)

25' Usually more than 192 ventrals in males and more than 211 in females; no tips or irregular, small tips present on red scales 26

26 Snout and/or supralabials white
.... *M. distans* (p. 161)

26' Snout black 27

27 Black nuchal band covers 7 to 10 dorsals
.... *M. fulvius* (p. 176)

27' Black nuchal band covers 3 to 5 dorsals
.... *M. nigrocinctus* (p. 201)

28 Many black bands incomplete ventrally (Pattern 38)
.... *M. proximans* (p. 209)

28' All or most black bands complete ventrally .. 29

29 Nuchal black band 7 to 10 dorsals long (Color 29)
.... *M. fulvius* (p. 176)

29' Nuchal black band less than 7 dorsals long .. 30

30 Dorsally the entire or almost the entire red band covered by irregular saddlelike black band (Pattern 27); red visible only ventrally and laterally
.... *M. ephippifer* (p. 169)

30' Red band visible dorsally; no saddlelike black band 31

31 No black tips or very small black dots on tips or just brownish overtones 32

31' Black tips clearly distinct and/or large irregular black spots on red 36

32 Twenty-three to 24 black bands in males and 26 to 28 in females; no supraanal tubercles in males
.... *M. nebularis* (p. 201)

32' Less than 24 black bands in males, but when there are more then males have supraanal tubercles; usually less than 26 black bands in females, but when more then small black spots on red tips 33

33 Ventrals less than 208 in males and less than 222 in females 34

33' Ventrals usually more than 207 in males and more than 221 in females; when less then small black spots on red tips 35

34 Males have supraanal tubercles; nuchal black band more than 3 dorsals long; black bands 3 or more dorsals long; first red band usually less than 13 dorsals long
.... *M. nigrocinctus* (p. 201)
34' No supraanal tubercles in males; nuchal black band covers 2 to 3 dorsals; black body bands usually less than 3 dorsals long; first red band 13 to 24 dorsals long
.... *M. hippocrepis* (p. 182)
35 Males have supraanal tubercles; females have 17 to 27 black body bands, usually more than 17
.... *M. browni* (p. 146)
35' Males without supraanal tubercles; females have 13 to 18 black body bands
.... *M. bogerti* (p. 146)
36 Regular black tips on all or almost all red dorsals clearly visible 37
36' Large spots or irregular tips not on all scales or mixture of both 42
37 Ventrals usually less than 206 in males and less than 223 in females 38
37' Ventrals usually more than 205 in males and more than 223 in females 40
38 Black body bands 8 to 17, usually less than 15; belly with many black spots or not; males without supraanal tubercles
.... *M. diastema* (p. 152)
38' 13 to 75 black body bands, usually more than 15; if less then males have supraanal tubercles; belly without or with few black spots 39
39 Males with supraanal tubercles; subcaudals 32 to 43 in females; 13 to 23 black body bands, usually 15 to 20
.... *M. nigrocinctus* (p. 201)
39' Males without supraanal tubercles; subcaudals 26 to 31 in females; 18 to 75 black body bands, usually more than 22
.... *M. annellatus* (p. 142)
40 Black tips large, somewhat irregular; some occupy almost 3/4 of red scales; nuchal black 6 to 8 dorsal rows, usually 7
.... *M. stuarti* (p. 221)
40' Black tips small, mostly regular, occupy 1/4 of red scale; nuchal band 4 to 6 dorsals long, usually 5 . . 41
41 Subcaudals 31 to 34 in females and 43 to 48 in males
.... *M. nigrocinctus* (p. 201)
41' Subcaudals 35 to 47 in females and 46 to 59, usually more than 48, in males
.... *M. browni* (p. 146)
42 Around 27 black dorsal bands in males and 40 to 41 in females; a black incomplete pseudoband between the regular bands
.... *M. diastema* (p. 152)
42' Less than 27 black bands in males, but if more then no black pseudoband present; less than 40 in females 43

43 216 to 218 ventrals in males and 226 to 231 in females; subcaudals 47 to 49 in males and 35 to 38 in females
.... *M. ephippifer* (p. 169)
43' Less than 216 ventrals in males and less than 226 in females; if more than less than 47 subcaudals in males and less than 35 in females 44
44 185 to 195 ventrals in males and 205 to 208 in females
.... *M. fulvius* (p. 176)
44' More than 195 in males and more than 208 in females 45
45 41 to 45 subcaudals in males and 3 to 5 tail bands in females
.... *M. fulvius* (p. 176)
45' 48 to 56 subcaudals in males and 6 to 9 tail bands in females
.... *M. diastema* (p. 152)
46 Head uniformly black including parietals and supralabials; no distinguishable nuchal black band 47
46' Black cap covers parietals. Black nuchal band, if present, frequently fused with black cap 48
47 206 to 226 ventrals in males and 219 to 245 in females
.... *Micruroides euryxanthus* (p. 136)
47' 186 to 191 ventrals in males and 203 to 210 in females .... *M. averyi* (p. 146)
48 Black cap covers parietals entirely or almost entirely, including tips; cap in contact with black nuchal band or not 51
48' Black cap reduced on parietals; it covers neither parietal tips nor its lateroposterior portion 49
49 Nuchal black band covers 6 or more dorsals and parietal tips
.... *M. diastema* (p. 152)
49' Nuchal black band 5 or less dorsals long; does not cover parietal tips 50
50 195 to 208 ventrals in males; 210 to 224 in females, usually less than 222; subcaudals 27 to 32 in females; black cap occupies most of parietals
.... *M. corallinus* (p. 149)
50' 210 to 224 ventrals in males; 222 to 240 in females; 32 to 43 subcaudals in females; black cap reduced to area between parietals
.... *M. alleni* (p. 139)
51 Ventrals less than 200 in males and usually less than 218 in females; if more then chin is white 52
51' Ventrals more than 199 in males and more than 217 in females 58
52 Chin all white with shields weakly outlined by grey
.... *M. clarki* (p. 149)
52' Chin with mental and several infralabials black or at least large black spots 53
53 Tubercles in males; black cap not in contact with nuchal band; black nuchal band sometimes reduced or absent; red not melanistic
.... *M. dumerilii* (p. 163)

53' Tubercles absent in males; black cap frequently in contact with nuchal band; black nuchal band not reduced; red frequently melanistic 54
54 Black bands are longer than the red; black nuchal bands extended 7 or more dorsals
.... *M. medemi* (p. 194)
54' Black bands shorter than red; black nuchal 5 or fewer dorsals 55
55 Black bands 20 or fewer
.... *M. paraensis* (p. 207)
55' Black bands 21 or more 56
56 Ventrals more than 202 in males and more than 213 in females
.... *M. remotus* (p. 213)
56' Ventrals less than 200 in males and 213 or less in females 57
57 Ventrals 188 to 196 in males, 203 to 212 in females; red usually obscured by black
.... *M. psyches* (p. 210)
57' Ventrals 178 to 187 in males, 192 to 205 in females; red bands distinct, sometimes with weak accessory bands
.... *M. circinalis* (p. 149)
58 Red bands melanistic or indistinct from black (Pattern 14) 59
58' Red and black clearly distinct (Pattern 18) ... 62

59 Black cap in contact with black nuchal band   60
59' Black cap not in contact with black nuchal band (Fig. 59) 61
60 Usually light spots on head shields
.... *M. langsdorffi* (p. 185)
60' No light spots on head shields
.... *M. steindachneri* (p. 219)
61 Less than 231 ventrals in females; more than 4 black tail bands
.... *M. langsdorffi* (p. 185)
61' More than 230 ventrals in females; less than 5 black tail bands
.... *M. petersi* (p. 208)
62 Light snout spots frequently present; when absent then more than 11 black tail bands in males and more than 8 in females
.... *M. langsdorffi* (p. 185)
62' No light snout spots on snout; less than 9 black tail bands in males and less than 8 in females 63
63 202 to 203 ventrals in males and 218 to 221 in females
.... *M. psyches* (p. 210)
63' 206 to 219 ventrals in males and 223 to 235 in females
.... *M. mertensi* (p. 195)

| P14 |
| 266 |
| P18 |
| 267 |

Chapter 15
Description of Species and Subspecies, with Keys to the Subspecies

The descriptions that follow summarize the characteristics of all species and subspecies of coral snakes. In addition to the scientific name, I have also included common names, and wherever it is known I used the name applied to the species by local people (see section on names and folklore). In most cases, I give a common name that refers to some outstanding characteristic or geographical area, particularly the country in which the coral snake is found. Many English common names correspond to those proposed by Campbell and Lamar (1989) in *The Venomous Reptiles of Latin America* but in other cases they are different. As their book is an important reference for venomous reptiles, I have included the English common name used by Campbell and Lamar in parentheses when it differed from the one I proposed. I have also suggested common names for all subspecies of coral snakes. The English common name is followed by the Spanish and/or Portuguese common names. It should be remembered that *cobra* in Portuguese simply means snake, not of course the deadly cobra of Africa and Asia.

Some information of interest mainly to systematic biologists is also included such as the original description and data on types. The characteristics and their terminology are discussed in the section on external features.

For species divided into subspecies, the species description includes its geographical *Distribution* and its *Definition*, which serves as a brief diagnosis for species recognition. These are followed by *Size, Remarks,* and *References*. The latter includes the authors (given in chronological sequence) who have dealt with the species and its subspecies in this century, usually clustered by countries for which they have been discussed, as well as other topics. Significant publications before 1900 are mentioned at the end of the more recent publications. Brief comments on earlier checklists and significant references that include coral snakes appear in the section on distribution of coral snakes by countries and selected references.

References are followed by a *Key* to the subspecies. When in doubt, after analyzing the characteristics given in the key, consult the distribution given in parentheses for each subspecies, as well as the more detailed description that appears for each subspecies.

For each subspecies *Range* includes the ecological environment, geographical area, and altitude. *Description* summarizes the principal characteristics and their variation necessary to identify a subspecies. Each range of number of ventrals, subcaudals, and black body bands is followed by the mean number of these characteristics in parentheses. For example, the males of *Micruroides euryxanthus euryxanthus* have from 212 to 230 (222.4) ventrals. I have also included the number of specimens that I have examined for each form as this offers an idea of the statistical validity of the variation of characteristics given in the descriptions. Obviously, the more specimens that are examined the better the range of variation will describe the species and subspecies. However, some exceptions and aberrations always occur. Some species of coral snakes are known from only one or a few specimens and the descriptions derived from these should be considered as only tentative.

Description is followed by *Remarks* and then by *Food*, where I give the diet I have observed in nature or found in museum specimens, as well as information from previous workers. The *References* include major authors who have dealt with the subspecies and the most recently published color photos, if any. *Etymology* gives the origin and meaning of the scientific name or names that have been given to the species and subspecies.

For species without subspecies, the same subheadings are maintained but combined where necessary. For example, *Distribution and range* combine geographical area and ecology, while other headings such as *Food* are incorporated in the treatment of the species.

To make the descriptions as complete as possible, I have examined approximately 80% of all the specimens of coral snakes collected in the world from 1758 on and deposited in different museums in the United States, Latin America, and Europe.

Genus *LEPTOMICRURUS*

The Black-backed Coral Snakes; Corales Espalda-negra; Cobras Coral Costas-Preta

Definition of the genus: Long and slender coral snakes, they have a short tail and their head is hardly distinguishable from their body. The head shields are similar to those of *Micrurus*, but the mental is in contact with the first pair of chin shields, separating the first infralabials. Dorsals are in 15 to 15 rows, without apical pits. Anal and the subcaudals are divided. Basic coloration is dorsum all black with yellow or reddish ventral spots. The first yellow spots might extend over the dorsum and form complete but narrow bands around the body. The head has a parietal or postparietal yellow or red band. The tail has several red ventral spots, some of which might form a complete band around the tail. Only the maxilla has fangs.

The hemipenis is bifurcated, with sulcus spermaticus also bifurcated. The base of the organ is naked, but the rest is spinose; the largest spines are around the zone of bifurcation. A naked fold extends from the base halfway up to the bifurcation of the organ.

Leptomicrurus collaris (Map 2)

Guianan Black-backed Coral Snake; Coral Espalda-Negra Guayanesa; Cobra Coral Costas-Preta Guianesa

Distribution: From southeastern Venezuela, Guyana, and Suriname, to French Guiana, and probably to northern Pará, Brazil.

Definition: A coral snake with a black body and yellow or reddish spots on the belly. The head and dorsal part is all black with a whitish or reddish nuchal band just behind the head. The anterior temporal shield is absent and the sixth supralabial usually touches the parietal, resulting in 0+1 temporals.

Size: This is one of the smallest coral snakes. The largest specimen measures only 456 mm, but most adults are less than 400 mm long.

Remarks: This species can be easily recognized by the absence of the first temporal shield and by the black head followed by a whitish or reddish nuchal band.

For a long time it was thought that this species lived in the Philippines. The original specimen, described by Schlegel (1837) in the Leiden Museum, Holland, did not have any locality information, as it is not unusual for specimens that arrived at the European museums from "exotic places" centuries ago. Two subspecies are recognized.

References: Schmidt (1937), Brongersma (1966), and Roze and Bernal-Carlo (1988) reviewed the literature and status of this species, which has an interesting but complicated taxonomic history. Campbell and Lamar (1989) gave a description and the distribution. Other significant contributions are those by Thompson (1913), Gomes (1918b), Schmidt (1939), Hoge and Romano (1966), and Sandner-Montilla (1985), as well as Roze (1967, 1983), and Romano (1972); Roze and Trebbau (1958) and Vetencourt Finol (1960), Hoge and Lancini (1962), Roze (1966a), and Lancini (1970, 1979) discussed it from Venezuela; Hoogmoed (1983) and Chippaux (1987) mentioned it for the Guianas, while Dixon and Rivero-Blanco (1979) discussed it from lowlands of South America. Roux-Estève (1983) gave data on a type specimen. A significant earlier reference is Kappler (1881).

Key to the Subspecies of *L. collaris*

1 Ventrals 212 to 219 in males; probably less than 247 in females
 .... *L. c. breviventris* (Venezuela and Guyana)
1' Ventrals 227 to 237 in males; about 247 in females
 ...... *L. c. collaris* (Guyana, Suriname and French Guiana, probably Para, Brazil)

Leptomicrurus collaris collaris (Color 1, 2)

Long Black-backed Coral Snake; Coral Espalda-Negra Larga Cobra; Coral Costas-Preta Longa

Elaps collaris Schlegel, 1837:448. (Holotype: ML 1444 [lectotype selected by Brongersma, 1966], a male from an unknown locality, but the type locality was designated by Hoge and Romano, 1966.)

Elaps gastrodelus Duméril, Bibron, and Duméril, 1854: 1212. (Holotype: MNHN 3930, a male from an unknown locality, collected by Keraudren.)

Leptomicrurus collaris collaris: Roze and Bernal-Carlo, 1988: 586.

Range: Lowland tropical rain forest and low montane wet forest in southern Guyana, Suriname, and French Guiana, and questionably in the Amazonian Pará region of Brazil, from sea level to about 700 m.

Description: Males have 227 to 237 (230.1) and females have approximately 247 ventrals; subcaudals 20 to 23 (21.4) in males and around 17 in females; 0+1 temporals, at least on one side of the head, and sixth supralabial in contact with the parietal. Examined: 8 males and 1 female, including the holotypes.

The head is all black except for occasional white or light spots on some snout shields and on the chin. A white or yellowish nuchal band barely touches the tips of the parietals. The body is all black above but on the belly there are yellowish or light orange-red ventral spots, 2 to 3 ventrals long. The light ventral spots extend on the first or second dorsal row where they cover only one dorsal. The black interspaces on the belly are 3 to 4 ventrals long. The red ventral spots form complete bands on the tail.

The males have 35 to 45 (40.5) and the females have approximately 45 light ventral spots on the body; both sexes have 2 to 3 red tail bands.

Remarks: Its distribution in Para, Brazil, still has to be confirmed. Cuhna and Nascimento (1978) collected quite intensively in that region without finding any specimens. As it is a rare species, it might still appear in northern Brazil, where it has presumably been found (Gomes, 1918b).

Food: Unknown.

References: Brongersma (1967) mentioned it for Suriname, Hoogmoed (1983) for the Guianas region, and Chippaux (1987) for French Guiana; Campbell and Lamar (1989) featured color photos. An earlier significant reference is that by Kappler (1881) from Suriname.

Etymology: Latin *collaris* means iron collar or chain for the neck. The name alludes to its conspicuous light collar or nuchal band, the only complete band on the body. The name *gastrodelus* is derived from the Greek words *gastr* meaning stomach or belly and *delo* meaning visible. This indicates that the yellow bands are visible only on the belly.

Leptomicrurus collaris breviventris (Fig. 51)
Short Black-backed Coral Snake; Coral Espalda-Negra Corta; Cobra Coral Costas-Preta Curta

Leptomicrurus collaris breviventris Roze and Bernal-Carlo, 1988:587. (Holotype: FMNH 26658, a male from Oko Mountains, Essequibo, northwestern Guyana, 400 m, collected by E. R. Blake on April 22, 1937.)

Range: Tropical low elevation rain forest in southeastern Venezuela and northwestern Guyana, from 400 to 600 m above sea level.

Description: Males have 212 to 219 (215.5) ventrals and around 24 subcaudals. Examined: the only known specimens, both males, including the holotype.

The head is black above, including the parietals, followed by a reddish nuchal band that covers 2 to 4 dorsals. One specimen has an irregular light crossband or spots on the snout. Below, the head is whitish but the

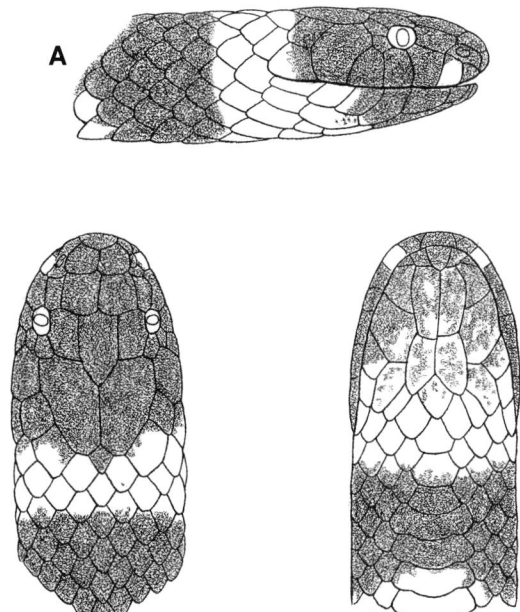

Figure 51. Head coloration of *Leptomicrurus collaris breviventris*, from Venezuela, 109th km on El Dorado road to Santa Elena, Bolivar: A) Lateral view, B) Dorsal view, C) Ventral view (MBUCV 8004, paratype).

anterior part, including the mental, some of the genials, and several infralabials, are black or heavily mottled with black. The body is all black dorsally, with orangy-yellow ventral spots 2 to 4 ventrals long. They extend over the first and second dorsal rows but are reduced in size. Occasionally, some yellowish spots continue as a series of very small dots, barely distinguishable, extending as a discontinuous row across the dorsum. On the ventral portion of the tail are large red spots that have fused together, making the tail all red below. The spots are much reduced in length dorsally, where they form short red bands.

The males have 40 to 45 (42.5) yellowish spots on the body and 2 to 3 red spots or bands on the tail.

Remarks: This is a little-known subspecies.

Food: Unknown.

References: Schmidt (1937) described one Guyanese specimen, Roze and Trebbau (1958) another from Venezuela. Vetencourt Finol (1960), Hoge and Lancini (1962), Roze (1966a, 1983), Lancini (1970, 1979) and Sandner-Montilla (1985) mentioned it for Venezuela under the name of *L. collaris*.

Etymology: Latin from *brevi-* for short and *venter* meaning belly, referring to the low number of ventrals, thus to the short body.

Leptomicrurus narduccii (Map 2)
Andean Black-backed Coral Snake; Coral Espalda Negra Andina; Cobra Coral Costas Preta Andina

Distribution: Amazonian slopes of the Andes and upper Amazon in eastern Ecuador, Peru, and northern Bolivia as well as in southern Colombia and probably in Acre, Brazil.

Definition: An all-black coral snake with yellow or reddish ventral spots, some of which occasionally may be complete dorsally, a yellow or white frontal-parietal crossband, somewhat irregular red bands on the tail, and a high number of ventrals: 261 to 379 in both sexes.

Size: A medium-large but slender coral snake. The longest specimen measures 1117 mm, but many adults range between 500 and 800 mm.

Remarks: This widely distributed, all-black coral snake with a white or yellowish-orange head crossband is still one of the least-known coral snakes. In some areas it lives together with the little black coral snake (*L. scutiventris*) from which, except for being much smaller, it can hardly be distinguished.

References: General comments on this species by Amaral (1925a, 1930b, 1930c), Schmidt (1936a), Cendrero et al (1972), Roze (1967, 1983), a complete description by Campbell and Lamar (1989), while Romano (1972) and Roze and Bernal-Carlo (1988) reviewed its generic status. Other references include for Bolivia: Griffin (1916) and Kempff-Mercado (1975); for Brazil: Gomes (1918a), Amaral (1948b), Hoge and Romano (1966), and Santos (1981); for Colombia: Nicéforo-María (1942), Dunn (1944a), Daniel (1949), Medem (1969), Angel (1983), and Silva and Rodríguez (1985); for Ecuador: Werner (1901a), Orcés (1943, 1948), J. A. Peters (1960), Duellman (1978), and Miyata (1982); for Peru: Dunn (1946) and Carrillo de Espinoza (1983). Earlier significant references include Cope (1870, 1876b) and Jan and Sordelli (1872).

Key to the Subspecies of *L. narduccii*

1 19 to 20 subcaudals in females and 25 to 27 in males; the black snout coloration usually does not cover the anterior part of the frontal
.... *L. n. narduccii* (Bolivia)

1' 21 to 27 subcaudals in females and more than 30 in males; the black snout coloration includes the anterior part of the frontal
.... *L. n. melanotus* (Southern Colombia, Ecuador, Peru, and northwestern Brazil)

 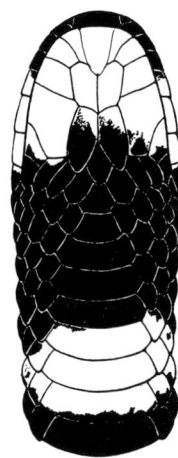

Figure 52. Head coloration of *Leptomicrurus narduccii narduccii*, from Bolivia: Sara, Río Sirubu, Santa Cruz: A) Dorsal view, B) Ventral view (UMNZ 67893).

Leptomicrurus narduccii narduccii (Fig. 52)
Bolivian Black Coral Snake; Coral Negra Boliviana

Elaps narduccii Jan, 1863b: 222. (Holotype: Lost in Milan Museum, from Bolivia, collected by Dr. Narducci.)
Leptomicrurus narduccii narduccii: Roze and Bernal-Carlo, 1988:591.

Range: Subtropical low altitude forest altered by humans and intermediate vegetation in the Santa Cruz region of Bolivia at altitudes between 300 and 600 m.

Description: Males have 261 to 278 (273.4) and females have 316 to 325 (320.0) ventrals; subcaudals 25 to 27 (26.0) in males and 19 to 20 (19.7) in females; 1-1, occasionally, 1-2 temporals. Examined: 11 males and 6 females.

The black snout does not reach or reaches but does not cover the anterior part of the frontal or supraoculars, but it includes the first three supralabials. The rest of the head is white or yellowish, including the parietals. The black dorsal coloration barely covers the tips of the parietals, part of the posterior temporal, and seventh supralabial. Below, the head is almost always white, including the genials. The rest of the body is all black dorsally with light (reddish or yellow?) ventral spots that are irregularly oval or almost square and include the first dorsal row. The light spots cover 2 to 4, usually 3 or 3.5, ventrals. On the tail is one complete but reduced red band, followed by a short black band that gives an impression of a tail all red ventrally crossed by a short black band, one or two ventrals long. Some specimens have the entire ventral part red, without a black crossband. In live specimens the red coloration of the tail is somewhat more intense than that of the body.

The males have 38 to 48 (41.6) and the females have

44 to 52 (47.2) red ventral spots. Most specimens have two large red spots on the tail; the first forms a complete red band.

Remarks: This is the southernmost species of the genus *Leptomicrurus*. Thus far, all the known specimens except the one used by Jan (1863b) to describe the species, now apparently lost, were collected by one avid collector, José Steinbach, who in the earlier part of this century sent valuable collections to European and North American museums.

Food: Snakelike teiid lizards (*Bachia dorbignyi*).

References: Roze and Bernal-Carlo (1988) clarified the status of this subspecies, Griffin (1916) described two specimens and Kempff-Mercado (1975) mentioned it for Bolivia.

Etymology: Named after Dr. Narducci from Milan who lived in the last century in Bolivia and sent snakes to the Milan Museum, including the type specimen of this coral snake.

Leptomicrurus narduccii melanotus (Color 3)
Slender Black Coral Snake: Coral Negra Esbelta; Cobra Coral Preta Esbelta

Elaps melanotus W. C. Peters, 1881:51 (Holotype: ZMB, presumably lost, from Sarayacú, Ecuador.)
Leptomicrurus narduccii melanotus: Roze and Bernal-Carlo, 1988: 592.

Range: Amazonian rain forest and wet forest of Andean foothills in southern Colombia, eastern Ecuador, northern Peru, and northwestern Brazil at altitudes between 150 and 1,300 m.

Description: Males have 261 to 376 (312.7) and females have 301 to 379 (346.0) ventrals; subcaudals 24 to 35 (29.8), usually 28 to 35 in males and 21 to 27 (23.1) in females; 1-1 temporals; genials in contact with the mental. Examined: 30 males and 20 females.

The black snout coloration usually includes part of the supraocular, anterior part of the frontal and part of the fourth supralabial. It is followed by a yellow band that covers 2 or 3 ventrals, sometimes more. The yellow or orangy ventral spots are usually sharply angular and project from the belly upwards, covering 2 or 3 dorsal rows, especially in specimens from eastern Ecuador. On the tail, the red spots are expanded and 1 or 2 are complete dorsally, forming intense-but-narrow red bands on the tail. On the posterior portion of the tail the black is reduced to short bands, 1 or 2 ventrals long.

The males have 37 to 60 (48.4) and the females have 38 to 62 (48.8) light ventral spots. On the tail are 2 to 4 red ventral spots in both sexes, some of which are complete dorsally.

Remarks: Because of loss of yellow and red pigmentation in preserved specimens, the older descriptions of this species are somewhat incorrect. The only description of color of a living specimen is by Duellman (1978). The light bands seem to vary in live specimens from white to golden yellow to reddish. The red tail spots are quite intense.

Food: Snakelike teiid lizards (*Bachia*)

References: Duellman (1978) commented on the variation and coloration of this coral snake, Almendariz mentioned it for Ecuador and Campbell and Lamar (1989) offered a color photo.

Etymology: Greek from *melano* meaning black and *melanotus* meaning the black-colored one, alluding to the predominantly black dorsal coloration of this coral snake.

Leptomicrurus scutiventris (Map 3)
Little Black Coral Snake; Coral Negra Pequeña; Cobra Coral Preta Pequena

| C3 |
| 247 |
| M3 |
| 232 |

Elaps scutiventris Cope, 1870: 156. (Holotype: ANSP 6801, a female from Pebas on the Amazon in Ecuador [= Peru], collected by James Orton.)
Leptomicrurus schmidti Hoge and Romano, 1966: 1. (Holotype: IB 22149, a male from Tapurucuara, Municipio Vaupés, State of Amazonas, Brazil, collected by F. M. Oliveira in June, 1962.)
Micrurus karlschmidti Romano, 1972: 112. (New name for *L. schmidti*)
Leptomicrurus scutiventris: Roze and Bernal-Carlo, 1988: 595.

Distribution and range: Amazonian rain forest, wet low montane forest in Andean valleys and intermediate vegetation altered by humans in southern and southeastern Colombia, northeastern Ecuador, northern Peru, east of the Andes, and northwestern Brazil, from 150 m to 1,200 m above sea level.

Definition: A small black coral snake with an orange or yellowish head band and red ventral spots that sometimes extend over the dorsum forming several narrow bands, and a low number of ventrals: 219 to 274 in both sexes.

Description: Males have 219 to 243 (231.6) and females have 253 to 274 (256.2) ventrals; subcaudals 21 to 27 (24.0) in males and 15 to 20 (18.0) in females; 1-1 temporals; Examined: 12 males and 3 females, including the type of *L. schmidti*.

The snout is black to the level of the eyes and may or may not include the anterior part of the frontal and supraoculars. The orangy-red or light head band covers the rest of the head, except the tip of the parietals and the seventh supralabial, which are black. Below the head is usually all light red including all the genials. Occasionally, some black spots are present on a few infralabials and the mental. The body is usually all black dorsally with red ventral spots. In some small specimens the ventral spots are reduced but complete dorsally, forming narrow body bands. The red ventral spots occupy 2 to 4 ventrals and extend on the first two dorsal rows. When the red spots become complete bands dorsally they cover one scale or less. The black ventral interspaces between the red spots are 4 to 8 ventrals long. On the tail, one or more red bands are always complete; ventrally they are longer than the red body bands.

The males have 26 to 34 (31.2) and the females have 24 to 35 (28.5) red ventral spots. On the tail are 2 to 4 reddish-orange ventral spots or bands.

Size: A very small species. The longest specimen, which is the type specimen, is 445 mm long, but adults are usually less than 400 mm long.

Remarks: This species is similar to and until 1988 was confused with *L. narduccii*, but is considerably smaller and shorter. They live in approximately the same regions even though *L. scutiventris* is found in the Brazilian Amazon where *L. narduccii* has not been found.

Food: Small, burrowing teiid lizards, probably including *Bachia*.

References: Dixon and Soini (1986) discussed its variation and ecology under the name of *M. narduccii*, Silva and Rodriguez (1985) and Silva (1994) described it for Colombia, Almendariz (1991) mentioned it for Ecuador, while Roze and Bernal-Carlo (1988) reviewed its status and variation.

Etymology: Latin from *scuti-* a shield or scale and *venter* meaning belly; *scutiventris*, one with ventral scales, probably alludes to the relatively high number of ventrals in this species. The names *schmidti* and *karlschmidti* are dedications to Karl P. Schmidt, the late curator of herpetology at the Field Museum of Natural History, Chicago.

Genus *MICRUROIDES*
The Western Coral Snakes

Definition of the genus: These are slender and small coral snakes, with a moderate to short tail and head hardly distinguishable from the body. The head shields are similar to those of *Micrurus*, but there is only one pair of small genials. Dorsals in 15-15 rows (except immediately behind the head where there usually are 17 rows) without apical pits. The anal and the subcaudals are divided. This basic coloration is a head that is all black to the tips of the parietals and a body covered by single red-yellow-black bands. Maxilla with fangs and 1 or 2 small, additional teeth.

The hemipenis is deeply bilobed, with sulcus spermaticus bifurcated. The base is up to one third of the length of the organ naked, but the rest is covered with spines that diminish in size toward the apex; the largest spines are around the zone of bifurcation. A small naked fold is at the base of the organ.

Micruroides euryxanthus (Map 4)
Western Coral Snake (Sonoran Coral Snake); Coralillo or Coralilla Occidental

Distribution: Central and southern Arizona and southwestern New Mexico, United States, and western Mexico from northern and western Chihuahua and Sonora, including Isla Tiburón, to Mazatlán, Sinaloa.

Definition: A single-banded coral snake with the entire head black, including parietals, followed by a yellow or white nuchal band. The yellow bands are immaculate. Males lack supraanal tubercles. They have only one pair of genials.

Remarks: The species can be easily recognized by the combination of the black head, immaculate yellow bands, and the presence of only one pair of genials. Three subspecies are recognized.

Size: This is one of the smallest coral snakes. The largest reported specimen was 560 mm long; most adults measure between 300 and 400 mm.

References: Roze (1974) and Campbell and Lamar (1989) reviewed the literature and offered descriptions of the species. General comments and descriptions appeared in Cope (1900), Stejneger (1902), Ruthven (1907), Van Denburg (1922, 1924), Ortenburger and Ortenburger (1927), Schmidt (1928), Schmidt and Davis (1944), Stejneger and Barbour (1943), Lowe (1948, 1955, 1964), Hensley (1950), Stebbins (1954, 1966, 1985), Romer (1956), Wright and Wright (1957), Roze (1967, 1983), Underwood (1967), Fowlie (1967), Nickerson and Mays (1970), Shaw (1971), Hahn and May (1972), Murphy (1983), Murphy and Ottley (1984), Lowe et al. (1986), and Gates (1956, 1957). General behavior and feeding were described by Vorhies (1929), Schmidt (1932a), Gloyd (1937), Woodin (1953), Bogert (1960), Lindner

(1962), Funk (1964), Bellairs (1970), Gehlbach (1972), Vitt and Hulse (1973), Greene (1973a and 1973b), and mimicry was described by Pope (1937), Hecht and Marien (1956), Mertens (1956), Parker (1963), and Greene and McDiarmid (1981). Comments on Mexican coral snakes were given by Mocquard (1908–1909), Cuesta Terrón (1932), Martin del Campo (1935), Bogert and Oliver (1945), H. M. Smith and Taylor (1945, 1966), Cliff (1954), Zweifel and Norris (1955), Duellman (1957), Soule and Sloan (1966), Hardy and McDiarmid (1969), Echternacht (1973), Murphy and Ottley (1984), Webb (1984), and Tanner (1985). Earlier significant references are those by Cope (1861, 1879, 1887, 1892, 1896), Coues (1875), Garman (1884), and Stejneger (1895).

Key to the Species of *M. euryxanthus*

1 42 to 93 red scales on middorsal line of body
    .... *M. e. euryxanthus* (Southern United States and northern Mexico)
1' 93 to 112 red scales on middorsal body 2
2 206 to 207 ventrals and 12 to 13 black body bands in males
    .... *M. e. neglectus* (Mazatlán, Sinaloa, Mexico)
2' 213 or more ventrals and 9 to 11 black body bands in males
    M. e. australis (Southern Sonora and southwestern Chihuahua, Mexico)

Micruroides euryxanthus euryxanthus (Color 4)
Arizona Coral Snake; Coralillo de Arizona

Elaps euryxanthus Kennicott, 1860: 337. (Holotype: USNM 1122, a male from Sonora, Mexico, received from T. Webb.)
Micruroides euryxanthus euryxanthus: Zweifel and Norris, 1955: 246.

Range: Arid and semiarid plateau region of central Arizona, southward and eastward into southwestern New Mexico, United States, and adjacent northwestern Chihuahua and northern Sonora, Mexico, including Isla Tiburón; from sea level to about 2,100 m. One questionable record from El Paso, Texas, United States.

Description: Males have 212 to 230 (222.4) and females have 219 to 245 (231.7) ventrals; subcaudals 23 to 32 (26.5) in males and 19 to 27 (24.1) in females. Examined: 83 males and 61 females, including holotype.
    The black head coloration usually includes all of the parietals, supralabials, and infralabials, but occasionally it is slightly reduced on the parietals. On the chin, the black becomes spotty. The yellow nuchal band is 4 to 8 dorsals long and the other yellow bands are 3 to 5 dorsals long; all are immaculate. The black bands are 4 to 6 dorsals and ventrals long. The number of red dorsal rows counted along the middorsal line on the body ranges between 42 an 93 (69.9) in both sexes. The black tail bands are about two times as long as the yellow bands.
    Males have 9 to 13 (11.4) and females have 9 to 16 (12.6) black body bands. Both sexes usually have 2 black tail bands.

Remarks: This subspecies probably integrates with *M. e. australis* in central Sonora, Mexico.

References: Roze (1974) reviewed the existing literature about this subspecies, and Campbell and Lamar (1989) offered color photos. Most of the other references appear under the name of *M. euryxanthus*.

Food: Predominant food is the western blind snake (*Leptotyphlops humilis*); occasionally it takes the banded sand snake (*Chilomeniscus cinctus*), and probably other snakes and lizards.

Etymology: The Greek name *euryxanthus* is derived from *eury* meaning broad or wide, and *xanthos* meaning yellow, alluding to the presence of the wide yellow bands.

Micruroides euryxanthus australis (Pattern 1)
Sonora Coral Snake; Coralillo de Sonora

Micruroides euryxanthus australis Zweifel and Norris, 1955: 246. (Holotype: MVZ 50839, a male from Guirocoba, Sonora, Mexico, obtained by R. Zweifel and K. Norris on August 10, 1950.)

Range: Tropical dry and desert formations in central and southern Sonora and southwestern Chihuahua, Mexico, from sea level to about 800 m.

Description: Males have 213 to 226 (220.3) and females have 224 to 228 (226.0) ventrals; subcaudals 25 to 31 (27.2) in males and 22 to 26 (23.5) in females. Examined: 8 males and 4 females, including the holotype.
    The head is black, including the parietals. The chin is also all black to the genials. The yellow or white nuchal band is 3 to 5 dorsals long, the others are 2.5 to 4 dorsals and ventrals long and immaculate. The black bands usually are 4 to 5 dorsals long. The red bands are immaculate, 5 to 14 dorsals long; the anterior bands are longer than the posterior. The number of dorsal rows counted along the middorsal line on the body ranges between 93 and 112 (100.6) in both sexes. The black tail bands are two or more times as long as the white bands.
    The males have 9 to 11 (10.2) and the females have

C4
247
P1
264

10 to 12 (11.0) black body bands. Both sexes have 2 black bands on the tail.

Remarks: This subspecies integrates with *M. e. euryxanthus* in central Sonora, Mexico.

References: In describing the subspecies Zweifel and Norris (1955) also commented on variation and distribution, and Campbell and Lamar (1989) featured a color photo.

Food: Probably blind snakes.

Etymology: The Latin name *australis*, meaning southern alludes to its southern distribution with respect to the nominal subspecies, *M. e. euryxanthus*.

Micruroides euryxanthus neglectus (Pattern 2)
Sinaloa Coral Snake; Coralillo de Sinaloa

Micruroides euryxanthus neglectus Roze, 1967: 4. (Holotype: UMMZ 114637, a male from 16.3 miles north-northwest of Mazatlán, Sinaloa, Mexico, collected by W. E. Duellman.)

Range: Tropical semiarid and dry thorn forest around Mazatlán, Sinaloa, Mexico, from sea level to about 200 m.

Description: Males have 206 to 207 (206.5) ventrals and 25 to 26 (25.5) subcaudals. Only two males, including the holotype, are known.
   The head and the chin, including the parietals and the genials, are black but the tips of the parietals can be white. The yellow or white nuchal band is 2 dorsals long; the others are only one half to 2 dorsals and ventrals long, and are immaculate. The black bands are 5 to 7 dorsals and 5 to 6 ventrals long. The red nuchal band is 14 to 17 dorsals long; the rest are shorter. The red bands are unspotted but the red scales have a slightly brownish border. Both males have 106 red dorsal rows on the midline.
   The males have 12 to 13 (12.5) black body bands and 2 to 3 black tail bands.

Remarks: Very little in known about this southernmost subspecies of the genus *Micruroides*.

Food: Unknown, probably snakes.

References: Hardy and McDiarmid (1969) reviewed the distribution of this coral snake, while Webb (1984) investigated its biogeography.

Etymology: The Latin name *neglectus* expresses the status of this subspecies, ignored by science until 1967.

Genus *MICRURUS*
American Coral Snakes

Definition of the genus: Long and slender coral snakes with a moderate to short tail and a head that is hardly distinguishable from the body. The head shields typically consist of 1 rostral, 2 nasals, usually divided, 2 internasals, 2 prefrontals, 2 supraoculars, 1 preocular (the loreal is absent), 2 postoculars (occasionally 1 postoccular), 1 frontal, 2 parietals, 1+1 or 1+2 temporals, and 7 supralabials, third and fourth in contact with the orbit (except *M. surinamensis* that has only one supralabial in contact with the orbit). Below, the head has one mental, 2 pairs of genials separated from the mental by the contact of the first pair of infralabials, and usually 7 infralabials. Dorsals are in 15 to 15 rows (except immediately behind the head where there usually are 17 rows), without apical pits. The anal is divided (except *M. hemprichi* that has an undivided anal plate). The subcaudals are also divided (except in some species where the first several are undivided). The basic color pattern consists of red, black, and yellow or white bands, but several species have only bicolor red-black or red-white body bands or a variation thereof. Only the maxilla bears fangs. The hemipenis is divided and is bilobed or bifurcated with a forked sulcus spermaticus; a naked longitudinal fold extends from the base to near the bifurcation of the organ. In species with bilobed organs, spines cover almost the entire organ while in species with bifurcated organs the base is naked and spines are of various sizes. Species with bifurcated organs also have a terminal spine on the apex of the hemipenis.

Micrurus albicinctus (Map 5, Color 5)
White-banded Coral Snake; Cobra Coral de Cinta Branca

Micrurus albicinctus Amaral, 1926b:26. (Holotype: MNR 376, a male from "northern or central Mato Grosso [Brazil]," collected by Comissão Rondon.)
Micrurus waehnerorum Meise, 1938: 20. (Holotype: originally in Dresden Museum but destroyed in World War II, from São Paulo de Olivença, Amazonas, Brazil.)

Distribution and range: Lowland forest from central Mato Grosso and Rondônia to the middle Amazon, Amazonas, Brazil, 100 to 250 m above sea level.

Definition: An all-black coral snake with white bands represented by a transverse series of white spots over the entire body. Light spots are usually present on the prefrontals and internasals and on some other head shields as well. Males lack supraanal tubercles.

Description: Males have 189 to 205 (197.4) ventrals and females have 210 to 218 (215.8); subcaudals range from 42 to 49 (45.3) in males and 32 to 40 (35.1) in the known females. Examined: 15 males and 5 females, including the holotype.

The head is black above with large white or grayish spots on the prefrontals and/or internasals. Occasionally additional spots are present on the other head scales. The chin region is white but the infralabials are at least partially black. The body is black with a transverse series of small white spots that occupy one dorsal separating the black bands. This coloration is apparently derived from the original coloration of alternating black and red bands. The venter is black with short white crossbands one ventral long or a similar transverse series of white spots. The white bands are longer on the tail and occupy about 2 dorsals and 2 ventrals.

The males have 67 to 90 (72.4) and the females have 77 to 91 (82.5) black body bands. On the tail, the males have 10 to 13 (11.4) and the females have 6 to 9 (7.6) black bands.

Size: This is a small species. Most adults range between 400 and 500 mm in total length; the largest specimen measured only 573 mm.

Remarks: This was a poorly-known black and white coral snake from Amazonian Brazil until several specimens were collected by Nelson da Silva and collaborators from the Universidade Católica Goiás in 1989 in an animal rescue operation at the Samuel hydroelectric power plant in Rondônia, Brazil.

References: In addition to the original descriptions, Amaral (1930a, 1930b, 1937a, 1948b, 1978), Roze (1967, 1970b, 1983) and Roze and Nelson da Silva (1990) gave additional comments, and Cunha and Nascimento (1982b and 1991) proposed to synonymize it with *M. ornatissimus*.

Etymology: Latin *albicinctus* comes from *alba* meaning white and *cinctus* meaning banded or girdled; thus, the white-banded one. The name *waehnerorum* is dedicated to Mr. and Mrs. Wahner, a German couple who collected snakes in the Amazon region and presented them to the Dresden Museum in Germany. Unfortunately, all of these specimens were destroyed during an air raid shortly before the end of World War II.

Micrurus alleni (Map 6, Color 6)
Arrow-headed Coral Snake (Allen's Coral Snake); Coral Cabeza Flecha

Micrurus nigrocinctus alleni Schmidt, 1936b: 209. (Holotype: UMMZ 79794, a female from Río Mico, 7 miles above Rama, Siquía District, Nicaragua, collected by M. J. Allen.)

Micrurus nigrocinctus yatesi Dunn, 1942: 8. (Holotype: ANSP 22564, from Farm Two, Chiriquí Land Co., near Puerto Armuelles, Chiriquí, Panama.)

Micrurus alleni richardi Taylor, 1951: 172. (Holotype: KU 25189, a female from Los Diamantes, 2 km south of Guapiles, Costa Rica.)

Micrurus alleni: Savage and Vial, 1974: 295.

Distribution and range: Tropical lowland rainforest and humid low montane forest of eastern Nicaragua, Honduras, and the Atlantic and Pacific side of Costa Rica and western Panama (probably to Darién), from sea level to 1,400 m altitude.

Definition: A single-banded coral snake with black, red, and yellow or white bands. The red dorsals have conspicuous black tips that tend to increase in intensity in larger individuals, at least partly obliterating the red coloration. The black snout coloration extends back along the suture between the parietals, producing a part-black cap pattern. The black nuchal band does not reach the tips of the parietals. On the tail, the yellow or white bands have large and irregular black scale tips or spots. Males have supraanal tubercles.

Description: Males have 211 to 224 (215.2) ventrals and females have 222 to 240 (231.7); subcaudals 48 to 60 (53.3) in males and 32 to 43 (38.4) in females. Occasional specimens have a few undivided subcaudals. Examination was made of 47 males and 31 females, including all holotypes.

The black snout color covers the supraoculars and frontal and projects back onto the parietals along the interparietal suture. The projection may extend to the posterior end of the suture, or it may be represented by one or more spots between the parietals, forming a partly black pattern. Some larger specimens (as for example one from the Volcán Chiriquí area of Panama) have the whole upper part of the head covered by a melanistic suffusion in which, however, the black interparietal projection still can be discerned. Occasionally, the snout has some lighter grayish spots. Below, the head is yellow or white with the mental and the first infralabials partly or entirely black and with occasional black spots on the genials. The black nuchal band is 5 to 8 dorsals long and starts about 1 dorsal behind the tips of the parietals. Ventrally, it does not cover the tips of the second pair of genials. The black body bands are 3 to 5 dorsals and 2 to 4 ventrals long. All the red scales have conspicuous black tips that frequently occupy one half or more of each scale. There is a general melanistic tendency in this species that increases with the size of the individual. In the specimens from the Pacific lowlands of southeastern Costa Rica and adjacent Panama, as well as from the drier low montane forests of Boquete and Volcán Chiriquí, the black coloration almost completely obliterates the red bands. Ventrally, the red bands may have irregular black spots or tips. The population from the Atlantic side has predominantly white bands while the Pacific population has yellow bands that are particularly intense in individuals from the southeastern part of Costa Rica and Panama. Surprisingly, individuals from the Bocas del Toro lowlands in eastern Panama have yellow bands. The yellow or white bands are one half to 2 dorsals and one half to 1.5 ventrals long. Some adults have black or at least darker tips on the white scales. On the tail, the black bands are 4 to 5 times longer than the light bands. The latter usually have irregular black spots or tips.

There are 14 to 24 (19.1) black body bands in males, and 15 to 26 (21.4) in females. The males have 5 to 9 (7.7) and the females have 4 to 6 (5.2) black tail bands.

Size: This a medium-large species. The longest specimen has an overall length of 1165 mm, but most adults measure between 500 and 700 mm.

Remarks: This species appears to be represented by two (possibly separate) populations, one on the Atlantic side and the other on the Pacific side of southern Central America. The population on the Pacific side is much darker overall than that on the Atlantic side. It is possible that these populations represent a distinct subspecies.

Food: The predominant food is the swamp eel (*Synbranchus marmoratus*) but lizards are also taken.

References: A complete description with a color photo and distribution of the species appeared in Campbell and Lamar (1989); general notes in Roze (1967, 1970b, 1983), Bolaños (1983, 1984), and Villa (1984). Several authors have reported on this species including for Costa Rica: E. H. Taylor (1951, 1954), Scott (1969), Savage and Vial (1974), Savage (1976, 1980); for Nicaragua: Gaige et al (1937), Villa (1983, 1984), and Villa et al (1988); for Panama: Dunn (1942), Grocott and Saddler (1958) and a report from Honduras by McCranie (1993). Gutiérrez and Bolaños (1979) and Gutiérrez et al (1988) described its chromosomes, R. T. Taylor et al (1974) its distribution, and Greene and McDiarmid (1981) commented on its mimicry.

Etymology: Named after Morrow J. Allen who collected the holotype as well as many other herpetological specimens in eastern Nicaragua. The name *richardi* was dedicated to Richard C. Taylor, brother of Edward Taylor, who helped to collect specimens in Costa Rica. The name *yatesi* is dedicated to Thomas Yates who obtained and sent specimens from Panama to the Academy of Natural Sciences of Philadelphia.

Micrurus ancoralis (Map 7)
Anchor Coral Snake (Regal Coral Snake); Coral Ancla

Distribution: From Darién, Panama, along the Pacific lowlands and western slopes of the Andes in Colombia to southwestern Ecuador.

Definition: A triad-type coral snake with a characteristic anchor-shaped black marking formed by the black nuchal band projecting onto the parietals and the angular forward projection of the central black band of the first triad. The first triad is complete and the triads are found on both the body and the tail. The head is red with a few black markings.

Size: This is one of the largest coral snakes. The longest measured specimen is 1486 mm long; many adults measure 900 mm or more.

Remarks: The anchor-shaped neck mark is unique among coral snakes and makes this species easily distinguishable. Two subspecies are recognized that intergrade in southwestern Colombia in the upper Saija River drainage, Cauca.

References: Schmidt (1936a) and Campbell and Lamar (1989) reviewed the variation and distribution of this subspecies. Other references include Roze (1967, 1970b, 1983); for Colombia: Amaral (1925a, 1927c, 1931b), Nicéforo-María (1942), Dunn (1944a), Daniel (1949), Medem (1969), Castro et al (1982), Angel (1983), and Pérez-Santos and Moreno (1986, 1988); for Ecuador: Amaral (1925a), Orcés (1943, 1948), J. A. Peters (1955, 1960), and Miyata (1982); for Panama: Dunn (1942), Grocott and Saddler (1958). Tiedemann and Haupl (1980) commented on one type specimen.

Key to the subspecies of *M. ancoralis*

1. Black body triads 16 to 20 in males and 17 to 21 in females; red bands about as long as the black bands .... *M. a. ancoralis* (Western Ecuador)
1'. Black body triads 12 to 17 in males and 14 to 16 in females; red bands at least twice as long as the black bands
..... *M. ancoralis jani* (Eastern Panama and western Colombia)

Micrurus ancoralis ancoralis (Pattern 3)
Ecuadorian Anchor Coral Snake; Coral Ancla Ecuadoriana

Elaps marcgravii var. *ancoralis* Jan, 1872. (Holotype: ZSBS 210/0, a male from Ecuador, collected by M. Wagner.)

Elaps rosenbergi Boulenger, 1898b: 117. (Holotype: BM 1946.1.23.74, a female from Paramba, Ecuador, collected by W. F. H. Rosenberg.)
Micrurus ancoralis ancoralis: Schmidt, 1936a: 197.

Range: Tropical rain forest and low mountain wet forest of the Pacific lowlands and western slopes of the Andes in northwestern and western Ecuador extending southward to Bahia de Caraquez from sea level to about 1,000 m. Earlier records from Canelos and Sarayacú in Pastaza, Ecuador, require confirmation.

Description: Males have 242 to 255 (250.7) and females have 266 to 284 (271) ventrals; subcaudals 31 to 37 (34.0) in males, 28 to 35 (30.5) in females. Very exceptionally the mental is in contact with the first pair of genials. Examined: 17 males and 20 females, including holotypes.

The upper part of the head is all red to the parietals. Some specimens have black spots or faint lines on the crown shields. Below, the head is almost invariably light red from the chin to beyond the second pair of genials. The sinuous, anchor-shaped anterior projection frequently covers more than half the parietals. The outer black bands of a triad are as long as or slightly longer than the central black band: 4 to 6 dorsals long on the anterior part of the body and about 4 on the posterior part of the body on the vertebral line. Ventrally, the outer black bands of a triad are 3 to 4 ventrals long anteriorly and 2 to 3 posteriorly. The white bands are usually one dorsal and 2 ventrals long, with occasional black tips on the dorsal scales. The red bands are equal to the black bands dorsally, occupying about 3 to 4 dorsals on the vertebral line. They become gradually longer laterally and ventrally, where they occupy 4 to 5 scales, occasionally even more. The red dorsal scales have conspicuous black tips. On the tail, the triads are clearly marked and the red bands are longer than the preceding first band of the triad. The black bands of the tail are somewhat irregular, occasionally broken, or occupying only half scale.

The males have 16 to 20 (17.5) and the females have 16 to 21 (19.4) black triads on the body. There are 1 to 1⅔ triads on the tail, regardless of sex.

Food: Probably snakes.

References: Orcés (1943, 1948), J. A. Peters (1955, 1960), Miyata (1982), and Almendariz (1991) gave its distribution in Ecuador, and Campbell and Lamar (1989) gave a color photo.

Etymology: From Latin *ancora*, an anchor. Actually *ancorale* means a cable belonging to an anchor and it refers to the anchor-shaped black nuchal band of this subspecies. The name *rosenbergi* is dedicated to an avid collector of amphibians and reptiles, W. F. H. Rosenberg in South America, who sent many specimens to the British Museum (Natural History) and also collected the type specimen.

Micrurus ancoralis jani (Color 7)
Choco Anchor Coral Snake; Coral Ancla Chocoana

Micrurus ancoralis jani Schmidt, 1936a: 197. (Holotype: MCZ 32722, a male from Andagoya, Chocó, Colombia, collected by H. G. F. Spurrell.)

Range: Tropical rain forest and humid low montane forest from Darién, Panama, to the Pacific lowlands of the Chocó region and the western slopes of the Andes of Colombia, from near sea level to about 1000 m or higher.

Description: Males have 244 to 262 (252.3) and females have 267 to 286 (274.5) ventrals; subcaudals 32 to 37 (35.5) in males and 30 to 35 (32.5) in females. Examined: 18 males and 14 females, including the holotype.

The upper and lower part of the head are red but some head scales may have black spots. The sinuous border of the anchor-shaped nuchal black marking covers at least half of the parietals in nearly all specimens. The red color below includes the second pair of genials. The central black band of the triad is as long as or slightly longer than the outer ones. The black bands are 3 or 4 dorsals long, but are reduced to 1 or 2 (occasionally 3) ventrals below. The white bands are 1 or 2 dorsals long with very large black areas that occupy up to three quarters of the white scales. Ventrally the white bands are as long as or longer than the black bands, occupying 1 to 3 ventrals. The red bands have black tips that occupy up to more than half the scale in some specimens. The first two rows of dorsals usually lack black tips.

The males have 12 to 17 (14.5) and the females have 14 to 16 (15.4) black triads on the body. There are 1 to 1⅓ black triads on the tail in both sexes.

Food: Known to feed on the small black colubrid snake, *Ninia atrata*.

References: Amaral (1927c, 1931b), Dunn (1944a), Nicéforo-María (1942), Daniel (1949), Schmidt (1955), Medem (1969), Castro et al (1982), Angel (1983), and Pérez-Santos and Moreno (1988) described its variation and distribution in Colombia; Grocott and Saddler (1958) described it in Panama; and Campbell and Laar (1989) featured a color photo.

Etymology: Named after the last-century Italian herpetologist, Giorgio Jan, because, as mentioned by Schmidt in the original description, "[his] early descriptions of species in this genus were more sound than those of subsequent writers."

Micrurus annellatus (Map 8)

Annellated Coral Snake: Coral Anillada; Cobra Coral Anelada

Distribution: Eastern slopes of the Andes and the upper Amazon of Ecuador, Peru, and Bolivia; questionable records from western Brazil.

Definition: A single-banded coral snake with a black snout and a white parietal crossband that may be long or short. Red bands have heavy black tips or red completely obliterated by black, resulting in a black-and-white coloration. Males do not have supraanal tubercles.

Size: This is a moderately small coral snake. The longest measured specimen is 728 mm. Many adults measure between 450 and 600 mm in total length.

Remarks: Three subspecies are recognized. *M. a. annellatus* and *M. a. balzani* intergrade around San Carlos in the eastern lowlands of Beni, Bolivia.

References: Schmidt (1954) revised this species and Campbell and Lamar (1989) gave a complete description, while Roze (1967, 1970b, 1983) reinterpreted it. Other mentions of the species include Amaral (1931b). Schmidt and Walker (1943a), Meneses (1974a), and Carrillo de Espinosa (1983) mentioned it for Peru; J. A. Peters (1960), Soini (1974b), Duellman (1979b), and Miyata (1982) mentioned it for Ecuador; and Hoge and Romano (1969) questioned it as probably from Brazil.

Key to the Subspecies of *M. annellatus*

1 Nearly always only one postocular; red bands clearly distinguishable
 .... *M. a. balzani* (north-central Bolivia)
1' Two postoculars; red bands distinguishable or not 2
2 Parietal white band two thirds or less of its length; black and white bands or black, white, and red bands on the body
 ... *M. a. annellatus* (eastern Ecuador, eastern and southern Peru, northern Bolivia)
2' Almost entire parietal white; black, white, and red body color
 .... *M. a. bolivianus* (Central Bolivia)

Micrurus annellatus annellatus (Pattern 4)

Common Annellated Coral Snake; Coral Anillada Común

Elaps annellatus W. C. Peters, 1871: 402 (Holotype: ZMB 7185, a female from Pozuzo, Peru, collected by R. Abendroth.)

Micrurus annellatus montanus Schmidt, 1954: 322. (Holotype: FMNH 40221, a male from Camp 4, about 10 km north of Santo Domingo Mine, Puno, Peru, 2,000 m, collected by Colin Campbell Sanborn on November 2, 1941.)

Micrurus annellatus annellatus: Schmidt, 1954: 322.

Range: Low montane rain forest and high montane humid forest of the upper Amazon in Ecuador, Peru, and Bolivia, and the eastern slopes of the Andes in central and southeastern Peru, between 600 to 2000 m above sea level. One questionable record from Leticia, Colombia (Pérez-Santos and Moreno, 1988).

Description: Males have 189 to 201 (194.3) and females have 203 to 216 (210.3) ventrals; subcaudals 40 to 47 (43.4) in males and 29 to 35 (32.1) in females; 2 postoculars; usually 1+1 temporals. Examined: 31 males and 19 females, including the holotype.

The snout is black and the parietal white band is short, covering one eighth to two thirds of the parietals; it never extends onto the tips of these scales. Laterally, the white band covers the temporals and 2 to 3 supralabials. The head is black below, including one or both pairs of genials and the fourth infralabial. The black nuchal band covers the posterior part of the parietals and 4 or 5 dorsals. In about 70% of the specimens the red bands have been completely obliterated by black. At least dorsally, this produces a color pattern of longer and shorter black dorsal bands. These are separated by white bands about 1 dorsal and 1 or 2 ventrals long. The original black bands are 3 or 4 dorsals long and the original red bands (black or not) are 3 to 5 dorsals long. Black and white bands of the same size as those of the body are found on the tail.

To count the number of black bands and give their variation is complicated by the fact that the red bands can be red or black. Counting the original black bands, the males have 17 to 31 (24.7) and the females have 18 to 33 (25.6) black body bands. Counting all the black bands (in black-and-white specimens) or black and red bands together (in black-white-red specimens), the males have 34 to 61 (49.9) and the females have 36 to 75 (56.6) black body bands. The males have 7 to 9 (8.1) and the females have 5 to 9 (6.7) black tail bands.

Remarks: Presence of the black-white-red and black-white color forms makes this subspecies quite difficult to define. In several areas both color variations coexist, as in Marcapata Valley, Peru.

Food: Small, secretive, limbless lizards (*Bachia*).

References: Schmidt (1954) described its variation and distribution, Carrillo de Espinoza (1983) included notes on food, Almendariz (1991) mentioned it for Ecuador, and Campbell and Lamar (1989) offered a color photo.

Etymology: Latin *annellatus* comes from *anellus* meaning little ring, thus covered with little rings, alluding to many short bands on the body of this coral snake. *Montanus* is Latin for inhabitant of mountains, alluding to its distribution in the Andean mountains.

Micrurus annellatus balzani (Color 8)
Yungas Coral Snake; Coral de Yungas

Elaps balzani Boulenger, 1898b: 130. (Holotype: presumably lost in the Genoa Museum, a male from Yungas, Bolivia, 1600 m, collected by M. L. Balzan.)
Elaps regularis Boulenger, 1902c: 402. (Holotype: BM 1946.1.17.22, a female from Chulumani, Bolivia, collected by E. O. Simmons in 1901.)
Micrurus annellatus balzani: Roze, 1967: 6.

Range: In humid and dry formations 500 and 2000 m above sea level in the eastern Andes in western Bolivia and upper Amazon humid valleys in northern Bolivia. It probably also extends into adjacent Peru.

Description: Males have 186 to 197 (190.8) and females have 204 to 213 (207.7) ventrals; subcaudals are 38 to 45 (40.6) in males and 26 to 31 (28.1) in females. Usually there is only one postocular; the third, fourth and fifth supralabials are in contact with the orbit at least on one side; 1+1 temporals. Examined: 7 males and 7 females, including one holotype.

The black snout coloration extends over the entire frontal and the anterior border of the parietals. The remainder of the parietals are white and so are the temporals and the last supralabials. The chin is white with some black spots on the mental and on several infralabials, and sometimes on the genials. The nuchal black band is 3 to 5 dorsals long. It reaches but does not cover the tips of the parietals. Below, it projects forward onto the second pair of genials. The body is covered by black-red-and-white or only black-red bands. Depending on their number, the black bands may be either longer or shorter than the red bands. The black bands are 3 to 6 dorsals long, whereas the red bands are 3 to 8 dorsals long and are about the same length ventrally. About half of the individuals have black ventral spots on the red bands. The white bands are about one half of a dorsal long and are barely distinguishable in preserved specimens. The black bands on the tail are about twice as long as the white bands.

The males have 21 to 28 (25.2) and the females have 24 to 34 (29.1) black body bands. The males have 6 to 8 (6.9) and the females have 3 to 5 (4.4) black bands on the tail.

Remarks: Easily recognizable by the presence of only one postocular. This is a little-known, high-altitude coral snake.

Food: Blind snakes (*Leptotyphlops melanotermus*).

References: Roze (1967) reinterpreted this subspecies and Campbell and Lamar (1989) illustrated it.

Etymology: Named after professor L. Balzan who collected extensively in Bolivia and sent the specimens to the Genoa Museum in Italy. Latin *regularis* comes from *regula*, a rule or pattern, denoting the fact that in this coral snake presence of only one postocular is the rule of the regular pattern of scutellation.

Micrurus annellatus bolivianus (Pattern 5)
Bolivian Coral Snake; Coral Boliviana

Micrurus annellatus bolivianus Roze, 1967: 7. (Holotype: ZMH 2706e, a female from Charobamba River, about 50 km northeast of Zudañez, Chuquisaca, Bolivia.)

Range: Medium to high montane humid or dry forests of the eastern Andes and high Amazonian valleys in central Bolivia, between 1,200 and 2,200 m altitude.

Description: No males are known; females have 209 to 215 (211.6) ventrals and 26 to 31 (29.0) subcaudals; 2 postoculars; usually 1+2 temporals. Examined: 3 females including the holotype.

The black snout coloration covers the anterior part of the parietals and may include the tip of the frontal. In some specimens the black projects backward along the suture between the parietals. Below, the head is white except for the mental and the upper part of the first three infralabials. There are small black spots on some other shields. The black nuchal band extends over the tips of the parietals and 5 or 6 dorsals. Below, it covers 4 to 6 ventrals and the tips of the second pair of genials. The black body bands are 3 to 4 dorsals in length and usually 2 ventrals long. Some of them may be interrupted ventrally. The red bands are 7 to 10 dorsals and ventrals long. The red scales have conspicuous black or dark brown tips dorsally and irregular black mottling or large spots ventrally. The white bands are barely distinguishable. The black bands are two to four times longer than the white bands; the scales of the latter have conspicuous black tips.

The females have 20 to 25 (22.0) black bands on the body and 5 on the tail.

Remarks: This race is poorly known.

Food: Unknown.

References: Only the original description and a brief mention in Campbell and Lamar (1989).

Etymology: Named to denote its distribution in Bolivia.

Micrurus averyi (Map 3, Color 9)
Black-headed Coral Snake; Coral Cabeza Negra; Cobra Coral Cabeça Preta

Micrurus averyi Schmidt, 1939: 45. (Holotype: FMNH 30956, a female from the head of Itabu Creek, "Boundary Camp," Courantyne District, near the Brazilian border at Latitude 1 40' N and Longitude 58 W (Guyana), collected by Emmett R. Blake on September 22, 1938.)

Distribution and range: Lowland and low montane, nonflooded rain forest in the central Amazon, from southern Guyana to Manaus, Amazonas, Brazil; probably also in Suriname; 100 to 700 m above sea level.

Definition: A single-banded coral snake with the head all black except for a light area on the third and fourth supralabials and temporals, and without a black nuchal band; the red band starts immediately behind the parietals. There are no supraanal tubercles in males.

Descriptions: The males have 190 to 198 (193.8) and females have 207 to 220 (212.0) ventrals; subcaudals 45 to 48 (46.7) in males and 29 to 34 (32.0) in females; 1+1 or 1+2 temporals. Examined 2 males and 3 females, including the holotype.

The head is black above and below except for light spots that cover several supralabials and temporals. A red spot is present on the genials. The black bands are usually 2 dorsals (sometimes one) and 2 ventrals long, occasionally reduced or interrupted on the first dorsal. The red bands occupy 12 to 28 dorsals and ventrals, without any black tips or slightly darkened borders. The white bands are frequently reduced to a length of one half a dorsal, so that they form an interrupted series of spots around the black bands. The black tail bands are subequal to the red bands that are obscured by heavy black spotting on each scale. The white tail bands are barely one scale long.

The males have 8 to 10 (9.3) and the females have 11 to 13 (11.4) black body bands. The males have 7 and the females have 4 to 5 (4.7) black tail bands.

Size: This is a medium-sized species. The longest specimen measures 715 mm in total length.

Remarks: The unique all-black head coloration and the absence of the black nuchal band, combined with the long, brilliant red bands without black scale tips are unique among South American coral snakes.

Food: Unknown.

References: Vanzolini (1985) reviewed the variation and distribution of this species, and Campbell and Lamar (1989) described it and offered a color photograph. Other mentions include Roze (1967, 1970b, 1983); Hoge and Romano (1981) and Zimmerman and Rodrigues (1990) mention it for Brazil; and Brongersma (1967) and Abuys (1987a, 1987b) for Suriname.

Etymology: Named after Sewell Avery, a trustee of the Field Museum of Natural History, Chicago.

Micrurus bernadi (Map 9, Pattern 7)
Saddled Coral Snake (Blotched Coral Snake); Coralillo Ensillado

Elaps bernadi Cope, 1887:87. (Holotype: ANSP 14767, a female from Zacualtipan, Hidalgo, Mexico, collected by Santiago Bernad.)
Micrurus bernadi: Schmidt, 1933: 40.

Distribution and range: Northern Veracruz, eastern Hidalgo, and northern Puebla, Mexico, in low humid montane and cloud montane forests from 50 to almost 2,000 m of altitude.

Definition: A red coral snake in which the single black bands are reduced to dorsal spots that usually do not form black bands. The head is black with a white parietal spot or a short white band that is usually interrupted ventrally, where most or all of the scales are black. Males have no supraanal tubercles.

Description: Males have 198 to 212 (205.0) and females 212 to 225 (219.7) ventrals; subcaudals are about 48 in males and 34 to 39 (36.39) in females; 1+1, occasionally 1+2, temporals. Examined: 2 males and 4 females, including the holotype.

The head is black except for a yellow or white parietal spot or a narrow band. Ventrally, the black extends onto the first ventrals, with occasional white spots on some shields. Both dorsally and ventrally the black nuchal band is fused with the black head coloration. The black dorsal spots or saddlelike bands on the red background color are usually 2 dorsals long. Rarely, a few bands may be complete ventrally but these are interrupted dorsally. The red spaces between the black spots are longer than the spots; they are immaculate or have a few irregularly-placed black tips. Ventrally, the red scales are immaculate or have small black dots. Usually there are no yellow bands around the black spots, but rarely there may be an inconspicuous yellow border. On the tail, the black bands may be complete or incomplete ventrally; they are longer than the yellow bands.

The males have 25 to 44 (34.5) and the females have 27 to 41 (33.0) black body spots. The males have 6 to 12 (9.0) and the females have 6 to 8 (6.5) black tail bands.

Size: This is a medium-sized species. The longest measured specimen is 826 mm in total length, with a tail length of 85 mm.

Remarks: The combination of the black dorsal spots or saddles and the mainly black head (at least on the lower part) makes this species distinctive.

Pérez-Higareda and Smith (1990) suggested that this species is subspecifically related to *M. diastema*. The main distinction between both are the black dorsal spots or incomplete bands in *M. bernadi*, a condition that occasionally appears in some other subspecies of *M. diastema* (cf, *M. d. alienus*). The authors might well be correct, but since so few specimens are known from this species, a decision must be postponed until its variation and distribution are better known.

Food: *Pliocercus elapoides*, which is a mimic or false coral snake. One preserved specimen had a knot of hair in its stomach. This was probably the remains of a meal of one of the snakes that *M. bernadi* had preyed upon.

References: Schmidt (1933a, 1958), reviewed the status of this unusual species and Campbell and Lamar (1989) offered a description and distribution; Greene and McDiarmid (1981) discussed its mimicry role. Mentions for Mexico include Martín del Campo (1935, 1950), H. M. Smith (1941), H. M. Smith and Taylor (1945), Neill (1963), and Roze (1967, 1983). An earlier reference is by Ferrari-Pérez (1886).

Etymology: Named after Santiago Bernad, collector of the holotype.

Micrurus bocourti (Map 5, Color 10)
False Triad Coral Snake (Ecuadorian Coral Snake)
Coral de Tríadas Falsas

Elaps bocourti Jan, 1872: pl. 6, Fig 2. (Holotype: MNHN 869, a male from an unknown locality, collected by Liataud in 1843. Type locality restricted to Río Daule, Guayas Province, Ecuador, by Roze, 1967.)
Micrurus ecuadorianus Schmidt, 1936a: 196. (Holotype: MCZ 3559, a male from Río Daule, western Ecuador.)
Micrurus bocourti: Roze, 1983: 316.

Distribution and range: Humid to dry lowland formations and dry western slopes of the Andes in southwestern Ecuador and northwestern Peru; from near sea level to about 1,500 m.

Definition: A coral snake with accessory black bands forming triads and with the first triad consisting of only two bands. A black cap is present on the top of the head. The red bands have both small and large black tips or spots. Males are without supraanal tubercles.

Description: Males have 197 to 206 (201.6) and females have 212 to 220 (215.9) ventrals; subcaudals 43 to 50 (46.2) in males and 32 to 35 (34.1) in females; usually 1+1, occasionally 1+2, temporals. Examined: 21 males and 19 females, including all holotypes.

The black cap is separated from the black nuchal band by an irregular white band. Occasionally, white spots are found on the parietal tips and the first dorsals. The last supralabials and temporals are white. Below, the mental and the first infralabials are partially or completely black. The rest of the head is white, but black tips may be present on some chin scales. In some specimens the chin is almost completely white. The nuchal black band is one of the original black bands, behind which an accessory band is formed so that the first triad consists of only 2 black bands. The other black triads consist of a central band, 3 to 5 dorsals long, and irregular outer bands 1 to 2 (sometimes 3) dorsals long. Ventrally, the bands of the triads are irregular, interrupted, or 1 ventral long. The red bands have irregular black tips or large black spots that are concentrated around the periphery to produce the accessory black bands. The red bands are 5 to 13 dorsals and ventrals long. Ventrally they have both large and small black smudges or spots. The white bands within a triad are 1 or 2 dorsals and ventrals long with small, poorly-defined black tips. There are black and white bands on the tail. The white bands have a large, irregular spot in the middle.

The males have ⅔ 14 to ⅔ 20 (15.8) and the females have ⅔ 15 to ⅔ 21 (17.9) black accessory triads on the body. On the tail, the males have 5 to 8 (6.8) and the females have 4 to 6 (5.1) black tail bands.

Size: This is a medium-sized species; the longest measured specimen is 820 mm, but many adults range between 450 and 700 mm in total length.

Food: Caecilians (limbless amphibians).

References: H. W. Parker (1938) and Campbell and Lamar (1989) discussed its variation and distribution, while Roze (1967, 1970b, 1983) summarized its status. Other references for Ecuador are by Almendariz (1991) and (as *M. ecuadorianus*) by Schmidt (1936a), Orcés (1943, 1948), J. A. Peters (1955, 1960), and Miyata (1982). Roux-Estève (1983) and Roze (1989) commented on the type specimens.

Etymology: Named after Marie-Fermin Bocourt, one of the remarkable 19th century French herpetologists. The name *ecuadorianus* indicates its distribution in Ecuador.

Micrurus bogerti (Map 9, Pattern 6)
Coastal Coral Snake (Bogert's Coral Snake); Coralillo Costanero

Micrurus bogerti Roze, 1967: 9. (Holotype: AMNH 96952, a male from Tangola-Tangola (Tangolunda), east of Puerto Angel, Oaxaca, Mexico, obtained by W. Beebe in 1937.)

Distribution and range: Dry coastal thorn and scrub formations and tropical deciduous forest between Puerto Angel and Tapanatepec on the Pacific side of Oaxaca, Mexico, from sea level to 400 m.

Definition: A single-banded coral snake with a black snout and a yellow parietal band that is followed by a black nuchal band that covers the tips of the parietals. It has 16 to 19 black body bands separated by red bands; the red bands are without (or with very few) black-tipped scales. Males are without supraanal tubercules.

Description: Males have 214 to 215 (214.5) and females have 224 to 230 (228.0) ventrals; subcaudals 52 to 56 (54.0) in males and 38 to 43 (41.0) in females; the first subcaudals frequently are undivided. Examined: 2 males and 3 females, including the holotype.

The snout and the anterior margin of the parietals are all black. The mental and the first three infralabials are black; the remainder of the chin region is yellow, with some black spots on the genials. The black nuchal band covers the parietal tips and 6 to 7 dorsals. The black bands on the body and 3 to 4 dorsals and usually 3 ventrals long. On the first dorsal row many black bands are reduced to a length of 2 to 2.5 scales. The yellow or white bands are 1 to 2 scales long anteriorly, and 1 scale long on the posterior part of the body. The red bands are 6 to 8 dorsals long, while the first red band is about 10 to 15 dorsals long. The red scales are immaculate or have a few black spots. The black tail bands are more than twice as long as the light bands that separate them.

The males have 16 to 19 (17.1) and the females have 13 to 18 (15.2) black body bands. The males have 5 to 6 (5.3) and females have 3 to 4 (3.5) black tail bands.

Size: This is a medium-sized species; the longest specimen measures 770 mm in total length; most adults range between 380 to 600 mm in total length.

Food: Unknown.

References: Campbell and Lamar (1989) reviewed the species; other records include Roze (1983), Johnson (1984), and Villa et al (1988).

Etymology: Named after Charles M. Bogert, curator emeritus of herpetology of the American Museum of Natural History, New York, who as the original description indicates, "has a remarkable understanding of and appreciation for the local conditions" of the region of Oaxaca.

Micrurus browni (Map 10)
Sierra Madre Coral Snake (Brown's Coral Snake); Coralilla de Sierra Madre

Distribution: From the Mexican plateau, at Mexico City and the state of Mexico southward to the Pacific coast from Acapulco, Guerrero, Oaxaca, and Chiapas, Mexico, to the western mountains of Guatemala.

Definition: A single-banded coral snake with white or yellow bands bordering the black bands. The snout, including the eyes, is black, followed by a black parietal band. The mental and the first infralabials are black. The black nuchal band covers the tips of the parietals. The red dorsal scales may or may not have black tips. The tail has black and white or yellow bands only; the black bands are wider than the white ones. Males usually have supraanal tubercles, but these may be reduced or absent. There are 1+1 or 1+2 temporals.

Size: This is a medium-sized coral snake; the overall length of the largest specimens 830 mm. Many adults measure between 450 and 700 mm.

Remarks: Three subspecies are recognized.

References: Roze (1967, 1970b, 1983) recognized and defined the subspecies and Campbell and Lamar (1989) gave description and distribution. Its variation and distribution in Guatemala is given by Campbell and Vannini (1989), and in Mexico by Taylor (1940), H. M. Smith and Taylor (1945, 1966); H. M. Smith (1947), Martin del Campo (1950), Davis and Dixon (1959), Lynch and Smith (1966), Alvarez del Toro (1972 and 1983), Johnson (1984), Blaney and Blaney (1978), Muñoz Alonso (1988), and Villa et al (1988) and McCranie and Wilson (1991). Guitiérrez et al (1988) described karyotypes.

Key to the Subspecies of *M. browni*

1 Males have 10 to 14 and females have 11 to 17 black body bands
 .... *M. b. taylori* (Acapulco region, Mexico)
1' More than 15 black bands in males and 17 or more in females 2

2 Females have 224 ventrals, 35 subcaudals, and 27 black bands; males have 53 to 59 subcaudals and 19 to 20 black body bands
.... *M. b. importunus* (Dueñas area, southern Guatemala)

2' Females have 224 to 230 ventrals, 36 to 45 subcaudals, and 17 to 29 black body bands; males 46 to 53 subcaudals and 14 to 26 black body bands
... *M. b. browni* (Mexico and Guerrero to Chiapas, Mexico, and western Guatemala)

Micrurus browni browni (Pattern 9)
Common Sierra Madre Coral Snake; Coralillo Común de Sierra Madre

Micrurus browni Schmidt and Smith, 1943a: 29. (Holotype: FMNH No. 38494, a male from Chilpancingo, Guerrero, Mexico, collected by W. W. Brown.)
Micrurus browni browni: Roze, 1967: 11.

Range: Subhumid to dry high and intermediate montane formations, including oak-pine and dry scrub assemblages on the Mexican Plateau from Mexico City, the state of Mexico, and central Guerrero eastward on the Pacific side of Sierra Madre del Sur to Oaxaca and Chiapas, Mexico, and the western mountains of Guatemala; from 500 to over 2,000 m in altitude.

Description: Males have 204 to 218 (209.2) and females 224 to 230 (226.7) ventrals; subcaudals 46 to 52 (48.5) in males, 36 to 45 (39.1) in females. Examined: 36 males and 24 females, including the holotype.

The black snout coloration extends over the supraoculars and usually forms a nearly straight posterior border that extends over the anterior part of the parietals and the frontal. Occasionally, the tip of the frontal is white. The mental and the first 2 to 4 infralabials are black. The nuchal black band covers the sixth and the seventh infralabials and the first few ventrals. The black body bands are 3 to 4 dorsals (up to 7 in specimens from Chiapas) and usually 3 ventrals long. The red bands vary in individual snakes; some lack black-tipped scales others have strong black tips or scattered scales without black tips. Ventrally, the red bands are usually immaculate, but occasional specimens have few small and irregular black spots. The white or yellow bands are 1 to 1.5 dorsals long, without black-tipped scales. The black tail bands are 2 or more times as long as the white ones.

There are 14 to 26 (22.1) black body bands in males and 17 to 26 (23.2) in females. The males have 5 to 8 (6.2) and the females have 4 to 5 (4.8) black tail bands.

Remarks: This subspecies intergrades with *M. browni taylori* between Chilpancingo and Acapulco, near Acahuizotla, Guerrero, below 1,000 m.

The distribution of this subspecies is quite extensive, somewhat fragmented, and exhibits some variation between the populations.

Food: Several species of snakes, including an Asian blind snake (*Typhlops braminus*) that has been introduced into southern Mexico.

References: Mittleman and Smith (1949) discussed its status in Mexico; Alvarez del Toro (1983) reviewed its morphology and Campbell and Lamar (1989) featured a color photo.

Etymology: Dedicated to W. W. Brown who, according to the authors of this name, is "a veteran collector" in Mexico who collected the holotype of this subspecies.

Micrurus browni importunus (Pattern 8)
Antigua Coral Snake: Coral de Antigua

Micrurus browni importunus Roze, 1967: 11. (Holotype: BM 64.1.26.41A, a male from Dueñas, about 25 km west-southwest of Guatemala City in the Antigua Basin, Sacatepequez, Guatemala, collected by Salvin and Goodman.)

Range: Known only from the region of Dueñas in the Antigua Basin, Sacatepequez, Guatemala, from 1,200 to 1,800 m above sea level.

Description: Males have 209 to 211 (210) and females have about 224 ventrals; subcaudals 51 to 58 (54.5) in males and about 35 in females. Examined: 2 males and 1 female, including the holotype.

The black color of the snout extends onto the supraoculars, covering almost the entire frontal and the upper postoculars. The black extends back from the mental as a heavy stripe, covering part of the first three infralabials on both sides of the head. The nuchal black band covers the posterior third of the parietals and the first 5 dorsals as well as ventrals. The black bands are 3 to 4 dorsals long (and usually 3 ventrals long), bordered by white bands 1 to 1.5 dorsals long. The red areas are immaculate or may have small black-tipped scales. The red bands are immaculate ventrally. The black tail bands are about twice as long as the white ones.

There are 19 to 20 (19.6) black body bands in males and about 27 in females. The males have 6 to 7 (6.7) black tail bands and the only known female has 6.

Food: Coffee snake (*Ninia sebae sebae*).

References: Roze (1970b, 1983) gave some information and a key.

Etymology: Latin *importunus* is intruder or troublesome, alluding to its surprising intrusion into the area of distribution of another coral snake, *M. nigrocinctus*.

Micrurus browni taylori (Pattern 10)
Acapulco Coral Snake; Coralillo de Acapulco

Micrurus nuchalis taylori Schmidt and Smith, 1943: 30. (Holotype: FMNH 100051, a male from Acapulco, Guerrero, Mexico, collected by E. H. Taylor in 1936.)
Micrurus browni taylori: Roze, 1967: 12.

Range: Subhumid coastal tropical lowlands altered by human use around Acapulco, Guerrero, Mexico, from sea level to 400 m.

Description: Males have 212 to 220 (217.1) and females 223 to 238 (231.2) ventrals; subcaudals in males 53 to 59 (55.3), in females 37 to 47 (43.1). Only 1+1 temporals. Examined: 12 males and 12 females, including holotype.

The black snout coloration extends onto the supraoculars, both postoculars, and the frontal except for its posterior tip; it does not have a straight, posterior border. The black nuchal band covers the tips of the parietals, 5 or 6 dorsals, and about 4 ventrals. The mental and the first 3 or 4 infralabials are black. The black bands are 2.5 or 3 dorsals and 1 or 2 ventrals long; they are bordered by white bands that are usually 1 dorsal long. A few specimens have the black bands reduced or interrupted ventrally. The red scales usually have black tips. Ventrally, the red areas are immaculate or have a few very small black dots. The black tail bands are about 4 times as long as the white ones.

There are 10 to 14 (11.4) black body bands in males and 11 to 17 (13.8) in females. The males have 4 to 6 (4.9) and the females 3 to 5 (3.9) black tail bands.

Remarks: Apparently, this subspecies is restricted to the coastal lowlands of Guerrero around Acapulco. It intergrades with *M. browni browni* in the region of Acahuizotla at an altitude of about 800 m.

Food: Several species of snakes, such as the blind worm snake (*Typhlops braminus*), slender blind snake (*Leptotyphlops goudoti blakewelli*), and colubrid snakes (*Tantilla*).

References: This subspecies was known from only one specimen until the Mexican biologist Gustavo Casas-Andreu and William López-Forment (1978) published information about its morphological variation, reproduction, feeding, and ecology.

Etymology: Named after Edward H. Taylor of the University of Kansas, a prolific collector and renowned herpetologist.

Micrurus catamayensis (Map 11, Color 11)
Catamayo Coral Snake; Coral Catamayense

Micrurus catamayensis Roze, 1989: 3. (Holotype BM 1935.11.3.103, a male from 2 km west of Loja, Catamayo Valley, Ecuador, 4,780 ft, collected by Carrion.)

Distribution and range: High montane dry scrub formations and subhumid gallery forest in Catamayo Valley, Loja, southern Ecuador, from 1,000 to 1,800 m above sea level.

Definition: A black-capped coral snake with weakly developed accessory bands that form poorly-defined triads. Males without supraanal tubercles.

Description: Males have 210 to 216 (213.0) and females 227 to 237 (232.0) ventrals; subcaudals 43 to 46 (44.5) in males and 31 to 36 (33.6) in females. Examined: 2 males and 8 females, including holotype.

The black cap covers the upper part of the head, including the parietals and most of the first 5 supralabials. It is separated from the black nuchal band by a narrow white band, 1 to 2 dorsals long; the scales of the white band have irregular black tips. The mental and the first 4 infralabials are black and some chin scales have dark borders. The black body bands are 3 to 5 dorsals long and a little shorter ventrally, where they are irregular and occasionally incomplete. The accessory black bands are poorly defined and are frequently incomplete ventrally. The white bands also are irregular, 1 to 2 dorsals long, and have irregular, faintly dark-tipped scales. The red bands are 4 to 7 dorsals and 3 to 4 ventrals long with irregular large black scale tips or spots; some dorsals lack black tips. Ventrally, the red bands have large black spots or smudges. The black and white tail bands are of variable length, but the black bands are always longer than the white bands that follow them.

The males have 22 to 24 (23.0) and the females have 27 to 32 (28.9) black (accessory type) triads. The males have 6 to 9 (7.5) and the females have 5 to 7 (5.8) black tail bands.

Size: This is a medium-sized coral snake; the longest specimen has a total length of 915 mm; many adults measure between 450 and 650 mm.

Food: Unknown.

References: Only the original description, but H. W. Parker (1938) described its variation under *M. ecua-*

dorianus and Almendariz (1991) mentioned its distribution in Ecuador.

Etymology: The name *catamayensis* is Latin for inhabitant or dweller of Catamayo, a valley in southern Ecuador.

Micrurus circinalis (Map 5, Pattern 11)
Trinidad Northern Coral Snake; Coral Norteña Trinitaria; Cobra Coral Septentrional de Trinidad

Elaps circinalis Duméril, Bibron and Duméril, 1854: 1210. (Holotype: lectotype [designated by Roze, 1989] MNHN 3912, a female from an unknown locality, collected by Geoffroy.)
Elaps riisei Jan, 1858: 525. (Holotype: originally in the Museo Civico di Storia Natural, Milan, Italy, from "St. Thomas, petites Antilles," apparently in error; destroyed in World War II.)
Micrurus circinalis: Schmidt, 1936a: 192.

Distribution and range: Lowland rain forest and low montane wet to intermediate forest in Trinidad, including Gasparee Island, northeastern Venezuela and northern Guyana, from sea level to 400 m.

Definition: A single-banded coral snake with a black cap, intensely red bands with black tips, and a tendency to form weak accessory black bands. The anterior temporal is either reduced or fused with the sixth supralabial. Males lack supraanal tubercles.

Description: Males have 178 to 187 (183.3) and females have 192 to 205 (196.1) ventrals; subcaudals 43 to 50 (45.9) in males and 30 to 35 (32.3) in females; 0+1 or 1+1 temporals; anterior temporal usually reduced in size or fused with the sixth supralabial. Examined: 29 males and 23 females, including the holotype.

The black cap may be fused or not with the black nuchal band. When not fused, a postparietal yellow or white band occupies one dorsal, the temporals, and the last supralabials. The chin is black with an irregular white crossband that covers the last infralabials and part of the genials. The black nuchal band is 3 to 4 dorsals and 2 to 3 ventrals long, and ventrally it projects forward onto the genials. The black bands are 2 to 3 dorsals and about 2 ventrals long and are somewhat irregular in shape. The red bands are clearly distinct, with black tips occupying usually not more than one half of a scale. In more than half of the specimens a weak accessory black band is present. When present, it is more conspicuous on the posterior part of the body. It seems there is an ontogenetic tendency as with an increase of size the black tips of the red scales become larger and the accessory blands become more conspicuous. Ventrally, many specimens have some irregular black spots on the red bands. The black tail bands are 2 to 3 times as long as the light interspaces, many of which have a darkish red dorsal spot or a complete, short, red band between the white bands, corresponding to the red body bands.

The males have 22 to 30 (25.5) and the females have 21 to 31 (27.2) black body bands. The males have 8 to 12 (9.8) and the females have 6 to 8 (6.8) black tail bands.

Size: This is one of the smallest species. The largest measured specimen is 537 mm long, while adults vary between 400 and 500 mm.

Remarks: This species has a unique condition in the reduced or absent anterior temporal and the presence of irregular, weak, black accessory bands. No specimen has been found with any tendency of the red bands to be melanistic. It was considered as a subspecies of *M. psyches* (Roze, 1967), but here it is considered as a full species (see note under *M. psyches*).

Food: Colubrid ground snakes (*Atractus trilineatus*) and snakelike teiid lizards (*Bachia*).

References: Lancini (1979) and Campbell and Lamar (1989) described it and provided color photos. General references of the species appeared in Amaral (1925a, 1927d, 1930c) and Schmidt (1936a). Mole (1914, 1924), Schmidt (1957), Wehekind (1960), Boos and Quesnel (1968), Boos (1975, 1984a, 1984b), and Emsley (1977) recorded it for Trinidad; and Mila de la Roca (1932), Briceño (1934), Vellard (1941), Rohl (1949), Marcuzzi (1950), Roze (1955, 1966a, 1967, 1970b, 1983), Vetencourt Finol (1960), Hoge and Lancini (1962), Lancini (1970, 1979) and Sandner-Montilla (1985) recorded it for Venezuela. Roux-Estève (1983) and Roze (1989) described type specimens. Earlier references include Günther (1858), Jan and Sordelli (1872). Ernst (1877), Mole and Urich (1894), Boulenger (1896) and Quelch (1898).

Etymology: Latin from *circin*, a ring or circle, and *-alis*, pertaining to; thus *circinalis* refers to this snake as belonging to ringed or banded snakes.

Micrurus clarki (Map 12, Color 12)
Clark's Coral Snake; Coral de Clark

Micrurus clarki Schmidt, 1936b: 211. (Holotype: MCZ 38390, a male from Yavisa, Darién, Panama, collected by H. C. Clark in 1934.)

Distribution and range: Intermediate and wet lowland forest and tropical rain forest from southeastern Costa Rica to Darién, Panama, from sea level to about 900 m. Unconfirmed records from western Colombia.

Definition: A single-banded coral snake with white or yellow bands one dorsal long bordering the black bands. Head with a black cap that extends over all or nearly all of the parietals. The black nuchal band does not reach the tips of the parietals. The chin scales are light; several are outlined by black or dark borders. The mental and the first infralabials are not black as they are in all the other single-banded Central American coral snakes. Males do not have supraanal tubercles.

Description: Males have 190 to 197 (193.6) and females have 203 to 221 (215.2) ventrals; subcaudals 53 to 58 (55.1) in males and 34 to 44 (38.2) in females; 1+1 temporals. Examined: 7 males and 6 females, plus 5 heads and the holotype.

The black head cap extends over all of the snout and the parietals. Occasionally, dark blue spots or borders are present on the internasals or prefrontals. The temporals and several supralabials have dark borders or diffused black edges. All infralabials are light, but many have narrow dark borders. The nuchal black band is 3 to 5 dorsals long. Ventrally, the nuchal band projects forward onto the second pair of genials. The black body bands are 3 to 4 dorsals and 2 to 3 ventrals long, bordered by a narrow white or yellow band that is 1 scale long. The white dorsals have black tips, or at least the tips of the scales are darkened. All the red dorsals have conspicuous black tips. The tail bands are black and yellow or black and white; the scales of the light bands have large black tips or spots.

There are 13 to 17 (14.8) black body bands in males and 14 to 19 (16.6) in females. Males have 6 to 9 (7.4) and females have 5 to 6 (5.7) black tail bands.

Size: This is a moderately small coral snake. The largest specimen measures 832 mm, but adults average 380 mm to 600 mm.

Remarks: This species can be distinguished from other single-banded Panama coral snakes by the absence of supraanal tubercles in males. It is as yet a little-known species and its presence in western Colombia has to be confirmed. Some individuals of *M. dumerilii transandinus* from the Pacific side of Colombia have been confused with this species.

Food: Unknown.

References: Dunn and Bailey (1939), Clark (1942), and Dunn (1942, 1949) commented on its presence and variation in Panama; Grocott and Sadler (1958) and Bolaños (1984) mentioned it as a venomous snake. Savage and Vial (1974), E. H. Taylor (1951), Scott (1969), and Solórzano and Cerdas (1984), discussed its presence in Costa Rica, while Roze (1967, 1970b, 1983), Villa et al (1988), and Campbell and Lamar (1989) gave variation and distribution; the latter featured a color photo. Castro et al (1982) and Pérez-Santos and Moreno (1988) suggested its presence in Colombia but this has yet to be verified.

Etymology: Named after H. C. Clark who, while director of the Gorgas Memorial Laboratory in Panama City, in the 1930s and 1940s, conducted a snake census of Panama that amassed more than 10,000 specimens.

Micrurus corallinus (Map 11, Color 13)
Painted Coral Snake; Cobra Coral Pintada; Coral Pintada

Elaps corallinus Merrem, 1820: 144. (Holotype: Lectotype AMNH 3911 [designated by Roze, 1966b], a female from Rio de Janeiro, Cabo Frio, Brazil, collected by Maximillian zu Wied-Neuwied.)
Elaps corallinus Wied-Neuwied, 1820: 108. (The same holotype as Merrem's *E. corallinus*.)
Micrurus corallinus: Amaral, 1925a: 20.

Distribution and range: Littoral and subtropical deciduous forest in eastern and central Brazil, from Minas Gerais and Espiritu Santo westward and southwestward to Rio Grande do Sul, and into eastern Paraguay and northeastern Misiones, Argentina; probably also in Uruguay.

Definition: A single-banded coral snake with a black cap that covers most, but not all of the parietals; its posterior border is usually angular. Males without supraanal tubercles.

Description: Males have 195 to 208 (203.9), usually more than 198, ventrals and females have 210 to 224 (215.4), usually less than 220; subcaudals 43 to 47 (44.4) in males and 27 to 32 (29.8) in females; 1+1 or 1+2 temporals. Examined: 216 males and 188 females, including holotype.

The black cap covers the snout and the greater part of the parietals. Usually, it does not cover the lateroposterior part of the parietals nor their tips, and is separated from the black nuchal band by a narrow yellow or white band. The chin is yellowish or white but part of the mental and the first infralabials are black. Occasional small black spots may be present on other scales. The black nuchal band is 3 to 4 dorsals and 4 to 6 ventrals long. In many specimens it projects slightly forward ventrally, reaching the posterior end of the genials. The black body bands are 3 to 4 dorsals and ventrals long. The red bands are about 3 times as long as the black bands and have black tips on all scales except those of the first dorsal row. The black tips of the dorsals are small and irregular, consisting of smaller black dots concentrated around the tips of the scales.

Ventrally, the red bands are usually immaculate. The yellow bands are about 1 dorsal long and have small black-tipped scales. The black tail bands are about 2 to 3 times as long as the yellow bands. The latter are about 2 dorsals long, but gradually expand laterally and ventrally where they occupy 3 to 4 ventrals.

The males have 15 to 21 (18.1), usually 17 to 20, and the females have 17 to 23 (19.3), usually 18 to 21, black body bands. The males have 5 to 7 (6.3) and the females have 3 to 5 black tail bands.

This is a medium-large species. The longest measured specimen is 987 mm long. Many adults measure 600 to 850 mm.

Remarks: This coral snake exhibits nervous and unpredictable behavior, almost an "angry" attitude that is dangerous to people handling it.

Food: Mostly amphisbaenid or "two-headed" lizards and caecilians, limbless amphibians.

References: General comments and distribution are given by Amaral (1925a, 1927d), Gliesch (1925), Mertens (1927), Schmidt (1936a), Roze (1967, 1970b, 1983), Cendrero et al (1972), and Freiberg (1984), while a complete description with a color photo and distribution is found in Campbell and Lamar (1989). Comments on the species are given for Argentina by Fernández Barrán and Freiberg (1951), Barrio and Miranda (1967), Freiberg (1968), Abalos y Mischis (1975), Cei (1987), Scrocchi (1990), and Martinez et al (1992); for Brazil, many references that include Gomes (1918a), Amaral (1925a, 1926d, 1926e, 1930b, 1930c, 1948a, 1974), L. Muller (1927), Prado (1945), Machado (1945), Azevedo (1964), P. Müller (1968), Lema and Fabian-Beurmann (1977), Santos (1981), Lema (1983), Vanzolini (1985), and Marques and Puorto (1991); for Paraguay by Bertoni (1914, 1939), Migone (1929), Schouten (1931, 1937), and Gatti (1955); and for Uruguay by Devicenzi (1925) and Vaz-Ferreira y Sierra de Soriano (1960). Roze (1966b) commented on the type specimen. Earlier important references include Wied-Neuwied (1821, 1824, 1825), Günther (1859), and Mathes (1860).

Etymology: Latin from *corallium* meaning red coral; *corallinus* means with the pattern of red coral.

Micrurus decoratus (Map 13, Color 14)
Decorated Coral Snake (Brazilian Coral Snake); Cobra Coral Decorada

Elaps decoratus Jan, 1858: 525. (Holotype: lost in Museum of Milano; type locality "Mexico" is an error.)
Elaps fischeri Amaral, 1921: 39. (Holotype: IB 1849, a male from Fazenda Bonito, Serra Bocaina, Valley of Mambucaba River, São Paulo, Brazil, 100 m.)
Elaps ezequieli Lutz and Mello, 1922: 235. (Holotype: In Instituto Oswaldo Cruz, Brazil, female from Caxambuy, Serra da Mantiqueira, Minas Gerais, Brazil.)
Micrurus decoratus: Amaral, 1926a: 32.

Distribution and range: Humid lowland and low montane subtropical formations frequently altered by humans in eastern and southeastern Brazil, from Minas Gerais, São Paulo and Rio de Janeiro southward to Rio Grande do Sul, from sea level to over 1,000 m.

Definition: A triad-type coral snake with the first triad consisting of only 2 black bands. The head is black with a yellow prefrontal band and a red parietal band. Usually, there are 0+1 temporals; the anterior temporal is fused with the sixth supralabial, which is in contact with the parietal and both postoculars.

Description: Males have 195 to 208 (202.3) and females have 209 to 218 (214.0) ventrals; subcaudals 19 to 22 (21.5) in males and 16 to 19 (17.4) in females; almost always 0+1 temporals, at least on one side. Examined: 20 males and 9 females.

The black snout coloration is followed by a yellow postfrontal band that varies in length; it is followed by a black frontal-parietal band that covers the anterior part of the parietals. The red parietal band extends beyond the tips of the parietals onto the first several dorsals, where the scales have occasional black tips. The red band is followed by a black band that represents the first black band of the incomplete first triad. Below, the mental and the first 3 to 4 infralabials are partially or completely black. The other chin scales are red, followed by the yellow band. The first triad consists of 2 distinct black bands, with the usual first black band absent or reduced to a few black tips on the red scales, rarely suggesting a very irregular first black band. The central black band of the triad is 3 to 5 dorsals long and up to 3 times as long as the outer bands, giving an impression of an accessory triad-type coloration. Ventrally, the outer black bands are reduced and irregular, 1 or less than 1 ventral long. The red bands are longer than the central black band and slightly shorter than the length of an entire triad. The red scales have conspicuous black tips, but in males they are smaller and less pronounced than in the females. The scales in the yellow bands are without black tips, and except for the first band that is somewhat longer, the bands are 1 to 2 dorsals long. Distinct triads are also found on the tail.

Including the first incomplete triad, the males have 15 to 19 (16.7) and the females have 15 to 19 (17.1) triads on the body. A more precise way of rendering the number of black triads is ⅔ 14 to ⅔ 19 in males and females. The males have 1 to 1⅔ and the females have one to 1⅓ triads on the tail.

Size: This is a moderately-small species. The longest specimen is 638 mm, but many adults are 430 to 600 mm in total length.

Remarks: Absence of the first temporal makes this species distinguishable from all other triad-type coral snakes.

Food: Unknown.

References: Amaral (1921) was misled by the abnormal contact between genials and the mental to describe *E. fisheri*. Other references of the species include: Amaral (1922, 1926e, 1930b, 1930c, 1978), Lutz and Mello (1922), Schmidt (1936a), Prado (1945), Azevedo (1962a), Roze (1967, 1970b, 1983), Lema and Azevedo (1969), Lema (1971a), Hoge and Romano (1973), Lema et al (1980), Hoge and Romano (1981), and Campbell and Lamar's (1989) description, illustrated with a color photo.

Etymology: Latin from *decorus* meaning adorned and beautiful, alluding to the very beautiful color pattern of this species; *fischeri*, dedicated to C. M. Fischer, employee of the Instituto Butantan who collected the holotype; and *ezequieli*, named after Ezequiel Dias who organized medical defense against venomous snakes and scorpions in Minas Gerais, Brazil.

Micrurus diana (Map 5, Pattern 12)
Diana's Coral Snake; Coral Diana

Micrurus frontalis diana Roze, 1983: 324 (Holotype: FMNH 159889, a male from the vicinity of Santiago, Provincia Chiquiticos, Departamento Santa Cruz, Bolivia, 700 meters, collected by Roy F. Steinbach, April 7–20, 1973.)
Micrurus diana: Roze, 1994: 179.

Distribution and range: Transition forest altered by humans in the Serranía de Santiago, eastern Bolivia, around 700 m high.

Definition: A triad-type coral snake with 9 to 11 complete triads and the first black band in contact with the black parietal coloration. Snout creamy white with plates outlined by black.

Description: Males have 215 to 224 (219.3) and females have about 224 ventrals; subcaudals 22 to 26 (23.8) in males, up to 11 of them undivided, and about 20 in females, all divided; 1+1 temporals. Examined: 4 males and one female, including the holotype.

The snout, including the frontal, supraoculars and postoculars, is creamy yellow with the individual plates outlined by irregular black borders. The parietals, posterior part of the frontal, and the supraoculars are black. There is a black spot below the eye, covering the upper part of the third and fourth supralabials. A narrow grayish white line is present on the suture between the parietals. The black parietal band fuses with the first black band of the first triad. The temporals and the last supralabials are red. Below, the mental and the first infralabials and the anterior part of the genials are creamy white. The remainder of the head is red to the posterior tip of the genials. A narrow black line runs on the suture between the anterior pair of genials. The black bands of each triad are of approximately the same length, covering 3 to 4 dorsals and ventrals. The white bands are longer than the black bands, covering 4 to 6 dorsals and ventrals. Most or all the white scales have irregular black tips and large irregular black spots that produce an impression of a feebly-marked additional black band. The red bands are longer than the white bands, covering 7 to 11 dorsals and ventrals, without black-tipped scales.

The males have 9 to 11 (9.3) and the females have about 9 black triads on the body. There are usually 1⅓ triads on the tail in both sexes.

Size: The longest measured specimen is 998 mm. Many adults vary between 600 and 900 mm in total length.

Remarks: Thus far, this species, originally described as subspecies of *M. frontalis*, is known only from the Serranía de Santiago, an isolated mountain chain surrounded by swampy lowlands in eastern Bolivia.

Fusion of the black parietal coloration with the first black band on the body is unique to this species, except for occasional specimens of *M. f. frontalis*.

Food: Colubrid ground snakes.

References: Only the original description and a comment by Campbell and Lamar (1989).

Etymology: As the original description states: "Dedicated to Diana, the goddess of forests, animals and moon who should be adored and invoked to protect the endangered nature, particularly animals."

Micrurus diastema (Map 14)
Diastema Coral Snake; (Variable Coral Snake); Coral Diastema

Distribution: From central Veracruz, eastern Puebla, and northern Oaxaca to the Isthmus of Tehuantepec and the Peninsula of Yucatán in Mexico, then southward to Belize and northern and central Guatemala, ranging into northwestern Honduras.

Definition: A single-banded coral snake with or without white bands delimiting the black bands. The snout is black to the anterior part of the parietals, but in several subspecies the point of the snout and several supralabials are white. Several subcaudals frequently are entirely white. The males have no supraanal tubercles; there are 1+1 or 1+2 temporals.

Size: This is a medium-sized coral snake. The longest specimen is 895 mm long. There is some difference in size among different subspecies, but many adults measure between 500 and 750 mm in total length.

Remarks: This is one of the most complex species, exhibiting considerable geographical variation. Its total distribution covers practically all the tropical and subtropical ecological zones from dry semidesert to tropical wet forest, from sea level to altitudes above 1500 m. As a result, seven subspecies are recognized, occupying geographically discrete areas. Once the large zones of intergradation are recognized between the subspecies, they can be clearly characterized by nonoverlapping characteristics. To use the key for subspecies, the locality of the specimen must be known, as locality allows identification of a specimen of a given subspecies or determines its intermediate status between two subspecies. In the latter case, only the species name can be known with certainty.

References: Numerous references and interpretations of this species and its subspecies have appeared, mostly due to its considerable variation. Before Roze (1967), it was dealt with under the name of *affinis*. The most recent description and distribution appeared in Campbell and Lamar (1989), while Fraser (1973) described its variation without recognizing the subspecies. Other more general publications are those by Schmidt (1933a, 1936b), Cendrero et al. (1972), Roze (1983), and Villa et al. (1988). It was described for Belize by Schmidt (1941), Neill and Allen (1959), Neill (1960), and Henderson and Hoevers (1975); for Honduras by Meyer (1969), Wilson (1983), and Wilson and Meyer (1982 and 1985); for Guatemala by Ahl (1927), Stuart (1934, 1935, 1948, 1950, 1958, 1963) and Campbell and Vannini (1989); for Mexico by Werner (1903), Gadow (1905), Mocquard (1908–1909), Ruthven (1912), Martín del Campo (1935, 1950), Gaige (1936), Schmidt and Andrews (1936), Andrews (1937), H. M. Smith (1938, 1960), E. H. Taylor (1940), Schmidt and Smith (1943), H. M. Smith and Taylor (1945), Werler and Smith (1952), J. A. Peters (1953), Barrera (1963), Duellman (1965a), Alvarez del Toro (1972, 1983), Blaney and Blaney (1978, 1979), Pérez-Higadera et al. (1978), Lee (1980), Pérez-Higareda (1980), Ramírez-Bautista et al. (1981), Johnson (1984), Dundee et al. (1986), and Flores Villela et al. (1987). Its defensive behavior and mimicry were described by Gehlbach (1972) and Greene and McDiarmid (1981) and one type specimen by Tiedemann and Haupl (1980), while Gutiérrez et al. (1988) described its karyotype. Earlier significant references include Günther (1859), Cope (1859, 1870, 1885, 1887), Garman (1884a, 1884b), and Ferrari-Pérez (1886).

Key to the Subspecies of *M. diastema*

1 More than 35 black body bands
   . . . . *M. d. apiatus* (Central Guatemala)
1' Less than 35 black body bands 2
2 Less than 7 black tail bands in males; less than 6 in females; regular black tips on all red dorsals . . . 3
2' Seven or more black tail bands in males and 6 or more in females; irregular black tips but not on all red dorsals 4
3 Ventrals with many black spots; black dorsal bands not more that 3 dorsals long; black snout covers only anterior half of parietals; subcaudals 44 to 49 in males and 32 to 38 in females
   . . . *M. d. diastema* (Central Veracruz and eastern Puebla, Mexico)
3' Ventrals nearly always without black markings; black dorsal bands 4 or more dorsals long; black snout coloration covers most of the parietals, frequently fused with the first (nuchal) black band; subcaudals 48 to 54 in males, 39 to 45 in females
   . . . . *M. d. alienus* (Northern Yucatán, Mexico)
4 Usually 22 or more black body bands in males, 23 or more in females 5
4' Usually less than 22 black body bands in males and 22 or less in females 6
5 An irregular black crossband formed by concentration of black spots in the middle of the red area between two black bands
   . . . . *M. d. aglaeope* (Northwestern Honduras)
5' Irregular black tips on many but not on all red scales; occasional black spots in the middle of red bands
   M. d. sapperi (Northeastern Chiapas, Mexico, northern Guatemala, and Belize)
6 Irregular black tips on all red scales; 19 to 22 black dorsal bands in males and 20 to 21 in females
   . . . . *M. d. affinis* (Northern Oaxaca, Mexico)
6' Many large irregular and occasional smaller black spots on several but not all red scales; 15 to 18 black dorsal bands in males
   . . . . . . *M. d. macdougalli* (Eastern Oaxaca, Mexico)

Note: Intergrades are not identified by this key; consult the distribution of intergrades in Map 14.

Micrurus diastema diastema (Fig. 53, Pattern 13)
Veracruz Coral Snake; Coralilla Veracruzana

Elaps diastema Duméril, Bibron, and Duméril, 1854: 1222. (Holotype: lectotype [selected by Schmidt,

Figure 53. Micrurus diastema diastema, from Mexico: Rancho Santa Fe, 4 km E of Hueyapán de Ocampo, Veracruz. (Photo by Roger and Isabelle Hunt Conant.)

1933a] MHNP 7657, a female from Mexico, collected by Ducommun in 1838.)

Elaps epistema Duméril, Bibron, and Duméril, 1854: 1222. (Holotype: MNHN 3992, a male from Mexico, collected by Verreaux.)

Elaps corallinus var. *crebripunctatus* W. C. Peters, 1896: 877. (Syntypes: ZMB 1660 [2 specimens] from Matamoros, Puebla, Mexico, obtained by Berkenbusch, specimens apparently lost.)

Micrurus diastema diastema: Roze, 1967: 14.

Range: Wet lowland tropical forest and humid low montane formations, partially modified by human influence, in central Veracruz and eastern Puebla, Mexico, from sea level to about 1,000 m.

Description: Males have 188 to 203 (196.1) and females have 203 to 217 (211.7) ventrals; subcaudals 44 to 49 (46.2) in males and 32 to 38 (35.1) in females; none or very few entire; 1+1 temporals, very rarely 1+2 on one side of the head only. Examined: 35 males and 30 females, including two holotypes.

The black snout color extends back to include the anterior part of the parietals and the first few supralabials. This is followed by a red parietal band. Rarely there are light spots on the snout. Below, the chin is light or mottled with black. The nuchal black band is usually complete, but occasional specimens have the black bands interrupted laterally or reduced to dorsal spots. The black bands are 2 to 3 dorsals and ventrals long. The white bands are one half to one scale long. The red bands are about 4 to 7 times as long as the black bands, with regular black tips on all scales. Ventrally, the red bands have black mottling; in some specimens this is quite heavy, but occasionally the red ventrals are nearly immaculate. On the tail, there are black and white bands only.

The males have 10 to 16 (13.4) and the females have 11 to 16 (13.6) black body bands, but most specimens have fewer than 14. Males have 4 to 6 (5.2) and females have 3 to 5 (3.7) black tail bands.

Remarks: This subspecies intergrades with *M. d. affinis* and *M. d. sapperi* in southeastern Veracruz.

Food: Several species of colubrid snakes including ground snakes, *Geophis* and *Ninia*.

References: See under species.

Etymology: From Greek, *diastema* means a space or interval, apparently alluding to the long interspaces of red between the black bands. *Epistema* comes from the Greek words *epi* meaning above or upon and *stema* meaning thread, probably alluding to the weavy, thread-like black ornaments on the head. *Crebripunctatus* is Latin from *crebri*, meaning frequent or close and *punctatus* meaning marked with small punctures or dots; thus the name means "marked with frequent spots," alluding to the regular black tips on the red scales.

Micrurus diastema affinis
Speckled Coral Snake; Coralilla Salpicada

Elaps affinis Jan, 1858: 525. (Holotype: MNHN 3921, a female from Mexico.)
Micrurus diastema affinis: Roze, 1967: 14.

Range: Humid medium-altitude forests in northern and central Oaxaca, Mexico, between 500 and 1300 m above sea level.

Description: Males have 207 to 211 (209) and females have 211 to 224 (222.1) ventrals; subcaudals are about 51 in males and 38 to 40 (38.7) in females; 1+1 temporals. Examined: 2 males and 3 females, including the holotype.

The black of the snout extends back to include the entire frontal and the anterior part of the parietals. The black nuchal band covers the parietal tips and is usually incomplete ventrally. Below, the chin is white. The black bands are 1½ to 2 dorsals and 2 ventrals long. They are reduced on the first or second dorsal row to 1 scale in length or may be interrupted or incomplete ventrally. The white bands are ½ to 1 dorsal long. The red bands are 5 to 6 times as long as the black bands, with irregular black tips on almost all scales. They are sometimes marked with larger black spots. Ventrally, the red scales have numerous black spots or mottling. On the tail there are only black and white bands.

The males have 19 to 22 (20.5) and the females 19 to 20 (19.60) black body bands. The males have 9 and the females have 6 black tail bands.

Remarks: This subspecies intergrades with *M. d. diastema* in Veracruz and with *M. d. macdougalli* in eastern Oaxaca, Mexico.

Food: Unknown, probably snakes.

References: Roze (1967) discussed the status of this subspecies.

Etymology: Latin *affinis* means related or allied, probably alluding to its similarity to other single-banded Mexican coral snakes.

Micrurus diastema aglaeope (Color 15)
Splendid Coral Snake; Coral Espléndida

Elaps aglaeope Cope, 1859: 344. (Holotype: ANSP 6858, a male from Honduras.)
Micrurus diastema aglaeope: Roze, 1967: 15.

Range: Dry formations in moderate elevations around Lago Yoja and the humid Ulua Valley of northwestern Honduras.

Description: Males have 204 and females have 216 to 217 (216.5) ventrals; subcaudals around 54 in males and 40 to 41 (40.5) in females; 1+1 or 1+2 temporals. Examined: 1 male and 2 females, including the holotype.

The snout has a large and irregular white spot covering at least the rostral and the internasals. The first supralabials may be either light or dark. The black snout color extends to the anterior end of the parietals. The black nuchal band covers the tips of the parietal and is complete ventrally. The chin is white with a few reduced, irregular spots on some scales. The black bands of the body are 2 to 3 dorsals long; the white bands are absent or poorly marked. The red bands are 2 to 3 times as long as the black bands, but an additional black band is equidistant between the 2 black bands. This additional band is partially interrupted and formed by large irregular black spots, while the red scales have no black tips. This coloration gives the impression that the black tips have been concentrated in the middle of the red band to form a central black band or spot. This additional, irregular, and partially interrupted black band does not cover the ventrals, although it may be represented by a few black ventral spots. Only black and white bands are found on the tail.

The males have about 27 black bands and the females have 31 to 34 (32.5). The males have about 10 black tail bands and the females have 7 to 10 (8.5).

Remarks: *M. d. aglaeope* can be easily distinguished by the presence of the additional black band in the middle of the red band. This subspecies intergrades with *M. d. sapperi* in the Motagua Valley of Guatemala.

Food: Probably snakes.

References: Schmidt (1936b) discussed its status and Campbell and Lamar (1989) featured a color photograph.

Etymology: Greek from *aglao* meaning splendor or beauty, apparently alluding to the splendor and beauty of this coral snake and its brilliantly red bands, undimmed by black tips.

Micrurus diastema alienus (Pattern 14)
Yucatán Coral Snake; Coralilla Yucateca

Elaps alienus Werner, 1903: 249 (Holotype: MHNB from Venezuela or Ecuador, restricted to Chichén Itzá, Yucatán [Mexico], by Roze, 1967.)
Micrurus affinis mayensis Schmidt, 1933a: 37. (Holotype: MCZ 31872, a male from Chizén Itzá, Yucatán [Mexico], collected by George H. Shattuck, March 17, 1930.)
Micrurus diastema alienus: Roze, 1967: 15.

Range: Dry and humid lowland forests modified by human influence of the Yucatán Peninsula in Yucatán and northern Quintana Roo, Mexico, up to about 300 m above sea level.

Description: Males have 193 to 203 (198.1) and females have 205 to 218 (211.8) ventrals; subcaudals 48 to 54 (52.7) in males and 39 to 45 (42.3) in females, up to 80% of the subcaudals undivided; always 1+2 temporals. Examined: 48 males and 30 females, including all holotypes.

The black snout coloration extends over at least one third of the parietals, but may also extend over the entire parietals, in which case it fuses with the nuchal black band. Usually there are no white spots on the snout. The chin is white or with occasional dark spots on the first infralabials. The black bands are 4 to 5 dorsals and ventrals long, delimited by white or yellow bands about 2 dorsals long. Occasional specimens have the black bands considerably reduced or nearly absent or only the black nuchal band present. The number of black bands in these cases is 2 to 6. On the other hand, 1 specimen out of 78 examined had 20 black body bands and irregular black-tipped red scales, an aberrant coloration. The red bands are 3 to 6 times longer than the black bands and have black tips on all scales. Ventrally, the red bands are usually immaculate. Only black and white bands are found on the tail.

The males have 8 to 17 (13.4) and the females have 9 to 16 (14.7) black body bands. However, more than 90% of the specimens have no more than 14 black bands. On the tail, the males have 3 to 6 (4.2) and the females have 2 to 5 (3.4) black bands.

Food: A large variety of snakes such as blind snakes (*Typhlops microstomus*), slug-eating snakes (*Sibon sanniola*), coffee snake (*Ninia sebae*), and other ground-dwelling snakes (*Stenorrhina freminvillei, Tantilla canula, Ficimia publia,* and *Elaphe phaescens*) as well as lizards (*Ameiva undulata*).

Remarks: This subspecies intergrades with *M. d. sapperi* in southern Quintana Roo, Mexico.

References: Schmidt and Andrews (1936), Duellman (1965), Blaney and Blaney (1979), and Lee (1980), among others, reviewed its distribution and morphological variation, while Campbell and Lamar (1989) offered a color photograph.

Etymology: Latin *alienus* is foreign or stranger, probably alluding to the foreign and strange appearance of the type specimen that has hardly any black bands as compared to the regularly black and red coral snakes. *Mayensis* means that the snake is from the region where Mayan Indians lived.

Micrurus diastema apiatus (Fig. 54)
Spotted Nose Coral Snake; Coralilla Hocico Manchado

Elaps apiatus Jan, 1858: 522 (Holotype: MNHN 3920, a male from Vera Cruz, corrected to Verapaz, Guatemala, by Schmidt, 1933a, collected by Morelet in 1849.)
Micrurus diastema apiatus: Roze, 1967: 15.

Range: Humid tropical montane forest and grasslands in Alta Verapaz and Huehuetenango, Guatemala, between 600 and 1300 m above sea level; possibly also in the mountains of eastern Chiapas, Mexico.

Description: Males have 195 to 213 (205.8) and females 217 to 227 (223.4) ventrals; subcaudals 48 to 57 (53.4) in males and 36 to 43 (40.1) in females; nearly all specimens have 15 or more undivided subcaudals; 1+1 or 1+2 temporals. Examined: 22 males and 18 females, including the holotype.

The snout is dark except the point of the snout, and the lower part of the supralabials are white. The chin is white or with a few reduced black spots. The nuchal black band reaches the parietal tips; occasionally there is an irregular black spot on the white parietal band. Black and red bands extend over the entire body; no white bands are present. The black bands are about 2 dorsals long; occasional bands may be interrupted or displaced along the midventral line. The red bands are up to 3 times as long as the black bands, but in some specimens they are only slightly longer. A few black spots are concentrated in the central area of the red bands, but they do not form a central black band as they frequently do in *M. d. aglaeope*. Occasionally, the black central spots may be very few, and in some specimens they are completely absent, producing a body pattern of simple red and black bands. Ventrally, the red bands are usually immaculate, but sometimes they have a very few small black spots. There are black and white bands only on the tail.

The males have 46 to 60 (46.9) and the females have 44 to 61 (49.3) black body bands. The males have 11 to 15 (13.1) and the females have 8 to 11 (9.8) black tail bands.

Remarks: This subspecies intergrades with *M. d. sapperi* in the lowlands of Petén, Guatemala, and in central Chiapas, Mexico. It intergrades with *M. d. aglaeope* in the area of low hills at the southwestern end of Lago Izabál, Guatemala. The red- and black-banded body coloration and the high number of black bands makes it easily distinguishable from other subspecies.

Food: A wide variety of amphibians and reptiles, including caecilians, night lizards (*Lepidophyma flavomaculatum*) and colubrid snakes (*Adelphicos quadrivirgatus*), *Geophis* sp., *Ninia diademata, Ninia sebae, Stenorrhina degenhardtii,* and other species).

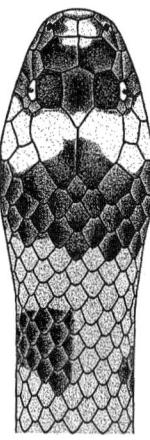

Figure 54. Head of *Micrurus diastema apiatus*, from Guatemala. Stippled area is red, and no white bands on the body.

References: Stuart (1948, 1950) described its habitat and distribution in Guatemala.

Etymology: The name can have several meanings in Latin. It could be from *apex* and *apicis* meaning a long mark, alluding to the black short bands or to its dwelling on high mountains, or from *apicatus* meaning adorned with a cap, alluding to its head marking.

Micrurus diastema macdougalli (Pattern 15)
MacDougall's Coral Snake; Coralilla de MacDougall

Micrurus diastema macdougalli Roze, 1967: 15. (Holotype: AMNH 65163, a male from El Modelo, Río Chalchijapa and Río del Corte, Oaxaca, Mexico, collected by T. C. MacDougall on March 5, 1944.)

Range: Subtropical broad-leaf and scrub forests in the Atlantic slopes of Sierra Madre del Sur in eastern Oaxaca, Mexico, about 600 m above sea level.

Description: Males have 200 to 206 (205.1) and females have 211 to 218 (215.0) ventrals; subcaudals 49 to 56 (52.6) in males and about 42 in females; about half of the specimens have up to 6 undivided subcaudals; 1+1 or 1+2 temporals. Examined: 5 males and 3 females, including the holotype.

The snout is black but part of the rostral and the lower parts of the supralabials are white. The chin is white or yellow with black spots on the first pair of genials and/or the first infralabials. The black nuchal band may extend over the parietal tips; it may be complete or interrupted ventrally. The black bands are 1 to 2½ dorsals long, delimited by yellow bands 1 to 2 dorsals long. The red bands are 4 to 5 times longer than the black bands; they have irregular black spots, but these are not found on all scales and they do not look like regular black-tipped scales. Ventrally, the red areas have some black spots. Black, white, or yellow bands are found on the tail.

The males have 15 to 18 (16.7) and the females have 13 to 19 (15.6) black body bands. The black tail bands may be longer (or not) than the yellow bands; the males have 7 to 9 (8.1) and the females have about 6 black tail bands.

Remarks: This subspecies intergrades with *M. d. affinis* near Buena Vista, in central Oaxaca, Mexico.

Food: Unknown, probably snakes.

References: Original description and a note by Powers (1984).

Etymology: Named after T. C. MacDougall "who has made valuable collections in the Tehuatepec region that have greatly facilitated the herpetological survey of that region," as stated in the original description.

Micrurus diastema sapperi (Color 16)
Irregular Coral Snake; Coralilla Irregular or Coral Irregular

P15
266
C16
250

Elaps fulvius var. *sapperi* Werner, 1903: 250. (Holotype: ZSBS from Guatemala, lost during the Second World War.)
Elaps guatemalensis Ahl, 1927: 251. (Holotype: ZMB 8160, a male from Guatemala.)
Micrurus affinis stantoni Schmidt, 1933a: 36. (Holotype: FMNH 4201, a male from Belize, British Honduras [=Belize], collected by W. A. Stanton.)
Micrurus diastema sapperi: Roze, 1967: 17.

Range: Humid tropical lowland forest, tropical secondary forest influenced by humans, and grasslands in Campeche, southwestern Quintana Roo, and eastern Tabasco, Mexico, western Guatemala, and Belize.

Description: Males have 197 to 207 (203.4) and females have 214 to 225 (218.9) ventrals; subcaudals 50 to 55 (52.9) in males and 37 to 42 (40.1) in females; usually 1+2, occasionally 1+1, temporals on one side. Examined: 32 males and 21 females, including two holotypes.

The snout is black to the anterior part of the parietals. About 70% of the specimens have a light spot on the snout that covers the rostral and internasals and occasionally the lower part of the first supralabials. The nuchal black band covers the tips of the parietals and 3 to 4 dorsals. It may be complete or interrupted ventrally. The black bands are 2 to 3 dorsals and ventrals long. The white or yellow bands are ½ to 1 scale long. The red bands are 4 to 7 times as long as the black bands; they have irregular black-tipped scales or small spots fused to form larger spots. Ventrally, the red bands usually lack black markings. On the tail, the black bands are longer than the white bands.

The males have 22 to 33 (26.4) and the females have 25 to 32 (28.7) black body bands. The males have 7 to 11 (8.6) and the females have 6 to 9 (7.2) black tail bands.

Remarks: This subspecies intergrades with *M. d. aglaeope* in eastern Guatemala; with *M. d. alienus* in central and southern Quintana Roo and northern Campeche, Mexico; with *M. d. apiatus* in northeastern Chiapas and central Guatemala; and with *M. d. diastema* in southeastern Veracruz and Tabasco. A gradual cline of some characteristics is found going from Guatemala to Mexico, which makes the interpretation of specimens from some areas quite complicated.

Food: Ground-dwelling colubrids (*Tropidodipsas sartorii*) and coffee snakes (*Ninia sebae*).

References: Schmidt (1941), Neill and Allen (1959), and Henderson and Hoevers (1975) reviewed its distribution, ecology, and variation in Belize and Campbell and Lamar (1989) offered a color photo.

Etymology: Sapperi is named after Professor Sapper, who collected and sent collections of reptiles from Guatemala to the Munich Museum. The name *guatemalensis* denotes its presence in Guatemala, while *stantoni* is dedicated to W. A. Stanton, a Jesuit priest who collected the holotype.

Micrurus dissoleucus (Map 13)
Pygmy Coral Snake; Candelilla

Distribution: Central Panama to northern and northeastern Colombia, and northern and eastern Venezuela.

Definition: A triad-type coral snake in which the black nuchal band that covers part of the parietals is the last black band of the first triad. The first two are absent. The head is black with a white parietal band. Red and white dorsal scales are outlined by black. The triads also are present on the tail. The prefrontals are as long as or longer than the frontal.

Size: This is the smallest species of coral snakes of the genus *Micrurus*, but the length varies from subspecies to subspecies. Size is given under the description of each subspecies.

Remarks: This species is easily recognizable by the fact that the first triad is represented by only one black band, which, is unique among the triad-type species of South America, and by the faint black outline of the red and white dorsal scales. Four subspecies are recognized.

References: General comments on the species are by Amaral (1925a), Schmidt (1936a), Roze (1966a, 1967, 1970b, 1983), P. Muller (1973), Rivero-Blanco and Dixon (1979), Cendrero et al. (1982), and Villa et al. (1988) and description and distribution with a color photograph by Campbell and Lamar (1989). Records for Colombia are by Ruthven (1922), Amaral (1928, 1931b), Nicéforo María (1942), Dunn (1944a), Daniel (1949), Schmidt (1955), Medem (1969), Dugand (1975), Castro et al. (1982), Angel (1983), Pérez-Santos (1986a), Pérez-Santos and Moreno (1986, 1988); for Panama by Barbour (1923), Barbour and Amaral (1924), Schmidt (1933b), Evans (1947), Dunn (1949), Grocott and Sadler (1958), and Smith and Grant (1958); and for Venezuela by Milá de la Roca (1932), Briceño (1934), Vellard (1941), Marcuzzi (1950), Roze (1955, 1966a, 1970a), Vetencourt Finol (1960), Hoge and Lancini (1962), Lancini (1970, 1979), and Sandner-Montilla (1985). Type specimens were discussed by McCoy and Richmond (1966) and Tiedemann and Haupl (1980).

Key to the Subspecies of *M. dissoleucus*

1 Males with 21 to 22 subcaudals; females with 17 to 19 subcaudals; chin all black or with a few light spots .... *M. d. melanogenys* (Santa Marta, Colombia)
1' More than 22 subcaudals in males and usually more than 19 in females; chin black or light 2
2 Frontal as wide as or narrower than supraoculars .... *M. d. dunni* (Panama)
2' Frontal wider than supraoculars 3
3 Chin entirely black or almost entirely black; usually only one full triad on the tail
...... *M. d. nigrirostris* (Lower Magdalena Valley, Colombia)
3' Chin white with some black on mental and first supralabials; usually 1⅓ triads on tail
... *M. d. dissoleucus* (northeastern Colombia and northern Venezuela)

Micrurus dissoleucus dissoleucus (Pattern 17)
Venezuelan Pygmy Coral Snake; Candelilla Venezolana

Elaps dissoleucus Cope, 1859: 345. (Holotype: ANSP 6781, a female from Venezuela, collected by Meigs. The type locality was restricted to Maracaibo, Zulia, Venezuela, by Roze, 1955.)
Micrurus dissoleucus dissoleucus: Schmidt, 1936a: 202.

Range: The llanos savanna and low montane dry and humid forest formations from Norte de Santander, Colombia, to Sucre and Delta Amacuro in eastern Venezuela, from sea level to 550 m. It has also penetrated as high as 1,000 m in places where the original low montane tropical forest has been eliminated by human activities, such as in the Valle de Caracas in the Cordillera de la Costa, Venezuela.

Description: Males have 171 to 190 (182.6) and females have 193 to 208 (202.1) ventrals; subcaudals 24 to 28 (25.9) in males and 20 to 23 (21.4) in females; the frontal is wider than the supraocular and about as long as or a little longer than the prefrontals. Examined: 20 males and 18 females, including the holotype.

The black snout coloration is followed by a parietal white or yellow band that extends over the anterior part of the parietals, the posterior part of the postoculars, the frontal, and most of the temporals, as well as the fifth to seventh supralabials. Below, the mental and the first infralabials are black and the remainder of the chin is white with occasional black spots that are usually concentrated around the sutures. The black nuchal band covers the posterior part of the parietals and 3 to 4 dorsals; it is usually interrupted ventrally. The black central band of a triad is slightly longer than the outer ones but shorter than the red bands. The latter are either immaculate or have a few poorly-marked borders or tips. The length of the red and black bands is directly related to the number of triads; the fewer the triads, the longer the bands are. The white bands, however, are always about 3 to 4 dorsals long. They are shorter than the outer black bands and have a few small black-tipped scales and a faint dark outline. The black triads on the tail are reduced ventrally; the red bands are as long as or shorter than the black outer bands.

Including the black nuchal band that represents the remnant of the first triad, the males have ⅓ 7 to ⅓ 10 (8.6), usually ⅓ 8 to ⅓ 9 triads on the body, and the females have ⅓ 6 to ⅓ 11 (8.8), usually ⅓ 7 to ⅓ 10. The males have from 1⅓ to 1⅔ and the females have 1 to 1⅓ black triads on the tail. In occasional specimens the cloaca lies in the middle of the last black band of the last body triad.

Size: This moderate to small coral snake is the largest subspecies of *M. dissoleucus*. The longest specimen measures 602 mm; most adults are between 320 to 450 mm long.

Food: Diurnal lizards (*Ameiva bifrontata*).

References: Nicéforo María (1942) reported on several specimens from Norte de Santander, Colombia, and Pérez-Santos and Moreno (1988) offered a color photograph, while Roze (1955, 1966a), Lancini (1970, 1979), and Campbell and Lamar (1989) gave description and distribution of this subspecies in Venezuela, including illustrations in color.

Etymology: Greek from *disso* meaning double and *leuco* meaning white, meaning "double white," which alludes to the double white bands between the black bands of a triad.

Micrurus dissoleucus dunni (Pattern 16)
Panama Pygmy Coral Snake; Candelilla Panameña

Micrurus dunni Barbour, 1923: 15. (Holotype: MCZ 16304, a female from Ancón, Panama Canal Zone, Panama.)
Micrurus dissoleucus dunni: Schmidt, 1936a: 203.

Range: Lowland dry and humid forest of the Canal Zone and modified humid forest and savanna westward to Coclé and Herrera, Panama, from sea level to about 250 m.

Description: Males have 182 to 195 (188.2) and females have 205 to 211 (209.8) ventrals; subcaudals 23 to 27 (25.5) in males and 19 to 23 (20.5) in females; the frontal narrower or at most as wide as the supraoculars; the prefrontal is usually longer, but occasionally only as long as the frontal. Examined: 13 males and 6 females, including the holotype.

The white parietal band is short but quite regular, extending over the tip of the frontal, the anterior one-third to two-thirds of the parietals, at least the upper postocular and anterior temporal, and 2 supralabials. The chin is white with the mental and the first infralabials black. The black nuchal band extends over the posterior part of the parietals and 4 or 5 dorsals and is complete ventrally. The black central band of the triads is approximately 1½ times as long as the outer band and longer than the red bands. The latter are a little longer than the outer black bands. The red dorsals are immaculate or have a very few small black-tipped scales. The white or yellow bands are about half the length of the outer black bands, with occasional black-tipped scales. The length of the tail bands is about the same as those on the body.

Including the black nuchal band which represents a remnant of the first triad, the males have ⅓ 8 to ⅓ 11 (9.2) and the females have ⅓ 10 to ⅓ 12 (10.5) triads. In occasional specimens, the cloaca lies in the middle of the last black band of the last triad. The males have 1⅓ to 1⅔ and the females have 1 to 1⅓ triads on the tail.

Size: This is a small subspecies; the longest specimen measured 376 mm, but most adults range between 280 and 350 mm.

Food: Unknown.

References: Schmidt (1955) and Smith and Grant (1958) commented on the status and distribution of this subspecies.

Etymology: Named after Emmett R. Dunn, one of the great American herpetologists of this century.

Micrurus dissoleucus melanogenys (Color 17)
Santa Marta Pygmy Coral Snake; Candelilla Santamartense

Elaps melanogenys Cope, 1860a: 72. (Holotype: ANSP 6807, a female from South America, restricted to Santa Marta region, Colombia, by Schmidt, 1955, collected by Wilson.)

Elaps hollandi Griffin, 1916: 218. (Holotype: CM 206, a male from Bonda, Colombia, collected by H. H. Smith in June 1901.)
Micrurus dissoleucus melanogenys: Schmidt, 1936a: 203.

Range: Low montane scrub formations and semi-desertic formations in the foothills of Sierra Nevada de Santa Marta region of Colombia, from sea level to about 200 m.

Description: Males have 185 to 193 (190.0) and females have 196 to 207 (198.4) ventrals; subcaudals 21 to 22 (21.6) in males and 17 to 19 (17.3) in females; the frontal is wider than the supraoculars and approximately as long as the prefrontals. Examined: 4 males and 5 females, including the holotype.

The white parietal band is quite regular and covers the posterior part of the frontal and the anterior part of the parietals, at least 1 temporal, and 1 or 2 supralabials. The chin is all black or black with small white spots on the genials. The black nuchal band extends over the posterior part of the parietals and 4 to 5 dorsals. Ventrally, it fuses completely with the black infracephalic coloration, making the chin and usually the first 3 ventrals all black. The central black band of the triads is longer than the outer ones and the latter are longer than the white bands. The red bands are up to twice as long as the central black bands and about 2 or more times longer than the outer black bands. The white bands are 2 to 3 dorsals long and have irregular small black tips on about one-third of the dorsals. The coloration of the tail has the same pattern as the body except that the red bands are about as long as the outer black bands.

Including the black nuchal band that represents a remnant of the first triad, the males have $1/3$ 7 to $1/3$ 9 (7.5) and females have $1/3$ 7 to $1/3$ 8 (7.3) triads on the body. Both sexes have only one full triad on the tail.

Size: This is probably the smallest subspecies of all coral snakes. The smallest specimen measures only 162 mm in total length. The largest specimen measures 366 mm but most adults range between 280 and 320 mm in total length.

Remarks: This subspecies intergrades with *M. d. nigrirostris* near Ciénaga, Magdalena, Colombia.

Food: Unknown.

References: Schmidt (1955) compared it with other subspecies of this species.

Etymology: Greek from *melanos* meaning black and *genys* meaning chin, thus alluding to the black chin of this species.

Micrurus dissoleucus nigrirostris
Barranquilla Pygmy Coral Snake; Candelilla Barranquillera

Elaps gravenhorsti Jan, 1858: 523. (Holotype unknown.)
Micrurus dissoleucus nigrirostris Schmidt, 1955: 355. (Holotype: SMF 20734, a male from Barranquilla, Colombia, collected by Fr. Regel in 1897.)

Range: Dry lowland forest and coastal scrub formation but also humid forest in Atlántico and the delta region of the lower Valle de Magdalena, Colombia, near sea level.

Description: Males have 189 to 205 (197.4) and females have 210 to 225 (219.6) ventrals; subcaudals 23 to 27 (24.8) in males and 19 to 23 (21.0) in females; the frontal is wider than or about as wide as the supraoculars, but longer or about as long as the prefrontals. Examined: 14 males and 8 females, including the holotype.

The white parietal band usually includes the posterior parts of the frontal and the supraoculars, the anterior part of the parietals, 1 or 2 postoculars, and at least 1 temporal and 2 supralabials; the sixth supralabial is always white. The chin and several ventrals are all black with occasional light spots on the genials. The black nuchal band extends over the posterior part of the parietals and 3 to 5 dorsals. Ventrally, it fuses with the black coloration of the head. Occasionally, the black nuchal band is interrupted ventrally. The central black band of the triads is longer than the outer bands. The white bands are 3 to 4 dorsals long, shorter than the outer black bands, and have black tips on about half of the scales. The red bands are approximately twice as long as the central black band, but are shorter toward the posterior part of the body. They are immaculate or have a few small black-tipped scales. The black tail bands are slightly reduced ventrally and the red bands are shorter than those on the body.

Including the first nuchal black band, the males have 1/3 6 to 1/3 8 (6.6) and the females have 1/3 7 to 1/3 8 (7.6) triads on the body. About half of the males have 1 tail triad and the balance has 1-1/3 triads, while females have a single, complete triad.

Size: This is a small subspecies, but a little larger than its neighbor, *M. d. melanogenys*. The longest specimen measured 381 mm in total length, and several adults range between 290 and 350 mm.

Remarks: This subspecies intergrades with *M. d. melanogenys* near the Ciénaga region, Magdalena, Colombia.

Food: Unknown.

References: Schmidt (1955), Medem (1968), Dugand (1975), Pérez-Santos (1986a), and Pérez-Santos and Moreno (1988) gave additional descriptions and distribution.

Etymology: Latin from *niger* meaning black and *rostrum* meaning snout; thus *nigrirostris* is black-snouted (snake). *Gravenhorsti* was named after J. L. C. Gravenhorst, an active herpetologist at the Breslau Museum in the middle of the last century.

Micrurus distans (Map 15)
Clear-banded Coral Snake (West Mexican Coral Snake) Coralilla Bandas Claras

Distribution: From southwestern Chihuahua and southern Sonora through Sinaloa, Nayarit, Colima, and Jalisco, southward to the Río Balsas basin in Michoacán and Guerrero, Mexico.

Definition: A single-banded coral snake with a black snout and a yellow or white parietal band and with light spots on the snout and/or supralabials. The chin is yellow with some scales bordered with black. The nuchal black band does not reach the tips of the parietals. The red scales lack black tips or have a few small black tips. There are no supraanal tubercles in males.

Size: This is a medium-large coral snake. The longest measured specimen is 1,075 mm; many adults range between 450 and 850 mm.

Remarks: It can be recognized by the long red and yellow bands that are usually not spotted. Four subspecies are recognized.

References: General notes on the species are by Schmidt (1933a, 1936b) and Roze (1967, 1983); Zweifel (1959) clarified its taxonomy and a complete description and distribution appeared in Campbell and Lamar (1989). General distribution in Mexico is given by Schmidt (1933a, 1936b), Martín del Campo (1935), H. M. Smith and Taylor (1945, 1966), and Croulet (1963); in Chihuahua by Tanner (1985); in Colima by Oliver (1937) and Duellman (1958); in Jalisco by Casas-Andreu (1981); in Michoacán by Schmidt and Shannon (1947) and Duellman (1954, 1961); in Nayarit by H. M. Smith and Chrapliwy (1958); in Sinaloa by E. H. Taylor (1938) and Hardy and McDiarmid (1969); and in Sonora by Bogert and Oliver (1945) and Zweifel and Norris (1955). H. M. Smith and Necker (1944) commented on type specimens. Earlier significant references include Kennicott (1860), Garman (1884a), Dugès (1891), and Mocquard (1899).

Key to the Subspecies of *M. distans*

1 Less than 10 black body bands
   ... *M. d. michoacanensis* (Guerrero and Michoacán, Mexico)
1' More than 10 black bands 2
2 Males with 17 to 19 and females with 19 to 20 black body bands.
   ...... *M. d. zweifeli* (Southern Nayarit and Jalisco, Mexico))
2' Less than 16 black bands in males and less than 18 in females 3
3 Males with 50 to 55 subcaudals and 198 to 209 ventrals; females with 43 to 44 subcaudals and 216 to 218 ventrals
   ... *M. d. oliveri* (Southwestern Jalisco and Colima, Mexico)
3' Males with 46 to 52 subcaudals and 208 to 214 ventrals; females with 37 to 41 subcaudals and 222 to 235 ventrals
   .... *M. d. distans* (Sonora and Chihuahua to northern Nayarit, Mexico)

Micrurus distans distans (Color 18)
Common Clear-banded Coral Snake; Coralilla Bandas Claras Común

Elaps distans Kennicott, 1860: 338. (Holotype: USNM 1144, a male from Batosegachie, Chihuahua, Mexico.)
Micrurus distans distans: Zweifel, 1959: 7.

Range: Tropical dry lowland and dry montane formations from southern Sonora, southern Chihuahua, and southwestern Sinaloa to northern Nayarit, Mexico, from about sea level to 1,500 m.

Description: Males have 208 to 214 (210.3) and females have 222 to 235 (228.8) ventrals; subcaudals 46 to 52 (49.7) in males and 38 to 41 (39.4) in females. Examined: 13 males and 10 females, including the holotype.

The black snout coloration extends over the anterior part of the parietals and postoculars. Light spots are present on the rostral and on the supralabials and occasionally also on the nasals and internasals. The chin is all white or has some small black spots on the infralabials and the genials. The nuchal black band begins 1 to 2 dorsals behind the parietals. The nuchal band is 4 to 7 dorsals long and often is interrupted or reduced ventrally. The black bands are 2 to 4 dorsals long in males and 3 to 6 in females; they are reduced by 1 to 2 scales ventrally. The yellow or white bands are ½ to 2 dorsals long, without black-tipped scales. The first red band is 18 to 25 dorsals long, and immaculate. The other red bands decrease in size toward the tail and occupy 13 to 18 dorsals in males and 6 to 13 in females. Thus, there is a sexual dimorphism in the length of the red and black bands. Only black and white bands are present on the tail; the black bands are about 4 times as long as the white bands.

The males have 11 to 15 (12.8) and the females have 12 to 17 (13.6), usually 12 to 14, black body bands. The males have 4 to 6 (5.1) and the females have 3 to 4 (3.5) black tail bands.

Remarks: This subspecies intergrades with *M. d. zweifeli* in central Nayarit, Mexico.

Food: Colubrid snakes.

References: See reference for *M. distans* for Sinaloa, Sonora and northern Nayarit. Campbell and Lamar (1989) include a color photograph.

Etymology: Latin from *dista* meaning stand apart; *distans* probably refers to the long distance between the black bands, unusual in coral snakes.

Micrurus distans michoacanensis
Michoacán Clear-banded Coral Snake; Coralilla Bandas Claras Michoacana

Elaps distans var. *michoacanensis* Dugès, 1891; 487. (Holotype: lost in Dugès Museum, Mexico.)
Micrurus distans michoacanensis: Zweifel, 1959: 9.

Range: Low dry montane tropical scrub forest in the Río Balsas basin of Michoacán and Guerrero, Mexico, from about 100 to 700 m above sea level.

Description: Males have 208 to 213 (209.5) and females have 224 to 230 (225.4) ventrals; subcaudals 47 to 50 (49.0) in males and 38 to 39 (38.8) in females. Examined: 6 males and 4 females.

The black snout coloration extends over the anterior part of the parietals, all of the frontal, the anterior temporals, and the postoculars. Light spots are present on the rostral, the internasals, and the first supralabials. The chin is all white. The black nuchal band begins 1 to 2 dorsals behind the parietals and is 4 to 8 dorsals and ventrals long. The black body bands are 3 to 4 dorsals and ventrals long. The remainder of the body is covered by red bands with or without short yellow bands. The general impression of this snake in life is that it is a brilliantly red-colored snake with a few black bands. The black tail bands are up to 4 times as long as the light bands.

The males have 6 to 7 (6.6) and the females 7 to 9 (7.8) black body bands. Except for one females that has only two bands, both sexes have 3 black tail bands.

Remarks: Found in the dry Balsas River basin, it looks similar to the previous subspecies.

Food: Probably colubrid snakes.

References: Schmidt and Smith (1943) discussed its status and type specimen and Duellman (1961) gave ecological and morphological data.

Etymology: Latin *michoacenensis* denotes belonging to or an inhabitant of Michoacán.

Micrurus distans oliveri (Pattern 18)
Colima Clear-banded Coral Snake; Coral Bandas Claras Colimense

Micrurus distans oliveri Roze, 1967: 18. (Holotype: AMNH 12780, a male from Periquillo, Colima, Mexico, obtained by P. D. R. Ruthling on March 28, 1919.)

Range: Dry lowland scrub forest in Colima and southwestern Jalisco, Mexico, from about sea level to 200 m.

Description: Males have 197 to 209 (203.0) and females have 216 to 218 (216.7) ventrals; subcaudals 50 to 55 (52.8) in males and 43 to 44 (43.7) in females. Examined: 3 males and 3 females, including the holotype.

The black snout coloration includes half of the parietals, but white spots are found on the first supralabials and usually also on the rostral and internasals. The chin is almost completely white but has some dark or black markings concentrated on the sutures of the first infralabials and the genials. The black nuchal band begins 1 to 2 dorsals behind the parietals and is 4 to 6 dorsals long. It is usually reduced but complete ventrally. The black body bands are 3 to 4 dorsals and 2 to 4 ventrals long. The faint yellow bands are ½ to 1 dorsal long. The red bands are usually immaculate, but occasional faint blackish tips are sometimes observed on the first few red bands. The white tail bands may be longer or shorter than the black bands that follow them.

The males have 11 to 13 (12.0) and the females have 13 to 14 (13.6) black body bands. The males have 3 to 6 (5.1) and the females have 4 to 5 (4.3) black tail bands.

Remarks: A little-known coral snake from western Mexico.

Food: Unknown.

References: The original description and Casas-Andreu (1981).

Etymology: Named after the late James A. Oliver, director of the American Museum of Natural History, New York, who made considerable contributions to herpetology.

Micrurus distans zweifeli (Pattern 19)
Zweifel's Coral Snake; Coralilla de Zweifel

Micrurus distans zweifeli Roze, 1967: 21. (Holotype: CAS 95769, a male from Laguna Santa María, Nayarit, Mexico, between elevations of 2,000 and 4,000 ft, collected by A. Green on July 19, 1964.)

Range: Dry to humid moderate montane tropical formations in southern Nayarit and adjacent Magdalena, Jalisco, Mexico, from 700 to 1,200 m above sea level.

Description: The only known male has 217 ventrals; females have 237 to 242 (239.5) ventrals; subcaudals around 48 in males and 39 to 41 (40.0) in females. Examined: 1 male and 2 females, including the holotype.

The black snout coloration extends over the anterior part of the parietals, the preoculars, and the anterior temporal, but light spots are found on the rostral and/or internasals and the first supralabials. The black nuchal band is 7 to 8 dorsals long, but is reduced to 2 to 5 scales ventrally. It begins behind the parietals. The black body bands are 4 to 6 dorsals and 3 to 5 ventrals long; they are bordered by yellow bands 1 to 2 dorsals and ventrals long. The red bands are 5 to 10 dorsals and ventrals long with small black or dark grey scale tips that decrease in size or may be absent on the last red bands. The black tail bands are 3 to 4 times as long as the white bands.

The only known male has 19 and the females have 19 to 20 (19.5) black body bands. The male has 6 and the females have 4 black tail bands.

Remarks: This subspecies intergrades with *M. d. distans* in southern Nayarit, Mexico.

Food: Unknown.

References: The original description.

Etymology: Named after Richard G. Zweifel, curator emeritus of herpetology of the American Museum of Natural History, New York, who did extensive research in western Mexico.

Micrurus dumerilii (Map 16)
Capuchin Coral Snake (Duméril's Coral Snake); Coral Capuchina

Distribution: Northern Colombia and northern Venezuela, southward to northwestern Ecuador; probably also in eastern Panama.

Definition: A single-banded coral snake in which several subspecies have developed accessory triad color patterns. When accessory triads are present, the first is represented by the nuchal band and a poorly developed posterior accessory black band. This means that the first "triad" is made up of only ⅔ of a full triad. The head has a black cap that is occasionally reduced in some subspecies. The black nuchal band may be present, reduced, or absent. The red bands have conspicuous black-tipped scales. On the tail there are only black and white bands, or in larger specimens most of the light bands can be red. Males have supraanal tubercles.

Size: This is a medium-sized coral snake. The longest measured specimen is 922 mm in total length, but many adults measure between 500 and 700 mm.

Remarks: Six subspecies are recognized, some of them still poorly defined. It is a somewhat confusing species as it contains both single-banded subspecies and subspecies with accessory triad color pattern.

References: General comments on the species are by Amaral (1925a), Schmidt (1936a), Roze (1967, 1970b, 1983), P. Müller (1973), and description and distribution by Campbell and Lamar (1989). Records for Colombia are: Ruthven (1922), Amaral (1928, 1931b), Rendahl and Vestergren (1940), Nicéforo-María (1942), Dunn (1944a, 1944b), Daniel (1949), Schmidt (1955), Medem (1969), Dugand (1975), Castro et al (1982), Angel (1983), Pérez-Santos (1986a, 1986b), Pérez-Santos and Moreno (1986, 1987, 1988); for Ecuador: Orcés (1942, 1943, 1948), J. A. Peters (1960) and Miyata (1982); and for Venezuela: D'Empaire et al (1921), Milá de la Roca (1932), Pifano (1935, 1938), Vellard (1941), Marcuzzi (1950), Roze (1955, 1966a), Vetencourt Finol (1960), Hoge and Lancini (1962), Lancini (1970, 1979), and Sandner-Montilla (1985). Type specimens were discussed by McCoy and Richmond (1966), Tiedemann and Haupl (1980), and Roux-Estève (1983).

Key to the Subspecies of *M. dumerilii*

1 Triads present; black bands are irregular ventrally 2
1' Single black bands, ventrally well defined 3
2 Ventrals 195 to 206 in males and 208 to 220 in females; black nuchal band 6 to 11 dorsals long
 . . . . *M. d. dumerilii* (Lower Magdalena Valley, Colombia)
2' Ventrals 170 to 192 in males and 198 to 208 in females; black nuchal 3 to 5 dorsals long
 . . . . . . *M. d. colombianus* (Santa Marta Mountains, Colombia)
3 Usually more than 191 ventrals in males and more than 203 in females 4
3' Ventrals 177 to 191 in males and 194 to 199 in females
 . . . . *M. d. venezuelensis* (Northern Venezuela)

4 Black nuchal band usually reduced to half or absent dorsally; black bands 10 to 17, usually no more than 13 in males and 13 to 16 in females
M. d. antioquiensis (Central Cauca Valley, Colombia)
4' Black nuchal present; black bands 11 to 19 in males and 15 to 23 in females 5
5 Black cap usually reduced or absent from parietals; snout all black; black bands 14 to 19, usually more than 16 in males; 19 to 23 in females
... *M. d. carinicauda* (Northwestern Venezuela and adjacent Colombia)
5' Black cap usually complete; frequently light spots on snout; black bands 11 to 16 in males; 15 to 20 in females
M. d. transandinus (Western Colombia and northwestern Ecuador)

Note: Intergrades from Cundinamarca and Boyacá, Colombia, and Falcón, Venezuela, are not identified with this key. See text for their identification as intergrades by localities.

Micrurus dumerilii dumerilii (Fig. 55)
Common Capuchin Coral Snake; Coral Capuchina Común

Elaps dumerilii Jan, 1858: 522. (Holotype: MNHN 3923, a male from Cartagena [Colombia], collected by Barot.)
Micrurus dumerilii dumerilii: Roze, 1970b: 207.

Range: Dry and intermediate tropical lowland formations in the lower Magdalena Valley in northern Colombia, from sea level to about 200 m.

Description: Males have 195 to 206 (198.9) and females have 208 to 220 (215.3) ventrals; subcaudals 49 to 53 (50.7) in males and 35 to 41 (37.2) in females. Examined: 685 males and 328 females, including the holotype.

A triad-type subspecies in which the black cap extends completely or almost completely over the parietals but is separated from the black nuchal band. The chin is heavily marked by irregular black spots. The black nuchal band is 6 to 11 dorsals long and 1 to 2 scales shorter ventrally. The black central band of the triads is 2 or more times as long as the irregular outer bands. The frequent lengths of the bands of the first full triad are 2-5-2 or 3-5-3 dorsals. Dorsally, the central black band is as long as ventrally or a little longer. The black outer bands are quite irregular dorsally and more so ventrally where they may be represented only by irregular black spots. The white bands are usually 1 dorsal and ventral long, except the first light band behind the black nuchal, which is usually 2 dorsals long. The white bands have irregular black-tipped scales. The red bands may be slightly longer or shorter than a complete triad, with irregular black tips on all dorsals, but ventrally they are usually immaculate. The black tail bands are 3 to 4 times as long as the white ones. The latter have very conspicuous black-tipped

Figure 55. *Micrurus dumerilii dumerilii*, from Colombia, around Barranquilla: A) Dorsal view, B) Ventral view. (Courtesy of Edward Seligmann.)

scales or a large black dorsal spot that at times fuses with the black bands.

The males have ⅔ 7 to ⅔ 10 (8.4) and the females have ⅔ 9 to ⅔ 13 triads. Males have 6 to 9 (8.4) and females have 5 to 7 (6.1) black tail bands.

Remarks: This subspecies intergrades with *M. d. colombianus* east of Barranquilla, Colombia. It is one of the most abundant coral snakes.

Food: Unknown, probably lizards.

References: See under species, especially those from northern Colombia.

Etymology: Named after Auguste M. C. Duméril, one of the great French herpetologists of the last century.

Micrurus dumerilii antioquiensis (Pattern 20)
Antioquian Coral Snake; Coral Antioqueña

Micrurus antioquiensis Schmidt, 1936a: 195. (Holotype: BM 1946. 1.17.23, a female from Santa Rita, north of Medellín, Antioquia, Colombia, collected by Pratt in 1898.)
Micrurus dumerilii antioquiensis: Roze, 1970b: 207.

Range: Humid to wet montane forest in Valle del Cauca from Medellín southward in central Colombia, from 900 to 2,600 m above sea level.

Description: Males have 189 to 204 (194.6) and females have 210 to 217 (214.0) ventrals; subcaudals 47 to 57 (53.4) in males and 36 to 42 (39.4) in females. Examined: 20 males and 20 females, including the holotype.

A single-banded subspecies in which the black cap covers almost the entire parietals but the black nuchal band is either absent or reduced to a half band that is interrupted either dorsally or laterally. The chin is completely black or is light with large black spots on the genials and the gular region and with smaller black spots on other infracephalic scales. The impression of this subspecies is that it "moved" the black pigment from the dorsal black nuchal region forward onto the ventral part of the head. The black bands are 2 to 3 dorsals and 2 to 4 ventrals long. The white bands are reduced to ½ dorsal and may be indistinct ventrally. The red bands are 8 to 12 dorsals and ventrals long, immaculate or with small dots concentrated along the borders. The black tail bands are only slightly longer than the white bands. The latter have scales with conspicuous black tips or large irregular black spots that fuse together in some specimens.

The males have 10 to 17 (12.5) black body bands, usually 11 to 13, and females have 13 to 16 (14.8). The males have 6 to 8 (7.0) and the female have 4 to 6 (5.2) black tail bands.

Remarks: This subspecies intergrades with *M. d. carinicauda* in Cundinamarca and Boyacá, Colombia.

Food: Unknown.

References: Nicéforo-María (1942), Schmidt (1955), Medem (1969), and Pérez-Santos and Moreno (1986, 1987, 1988) provided additional comments on this subspecies.

Etymology: The name *antioquiensis* denotes its presence in Antioquia, Colombia.

Micrurus dumerilii carinicauda
Intermediate Capuchin Coral Snake; Coral Capuchina Intermedia

Micrurus carinicauda Schmidt, 1936a: 194. (Holotype: FMNH 2587, a male from Orope, Zulia, Venezuela [corrected to Orope, Táchira, Venezuela, by Hoge and Lancini, 1962, as Orope actually lies in Táchira and not in Zulia], collected by Ned Dearborn in 1909.)
Micrurus dumerilii carinicauda: Roze, 1970b: 207.

Range: Savanna and intermediate tropical formations in Norte de Santander and Santander, Colombia, and adjacent Zulia, Táchira, and Apure in western Venezuela, from 100 to 800 m above sea level.

Description: Males have 192 to 197 (193.6) and females have 204 to 212 (208.2) ventrals; subcaudals 48 to 55 (51.0) in males and 33 to 42 (35.1) in females. Examined: 8 males and 11 females, including the holotype.

A single-banded subspecies in which the black cap covers most of the parietals or is reduced and covers about one half the length of the parietals. The chin is white with several black scales, usually the mental and the first infralabials. The black nuchal band is complete and 4 to 6 dorsals long. The white or yellow bands are ½ to 1 dorsal and ventral long. The red bands are 6 to 13 dorsals and ventrals long; the anterior bands are longer than the posterior bands and all red scales have regular black tips. The red bands are usually immaculate ventrally. The black tail bands are about twice as long as the white bands; the latter have irregular black-tipped scales.

The males have 14 to 19 (17.1) and the females have 19 to 23 (20.7) black body bands. The males have 6 to 9 (7.7) and the females have 4 to 7 (4.9) black tail bands.

Remarks: This subspecies intergrades with *M. d. antioquiensis* in Cundinamarca and Boyacá, Colombia, and with *M. d. venezuelensis* in Falcón, Venezuela.

Food: Swamp eels (*Synbranchus marmoratus*) and snakelike lizards (*Bachia cuvieri*).

References: Roze (1955, 1966a), Hoge and Lancini (1962), and Lancini (1979) commented on diverse aspects of this subspecies in Venezuela, including some illustrations; Schmidt (1932a) described food.

Etymology: Latin from *carina* meaning a keel and *cauda* meaning tail; the keeled-tail (snake), denoting the presence of supraanal keels or tubercles in males.

Micrurus dumerilii colombianus
Santa Marta Capuchin Coral Snake; Coral Capuchina Santamartense

Elaps colombianus Griffin, 1916: 216. (Holotype: CM 197, a female from Minca, Colombia, collected by H. H. Smith in June [no year given, probably 1901].)
Micrurus dumerilii colombianus: Roze, 1970b: 207.

Range: Tropical dry montane scrub formations and wet forest in the Santa Marta Mountains of northern Colombia, between 300 and 2,200 m above sea level.

Description: Males have 179 to 192 (185.2) and females have 198 to 207 (203.5) ventrals; subcaudals 44 to 51 (47.1) in males and 31 to 37 (34.4) in females. Examined: 7 males and 4 females, including the holotype.

An accessory triad-type subspecies in which the black cap may be either complete or reduced. Occasional light spots are present on the snout. The chin is mostly black or is white with some irregular black spots. The nuchal black band, 3 to 5 dorsals long, is followed by a white band 1 dorsal long and by a poorly-defined accessory black band, formed by the concentration of black-tipped scales but without forming a clearly defined band. In this accessory triad-type pattern, the central black bands are 2 to 3 dorsals and ventrals long. The outer bands, formed by the concentration of black-tipped scales, become better defined on the posterior part of the body where they are 1 to 2 dorsals long. They are absent on the venter or are represented by irregular black spots. The white bands are ½ to 1 dorsal and ventral long. The first red band is 19 to 21 dorsals long; the others are 11 to 15 dorsals and ventrals long. They become shorter toward the posterior part of the body. The red scales have conspicuous or feebly-defined black tips. The tail has irregular black and white spots, barely distinguishable as bands.

The males have ⅔ 10 to ⅔ 13 (11.4) and the females have ⅔ 11 to ⅔ 14 (12.5) triads. The males have 6 to 10 (7.3) and the females have 4 to 6 (4.7) irregular black tail bands.

Remarks: This subspecies intergrades with *M. d. dumerilii* east of Barranquilla, northern Colombia.

Food: Unknown.

References: Ruthven (1922) commented on the variation of this subspecies.

Etymology: The name *colombianus* denotes its exclusive presence in Colombia.

Micrurus dumerilii transandinus (Color 19)
Transandean Capuchin Coral Snake; Coral Capuchina Transandina

Micrurus transandinus Schmidt, 1936a: 195. (Holotype: MCZ 32744, a male from Andagoya, Chocó, Colombia, collected by H. G. F. Spurrell in 1915.)
Micrurus dumerilii transandinus: Roze, 1970b: 207.

Range: Tropical lowland rain forest and wet montane forest of the Pacific side of the Andes in western Colombia and northwestern Ecuador, from sea level to about 1,500 m. One record was from Panama.

Description: Males have 190 to 204 (196.3) and females have 205 to 217 (212.1) ventrals; subcaudals 48 to 58 (53.4) in males and 36 to 41 (39.2) in females. Examined: 32 males and 34 females, including the holotype.

A single-banded subspecies with a complete or nearly complete black cap that covers the tips of the parietals. The chin is white but most of the infracephalic scales are outlined by black, and occasionally the upper part of the mental and the first infralabials also are black. The black nuchal band is 3 to 5 dorsals and ventrals long. In occasional specimens the black bands are irregularly expanded ventrally. The white bands are ½ to 1 dorsal and ventral long. The red bands have regular black-tipped scales and they diminish in length toward the tail. The first red band is 13 to 17 dorsals long, but near the tail they are only 5 to 7 dorsals and ventrals long. Ventrally, occasional specimens have 1 or 2 large black spots in the red areas. Black and white tail bands are found in small to medium-sized individuals, but larger specimens have black, red, and white bands with conspicuous irregular black-tipped scales in the middle of the red bands.

The males have 11 to 16 (14.3) and the females 15 to 21 (17.4) black bands. The males have 6 to 9 (7.5), usually 7 to 8, the females have 5 to 7 (5.6), usually 5 to 6, black tail bands.

Remarks: A single specimen is said to have come from the Isthmus of Panama and it is probable that this coral snake is found in the Darién region of Panama.

References: See under the species; Campbell and Lamar (1989) featured color photos and Alemdariz (1991) gave its distribution in Ecuador.

Etymology: Name denotes its transandean distribution; Latin *transandinus* meaning inhabitant of regions across or "on the other side or beyond" the Andes.

Micrurus dumerilii venezuelensis (Pattern 21)
Venezuelan Capuchin Coral Snake; Coral Capuchina Venezolana

Micrurus dumerilii venezuelensis Roze, 1989: 7. (Holotype: AMNH 59392, a female from El Valle, Distrito Federal, Venezuela, collected by Edgardo Mondolfi, July 20, 1938)

Range: Tropical lowland and humid montane forest altered by humans in the Cordillera de la Costa in north-central Venezuela, from sea level to about 1,100 m.

Description: Males have 177 to 191 (183.4) and females have 194 to 199 (197.0) ventrals; subcaudals 47 to 51 (48.6) in males and 33 to 35 (34.3) in females. Examined: 7 males and 4 females, including the holotype.

This is a single-banded subspecies with the black cap usually reduced, covering only half the length of the parietals. Occasionally the black cap reaches almost to the tips of the parietals. Below, the mental and the first infralabials are black; the rest of the chin is white. The black nuchal band covers 3 to 6 dorsals and ventrals. The black bands cover 2 to 4 dorsals and 2 to 3 ventrals. The yellow or white band is ½ to 1 dorsal and ventral long, usually without black tips. The red bands have scales with regular black tips and are 5 to 10 dorsals and ventrals long; the longest ones are on the anterior part of the body. They are usually immaculate ventrally. The black tail bands are 2 to 3 times longer than the white or yellow bands.

The males have 17 to 24 (20.1) black body bands and the females have 24 to 26 (25.0). The males have 8 to 10 (8.4) and the females have 6 to 7 (6.5) black tail bands.

Remarks: This subspecies intergrades with *M. d. carinicauda* in Falcón, Venezuela, and its exact distribution has yet to be defined.

Food: Unknown.

References: Only the original description and Roze (1955) and Lancini (1979) published color photos under the name of *M. carinicauda* and *M. dumerilii carinicaudus*, respectively.

Etymology: In Latin the ending *-ensis* means belonging to or inhabitant of; thus *venezuelensis* denotes its presence in Venezuela.

Micrurus elegans (Map 17)
Elegant Coral Snake; Coral Elegante or Coralilla Elegante

Distribution: Mexico from central Veracruz and northern Oaxaca to Tabasco and Chiapas, southward to Alta Verapaz, Guatemala.

Definition: A triad-type coral snake in which the white or yellow and the red or yellowish-brown bands are partially split in two by an irregular series of transverse black dorsal spots. The head is black with a narrow, irregular white or yellow parietal band (usually interrupted on the parietal suture) that extends irregularly onto the lower part of the head. The first body triad consists of only 2 black bands. It is the only species with triad-type coloration that has supraanal tubercles and in which the red is occasionally replaced by an orangy-yellow or yellowish-brown color.

Size: This is a medium-small sized coral snake. The largest specimen measures 733 mm in total length; many adults range between 400 and 600 mm.

Remarks: The unique, disrupted triad-type coloration distinguishes this species. Two subspecies are recognized.

References: General notes on species and/or subspecies are found in Mocquard (1908–1909), Schmidt (1932, 1933a, 1936b, 1958), Roze (1967, 1970b, 1983), Villa et al. (1988), and full description in Campbell and Lamar (1989); for Mexico in Gadow (1905), Ocaranza (1930), Cuesta Terrón (1932), H. M. Smith and Taylor (1945), Martín del Campo (1950), Alvarez del Toro and Smith (1956), Baker et al. (1971), Alvarez del Toro (1972, 1983), Blaney and Blaney (1978), Ramirez-Bautista et al. (1981), Johnson (1984), Flores Villela et al. (1987), and Pérez-Higadera et al. (1987); for Guatemala in Stuart (1948, 1950, 1963) and Campbell and Vannini (1989). Comments related to mimicry were by H. M. Smith (1941, 1942), H. M. Smith and Landy (1965), and Greene and McDiarmid (1981) and comments about karyotypes were by Gutiérrez et al. (1988). Significant earlier references include Jan (1859a), Jan and Sordelli (1872), Cope (1861, 1887), Sumichrast (1881–1882), Garman (1884a, 1884b), and Werner (1896).

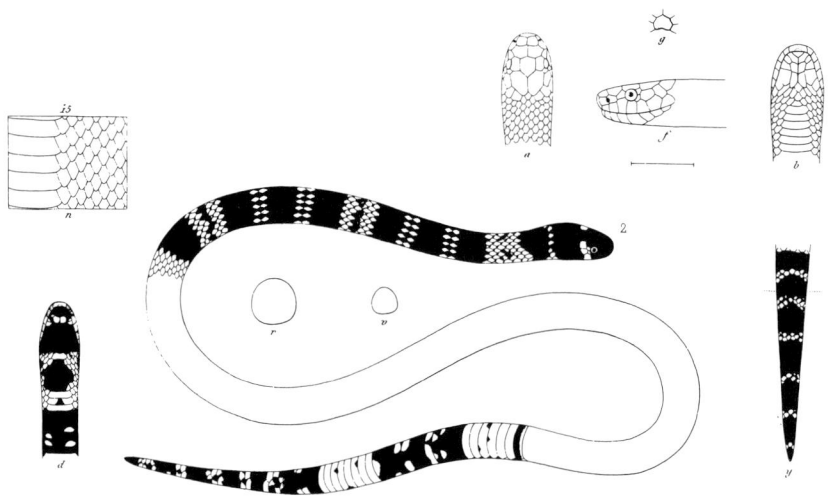

Figure 56. Micrurus elegans, a figure from Jan 1858 and 1859a, Jan and Sordelli 1872 (Livr. 42, pl. 5, fig. 2) depicting a specimen from Mexico. This figure serves as lectotype for *M. elegans*.

Key to the Subspecies of *M. elegans*

1. Males have 187 to 197 and females 203 to 216 ventrals; red bands distinct or reddish brown
..... *M. e. elegans* (Veracruz and Oaxaca, Mexico)
1'. Males have 202 to 212 and females 218 to 226 ventrals; "red" bands frequently yellowish brown
.. *M. e. veraepacis* (Tabasco, Mexico to Guatemala)

Micrurus elegans elegans (Fig. 56, Pattern 22)
Western Elegant Coral Snake; Coralilla Elegante Occidental

Elaps elegans Jan, 1858: 524. (Holotype: the lectotype, a female from Mexico, designated by Schmidt, 1958, in Museo di Storia Naturale, Milan, was destroyed during World War II. As the specimen was illustrated by Jan, 1858 and 1859a, and by Jan and Sordelli, 1872, the illustration in the latter work [Livr. 42, pl. 5, Fig. 2] may serve as the lectotype (Fig. 56). The type locality was restricted to Jalapa, Veracruz, Mexico, by H. M. Smith and Taylor, 1945.)

Micrurus elegans elegans: Schmidt, 1933a: 32.

Range: Wet and dry montane forest and cloud forest in central Veracruz and northern Oaxaca, at altitudes between 800 and 1,700 m.

Description: Males have 187 to 197 (192.9) and females have 203 to 214 (206.8) ventrals; subcaudals 39 to 44 (41.2) in males and 29 to 31 (30) in females. Many specimens have up to 22 undivided subcaudals. Examined: 13 males and 7 females.

The head is black including the first dorsals and ventrals, except for a narrow, irregular yellow parietal crossband that is interrupted on the parietal suture. It covers the central part of the parietals, one or more temporals, and part of the supraoculars. There are some yellow spots on one or more infralabials and on part of the genials. An irregular yellow band consisting of a series of individual yellow or brownish dorsal spots is found several dorsals behind the parietals. The first red band is behind the second black neck band. The body is covered by a peculiarly modified triad-type coloration. The red and yellow bands are interrupted transversely by an irregular series of black spots that frequently are not continuous, particularly on the red bands. The red bands are usually longer than the black bands, occupying 4 to 6 dorsals. However, they are so irregular that their actual length is difficult to define. The central black band is slightly longer than the outer bands. Approximately the same irregular pattern is present on the venter. The anal plate is usually situated at the level of the central black band of the last body triad, so that the formula for a complete sequence of body triads is $2/3 \times 1/3$. Only single black and irregular yellow bands are present on the tail.

The males had $2/3\ 10$ to $2/3\ 13\ 1/3$ (10.9) and the females have $2/3\ 11\ 1/3$ to $2/3\ 13\ 1/3$ black body triads. The males have 7 to 8 (7.7) and the females have 5 to 7 (6.0) black tail bands.

This subspecies seems to be the smaller one. The largest measured specimen is 555 mm long, while adults have an overall length between 450 and 500 mm.

Food: Litter-dwelling colubrid snakes (*Geophis semidoliatus*) and blind snakes (*Leptotyphlops*).

References: Ramírez-Bautista et al. (1981), Pérez-Higadera (sic) (1987), Flores Villela et al. (1987) and Pérez-Higareda and Smith (1990) mentioned this subspecies for the Tuxtla region of Veracruz, Mexico.

Etymology: Latin *elegans* means elegant or fine, alluding to its very rich color pattern.

Micrurus elegans veraepacis (Color 20)
Verapaz Elegant Coral Snake; Coral Elegante Verapazense

Micrurus elegans verae-pacis Schmidt, 1933a: 32. (Holotype: ZSBS 2247/0, a male from Campur, Alta Verapaz, Guatemala, collected by Karl Sapper.)

Range: Humid and dry montane formations from southern Tabasco and Chiapas, Mexico, to Alta Verapaz and Huehuetenango, Guatemala, at altitudes between 600 and 1700 m above sea level.

Description: Males have 202 to 212 (207.2) and females have 218 to 226 (222.7) ventrals; subcaudals 46 to 49 (47.6) in males and 32 to 37 (34.0) in females. A few specimens have 1 or 2 undivided subcaudals. Examined: 10 males and 12 females, including the holotype.

The head is black and extends over several dorsals behind the parietals. The yellow parietal crossband is somewhat wider than in the previous subspecies but is irregular and interrupted on the parietal suture. Ventrally, it is represented by a few irregular yellow spots on some infralabials and on the genials. The head coloration is similar to that of *M. e. elegans*. The original red bands frequently are yellowish brown, equal to or shorter than the black bands, and are usually 2 to 3 dorsals long. They have only a few irregular black spots that do not form black crossbands on the "red" (yellowish or orange-brown) bands. The black bands are 4 to 5 dorsals long and are approximately the same length. The white bands have an irregular black crossband, splitting them into two. On the venter the black bands are irregular and somewhat expanded, suggesting only an approximate triad-type coloration. The overall impression of specimens of this subspecies is that of a black, yellowish-brown and white-colored coral snake.

The males have $2/3$ 12 $1/3$ to $2/3$ 14 $1/3$ (13.0) and the females have $2/3$ 14 $1/3$ to $2/3$ 19 $1/3$ (16.2) black triads on the body. The males have 6 to 10 (7.8) and the females have 4 to 12 (7.3) irregular black tail bands.

Food: Ground-dwelling colubrid snakes (*Stenorrhina degenhardtii*).

References: Stuart (1948, 1950) described them from the Alta Verapaz region of Guatemala, while Campbell and Lamar (1989) featured a color photo.

Etymology: The name *veraepacis* denotes its distribution or presence in Verapaz, Guatemala, from where it was originally described.

Micrurus ephippifer (Map 17)
Double Black Coral Snake (Oaxacan Coral Snake); Coralilla Doble Negra

Distribution: From the Isthmus of Tehunatepec to central Oaxaca, Mexico.

Definition: A single-banded coral snake with a black snout followed by a white parietal band. The mental and the first infralabials are black. The nuchal black band covers the parietal tips. Dorsally the red bands have irregular black-tipped scales, spots, or a large saddlelike band that covers all or most of the red bands. The tail has black and white bands. Males lack supraanal tubercles.

Size: The is a medium-sized coral snake. The longest measured specimen is 926 mm; most adults measure between 500 and 730 mm.

Remarks: It can be easily recognized by the large black spots on the red scales. Two subspecies are recognized.

References: Data on distribution and variation from Oaxaca, Mexico are given by Schmidt (1933a, 1958), Martin del Campo (1935), H. M. Smith (1943), Woodbury and Woodbury (1944), H. M. Smith and Taylor (1945), H. M. Smith and Langebartel (1949), Lynch and Smith (1965), and Roze (1967, 1970b, 1983, 1989); a complete description with a color photo appeared in Campbell and Lamar (1989), while discussion of mimicry in Greene and McDiarmid (1981). Earlier significant references include Cope (1887).

Key to the Subspecies of *M. ephippifer*

1 Saddlelike black bands or spots on red bands; males have 15 to 21, females 17 to 23 black bands
    ... *M. e. ephippifer* (Tehuantepec, Oaxaca, Mexico)
1' Red bands have irregular black-tipped scales or spots occasionally fuse to form larger blotches; males have 22 to 26 and females 27 to 29 black bands
    .... *M. e. zapotecus* (Sierra Madre del Sur, Oaxaca, Mexico)

Micrurus ephippifer ephippifer (Pattern 27)
Tehuantepec Coral Snake; Coralilla Tehuantepeca

Elaps ephippifer Cope, 1886: 281. (Holotype: USNM 3085, a female from the Pacific side of the Isthmus of Tehuantepec [Oaxaca, Mexico] collected by Sumichrast.)
Micrurus ephippifer ephippifer: Roze, 1989: 11.

Range: Dry lowlands and dry scrub montane formations in the Isthmus of Tehuantepec and the dry mountains to the west in Quiengola, Oaxaca, Mexico, from sea level to about 1500 m.

Description: Males have 209 to 219 (215.7) and females have 225 to 239 (232.2) ventrals; subcaudals 49 to 57 (53.4) in males and 39 to 44 (41.5) in females. Examined: 21 males and 18 females, including the holotype.

The black snout coloration extends to the anterior part of the parietals and includes most of the frontal. The nuchal black band is 6 to 7 dorsals and about 5 to 6 ventrals long. It usually does not project forward onto the genials. Usually, the chin is yellow or white without or with very few black markings. The black bands are 4 to 6 dorsals and usually 4 ventrals long. The red bands dorsally are almost completely covered by a saddlelike black pattern. The impression is that of a black and white or black and yellow snake. The saddlelike black band either extends to ventrals or to the first rows of dorsals, which are still red. Ventrally, the red bands usually have some large black spots. The yellow bands are 1½ to 2 dorsals long. The black tail bands are about 2 or more times as long as the yellow or white bands.

The males have 15 to 21 (17.9) and females have 17 to 23 (20.5) black body bands. These counts include the original black bands only, not the saddlelike black bands that almost cover the red bands. The males have 5 to 6 (5.6) and the females have 4 to 6 (4.6) black tail bands.

Remarks: The saddlelike bands that cover the red areas make this subspecies easily distinguishable. It intergrades with *M. e. zapotecus* in the dry valleys east of Oaxaca and around Cerro San Felipe, Oaxaca, Mexico.

Food: Blind snakes (*Leptotyphlops phenops*).

References: Smith and Langebartel (1949) and Schmidt (1958) summarized the characteristics of the subspecies.

Etymology: Greek from *ephippi* meaning saddle, alluding to the saddlelike black dorsal spots, or *ephippifer* meaning bearer of saddle.

Micrurus ephippifer zapotecus (Fig. 57, Color 21)
Zapotec Coral Snake; Coralilla Zapoteca

Micrurus ephippifer zapotecus Roze, 1989b: 11. (Holotype AMNH 103119, a male from Tejocotes, Distrito de Etla, Oaxaca, Mexico, 2286 m, collected by Charles M. Bogert on September 10, 1968.)

Range: In humid and high mountain woodlands, pine-oak and oak-madroño formations in Sierra Madre del Sur, west of Oaxaca, Mexico, at altitudes between 1,700 and 2,400 m.

Figure 57. *Micrurus ephippifer zapotecus*, from Mexico: Tejocotes, Oaxaca (AMNH 103120, paratype).

Description: Males have 216 to 218 (217.0) and females 226 to 231 (228.5) ventrals; subcaudals are 47 to 49 (48.0) in males and 35 to 38 (36.5) in females. Examined: 2 males and 2 females, including the holotype.

The black snout coloration extends to the anterior part of the parietals and includes most of the frontal. The nuchal black band is 5 to 6 dorsals long and projects forward ventrally where it usually covers part of one or both pairs of genials, or there are at least some black spots on these shields. The black bands are 3 to 4 dorsals and 2 to 3 ventrals long. The red bands vary from having few black-tipped scales plus some larger spots to having a large black central band. However, the black on the red never occupies the entire red band. Ventrally, the red bands are either immaculate or have some small black tips or spots on the shields. The yellow bands are 1½ to 2 dorsals and 1 ventral long. The black tail bands are about twice as long as the yellow bands.

The males have 22 to 26 (24.0) and the females 27 to 29 black body bands. The males have 6 to 7 (6.5) black tail bands and the females have 5 to 6 (5.5).

Remarks: This subspecies intergrades with *M. e. ephippifer* to the east and in the vicinity of Oaxaca, and in Cerro San Felipie, Oaxaca, Mexico.

Food: Ground snakes, (*Rhadinaea taeniata aemula*).

References: Roze (1989) commented on the habitat and feeding of this subspecies.

Etymology: The name *zapotecus* indicates this coral snake dwells in the area where the Zapotec culture flourished several hundred years ago.

Micrurus filiformis (Map 11, Color 22)
Thread Coral Snake (Slender Coral Snake); Coral Hebra; Cobra Coral Fio

Elaps filiformis Günther, 1859: 86. (Holotype: BM 1946.1.20.13, a male from Pará, Brazil, collected by Higgins.)

Micrurus filiformis: Amaral, 1925a: 19.

Micrurus filiformis subtilis Roze, 1967: 22. (Holotype: AMNH 4461, a male from Carurú, Río Vaupés, Colombia-Brazil boundary, obtained by H. Schmidt and S. Weiss in November 1906).

Distribution and range: Tropical lowland rain forest, secondary forest, low montane forest, and open fields, usually near waters in the Amazon basin from southeastern and southern Colombia and northeastern Peru to Pará and Maranhão in northern Brazil; probably also found in the southern tip of Venezuela and Suriname from sea level to about 500 m.

Definition: A triad-type coral snake in which the first triad is complete. The snout is black, followed by a white prefrontal band, a frontal black band, and a red parietal-postparietal band. The red bands are nearly immaculate. Ventrals in both sexes are 271 to 333, a uniquely high number among species with a triad-type coloration. There are 1 or 2 postoculars and 6 or 7 infralabials. The internasals are reduced and the nostrils are directed more upward than toward the sides.

Description: Males have 270 to 316 (281.6) and females have 275 to 333 (302.8) ventrals; subcaudals 33 to 45 (39.2) in males and 30 to 41 (34.8) in females; 1 or 2 postoculars; 6 or 7 infralabials. Examined: 23 males and 9 females, including all holotypes.

The snout is black. The white prefrontal band forms a semiundulated figure covering part of the internasals and 2 supralabials, but its shape and length may be irregular or reduced to a white internasal spot. The black frontal band that follows extends over the frontal and anterior part of the parietals. It is followed by a red band that covers 1 to 6 dorsals. The chin is mostly red, with the mental and 3 to 4 infralabials black. The central black band of the triad is 3 to 6 dorsals and 3 to 5 ventrals long. The outer black bands are 2 to 4 dorsals and ventrals long. The white bands are immaculate, 1 to 3 dorsals (usually 2) and 2 to 4 ventrals long. The black triads are somewhat more irregular ventrally than they are dorsally. The red bands are 3 to 6 dorsals and 3 to 8 ventrals long. Dorsally, the red scales may be immaculate, or a very few scales have small and irregular black tips. On the tail the red bands and the triads are approximately the same length as on the body.

The males have 13 to 20 (17.1) and the females have 14 to 19 (17.7) body triads. The males have 1⅔ to 2⅔ and the females have 1⅓ to 2 black triads on the tail.

Size: This is medium-sized coral snake. The longest specimen reported by Cunha and Nascimento (1973) is 960 mm long, but most adults measure between 450 and 580 mm.

Remarks: This an exceptionally slender species, more so than most of the generally recognized slender coral snakes. It approaches the black-backed coral snakes (*Leptomicrurus*) in its slender form and in its strongly bent venom gland. The subspecies I described as *M. filiformis subtilis* (Roze, 1967), is not a clearly-defined one, as shown by Cunha and Nascimento (1982), even though the western populations have a lower number of ventrals. Bill Lamar has collected several specimens in Colombia near or in rivers (Lamar, personal communication) and it is quite possible that this species is much more dependent on the presence of water than other coral snakes, except the aquatic coral snake.

Food: Unknown; probably lizards and snakes; some invertebrates reported by Dixon and Soini (1977) may have been food taken by the coral snake's ingested prey.

References: General references of the species appeared in Schmidt (1936a), Roze (1967, 1970b, 1983), and a description with a color photo in Campbell and Lamar (1989) and Silva (1994); Greene (1973b) described its behavior. Amaral (1925a, 1930a, 1930b, 1930c, 1948b), Prado (1945), Machado (1945), Cuhna and Nascimento (1973, 1978, 1982a), Hoge and Romano (1973), Hoge et al. (1973), and Santos (1981) described it for Brazil; Amaral (1931b), Nicéforo-María (1942), Dunn (1944a), Daniel (1949), Schmidt (1955), Silva and Rodríquez (1985), and Pérez-Santos and Moreno (1986, 1987, 1988) for Colombia; Orcés (1943, 1948), J. A. Peters (1960), Miyata (1982), and Almendariz (1991) for Ecuador, while Meneses (1974), Soini (1974b), Carrillo de Espinoza (1983), and Dixon and Soini (1986) described it for Peru. Chippaux (1987) mentioned its possible presence in French Guiana. Earlier references include Cope (1860).

Etymology: Latin from *filum* meaning thread and *forma* meaning shape or figure; thus *filiformis* means thread-like or in the form of a thread, describing well this slender species. *Subtilis* is a Latin word for slender or thin.

Micrurus frontalis (Map 18)
Short-tailed Coral Snake (Southern Coral Snake); Cobra Coral de Rabo Curto; Coral Cola Corta

Distribution: Central and southern Brazil south of the Amazon basin, southern Bolivia, Paraguay, Uruguay, and northeastern Argentina south of the Amazon basin.

Definition: A triad-type coral snake with head irregular black, white, and red ranging from mostly black with some head scales outlined in white to mostly white and red, including the parietals; the snout has irregular black and white spots. The last three supralabials are usually red or red with a few black markings. The triads cover both the body and the tail and the white bands usually have black-tipped scales and/or black spots. The tail is short and stout.

Size: This is a medium-large coral snake in which the subspecies vary in size. The size is given under each subspecies.

Remarks: This is one of the most complex of the South American coral snakes. It is quite possible that several species can be distinguished in this assemblage of coral snakes. Five subspecies are recognized but they show considerable geographical variation and intergradation. Further information from less-studied areas such as the Mato Grosso of Brazil, southern Bolivia, Paraguay, and Misiones, Argentina, would permit a more precise definition and redefinition of the existing subspecies and of their distribution.

References: General comments on the species appeared in Amaral (1925b, 1944), Schmidt (1936a), Shreve (1953), Roze (1967, 1970b, 1983), Minton et al. (1968), and Cendrero et al. (1972); on distribution by Cei (1979, 1987) and Gallardo (1979); behavior by Lankes (1928), Schneider (1938), Allen (1940), Gehlbach (1972), and Sazima and Abe (1991); on mimicry by Mertens (1956, 1957), Marques and Puorto (1991) and Sazima and Abe (1991); Vanzolini (1953) and Roux-Estève (1983) on type specimens and their localities and a complete description and distribution by Campbell and Lamar (1989). In Bolivia by Kempff-Mercado (1975); in Brazil by Ihering (1911), Griffin (1916), Gliesch (1925), Amaral (1926d, 1930b, 1930c, 1944d, 1948a, 1974, 1978), Machado (1945), Vanzolini (1953), Magalhães (1959), Azevedo (1960, 1962a, 1962b), P. Müller (1971), Lema (1971b), Hoge and Romano (1973, 1981), Hoge et al. (1975), Cordeiro and Hoge (1974), Lema and Fabian-Beurmann (1977), Lema et al. (1980), and Santos (1981); in Paraguay by Bertoni (1914, 1939), Migone (1929), Schouten (1931, 1937); and in Uruguay by Devincenzi (1925), Vaz-Ferreira and Sierra de Soriano (1960), Klappenbach and Orejas-Miranda (1969), Achaval (1976), and Achaval et al. (1976, 1978). Earlier significant descriptions include publications by Günther (1859), Cope (1860a, 1862), and Koslowsky (1895, 1898).

Key to the Subspecies of *M. frontalis*

1 Ventrals 194 to 208 in males and 205 to 212 in females; parietals partially red
.... *M. f. altirostris* (southern Brazil, eastern Uruguay and northeastern Argentina)
1' More than 208 ventrals in males and more than 212 in females 2

2 White bands as long as or longer than black bands; snout light with irregular black borders; parietals mostly red
.... *M. f. brasiliensis* (Bahia, Goias, to northern Minas Gerais, Brazil)
2' White bands as long as or shorter than black bands, or if not, snout and parietals mostly black 3
3 Parietals, supraoculars, and frontals black, at most outlined or spotted with white
.... *M. f. frontalis* (south-central Brazil and southern Paraguay)
3' Light prefrontal band and/or parietals partially light (red) 4
4 10 to 14 triads; first white body band immaculate
.... *M. f. baliocoryphus* (Mesopotamic region of northeastern Argentina)
4' 12 to 19 triads; first white body band with black tips
.... *M. f. multicinctus* (southeastern Brazil)
Note: This key is not accurate for intergrades. Consult other characteristics and distribution under the description of subspecies. Moreover, the subspecies and their distribution are only tentatively determined.

Micrurus frontalis frontalis (Color 23)
Brazilian Giant Coral Snake; Cobra Coral Brasileira Gigante; Coral Brasileña Gigante

Elaps frontalis Duméril, Bibron, and Duméril, 1854: 1223. (Holotype: The only syntype left, MNHN 854, a male from Brazil, collected by Claussen may serve as lectotype.)
Micrurus frontalis frontalis: Schmidt, 1936a: 199.

Range: Lowland and low montane humid and deciduous forest altered by humans from southern Minas Gerais, Goiás, Mato Grosso, and São Paulo (probably also in northwestern Parana), to southern Paraguay, from near sea level to about 700 m.

Description: Males have 213 to 230 (224.4) and females have 218 to 232 (225.8) ventrals; subcaudals 19 to 25 (22.9) in males and 19 to 22 (20.3) in females; 1+1, occasionally 1+2, temporals. Examined: 143 males and 131 females, including the type.
 The upper head coloration is quite varied. The head shields are normally black, including the parietals, but there are some irregular white spots on the snout, especially on the supraoculars, prefrontals, and internasals, and/or with several snout shields outlined in white. The rostral is white or white with some black spots. The parietals are almost always completely black. The first three supralabials are black or have large white spots or white borders. The chin is only white and red or has some irregular grey or black spots on some shields. The nuchal red band is up to 3 dorsals long, followed by the first triad; rarely, the red band is

interrupted by the contact of the parietal black and the first black band of the first triad. The black bands in a triad are approximately of equal length to the white bands, sometimes a little longer or shorter. In some specimens the black bands expand over the middorsal or midventral region, thus decreasing the length of the white bands. The white (sometimes creamy-yellowish) bands are usually 3 dorsals long with conspicuous black tips. The red bands are longer than either the black or the white bands, 6 to 10 dorsals and ventrals long, with small black-tipped scales that are frequently absent from the first dorsal row. In large adults the red and white bands may have brownish overtones, making the red bands less brilliant. The tail has a slightly angular shape, forming an inconspicuous, inverted "V", and has a triad pattern.

The males have 10 to 13 (11.7) and females 12 to 14 (12.6) black triads. The males usually have 1⅔ and the females 1⅓ to 1⅔ triads on the tail.

Size: The longest measured specimen is 1190 mm, but many adults measure between 650 and 1000 mm in overall length.

Remarks: The Paraguayan specimens have a slightly higher number of black triads. This subspecies intergrades with *M. f. multicinctus* in northern Parana and probably in eastern São Paulo, Brazil.

Food: Limbless amphisbaenid lizards (*Leposternon microcephalum, Amphisbaena*) colubrid snakes (*Sibynomorphus mikanii*), and false coral snakes (*Erythrolamprus*), as well as probably *Amphisbaena roberti*, *A. mertensi*, and *A. steindachneri* (Sazima and Abe, 1991), and reported to be cannibalistic.

References: Description and variation is found in Shreve (1953) and color photos by Mertens (1956, 1957) and Campbell and Lamar (1989); also see under the species description.

Etymology: Latin from *frons* meaning forehead and *-alis* meaning pertaining to; frontalis means pertaining or related to forehead, probably alluding to the spotted snout and upper head shields of the holotype.

Micrurus frontalis altirostris (Color 26)
Uruguayan Coral Snake; Coral Uruguaya; Cobra Coral Uruguaia

Elaps altirostris Cope, 1859: 345. (Holotype: ANSP 6857, a male from "South America.")
Elaps heterochilus Mocquard, 1877: 39. (Holotype: MNHN 1889, a male from Brazil, collected by Pougnet.)
Micrurus frontalis altirostris: Schmidt, 1936a: 199.

Range: Pampas, savanna, and lowland deciduous forest and open fields, frequently altered by humans, in Uruguay and adjacent southern Rio Grande do Sul, Brazil, and probably in central Misiones, Argentina, from sea level to about 400 m.

Description: Males have 194 to 208 (200.9) and females have 202 to 212 (206.1) ventrals; subcaudals 17 to 24 (18.8) in males and 16 to 22 (18.1) in females; 1+1 temporals. Examined: 14 males and 11 females, including all holotypes.

The snout is black to the parietals, with occasional small white spots on some sutures. Most of the anterior part of the parietals is red, together with 1 or 2 rows of dorsals. The tips of the parietals have large or small irregular black spots. The chin is heavily blackened with some irregular light, white, or creamy white spots on several shields. The first triad begins 1 to 2 scales behind the parietals. The central black band is somewhat longer than the outer ones, and all are longer than the white bands. The latter are about 2 dorsals long with large black tips on the scales. The red bands, 4 to 6 dorsals long, are as long as or longer than the central black bands and have small black-tipped scales. Ventrally, the white and red bands are frequently obscured by an irregular invasion of black coloration.

The males have 11 to 15 (13.8) and females have 12 to 16 (14.5) body bands. The tail triads range from 1 to 1⅔ in both sexes.

Size: The longest measured specimen is 878 mm long. Many adults measure between 500 and 700 mm in overall length.

Remarks: The red parietal coloration and the blackened chin scales makes this an easily identified subspecies. It intergrades with *M. f. multicinctus* in northern Rio Grande do Sul, Brazil, and with *M. f. baliocoryphus* in northern Misiones, Argentina. The remaining distribution of the intergrades is still not defined.

Food: Blind snakes (*Leptotyphlops muñoai*) and limbless amphisbaenid lizards (*Amphisbaena darwini*), also *Ophioides*.

References: General comments are by Barrio and Miranda (1967), Scrocchi (1990), and Martinez et al. (1992) for Argentina, and by Lema and Fabian-Beurmann (1977) for Brazil. Vaz-Ferreira et al. (1970) described the reproduction and Achaval et al. (1976) offered general characteristics for the Uruguayan populations. Campbell and Lamar (1989) featured color photos.

Etymology: Latin from *alti-* meaning high and *rostris* meaning snout, probably alluding to the black coloration of the snout that extends to the parietals.

Micrurus frontalis baliocoryphus (Pattern 28)
Mesopotamian Coral Snake; Coral Mesopotámica; Cobra Coral Mesopotamica

Elaps baliocoryphus Cope, 1859: 346 (Holotype: ANSP 6842, collected by Mr. Kennedy from Buenos Aires, Argentina. Type locality restricted to Villa Federal, Entre Ríos, Argentina by Roze, 1983.)
Micrurus frontalis mesopotamicus Barrio and Miranda, 1967: 872 (Holotype: CHINM 1823, a male from Villa Federal, Entre Ríos, Argentina, collected by J. Vermeersch.)
Micrurus frontalis baliocoryphus: Hoge and Romano, 1981: 396.

Range: Lowland pampas and deciduous formations in Entre Ríos, Corrientes, and southern Misiones in the Argentinian mesopotamic region between the Río Paraná and the Río Uruguay, Argentina, from sea level to about 200 m above sea level.

Description: Males have 218 to 223 (220.6) and females have 213 to 225 (218.9) ventrals; subcaudals 22 to 27 (25.1) in males and 19 to 26 (24.2) in females; 1+1 temporals. Examined: 12 males and 9 females, including all holotypes.

The snout is almost black, with the rostral and the internasals outlined by white. The prefrontals are almost completely white or whitish with irregular black spots. The remainder of the head, including the parietals, is black with a short white or whitish with irregular black spots. The remainder of the head, including the parietals, is black with a short white, slightly v-shaped crossband on the anterior part of the parietals. The first 2 to 4 dorsal rows are covered by a red nuchal band. The anterior supralabials are white and the posterior supralabials are red, usually with some irregular black spots. The chin is white with large black spots on several infralabials and other shields. The black central band of the triad is approximately twice as long as the outer ones. The white bands are a little shorter than the outer black bands, about 2 dorsals and ventrals long. The white bands of the first 2 triads are immaculate; the others have black-tipped scales. The red bands are slightly longer or shorter than the central black bands and have conspicuous black-tipped scales.

The males have 12 to 14 (12.8) and the females have 10 to 14 (12.4) black triads on the body. Both sexes have 1⅓ to 1⅔ triads on the tail.

Size: The longest known specimen is 826 mm.

Remarks: A special characteristic of this subspecies is the well-defined, slightly v-shaped, white parietal crossband. It intergrades with *M. f. altirostris* in northern Argentina.

Food: Probably amphisbaenid lizards.

References: Scrocchi (1990) summarized its characteristics and distribution, and Allen (1940) described its behavior.

Etymology: Greek from *bali-* meaning spotted and *coryph* meaning head; *baliocoryphus*, meaning snake with spotted head, alluding to the red and black head. *Mesopotamicus* alludes to its distribution in the Argentinean mesopotamic region in Entre Ríos.

Micrurus frontalis brasiliensis (Color 27)
Brazilian Short-tailed Coral Snake; Cobra Coral Rabo Curto Brasileira; Coral Cola Corta Brasileña

Micrurus frontalis brasiliensis Roze, 1967: 25. (Holotype: UMMZ 108880, a male from Barreiras, Bahia, Brazil, obtained by J. R. Bailey in 1942.)

Range: Cerrado savannas, scrub-palm, and deciduous subtropical and tropical forest from eastern Bahia and Goiás to northeastern Mato Grosso and southward to northern Minas Gerais, Brazil, from 100 to 600 m above sea level.

Description: Males have 220 to 236 (226.7) and females have 224 to 238 (229.4) ventrals; subcaudals 20 to 25 (22.1) in males and 16 to 19 (17.9) in females; 1+1 temporals. Examined: 38 males and 36 females, including the holotype.

The snout, back to the anterior part of the frontal and supraoculars, is light with irregular black spots or borders. A black interorbital band covers the supraoculars and the frontal and extends back irregularly over the central part of the parietals. There is usually a light spot on the suture between the parietals. The posterior part of the parietals and the postparietal scale are red; this color extends over several dorsal scales. The chin is light, white and red with black spots on the mental and first infralabials. The black bands are of equal length, as long as or a little shorter than the white bands. The light bands, including the first ones, have regular and conspicuous black borders. The red bands are more than twice as long as the black bands, with very few or no black-tipped scales.

The males have 11 to 14 (12.3) and the females have 11 to 12 (11.6) black triads on the body. Both sexes have 1⅓ to 1⅔ black tail bands.

Size: The longest measured specimen is 1122 mm in total length; many adults measure between 650 and 850 mm.

Remarks: This is the northernmost subspecies.

Food: Unknown, probably amphisbaenid lizards and snakes.

References: Magalhães (1959) summarized the distribution and venom of this subspecies in Minas Gerais, Brazil, under the name of *M. frontalis*.

Etymology: The name *brasiliensis* indicates its presence in Brazil.

Micrurus frontalis multicinctus
Many-banded Coral Snake; Cobra Coral de Muitos Aneis

Micrurus lemniscatus multicinctus Amaral, 1944: 91. (Holotype: IB 8877, a female from Texeira Soares, Paraná Brazil.)
Micrurus frontalis multicinctus: Roze, 1983: 325.

Range: Low to intermediate altitude coastal mountains with deciduous subtropical, evergreen, and mixed vegetation and araucaria forests in eastern São Paulo, Paraná, Santa Catarina; probably also in northern Rio Grande do Sul, Brazil.

Description: Males have 210 to 222 (214.7) and females have 213 to 230 (219.8) ventrals; subcaudals 20 to 24 (22.3) in males and 18 to 23 (20.2) in females; 1+1 temporals. Examined: 28 males and 17 females, including the holotype.

The snout is black with some light spots. A short, irregular white crossband covers the anterior part of the frontal, the supraoculars, and preoculars. It is followed by an irregular black interorbital band. The parietals are red with black lateral and posterior borders; sometimes the black may occupy half of the parietals. The red head band extends onto the first dorsal row. The anterior supralabials are white, and the posterior are red with irregular black spots. Below, the mental and the first infralabials are black. The remainder of the chin is white and red with large black spots on several shields. The central black band of the triad is slightly longer than the outer ones. The white bands are shorter than the black bands, 1 to 2 dorsals long; they have black-tipped scales. The red bands are longer than the black central bands, but have smaller black tips than do the white bands.

The males have 13 to 18 (14.9) and the females 13 to 18 (15.2) black triads on the body. Both sexes have 1⅓ to 1⅔ triads on the tail.

Size: The longest measured specimen is 687 mm long; most adults are slightly shorter.

Remarks: This subspecies intergrades with *M. f. frontalis* in northern Parana, and probably in western São Paulo, Brazil, and with *M. f. altirostris* in Santa Catarina. The exact areas of intergradation still have to be defined.

Food: Limbless amphisbaenid lizards.

References: See under the species.

Etymology: Latin from *multi-* meaning many and *cinctus* meaning girdled, alluding to the many bands around its body.

Micrurus frontifasciatus (Map 19, Color 28)
Bolivian Triad Coral Snake (Bolivian Coral Snake); Coral Tricolor Boliviana

Elaps frontifasciatus Werner, 1927: 250. (Holotype: NMW [no number], from Bolivia, collected by Staudinger.)
Micrurus frontifasciatus: Roze, 1983: 326.

Distribution and range: Low and high mountain dry forest, cloud forest and lowland gallery forest on the eastern slopes of the Andes in southeastern Peru and northern Bolivia, between about 600 and 2500 m above sea level.

Definition: A triad-type coral snake with triads on both body and tail and with the first triad complete. The head has a black snout, a white prefrontal band, and a black frontal band, followed by a red band that covers the parietals and several dorsals. The central black band of a triad is longer than the outer ones. The scales of the white and the red bands usually have black tips.

Description: Males have 210 to 222 (214.0) and females have 224 to 248 (234.2) ventrals; subcaudals 31 to 34 (32.8) in males and 30 to 33 (32.2) in females. Examined: 6 males and 4 females, including the holotype.

The snout, including the internasals, is all black. The white band that follows covers the prefrontals, usually the anterior part of the frontal, and 2 or 3 supralabials. The black frontal band also includes the anterior part of the parietals, all the postoculars, part of the first temporal, and 2 to 3 supralabials. The red parietal band also extends over 4 dorsals. Occasionally there are some black spots on the parietals and the dorsals. The chin is either all white and red or has some black spots on the mental and the first infralabials.

The central black band of each triad is less than twice as long as the outer bands. The central band of the first triad is 9 to 11 dorsals and 7 to 9 ventrals long. The other central black bands vary in length between 4 to 6 dorsals and 3 to 6 ventrals. The outer black bands are 3 to 5 dorsals and 3 to 4 ventrals long. The white bands are 2 to 3 dorsals and ventrals long with irregular black-tipped scales. The red bands are as long as or longer than the black outer bands, occupying 3 to 7 dorsals and ventrals. In small specimens the red bands are immaculate, but in adults many of the red dorsals have irregular black tips.

The males have 8 to 9 (8.7) and the females 9 to 10 (9.7) triads on the body. Both sexes have 1⅓ to 1⅔ triads on the tail.

Size: This is a medium to long species. The longest measured specimen, which is the holotype, measures 1,040 mm in total length.

Remarks: This species looks similar to *M. lemniscatus helleri*, with which it is partially sympatric in Bolivia and Peru, but the few records indicate that this species prefers somewhat higher elevations.

Food: Unknown.

References: There is a brief description and color photo in Campbell and Lamar (1989) and comments in Roze (1967, 1970b, 1983) on the systematics of this little-known species.

Etymology: Latin from *front*, forehead, and *fascia*, band, thus *frontifasciatus* is forehead-banded, indicating the presence of the black frontal band.

Micrurus fulvius (Map 20)
North American Coral Snake (Harlequin Coral Snake) Coralillo o Coralilla Norteamericana

Distribution: The eastern and southern United States from southeastern North Carolina to the southern tip of Florida, westward to southern Arkansas and eastern and southern Texas, and southward to northeastern and central Mexico, from Coahuila, Nuevo León, and Tamaulipas, to Aguas Calientes, Querétaro, Guanajuato, and Morelos.

Definition: A single-banded coral snake with yellow or white bands bordering the black bands. The snout is black, followed by a yellow or white crossband that includes the parietal, which is followed in turn by a black nuchal band. The chin is yellow or white, but the mental and the first infralabials are black. The red dorsals have large or small irregular black tips; in some specimens they are reduced or absent. Only black and yellow or white bands are on the tail. Males have no supraanal tubercles.

Size: This is a medium-sized coral snake. Even though the longest reported specimen measures 1295 mm in total length, adults usually measure between 450 and 700 mm.

Remarks: Five subspecies are recognized. Although the United States subspecies are the most-studied coral snakes, the Mexican subspecies and their distribution are less well known.

References: There are many references, especially for the United States subspecies. They have been summarized by Roze and Tilger (1983) and Campbell and Lamar (1989). General notes on classification and variation are those by Schmidt (1928), Wright and Wright (1957), Roze (1967, 1983), Shaw (1971), and Connant (1975); notes on distribution by Mitchell (1903), Stejneger and Barbour (1943), Mittleman (1947), H. M. Smith and Buechner (1947), Milstead et al. (1950), Link (1951), Martín del Campo (1953), Milstead (1960), Robison (1972), Liner and Chaney (1974), Palmer et al. (1974) and Tennant (1984); color variation by Gloyd (1938), Meachem and Myers (1961), and Neill (1963); mimicry by Brattstrom (1955), Hecht and Marien (1956), Martin (1958), Wickler (1968), Gehlbach (1972), Greene and Pyburn (1973), Grobman (1978), Greene and McDiarmid (1981), and Roze (1983). The most comprehensive references to date on food and feeding are those by Greene (1973a, 1984); others include Ditmars (1907, 1912), Strecker (1908), Schmidt (1932a), Clark (1939), J. E. Minton (1949), Curtis (1952), Kennedy (1964), Chance (1970), Malloy (1971), and Fisher (1973), while cannibalism is mentioned by Loveridge (1938, 1944), Curtis (1952), and Chance (1970). Behavior is described in Engelhardt (1932), Ruick (1948), Neill (1951, 1957), Sochurek (1955), and Gehlbach (1970); reproduction in Quinn (1979), Allen and Neill (1950), Sabath and Worthington (1959), Werler (1970), Campbell (1973), Zegel (1975), Jackson and Franz (1981), and Tyron and McCrystal (1982). Graham (1977) described the karyotype. Description and distribution of Mexican subspecies are found in Cuesta Terrón (1932), Martín del Campo (1935, 1950, 1955), E. H. Taylor (1940, 1949, 1950), H. M. Smith and Taylor (1945), Martin (1958), Booth (1959), Milstead (1960), Schmidt and Owens (1944), Hensley and Smith (1962), Brown and Brown (1967), Dixon et al. (1972), Minton de Cervantes and Minton (1975), Minton and Cervantes (1977), and McCoy (1984). Additional references are found under subspecies, particularly for Mexican forms. Earlier references include Günther (1859), Cope (1859, 1879, 1887, 1892), Mathes (1860), Jan and Sordelli (1872), Dugés (1885, 1890, 1896), Velasco (1890), Stejneger (1895), and Grijs (1898).

Key to the Subspecies of *M. fulvius*

1 Black nuchal band does not reach or cover the parietal tips
   M. f. fulvius (North Carolina to Florida and west to Mississippi River, United States)
1' Black nuchal band usually covers the parietal tips 2

2   Ventrals 185 to 195 in males and 203 to 208 in females
    ... *M. f. maculatus* (Tampico, Tamaulipas, Mexico)
2' More than 196 ventrals in males and more than 216 in females 3
3   Males with 10 to 14 and females with 10 to 15 black body bands
    M. f. tenere (Louisiana to Texas, United States, to northern Mexico)
3' More than 14 bands in males and more than 15 in females.
4   Males have 198 to 204 and females 216 to 225 ventrals; chin usually heavily mottled with black
    ... *M. f. microgalbineus* (Southern Tamaulipas and San Luís Potosí, Mexico)
4' Males have 208 to 216 and females 222 to 231 ventrals; little or no grey mottling on the chin
    ...... *M. f. fitzingeri* (Agua Calientes, Guanajuato, Querétaro to Morelos, Mexico)

Micrurus fulvius fulvius (Color 29, Pattern 23)
Eastern Coral Snake

Coluber fulvius Linnaeus, 1766: 381. (Holotype: Not known to exist. A female from "Carolina" [restricted to Charleston, South Carolina, United States, by Schmidt, 1953; see also Roze and Tilger, 1983].)
Micrurus fulvius barbouri Schmidt, 1928: 64. (Holotype: MCZ 13658, a male from Paradise Key, Dade County, Florida, United States, obtained by T. Barbour in 1920.)
Micrurus fulvius fulvius: Schmidt, 1928: 64.

Range: In a variety of dry and humid lowland habitats in eastern and southeastern United States, from southeastern North Carolina to the southern tip of Florida, east of the Mississippi River, including coastal South Carolina, southern Georgia, southern Alabama, and eastern Mississippi, from sea level to about 300 m.

Description: Males have 197 to 217 (206.3) and females have 219 to 233 (225.8) ventrals; subcaudals 40 to 47 (43.6) in males and 30 to 37 (34.0) in females; 1+1 or 1+2 temporals. Examined: 83 males and 54 females, including one holotype.

The black snout coloration extends over the supraoculars, one or both postoculars, and almost the entire frontal, forming a slightly convex border over the anterior part of the parietals. It is followed by the light parietal crossband that covers the tips of the parietals and one dorsal. Below, the mental and the first three infralabials are black. Both pairs of genials are yellow; occasionally their tips are black. The nuchal black band is 7 to 10 dorsals and ventrals long and does not reach the parietal tips. The black body bands are 7 to 11 dorsals and 6 to 9 ventrals long. The red bands usually have very irregular black-tipped scales and/or black spots, with a tendency to form a pair of large black spots in at least some specimens. Some red scales may lack black tips. Specimens in the southern tip of Florida have practically no black-tipped scales (Pattern 3). Ventrally, the red bands have larger or smaller black spots; occasional specimens are without black spots. The yellow bands usually are of an intense yellow and are 1½ dorsals and 1 ventral long; in occasional specimens the yellow bands are white or creamy white. The black bands on the tail are about 3 times as long as the yellow bands.

The males have 11 to 17 (13.7) and the females have 12 to 19 (14.8) black body bands. The males have 3 to 5 (3.9), usually 4 black tail bands, and the females have 3 to 4 (3.2), usually 3.

Remarks: The Mississippi River has been considered the dividing line between the distribution of the two coral snakes in the United States: *M. f. fulvius* and *M. f. tenere*. However, no intergrades have been identified and the distribution seems to be separated by a broad zone, at places more than 100 km wide, along the Mississippi Valley. An even wider gap exists in the Mississippi delta region. Except for the fringe areas, no coral snakes have been reported from that region, except for specimens introduced by humans. In the southern tip of Florida a somewhat isolated population that was described as *M. fulvius barbouri* is characterized by the absence or nearly complete absence of any black markings on the red dorsals.

This is the only subspecies of *M. fulvius* in which the black nuchal band does not reach the parietal tips. This feature easily distinguishes it not only from *M. f. tenere* but from the other subspecies as well. *M. f. fulvius*, moreover, has nearly twice as much protein in its venom as *M. f. tenere*. All this raises an uncomfortable question: are these two forms really subspecifically related or are we dealing with two different species? Studies of karyotypes, blood serum, and DNA might shed some light on the question.

Food: A great variety of lizards and snakes, but the latter predominate. The lizards include the ground skink (*Scincella laterale*), the five-lined skink (*Eumeces fasciatus*), and the glass lizard (*Ophisaurus*). Preferred ground snakes are the black racer (*Coluber constrictor*), the ringneck snake (*Diadophis punctatus*), the brown snake (*Storeria dekayi*), the mud snake (*Farancia abacura*), and the crowned snakes (*Tantilla coronata* and *Tantilla gracilis*). Other known snake food includes the corn snake (*Elaphe guttata*), the king snake (*Lampropeltis getulus*), the rough green snake (*Opheodrys aestivus*), the earth snakes (*Virginia striatula* and *Virginia valeriae*), and the red-bellied snake (*Storeria occipitomaculata*). It is also cannibalistic. In captivity, the coral snake will eat a variety of lizards and other snakes.

| C29 |
| 254 |
| P23 |
| 268 |

References: No less than 110 publications have dealt with different aspects of this subspecies and are listed under the species. Some of the more important references about this subspecies are those by Carr (1940), Wright and Wright (1957), Duellman and Schwartz (1958), Shaw (1971), Palmer et al (1974), Mount (1975), Conant (1975), and Jackson and Franz (1981).

Etymology: The name *fulvius* is derived from Latin for orange or orange-yellow. It was given, apparently, upon observation of preserved specimens in which the coral red pattern had faded to yellowish orange.

Micrurus fulvius fitzingeri (Pattern 24)
Guanajuato Coral Snake; Coralillo de Guanajuato

Elaps fitzingeri Jan, 1858: 521. (Holotype: Syntype NMW 18297 is a female from Mexico purchased from Baron von Karwinsky by Josef Natterer in June 1834. Other syntypes previously in the museums of Milano and Torino, Italy, and in Hamburg, Germany, have been lost. The type locality was restricted to Guanajuato, Mexico, by Smith and Taylor, 1950.)
Micrurus fulvius fitzingeri: Roze, 1983: 326.

Range: Dry desertic Mexican plateau in Guanajuato and Querétaro southward to Morelos, Mexico, at altitudes between 1,000 and 3,000 m above sea level. Probably also in Zacatecas, Aguas Calientes, and southern Coahuila, Mexico.

Description: Males have 208 to 216 (212.0) and females have 222 to 231 (225.4) ventrals; subcaudals 41 to 44 (42.5) in males and 31 to 35 (33.3) in females; 1+1 temporals. Examined: 3 males and 6 females, including the syntype.

The black snout coloration covers the supraoculars and the anterior part of the parietals. It is followed by a yellow parietal crossband that includes the frontal tip. The mental and the first 3 infralabials are black and there are some irregular gray smudges on several other chin shields. The nuchal black band reaches and usually covers the tips of the parietals as well as 5 to 6 dorsals and 4 to 5 ventrals. The black bands are 4 to 5 dorsals and ventrals long. The red bands have irregular black tips on many scales, without larger black spots. Ventrally, the red bands are immaculate or occasionally have a few small black spots. The yellow or white bands are 1 to 2, usually 1½ scales long and are immaculate. The black tail bands are 2 times or more as long as the white ones.

There are 19 to 22 (20.5) black body bands in males and 19 to 26 (22.7) in females. The males have 5 to 6 (5.5) and the females have 3 to 6 (4.2) black tail bands.

Remarks: This subspecies is restricted to the central plateau of Mexico and intergrades with *M. f. microgalbineus* along the southern border between Hidalgo and Querétaro.

References: Brief notes by Schmidt (1933a), Brown and Smith (1942), Hensley and Smith (1962), Dixon et al (1972), Greene (1972), and Minton and Cervantes (1977); Roze (1967, 1983) clarified the systematics.

Etymology: This subspecies was named after one of the great 19th century German herpetologists, Leopoldo J. F. J. Fiztzinger.

Micrurus fulvius maculatus (Pattern 25)
Tampico Coral Snake, Coralillo de Tampico

Micrurus fulvius maculatus Roze, 1967: 27. Holotype: ZMH 5685, a male from Tampico, Tamaulipas, Mexico, collected by E. Kallert, on February 10, 1930.

Range: Swampy and humid lowlands around Tampico, Tamaulipas, Mexico, at near sea level.

Description: Males have 185 to 195 (190.0) and females have 205 to 208 (206.5) ventrals; subcaudals 43 to 45 (44.0) in males and about 31 in females; 1+1 temporals. Examined: 2 males and 2 females, including the holotype.

The black snout coloration forms an irregular posterior border covering the supraoculars and the anterior part of the parietals. The mental and the first 3 infralabials are black. Some black or dark mottling is present in some chin shields. The nuchal black band covers the parietal tips and 6 to 7 dorsals and 6 ventrals. The black body bands are 5 dorsals and 4 ventrals long. The red bands have most of the black scale tips fused to form larger spots; about half of the red scales, however, lack black markings. Ventrally, the red bands have irregular black dots. The black tail bands are about 3 times or more longer than the yellow bands.

The males have 15 to 17 (16) and the females have 13 to 17 (15) black body bands. There are 5 to 7 (6) black tail bands in males and 4 to 5 (4.5) in females.

Remarks: This subspecies apparently intergrades with *M. f. microgalbineus* north and west of Tampico, Tamaulipas, Mexico.

Food: Unknown, probably snakes.

References: Only the original description and a brief mention in Campbell and Lamar (1989).

Etymology: The name *maculatus* (Latin for spotted) refers to the presence of some large black spots in the red bands.

Micrurus fulvius microgalbineus (Pattern 26)
Spotted Coral Snake; Coralillo Manchado

Micrurus fitzingeri microgalbineus Brown and Smith, 1942: 63. (Holotype: Bryce C. Brown private collection, deposited in Strecker Museum, Baylor University [BCB 5381], a female from 7 km south of Antiguo Morelos, Tamaulipas, Mexico, collected by B. C. Brown on June 21, 1941. The specimen originally was No. 27847 in the E. H. Taylor-H. M. Smith Collection.)
Micrurus fulvius microgalbineus: Roze, 1967: 29.

Range: Dry subtropical and tropical deciduous and humid forests in southern and southwestern Tamaulipas to central and eastern San Luís Potosí, Mexico, at altitudes between 80 and 500 m above sea level.

Description: Males have 198 to 204 (200.6) and females have 216 to 225 (221.1) ventrals; subcaudals 41 to 45 (43.2) in males and 32 to 38 (34.6) in females; 1+1 temporals. Examined: 8 males and 5 females, including the holotype.

The black snout coloration includes the entire frontal and the anterior part of the parietals. The mental and the first several infralabials are black. The rest of the chin shields are usually heavily mottled with black. The yellow parietal band is short, about 1½ to 2 times shorter than the black snout coloration. The nuchal black band covers about one fourth of the parietals, 5 to 6 dorsals, and 3 to 5 ventrals. The black body bands are 3 to 5 dorsals and 2 to 4 ventrals long. The specimens from Tamaulipas have slightly longer black bands than those farther south. The red bands have scales with irregular black tips that occasionally occupy an entire scale. Some red scales are without black markings. Ventrally, the red bands have many larger and smaller black spots. The yellow bands are 1 to 1½ dorsals and 1 ventral long. The black tail bands are about 3 times longer than the white ones.

There are 18 to 22 (20.8) (one specimen has 27) black body bands in males and 17 to 25 (22.4) in females. The males have 5 to 7 (6.1) and the females 4 to 5 (4.6) black tail bands.

Remarks: This subspecies intergrades with *M. f. tenere* in central Tamaulipas, with *M. f. maculatus* north and west of Tampico, Tamaulipas, and with *M. f. fitzingeri* along the southern border between the Mexican states of Hidalgo and Querétaro.

Food: Hooknose snakes (*Ficimia olivaceae*), blackheaded snakes (*Tantilla ruber*), and the Mexican snail-eater (*Tropidodipsas sartorii*).

References: E. H. Taylor (1950) offered taxonomic notes and a photo; Martin (1958), Hensley and Smith (1962), and Minton de Cervantes and Minton (1975) dealt with intergradation; and Campbell and Lamar (1989) offered a color photo.

Etymology: The name is derived from a modern Latin adaptation of the original Greek word *micro* meaning small and tiny and *galbineus*, Latin for greenish yellow. The name *microgalbineus* alludes to the short yellowish bands of this subspecies.

Micrurus fulvius tenere (Color 30)
Texas Coral Snake; Coralillo Tejano

Elaps tenere Baird and Girard, 1853: 22. (Holotype: syntype designated as lectoholotype, USNM 1119, a female from "San Pedro of Rio Grande," collected by J. D. Graham [two syntypes, USNM 1121, from "New Braunfels, Texas," collected by F. Lindheimer have been lost]. The type locality was restricted to New Braunfels, Texas, United States by Smith and Taylor, 1950. See also Roze and Tilger, 1983.)
Elaps tristis Baird and Girard, 1853: 23. (Holotype: syntypes USNM [2 specimens], males from Rio Grande, west of San Antonio, Texas, United States, collected by S. Churchill, and USNM 1124, a male from Kemper County, Mississippi, United States, collected by D. C. Lloyd.)
Micrurus fulvius tenere: Schmidt, 1933a: 40.

Range: In dry to humid lowland habitats west of the Mississippi River from Louisiana, southern Arkansas, and Texas to northern Coahuila, Nuevo León, and Tamaulipas, Mexico, from sea level to 300 m. One unconfirmed record from Sonora, Mexico.

Description: Males have 200 to 211 (206.8) and females 219 to 227 (223.9) ventrals; subcaudals 38 to 46 (42.6) in males and 26 to 34 (31.8) in females; 1+1 or 1+2 temporals. Examined: 39 males and 24 females, including several types.

The black snout coloration covers the supraoculars and the anterior part of the parietals, forming a slightly sinuous posterior border that is slightly concave over the tip of the frontal. The mental and upper part of the first three infralabials are black. Many specimens have a small black spot on the suture between the chin shields. The nuchal black band covers the parietal tips and is 7 to 10 dorsals and 6 to 9 ventrals long. In occasional specimens the nuchal black band projects anteriorly to fuse with the black spot between the chin shields. The nuchal black band has a very slight middorsal loop that extends forward to cover the parietal tips. The red bands have many irregular black spots and black scale tips with a tendency for them to concentrate along the border of the yellow bands, occasionally forming a solid "accessory" black band.

Ventrally, the red bands have irregular black dots frequently forming larger spots. The intensely yellow bands are immaculate, 1½ to 2 dorsals and usually 1 ventral long. On the tail, the black bands are 3 or more times as long as the yellow bands.

There are 10 to 14 (12.2) black body bands in males and 10 to 15 (12.7) in females. The males have 3 to 4 (3.4) and the females have 2 to 3 (2.9), usually 3, black tail bands.

Remarks: This subspecies intergrades with *M. f. microgalbineus* in central Tamaulipas and with *M. f. fitzingeri* in central Coahuila, Mexico.

Food: A variety of snakes and lizards. Preferred lizards are the five-lined skink (*Eumeces fasciatus*), short-lined skink (*Eumeces tetragrammus brevilineatus*), and ground skink (*Scincella laterale*). Other lizards include the fence lizard (*Sceloporus undulatus*) and the spotted whiptail (*Cnemidophorus gularis*). The most common snake food is the rough earth snake (*Virginia striatula*). Other frequent food snakes include the Texas rat snake (*Elaphe obsoleta*), the rough green snake (*Opheodrys aestivus*), the ground snake (*Sonora episcopa*), the lined snake (*Tropidoclonion lineatum*), and the brown snake (*Storeria dekayi*). Other snake prey include the ring neck snake (*Diadophis punctatus*, king snakes (*Lampropeltis getulus, L. calligaster*), the Texas blind snake (*Leptotyphlops dulcis*), the coachwhip (*Masticophis flagellum*), the diamondback water snake (*Nerodia taxispilota*), the patchnose snake (*Salvadora grahamiae*), the black-headed snakes (*Tantilla atriceps, T. gracilis*), the checkered garter snake (*Thamnophis marcianus*), the smooth earth snake (*Virginia valeriae*), and also the venomous copperhead (*Agkistrodon contortix*). Occasionally frogs and remnants of small mammals also have been found in the stomach of the Texas coral snake. They may have been in the stomach of the prey snake when it was devoured by the coral snake. The Texas coral snake is known to be cannibalistic as well.

References: Many of the 80 or more publications dealing with this subspecies are summarized by Roze and Tilger (1983). A recent description is found in Tennant (1984); Quinn (1979) described reproduction, while Gloyd (1938) an aberrant color pattern. See also under the species description.

Etymology: The Latin name, *tenere*, is used as an adverb in the comparative or superlative of *tener*, tender, delicate, meaning tenderly or delicately, in allusion to the delicate features of this slender subspecies. Frost and Collins (1988) showed that this name is incorrect gramatically and should be replaced by *tener*. They are technically correct, but I retained the older name as it also could be considered a "proper" name for the species, since its original description and much of the venom and accident literature goes under *tenere*.

Micrurus hemprichii (Map 21)
Worm-eating Coral Snake (Hemprich's Coral Snake); Coral Lombricera; Cobra Coral Lombrigueira

Distribution: Southern Venezuela, the Guianas, and the upper Amazon and eastern slopes of the Andes in southern Colombia; eastern Ecuador, Peru, northern Bolivia, and the Amazon region of Brazil from Rondônia to Pará.

Definition: A triad-type coral snake in which the first triad is complete and the bands that separate them are not red but usually brownish or orangish-yellow. The black bands of the triads are very long, several times longer than the orangish-red and white bands. This species gives the impression of a black coral snake with small brownish and white crossbands. It is the only species of *Micrurus* in which the anal plate is undivided.

Size: This is a medium-sized species. The longest measured specimen is 917 mm long. Many adults measure between 450 and 700 mm.

Remarks: This species is distinguished by the undivided anal plate and by the very long triads. Three subspecies are recognized.

References: Schmidt (1953a) reviewed the subspecies and Campbell and Lamar (1989) gave description and distribution. General references of the species appeared in Schmidt (1936a), Roze (1967, 1970b, 1983). Amaral (1925a, 1930b, 1948b), Machado (1945), Hoge and Romano (1971a, 1971b, 1981), Cuhna and Nascimento (1973, 1978, 1982a), Santos (1981), Vanzolini (1986), and Nascimento et al. (1987) and Zimmerman and Rodrigues (1990), gave it for Brazil; Amaral (1931b), Nicéforo-María (1942), Dunn (1944a), Daniel (1949), Schmidt (1955), Silva and Rodríguez (1985), Pérez-Santos and Moreno (1988) and Silva (1994) gave it for Colombia; Orcés (1943, 1948), J. A. Peters (1960a), Miyata (1982), and Almendariz (1991) for Ecuador; H. W. Parker (1935) and Beebe (1946) described it for Guyana under the name of *M. psyches*; Gasc and Rodrigues (1980) and

Chippaux (1987) mentioned its presence in French Guiana; Schmidt and Walker (1953a), Meneses (1974), Soini (1974b), Carrillo de Espinoza (1983), and Dixon and Soini (1986) described it for Peru; Brongersma (1967) and Abuys (1987b) mentioned it for Suriname; and Roze (1954, 1955, 1957, 1966a, 1987), Vetencourt Finol (1960), Hoge and Lancini (1962), Lancini (1970, 1979) and Sandner-Montilla (1985) described it for Venezuela. Earlier references include Cope (1860a) and Boulenger (1898b).

Key to the Subspecies of *M. hemprichii*

1 Triads invisible or almost invisible dorsally
..... *M. h. rondonianus* (State of Rondônia, Brazil)
1' Triads clearly distinguishable 2
2 Triads 7 to 10 in males and usually 7 to 9 in females; 156 to 181 ventrals in males and 160 to 182 in females
..... *M. h. hemprichii* (southeastern Venezuela, the Guianas, and northern Brazil)
2' Triads 5 to 6 in both sexes; ventrals 177 to 193 in males and 178 to 185 in females
.. *M. h. ortoni* (southern Colombia and Venezuela, eastern Ecuador and Peru, western Brazil, and northern Bolivia)

Micrurus hemprichii hemprichii (Color 31)
Eastern Worm-eating Coral Snake; Coral Lombricera Oriental
Cobra Coral Lombrigueira Oriental

Elaps hemprichii Jan, 1858: 523. (Holotype: originally in MSNM, but lost during World WAR II. Originally from "Colombia," but restricted to the vicinity of Bartica, Guyana, by Schmidt, 1933a.)
Micrurus hemprichii hemprichii: Schmidt, 1953a: 166.

Range: Lowland and low altitude tropical rain forest and humid forests in southeastern Venezuela and the Guianas to Manaus and Belém, Pará, Brazil, from sea level to 250 m.

Description: Males have 156 to 181 (173.6) and females have 160 to 182 (178.0) ventrals; subcaudals 26 to 29 (27.7) in males and 22 to 28 (24.3) in females; 90% of specimens have 1 to 10 undivided subcaudals. Examined: 16 males and 6 females.
 The black cap includes all the parietals or is reduced, covering only the anterior part of the parietals and forming an irregular, posterior border. The chin is yellowish with small black spots on the mental. The black central band of the triads is about the same length as the outer bands, covering 4 to 8 dorsals and 3 to 5 ventrals. The red (or dark yellow) bands are 2 to 4 dorsals and ventrals long. The white bands are 1 to 1½ dorsals and 2 ventrals long. The red bands on the tail are twice as long as those on the body.
 The males have 7 to 10 (8.5) and the females have 7 to 9 (one specimen has 6) (8.4) triads on the body. Both sexes have 1 to 1⅓ triads on the tail.

Remarks: This subspecies intergrades with *M. h. ortoni* in the upper Orinoco basin in southern Venezuela and in the central Amazon region of Brazil.

Food: Invertebrate onychophorans (*Peripatus*) and limbless amphisbaenid lizards (*Amphisbaena mitchelli*).

References: Cunha and Nascimento (1973, 1978) and Hoge and Romano (1971b) gave data on ecology, variation, and distribution of this subspecies for the Belem region, Pará, Brazil; Lancini (1979) and Campbell and Lamar (1989) offered color photos. Other references are from the Guianas (see under the species).

Etymology: Named after W. Hemprichi, a German naturalist who wrote several major works on natural history beginning in 1820.

Micrurus hemprichii ortoni
Western Worm-eating Coral Snake; Coral Lombricera Occidental; Cobra Coral Lombrigueira Occidental

Micrurus hemprichii ortoni Schmidt, 1953a: 166. (Holotype: MCZ 12423, a male from Pebas, Peru, collected by James Orton, December 1867.)

Range: Lowland and low montane tropical rain forest or humid forest of the upper Amazonian region and the eastern slopes of the Andes in southern Colombia and Venezuela, northwestern Brazil, eastern Ecuador, and Peru, and northern Bolivia, from 100 to 1,200 m above sea level.

Description: Males have 177 to 193 (183.9) and females have 178 to 185 (181.3) ventrals; subcaudals 29 to 31 (29.9) in males and 21 to 26 (25.1) in females; occasional specimens have a few undivided subcaudals. Examined: 10 males and 7 females, including the holotype.
 The black cap of the head is not reduced in 60% of the specimens. The remainder have some reduction of the black head coloration, varying from speckled brown or black on the posterior part of the parietals to red on more than half of the parietals. The chin is red with small black spots on several scales. The black bands vary in length from 6 to 13 dorsals. The first triad is the longest and the last triad is the shortest. The white bands are usually 1 dorsal and 2 to 3 ventrals long. The red bands are 2 to 3 dorsals and 3 to 12 ventrals long. The white and red scales are outlined

with black; some specimens have small black tips on the scales. The only red band on the tail is longer than those on the body, extending over 8 to 12 dorsals, and it is usually longer than the last black band on the body.

The males have 5 to 6 (5.5) and the females have 5 to 6 (5.6) triads on the body. About 70% of the specimens of both sexes have ⅔ of a triad on the tail. The rest have 1 full triad on the tail.

Remarks: This subspecies intergrades with *M. h. hemprichii* in Amazonas, Venezuela, and in the central Amazon, Brazil.

Food: The predominant food is invertebrate onychophorans (*Peripatus*); also small colubrid snakes.

References: Dixon and Soini (1986) described variation, ecology, and other data from the Iquitos region, Peru. Roze (1987) described it from the southern tip of Venezuela, while Silva (1994) offered data from Colombia. Almendariz (1991) gave its distribution in Ecuador, and Campbell and Lamar (1989) offered a color photo. A specimen mentioned by Schmidt (1953a) from Pará, Brazil, belongs to *M. h. hemprichii*; the locality may be in error. Other references from Colombia, Ecuador, and Peru belong here (see under species).

Etymology: Named after James Orton, an early American explorer of natural history who studied the Andes and the Amazon region in the 19th century.

Micrurus hemprichii rondonianus (Color 32)
Rondonian Coral Snake; Cobra Coral de Rondônia

Micrurus rondonianus Roze and Silva, 1990: 170. (Holotype: UCG 3299, a male from the Hydroelectric Power Plant of Samuel [Usina Hidroeletrica Samuel], Rondônia, Brazil, 85 m above sea level, collected by Nelson Jorge da Silva and the animal rescue team of the Universidade Católica Goiás, Brazil, between December 1988 and March 1989.)
Micrurus hemprichii rondonianus: Roze, 1994: 180.

Range: Tropical rain forest in the area of Hydroelectric Power Plant, Rondônia, Brazil, 80 to 100 m above sea level.

Description: Males have 173 to 183 (176.2) ventrals and females have 174 to 183 (180.2); subcaudals 26 to 32 (27.9) in males and 22 to 28 (25.1) in females; anal plate undivided. Examined: 23 males and 13 females, including the holotype.

The snout is black including the frontal and anterior part of the parietals, followed by a brownish sepia band that covers the first dorsals. The borders of the parietals, the temporals, and the first dorsals are black. Below, the head is all white including the first three scales behind the tips of the genials. The body is covered by large black bands, 27 to 32 dorsals long, separated by sepia bands about 2 to 3 dorsals and 5 to 6 ventrals long. Ventrally, between the sepia bands are 2 white spots, 3 to 4 ventrals long, that are reduced in size ventrolaterally, but extend onto the first dorsals. The ventral coloration is suggestive of black triads, distinguishable only ventrally and separated by the brownish sepia bands. In some specimens, the white ventral bands continue over the dorsum as white dots occupying less than 1 dorsal scale forming interrupted pearly rings visible on the first or second black body band.

Counting the complete triads, distinguishable ventrally, the males have 5 to 7 black triads (or 5 to 7 long black bands on the dorsum, separated by yellowish sepia bands) and females also have 5 to 7 black triads, distributed in the following way:

Number of triads in *Micrurus hemprichii rondonianus*

Sex	n	5	5⅔	6	6⅔	7	7⅔	Mean
Males	23	—	7	—	10	3	2	6.43
Females	13	2	6	2	2	2	—	5.91

On the tail is at least one brownish sepia-band, but the anal plate in 28 specimens is situated before it, and in 9 specimens approximately within or slightly behind the brownish band, producing such formulas as 5⅔ or 6⅔ triads.

Remarks: This subspecies differs from the others in absence or near absence of black triads dorsally. It could be considered a melanistic form of an already very dark species.

Food: Unknown.

References: Only the original description.

Etymology: *Rondonianus*, dweller or inhabitant of Rondônia, state of Brazil, where it is found.

Micrurus hippocrepis (Map 22, Color 33)
Belize Coral Snake; Coral or Coralillo de Belize

Elaps hippocrepis: W. C. Peters, 1862: 925. (Holotype: ZMB 4065, a female from Santo Tomás [presently near Puerto Matías de Galvez].)
Micrurus hippocrepis: Roze, 1967: 29.

Distribution and range: Lowland rain forest and low montane humid valleys and pine forests on the Caribbean side of Belize and northern Guatemala from sea level to about 600 m.

Definition: A single-banded coral snake with the upper part of the head black, followed by a white parietal band. The red bands are long; the first is 13 to 24 dorsals long, usually without black-tipped scales or with a few small and irregular black tips on some scales. Black and immaculate white bands are found on the tail. Males lack supraanal tubercles.

Description: Males have 196 to 207 (201.5) and females have 213 to 226 (220.4) ventrals; subcaudals 49 to 55 (52.6) in males and 37 to 41 (38.2) in females; usually 1+2 temporals. Examined: 6 males and 6 females, including the holotype.

The snout is usually black, including the supraoculars and most of the frontal. The rostrum is occasionally light. The white or creamy-yellow parietal band extends over the parietals, the posterior tip of the frontal, and 3 to 5 supralabials. The chin is white with small black spots on the mental and first infralabials. The black nuchal band covers the tips of the parietals and 2 to 3 dorsals. It is usually reduced or interrupted ventrally. The black bands usually are 2 to 2½ dorsals and ventrals long; they are sometimes interrupted ventrally. The red bands are long, encompassing 10 to 23 dorsals and ventrals. They are usually immaculate or have small, irregular black tips on some scales. The white or creamy-white bands are immaculate and 1 to 1½ dorsals and 1 ventral long. The black bands of the tail are longer than the white bands. The anterior white tail bands may have a red spot or a narrow red band with some black spots or irregular, black-tipped scales.

The males have 9 to 13 (11.7) and the females 14 to 18 (16.3) black body bands. The males have 5 to 6 (5.3) and the females have 4 to 5 (4.6) black tail bands.

Size: This is a medium-sized species. The longest measured specimen is 710 mm long, but average adults measure between 470 and 650 mm.

Remarks: The general impression of this species is a brilliantly red-colored snake with only a few short black bands. Some specimens have some black spots or black-tipped scales that approach the coloration of the sympatric *Micrurus diastema sapperi*, with which it probably has developed a system of Mullerian mimicry.

Food: Coffee snake (*Ninia sebae*) and other colubrid snakes.

References: General comments in Schmidt (1933a, 1936b, 1941), Roze (1967, 1970b, 1983), P. Müller (1973), Lee (1980), and Villa et al. (1988). Neill (1955), Neill and Allen (1959a), McCoy (1971), Henderson and Hoevers (1975), and Campbell and Vannini (1989) offered some data on its ecology and distribution in Belize, and Stuart (1948, 1963) in Guatemala. Campbell and Lamar (1989) provided a description and a color photo and Gutiérrez et al. (1988) described its karyotype.

Etymology: Greek from *hippus* meaning horse and *crepis* meaning a boot or sandal, apparently alluding to the horseshoe type of head coloration, formed by the white parietal band and black nostril band, reduced on the supralabials, that somewhat reminds one of a horseshoe.

Micrurus ibiboboca (Map 19, Color 34)
Ibiboboca (Caatinga Coral Snake)

Elaps ibiboboca Merrem, 1820: 142. (Holotype: AMNH 3937, a male from "Brazil," obtained by Wied-Neuwied, later specified by Wied-Neuwied (1825) as "mouth of Rio Belmonte" [State of Bahia, Brazil], as explained by Roze, 1966b.)
Elaps marcgravii Wied-Neuwied, 1820: 109. (Holotype: the same as that for *M. ibiboboca*; see Roze, 1966b.)
Micrurus ibiboboca: Amaral, 1925b: 29.

Distribution and range: Eastern Brazil from Maranhão, Piaui, and Ceará to Goiás and Rio de Janeiro, Brazil, in a variety of environments from lowland humid forest, caatinga scrub, and semideciduous upland forest; penetrating only marginally into cerrado savanna, from sea level to about 1,200 m. Isolated populations are probably also found in Suriname and French Guiana.

Definition: A triad-type coral snake in which the first triad is complete. It has a white or yellow prefrontal band that occasionally covers the entire snout. The chin is all light (white and red) or has a black spot on the mental and the first infralabial. It has a low number of subcaudals: 20 to 28 in males and 19 to 27 in females.

Description: Males have 206 to 247 (224.5) and females have 216 to 254 (228.8) ventrals; subcaudals 20 to 28 (24.2) in males and 19 to 27 (23.8) in females; 1+1 temporals. Examined: 35 males and 25 females, including the holotype.

The head is covered by black, white, black, and red bands. The black snout coloration is quite variable, ranging from practically no black at all to a large spot that includes the anterior part of the prefrontals, the nasals, and several supralabials. The white prefrontal band that follows sometimes also includes the anterior part of the frontal and the supraoculars. The black frontal band also includes part of the parietals and occasionally has a posterior projection on each parietal scale, forming a butterflylike figure. The red parietal band that follows also covers the first 2 to 4 dorsals. The chin is either all light or has a black mental spot. The central black band of a triad is normally longer than the outer bands, especially in the first triad where it covers 4 to 8 dorsals and 1 scale less on the venter. The outer black bands cover 3 to 5 dorsals and 2 to 4 ventrals. In some specimens all 3 black bands of a triad are of the same length. The white bands are 2 to 4 dorsals and ventrals long, with regular black-tipped scales. The length of the red bands is quite variable, ranging from 8 to 13 dorsals, but the red bands are always longer than the black central bands of the triads. Ventrally, the red bands are 1 or 2 scales longer. The red dorsals are either immaculate or have somewhat irregular, black-tipped scales, but these always have smaller tips than the ones on the white dorsals.

The males have 7 to 13 (10.1) and the females 8 to 13 (10.8) black triads on the body. Both sexes have 1⅓ to 1⅔ triads on the tail, but in the females the first count predominates.

Size: This is a large species. The longest specimen measured 1330 mm in overall length; many adults reach total lengths of 700 to 850 mm.

Remarks: The species shows considerable variation from region to region, and it is quite possible that several subspecies will be distinguishable once larger collections are available from several crucial regions of eastern Brazil. Moreover, the relationship of this species to *M. lemniscatus*, *M. isozonus*, and *M. frontalis* has yet to be clarified. It is possible that the Suriname and French Guyana populations actually represent *M. isozonus*, or they represent extension of this species into northeastern South America.

Food: A variety of snakelike lizards and snakes, including the limbless amphisbaenid lizards (*Leposternon polystegum*, *Amphisbaena vermicularis*), colubrid snakes (*Sibynomorphus mikanii*) and caecilians (*Siphonops annulatus*). It is also reported to be cannibalistic.

References: This is one of the first coral snakes known to the Old World, described by Marcgravius in 1648 from Brazil, more than 100 years before the modern classification of zoology was established by Linnaeus in 1758. In more recent times, it was discussed for Brazil by Amaral (1925b, 1926d, 1944), Schmidt (1936a, 1957), Prado (1945), Vanzolini (1948), Schmidt and Inger (1951), Azevedo (1962a), Roze (1967, 1970b, 1983), Cordeiro and Hoge (1974), Hoge and Romano (1973, 1981), Vanzolini et al (1980), Williams and Vanzolini (1980), Hoge et al (1981) and Vitt and Vangilder (1983). For French Guyana it was reported by Chippaux (1987), for Suriname by Abuys (1982, 1987b), and for the Guyana region by Hoogmoed (1979). Roze (1966b) commented on the type specimen. A recent description with color photo appeared in Campbell and Lamar (1989). Records given by Bertoni (1939) and Gatti (1955) for Paraguay are most probably based on specimens of *M.*

frontalis. Earlier references include Günther (1859) and others mentioned in the synonymy.

Etymology: *Ibiboboca* is the indigenous name given to this species in Brazil; it is not of Portuguese origin.

Micrurus isozonus (Map 19, Color 35)
Equal-banded Coral Snake; Coral de Franjas Iguales; Cobra Coral de Faixas Iguais

E. [laps] isozonus Cope, 1860a: 73. (Holotype: Syntypes ANSP 6804, a female, and 6805, a male, no locality, collected by Wilson. The type locality was restricted to Caracas, Venezuela, by Roze, 1955.)
Elaps omissus Boulenger, 1920: 109. (Holotype: BM 1946.1.17.15, a male from Venezuela collected by Werner.)
Micrurus isozonus: Schmidt, 1936a: 198.

Distribution and range: Llanos savanna in Meta, eastern Colombia, humid forests of the Cordillera de la Costa in northern and Central Venezuela, Isla Margarita, the llanos of central eastern and southeastern Venezuela, and the adjacent Rio Cotinga region in Roraima, Brazil, from near sea level to 1,200 m.

Definition: A triad-type coral snake with a spotted snout of black and white, followed by an interorbital black band and by a red parietal band. The first triad is complete and the white or yellow bands are usually longer than the black bands. The red and white bands have conspicuous, black-tipped scales.

Description: Males have 199 to 217 (207.8) and females have 215 to 225 (219.3) ventrals; subcaudals 26 to 33 (29.2) in males and 25 to 29 (27.3) in females; usually several subcaudals are undivided. Examined: 41 males and 24 females, including the 3 type specimens.

The snout is spotted with black and white; frequently the internasals are covered by an irregular black band. The prefrontals are either blackish or white with black posterior borders. The black interorbital band is irregular and usually projects backward to include the anterior tip of the frontal. The red parietal band has occasional black spots. The chin is white and red with irregular black spots on the mental and the first infralabials. The outer black band of the first triad usually reaches the posterior tips of the parietals. The black central band of the triads is slightly longer than the outer bands. It extends over about 3 dorsals but is generally shorter than the white bands; very rarely they are of equal length. The white bands are 3 to 5 dorsals and ventrals long, with conspicuous, black-tipped scales and occasional light brownish overtones, especially in large specimens. The triads have approximately the same proportions on the tail.

The males have 10 to 13 (11.2) (one specimen from Colombia has 9) and the females have 10 to 14 (11.8) black triads. Both sexes have 1 to 1⅓ triads, very rarely 1⅔ triads.

Size: This is a medium-sized species. The longest measured specimen is 885 mm long, but many adults measure between 480 and 700 mm in total length.

Remarks: This species is closely related to *M. frontalis* and it may be its representative north of the Amazon Basin. It can be easily recognized in northern South America by the combinations of an irregular head coloration and clearly defined triads.

Food: Litter-dwelling lizards (*Bachia*) and colubrid snakes.

References: Mostly for Venezuela by Schmidt (1936a), Vellard (1941, under *M. lemniscatus*), Marcuzzi (1950), Roze (1952, 1955, 1964, 1966a, 1967, 1970b, 1983), Alemán (1952), Vetencourt Finol (1960), Hoge and Lancini (1961, 1962), Lancini (1962c, 1970, 1979), Test et al. (1966), and Sandner-Montilla (1985). Medem (1969) mentioned it for Colombia, and P. Müller (1973) and Rivero-Blanco and Dixon (1979) discussed its distribution. Description with color photo appeared in Campbell and Lamar (1989). Earlier references include Günther (1859) and Cope (1876b).

Etymology: The name *isozonus*, Latin for equal areas or zones, alludes to the approximately equal length of the black and white bands.

Micrurus langsdorffi (Map 19, Color 36, 37)
Confused Coral Snake (Langsdorff's Coral Snake); Coral Confundida; Cobra Coral Confusa

Micrurus langsdorffi Wagler, 1824: 10. (Holotype: ZSBS 2250/0, a male from Rio Japurá, Amazonas [Brazil], obtained by Spix.)
Elaps imperator Cope, 1868: 110 (Holotype: ANSP 6793, a female from Napo and Marañon, Peru, collected in 1868).
Elaps batesi Günther, 1868: 428. (Holotype: BM 1946.1.17.21, a male from Pebas, northeastern Peru, collected by Hauxwell.)
Micrurus mimosus Amaral, 1935: 221. (Holotype: IB 8902, a female from Río Putumayo, Colombia, collected by Fray Miguel in 1934.)

Distribution and range: Lowland tropical rain forest or altered secondary formations in southern Colombia, adjacent northeastern Ecuador, northwestern Brazil, and northeastern Peru from 80 to 450 m above sea level.

Definition: A single-banded coral snake with a black cap and a basic black-white-red color pattern but with a complex polychromatic polymorphism. The black bands may be absent altogether, absent only ventrally, or only black and white bands may be present. Frequently, white or light spots are present on some upper head shields. Males have no supraanal tubercles.

Description: Males have 202 to 210 (205.9) and females have 218 to 229 (224.1) ventrals; subcaudals 46 to 56 (50.4) in males and 32 to 37 (34.6) in females; 1+1, occasionally 1+2, temporals. Examined: 26 males and 26 females, including all holotypes.

The single-banded coloration shows a remarkable variation, representing a polymorphic variety of color patterns, particularly in the Iquitos region of the Peruvian Amazon. It nearly defies a systematic description. The "normal" color pattern consists of a black head cap that occupies the parietals and sides of the head. Light spots may be present or absent on the internasals and prefrontals. The body is covered by black bands alternating with red bands and delimited by a series of white or yellowish spots, like pearly crossbands. The latter occupy one dorsal or less and at times form a poorly defined white band on the venter. In one variation, the red bands are completely obliterated by black and the body is black dorsally with nearly white crossbands. In many cases of the all-black coloration, the venter is red and white only or only white. In another variation, the black bands are replaced by yellow or brown bands, producing a yellow and red or brown and red body pattern with the pearly bands present or absent. Irregular black, brown, or grey-tipped scales or spots are present on all dorsal bands. In the yellow-red or yellow-reddish-white color pattern, the snout also is yellow or brownish yellow and so are most of the supralabials. The first nuchal "black" band is black, or yellow, or brown, depending on the color pattern. The nuchal band does not cover the tips of the parietals and it usually is incomplete ventrally. The chin, depending on the color pattern, may be white and red, or white with black spots on the mental, infralabials, and genials, or the chin can be almost entirely black with a few white, grayish, yellowish, or reddish spots. The original black bands are 2 to 4 dorsals and 2 to 3 ventrals long, if present. The red bands are 2 to 6, up to 10 dorsals long with irregular but conspicuous black-tipped scales. The last body band is red, followed by black and white (or some variation thereof) tail bands. In some specimens a red spot is present on each white tail band.

Counting the original black bands, the males have 18 to 37 (30.2) and females 29 to 47 (37.3) black body bands. This count doubles in specimens in which the "red" bands are also black. The males have 6 to 11 (8.1), usually less than 11, and the females have 5 to 8 (6.3), usually less than 8, black tail bands.

Size: This is a medium-small coral snake. The longest measured specimen is 770 mm, but many adults range between 450 and 600 mm.

Remarks: Due to the array of color patterns that may not even resemble one another, this is a confusing species. One possible explanation of this chromatic polymorphism has to do with mimicry systems. In the upper Amazon of Peru this subspecies has no clear Mullerian mimicry pattern with which to associate. It is also possible than some Batesian mimics of the genus *Atractus* have forced a polymorphic "escape" from the disadvantageous association of their color patterns. In areas where other single-banded venomous coral snake exist, such as in the southern Colombia, the regular single-banded color pattern predominates. The variety of color patterns also has caused repeated descriptions of this subspecies under different names.

Cunha and Nascimento (1982b) synonymized it with *M. albicinctus*. The latter is a clearly distinct species. Campbell and Lamar (1989) included in its distribution Bolivia and Rondônia and Mato Grosso, Brazil, but this corresponds to the distribution of *M. albicinctus*. Roze (1967, 1970b, 1983) recognized two subspecies, *M. l. langsdorffi* and *M. l. ornatissimus*, but Cunha and Nascimento (1982b) recognized both forms as different species.

References: Soini (1974a) described its polychromatism, Campbell and Lamar (1989) gave description and distribution, while Duellman (1978) and Silva (1994) offered a description and color drawing of the regular red and black color pattern in Ecuador and Colombia. General references of the species appeared in Ihering (1911), Amaral (1925a, 1930b), and Schmidt (1936a). Prado (1945), Machado (1945), Hoge and Romano (1973, 1981), and Santos (1981) gave it for Brazil; Amaral (1935, 1937a), Rendahl and Vertergren (1941), Nicéforo-María (1942), Dunn (1944a), Daniel (1949), Schmidt (1955), Medem (1969), Silva and Rodríguez (1985), and Pérez-Santos and Moreno (1988) gave it for Colombia; Almendariz (1991) mentioned it for Ecuador; Dunn (1946), Schmidt and Walker (1953a), Meneses (1974), Carrillo de Espinoza (1983), Dixon and Soini (1986), and Henderson, Dixon, and Soini (1979) described it for Peru. Greene and McDiarmid (1981) and Roze (1983) dealt with mimicry, while Hoogmoed and Gruber (1983) commented on type specimens. Earlier significant references are those by Günther (1859, 1868), Jan (1858, 1859c), Cope (1868), Jan and Sordelli (1872), Orton (1876), and Boulenger (1898).

Food: Blind snakes (*Typhlops reticulatus*; *Leptotyphlops*) and colubrid snakes.

Etymology: Named after the 19th century naturalist Langsdorff. *Batesi* is probably dedicated to H. W. Bates, a British naturalist who traveled and collected in South America in the 19th century. The name *mimosus* is from Greek *mim-* meaning imitator or actor, and *-osus*, a Latin suffix for prone to or inclined to; thus the name would suggest inclined to imitate, probably alluding to the similarity of this species to other Colombian coral snakes of similar color pattern. The name *imperator* comes from the Latin word *imperare* meaning to command; thus the name means ruler or emperor, probably indicating its royal coloration.

Micrurus laticollaris (Map 22)
Double Collar Coral Snake (Balsan Coral Snake); Coralillo de Doble Collar

Distribution: The states of Colima and Jalisco and the Río Balsas basin in Michoacán, Guerrero, Morelos, Puebla, and Oaxaca, Mexico.

Definition: A triad-type coral snake with the triads only on the body. The tail is ornamented with single black and yellow or white bands. The first and last "triad" consist only of 2 black bands; the first band is absent from the first triad and the last band is absent from the last. The snout is black, followed by a yellow parietal-postparietal band. There are 1+2 temporals.

Size: This is a medium-sized species. The longest measured specimen is 728 mm long. Most adults measure between 500 and 700 mm.

Remarks: The presence of single black and yellow bands on the tail is unique among triad-type coral snakes. Two subspecies are recognized.

References: Roze (1967) defined both subspecies; Frost and Aird (1978) described its distribution; Schmidt (1958) and Campbell and Lamar (1989) gave a complete description and distribution. Other references include Schmidt (1933a, 1936b), Martín del Campo (1935), E. H. Taylor (1940), H. M. Smith and Taylor (1945, 1950), Davis and Smith (1953), Duellman (1958, 1961, 1965b), Dixon and Webb (1965), Webb (1966), and Roze (1970b, 1983, 1989).

Key to the Subspecies of *M. laticollaris*

1 Subcaudals 40 to 43 in males and 35 to 38 in females; usually no light spots on snout or supralabials

.... *M. l. laticollaris* (Michoacán to Oaxaca and Puebla, Mexico)
1' Subcaudals 44 to 47 in males and 39 to 41 in females; light spots on snout and supralabials
 ... *M. l. maculirostris* (Puebla and Jalisco, Mexico)

Micrurus laticollaris laticollaris
Eastern Double Collar Coral Snake; Coralillo Oriental de Doble Collar

Elaps marcgravii var. *laticollaris* Peters, 1869: 877. (Holotype: lectotype [designated by Schmidt, 1958] ZMB 6659, a male from "Mexico" collected by Berkenbusch. The type locality was restricted to Izúcar de Matamoros, Puebla, Mexico, by H. M. Smith and Taylor, 1950.)
Micrurus laticollaris laticollaris: Roze, 1967: 30.

Range: Dry low montane and transition humid formations in the Telpalcatepec-Balsas Basin in Michoacán, Guerrero, Morelos, and Puebla, also extending into western Oaxaca, Mexico, at elevations between 400 and 1,800 m above sea level.

Description: Males have 206 to 211 (209.8) and females have 219 to 220 (217.6) ventrals; subcaudals 40 to 43 (41.1) in males and 35 to 38 (36.1) in females. Examined: 6 males and 12 females, including the holotype.
 The snout is black with a yellow or white parietal band that covers one half or more of the parietals, the temporal, and the last 2 or 3 supralabials, as well as 1 or 2 dorsal rows. Occasionally the tip of the frontal is included in the parietal band. The chin is all yellow, including the mental, but occasionally there are a few small grayish spots on the other scales. The black nuchal band is the second band of the first triad and covers 9 to 11 dorsals. The central black band of the complete triads is 5 to 8 dorsals long, and the outer bands are 3 to 4 dorsals long. Ventrally, the outer black bands are 1 or 2 ventrals shorter and frequently unite irregularly or are reduced or invaded by the white bands. The yellow or white bands are immaculate and 3 to 4 dorsals long. The red bands, 4 to 9 dorsals long, have a few scattered black-tipped scales and they may be either longer or shorter than the central black band. The black tail bands are longer than the yellow ones.
 The males have $\frac{2}{3}+5+\frac{2}{3}$ to $\frac{2}{3}+6+\frac{2}{3}$ (5.3 complete) triads, and the females have $\frac{2}{3}+5+\frac{2}{3}$ to $\frac{2}{3}+7+\frac{2}{3}$ (6.0 complete) triads on the body. One female has 4 black tail bands; all other specimens have 3.

Food: Unknown.

References: Duellman (1961, 1965b) gave ecological and distributional data.

Etymology: Latin from *lati-* meaning broad or wide and *collari* meaning of the collar, referring to the long black nuchal band.

Micrurus laticollaris maculirostris (Pattern 29)
Western Double Collar Coral Snake; Coralillo Occidental de Doble Collar

Micrurus laticollaris maculirostris Roze, 1967: 31. (Holotype: KU 32546, a male from the vicinity of Colima, Colima, Mexico, collected in the spring of 1951.)

Range: Dry montane and scrub formations in Colima and southern Jalisco, Mexico, at elevations between 300 and 800 m above sea level.

Description: Males have 207 to 215 (211.1) and females have 219 to 220 (219.5) ventrals; subcaudals 44 to 47 (45.3) in males and 39 to 41 (40.0) in females. Examined: 8 males and 2 females.
 The black snout coloration covers ½ to ¾ of the parietals, but there are light spots on the rostral and on several supralabials. The chin is light with occasional small, grayish spots. The black nuchal band is 11 to 12 dorsals long and does not reach the tips of the parietals. The central black band of the triad is longer than the outer ones but is shorter than the red bands. The triads are clearly defined, both dorsally and ventrally. Most yellow bands are 3 dorsals and ventrals long and immaculate. The red bands are 7 to 12 dorsals long, with irregular black-tipped scales. A sample of the lengths of the red-black-yellow-black-yellow sequence at midbody is 12-4-3-6-3-4.
 The males have $\frac{2}{3}+5+\frac{2}{3}$ to $\frac{2}{3}+7+\frac{2}{3}$ (5.6 complete) triads, and the females have $\frac{2}{3}+5+\frac{2}{3}$ to $\frac{2}{3}+6+\frac{2}{3}$ (5.5 complete) triads on the body. Both sexes have 3 black tail bands.

Food: Unknown.

References: Dixon and Webb (1965) gave data on distribution in Jalisco and Campbell and Lamar (1989) featured a color photo.

Etymology: The Latin word *maculirostris* alludes to the light dots on the snout.

Micrurus latifasciatus (Map 23, Pattern 32)
Long-banded Coral Snake (Broad-ringed Coral Snake); Coralillo de Bandas Largas

Micrurus latifasciatus Schmidt, 1933a: 35. (Holotype: MCZ 22135, a female from Finca El Ciprés, Volcán Zunil, Suchitepequez, Guatemala, collected by A. W. Anthony in 1925.)

Micrurus nuchalis Schmidt, 1933a: 35. (Holotype: MCZ 27830, a female from Tapanatepec, Oaxaca, Mexico, collected by W. W. Brown on November 7, 1927.)

Distribution and range: Dry tropical lowlands to moderate and high dry to humid montane formations on the Pacific side of Oaxaca and Chiapas, Mexico, to eastern Guatemala, from near sea level up to 1,350 m.

Definition: A single-banded coral snake with 6 to 9 black body bands and 2 or 3 tail bands. The snout is black, followed by a yellow or white parietal band and then by a black nuchal band that is 8 to 13 dorsals long. The red bands have conspicuous, black-tipped scales. The males have supraanal tubercles; some females have feeble supraanal keels.

Description: Males have 186 to 200 (192.7) and the females have 201 to 212 (206.6) ventrals; subcaudals 48 to 56 (53.0) in males and 37 to 46 (40.4) in females. About one third of the specimens have 3 to 11 undivided subcaudals. Examined: 32 males and 25 females, including the holotypes.

The black snout coloration may or may not include the tip of the frontal and covers the anterior part of the parietals and the first 4 supralabials. The chin has the mental and the first 3 infralabials partially or totally black. The black nuchal band usually covers the tips of the parietals, the first 8 to 13 dorsals, and 6 to 11 ventrals as well as the genials. The black body bands are 4 to 9 dorsals long, the anterior longer than the posterior. The red bands are 15 to 35 dorsals long, the anterior longer than the posterior. All dorsal red scales have conspicuous black tips that cover up to one half of the scale. About half of the specimens from Oaxaca have the black-tipped scales concentrated around the border of the yellow or white bands beginning with the second black band, thus producing a poorly-defined black accessory band. The red bands are usually immaculate ventrally. The white or yellow bands are 1 to 4 dorsals long. The black tail bands are 3 or more times as long as the white bands.

The males have 5 to 9 (6.9), usually more than 8, black body bands and females have 7 to 9 (8.1). Both sexes have 2 to 3 black tail bands.

Size: This is a medium-large species. The longest specimen measured 1140 mm; most adults range between 600 and 900 mm.

Remarks: This species is easily recognizable by its very long red bands on the body and the very long black bands on the tail. The brilliance of the long red bands is somewhat obscured, however, by the conspicuous black-tipped scales and by the brownish overtones present in the larger specimens.

Food: Caecilians (e.g., *Dermophis mexicanus*) and a variety of colubrid snakes (*Ninia sebae*, *Geophis nasalis*, and *Adelphicos quadrivirgatus*).

References: Description with a color photo and distribution appeared in Campbell and Lamar (1989) and general comments on the species in Roze (1967, 1970a, 1983) and in Villa et al. (1988). Distribution in Guatemala was given by Stuart (1963) and Campbell and Vannini (1988, 1989), while information on Mexican specimens is offered by Schmidt (1933a, 1958), Martín del Campo (1935, 1950), Schmidt and Smith (1943), H. M. Smith and Taylor (1945), Landi et al. (1966), Lynch and Smith (1966), Alvarez del Toro (1983), and Johnson (1984); Greene and McDiarmid (1983) commented on mimicry and Tiedemann and Haupl (1980) on type specimens.

Etymology: Latin from *lati-* meaning broad or wide and *fasciatus* meaning banded, alluding to the long body bands.

Micrurus lemniscatus (Map 24)
Ribbon Coral Snake (South American Coral Snake); Coral Acintada; Cobra Coral de Faixas

Distribution: Amazon region east of Andes, except middle Amazon, in southern Colombia, Ecuador, Peru, and Bolivia; also eastern and southern Venezuela, Trinidad, the Guianas, and Brazil; probably also Paraguay.

Definition: A triad-type coral snake in which the first triad is complete. The snout is black, followed by a white crossband, a black crossband which covers the frontal, and finally a red parietal band that covers several dorsals.

Size: This is a large-size coral snake. The longest measured specimen is 1,390 mm long. Many adults measure between 500 and 900 mm.

Remarks: In spite of the vast distribution, the basic head and body coloration is surprisingly uniform, having only minor variations. The white and red head crossbands distinguish it from all coral snakes in northern South America except *M. filiformis*. The range of variation in number of ventrals and subcaudals and in number of triads permits recognition of at least 4 subspecies. Lack of specimens from several crucial areas in Brazil, Bolivia, and Venezuela makes our knowledge of the variation and distribution of this species inadequate. It is possible that more than one species is included among the subspecies.

References: Numerous references. The most recent description and distribution with color photos is by Campbell and Lamar (1989) and Silva (1994). A general overview was given by Schmidt (1936a) and Roze (1967, 1970b, 1983); other general remarks by Cendrero et al. (1972). Its presence in Bolivia is discussed by Kempff-Mercado (1975); in Brazil by Gomes (1918b), Amaral (1925b, 1926b, 1930b, 1944, 1948b, 1974), Gliesch (1925, probably refers to *M. frontalis*), Prado (1945), Machado (1945), Vanzolini (1948), Hoge (1953, 1967), Hoge and Romano (1973, 1981), Cunha and Nascimento (1973, 1978, 1982a, 1988), Santos (1981), Cunha et al. (1985), Vanzolini (1986), Nascimento et al. (1988), Zimmerman and Rodriguez (1990), and Roze and da Silva (1990); in Colombia by Amaral (1931b, 1937b), Nicéforo-María (1933, 1942), Dunn (1944a), Daniel (1949), Schmidt (1955), Medem (1969), Silva and Rodríguez (1985), and Pérez-Santos and Moreno (1986, 1988); in Ecuador by Orcés (1942, 1943, 1948), J. A. Peters (1960), Duellman (1978), Fugler and Walls (1978), and Miyata (1982); in French Guiana by Gasc and Rodrigues (1980) and Chippaux (1987); in Guyana by Parker (1935) and Beebe (1946); in Paraguay questionable records are by Bertoni (1914, 1939), Schouten (1931, 1937), and Gatti (1955); in Peru by Schmidt and Schmidt (1925), Schmidt and Walker (1943a), Meneses (1974), Soini (1974b), Carrillo de Espinoza (1983), Dixon and Soini (1986), and Rodríguez and Cadle (1990); in Suriname by Brongersma (1967), Moonen et al. (1978), and Abuys (1987b); in Trinidad by Werner (1900), Mole (1914, 1924), Burger (1955), Schmidt (1957), Wehekind (1955, 1960), Boos and Quesnel (1968), Boos (1974, 1984a, 1984b), Emsley (1977), and Welch (1980); in Venezuela by Milá de la Roca (1932), Vellard (1941), Marcuzzi (1950), Roze (1955, 1966a, 1987), Vetencourt Finol (1960), Hoge and Lancini (1962), Lancini (1979), and Sandner-Montilla (1985). Type specimens were discussed by Andersson (1899), Tiedemann and Haupl (1980), and Roze (1989); general distribution by Rivero-Blanco and Dixon (1979); ecology and behavior by Sazima and Abe (1991); behavior by Lankes (1938) and Schmidt and Inger (1951); karyotype by Beçak and Beçak (1969); and mimicry by Mertens (1956), Roze (1983), Marques and Puorto (1991), and Sazima and Abe (1991). Earlier references include publications as far back as Bancroft (1796), Gray (1829), Günther (1859), Cope (1859, 1870, 1876b), Urich (1894, 1898), and Quelch (1898).

Key to the Subspecies of *M. lemniscatus*

1 White bands usually 1½ dorsals long with conspicuous black tips forming transverse interrupted rows
.... *M. lemniscatus carvalhoi* (eastern and southern Brazil)
1' White bands usually 2 or more dorsals long, with or without scattered irregular black tips 2
2 212 to 225 ventrals in males and more than 242 in females
.... *M. lemniscatus diutius* (Trinidad, eastern Venezuela, the Guianas, and northern Brazil)
2' Usually more than 228 ventrals in males and more than 242 in females 3
3 12 to 15 (usually 13 to 15) black triads in males and 11 to 14 in females (11 only rarely)
..... *M. lemniscatus lemniscatus* (The Guianas and Amapá, Brazil)
3' 9 to 11 black triads in males and 8 to 11 in females
...... *M. lemniscatus helleri* (Venezuela, Colombia, western Brazil, Ecuador, Peru, and Bolivia)

Micrurus lemniscatus lemniscatus
Guiana's Ribbon Coral Snake: Coral Acintada Guayanesa; Cobra Coral de Faixas de Guianas

Coluber lemniscatus Linnaeus, 1758: 224. (Holotype: lectotype [designated by Roze, 1989] NRS No. L-93, a male from "Asia" [in error]; restricted to Belém, Pará, Brazil, by Schmidt and Walker, 1943a.)
Micrurus lemniscatus lemniscatus: Burger, 1955: 40.

Range: Lowland rain forest, open humid forest, and drier cultivated lands in northern parts in Guyana, Suriname, and French Guiana, reaching northern Pará and Maranhão, Brazil, from sea level to about 600 m.

Description: Males have 235 to 246 (240.8) and females have 242 to 264 (256) ventrals; subcaudals 36 to 40 (37.4) in males and 31 to 39 (35.1) in females. Examined: 20 males and 15 females, including the types.
The snout is invariably black, including internasals. The prefrontal band is irregular and also covers the second and third supralabials. The black frontal band also covers the anterior part of the parietals where it forms a straight or nearly straight posterior border. The frontal band includes 2 to 4 dorsals, some of which have irregular black tips. The chin has either a few black scales or the entire anterior part of the head is black, including 3 to 4 infralabials. The central black band is longer than the outer ones, 4 to 6 dorsals and 3 to 5 ventrals long. The red bands are shorter than the central black bands; the red scales are usually outlined by dark brown or grey and some have irregular black tips. The white bands are 1½ to 2 dorsals long and wider on the belly where they occupy 2 to 3 ventrals. They have smudgy brownish black spots or irregular blackish borders.
The males have 12 to 15 (13.9) and the females have 11 to 14 (13.0) black triads on the body. In both sexes, more than 90% of the specimens have 1⅔ triads on the tail.

Remarks: The exact distribution of this subspecies and the adjacent *M. lemniscatus diutius* is not well known. This is particularly due to the fact that older specimens, especially in European museums, bear geographically vague localities such as "British Guiana, Surinam, and French Guiana." One of the first collections with precise localities was made by the well-known American naturalist, William Beebe (1946), in the Kartabo region of Guyana, and is presently deposited in the American Museum of Natural History, New York. Recently, two Brazilian herpetologists, Cunha and Nascimento (1973, 1978), have collected and reported on significant collections from northeastern Brazil.

Its intergradation with *M. l. diutius* is unclear.

Food: In the Guianas it feeds exclusively on swamp eels (*Synbranchus marmoratus*), but in Brazil its food includes the aquatic false coral snake (*Hydrops*), litter-dwelling snakes (*Liophis*), and a limbless amphisbaenid lizard (*Leposternon*).

References: Beebe (1946) offered ecological and morphological data from the Kartabo region, Guyana; Roze (1970b) offered keys to the subspecies, and Cunha and Nascimento (1973, 1978, 1982a) provided data on ecology and variation.

Etymology: In Latin *lemniscatus* means adorned with ribbons, referring to the red, black, and white bands.

Micrurus lemniscatus carvalhoi (Color 38)
Brazilian Ribbon Coral Snake; Cobra Coral de Faixas Brasileira; Coral Acintada Brasilera

Micrurus lemniscatus carvalhoi Roze: 1967: 33. (Holotype: USNM 76341, a male from Catanduva, São Paulo, Brazil.)

Range: In lowland dry forest and low montane semideciduous or humid forest, marginally also in cerrado savanna in Parana, São Paulo, Minas Gerais, and Mato Grosso; extending along the coast north to Bahia and Rio Grande do Norte, Brazil; probably also in Paraguay.

Description: Males have 228 to 254 (236.7) and females have 250 to 263 (256.9) ventrals; subcaudals 29 to 36 (33.2) in males and 27 to 34 (32.4) in females. Examined: 92 males and 51 females, including the holotype.

The posterior border of the black snout coloration is quite irregular, usually projecting backward along the internasal suture and also on the nasal opening. The white prefrontal band forms an irregular, slightly V-shaped band, usually covering the anterior part of the frontal. The black fronto-parietal band usually extends also on one half to three quarters of the parietals. The chin is white and red. The first 3 to 4 infralabials are black. Below, the rest of the head is white anteriorly, gradually changing to red on the throat. The central black bands are 4 to 6 dorsals long, slightly longer than the outer ones that are 2 to 5 dorsals long. On the venter, the black bands are irregular and about 1 scale shorter than on the dorsum. The red bands are longer than the black bands, covering 7 to 13 dorsals. They have from a few to more than 20 black tips or spots irregularly distributed but concentrated on the dorsal area. The white bands are usually not more than 1½ scales long on the midvertebral line. Most of them have conspicuous black tips that either fuse with the following black band or form a transverse row of black spots on the posterior part of the white band.

The males have 10 to 15 (12.9) and the females have 9 to 16 (13.4) black triads. Both sexes have 1 to 2 triads on the tail.

Remarks: The distribution of this subspecies has not been clearly determined.

Food: Feeds on swamp eel (*Synbranchus marmoratus*), *Gymnotus* sp., and snakes (*Sibynomorphus mikani*), as well as amphisbaenid, *Amphisbaena roberti*, as reported by Sazima and Abe (1991).

References: Roze (1967) gave its variation and Beçak and Beçak (1969) described the karyotype; Mertens (1956) and Campbell and Lamar (1989) offered color photos and dealt with mimicry and Vanzolini (1948) mentioned food.

Etymology: Named after the Brazilian herpetologist, Antenor Leitão de Carvalho, "whose friendly cooperation is well known and appreciated within and outside Brazil," as is stated in the original description.

Micrurus lemniscatus diutius (Fig. 58)
Trinidad Ribbon Coral Snake; Coral Acintada Trinitaria; Cobra Coral de Faixas de Trinidad

Micrurus lemniscatus diutius Burger, 1955: 8. (Holotype: FMNH 34472, a male from Tunapuna, collected by N. A. Weber.)

Range: In lowland rain forest and low montane humid forests, occasionally also in more open cultivated lands and marginally penetrating into savanna; in Trinidad, eastern and southeastern Venezuela, southern Guyana, Suriname, and French Guiana southward to Amazonas and to the central Amazon region in Brazil.

Description: Males have 212 to 225 (218.6) and females have 225 to 242 (233.1) ventrals; subcaudals 31 to 38 (35.6) in males and 31 to 37 (34.8) in females. Examined: 28 males and 21 females, including the holotype.

Figure 58. Micrurus lemniscatus diutius, from Trinidad: N of Sangre Grande (AMNH 78987).

The black snout coloration is irregular, sometimes reduced to a rostral spot. The white prefrontal band has irregular anterior and posterior borders. The black frontal band is also of irregular shape, usually not forming a regular posterior border. With considerable variations, it covers the ocular and 2 to 3 supralabials. The red parietal band includes one half or more of the parietals and usually 3 dorsals. Usually there are no black tips or spots on the red nuchal scales, at least not very conspicuous ones. Inferiorly, the coloration varies from nearly immaculate white and red to black covering the mental and the first infralabials. The central black bands are about twice as long as the outer ones, sometimes a little less. They cover 7 to 12 dorsals on the middorsal line and 5 to 10 ventrals. The anterior triads have the central black band longer than the posterior triads. The black outer bands cover 4 to 7 dorsals. The lengths of the red bands vary considerably, covering 2 to 10 dorsals and 4 to 12 ventrals. The red dorsals have a few to many irregular black tips. The white bands are usually 2 or more dorsals long on the middorsal line and 2 to 5 scales long ventrally. The white dorsals have irregular dark brown or smudgy black tips or are irregularly outlined by brownish black.

The males have 7 to 11 (9.5) and the females have 8 to 11 (9.6) triads. Nearly all specimens of both sexes have 1⅔ triads on the tail.

Remarks: The variation and distribution of this coral snake is not well established.

Food: A wide variety of food including swamp eel (*Synbranchus marmoratus*), aquatic false coral snake (*Hydrops triangularis triangularis*), and the snakes from humid and inundated forests (*Liophis*); also litter-dwelling lizards (*Bachia*), legless amphisbaenid lizards (*Leposternon polystegum*), and snakes (*Atractus trilineatus*), including other coral snakes (*Micrurus circinalis*) and even individuals of its own kind. Thus, it is truly cannibalistic.

References: Many references particularly from Trinidad, starting with Urich (1894, 1898), Mole and Urich (1894), Boettger (1898), Mole (1924), Schmidt (1957), Wehekind (1960), and Emsley (1977); from Venezuela, Roze, (1955, 1966a) and Lancini (1979) offered color pictures; and from Pará, Brazil, Cunha and Nascimento (1973, 1978). Campbell and Lamar (1989) also featured color photos.

Etymology: The Latin word *diutius* is a comparative for "longer or too long," and the name is intended to convey, as proposed in the original description, a sense of "too long, from the point of view of potential victims, a meter-long venomous snake is certainly too long."

Micrurus lemniscatus helleri (Color 40)
Western Ribbon Coral Snake; Coral Acintada Occidental; Cobra Coral de Faixas Occidental

Micrurus helleri Schmidt and Schmidt, 1925: 129. (Holotype: FMNH 5577, a male from Pozuzo, Huanuco, Peru, collected by Edmund Heller in 1922.)
Micrurus lemniscatus helleri: Roze, 1967: 35.

Range: In humid and rain forest from the eastern slopes of the Andes on both sides of the Amazon from southern Venezuela and Colombia to Ecuador, Peru, and Bolivia, and in western Brazil where its distribution is uncertain, from 80 m to about 1,500 m above sea level.

Description: Males have 230 to 248 (238.9) and females have 240 to 260 (252.3) ventrals; subcaudals 33 to 41 (36.7) in males and 34 to 43 (36.2) in females. Examined: 112 males and 73 females, including the holotype.

The snout is black. The white prefrontal band varies in size and shape and occasionally also includes part of the internasals and frontal. The black frontal band usually covers 2 to 3 supralabials, the oculars, and the anterior part of the parietals. The red parietal band includes 2 to 5 dorsals as well. Inferiorly, the mental and up to 3 or 4 infralabials are black. The black bands of the first triad are longer than the black bands of more posterior triads. The central black band is 4 to 8 dorsals long and the outer black bands are 3 to 7 dorsals. Ventrally, all black bands are about 1 ventral shorter than dorsal black bands. The red bands are 4 to 8 dorsals and ventrals long, usually without black tips or with a few markings. The white bands are 2 to 3 dorsals long and a scale longer ventrally.

The males have 9 to 11 (9.8) and the females have 8 to 11 (9.6) triads. Only 1 female out of 40 has 12 triads. Most of the specimens of both sexes have 1⅔ triads on the tail; the rest have 1⅓ or 2.

Remarks: The distribution of this subspecies has not yet been clearly defined. Because it shows considerable variation within its vast range, Cunha et al. (1987) questioned its validity. On the other hand, it is possible that more than one subspecies is included under this name.

Food: A wide variety of food, including swamp eel (*Synbranchus marmoratus*), which is preferred by larger adults. Smaller specimens feed on caecilians (*Oscaecilia bassleri*), litter-dwelling teiid lizards (*Bachia trinasale*), blind snakes (*Typhlops brongersmianus*), and colubrid snakes.

References: Diverse aspects of this coral snake are reported by Schmidt (1955), Nicéforo María (1942), and Medem (1969) for Colombia; Duellman (1978) and Almendariz (1991) for Ecuador; Dixon and Soini (1986) and Carrillo de Espinosa (1983) for Peru; and Roze (1987) for the southern tip of Venezuela. Campbell and Lamar (1989) and Silva (1994) featured a color photo.

Etymology: Named after Edmund Heller, collector of the type specimen and participant in the Marshall Field Expedition to Peru in 1922 to 1923.

Micrurus limbatus (Map 23)
Tuxtlan Coral Snake; Coralillo de Tuxtla

Distribution: Los Tuxtlas region of southern Veracruz, Mexico.

Definition: A bicolored red and black coral snake in which the black body bands are either complete or are represented by black dorsal and ventral spots or irregular blothes; only the black nuchal band is always complete. Males do not have supraanal tubercles.

Size: This is a small species. The longest specimen I have measured was 585 mm long. Most adults measure between 400 and 550 mm.

Remarks: This species can be easily recognized by its irregular black spots or black bands without any white or yellow bands. It seems to be endemic in the San Andrés Tuxtla region of Mexico. Recently, Pérez-Higareda and Smith (1990) recognized two subspecies distributed in two limited, but geographically distinct areas in Los Tuxtlas region, Mexico.

References: In addition to the original description and the definition of the two subspecies by Pérez-Higareda and Smith (1990), the most recent description with color photos of both subspecies is that of Campbell and Lamar (1989). H. M. Smith and Taylor (1966), Roze (1967, 1983), Fraser (1973), Pérez-Higareda (1980), Ramírez-Bautista et al. (1981), and Pérez-Higadera et al. (1987), Flores Villela et al. (1987) provided some additional information about this little-known species. Several reports have been prepared working out of the Estación de Biología Tropical "Los Tuxtla" of the Universidad Nacional Autónoma of Mexico. Mimicry and behavior are discussed by Greene (1973), Greene and Pyburn (1973), and Greene and McDiarmid (1981).

Key to the Subspecies of *M. limbatus*

1 Black body bands always complete
  .. *M. l. limbatus* (northwestern Los Tuxtlas, Mexico)
1' Black dorsal and ventral spots or blotches
  .... *M. L. spilosomus* (eastern Los Tuxtlas, Mexico)

Micrurus limbatus limbatus (Pattern 30)
Tuxtlan Banded Coral Snake; Coralillo Anillado de Tuxtla

Micrurus limbatus Fraser, 1964: 570. (Holotype: UMMZ 123858, a female from the southern slope of Volcán San Martín, 7 airline miles north of San Andrés Tuxtla, at 1,050 m altitude, Veracruz, Mexico, collected by D. C. Robinson on July 11, 1959.)
Micrurus limbatus limbatus: Pérez-Higareda and Smith, 1990: 5.

Range: Tropical rain forest and low montane wet forest and patchy grassland in the northwestern region of Los Tuxtlas around Volcán San Martín, Veracruz, Mexico, from 10 to 1500 m of altitude.

Description: Males have 189 to 191 (191.2) and females have 198 to 206 (202.5) ventrals; subcaudals 37 to 42 (37.5) in males and 25 to 30 (27.3) in females. Examined: 3 males and 2 females, including the holotype, but variation of 8 males and 10 females, as reported by Pérez-Higareda and Smith (1990), has been added.

The black snout coloration includes the frontal and projects backward between the suture of the parietals. The red or pink parietal band includes several supralabials, temporals, and the first dorsal row behind the parietals. The chin is white or reddish white with some irregular black spots on the infralabials and some other shields. The black bands are complete. The red scales on the body are irregularly outlined by black or have small blackish-brown tips. Occasionally, there are some black spots at times the size of a band on the reddish-orange bands between them. On the tail, the black bands are regular, 2 to 4 dorsals and 3 to 5 subcaudals long. The red bands on the tail have small, irregular black spots. In some specimens the complete black bands alternate dorsally and ventrally with black spots. The males have 25 to 45 black bands and/or spots combined. The females have 37 to 41 complete bands. All specimens except one have 4 black tail bands.

Remarks: This subspecies probably intergrades with *M. l. spilosomus* in the Coyame of Los Tuxta region.

Food: Colubrid snakes.

References: Campbell and Lamar (1989) featured a color photo of this subspecies and Pelaste-Villafuerte and Flores-Villela (1992) mentioned it for Veracruz.

Etymology: The name *limbatus* is derived from the Latin *limbus* meaning a fringe or border, alluding, possibly, to the black borders or margins outlining the red scales.

Micrurus limbatus spilosomus (Color 41)
Tuxtlan Spotted Coral Snake; Coralillo Manchado de Tuxtla

Micrurus limbatus spilosomus Pérez-Higareda and Smith, 1990: 6. (Holotype: UNAM-LT [Universidad Nacional Autonoma de Mexico, Los Tuxtlas] 2733, a female from Bastonal, Sierra de Santa Marta, municipality of Catemaco, Veracruz, Mexico, 900 m, collected by G. Pérez-Higareda.)

Range: Low montane wet forest, in Sierra de Santa Marta, Los Tuxtlas region, Veracruz, Mexico, 900 to 1000 m of altitude.

Description: Males have 189 to 192 and females have 200 to 203 ventrals; subcaudals 41 to 42 in males and 27 to 29 in females. Examined: 1 male and 2 males, but data from the original description by Pérez-Higareda and Smith (1990) have been added.

The snout is black and extends from the prefrontals to the center of the parietals and includes the preoculars and first two or more supralabials. The rest of the head is light, pale red in life; below, the head is immaculate. The black nuchal band is complete, but the rest of the body is covered by alternating larger and smaller irregular black dorsal and ventral spots. The dorsal spots are round or oval and somewhat irregular, while the ventral blotches or spots are highly irregular and concentrated around the midventral region, frequently with no correspondence to the dorsal spots. On the tail are complete black bands.

There are 14 to 21 dorsal spots in both sexes and almost invariably 4 black tail bands.

Remarks: This subspecies can be easily recognized by its irregular black markings and by the absence of any white or yellow bands. *M. bernadi* from Mexico also has black dorsal spots, but they are more numerous (24 to 42) than in this subspecies. This subspecies probably intergrades in the region of Coyame, between the Santa Marta and San Martín areas in Veracruz.

Food: Unknown.

References: Only the original description by Pérez-Higareda and Smith (1990), a mention for Veracruz by Pelaste-Villafuerte (1992), and a color photo by Campbell and Lamar (1989).

Etymology: From Greek *spilo* meaning spot or spotted as adjective and *somus* meaning body; thus, the one with spotted body, alluding to the black body spots of this subspecies.

Micrurus margaritiferus (Map 25, Pattern 31)
Speckled Coral Snake; Coral Salpicada

| C41 |
| 256 |
| M25 |
| 240 |
| P31 |
| 269 |

Micrurus margaritiferus Roze, 1967: 35. (Holotype: AMNH 533362, a female from Boca Río Santiago-Río Marañón, Peru, obtained by H. Bassler in August 1929.)

Distribution and range: Tropical rain forest of Marañón and Santiago valley on the eastern slopes of the Andes of Peru, 200 to 400 m above sea level.

Definition: A black coral snake with a transverse series of white spots that form interrupted bands around the body, poorly outlining the black bands between them. Red bands are absent or found only on the venter.

Description: Males have around 205 and females have 221 to 225 (223.0) ventrals; subcaudals around 45 in males and 33 to 38 (35.5) in females; 1+1 temporals. Examined: 1 male and 2 females, including the holotype.

Head, body, and tail are all black above with small white spots that form crossbands. A few white spots are present on several supralabials and on few shields below. The body has a poorly defined transverse series of white spots, less than one dorsal and ventral long. The crossbands formed by the pearly white spots define the black areas as black bands on the body and on the tail. The black bands are alternately longer and shorter and correspond to the original shorter black bands and the original longer red bands that are now black. Ventrally, red bands can be red or white.

The males have around 68 and the females have 110 to 141 (125.5) poorly defined black body bands and 10 to 13 tail bands.

Size: This is a medium-sized species. The longest female measures 735 mm, as reported by Campbell and Lamar (1989).

Remarks: The absence of any red coloration on the dorsum and the pattern of white-sprinkled body makes this an easily recognizable species.

Food: Unknown.

References: In addition to the original description, the species has been mentioned from Peru by Meneses (1974), Soini (1974b), and Carrillo de Espinoza (1983), while Campbell and Lamar (1989) gave a description, distribution, and color photos. Greene and McDiarmid (1981) and Roze (1983) discussed mimicry of this very unusually colored species.

Etymology: Greek from *margarita* meaning pearl, and *margaritiferus*, meaning carrier or bearer of pearls, alluding to the sprinklings of pearly spots on the black body.

Micrurus medemi (Map 25, Pattern 33)
Villavicencio Coral Snake; Coral de Villavicencio Cobra Coral do Villavicencio

Micrurus psyches medemi Roze, 1967: 41. (Holotype: AMNH 96998, a male from Villavicencio, Meta, Colombia, obtained by Nicéforo María).
Micrurus medemi: Roze, 1994: 178.

Distribution and range: The region of Villavicencio, Meta, Colombia, in an ecologically interesting region where lowland humid montane forest is surrounded by drier savanna—a lowland llanos formation, between 250 and 600 m above sea level.

Definition: A single-banded coral snake with the black cap fused with the black nuchal band that is 7 to 9 dorsals long. The black body bands are 7 to 10 dorsals long and the red bands are melanistic: dark red, purple or almost black. Males do not have supraanal tubercles.

Description: Males have 193 to 198 (195.0) and females have 211 to 218 (215.0) ventrals; subcaudals 45 to 49 (46.8) in males and 31 to 33 (32.5) in females; 1+1, occasionally 1+2, temporals. Examined: 6 males and 3 females, including the holotype.

The black cap is fused with the black nuchal band. The latter is 7 to 9 dorsals and ventrals long. The chin is mostly black with short light bands over the genials. The black bands are 7 to 11 dorsals and 4 to 10 ventrals long. The white bands are 1 dorsal long on the midvertebral region, and 1 to 2 dorsals long laterally and ventrally, with brownish black tips. The original red bands are melanistic, brownish black, 4 to 8 dorsals and ventrals long. In some specimens they are completely black, thus indistinguishable from the black bands. Only black and white bands are found on the tail; the latter are 1 to 2 subcaudals long.

The males have 15 to 22 (18.7) and the females have 22 to 25 (23.3) black body bands. The males have 7 to 9 (7.8) and the females have 5 to 6 (5.7) black tail bands.

Remarks: Previously, this species was considered a subspecies of *M. psyches*.

Food: Litter-dwelling snakes (*Ninia atrata*).

References: Nicéforo María (1933 and 1942, as *M. psyches*), Roze (1967, 1970b, 1983) treated it as subspecies of *M. psyches*, and Medem (1969) and Pérez-Santos and Moreno (1988) mentioned it for Colombia; Campbell and Lamar (1989) featured a color photo.

Etymology: Named for Federico Medem, the late well-known Colombian herpetologist, who collected and studied many coral snakes.

Micrurus meridensis (Map 25, Pattern 34)
Merida Pygmy Coral Snake; Candelilla Merideña

Micrurus dissolecus meridensis Roze, 1989: 5. (Holotype: USNM 217256, a male from 1 km northeast of Lagunilla, Mérida, Venezuela, 915 m, collected on March 27, 1966.)
Micrurus meridensis: Roze, 1994: 180.

Distribution and range: Humid montane vegetation altered by humans around Lagunilla on the western slopes of the Andes de Mérida, Venezuela, around 900 m above sea level.

Definition: A triad-type coral snake in which the black nuchal band is single and the body triads consist of somewhat irregular black bands; the central band is longer than the outer bands.

Description: The only known specimens, a male, has 176 ventrals and 27 subcaudals; 1+1 temporals.

The snout and most of the head below are black, including the supraoculars and most of the frontal. It is followed by a white parietal crossband, but a black spot is present on the suture between the parietals. The nuchal black band is 3 dorsals long and covers the tips of the parietals. The black triads are irregular and several black bands are reduced or interrupted. The central black bands are 2 to 3 dorsals and ventrals long. The outer black bands are 1 to 2 dorsals and ventrals long but quite irregular. The white bands are also irregular, 1 to 2 dorsals long with the scales outlined by black borders. The red bands are 3 to 4 dorsals and ventrals long with small black tips. On the tail, the black bands are longer than on the body. The black bands are 3 to 4 dorsals long.

The male has 18 complete triads on the body plus the single black nuchal band, and 2⅓ triads on the tail.

Size: The only known specimen is 390 mm long.

Remarks: The irregular triads make it easily recognizable. As only one specimen is known, its variation and distribution still has to be determined. It belongs to the *M. dissoleucus* group; it was originally described as a subspecies of the latter, but the irregularity and the high number of the triads make it quite distinct.

Food: Unknown.

References: Only the original description.

Etymology: The name *meridensis* denotes its presence in the state of Mérida, Venezuela.

Micrurus mertensi (Map 25, Pattern 36)
Peruvian Desert Coral Snake (Merten's Coral Snake); Coral Peruana del Desierto

Micrurus mertensi Schmidt, 1936a: 192. (Holotype: SMF 9420B, a male from Pacasmayo, Peru, collected by M. Bamberger in 1887.)

Distribution and range: Lowland desert and dry shrub valleys in southwestern Ecuador and western Peru, from sea level up to about 1,700 m.

Definition: A single-banded black-red-white (yellow) coral snake with a black cap and without supraanal tubercles in males. The black snout may or may not be separated from the black nuchal band and the red dorsals have regular black tips.

Description: Males have 206 to 219 (212.4) and females have 223 to 235 (228.9) ventrals; subcaudals 45 to 51 (48.6) in males and 31 to 37 (33.9) in females; 1+1 or 1+2 temporals. Examined: 12 males and 13 females, including the holotype.

The black cap covers all of the parietals and is or is not in contact with the black nuchal band. The chin is white but the mental and the first 4 or 5 infralabials are partially or completely black. Irregular black spots or borders are present on some other shields. The nuchal black band starts 1 dorsal behind the tips of the parietals and is 5 to 7 dorsals and 4 to 6 ventrals long. The remainder of the black bands are 3 to 4 scales longer than the black bands, with conspicuous black tips on all dorsals. Ventrally, the red scales can have some irregular black spots. The first white or yellow band is 1.5 to 2 dorsals long; the rest are 1 dorsal and ventral long and are immaculate. The black tail bands are 2 or more times longer than the white bands.

The males have 22 to 28 (25.1) and the females have 26 to 31 (28.7) black body bands. On the tail the males have 7 to 9 (7.8) and females have 5 to 6 (5.6) black bands.

Size: This is a medium-large species. The longest specimen is 1,115 mm long, but adults measure between 500 and 800 mm.

Remarks: This coral snake is found in the desert of western Peru.

Food: Snakes, including blind snakes (*Leptotyphlops subcrotillus*) and desert pit-viper (*Bothrops pictus*). Some specimens had sand in their stomachs.

References: A description appeared in Campbell and Lamar (1989) and general notes were in Roze (1967, 1970b). H. W. Parker (1938), Orcés (1948), J. A. Peters (1960a), Miyata (1982), and Almendariz (1991) mentioned it for Ecuador; Schmidt and Walker (1943b), Meneses (1974), and Carrillo de Espinoza (1983) mentioned it for Peru. L. Müller (1973) commented on its distribution, Roze (1983) discussed mimicry, and Tiedemann and Haupl (1980) described type specimens.

Etymology: Named after the versatile 20th-century German herpetologist, the late Robert Mertens.

Micrurus mipartitus (Map 26)
Red-tailed Coral Snake; Rabo de Candela

Distribution: From Darién, Panama, into Colombia, and northern and northwestern Venezuela to western Ecuador and probably Peru.

Definition: A black and yellow- or white-banded coral snake with a red head band and several red tail bands.

Size: This is a medium-large but slender species. The largest measured specimen is 1,005 mm long, but many adults range between 500 and 800 mm.

Remarks: The red-tailed coral snake is easily recognizable by its black and yellow bands and intensely red head and tail bands. With its slender body and unique coloration, Rabo de Candela, also called Rabo de Ají, might be more closely related to *Leptomicrurus* than to *Micrurus*, but much more study is required to decide this. Five subspecies are recognized here, but more might be defined, particularly in Colombia.

References: Analysis of the variation appeared in Amaral (1926c), description and distribution in Campbell and Lamar (1989), and general comments on the species in Mocquard (1908–1909), Amaral (1925b, 1930a), Schmidt (1936a), Beebe (1947), Roze (1967, 1970b, 1983), Cendrero et al. (1972), P. Müller (1973), Duellman (1979), and Ayerbe et al. (1990). Records for Colombia are by Werner (1900), Griffin (1916), Ruthven (1922), H. W. Parker (1926), Amaral (1927d, 1928, 1931b), Rendahl and Vestergren (1940), Nicéforo-María (1933, 1942), Dunn (1944a, 1944b), Daniel (1949), Schmidt (1955), Medem (1965, 1969, 1979), Díaz-Gómez (1971), Dugand (1975), Ayerbe et al. (1977, 1979), Ayerbe (1979), Castro et al. (1982), Angel (1983), Pérez-Santos (1986b), Pérez-Santos and Moreno (1986, 1987, 1988), and Ayerbe et al. (1990); for Ecuador by Werner (1901a, 1903, 1927), Rendahl (1937), H. W. Parker (1938), Orcés (1942, 1943, 1948), Acosta-Solís (1944), J. A. Peters (1955, 1960), and Miyata (1982); for Panama by Schmidt (1933b), Dunn and Bailey (1939), Breder (1946), Grocott and Sadler (1958), and Villa et al. (1988); probable for Peru by Carrillo de Espinoza (1983); and for Venezuela by Milá de la Roca (1932), Briceño (1934), Pifano (1935, 1938), Vellard (1941), Marcuzzi (1950), Roze (1952, 1955, 1966a, 1970a), Alemán (1952, 1953), Vetencourt Finol (1960), Hoge and Lancini (1962), Lancini (1962c, 1970, 1979), Test et al. (1966), and Sandner-Montilla (1975, 1985). Mimicry was discussed by Greene and McDiarmid (1981) and type specimens by Roux-Estève (1983). A questionable record by Vanzolini (1986) from Rondônia, Brazil, must be confirmed. Earlier significant references include Jan (1863), Cope (1868), Jan and Sordelli (1872), Boulenger (1896), and García (1896).

Key to the Subspecies of *M. mipartitus*

1 Ventrals more than 223 in males and usually more than 251 in females 2
1' Ventrals 197 to 222 in males and 225 to 251 in females
.... *M. m. semipartitus* (northern Venezuela)
2 Males with 254 to 284 and females with 279 to 326 ventrals 4
2' Less than 250 ventrals in males and usually less than 279 in females 3
3 Black snout coloration covers less than half of supraoculars; mental and infralabials usually white; 242 to 249 ventrals in males and 270 to 281 in females
... *M. m. mipartitus* (eastern Panama and western Colombia)
3' Black snout coloration covers more than half of supraoculars; mental and infralabials usually blackish; 223 to 247 ventrals in males and 244 to 271 in females
.. *M. m. anomalus* (northern and central Colombia and northwestern Venezuela)
4 Light body bands with heavy black spots or tips that cover half or more of the scale; black nuchal usually incomplete
.... *M. m. popayanensis* (upper Cauca valley, Colombia)
4' Light bands usually with few small black spots or tips; nuchal black usually complete
.. *M. m. decussatus* (Andes of Colombia, Ecuador, and Peru, except upper Cauca valley)

Micrurus mipartitus mipartitus (Color 42)
Pacific Red-tailed Coral Snake; Rabo de Candela del Pacífico

Elaps mipartitus Duméril, Bibron, and Duméril, 1854: 1220. (Holotype: MNHN 3915, a female from Río Sucio or Senio [Sinu?], Colombia, collected by Goudot.)
Elaps aequicinctus Werner, 1903: 249. (Holotype: IRSNB 2919, a male from "Venezuela or Ecuador.")
Elaps microps Boulenger, 1913: 1036. (Holotype: BM 1946.1.17.33, a male from Peña Lisa, Condoto, Chocó, Colombia, collected by H. G. F. Spurrell.)
Micrurus mipartitus mipartitus: Roze, 1955: 467.

Range: Lowland tropical rain forest and moderate altitude humid forest from Darién, Panama, southward to the Pacific lowlands of western Colombia, from sea level to 850 m.

Description: Males have 242 to 249 (244.7) and females have 270 to 281 (276.5) ventrals; subcaudals 25 to 33 (29.1) in males and 23 to 28 (26.1) in females. Examined: 8 males and 6 females, including the holotypes.
The black snout coloration covers less than half of the supraoculars and the frontal and barely touches the upper postocular. It is followed by a red parietal band. The black nuchal band reaches the tips of the parietals and is 4 to 6 dorsals long. Below, the head is either white or has some irregular black dots or spots concentrated around the genials. The black bands are 4 to 6 dorsals long middorsally, 3 to 5 laterally, and 2 to 4 ventrally. The yellow or white bands are usually 1 dorsal long middorsally, but expand laterally where they occupy 2 dorsals and 2 to 3 ventrals. The yellow scales usually have irregular black tips, at least laterally, but are immaculate ventrally. The red tail bands are as long as or longer than the black tail bands. Some black tail bands may be interrupted ventrally. The tip of the tail may be either black or red.
The males have 43 to 59 (49.0) and the females have 50 to 77 (61.2) black body bands. On the tail, the males have 1 to 5 and the females have 2 to 4 black bands.

Remarks: This is the Candelilla of the Colombian Chocó region and it is also found in eastern Panama. It probably coexists with the Gargantilla (*M. multifasciatus*) in the Darién region, Panama.

References: Schmidt (1955) and Medem (1965) discussed it from Colombia; other references are from Panama, but they might also refer to *M. multifasciatus*. A color photo appeared in Campbell and Lamar (1989).

Etymology: Probably *mipartitus* is abbreviated Latin for *semi* meaning half and *parti* meaning divided. It refers to the half black and half white bands of this coral snake. *Aequicinctus* comes from the Latin word *aequa* meaning equal and *cinctus* meaning girdle; thus girdled or surrounded by bands of equal size. *Microps* is from the Greek word *micro* meaning small or minute, probably alluding to the small size of the head and eyes.

Micrurus mipartitus anomalus
Santa Marta Red-tailed Coral Snake; Rabo de Ají or Rabo de Candela Santamartense

Elaps anomalus Boulenger, 1896: 417. (Holotype: BM 1946.1.17.30, a males from Colombia obtained by F. A. Simmons.)
Micrurus mipartitus anomalus: Roze, 1967: 37.

Range: Humid mountain forest and humid median altitude savanna in Sierra Nevada de Santa Marta, Cordillera Oriental to Villavicencio, Colombia, the Andes of Mérida and the Sierra Perijá, Venezuela, from 500 to 2,000 m above sea level.

Description: Males have 223 to 247 (233.0) and the females have 244 to 271 (259.9) ventrals; subcaudals 27 to 33 (29.7) in males and 25 to 31 (26.8) in females; many specimens have 1 to 8 undivided subcaudals. In Santa Marta, half of the specimens had 1+2 temporals; other populations have 1+1 temporals. Examined: 5 males and 11 females, including the holotype.

The black snout coloration covers more than half of the supraoculars and the frontal, most of the postoculars, and the first five supralabials. The posterior border of the black snout coloration is either a straight line or it projects over the supraoculars to produce a sinuous border. It is followed by the red parietal band. Below, some solid black is on the mental and the first infralabials. The black nuchal band is 1 to 2 ventrals long in specimens that have a complete band. The black body bands are 3 to 5 dorsals long on the middorsal region, about 2 to 4 laterally, and 1 to 3 ventrally. The yellow or white bands are usually 1 dorsal long on the middorsal region, 2 laterally, and 2 to 3 ventrally. Black tips are present, especially laterally. The red tail bands are usually longer than the black bands; the latter are sometimes interrupted ventrally.

The males have 43 to 70 (57.3) and the females have 47 to 76 (67.6) black body bands. On the tail, the males have 3 to 6 and the females have 3 to 5 black bands.

Remarks: This subspecies intergrades with *M. m. semipartitus* in Falcón, Venezuela, and with *M. m. decussatus* in central and southern Cordillera Oriental, Colombia. The population in the Andes of Mérida may represent a different subspecies.

Food: Limbless amphisbaenid lizards (*Amphisbaena*), litter-dwelling gekkonid lizards (*Lepidoblepharis sanctaemartae*), colubrid snakes (*Atractus sanctaemartae*), and other snakes.

References: Amaral (1928) and Ruthven (1922) commented on its distribution and ecology from Santa Marta, and Campbell and Lamar (1989) featured a color photo.

Etymology: Greek from *anomalo* meaning uneven or irregular, alluding to the abnormal condition of the contact of the mental with the genials found in the type specimen.

Micrurus mipartitus decussatus (Color 43)
Andean Red-tailed Coral Snake; Rabo de Ají or Rabo de Candela Andina

Elaps decussatus Duméril, Bibron, and Duméril, 1854: 1221. (Holotype: 3 syntypes in MNHN 3916, 3916A, and 3916B, from "Nouvelle Grenade" [= Colombia].)
Elaps fraseri Boulenger, 1896: 432. (Holotype: BM 1946.1.17.34, a female from western Ecuador, collected by Fraser.)
Elaps mentalis Boulenger, 1896: 432. (Holotype: 2 syntypes BM 1946.1.17.16, a male from Pallatanga, eastern Ecuador, collected by Buckley, and BM 1946.1.14.27, a male from Cali, Colombia, 3,200 ft, collected by W. F. H. Rosenberg.)
Elaps calamus Boulenger, 1902: 57. (Holotype: BM 1946.1.20.25, a female from San Javier, northwestern Ecuador, collected by W. F. H. Rosenberg.)

Range: Low to high humid forest and valleys in the Cordilleras Occidental and Central in Colombia (also in Isla Gorgona) to western slopes and Pacific lowland in Ecuador and probably Peru, from almost sea level to 2,700 m.

Description: Males have 254 to 284 (267.8) and females have 279 to 326 (297.4) ventrals; subcaudals 26 to 34 (30.2) in males and 23 to 31 (26.8) in females. Examined: 56 males and 51 females, including the holotypes.

The black snout coloration extends over less than half of the frontal and supraoculars and first 4 supralabials. It is followed by a red band. Below, the head is mostly white in males but is covered with small, irregular smudges in females. Very few specimens have the mental and first infralabials black. The black nuchal band reaches, but rarely covers, the tips of the parietals. It is 3 to 6 dorsals long and is usually complete ventrally. The black bands are 2 to 6 dorsals long and are usually complete ventrally. The black bands are 2 to 6 dorsals long in the middorsal region, 2 to 4 laterally, and reduced to 1 to 3 ventrally. The white bands are usually 1 dorsal long on the middorsal line, 2 to 3 laterally, and 2 to 4 ventrally, with irregular, black-tipped scales at least on the lateral rows. The red tail bands are as long as or longer than the black bands; the latter are reduced or interrupted ventrally.

The males have 41 to 76 (60.4) and the females have 52 to 84 (66.7) black body bands. Both sexes have 2 to 5 black tail bands.

Remarks: Due to its variation, this subspecies has more synonyms than any other coral snake. It intergrades with *M. m. anomalus* in the southern Cordillera Oriental, Colombia. This is the most widespread Andean coral snake and several more subspecies may be recognized when more data are available.

Food: Blind snakes (*Leptotyphlops*), litter-dwelling colubrid snakes (*Atractus*), and other colubrid snakes.

References: Many references including Amaral (1931), Nicéforo María (1942), Schmidt (1955), Medem (1969), Almendariz (1991), and many more; color photos by Pérez-Santos and Moreno (1988) and Campbell and Lamar (1989).

Etymology: From *decusso*, Latin for crosswise, in the shape of the letter X; thus *decussatus* means marked with crosswise markings, alluding to its black crossbands. *Fraseri* is named after Mr. Fraser, who collected specimens, including this holotype, for the British Museum. *Calamus* is Latin for reed or reed-shaped stalk, alluding to the elongate body of this coral snake. *Mentalis* refers to the fact that in the type specimen the mental shield is in contact with the genials.

Micrurus mipartitus popayanensis
Popayán Red-tailed Coral Snake; Rabo de Ají Payanés

Micrurus mipartitus popayanensis Ayerbe, Tidwell, and Tidwell, 1990: 33. (Holotype: CSA 85, a male from Finca "Las Cascadas," Corregimiento de Sucre, Municipio de Bolivar, departamento de Cauca (Colombia), 1,400 m, collected by Henry and Arcelay Muñóz near a sugar trapiche on January 11, 1980.)

Range: Wet montane forest in the upper Rio Cauca valley around Popayán, south of Río Vinagre, Cauca, Colombia, between 1,300 and 1,500 m above sea level.

Description: Males have 255 to 259 (256.0) and females have 284 to 304 (291.3) ventrals; subcaudals 27 to 32 (29.0) in males and 24 to 26 (25.3) in females. Examined: 5 males and 4 females, including the holotype. Additional information is from Ayerbe et al (1990).

The snout is all black including ⅔ of the prefrontals, the first 3 and part of the fourth supralabial, and the prefrontal. The red parietal band that follows covers the entire parietals. The black nuchal band is 7 to 9 dorsals long in about 80% of specimens interrupted ventrally. The black body bands are 3½ to 5 dorsals and 2 to 3½ ventrals long. The light bands are creamy to light greenish, about 2 dorsals and 3 to 4 ventrals long, with conspicuous black spots on each scale or black tips. On the tail are red and black bands.

The males have 43 to 66 (51) and the females have 53 to 70 (60) black body bands. Both sexes have 2 to 3 red tail bands.

Remarks: This subspecies was recently described from an intriguing region of Popayán. The region is isolated from the lower Cauca valley by the highly acidic waters of Rio Cauca itself. The acidity comes from a tributary, Rio Vinagre, that originates near Volcano Puracé and carries considerable quantities of natural suphuric and hydrochloric acids that enter Río Cauca at an altitude of 2,000 m. For the last 1½ million years, it has produced a natural barrier between the upper and lower Cauca valley, especially for terrestrial fauna including amphibians and reptiles; moreover, no fish seem to be able to live in these highly acidic waters.

This subspecies is barely distinct from *M. m. decussatus* and might be a synonym of it. However, the color pattern seems to be distinct, at least from the population of *M. mipartitus* on the left side and lower valley of Río Cauca. Pending further studies, this subspecies might be recognized as a distinct taxonomic unit.

Food: Unknown, but Ayerbe et al. (1990) successfully fed this coral snake in captivity with juvenile *Leptophis ahaetulla, Atractus* sp. and *Dendrophidion bivittatus*, known from the same region.

References: Only the original description.

Etymology: Inhabitant of Popayán (Colombia).

Micrurus mipartitus semipartitus (Color 44)
Venezuelan Red-tailed Coral Snake; Rabo de Candela Venezolana

Elaps semipartitus Jan, 1858: 516. (Holotype: Lost from MSNM and MNHN, from "Cayenne". Type locality restricted to Caracas, Venezuela, by Roze, 1955.)
Micrurus mipartitus semipartitus: Roze, 1955: 465.

Range: Humid and cloud forest of the Cordillera de la Costa in northern Venezuela to valleys around San Felipe, Yaracuy, from about 800 to 2,000 m above sea level; occasional specimens are found below 800 m.

Description: Males have 197 to 222 (209.4) and females have 225 to 251 (241.5) ventrals; subcaudals 26 to 34 (29.8) in males and 24 to 30 (27.3) in females; 1+1 temporals. Examined: 33 males and 24 females.

The black snout coloration covers up to half of the supraoculars and the frontal and first 3 or 4 supralabials. It is followed by the red band. Below, the head is almost white in males but has some black spots or dots in females. The black nuchal band reaches the tips of the parietals and is 4 to 6 dorsals, but only 1 to 2 ventrals, long. The black body bands are 4 to 5 dorsals long on the middorsal line and 2 to 3 ventrally. The white bands are usually 1 dorsal long on the middorsal line and 2 to 3 ventrals long; they have some black-tipped scales, especially laterally. The red tail bands are longer than the black bands.

The males have 36 to 65 (45.0) and the females have 37 to 66 (50.7) black body bands. On the tail, the males have 2 to 5 and the females have 2 to 4 black bands.

Remarks: This subspecies is restricted to northern Venezuela and intergrades with *M. m. anomalus* in Falcón, Venezuela.

Food: Limbless amphisbaenid lizards (*Amphisbaena*) and colubrid snakes.

References: Roze (1955, 1970a) and Lancini (1976, 1979) provided data from Venezuela. Test et al. (1966) described its behavior, and Lancini (1979) and Campbell and Lamar (1989) gave color photos.

Etymology: Latin from *semi* meaning half and *parti* meaning divided, alluding to the coloration divided between black and white bands.

Micrurus multifasciatus (Map 27)
Gargantilla (Many-banded Coral Snake)

Distribution: Central America from Caribbean side of Nicaragua and Costa Rica to the Canal Zone of Panama.

Definition: A coral snake with only red and black bands. It has a black snout and a large parietal red crossband. The black bands are larger than the red bands and the black nuchal band usually does not reach the tips of the parietals.

Size: A medium-large species. The longest reported specimen is 1,130 mm long (Picado, 1931), but many adults range between 500 and 800 mm.

Remarks: The Gargantilla can be easily recognized by the simple black and red bands. Two subspecies are recognized.

References: This form was only recently recognized as a species distinct from *M. mipartitus* (Roze, 1983). Until then, this species appeared as *M. mipartitus* in Central America. A description and distribution with color photos appeared in Campbell and Lamar (1989); general notes for Central America are by Amaral (1926c), Schmidt (1928a), Roze (1967, 1970b), Bolaños (1971, 1983, 1984), Cendrero et al. (1972), Villa (1984), and Villa et al. (1988); for Costa Rica by Picado (1931), Wettstein (1934), Trejos (1937), E. H. Taylor (1951, 1954), Scott (1969), R. T. Taylor et al. (1974), Savage and Vial (1974), Van Devender (1980), Savage (1980), and Savage and Villa (1986); for Nicaragua by Villa (1962, 1972a, 1984); for Panama by Bates (1928), Dunn (1940a), Grocott and Sadler (1958), Myers and Rand (1969), and Rand and Myers (1990). Mimicry was considered by Greene and McDiarmid (1981) and karyotypes by Gutiérrez et al. (1979, 1988). Earlier references include Cope (1876, 1886, 1887) and Garman (1877).

Key to the Subspecies of *M. multifasciatus*

1 Males with 250 to 265 and females with 280 to 311 ventrals
   .... *M. m. multifasciatus* (Central Panama)
1' Males with 237 to 244 and females with 256 to 274 ventrals
   .... *M. m. hertwigi* (Nicaragua, Costa Rica, and northwestern Panama)

Micrurus multifasciatus multifasciatus (Color 45)
Panama Gargantilla; Gargantilla Panameña

Elaps multifasciatus Jan, 1858: 521. (Holotype: originally in Milan Museum; destroyed during World War II, probably a female from Central America.)
Micrurus multifasciatus multifasciatus: Roze, 1983: 330.

Range: Humid to wet tropical forest, also in areas altered by humans, in central Panama around the Canal Zone to Darién, from sea level to 400 m.

Description: Males have 250 to 265 (257.7) and females have 280 to 311 (294.1) ventrals; subcaudals 29 to 33 (31.2) in males and 25 to 29 (26.9) in females. Examined: 16 males and 13 females.

The snout is black to the frontal and supraoculars, followed by a large red crossband that includes the parietals and seventh supralabial. The chin is reddish or whitish, usually with smokey-blackish spots. The black nuchal band usually does not reach the parietals and is 4 to 6 dorsals and 2 to 4 ventrals long. The red bands are 1 to 2 dorsals long on the middorsal line and 2 to 3 scales long ventrally, with or without small black spots. The red tail bands are longer than the black bands that follow them.

The males have 40 to 55 (48.6) and the females have 48 to 64 (56.3) black body bands. On the tail, the males have 3 to 5 and females have 2 to 4 black bands.

Remarks: In the Darién region of Panama this subspecies probably coexists with the predominantly South American *M. mipartitus*.

Food: Unknown, probably limbless caecilians and snakes.

References: Dunn (1949) described its relative abundance in Panama, and Rand and Myers (1990) commented on mimicry (as *M. mipartitus*).

Etymology: Latin from *multi* meaning many and *fascia* meaning a band; *multifasciatus* is the one covered with many bands.

Micrurus multifasciatus hertwigi (Color 46)
Costa Rican Gargantilla; Gargantilla Costarricense

Elaps hertwigi Werner, 1897: 354. (Holotype: ZSBS 22680, a female from Central America, collected by M. Wagner.)
Micrurus multifasciatus hertwigi: Roze, 1983: 331.

Range: Tropical lowland rain forest and humid moderate altitudes on the Atlantic side of Nicaragua and Costa Rica to northwestern Panama, from sea level to 1,200 m.

Description: Males have 235 to 244 (239.6) and females have 256 to 274 (265.8) ventrals; subcaudals 31 to 38 (33.9) in males and 24 to 29 (26.4) in females. Examined: 10 males and 27 females.

The black snout coloration barely reaches the anterior border of the frontal and supralabials, followed by a large red crossband that includes all of the parietals. Below, the head is usually whitish or reddish, immaculate or with a few dark spots. The black nuchal band usually does not reach the parietals and is 5 to 7 dorsals and 3 to 4 ventrals long. The black bands are 4 to 5 dorsals and 3 to 4 ventrals long. The red bands may sometimes be pale orange or white; they are 2 to 3 middorsals long and 3 to 4 ventrals long. The red bands are usually immaculate, but may have a few black spots or tips. On the tail, the red bands are longer or shorter than the black bands.

The males have 40 to 59 (50.2) and the females have 45 to 73 (57.3) black body bands. On the tail, the males have 3 to 5 and females have 2 to 4 black bands.

Remarks: No intergradation is known between the two subspecies.

Food: Unknown, probably snakes.

References: Numerous references for Costa Rica and Nicaragua; see under the species description. Savage and Vial (1974) analyzed its variation in Costa Rica under *M. mipartitus*.

Etymology: Named after Wilhelm A. O. Hertwig, a notable German biologist at the Munich Museum at the turn of the century.

Micrurus multiscutatus (Map 28, Color 47)
Cauca Coral Snake; Coral Caucana

Micrurus multiscutatus Rendahl and Vestergren, 1940: 9. (Holotype: NRS 3131a, a female from El Tambo, Cauca, Colombia, 1745 m, collected by Kjell von Sneidern.)

Distribution and Range: Tropical lowland rain forest to moderate altitude humid forest on the Pacific side of the Cordillera Occidental in Cauca, Colombia, from 150 to 900 m above sea level.

Definition: A bicolor coral snake with only red and black bands on the body and tail and a large red frontoparietal band.

Description: Males have 295 and females have 325 to 329 (327.3) ventrals; subcaudals about 30 in males and 26 to 31 (28) in females. Examined: the only four known specimens: 1 male and 3 females, including the holotype.

The snout is black up to the frontal, followed by a red fronto-parietal band. Below, the head is red, but heavily mottled with black. The black nuchal band is 6 dorsals long and barely reaches the tips of the parietals. The body is covered by alternating red and black bands. The black bands are 3 to 4 dorsals and 2 to 3 ventrals long. The red bands are 2 to 3 dorsals and 3 to 4 ventrals long, with irregularly black-tipped scales.

The males have about 59 and the females have 65 to 68 (66.7) black body bands. Both sexes have 3 to 4 black tail bands.

Size: This is a medium-sized snake. The longest measured specimen, which is the holotype, is 842 mm long.

Remarks: This little-known species can be easily recognized by the presence of simple red and black bands and the large red parietal band. As noted on the labels in the Stockholm Museum, the specimens were collected at an altitude lower than that given in the original description. Roze (1983) recognized the validity of this species based on an additional specimen (AMNH 109781) from Quebrada Canguí, Saija drainage, Cauca, Colombia, collected by Charles Myers. It showed that the color pattern consists of only red-black bands.

Food: Unknown.

References: In addition to the original description, only Roze (1983), Pérez-Santos and Moreno (1986, 1988), and Campbell and Lamar (1989) recognized its species status; the latter authors offered a description and color photo.

Etymology: Latin from *multi* meaning many, and *scutum* meaning shield or scale; thus *multiscutatus* means with many shields or scales, alluding to the high number of ventrals.

Micrurus nebularis (Map 29, Pattern 35)
Neblina Coral Snake; Coralilla Neblinense

Micrurus nebularis Roze, 1987: 9. (Holotype: AMNH 103118, a male from Vivero Rancho Teja, 3 km east of Ixtlan de Juárez, Oaxaca, Mexico, 2,255 m, in pine-oak and humid woodlands, collected by Boone Hallberg on July 13, 1968.)

Distribution and range: In high mountain pine-oak and humid forest woodlands in the Sierra de Juárez of the Sierra Madre del Sur in central Oaxaca, Mexico, from 2,100 to 2,300 m above sea level.

Definition: A single-banded coral snake with a black snout and a large yellow parietal band and without any black tips on red scales, or only a very few; the red bands have brownish overtones. The nuchal band covers the parietal tips and the males have no supraanal tubercles.

Description: Males have 203 to 208 (205.5) and females have 218 to 223 (222.3) ventrals; subcaudals 45 to 47 (46.0) in males and 35 to 37 (35.8) in females. Examined: 2 males and 4 females, which are the only known specimens, including the holotype.

The snout is black up to the frontal, followed by a yellow parietal band. The nuchal black band touches and covers the tips of the parietals. Below, the chin is yellow, but the first three infralabials and the anterior part of the chin shields are black. The black body bands are 4 dorsals and 3 to 4 ventrals long. The red bands are 3 to 4 dorsals long, usually immaculate or with a few black tips, but with brownish overtones. The yellow bands are 1 ventral and 1 dorsal long. On the tail the bands are only black and yellow and the black bands are twice as long as the yellow bands.

The males have 23 to 24 (23.5) and the females have 26 to 28 (27.0) black body bands. On the tail, the males have 7 and the females have 5 or 6 black tail bands.

Size: This is a small species; the longest measured specimen, which is the holotype, is only 557 mm long.

Remarks: This species seems to be endemic to the high altitudes of Sierra Juárez around Oaxaca.

Food: Ground-dwelling snakes (*Geophis dubius*).

Reference: Only the original description.

Etymology: Latin from *nebula* meaning clouds; *nebularis* means pertaining to clouds.

Micrurus nigrocinctus (Map 30)
Central American Coral Snake: Coral Centroamericana

Distribution: From southern Chiapas, Mexico, and Belize covering Guatemala, Honduras, Nicaragua, Costa Rica, and Panama to the northwestern tip of Colombia; also several Central American islands: Isla del Maíz Grande, Nicaragua, and Coiba, Taboga, San José, and San Miguel, Panama.

Definition: A single-banded coral snake with black snout followed by a yellow parietal band and a black nuchal band that might or might not cover the tips of the parietals. The males have supraanal tubercles.

Size: This is a medium-large coral snake. An exceptionally large specimen measures 1,150 mm in overall length. Most adults, however, range between 500 and 750 mm.

Remarks: This is the most common Central American coral snake. It shows a considerable variation and large zones of intergradation between the subspecies, 6 of which are recognized here.

References: Numerous publications. General notes on the species appeared in Amaral (1927c), Schmidt (1928a, 1933a, 1936b), Ditmars (1932), Clark (1942), Fonseca (1949), Dunn (1951), Pope (1955), Roze (1967, 1970b, 1983), Bolaños (1982, 1983, 1984), Villa et al (1988), and a complete description with color photos appeared in Campbell and Lamar (1989). Belize specimens were commented on by Neill (1965) and Henderson and Hoevers (1975); Colombian specimens by Nicéforo María (1942), Dunn (1944a), Schmidt (1955), Pérez-Santos (1986a), and Pérez-Santos and Moreno (1986, 1988); Costa Rican specimens by Picado (1931, 1936), Wettstein (1934), E. H. Taylor (1951, 1954), Heyer (1967), Scott (1969), R. T. Taylor et al (1974), Savage and Vial (1974), Savage (1980), Van Devender (1980), Timmerman and Hayes (1981), Greene and Seib (1983), Mudde and Van Dijk (1985), and Savage and Villa (1986); El Salvadoran specimens by Mertens (1952); Guatemalan specimens by Schmidt (1932), Slevin (1939), and Stuart (1963) and Campbell and Vannini (1988, 1989); Honduran specimens by Clark (1925), Wilson and Meyer (1972, 1982, 1985) and Wilson (1983); Mexican specimens by H. M. Smith (1943), H. M. Smith and Taylor (1945, 1966), Mittleman and Smith (1949), Martín del Campo (1950), Landy et al (1966), Greene (1972), Lee (1980), Alvarez del Toro (1983), and Johnson (1984); Nicaraguan specimens by Barbour and Loveridge (1929) and Villa (1962, 1969, 1972b, 1983, 1984); Panama specimens by Barbour (1906), Bates (1928), Dunn (1933, 1947), Schmidt (1933b), Cochran (1946), Evans (1947), Elton (1948), Grocott and Saddle (1958), Sexton and Heathwole (1965), Nemuras (1967), Myers and Rand (1969), and Rand and Myers (1990). Behavior and mimicry was dealt with by Gehlbach (1970, 1972), abundance by Dunn (1949), food and feeding by Schmidt (1932a) and Greene (1973a), types by Tiedemann and Haupl (1980), and karyotypes by Gutiérrez and Bolaños (1979, 1981). Earlier significant references include Troschel (1855), Cope (1859, 1874, 1876a, 1886), Garman (1877, 1884), Dugès (1885), and Ferrari-Pérez (1886).

Key to the Subspecies of *M. nigrocinctus*

1 Black nuchal band does not reach parietals 2
1' Black nuchal band covers at least parietal tips .. 3
2 Black nuchal band 7 to 11 dorsals long; ventrals 180 to 192, usually less than 190 in males; 199 to 211, usually less than 205, in females
...... *M. n. mosquitensis* (southeastern Nicaragua, eastern Costa Rica and northwestern Panama)
2' Black nuchal band 3 to 5, exceptionally 7, dorsals long; ventrals 190 to 210, usually more than 190, in males; 206 to 221, usually more than 211, in females
.... *M. n. divaricatus* (Honduras, probably Belize)
3 Ventrals fewer than 210 in males and fewer than 225 in females 4
3' Ventrals 213 to 217 in males and 228 to 230 in females
.... *M. n. coibensis* (Isla Coiba, Panama)
4 Usually no black tips on red scales; no white bands or barely visible (when visible then no more than 14 black bands)
...... *M. n. zunilensis* (southern Chiapas, Mexico, southern Guatemala and western El Salvador)
4' At least some black tips on red present; white bands usually well distinct (when indistinct, then more than 14 black body bands) 5
5 Large regular black tips on all red scales; ventrals around 193 in males and 205 to 209 in females; 21 to 23 black bands in females
.... *M. n. babaspul* (Isla del Maíz, Nicaragua)
5' Black tips usually small and irregular; usually not present on all red scales; ventrals usually more than 193 in males and usually more than 209 in females 6
6 Black bands usually more than 19, up to 29; when less than 19, the black nuchal band does not reach parietals; red bands with few, irregular black tips, or large black spots
.... *M. n. divaricatus* (Honduras, probably Belize)
6' Black bands 13 to 23, usually less than 20; black nuchal band covers parietal tips; usually small black tips on most or all red scales; no large black spots on red
..... *M. n. nigrocinctus* (Pacific side of Nicaragua, Costa Rica and Panama to adjacent Colombia)

Micrurus nigrocinctus nigrocinctus (Color 48)
Common Central American Coral Snake; Coral Centroamericana Común

Elaps nigrocinctus Girard, 1854: 226. (Holotype: USNM 7347, a female from Taboga Island, Panama.)
Elaps melanocephalus Hallowell, 1860: 226. (Holotype: USNM 7331, a male from Omotepec, Nicaragua.)
Micrurus pachecoi Taylor, 1951: 165. (Holotype: KU 25188, a female from Guanacaste, Costa Rica, collector unknown.)
Micrurus nigrocinctus nigrocinctus: Schmidt, 1933a: 33.

Range: In a variety of habitats mostly in dry tropical to humid low montane and wet moderate montane formations; also in areas altered by humans on the Pacific side of Nicaragua, Costa Rica, and Panama to adjacent northwestern Colombia, from sea level to about 1,400 m.

Description: Males have 191 to 209 (203.2) ventrals, usually 193 to 203, and females have 207 to 225 (214.8), usually 210 to 223; subcaudals 42 to 51 (46.8) in males and 32 to 43 (38.3) in females; 1+1 temporals. Examined: 162 males and 126 females, including the holotypes.

The snout is black, including the supraoculars and the frontal, followed by a short or broad yellow or white parietal band. It might cover the tip of the frontal and the supraoculars, most of the parietals, the temporals, and about 4 supralabials. Below, the head is yellow or white with the mental and the first 3 infralabials black. The black nuchal band covers the tips of the parietals and the seventh supralabial. It is usually 4 to 6 ventrals long. Sometimes, it can be interrupted ventrally. The black body bands are 3 to 5 dorsals and 2 to 4 ventrals long. The red bands are 3 to 5 times longer than the black bands, and there is a considerable variation in the amount, size, and regularity of black tips. They vary from very few and small to fairly large, though they are somewhat irregular in size and distribution; exceptional specimens can be practically without black tips. The most common pattern is small black tips of irregular size present on many, but not all, red scales. Ventrally, the red bands are usually immaculate or sometimes have a few black spots. The yellow or white bands are usually ½ to 1 dorsal and 1 ventral long, sometimes inconspicuous or barely perceptible. The tail has only black and yellow bands; the black bands are 2 to 3 times longer than the yellow ones.

The males have 13 to 21 (17.7), usually 15 to 20, and the females have 13 to 23 (18.6), usually 15 to 21, black body bands. On the tail, the males have 4 to 8 (6.1) and the females have 3 to 6 (5.9) black tail bands, but the most frequent number of tail bands in both sexes is between 5 and 7.

Remarks: As this is the most common coral snake of Central America, well over 300 specimens have been available for studies from different regions. The specimens from the Pacific side of Costa Rica have a tendency to have a reduced or sinuous yellowish-brownish parietal band and this has led to consideration of this population as subspecifically different, under the name of *M. n. melanocephalus*. On the other hand, specimens from southwestern Nicaragua have a somewhat higher number of ventrals and subcaudals. In a collection made by the Nicaraguan herpetologist, Jaime Villa, the number of ventrals varies from 200 to 209 in males and from 217 to 223 in females as compared to 191 to 206 and from 207 to 221 for the males and females, respectively, of the Panama population. These numbers overlap and many specimens from Nicaragua have a reduced, but otherwise "normal" parietal band that makes it difficult to distinguish between the populations. There is a gradual increase in number of ventrals going from southeast to northwest, even though the Costa Rica Pacific-side populations are much closer to the Panamanian ones in their characteristics.

The subspecies intergrades with *M. n. divaricatus* and probably also with *M. d. zunilensis* over a broad area between Nicaragua and Honduras.

Food: A wide range of food items encompasses many amphibians and reptiles. These include caecilians; small, litter-dwelling lizards (*Gymnophthalmus speciosus*) and skinks (*Mabuya*); active whiptail lizards (*Cnemidophorus deppii deppii*); small iguanas (*Ctenosaurus similis*); and some teiid lizards (*Ameiva*). Even lizard eggs have been eaten by some coral snakes. Their food also includes blind snakes (*Anomalepis mexicanus* and *Helminthophis*) and striped snakes (*Coniophanes*). One specimen of colubrid snake that Schmidt (1932) extracted from a stomach served as a type specimen for an unknown species, subsequently named *Geophis dunni*.

References: See under species; Villa (1984) reviewed the systematics; color photos by Campbell and Lamar (1989).

Etymology: Latin from *niger* meaning black and *cinctus* meaning a girdle or band; thus black-banded coral snake, alluding to the black single bands. *Melanocephalus* is derived from the Greek words *melano* meaning black and *cephalus* meaning head, thus the black-headed species. The name *pachecoi* is dedicated to Marco Tulio Pacheco, a Costa Rican scientist.

Micrurus nigrocinctus babaspul
Babaspul

Micrurus nigrocinctus babaspul Roze, 1967: 38. (Holotype: AMNH 96996, a male from Little Hill, Great Corn Island (Isla del Maíz Grande) in the Caribbean Sea, about 55 km east-northeast of Bluefields, Nicaragua, collected by Seligmann, Zweifel, Villa, and Roze on January 27, 1966).

Range: Island rain forest of the Corn Islands (Islas del Maíz), Nicaragua, currently only on Isla del Maíz Grande.

Description: Males have around 193 and females have 205 to 209 (207.0) ventrals; subcaudals around 47 in males and 35 to 36 (35.5) in females. Examined: the only three known specimens: 1 male and 2 females, including the holotype.

The black snout covers the anterior tips of the parietals but the frontal tip is white. The mental and the upper part of the first 3 infralabials are black and there are a few small, black spots on the genials, or the black nuchal band projects forward ventrally onto the second pair of genials. The nuchal black band covers the tips of the parietals and 4 dorsals. The black bands are 2 to 3 dorsals and ventrals long. The red bands have conspicuous, regular black tips on all scales. Ventrally, the red bands have a few scattered black spots. The white bands are ½ to 1 dorsal long. On the tail, the black bands are about 3 times longer than the white bands; the latter have a few large dorsal spots.

The males have around 18 and the females have 21 to 23 (22.0) black body bands. The black tail bands vary around 7.

Remarks: It seems that the Babaspul is just about to become extinct due to high density human population on the Great Corn Island and active agriculture that has destroyed its natural habitat. Inhabitants of Little Corn Island (Isla del Maíz Pequeña) insist they do not have Babaspul, but older people still remember having seen it about 40 years ago.

Food: Unknown, probably island snakes and lizards.

References: Records were by Barbour and Loveridge (1929) and Villa (1969, 1972, 1984). Roze (1983) discussed the endangered status of Babaspul.

Etymology: Name derived from its common name in Creole English spoken on the islands where the coral snake is found. The name, *babaspul*, refers to barber's pole, in allusion to its black, white, and red bands that are used to advertise barber shops throughout the Western world.

Micrurus nigrocinctus coibensis (Pattern 39)
Coiba Coral Snake; Coral de Coiba

Micrurus nigrocinctus coibensis Schmidt, 1936b: 209. (Holotype: BM 1946.1.20.6, a male from Coiba Island, Panama, obtained by St. George Expedition.)

Range: Island vegetation in Coiba Island, Panama.

Description: Males have 213 to 217 (215.1) and females have 228 to 230 (228.9) ventrals; subcaudals 43 to 48 (46.0) in males and 31 to 34 (32.5) in females. Examined: 3 males and 4 females, including the holotype.

The black snout coloration covers all the supraoculars but usually does not cover the anterior part of the parietals nor the posterior part of the frontal. The mental and the first 3 or 4 infralabials are black. The black nuchal band covers the tips of the parietals and 7 dorsals. The black body bands are 3 to 4 dorsals and 2 to 3 ventrals long. The red bands have a few small, irregular black tips, no more than 12 per band. Ventrally, the red bands have a few small black spots. The white or yellow bands are barely visible, about 1 dorsal long. On the tail, the black bands are about 2 or more times longer than the white bands.

The males have 17 to 22 (18.8) and the females have 19 to 23 (20.6) black body bands. The males have 6 and the females have 4 to 5 black tail bands.

Remarks: This subspecies has the highest ventral and subcaudal count of all *M. nigrocinctus* and is restricted to Coiba Island, Panama. It seems to be a general phenomenon that island subspecies or populations of snakes tend to have a higher number of ventrals and subcaudals.

Food: Unknown.

References: No additional data after the original description.

Etymology: Latin *coibensis* means inhabitant of Coiba.

Micrurus nigrocinctus divaricatus (Color 49)
Honduras Coral Snake; Coral Hondureña

Elaps divaricatus Hallowell, 1855: 36. (Holotype: ANSP 6843, a male from Honduras, collected by Amory Edwards.)
Micrurus nigrocinctus divaricatus: Schmidt, 1933a: 33.

Range: Humid and wet lowland and wet low montane formations; also short-tree savanna and even dry lowlands in northern and central Honduras from sea level to about 1,300 m. One report from Belize.

Description: Males have 190 to 206 (198.3) and females have 206 to 221 (213.1) ventrals; subcaudals 45 to 52 (49.4) in males and 32 to 39 (37.2) in females; usually 1+2 temporals. Examined: 72 males and 49 females, including the holotype.

The black snout coloration is reduced and in many specimens it covers only part of the frontal and the supraoculars and has a somewhat irregular posterior border. The white parietal band usually includes the entire parietals and the seventh supralabial. Below the head is white, except part of the mental and the first infralabials that are black. The black nuchal band usually does not reach nor cover the tips of the parietals, or it might barely cover them. It is 3 to 5 dorsals and 2 to 4 ventrals long, but it can also be interrupted ventrally. The black bands are usually 3 to 4 dorsals and 2 to 4 ventrals long. The black tips on the red bands are irregular and vary considerably, from nearly nonexistent to larger and smaller black spots, reaching the extreme of forming an intermediate black band on the red bands. Ventrally, the red bands are immaculate or with a few small or large black spots. The yellow bands also vary from about 2 dorsals long to nearly or entirely absent. Only black and white bands are on the tail. The black bands are shorter than the white bands in the northern Honduras populations, but longer than the white bands in the inland Honduras populations.

Males have 11 to 24 (16.1) and females have 12 to 23 (18.2) black body bands. One specimen has 29 black body bands, but this includes the intermediate additional black bands formed on the red bands. The black tail bands vary from 3 to 8 in males and 3 to 7 in females.

Remarks: This is a highly variable coral snake and it is possible that some changes in its status have to be made once it is compared to populations in Guatemala and El Salvador. It intergrades with *M. n. mosquitensis* in northern Nicaragua and, probably, in eastern Honduras; it also intergrades with *M. n. zunilensis* in El Salvador and in southern Guatemala.

Food: Small litter-dwelling lizards (*Gymnophthalmus speciosus*) and colubrid snakes, including the coffee snake (*Ninia sebae*) and a mildly venomous snake (*Leptodeira nigrofasciata*).

References: Wilson and associates, particularly Wilson and Meyer (1972, 1985), discussed its variation in Honduras; color photos by Campbell and Lamar (1989).

Etymology: Latin from *divarica* meaning to spread out, probably referring to the extended red bands on the body.

Micrurus nigrocinctus mosquitensis (Color 50)
Misquito Coral Snake; Coral Misquita

Micrurus nigrocinctus mosquitensis Schmidt, 1933a: 33. (Holotype: MCZ 19741, a male from Limón, Costa Rica, collected by Samuel Kress in 1934.)

Range: Wet tropical lowland forest and wet to humid montane forest in the Atlantic side in eastern and southeastern Nicaragua, Costa Rica, and northwestern Panama, from sea level to about 1200 m.

Description: Males have 182 to 192 (186.4) and females have 197 to 211 (206.2) ventrals; subcaudals 46 to 52 (48.1) in males and 35 to 43 (38.7) in females; 1+1 temporals. Examined: 61 males and 43 females, including the holotype.

The black snout coloration does not reach the parietals and has an irregular posterior border across the posterior part of the frontal and the supraoculars. It is followed by a broad yellow parietal band that can be brownish yellow and extends over the first or first and second dorsals. Below, the head is yellow or white with the mental and the first several infralabials black; sometimes black mottling is present on other shields. The black nuchal band is 1 to 2 dorsals behind the tips of the parietals. It is 7 to 11 dorsals and 6 to 10 ventrals long. Below, it frequently extends toward the snout onto the second pair of genials. The black bands are 4 to 8 dorsals and ventrals long. The red bands have large, more or less regular black tips on all scales, but are mostly immaculate ventrally. The yellow bands are long and conspicuous, about 1½ to 2 dorsals and ventrals long, without black tips. Only black and yellow bands are on the tail. In larger specimens the red and yellow bands are brownish dorsally.

The males have 10 to 13 (11.7) and the females have 10 to 15 (13.2) black body bands. On the tail, males have 4 to 5, nearly always 4, and the females have 3 to 4 (3.2) black bands.

Remarks: The wide black and white or yellow bands and the conspicuous black tips on the red dorsals make it easily distinguishable from the other subspecies of *M. nigrocinctus*. It intergrades with *M. n. divaricatus* in a broad area in eastern Honduras and northeastern Nicaragua. Its intergradation with *M. n. nigrocinctus* is uncertain. It is possible that this subspecies is not related to *M. n. nigrocinctus* but is a species apart.

Food: Predominant food is a skink (*Sphenomorphus cherriei lampropholis*), but it also feeds on whiptail lizards (*Cnemidophorus*) and lizard eggs, as well as ground snakes (*Ninia maculata*) and *Coniophanes fissidens punctigularis*).

References: See under species; color photo by Campbell and Lamar (1989).

Etymology: Mosquitensis in Latin is inhabitant of the Misquito coast on the Atlantic side of Nicaragua and Honduras in which the Mosquito, or Misquito, or Miskito Kingdom existed until the beginning of this century.

Micrurus nigrocinctus zunilensis (Pattern 40)
Zunil Coral Snake; Coral Zunilense

Micrurus nigrocinctus zunilensis Schmidt, 1932: 266. (Holotype: CAS 66001, a male from Finca El Ciprés, on the lower slopes of the Volcán Zunil, provincia Suchitepequez, Guatemala, collected by J. R. Slevin.)
Micrurus nigrocinctus wagneri Mertens, 1941: 216. (Holotype: SMF 34190, a male from Finca Germania, Sierra

Madre, Chiapas, Mexico, 400 to 1,000 m, collected by H. O. Wagner, October 1, 1940.)

Micrurus nigrocinctus ovandoensis Schmidt and Smith, 1943: 26. (Holotype: USNM 111331, a male from Salto de Agua, Mt. Ovando, about 15 miles northeast of Escuintla, Chiapas, Mexico, 1,200 ft, collected by Hobart Smith on May 19, 1940.)

Range: Wet and humid montane and lowland tropical forest in southern Chiapas, southern Guatemala, and western El Salvador; probably also in southern Honduras, from sea level to about 1,500 m.

Description: Males have 194 to 207 (197.1) and females have 210 to 221 (217.4) ventrals; subcaudals 45 to 53 (47.7) in males and 35 to 40 (38.1) in females. Examined: 58 males and 47 females, including all holotypes.

The black snout coloration extends to and usually includes the entire supraoculars and all or most of the frontal. The yellow parietal band is short, covering less than half to two thirds of the parietals, part of the temporals, and several supralabials. Below, the head is all yellow or white with the mental and usually the first 3 infralabials black. The black nuchal band covers about one third of the parietals, sometimes more or less, and 3 to 5 dorsals. Ventrally, it frequently extends forward onto the genials. The black bands are usually 3 to 5 and 2 to 4 ventrals long. The red bands are 3 to 6 times longer than the black bands, usually without black tips, but occasional specimens can have small irregular black tips but not on all scales. The red bands as well as the light parietal band frequently have brownish overtones that dull the red or white bands dorsally. The yellow or white bands are usually absent or quite inconspicuous. When present, they are 1 or less dorsal long. Only black and white bands are present on the tail; the former are about 2 times or more longer than the latter.

The males have 12 to 19 (17.1), usually 15 to 18, and the females have 12 to 22 (17.7), usually 15 to 19, black body bands. On the tail, the males have 5 to 7 (6.3) and the females have 4 to 6 (4.9) black bands.

Remarks: This subspecies intergrades in a wide zone in western and central Honduras and, probably, in eastern Guatemala with *M. n. divaricatus*. The intergrades have yellow bands of various lengths and a longer, yellow parietal band. The nuchal black band barely covers the tips of the parietals and the red scales usually have black tips.

Food: Predominant food is two ground snakes (*Geophis nasalis* and *Ninia sebae*), but skink lizards, teiid litter-dwelling lizards (*Gymnophthalmus speciosus*), as well as reptile eggs have been found in their stomachs.

References: Schmidt (1936b), Mittleman and Smith (1949), Alvarez del Toro (1972, 1983), and Stuart (1963) gave data on distribution and variation; a color photo was provided by Campbell and Lamar (1989).

Etymology: *Zunilensis*, Latin for inhabitant of Volcán Zunil; *wagneri* is dedicated to H. O. Wagner, collector of the holotype, and *ovandoensis* is Latin for dweller of Mt. Ovando.

Micrurus ornatissimus (Map 31, Pattern 37)
Ornated Coral Snake; Coral Ornamentada; Cobra Coral Ornamentada

Elaps ornatissimus Jan, 1858: 521. (Holotype: Originally in MSNM, probably a male, from "Mexico," apparently in error [corrected to Ecuador or Peru by Cunha and Nascimento, 1982b]. Destroyed during World War II.)

Elaps buckleyi Boulenger, 1896: 416. (Holotype: Syntypes, BM 1946.1.17.17, a female from Canelos, Ecuador, collected by Buckley, and BM 1946.1.17.18, a male from Pará [Brazil] collected by Stevens.)

Micrurus ornatissimus: Schmidt, 1936a: 191.

Distribution and range: Tropical lowland and low montane rain forest and altered secondary formations in the Amazonian basin of southern Colombia, eastern Ecuador and southeastern Peru, from about 500 to 1,200 m above sea level. A questionable record from Pará, Brazil.

Definition: A single-banded coral snake with a black cap in contact with the black nuchal and usually with some light spots on the snout. The black body bands range from 38 to 67 and are outlined by pearly dots of white; the red scales have black tips and the males have no supraanal tubercles.

Description: Males have 201 to 211 (204.7) and females have 218 to 230 (225.1) ventrals; subcaudals 47 to 52 (49.2) in males and 33 to 38 (34.2) in females; 1+1 or 1+2 temporals. Examined: 16 males and 19 females, including the 2 extant syntypes.

The black cap extends over all of the parietal region and usually is in contact with the nuchal band. The latter is complete ventrally. The temporals and several supralabials are red with black spots or dots. Usually, a light spot is present on supraoculars or on some other head scutes. The chin is black with large white spots or white with irregular black spots, particularly on the mental and several infralabials. The body is covered by distinct red and black bands, the latter outlined by pearly white bands that occupy half dorsals and usually one ventral. The black bands usually are 2 dorsals and 1 to 2 ventrals long, a little constricted on the first dorsal row. The red bands are approximately of the same length as the black bands dorsally, but approximately of equal length ventrally.

The males have 38 to 60 (51.8) and the females 40 to 67 (54.4) black body bands. The males have 11 to 17 (14.8), usually more than 11, and the females have 8 to 12 (9.7) black tail bands.

Size: This is a medium-sized species. The longest measured specimen is 848 mm long, but adults usually range between 450 and 700 mm.

Remarks: One syntype of M. buckleyi is said to come from Pará, but this is either an error or the specimen was transported there by the river. Cunha and Nascimento (1973, 1978) made excellent surveys of the snakes of the region without finding any specimens of this coral snake. This form was little known until Professor Gustavo Orcés from the Instituto Politécnico of Quito, Ecuador, gathered a considerable collection of this subspecies from eastern Ecuador. This collection of 20 specimens was more than the combined number of specimens in all the rest of the museums of the world.

Food: Probably blind snakes.

References: Schmidt (1936a), Roze (1967, 1970b, 1983), and Cunha and Nascimento (1982b) discussed its status. Silva (1994) described and offered a color photo from Colombia. Orcés (1943, 1948), J. A. Peters (1960a), Duellman (1978), Fugler and Walls (1978), and Miyata (1982) described it for Ecuador.

Etymology: The name *ornatissimus* is Latin for very ornate or decorated, probably alluding to the light head spots and the pearly white crossbands that, in combination with the brilliant red bands, make it look quite "ornamentissimus" in life. This also makes it easily recognizable. *Buckleyi* is dedicated to Mr. Buckley, collector of the holotype, who presented it to the British Museum (Natural History).

Micrurus paraensis (Map 32, Color 51)
Pará Coral Snake; Cobra Coral do Pará; Coral de Pará

Micrurus psiches (sic) *paraensis* Cunha and Nascimento, 1973: 276. (Holotype: MPEG 851, a male from Icoraci, Belém, Pará [Brazil] obtained by O. Cunha and F. Nascimento in 1972.)
Micrurus donosoi Hoge, Cordeiro and Romano, 1976: 417. (Holotype: IB 40155, a male from Minera ção Serra do Sul Ltda, 60 km north of São Felix do Xingú, Long. 51 55' W. Lat. 6 10' S Pará, Brazil.)

Micrurus psyches debruini Abuys, 1987a: 215. (Holotype: a specimen from the surroundings of Kwamalsamoetoe [south Suriname] collected in 1982 and seen in the collection of an animal dealer, T. Henzen, in Paramaribo, not deposited in any museum. In a later publication, Abuys [1988] mentioned that the holotype has been deposited in the collection of the University of Texas at Arlington under WWL-3100.)
Micrurus paraensis: Hoge and Romano-Hoge, 1981: 400.

Distribution and range: In coastal secondary forest vegetation and remnants of tropical rain forest in southern Suriname, in Pará and western Maranhão to Rondônia, Brazil, from sea level to about 400 m.

Definition: A single-banded coral snake with a black cap in broad contact with the black nuchal band 3 to 4 dorsals long. The number of black body bands range from 13 to 18 in males and 10 to 20 in females. The red bands are frequently melanistic, and males have no supraanal tubercles.

Description: Males have 188 to 200 and females have 194 to 213 ventrals; subcaudals 42 to 52 in males and 30 to 38 in females; 1+1 or 1+2 temporals. Examined: 6 males and 3 females, including the holotypes of *M. paraensis* and *M. donosoi*. The data on variation of scale counts include those given by Cunha and Nascimento (1973, 1978, 1982b).

The black cap is in broad contact with the black nuchal band, but several supralabials are white. Below, the mental, first infralabials, and the anterior part of the genials are black, followed by a white band that reaches the first dorsals. Some specimens have almost the entire chin black. The black nuchal band covers 3 to 4 dorsals. The black body bands are 2 to 3 dorsals and ventrals long, delimited by 1 scale long white bands. The red bands are 5 or more times as long as the black bands, with black or blackish brown tips on the dorsals that occasionally occupy more than half of the scale. Some specimens have red bands quite melanistic. Ventrally, some specimens have black spots. The black tail bands are longer than the white interspaces. The latter have black-tipped scales or brownish overtones.

The males have 13 to 18 and the females have 10 to 20 black body bands. Both sexes have 5 to 14 black tail bands.

Remarks: Its status and total distribution still have to be determined; apparently, it is wider than originally anticipated.

Food: Colubrid snakes (*Tantilla melanocephala*). Some stomachs also contained centipedes, but they may have been in the stomach of the prey snakes.

References: Cunha and Nascimento (1973, 1977, 1982a, 1988), Hoge and Romano-Hoge (1981), and Nascimento et al. (1987, 1988) offered taxonomic notes and natural history observations. Records from Rondônia are by Nascimento et al. (1988) and by Roze and Jorge da Silva (1990). A color photo was provided by Campbell and Lamar (1989).

Etymology: The Latin name *paraensis* means dweller of Pará. The species *donosoi* was named after the late Roberto Donoso Barros, a Chilean herpetologist. The name *debruini* was dedicated to the enthusiastic student of herpetology and teacher in Lelydorp, Suriname, John de Bruin.

Micrurus peruvianus (Map 28, Pattern 41)
Peruvian Coral Snake; Coral Peruviana

Micrurus peruvianus Schmidt, 1936a: 193. (Holotype: MCZ 17385, a male from Perico, Department of Cajamarca, Peru, collected by G. K. Noble, in 1916.)

Distribution and range: Dry scrub formations on the eastern slopes of the Andes in the Chinchipe-Marañón valleys of Cajamarca and in Amazonas, Peru, from about 450 to 1,500 m above sea level.

Definition: A single-banded coral snake with a black head cap and without supraanal tubercles in males. The red dorsals have regular black tips.

Description: Males have 186 to 194 (190.0) and females have 196 to 207 (202.4) ventrals; subcaudals 37 to 40 (38.2) in males and 26 to 30 (28.1) in females; 1+1 or 0+1 temporals. Examined: 3 males and 4 females, including the holotype.

The black cap usually covers almost the entire parietal and usually is in contact with the black nuchal band, interrupting the white postparietal band. The chin is white with irregular spots on some shields, particularly around their posterior borders. The nuchal black band begins 1 dorsal behind the parietals and is 4 to 6 dorsals and ventrals long. The remainder of the black bands are 3 to 4 dorsals and 2 to 3 ventrals long. The red bands are as long as or longer than the black bands, with irregular black tips on all dorsals. On the venter, the red scales have irregular black spots concentrated around their posterior borders. The white bands are 1 to 1½ dorsals long and are immaculate. The black tail bands are twice as long as the white ones.

The males have 20 to 26 (24.2) and the females have 18 to 27 (24.7) black body bands. The black tail bands are 6 to 9 (7.8) in males and 4 to 5 (4.6) in females.

Size: This is a small species. The longest measured specimen is only 433 mm.

Remarks: This species seems to be endemic to the Andean valleys of Cajamarca, Peru.

Food: Unknown.

References: Shreve (1947), Roze (1967, 1970b, 1983), Meneses (1974a), Duellman (1979), and Carrillo de Espinoza (1983) mentioned it for Peru, while Dunn (1923) mentioned it under the name of *M. corallinus*; description and color photo by Campbell and Lamar (1989).

Etymology: The name in Latin means "dweller of Peru."

Figure 59. *Micrurus petersi*, from Ecuador: Plan de Milagro, Morona-Santiago (USNM 158295, holotype).

Micrurus petersi (Fig. 59, Map 28)
Mountain Coral Snake (Peter's Coral Snake); Coral Montañera

Micrurus steindachneri petersi Roze, 1967: 45. (Holotype: USNM 158295, a female from 1 mile south of Plan de Milagro on the trail to Pan de Azúcar, Morona-Santiago Province, Ecuador, 5,600 ft, collected by J. A. Peters on August 1, 1962.)
Micrurus petersi: Roze, 1983: 333.

Distribution and range: Endemic to humid moderate and high mountain forest in eastern slopes of Andes in Ecuador in Santiago-Morona Province, from 1,000 to 2,800 m above sea level.

Definition: A single-banded coral snake with a black cap but with a light blue snout. Posteriorly, the black head and parietals are surrounded by a row of light scales. The red bands are longer than the black bands but obscured by large grayish or black tips. Males probably lack supraanal tubercles.

Description: Males unknown; females have 231 to 232 (231.5) ventrals; subcaudals are around 31 in females; 1+1 temporals. Examined: 2 females, one of which is the holotype.

The head is all black to the parietal tips but the snout has light blue spots on the rostral, internasals, and prefrontals as well as on the first supralabials. Temporals and postparietals are yellowish or whitish with dark tips or dark borders. The chin is white except for the first 3 infralabials, which are black. There are black spots on the mental and genials. The black nuchal band starts 1 dorsal behind the parietals, forming a black arch around them. Below, the nuchal band projects forward onto the genials. The black bands are 4 to 5 dorsals and 2 to 4 ventrals long. They are bordered by yellow or white scales, forming an irregular band about 1 dorsal long, giving an impression of a string of alternating light spots around the body. The red bands are darkened dorsally by large grayish-black tips and grayish-blue overtones that make them appear grayish-bluish-red. They are 5 to 7 dorsals and ventrals long, but the first red band is about 9 dorsals long. Ventrally, the red is pale or yellowish white. The black bands on the tail are about 3 times longer than the light bands.

The only 2 known females have 20 and 21 body bands and 4 black bands on the tail.

Size: This is medium-sized species. The longest female is 667 mm long.

Remarks: More specimens, especially males, need to be studied to better define this species and its distribution.

Food: Unknown.

References: Roze (1970b, 1983), Miyata (1982), and Almendariz (1991) mentioned it for Ecuador; general description and color photo in Campbell and Lamar (1989).

Etymology: Named after James A. Peters, the late curator of amphibians and reptiles of the National Museum of Natural History, Washington, D.C., who traveled extensively in Ecuador and contributed more than anybody else to the knowledge of the herpetofauna of that country.

Micrurus proximans (Map 29, Pattern 38)
Nayarit Coral Snake; Coralillo de Nayarit

Micrurus diastema proximans Smith and Chrapliwy, 1958: 270. (Holotype: UIMNH 40369, a female from 4 miles north of San Blas, Nayarit, Mexico, collected by Davis, Lidiker, and Winkelmann on July 16, 1956.)
Micrurus proximans: Roze, 1967: 40.

Distribution and range: In dry lowland and coastal thorn formations in Nayarit, Mexico, up to 100 m above sea level.

Definition: A single-banded coral snake with black, red, and white or yellow bands in which the females have several black bands interrupted ventrally. It has a black snout and a white parietal band followed by a black nuchal band. The red dorsal scales have small black tips, but not on all scales. Males have supraanal tubercles.

Description: Males have 202 to 207 (204.8) and females have 210 to 218 (214.4) ventrals; subcaudals 47 to 53 (48.7) in males and 36 to 42 (38.3) in females. Usually 1+2 temporals, at least on one side. Examined: 7 males and 5 females, including the holotype.

The snout is black, including most of the frontal and anterior part of the parietals, followed by a yellow or white band that includes 3 or 4 supralabials. Below, the head is white with the mental and first infralabials black and with some black borders on several additional shields. The black nuchal band covers the tips of the parietals, 4 to 5 dorsals, and 3 to 4 ventrals, including the tips of the second pair of genials. The single black body bands are 2 to 3 dorsals and ventrals long. In females, several black bands are interrupted ventrally. The yellow or white bands are barely 1 dorsal and ventral long. The red bands are 2 or more times longer than the black bands. They are 7 to 9 dorsals and ventrals long, with small black tips present on several, but not all, dorsals. Only black and white bands are on the tail; the first are 2 or 3 times longer than the white bands.

The males have 17 to 22 (18.6) and the females have 21 to 24 (23.2) black body bands. In females only 3 to 10 bands are complete. Both sexes have 5 to 7 black tail bands.

Size: This is a small species. The longest specimen is 565 mm long, and adults measure between 400 and 500 mm.

Remarks: This is the westernmost species of single-banded coral snakes with supraanal tubercles in Mexico. It can be distinguished from other species by the incomplete black bands in females.

Food: A slender blind snake (*Leptotyphlops humilis dugesi*).

References: Zweifel (1959), H. M. Smith and Taylor (1966), and Roze (1967, 1983) offered brief comments on this species and Campbell and Lamar (1989) a general description.

Etymology: Latin from *proximatus* meaning near relationship or proximity, probably alluding to its close relationship to another coral snake from the same region, as interpreted by the authors of its original description.

Micrurus psyches (Map 31, Color 52)
Northern Coral Snake (Carib Coral Snake); Coral Norteña; Cobra Coral Septentrional

Vipera psyches Daudin, 1803: 320. (Holotype: MNHN 7654, a male from Suriname, collected by Le Vaillant.)
Micrurus psyches: Beebe, 1919: 216.

Distribution and range: The rain forest, low montane wet forest, and gallery forest in the fringes of savanna in southeastern Venezuela, northern Guyana, Suriname, and French Guiana, from 50 to about 500 m above sea level.

Definition: A single-banded coral snake with a black head cap that usually fuses with the black nuchal band, interrupting or nearly interrupting the white postparietal band. Black body bands range from 22 to 41; the red bands are partially or completely obliterated with black or dark brown. Black and white, or black, red, and white bands are found on the tail. Males lack supraanal tubercles.

Description: Males have 188 to 196 (192.9) and females have 203 to 212 (208.1) ventrals; subcaudals 44 to 49 (46.4) in males and 30 to 33 (31.9) in females; 1+1, occasionally 1+2, temporals; some subcaudals occasionally undivided. Examined: 14 males and 15 females, including the holotype.

The black cap is usually in contact with the black nuchal band; occasionally separated by a white postparietal band, 1 dorsal or less long. The chin is either all black or the genials and most of the infralabials are black. The black nuchal band is 3 to 5 dorsals and ventrals long. In most specimens the red bands are partially or totally obliterated by black. In the first case, the specimens have the original red bands purplish or blackish red. This gives the specimens a general appearance of a black or purplish black and white snake. The original black bands are 3 to 4 dorsals and ventrals long, outlined by short white bands 1 or less dorsals long. Sometimes the white bands also are dark, but they always can be distinguished ventrally. The original red bands are 3 to 7 dorsals and ventrals long. Ventrally, they can be distinguished, even in the darkest specimens, as purplish or reddish-black bands. Black and irregular red and white bands are found on the tail.

Counting the original black body bands, the males have 22 to 29 (25.8) and the females have 27 to 41 (30.7) bands. If the black and the original red bands that are blackish are counted as black, the males have 44 to 57 (51.2) and the females have 51 to 81 (63.0) bands. The males have 7 to 10 (8.8) and the females have 5 to 7 (6.2) black tail bands.

Food: Snakelike teiid lizards (*Bachia*).

Size: This is a medium-small species. The longest specimen measures 910 mm, but many adults range between 450 and 600 mm in total length.

Remarks: No less than 6 subspecies were considered part of this species (Roze, 1967, 1970, 1983, 1987; Cunha and Nascimento, 1973, 1978; Campbell and Lamar, 1989): *psyches, circinalis, medemi, paraensis, remotus*, and *donosoi*. The first 5 are considered as full species in this book and the sixth has been found to be a synonym of *paraensis* (Cunha and Nascimento, 1982a). No intergrades have been found and the species have quite distinctive characters. They are considered to be a natural species group, characterized by mostly single-banded color pattern and absence of any supraanal tubercles (Roze, 1994). Moreover, they have a somewhat discontinuous distribution.

References: Roze (1967, 1970b, 1983) mentioned it as subspecies and Campbell and Lamar (1989) gave a description and distribution with a color photo. General references to the species appeared in Amaral (1925a) and Schmidt (1936a); its distribution by P. Müller (1973), Rivero-Blanco and Dixon (1979), and Duellman (1979). Gasc and Rodrigues (1980) and Chippaux (1987) mentioned its presence in French Guiana; H. W. Parker (1935) and Beebe (1946) described it for Guyana; Brongersma (1967) and Moonen et al. (1978) mentioned it for Suriname, while Beebe (1946), Roze (1955, 1966) described it from Venezuela. Earlier references include Jan and Sordelli (1872), Cope (1876b), and Boulenger (1898).

Etymology: In Greek *psyche* means soul; it also means butterfly. It is difficult to interpret this name; perhaps it refers to a butterflylike head pattern found in some specimens.

Micrurus putumayensis (Fig. 60, Map 33)
Putumayo Coral Snake; Coral Putumayense; Cobra Coral do Putumayo

Micrurus schmidti Lancini, 1962a: 1. (Preoccupied by *Micrurus schmidti* Dunn, 1940). (Holotype: AMNH 1100058 [ex. MCN 1117], a female from Puerto Socorro, 270 km northeast of Iquitos, Rio Putumayo, Depto. de Loreto, Peru, collected by Julio Cáceres M. in March 1959.)

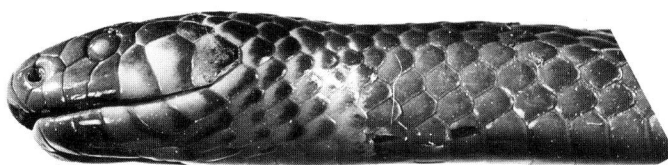

Figure 60. Micrurus putumayensis, from Peru: Puerto Socorro, 270 mi NE Iquitos (AMNH, holotype).

Micrurus putumayensis Lancini, 1962b: 1. (replacement name for *Micrurus schmidti* Lancini, 1962.)

Distribution and range: Tropical rain forest of the upper Amazon from Iquitos, eastern Peru, to the southern tip of Colombia and adjacent northwestern Brazil, at altitudes between 100 and 300 m above sea level.

Definition: A coral snake with alternating black and yellow bands only; 7 to 12 black body bands in both sexes. All the yellow scales are almost entirely invaded by black or dark brown coloration. A black cap covers the head.

Description: Males have 197 to 208 (201.6) and females have 216 to 226 (221.9) ventrals; subcaudals 47 to 51 (48.6) in males and 32 to 35 (33.6) in females; 1+1 or 1+2 temporals. Examined: 11 males and 7 females, including the holotype.

The body is covered by single, black and yellow bands, without any red bands. The black cap covers all of the upper part of the head to the parietal tips and most of the chin shields. The nuchal yellow band is 3 to 5 dorsals long. The black bands are 8 to 35 dorsals and ventrals long. In several specimens every second black band is somewhat irregular and reduced ventrally. The yellow bands are 4 to 11 dorsals and ventrals long; they are somewhat melanistic dorsally. Usually only the posterior border of each yellow scale is completely yellow. Ventrally, the yellow scales are immaculate or have black borders. Some scales have a trace of reddish or pink overtone.

The males have 7 to 11 (9.2) and the females have 9 to 14 (11.1) black body bands. The males have 2 to 3 and the females have 2 black tail bands.

Size: This is a medium-sized coral snake. The largest specimen measures 805 mm in total length; most adults a reach total length of about 700 mm.

Remarks: The absence of red bands, combined with the very long black bands, distinguishes this species from the other species of coral snakes. Its coloration may have been derived from a basic single red-yellow-black-yellow pattern in which the red bands have become completely obliterated by black. Traces of reddish or pinkish spots on the ventral side of the yellow bands of some specimens supports this possibility. In the type specimen, every second black band is irregular and reduced or nearly absent ventrally, suggesting that they represent the original red bands. This species is from the Amazon region in which melanistic tendencies are known in several species of coral snakes, such as *M. albicinctus*, *M. langsdorffi*, *M. psyches*, *M. margaritiferus*, and *M. annellatus*.

Food: Colubrid snakes.

References: Distribution is found in Roze (1967, 1970b, 1983) and a complete description in Campbell and Lamar (1989); for Brazil by Lema (1972), for Colombia by Medem (1969), and for Peru by Soini (1973, 1974b), Meneses (1974a), Carrillo de Espinoza (1983), and Dixon and Soini (1986).

Etymology: The Latin name *putumayensis*, meaning inhabitant of Putumayo, alludes to its presence in the region around the Putumayo River, while *schmidti* was dedicated to the great coral snake specialist, Karl P. Schmidt, from the Field Museum of Natural History, Chicago, United States.

Micrurus pyrrhocryptus (Map 34)
Southern Coral Snake; Coral Sureña; Cobra Coral Meridional

Distribution: From southeastern Brazil in Mato Grosso, Paraguay, and southern Bolivia to northern and central Argentina to Río Negro and Neuquén.

Definition: A triad-type coral snake with 5 to 11 (occasionally 12) triads. The nuchal red band is 5 to 23 dorsals long, and the central black band of a triad is 17 to 35 dorsals long.

Size: This is a large coral snake. The longest known specimen measures 1,240 mm in total length, but many adults average between 700 mm and 900 mm.

Remarks: This species was considered as a subspecies of *M. frontalis* (Shreve, 1953; Roze, 1983; Campbell and Lamar, 1989), but it has characteristics that separates it as a different species (Roze, 1994). Two subspecies are recognized, but it is quite possible that additional ones will be recognized since the status of coral snakes in southern South America, particularly in southern and southeastern Brazil, are poorly understood (see also comments under *M. frontalis* and *M. diana*).

References: General comments on the species (mostly as *M. frontalis pyrrhocryptus*) appeared in Schmidt (1936a), Amaral (1944), Shreve (1953), Roze (1967, 1970b,

1983, 1994), Hoge and Lancini (1960), and Hoge and Romano (1981); on distribution by Cei (1979) and Gallardo (1979) and a reference by Campbell and Lamar (1989). Data and distribution in Argentina are by Fernández Barrán and Freiberg (1951), Abalos (1961 and 1977), Abalos et al. (1964), Barrio and Miranda (1967), Freiberg (1968, 1984), Abalos and Bucher (1970), Abalos and Mischis (1975), Gallardo (1977), Cei (1987), Yanosky (1989) and Scrocchi (1990); in Bolivia by Kempff-Mercado (1975); in Brazil by Hoge (1956), Hoge and Romano (1973, 1981); in Paraguay by Bertoni (1914, 1939), Migone (1929), Schouten (1931, 1937), and Scott and Lovett (1975). Significant earlier descriptions include publications by Günther (1859), Cope (1860a, 1862), and Koslowsky (1895, 1898).

Key to the Subspecies of *M. pyrrhocryptus*

1 Triads mostly 5 to 9 (occasionally 10); first white band with at least some black-tipped scales
   .... *M. p. pyrrhocryptus* (southeastern Bolivia and northern Argentina)
1' Triads 10–11; first white band immaculate
   ..... *M. p. tricolor* (Paraguay and southern Brazil)

Micrurus pyrrhocryptus pyrrhocryptus (Pattern 2)
Argentinean Coral Snake; Coral Argentina; Cobra Coral Argentina

Elaps pyrrhocryptus Cope, 1862: 347. (Holotype: not known, from Vermejo River, Argentine Chaco, as designated by Schmidt, 1936a, collected during the Captain Page Expedition in 1853.)
Elaps simonsi Boulenger, 1902b: 338. (Holotype: BM 1946.1.21.33, a female from Cruz del Eje, Córdoba, Argentina, collected by P. O. Simons.)
Micrurus pyrrhocryptus pyrrhocryptus: Roze, 1994: 179.

Range: Pampas, dry forest, and scrub steppes as well as piedmont deciduous forest from southeastern Bolivia, southward to Mendoza and San Luís, and probably also in southern Paraguay, at low elevations to about 450 m.

Description: Males have 214 to 238 (231.3) and females have 216 to 238 (233.2) ventrals; subcaudals 25 to 30 (26.1) in males and 23 to 29 (25.4) in females; usually 1+1 temporals. Examined: 41 males and 34 females, including one holotype.

The head, including the parietals and the first 3 or 4 supralabials, is black and each plate is outlined by white or yellowish white borders. The chin may be immaculate white or yellowish white or light with irregular small to medium-sized black spots. The nuchal red band occupies 7 to 23, usually more than 11 dorsals, followed by the first triad. The central black band of a triad is usually more than twice as long as the outer bands. The first central band is 17 to 35 dorsals long, usually more than 20. About 10% of the specimens have 2 triads fused to form a quincad. The white, occasionally yellowish or creamy-white bands have black-tipped scales. The length of the red bands varies considerably according to the number of triads: the fewer triads, the longer the red bands are. The length of the red bands varies between 13 and 60 dorsals; all have conspicuous, regular black-tipped scales.

The males have 6 to 8 (7.1) and the females have 5 to 8 (7.2), occasionally 9, rarely 10, black triads on the body. The males have 1 to 1⅔ and the females have 1 to 1⅓, usually 1, black triads on the tail.

Remarks: It is the southernmost coral snake in South America, its distribution extending to a latitude about 35 degrees south.

Food: Limbless amphisbaenid lizards (*Amphisbaena leposternon*), also cannibalistic, at least as observed in captivity.

References: General observations and information on the distribution and variation are described by Abalos (1949), Shreve (1953), Abalos and Nader (1962), Abalos et al. (1964), Freiberg (1968), Barrio and Miranda (1968), and all the other references that appear in species references under Argentina; Kempff-Mercado (1975) mentioned it for Bolivia.

Etymology: Greek from *pyrrho* meaning red or reddish and *cryptus* meaning hidden or concealed, perhaps meaning that this large coral snake hides its venomous nature behind its lovely coloration. *Simonsi* was named after P. O. Simons, who collected the holotype.

Micrurus pyrrhocryptus tricolor (Pattern 43)
Pantanal Coral Snake; Coral de Pantanal; Cobra Coral do Pantanal

Micrurus tricolor Hoge, 1956: 67. (Holotype: IB 16290, a male from Garandazal, Mato Grosso, Brazil obtained by O. Lemos Alves.)
Micrurus pyrrhocryptus tricolor: Roze, 1994: 179.

Range: Savanna and dry tropical deciduous forests, and mixed formations including pantanal in southwestern Mato Grosso and Mato Grosso do Sul, Brazil, and the central Chaco dry lowlands in central Paraguay, from 100 to 500 m above sea level.

Description: Males have 217 to 229 (224.7) and females have 218 to 232 (225.9) ventrals; subcaudals 25 to 30

(28.1) in males and 20 to 29 (26.3) in females; 1+1 temporals. Examined: 6 males and 5 females, including the holotype.

The upper part of the head, including the parietals and the first 4 or 5 supralabials, are black, with individual shields outlined in white. The chin is white with irregular black spots on several shields. The nuchal red band is 5 to 9 dorsals long, followed by the first triad. The central black band of triad is usually less than twice as long as the outer ones. The central band of the first triad is 6 to 10 dorsals long. The dorsals of the first several white bands either lack black tips or have only a few. The other white bands have black tips on most or all of the scales. The red bands vary considerably in size, but all have irregular conspicuous black-tipped scales.

The males have 9 to 11 (9.8) and the females have 8 to 11 (9.6) black triads on the body. Both sexes have 1⅓ to 1⅔ (occasionally only 1), black triad on the tail.

Remarks: This subspecies probably intergrades with *M. p. pyrrhocryptus* along the Paraguay-Argentina border.

Food: Unknown.

References: In addition to the original description and a brief mention by Hoge and Lancini (1960), Scott and Lovett (1975) and Roze (1983) offered some data on this little known coral snake.

Etymology: *Tricolor*, Latin for three colors, denotes the black, white, and red bands that are conspicuous in this subspecies.

Micrurus remotus (Map 32, Color 53)
Remote Coral Snake; Coral Remota; Cobra Coral Remota

Micrurus psyches remotus Roze, 1987: 110. (Holotype: USNM 2661000, a male from Base Camp of Cerro de la Neblina, Territorio Federal Amazonas, Venezuela, 0 55' N, 66 10' W, 90 m, collected by Roy W. McDiarmid in forest 20 cm deep, on 6 February, 1985.)
Micrurus remotus: Roze, 1994: 178.

Distribution and range: Lowland and low montane rain forest, probably also cloud forest, in eastern Colombia, southern Venezuela and adjacent Amazonas, Brazil, from 90 to 1500 m above sea level.

Definition: A single-banded coral snake with a black cap that fuses with the black nuchal band that is about 4 dorsals long. The black body bands range from 25 to 40. The red bands are black-tipped and with brownish overtones, and the males lack supraanal tubercles.

Description: Males have 202 to 203 (202.3) and females have 214 to 225 (219.3) ventrals; subcaudals 42 to 49 (46.3) in males and 32 to 37 (35.3) in females; 1+2 or 1+1 temporals. Examined: 3 males and 4 females, including the holotype.

The black cap is fused with the black nuchal band. The temporals and the last supralabials are yellowish with brownish or dark spots and dots. The chin may be covered by an irregular mottling of white and black, or the black may be more concentrated on the mental and the first infralabials. The black nuchal band is 4 dorsals and 3 ventrals long and projects onto the second pair of genials. The black bands are 2 to 3 dorsals and ventrals long and are somewhat irregular ventrally. The red bands are distinct, with black-tipped scales and brownish overtones. Ventrally they are immaculate red or have some irregular black mottling. The yellowish-white bands are about half a dorsal long, forming interrupted and irregular crossbands bordering the black bands. Ventrally, the white bands are a full scale long. Only black and yellowish-white bands are found on the tail, but the latter usually have a small, reddish-brown dorsal spot.

The males have 25 to 29 (27.3) and the females have 29 to 40 (34.0) black body bands; 7 to 8 (8.7) black tail bands in males and 6 to 8 (7.0) in females.

Remarks: This coral snake was recently discovered in the little-explored regions of Venezuela, Colombia, and Brazil. It was described as a subspecies of *M. psyches* but here it is considered a full species (see note under *M. psyches*).

Food: Unknown.

References: Only the original description with a color photo and brief remarks and a color photo in Campbell and Lamar (1989).

Etymology: *Remotus*, Latin for distant, alludes to the distribution of this snake in little-traveled regions where only Indians and occasional naturalists venture.

Micrurus ruatanus (Map 35, Color 54)
Roatán Coral Snake; Coral Roatanense

Elaps ruatanus Günther, 1895: 185. (Holotype: BM 1946.1.21.20, a male from Roatán Island, Honduras, collected by G. F. Gaumer.)
Micrurus ruatanus: Schmidt, 1933a: 34.

Distribution and range: Tropical island vegetation altered by humans in Roatán Island in the Departamento de Islas de Bahía, Honduras.

Definition: A two-colored coral snake with alternating long and short black and red bands. The snout it black followed by a red parietal band. The nuchal black band does not reach the parietals and the males have supraanal tubercles.

Description: Males have 178 to 188 (183.7) and females have 193 to 203 (198.7) ventrals; subcaudals 46 to 48 (46.3) in males and 34 to 38 (36.9) in females. About half of the specimens have 2 to 10 undivided subcaudals; 1+1 temporals. Examined: 10 males and 5 females, including the holotype.

The black snout coloration reaches up to the anterior part of the supraoculars and half of the frontal. The rest of the head, including the last 4 supralabials and parietals, is red. The black nuchal band does not reach the parietals, and is 3 to 5 dorsals long. Below, the head is white, except the mental and first 2 or 3 infralabials which are black. The rest of the body is covered by black and red bands. Longer and shorter black bands alternate, in some specimens more than in others. The long black bands are usually 3 dorsals and 2 to 3 ventrals long, while the short black bands are 1 to 2½ dorsals long; some of them are interrupted laterally or ventrally. The long black bands are equal to or longer than the red bands. The red bands are immaculate. On the tail, the red bands are as long as or longer than the black bands.

The males have 33 to 39 (36.1) and the females have 41 to 45 (43.3) black body bands. Males have 5 to 7 (5.9) and the females have 2 to 6 (5.0) black tail bands.

Size: This is a medium-sized species. The largest-known specimen is 681 mm long, and adults range between 450 and 600 mm.

Remarks: This species is endemic to the Islas de Bahía (Bay Islands), Honduras, and is in danger of extinction. It can be easily distinguished by the presence of only red and alternating longer and shorter black bands.

Food: Roatán whiptail lizard (*Cnemidophorus lemniscatus ruatanus*).

References: Comments and data are by Barbour (1928), Dunn (1940), Roze (1967, 1970b, 1983), Wilson and Meyer (1972, 1982, 1985), Wilson and Hahn (1973), Wilson (1984), and Villa et al. (1988). A complete description was given by Campbell and Lamar (1989).

Etymology: Ruatanus, Latin for inhabitant of Roatán Island.

Micrurus sangilensis (Map 33, Pattern 45)
San Gil Coral Snake; Coral Sangilense

Micrurus ecuadorianus sangilensis Nicéforo María, 1942: 98. (Holotype: Colegio San José de Guaneta, Colombia, No. 2A, a male from San Gil, Departamento de Santander [Colombia], collected by R. H. Silvano Jorge in August 1937.)
Micrurus sangilensis: Roze, 1983: 334.

Distribution and range: Cloud forest and humid high montane forest, also altered by humans, of Cordillera of eastern Andes in Santander, Boyacá, and northern Cundinamarca, Colombia, at elevations between 1,000 and 2,000 m.

Definition: An accessory triad-type coral snake with a black cap on the head and with central black bands of a triad 2 to 3 times longer than the outer bands. The black nuchal band is the central band of the first triad. Males lack supraanal tubercles.

Description: Males have 190 to 196 (192.7) and females have 207 to 215 (209.8) ventrals; subcaudals 47 to 53 (48.3) in males and 35 to 37 (36.4) in females. Examined: 3 males and 5 females.

The black cap covers all the upper part of the head, including the entire parietals. The last supralabials and temporals are yellow with irregular black borders. The chin is yellow or white with irregular black spots. The nuchal black band, which is the second band of the first triad, starts 2 to 3 dorsals behind the parietals. It is 4 to 6 dorsals and ventrals long. The black central band of the triad is 3 to 4 dorsals and ventrals long and the outer black bands are 1 to 2 dorsals and ventrals long. The white bands are irregular, about 1 to 1½ dorsals long, and are covered with occasional black spots. The red bands are 4 to 10 dorsals and ventrals long; they can be long and short in the same specimen. The red scales have irregular black tips. On the tail are only single black and white bands, not triads.

The males have 17 to 22 (19.2) and the females have 17 to 21 (19.2) complete black triads on the body, plus the anterior ⅔ of a triad, so that the complete triad formula is, for example, ⅔ 17 triads. On the tail, the males have 7 to 10 and the females have 5 to 7 single black bands.

Size: This is a medium-sized species. The longest specimen is 600 mm long; many adults measure between 450 and 550 mm.

Remarks: The combination of the black cap and accessory triads in which the black central bands are much longer than the outer bands makes this species readily distinguishable. All the known specimens except one are located in Colombian museums.

Food: Unknown.

References: After the original description, only Schmidt (1955), Roze (1967, 1970b, 1983), Medem (1969), and Pérez-Santos and Moreno (1986, 1988) commented on this species.

Etymology: The name in Latin means pertaining to or inhabitant of San Gil, which is in Santander, Colombia.

Micrurus spixii (Map 36)
Amazonian Coral Snake; Coral Amazónica; Cobra Coral Amazonica

Distribution: Amazonian region of Colombia, Venezuela, Ecuador, Peru, Brazil, Bolivia, and northern Paraguay.

Definition: A triad-type coral snake in which the first triad consists of only two black bands, and the white, yellow, or greenish bands are as long as or longer than the black bands, except occasionally the black nuchal band. The anal is usually located in the middle of the last body triad, making it incomplete, but it continues on the tail.

Size: This is the largest coral snake. The longest measured specimen is 1,602 mm long, but many adults measure between 800 and 1,200 mm.

Remarks: This species can be easily recognized by the long triads in which the white and red bands are longer than the black bands and by the fact that, except in one subspecies, only two black bands are present before the first complete triad. The live snakes give an impression of a coral snake with very few red bands. It shows almost no sexual dimorphism. This is not only the largest but also the most abundant coral snake in the Amazon region. Four subspecies are recognized.

References: Many articles and books have been published. The two most complete descriptions are by Schmidt (1953b) and Campbell and Lamar (1989). Other general notes are by Boulenger (1905), Amaral (1925b), Schmidt (1936a), Roze (1967, 1970b, 1983), and Cendrero et al. (1972); for Bolivia by Griffin (1916) and Kempff-Mercado (1975); for Brazil by L. Müller (1927), Amaral (1930b, 1948b, 1978), Machado (1945), Prado (1945), P. Müller (1973), Cuhna and Nascimento (1973, 1978, 1982a), Hoge and Romano (1973, 1981), Hoge et al. (1973), Santos (1981), Cunha et al. (1985), Vanzolini (1986), Nascimento et al. (1988), Zimmerman and Rodrigues (1990), and Roze and da Silva (1990); for Colombia by Niceforo Maria (1942), Dunn (1944a), Daniel (1949), Schmidt (1955), Medem (1969), Silva and Rodríguez (1985), Pérez-Santos and Moreno (1986, 1988) and Silva (1994); for Ecuador by Orcés (1943, 1948), J. A. Peters (1960), Duellman (1978), and Miyata (1982); for French Guiana by Chippaux (1987); for Peru by Barbour and Noble (1920), Prado and Hoge (1948), Meneses (1974a), Soini (1974b), Carrillo de Espinoza (1983), and Dixon and Soini (1986); and for Venezuela those by Milá de la Roca (1932), Veillard (1941), Roze (1954, 1955, 1957, 1966a, 1987), Vetencourt Finol (1960), Hoge and Lancini (1962), Lancini (1970, 1979), and Sandner-Montilla (1975, 1985). Roux-Estève (1983) and Hoogmoed and Gruber (1983) dealt with some type specimens. Earlier significant references include Gray (1829) and Jan (1859a, 1959b).

Key to the Subspecies of *M. spixii*

1 Nuchal black band elongated and usually projecting forward, covering 8 or more dorsals
  ..... *M. s. obscurus* (Upper Amazon of Colombia, Venezuela, Brazil, Ecuador and Peru)
1' Nuchal black band not projecting forward; less than 7 dorsals long 2
2 Four to 6 (usually 5) complete triads on body
  .... *M. s. spixii* (Central Amazon, Brazil)
2' Six to 8 (usually more than 6) complete triads .. 3
3 Head all black or with small light spots on snout; parietals mostly black
  .... *M. s. martiusi* (lower Amazon in Brazil; probably Paraguay)
3' Head with large white spots; parietals mostly red
  .... *M. s. princeps* (Bolivia)

Micrurus spixii spixii
Central Amazon Coral Snake; Cobra Coral da Amazonia Central

Micrurus spixii Wagler, 1824: 48. (Holotype: ZSBS 209/0, a male from the region of Solimoēs, Amazonas, Brazil, collected by the Spix and Martius Expedition, 1817–1820.)
Elaps ehrhardti L. Müller, 1926: 198. (Holotype: ZSBS 203/1925, a female from Manacapurú, Rio Solimoēs, Brazil, collected by W. Ehrhardt on June 8, 1915.)
Micrurus spixii spixii: Schmidt and Walker, 1943: 294.

Range: Lowland tropical rain forest and humid forest of the middle Amazon region of Brazil, in Amazonas and Rondônia, from 50 to 150 m above sea level.

Description: Males have 206 to 217 (212.8) and females have 212 to 222 (216.7) ventrals; subcaudals 19 to 24 (21.8) in males and 19 to 23 (21.1) in females; almost all specimens have 1 to 17 undivided subcaudals; 1+1 temporals. Examined: 10 males and 9 females, including the types.

The upper head is almost entirely black with a few light gray borders on some shields. The first supralabials are creamy white with large black spots and borders, followed by a lateral red postocular area that extends below also over the throat. The black head coloration continues as the black nuchal band that is the second band of the first triad, about 2 to 4 dorsals long. The black bands are about half the length of the white or yellow bands and about one third the length of the red bands. The red bands are 7 to 12 dorsals and ventrals long and are immaculate. In the largest specimens some dark tips appear on the red scales. The yellow bands are 5 to 8 dorsals and ventrals long, with small black tips and faint dark borders. The last incomplete body triad continues on the tail.

Both males and females have 4 to 6 (5.3) complete triads on the body. Actually, most specimens have ⅓ of a triad more, so a complete triad formula is ⅔ 5 ⅓ + ⅔ on the body and tail. Almost all specimens of both sexes have ⅔ triads on the tail.

Remarks: This subspecies intergrades with *M. s. princeps* around the frontier between Brazil and Bolivia and with *M. s. obscurus* in central Rio Negro, Brazil.

Food: Snakes and lizards.

References: See the list under species; most recent description by Campbell and Lamar (1989) with color photos.

Etymology: Named after Spix, one of the great German explorers who led a remarkable Brazilian expedition from 1817 to 1820. The name *ehrhardti* was given to honor another German traveler, W. Ehrhardt, who collected one of the type specimens.

Micrurus spixii martiusi (Color 55)
Black-headed Amazonian Coral Snake; Cobra Coral Amazonica de Cabeça Preta; Coral Amazónica de Cabeza Negra

Micrurus spixii martiusi Schmidt, 1953b: 175. (Holotype: MCZ 2612, a male from Santarem, Pará, Brazil, collected by D. Bouraget in 1866.)

Range: Tropical rain forest and humid secondary forest, altered by humans, in lower Amazon from Pará to Goiás and Mato Grosso, Brazil, from sea level to 300 m. One unverified record from Paraguay.

Description: Males have 208 to 226 (217.4) and females have 211 to 226 (216.8) ventrals; subcaudals 21 to 25 (22.6) in males and 19 to 24 (21.8) in females; both sexes have the first 3 to 13 subcaudals undivided; 1+1 temporals. Examined: 21 males and 11 females, including the holotype.

The upper head is all black, with shields anterior to parietals with light borders or spots. The first supralabials are white with dark posterior borders or spots. The nuchal black band covers entire parietals and continues on the first 2 or 3 dorsals. It is complete around the neck. The last supralabials and infralabials and the chin are red. The black bands are about equal in size, 4 to 6 dorsals and 2 to 6 ventrals long. The white or yellow bands are 3 to 5 dorsals and ventrals long, with conspicuous black tips. The red bands are immaculate, longer than the white and black bands, especially the last red band, which may be up to twice as long as the previous bands. They are 6 to 12 dorsals and ventrals long, and in very large specimens they are darkish, covered by brownish gray. Triads continue onto the tail.

The males have 6 to 9 (7.8), usually 7 or more, and the females have 7 to 9 (8.1) complete bands. As the first triad consists of ⅔ of a triad, a typical formula for a specimen with 7 complete triads is ⅔ 7 ⅓ + ⅔. Almost all specimens of both sexes have ⅔ of a triad and occasionally ⅔ ½ on the tail.

Remarks: There is only one record from Paraguay. It has to be confirmed as it is outside the range of this subspecies.

Food: Litter-dwelling snakes (*Apostolepis quinquelineatus*) and limbless lizards (*Aulura anomala*), as well as other snakes.

References: Cunha and Nascimento (1973, 1978, 1982b, 1985) described variation and natural history of this subspecies and Campbell and Lamar (1989) offered a color photo.

Etymology: Named after the German explorer Martius, the traveling companion of Spix during their 1817–1820 South American expedition.

Micrurus spixii obscurus (Color 56)
Black-neck Amazonian Coral Snake; Coral Amazónica Cuello Negro; Cobra Coral Amazonica Pescoço Preto

Elaps corallinus var. *obscura* Jan, 1972: 4, pl. 6-3. (Holotype lost, from "Lima", in error, designated as Iquitos, Peru, by Schmidt, 1953b.)
Micrurus spixii obscura: Schmidt and Walker, 1943a: 294.

Range: Lowland tropical and low montane rain forest and humid forest altered by humans in upper Amazon and Orinoco basins in southern Colombia and Venezuela, eastern Ecuador and Peru, and probably in northern Bolivia, east of Andes, and northwestern Brazil, from 100 to 600 m above sea level.

Description: Males have 200 to 228 (215.6) and females have 207 to 225 (215.6) ventrals; subcaudals 17 to 22 (20.1) in males and 16 to 22 (18.5) in females; almost all specimens have several undivided subcaudals; 1+1 temporals. Examined: 74 males and 37 females.

The snout is marked with irregular black and white spots followed by an irregular black frontal crossband. The parietals are red, marked with black spots that vary from only one black spot on each parietal to heavy irregular black spots on all shields, including the temporals, supralabials, and infralabials. Below, the chin is white anteriorly, followed by a red band marked with irregular black spots. The nuchal black band is 8 or more dorsals and 4 or more ventrals long. The anterior border of the nuchal black band is somewhat roundish. The black body bands are as long as or shorter than the white or yellow bands. They are 4 to 7 dorsals and 3 to 5 ventrals long. The white bands can also be creamy white, yellow or greenish; they are 4 to 8 dorsals and 5 to 9 ventrals long, with black tips that are heavier in large specimens. The red bands are longer than the white bands, 7 to 15 dorsals and ventrals long, and immaculate or with very few small black tips in larger specimens. Triads continue onto the tail.

The males have 4 to 6 (5.1), rarely 7, and the females have 4 to 6 (5.2) complete body triads. Most specimens in both sexes have ⅔ triads on the tail. A frequent triad formula for specimens with 5 complete triads is ⅔ 5 ⅓ + ⅔.

Remarks: This is the most widely distributed and variable subspecies, easily recognized by its nuchal black band that projects forward, but it shows a considerable variation in its size and shape. For example, the population from the Orinoco drainage in Colombia, among other things, has the first triad irregularly complete and the second (central) black band does not project forward. They also have a slightly higher number of triads. Their head coloration is somewhat more regular and, as noted by Campbell and Lamar (1989), approaches that of *M. isozonus* found in the same area. It is possible there is a mimicry relationship yet to be studied.

Food: Feeds on a wide variety of animals that include burrowing, litter-dwelling species and also active surface runners. Food includes caecilians, active diurnal lizards (*Kentropix pelviceps*), litter-dwelling snakes (*Atractus collaris*), and other species that are frequently found in cultivated fields, such as the snail-eating snakes (*Dipsas*) as well as other ground snakes (*Liophis reginae, Liophis chrysostomus*) and other coral snakes. A specimen of this subspecies in the Vienna Museum had a *Micrurus a. annellatus* in its stomach.

References: Much has been published about these snakes. Among the most important writings are those by Schmidt (1955), Medem (1969), Duellman (1978), Lancini (1979), and Dixon and Soini (1986); Almendariz (1991) offered distribution in Ecuador and Campbell and Lamar (1989) and Silva (1994) provided color photographs. See also list under the species.

Etymology: Latin *obscurus* means dark and obscure and probably alludes to the darkened head and the long black nuchal band. When describing this subspecies Jan used a darkened, large adult specimen that apparently gave the impression of an "obscurus" snake.

Micrurus spixii princeps (Pattern 44)
Bolivian Amazonian Coral Snake; Coral Amazónica Boliviana; Cobra Coral Amazonica Boliviana

Elaps princeps Boulenger, 1914; 817. (Holotype: BM 1946.1.20.44, a male from Prov. Sara, Dept. Santa Cruz de la Sierra, Bolivia, collected by José Steinbach in 1904.)
Micrurus spixii princeps: Schmidt, 1953b: 175.

Range: Intermediate altitude humid forest, also forest altered by humans, including plantations in the Amazon region and in valleys of the eastern Andes of Bolivia, from 500 to 1,200 m above sea level.

Description: Males have 214 to 224 (218.9) and females have 215 to 227 (221.1) ventrals; subcaudals 19 to 24 (21.8) in males and 19 to 23 (21.2) in females; 1+1 or 1+2 temporals. Most specimens have several undivided subcaudals. Examined: 26 males and 17 females, including the holotype.

The head is light except for the poorly defined frontal band and a few small black spots on other head shields. The black nuchal band is short and barely reaches the tips of the parietals. The black bands are 3 to 6 dorsals and 2 to 4 ventrals long, shorter than the white bands. The latter, white or yellow, are 5 to 7 dorsals and 5 to 8 ventrals long, with black tips. The red bands are the longest, encompassing 7 to 12 dorsals and 8 to 13 ventrals; they are usually immaculate. The triads continue onto the tail.

The males have 6 to 8 (7.1) and the females also have 6 to 8 (6.9) complete triads on the body and usually ⅔ on the tail in both sexes. In this subspecies the first body triad is partly complete, so that the triad formula is usually 6 + ⅔ or 7 + ⅔.

Remarks: This subspecies appears to live in a higher and drier environment than the other subspecies. It intergrades with *M. s. obscurus* in western Bolivia and with *M. s. spixii* along the Brazil-Bolivia border. At least 33 specimens of the total of 43 specimens known in the museums were collected by José Steinbach, who for several years collected and distributed them to several European and American museums.

Food: Active teiid lizards.

References: Only Schmidt (1953b) and Kempff-Mercado (1975) offered some data on this little-known coral snake.

Etymology: In Latin *princeps* means distinguished, the chief or most distinguished, probably referring to the unusual coloration of this subspecies.

Micrurus spurrelli (Map 37, Pattern 47)
Butterfly-head Coral Snake (Colombian Coral Snake); Coral Cabeza Mariposa

Elaps spurrelli Boulenger, 1914: 817. (Holotype: BM 1946.1.17.19, a female from Peña Lisa, Condoto River, Colombia, collected by H. G. F. Spurrell.)
Micrurus nicefori Schmidt, 1955: 346. (Holotype: MLS 571, a male from "Villavicencio, Cundinamarca, Colombia" (probably error) collected by Nicéforo María in 1937.)
Micrurus spurrelli: Roze, 1967: 43.

Distribution and range: Lowland and low altitude rain forest of the Pacific side of the Chocó region in western Colombia, from sea level to about 400 m. A questionable report also from the llanos savanna region of Villavicencio, east of the Andes of Colombia.

Definition: A light (red?) and black coral snake, with two irregular light (red?) head crossbands—one on the prefrontal region and the other on the posterior part of the parietals—and sinuously-irregular black frontal-supraocular band somewhat resembling the shape of the butterfly. The body is covered by alternating light (red?) and black bands. The light bands have moderate to heavy black tips and they are shorter than the black bands. The color of the light bands in live specimens is unknown but it could be red. Red bands seem to be on the tail.

Description: Males have 234 to 241 (236.7) and females have 252 to 267 (259.5) ventrals; subcaudals 35 to 37 (36.3) in males and 26 to 30 (28.0) in females, usually 1+1 temporals. Examined: 3 males and 2 females, including the holotypes.

The snout is black, followed by a light supranasal-prefrontal band and by an irregular sinuous butterfly-like black band that covers the region between eyes and the anterior part of the parietals and extends onto supralabials. It is followed by a light parietal band that includes the tips of the parietals. Below, the head is light with irregular black spots on the mental and several infralabials, as well as small black dots on the chin. The black nuchal band starts 1 to 2 dorsals behind the tips of the parietals and is 5 to 7 dorsals long, reduced or interrupted on the ventral side. The black bands are 3 to 4 dorsals and 2 to 4 ventrals long. The light (red?) bands are 2 dorsals and 2 to 3 ventrals long. Irregular black tips are present on many, but not all, light dorsals. In larger specimens the light bands can be almost completely obliterated by black so that they are almost indistinguishable. On the tail, the black bands are up to 2 times longer than the (most probably) red bands.

The males have 47 to 53 (52.2) and the females have 52 to 53 (52.5) black body bands. The males have 6 to 7 (6.2) and the females have 4 to 6 (5.0) black tail bands.

Size: This is a small species. The longest measured specimen is 633 mm long, but adults measure around 400 mm.

Remarks: This little-known species can be easily recognized by the butterflylike black spot on the head, combined with the alternating, simple black and light body bands. No one has reported on the color of the light bands that fade in preserved specimens and could be red or white. The indefatigable Colombian herpetologist, the late Brother Nicéforo María, who is said to have obtained one of the specimens of this species, has given Villavicencio as its origin. This is a doubtful locality and is probably a mislabeled specimen in the collection of the Museo de La Salle, Bogotá.

Only 5 specimens have reached museums, 4 of them from the Colombian Chocó region.

Food: Unknown.

References: In addition to the original descriptions, only Nicéforo María (1942), Roze (1967, 1970b, 1983), and Medem (1969) mention it; a full description is found in Campbell and Lamar (1989).

Etymology: *Spurrelli* is named after H. G. F. Spurrell, fellow of the Zoological Society of London, an avid collector of amphibians and reptiles in South America, including this holotype. The name *nicefori* was dedicated to the remarkable Colombian herpetologist, Brother Nicéforo María.

Description of Species and Subspecies, with Keys to the Subspecies

Micrurus steindachneri (Map 37)
Piedmont Coral Snake, Steindachner's Coral Snake; Coral de Laderas

Distribution: Eastern slopes of Andes of Ecuador and adjacent Peru.

Definition: A single-banded coral snake with a black cap and red bands partially or nearly completely obliterated by black dorsally. The males have no supraanal tubercles.

Size: This is a medium-sized coral snake. The longest specimen is 880 mm long, but adults measure between 550 and 700 mm.

Remarks: This is one of the poorly known coral snakes of the eastern slopes of the Ecuadorian Andes. Two subspecies are recognized.

References: A complete description is given in Campbell and Lamar (1989); Roze (1967, 1970b, 1983), Duellman (1979), and Miyata (1982) offered some comments; Greene and McDiarmid (1981) commented on mimicry, Almendariz (1991) on the distribution of both subspecies in Ecuador, and Tiedemann and Haupl (1980) on type specimen.

Key to the Subspecies of *M. steindachneri*

1 Males with 214 to 216 ventrals; females with 30 to 37 black body bands
    .... *M. s. orcesi* (Río Pastaza basin in Ecuador)
1' Males with 200 to 210 ventrals and females with 38 to 42 black body bands
    .... *M. s. steindachneri* (Rio Santiago system in Ecuador and Peru)

Micrurus steindachneri steindachneri
Santiago Piedmont Coral Snake; Coral Santiagueña Montuna

Elaps steindachneri Werner, 1901: 599. (Holotype: NMW 15750, a male from Ecuador).
Elaps fasslii Werner, 1927: 249. (Holotype: the same as for *E. steindachneri*, but locality given as "Colombia.")
Micrurus steindachneri steindachneri: Roze, 1967: 43.

Range: Humid and wet low and median montane formations from the valleys of Río Upano and Río Ayambis, both tributaries of Río Santiago in the eastern slopes of Andes in Ecuador and adjacent Peru, between 650 and 1100 m above sea level.

Description: Males have 200 to 210 (204.1) and females have 227 to 231 (229.0) ventrals; subcaudals 42 to 48 (44.8) in males and 35 to 38 (35.5) in females. Examined: 6 males and 2 females, including the holotype.

The black cap is in contact with the black nuchal band; the latter is about 5 dorsals long and projects forward ventrally onto the second pair of genials. The temporals are light red and brownish, with dark spots. Mental and the first infralabials are black; the rest of the chin is mottled with blackish, brownish, and yellowish spots. The black body bands are 3 to 5 dorsals and 3 to 4 ventrals long. The red bands are 3 to 4 dorsals and ventrals long. They are heavily mottled with black so that the posterior bands are almost completely black, but ventrally they are immaculate. The white body bands are ½ to 1 dorsal and ventral long. The tail is almost completely black dorsally with irregular light bands or series of transversal white spots.

The males have 28 to 38 (34.2) and the females have 38 to 42 (40.0) black body bands. On the tail, the males have 8 to 12 (9.6) and the females have 7 black bands.

Remarks: This subspecies is found in the Río Santiago basin, while thus far *M. s. orcesi* is known only from the upper Río Pastaza basin.

Food: Unknown.

References: See under the species.

Etymology: Steindachneri is named after Franz Steindachner, a noted European herpetologist and curator at the Vienna Museum at the turn of the last century. *Fassli* is named after Mr. Fassl, an Austrian who collected the type specimen.

Micrurus steindachneri orcesi (Pattern 46)
Pastaza Piedmont Coral Snake; Coral Montuna de Pastaza

Micrurus steindachneri orcesi Roze, 1967: 43. (Holotype: UMMZ 88922, a female from Meta Trail, Baños, Ecuador, 1,200 m, obtained by Clarke McIntyre.)

Range: Humid medium-high montane forests on the eastern slopes of the Andes in the upper Río Pastaza basin, Ecuador, from 1,200 to 2,000 m above sea level.

Description: Males have 214 to 216 (215.0) and females have 224 to 231 (226.8) ventrals; subcaudals 47 to 49 (48.0) in males and 29 to 33 (30.8) in females. Examined: 3 males and 5 females, including the holotype.

The black cap is occasionally reduced on the parietal tips, but it is always in contact with the black nuchal band. Below, the mental and the first infralabials are black, and there are black spots on several other shields. A black spot is usually present on the anterior part of the second pair of genials. The black nuchal band projects forward ventrally but usually does not cover the second pair of genials. The black body bands are 3 to 7 dorsals and 2 to 4 ventrals long. The red bands are usually 3 to 4 dorsals and 2 to 4 ventrals long, partially obliterated by black dorsally but immaculate ventrally. The white bands are faintly indicated by a series of transverse rows of white scales. The tail is black with faintly distinguishable, irregular white crossbands.

The males have 24 to 37 (31.1) and the females have 30 to 37 (33.5) black body bands. On the tail, the males have 7 to 9 and females have 4 to 6 black bands; at times these are difficult to distinguish.

Remarks: This is a little-known subspecies.

Food: Unknown.

References: Only the original description; see under the species, but Campbell and Lamar (1989) featured a color photograph.

Etymology: Named after Professor Gustavo Orcés-Villagomez, an Ecuadorian biologist and educator who has contributed considerably to the knowledge of snakes of Ecuador.

Micrurus stewarti (Map 35, Pattern 48)
Panamanian Coral Snake; Coral Panameña

Micrurus stewarti Barbour and Amaral, 1928: 100. (Holotype: MCZ 24924, a male from Nombre de Dios, Serranía de la Bruja, Panama, collected by Thomas H. Stewart, 1926.)

Micrurus schmidti Dunn, 1940: 119. (Holotype: ANSP 21645, a male from Valle de Antón, 50 miles west of the Canal Zone, Panama.)

Distribution and range: Low to moderate elevation tropical rain forest and humid forest in central Panama, from 500 to 1,200 m above sea level.

Definition: A coral snake with only red and black bands over the entire body and with alternating longer and shorter bands. It has a large, red parietal band and the black nuchal band is 1 to 2 dorsals behind the parietals. The scales of the red bands have large black tips. Males have supraanal tubercles and females have weak keels or small tubercles.

Description: Males have 200 to 207 (204.5) and females have 224 to 228 (255.3) ventrals; subcaudals 50 to 55 (52.5) in males and 36 to 40 (38.3) in females; temporals usually 1+1. Examined: 4 males and 4 females, including the holotypes.

The snout is black to the frontal, followed by a parietal red band that covers the temporals and supralabials and extends beyond the tips of the parietals. Below, the head is predominantly red, including the genials, except for small black spots on the mental and the first two infralabials and a few black smudges on some other shields. The nuchal black bands are 12 to 16 dorsals and ventrals long and does not reach the parietals. The body is covered with red and black bands. The latter are usually of unequal size: alternating longer and shorter bands. The longer black bands are 8 to 14 dorsals and 7 to 12 ventrals long. The shorter black bands are 2 to 4 dorsals shorter and are usually reduced on the ventral side. The red bands are 2 to 4 dorsals and 3 to 6 ventrals long, with large, irregular black tips that are heavier and more conspicuous around each second black band. Red and black bands also alternate on the tail.

The males have 13 to 25 (18.2) and the females have around 21 black body bands. On the tail, the males have 3 to 5 (3.5) and the females 3 to 4 (3.5) black bands.

Size: This is a medium-large coral snake. The longest measured specimen is 833 mm long, but the average size is between 500 and 700 mm.

Remarks: This species can be easily recognized by the alternating black and red body bands; the black bands are much longer than the red bands, and the red scales have heavy black tips and spots. This coloration apparently has been produced by the invasion of black on the red bands. This is why the black bands are of unequal length. On both sides of a black band that occupies the position of an original red band, the black tips on the red are much heavier, somewhat blurring the clear distinction between red and black bands. The original black bands have clearly marked anterior and posterior borders.

This is a rare species: only 8 specimens have reached museums and nothing is known about its way of life.

Food: Unknown.

References: Brief comments by Schmidt (1933b), Dunn and Bailey (1939), Clark (1942), Evans (1947), Grocott and Sadler (1958), Smith (1958), Roze (1967, 1970b, 1983), Savage and Vial (1974), and Villa et al. (1988). Notes on mimicry are in Greene and McDiarmid (1981) and a complete description is in Campbell and Lamar (1989).

Etymology: Named after Thomas H. Stewart, collector of the holotype. The other name is dedicated to Karl P. Schmidt, one of the great American herpetologists and ecologists of the first half of this century, who had a special interest in coral snakes.

Micrurus stuarti (Map 35)
Volcano Coral Snake (Stuart's Coral Snake); Coral de los Volcanes

Micrurus stuarti Roze, 1967: 47. (Holotype: UMMZ 106708, a male from Finca La Paz, San Marcos, Guatemala, 1345 meters, obtained by L. C. Stuart.)

Distribution and range: At moderate elevations in humid montane and cloud forest altered by humans in southwestern Guatemala, from 800 to 1,600 m above sea level.

Definition: A single-banded coral snake with a black snout and large, yellow parietal crossband. The nuchal black band covers the tips of the parietals and the red body bands have scales with large, irregular black tips. Males have supraanal tubercles.

Description: Males have 210 to 215 (212.5) and females have 224 to 231 (226.7) ventrals; subcaudals 45 to 49 (47.0) in males and 37 to 39 (37.7) in females; invariably 1+2 temporals. Examined: 2 males and 3 females, including the holotype.

The snout is black, as are part of the frontal and the supraoculars. This is followed by a yellow or yellowish-brown parietal band that extends below onto the chin. The throat is mostly spotted grayish black. The nuchal black band extends to the parietals and is 6 to 8 dorsals long. The black body bands are 3 to 5 dorsals and 3 to 4 ventrals long. They are bordered by poorly developed whitish or sepia-whitish bands about 1 scale long dorsally and ventrally. The red bands are 8 to 15 dorsals long with large, irregular black tips on the scales, which are almost spots. Ventrally, the red bands are practically immaculate. The black bands on the tail are more than twice as long as the light bands. The latter also have large, black-tipped scales or spots.

The males have 13 to 14 (13.5) and the females have 16 to 19 (17.5) black body bands. On the tail, the males have 4 and the females have 3 to 4 (3.4) black bands.

Size: The largest specimen of this medium-sized coral snake is 745 mm long.

Remarks: Only 5 specimens are known to exist.

Food: Unknown.

References: Mentioned by Roze (1967, 1970b, 1983) and Villa et al. (1988), Campbell and Vannini (1989), and a complete description is in Campbell and Lamar (1989).

Etymology: Named after Laurence C. Stuart, the late biologist from the University of Michigan, whose contributions to the natural history of Guatemala and Central America are among the best for any Latin American country.

Micrurus surinamensis (Fig. 61, Map 38)
Aquatic Coral Snake; Coral de Agua; Cobra Coral Aquatica

Distribution: The Guianas, Orinoco, and Amazonian drainages in southern Colombia and Venezuela, Brazil from Amapá, Pará, and Roraima to Rondônia and Acre, and eastern Ecuador, Peru, and northern Bolivia.

Definition: A triad-type coral snake with the first triad complete and the upper head shields red, outlined by black borders. The frontal is narrower than the supraoculars and only one supralabial is in contact with the eye. The head is somewhat flattened with the nasal openings and eyes directed partially upwards. These are adaptations to its semiaquatic and aquatic life style.

Size: This is a large species. The longest specimen reported by Silva (1994) is 1350 mm long. Many adults measure between 600 and 900 mm.

Remarks: This wetland and river-dwelling coral snake can be easily recognized by its large and somewhat flattened head covered by red shields outlined by black. It is the only species in which only the fourth supralabial is in contact with the eye.

The story of this species and its description is interesting. It is the only coral snake whose original description is based not on a specimen, but apparently on a picture that appeared in the magnificent old treatise on nature by Seba in 1735 (Fig. 61), 82 years before its scientific description by Cuvier (1817). Even the type locality was not known but implied in the name given by Cuvier as Suriname, which apparently is correct.

Figure 61. Seba's plate of *Micrurus surinamensis*, possibly from Suriname, serving as lectotype of this species.

The aquatic coral snake apparently serves as a mimicry model imitated by several species of false aquatic coral snakes including *Hydrops*, *Helicops* and *Hydrodynastes*.

References: Many writings have been published; the three most complete descriptions are by Schmidt (1952), Campbell and Lamar (1989) and Silva (1994). Other general notes are by Amaral (1925b), Schmidt (1936a), Roze (1967, 1970b, 1983), Cendrero et al. (1972), and Hoogmoed (1979); for Bolivia by Griffin (1916) and Kempff-Mercado (1975); for Brazil those by Amaral (1930b, 1948b, 1978), Machado (1945), Prado (1945), P. Müller (1975), Cuhna and Nascimento (1973, 1978, 1982a), Hoge and Romano (1973, 1981), Hoge et al. (1973), Santos (1981), Cunha et al. (1985), Zimmerman and Rodrigues (1990), and Roze and da Silva (1990); for Colombia those by Nicéforo María (1942), Dunn (1944a), Daniel (1949), Schmidt (1955), Medem (1969), Silva and Rodríguez (1985), and Pérez-Santos and Moreno (1986, 1988); for Ecuador those by Orcés (1943, 1948), J. A. Peters (1960), Duellman (1978), Miyata (1982), and Almendarez (1991); for French Guiana those by Chippaux (1987); for Peru those by Barbour and Noble (1920), Prado and Hoge (1948), Meneses (1974a), Soini (1974b), Carrillo de Espinoza (1983), Dixon and Soini (1986), and Rodríguez and Cadle (1990); for Suriname those by Brongersma (1967), Moonen et al. (1978), Abuys (1987b); and for Venezuela those by Mila de la Roca (1932), Veillard (1941), Roze (1954, 1955, 1957, 1966a, 1987), Vetencourt Finol (1960), Hoge and Lancini (1962), Lancini (1970, 1979), and Sandner-Montilla (1975, 1985). Roux-Estève (1983) and Hoogmoed and Gruber (1983) dealt with some type specimens and Gutiérrez et al. (1988) with karyotypes. Earlier significant references include Gray (1829) and Jan (1859a, 1959b) and Cope (1859, 1876b).

Key to the Subspecies of *M. surinamensis*

1   156 to 174 ventrals in males and 170 to 187 in females
 . . . .*M. s. surinamensis* (Guianas and Amazon region of South America)
1' 182 to 193 ventrals in males and 197 to 206 in females
 . . . . *M. s. nattereri* (southern Venezuela and adjacent Brazil and Colombia)

Micrurus surinamensis surinamensis (Fig. 61, Color 57, 58)

Amazonian Aquatic Coral Snake; Coral de Agua Amazónica; Cobra Coral Aquatica Amazonica

Elaps surinamensis Cuvier, 1817: 84. (Picture of Seba, 1732, Fig. 61, from Suriname; holotype: lectotype MNHN 3926, a male from Suriname, collected by Levaillant, designated as lectotype by Schmidt, 1952.)
Micrurus surinamensis surinamensis: Schmidt, 1952: 29.

Range: Lowland tropical rain forest and humid forests in or near rivers and other waters in the Amazon region and southern Orinoco drainage in northern and central South America, including southern Colombia to Villavicencio, and the Amazon region of eastern Ecuador and Peru to northern Bolivia, and in Brazil from Amapá, Pará, Maranhão, and Roraima to Mato Grosso, Amazonia, Rondônia, and Acre; also Guyana, Suriname, and French Guiana, from sea level to about 500 m.

Description: Males have 156 to 174 (165.1) and females have 170 to 187 (177.5) ventrals; subcaudals 33 to 38 (35.5) in males and 31 to 34 (32.1) in females. Temporals 1+1 or 1+2. Large males occasionally have a few supra-anal tubercles. Examined: 34 males and 27 females, including the holotype.

The red shields are outlined by black that is particularly concentrated on the posterior border of the head shields. Below, the head is also red with a few black spots and borders on some shields. The first triad is complete and the first black band is in contact with or covers the tips of the parietals. The central black band of a triad is 2 or more times longer than the outer bands and with somewhat-roundish anterior and posterior borders, which makes them shorter ventrally than dorsally. The central black bands are 5 to 7 dorsals and 3 to 6 ventrals long. The yellowish or creamy-white bands within a triad are 1 to 2 dorsals and 2 to 4 ventrals long. Dorsally, they are immaculate, but larger specimens have blackish tips or irregular blackish borders, except the first dorsal row. The red bands are usually longer than the black central bands, about 7 to 13 dorsals and ventrals long, with irregular black tips or small spots on dorsals. Triads also continue on the tail, but the anal is usually in the middle of the last triad of the body, making it incomplete or split between the body and the tail.

The males have 5 to 8 (6.2), usually 5 to 7, and the females have 6 to 8 (6.9) complete triads on the body. As the anal plate splits a triad, the actual number of body and tail triads would be 6 ⅔ + ⅓ 1. Both sexes have ⅔ to 1⅓ triads on the tail.

Remarks: This subspecies is found throughout the entire Amazon region.

Food: In concordance with its aquatic lifestyle, it feeds on several species of bony fishes and eels, such as Sarapo or Carapo (*Gymnotus carapo*), a species of knife fish, Tamuata (*Callichthys callichthys*), an armored catfish, (*Synbranchus marmoratus*), a swamp eel, and other species.

Apparently, even the newly hatched of the Amazonian Aquatic Coral Snake (*M. surinamensis*) start hunting for small fishes very soon after birth. In Peru, I found remnants of fish bones in the stomach of a 266 mm long coral snake from Quistococha, near Iquitos (see also chapter on Food).

References: See under species; color photos by Campbell and Lamar (1989) and Silva (1994).

Etymology: *Surinamensis* in Latin is dweller or inhabitant of Suriname.

Micrurus surinamensis nattereri
Venezuelan Aquatic Coral Snake; Coral de Agua Venezolana; Cobra Coral Aquatica Venezuelana

Micrurus surinamensis nattereri Schmidt, 1952: 27. (Holotype: SMF 20708, a female from between Guaramoca and San Fernando, Venezuela [corrected to "Guaramaco and San Fernando de Atabapo in Upper Orinoco," Venezuela, by Hoge and Lancini, [1960], collected by G. Hübner in 1895.)

Range: In or around rivers, lakes, streams, and swampy areas in lowland tropical rain forest and humid forest in upper Orinoco and Río Negro basin in southern Venezuela and adjacent Brazil and Colombia, from 50 to 250 m above sea level.

Description: Males have 186 to 193 (190.0) and females have 197 to 206 (202.2) ventrals; subcaudals 38 to 40 (39.2) in males and 37 to 38 (37.6) in females. Examined: 7 males and 3 females, including the holotype.
   The red head shields are outlined by black and the first black band of the first triad covers part of the parietals. The central black band of a triad is 2 to 3 times longer than the outer black bands, but shorter than the red bands that separate the triads. The black central band is 6 to 8 dorsals and 4 to 5 ventrals long. The outer black bands are 2 to 3 dorsals and ventrals long. The red bands are 8 to 10 dorsals and ventrals long with black tips or irregular black spots. The creamy white bands are about 2 dorsals and 4 to 5 ventrals long, usually immaculate or with faint dark borders.
   The males have 6 to 8 (6.3) and the females have 6 to 8 (7.7) complete triads on the body, plus ⅓ of the following triad. On the tail, the triads vary from ⅔ 1 to ⅔ 1 ⅔ in both sexes.

Remarks: A little-known subspecies, similar to the much better-known Amazonian aquatic coral snake.

Food: Swamp eel (*Synbranchus marmoratus*) and probably other fishes.

References: Roze (1955, 1966a, 1987), Hoge and Lancini (1960, 1962), Vetencourt Finol (1960), and Lancini (1970, 1979) provided data on variation, distribution, and some pictures; color photo was given in Campbell and Lamar (1989).

Etymology: Named after Johann Natterer, a German ornithologist and active traveler, who collected zoological specimens in the Río Negro region in the last century.

Micrurus tschudii (Map 32)
Desert Coral Snake; Coral del Desierto

Distribution: Pacific slopes from southern Ecuador to southern Peru; probably also in northwestern Bolivia.

Definition: A triad-type coral snake with the first triad complete and the black head crossed by an irregular, frontoparietal red band. The first black band of the first triad covers the posterior part of the parietals. The black bands are usually as long as or longer than the white or yellow and red bands.

Size: This is a small coral snake. The longest measured specimen is 730 mm long, but many adults measure between 350 and 500 mm.

Remarks: This species can be recognized by the black head with red crossband and by the fact that the first black band of the first triad partially covers the head. Some of its morphological features make this species rather unique among coral snakes. Due to its short and numerous black, red, and white or yellow bands, it looks like a crawling ribbon or belt. Two subspecies are recognized.

References: Schmidt (1936a) recognized the subspecies, Greene and McDiarmid (1981) dealt with mimicry, and Campbell and Lamar (1989) offered a complete description. Other general references are by Amaral (1925b), and Roze (1967, 1970b, 1983), while Kempff-Mercado (1975) mentioned it for Bolivia (a doubtful possibility). H. W. Parker (1938), Orcés (1948), J. A. Peters (1960), and Miyata (1982) mentioned it for Ecuador and Schmidt and Schmidt (1925), Schmidt and Walker (1943b), Meneses (1974a, 1974b), and Carrillo de Espinoza (1977, 1983) mentioned it for Peru. Earlier significant references include Cope (1876b, 1877) for Peru.

Key for the Subspecies of *M. tschudii*

1 Snout usually with light spots; males with 10 to 12 and females with 10 to 13 triads; head below all light or with few black dots
   .... *M. tschudii olssoni* (northwestern Peru and southern Ecuador)

1' Snout usually black; males with 13 to 20 and females usually 14 to 22, rarely 13, triads; head below black or with large black spots
.... *M. t. tschudii* (western Peru and possibly northern Bolivia)

Micrurus tschudii tschudii (Color 59, Pattern 49A)
Southern Desert Coral Snake; Coral Sureña del Desierto

Elaps tschudii Jan, 1858: 524. (Holotype: unknown, originally in Vienna Museum from Peru; apparently lost.)
Micrurus tschudii tschudii: Schmidt, 1936a: 202.

Range: Desert and dry coastal valleys in western Peru and, probably, in northwestern Bolivia, from sea level to 400 m above sea level.

Description: Males have 188 to 213 (207.1) and females have 206 to 224 (214.3) ventrals; subcaudals 27 to 33 (30.0) in males and 25 to 31 (27.8) in females; occasional subcaudals are undivided; 1+1 temporals. Examined: 29 males and 24 females.

The head is all black with a red frontoparietal crossband. Most infralabials and genials are also black or black with some light borders. The first black band of the first triad covers half of the parietals and the first 2 to 3 dorsals; it is usually complete below. The black bands are of equal length, or the central black band is longer than the outer ones; they are usually 3 to 5 dorsals and ventrals long. The white or yellow bands are 2 to 3 dorsals and ventrals long, with or without black tips. The red bands are also usually shorter than the black bands, frequently with black tips. Ventrally, the red and white bands are immaculate. Triads also continue onto the tail.

The males have 13 to 20 (15.6) and the females have 14 to 22 (15.9), rarely 13, black triads on the body. On the tail, the males have 1⅓ to 2⅓ and the females have 1 to 2 black triads.

Remarks: This subspecies intergrades with *M. t. olssoni* in northern Peru.

Food: Limbless amphisbaenid lizards (*Amphisbaena occidentalis*); sand frequently found in empty stomachs.

References: See under species; color photo by Campbell and Lamar (1989).

Etymology: Named after the Swiss zoologist J. J. von Tschudi who in earlier times made considerable contributions to the natural history of Peru in middle of the 19th century.

Micrurus tschudii olssoni (Pattern 49B)
Northern Desert Coral Snake; Coral Norteña del Desierto

Micrurus olssoni Schmidt and Schmidt, 1925: 130 (Holotype: FMNH 5724, a male from Negritos, Piura, Peru, collected by Axel A. Olsson in July 1923.)
Micrurus tschudii olssoni: Schmidt, 1936a: 202.

Range: Desert and dry valleys on the Pacific side in southern Ecuador and northwestern Peru, from sea level to 1,500 m.

Description: Males have 187 to 203 (194.8) and females have 197 to 209 (201.9) ventrals; subcaudals 24 to 30 (26.8) in males and 25 to 29 (26.4) in females; occasional subcaudals are undivided; 1+1 temporals. Examined: 26 males and 22 females, including the holotype.

The snout is black with light spots. After the red frontoparietal band, the head is black, but this band is frequently interrupted below. The chin is all light, whitish yellowish or light pink, and immaculate or with few small black spots on some shields. The central black band is as long as or a little longer than the outer bands, 3 to 5 dorsals and ventrals long. The white or yellow bands are 2 to 4 dorsals and ventrals long and immaculate or with a few black tips. The red bands are 3 to 5 dorsals and ventrals long, usually as long as the black bands. The triads also continue on the tail.

The males have 10 to 12 (11.3) and the females have 10 to 13 (11.7) triads on the body. On the tail, both sexes have 1⅓ to 2 triads.

Remarks: This subspecies seems to be of a larger size than the previous subspecies and the population from the Catamayo Valley might turn out to be different from this subspecies. Catamayo in Ecuador is one of the biologically most interesting areas in South America. In northern Peru this subspecies intergrades with *M. t. tschudii*.

Food: Known to feed on gekko lizards (*Phyllodactylus*); sand also found in the stomach of several specimens.

References: Except for brief notes on distribution and variation by Schmidt (1936a) and H. W. Parker (1938) and its distribution in Ecuador by Almendariz (1991) in Ecuador, little else has been reported on this subspecies; color photo provided by Campbell and Lamar (1989).

Etymology: Named after Axel A. Olsson, collector of the holotype and member of the Field Museum of Natural History, Chicago, United States.

Chapter 16
Distribution by Countries

This chapter offers a list of species and subspecies of coral snakes found in every country, with their distribution.

The most updated publication on *The Venomous Reptiles of Latin America* (1989) by Jonathan Campbell and William Lamar includes a wealth of information on coral snakes and their distribution. It must be consulted by anybody seriously interested in the venomous reptiles of Latin America. In addition to descriptions of species, it includes a thorough review of ecological distribution and ecological maps for Latin America.

A significant overall publication on Latin American snakes was authored by James Peters and Braulio Orejas Miranda, *Catalogue of Neotropical Squamata* (1970), Part I Snakes. I contributed the section on coral snakes, genus *Micrurus*, with keys for their identification. This publication was updated with a supplement by Paulo Vanzolini (1988). A summary of New World coral snakes with checklists and biology appeared in two of my earlier publications (Roze, 1967, 1983), which served as background papers for this book. A useful checklist and key for identification of coral snakes is included in the book *Checklist and Keys to the Terrestrial Proteroglyphs of the World* by the Swiss herpetologist Philipe Golay (1985) and in an earlier book by the German herpetologist Konrad Klemmer (1963), *Liste der rezenten Giftschlangen: Elapidae, Hydropheidae, Viperidae und Crotalidae*. I did not include these publications under every species, but they mention most of the species dealt with here.

World checklists of snakes that include coral snakes are also found in the publication by Harding and Welch (1980) and in *Poisonous Snakes of the World*, a manual for the Department of Navy from the pens of Herndon Dowling, Sherman Minton, and Findlay Russell (1979), three well-known American scientists. This manual includes the most dangerous coral snakes and medical aspects of snakebites. Earlier checklists include those by Brazilians Afranio do Amaral (1930c), Alphonse Hoge and Alma Romano (1971a), and several more.

By far the most important contributions are those by Karl Schmidt. In about 30 years of active research he "rescued" coral snakes from earlier taxonomic confusions and systematically proceeded to survey, update, and describe many new coral snakes. Among his most significant papers are several Preliminary Accounts (1933a, 1936a), notes on the New World coral snakes (1936b), and several more papers mentioned under the appropriate species descriptions.

Distribution of Species by Countries

North America

United States
Micruroides euryxanthus euryxanthus	Southern Arizona and New Mexico, doubtfully in Texas (also in Mexico).
M. fulvius fulvius	Southern United States, North Carolina to Florida and Louisiana.
M. fulvius tenere	Southern United States in Louisiana, Arkansas, and Texas (also in Mexico).

Mexico
Micruroides euryxanthus euryxanthus	Northwestern Mexico (also in the United States)
M. euryxanthus australis	Southern Chihuahua and Sonora.
M. euryxanthus neglectus	Sinaloa.
Micrurus bernadi	Central-eastern Mexico.
M. bogerti	Southern Oaxaca.
M. browni browni	Central plateau to Chiapas (also in Guatemala).
M. browni taylori	Around Acapulco.
M. diastema diastema	Puebla, Veracruz.
M. diastema affinis	Northern Oaxaca.

M. diastema alienus	Yucatán.
M. diastema apiatus	Probably eastern Chiapas (also in Guatemala).
M. diastema macdougalli	Central Oaxaca.
M. diastema sapperi	Southeastern Mexico (also in Guatemala and Belize).
M. distans distans	Northwestern Mexico.
M. distans michoacanensis	Michoacán, Guerrero.
M. distans oliveri	Colima, Jalisco.
M. distans zweifeli	Nayarit.
M. elegans elegans	Veracruz, Oaxaca.
M. elegans veraepacis	Tabasco, Chiapas (also in Guatemala).
M. ephippifer ephippifer	Southeastern Oaxaca.
M. ephippifer zapotecus	Central Oaxaca.
M. fulvius fitzingeri	Central plateau.
M. fulvius maculatus	Tampico.
M. fulvius microgalbineus	Northwestern Mexico.
M. fulvius tenere	Northeastern and central Mexico (also in United States).
M. laticollaris laticollaris	Southern Mexico.
M. laticollaris maculirostris	Colima, Jalisco.
M. latifasciatus	Oaxaca, Chiapas (also in Guatemala).
M. limbatus limbatus	San Martín region, Los Tuxtla, Veracruz.
M. limbatus spilosomus	Santa Marta region, Los Tuxtla, Veracruz.
M. nebularis	Central Oaxaca.
M. nigrocinctus zunilensis	Southern Chiapas (also in Guatemala, El Salvador, Honduras).
M. proximans	Nayarit.

Central America

Belize
M. diastema sapperi	Entire country (also in Mexico).
M. hippocrepis	Entire country (also in Guatemala).
M. nigrocinctus divaricatus	Southeastern region (also in Honduras and Nicaragua).

Guatemala
M. browni browni	Western Guatemala (also in Mexico).
M. browni importunus	Antigua Basin.
M. diastema apiatus	Central Guatemala (also in Mexico).
M. diastema sapperi	Lowlands of northern Guatemala (also in Mexico and Belize).
M. elegans veraepacis	Alta Verapaz (also in Mexico).
M. hippocrepis	Eastern Guatemala (also in Belize).
M. latifasciatus	Southwestern Guatemala (also in Mexico).
M. nigrocinctus zunilensis	Pacific slopes in southern Guatemala (also in Mexico, El Salvador, and Honduras).
M. stuarti	Volcán Santa Clara region.

Honduras
M. alleni	Eastern Honduras (also in Nicaragua, Costa Rica and Panama)
M. browni browni(?)	Western Honduras (also in Mexico and Guatemala)
M. diastema aglaeope	Northern Honduras.
M. nigrocinctus zunilensis	Southern Honduras (also in Guatemala, El Salvador, and Mexico).
M. nigrocinctus divaricatus	Northwestern Honduras (also in Nicaragua and Belize).
M. ruatanus	Roatán Island.

El Salvador
M. nigrocinctus zunilensis	Entire country (also in Guatemala Mexico, and Honduras).

Nicaragua
M. alleni	Eastern Nicaragua (also in Costa Rica and Panama).
M. multifasciatus hertwigi	Eastern Nicaragua (also in Costa Rica and Panama).
M. nigrocinctus nigrocinctus	Western Nicaragua (also in Costa Rica, Panama, and Colombia).

Distribution by Countries

M. nigrocinctus babaspul	Corn Island
M. nigrocintus mosquitensis	Eastern Nicaragua (also in Costa Rica and Panama).

Costa Rica
M. alleni	Northwestern and eastern Costa Rica (also in Nicaragua and Panama).
M. clarki	Border with Panama (also in Panama).
M. multifasciatus hertwigi	Atlantic side of Costa Rica (also in Nicaragua and Panama)
M. nigrocinctus nigrocinctus	Pacific Side of Costa Rica, also in Nicaragua, Panama, and Colombia).
M. nigrocinctus mosquitensis	Atlantic side of Costa Rica (also in Nicaragua and Panama).

Panama
M. alleni	Western Panama (also in Costa Rica and Nicaragua).
M. ancoralis jani	Eastern Panama (also in Colombia).
M. clarki	Western and central Panama (also in Costa Rica).
M. dissoleucus dunni	Eastern Panama.
M. mipartitus mipartitus	Eastern Panama (also in Colombia).
M. multifasciatus multifasciatus	Central Panama.
M. multifasciatus hertwigi	Northwestern Panama (also in Costa Rica and Nicaragua).
M. nigrocinctus nigrocinctus	Entire country (also in Costa Rica, Nicaragua, and Colombia).
M. nigrocinctus coibensis	Isla Coiba.
M. nigrocinctus mosquitensis	Northwestern Panama (also in Costa Rica and Nicaragua).
M. stewarti	Central Panama.

South America

Colombia
Leptomicrurus narduccii melanotus	Southern Colombia (also in Brazil, Peru, and Ecuador).
L. scutiventris	Southern Colombia (also in Brazil, Peru and Ecuador).
Micrurus ancoralis jani	Pacific side (also in Panama and probably in Ecuador).
M. dissoleucus dissoleucus	Northeastern Colombia (also in Venezuela).
M. dissoleucus melanogenys	Santa Marta region.
M. dissoleucus nigrirostris	Northern Colombia.
M. dumerilii dumerilii	Northern Colombia.
M. dumerilii antioquiensis	Andes of Colombia.
M. dumerilii colombianus	Santa Marta region.
M. dumerilii transandinus	Western Colombia (also in Ecuador and Panama).
M. filiformis	Southeastern Colombia (also in Brazil and Peru).
M. hemprichii ortoni	Southern Colombia (also in Bolivia, Peru, and Ecuador).
M. isozonus	Eastern Colombia (also in Venezuela and Brazil).
M. langsdorffi	Southern Colombia (also in Ecuador, Peru, and Brazil).
M. lemniscatus helleri	Southern Colombia (also in Brazil, Ecuador, Peru, Bolivia, and Venezuela).
M. medemi	Around Villavicencio, Colombia.
M. mipartitus mipartitus	Northwestern Colombia (also in Panama).
M. mipartitus anomalus	Northern Colombia (also in Venezuela).
M. mipartitus decussatus	Andes of Colombia (also in Ecuador and Peru).
M. mipartitus popayanensis	Andes of Colombia
M. multiscutatus	Andes of Colombia.
M. nigrocinctus nigrocinctus	Northern Colombia (also in Panama, Costa Rica, and Nicaragua).
M. putumayensis	Southern Colombia (also in Peru and Brazil).
M. remotus	Eastern Colombia (also in Venezuela and Brazil).
M. sangilensis	Northeastern Colombia.
M. spixii obscurus	Southern Colombia (also in Venezuela, Ecuador, Peru, and Brazil).
M. spurrelli	Western Colombia.
M. surinamensis surinamensis	Southern Colombia (also in Ecuador, Peru, Brazil, and the Guianas).
M. surinamensis nattereri	Vaupés (also in Venezuela and Brazil).

Venezuela
Leptomicrurus collaris breviventris	Southeastern Venezuela (also in Guyana).
M. circinalis	Northeastern Venezuela (also in Trinidad).

M. dissoleucus dissoleucus	Northern Venezuela (also in Colombia).
Micrurus dumerilii carinicauda	Northwestern Venezuela (also in Colombia).
M. dumerilii venezuelensis	North-central Venezuela.
M. hemprichii hemprichii	Southern Venezuela (also in the Guianas and Brazil).
M. isozonus	Northern Venezuela (also in Colombia and Brazil).
M. lemniscatus diutius	Eastern Venezuela (also in Guianas, Trinidad, and Brazil).
M. lemniscatus helleri	Southern Venezuela (also in Brazil, Colombia, Ecuador, Peru, and Bolivia).
M. meridensis	Andes of Mérida.
M. mipartitus anomalus	Andes of Mérida (also in Colombia).
M. mipartitus semipartitus	Northern Venezuela.
M. psyches	Southeastern Venezuela (also in the Guianas).
M. remotus	Venezuelan Amazonia (also in Brazil and Colombia).
M. spixii obscurus	Venezuelan Amazonia (also in Colombia, Ecuador, Peru, and Brazil).
M. surinamensis nattereri	Venezuelan Amazonia (also in Brazil and Colombia).

Trinidad

Micrurus lemniscatus diutius	Entire island (also in Venezuela, the Guianas, and Brazil).
M. circinalis	Entire island (also in Venezuela).

Guyana

Leptomicrurus collaris collaris	Southern Guyana (also in Suriname, French Guiana, and Brazil).
L. collaris breviventris	Northeastern region (also in Venezuela).
Micrurus averyi	Southern region (also in Brazil).
M. hemprichii hemprichii	Most of the country (also in Venezuela, Suriname, French Guiana, and Brazil).
M. lemniscatus lemniscatus	Northern Guyana (also in French Guiana, Suriname, and Brazil).
M. lemniscatus diutius	Southern Guyana (also in Suriname, French Guiana, and Brazil).
M. psyches	Northern Guyana (also in Venezuela, Suriname, and French Guiana).
M. surinamensis surinamensis	Central and southern Guyana (also in the Amazonian countries).

Suriname

Leptomicrurus collaris collaris	Entire country (also in Guyana, French Guiana, and Brazil).
Micrurus hemprichii hemprichii	Southern and central regions (also in Venezuela, Guyana, French Guiana, and Brazil).
M. ibiboboca	Probably in southern region.
M. lemniscatus lemniscatus	Northern and central regions (also in Guyana, French Guiana, and Brazil).
M. lemniscatus diutius	Southern Suriname (also in Trinidad, Venezuela, Guyana, French Guiana, and Brazil).
M. psyches	Entire country (also in Venezuela, Guyana, and French Guiana).
M. surinamensis surinamensis	Southern region (also in several Amazonian countries)

French Guiana

Leptomicrurus collaris collaris	Southern region (also in Guyana, Suriname, and Brazil).
Micrurus hemprichii hemprichii	Northern and central region (also in Venezuela, Guyana, Suriname, and Brazil).
M. lemniscatus lemniscatus	Northern and central region (also in Guyana, Suriname, and Brazil).
M. lemniscatus diutius	Southern region (also in Trinidad, Venezuela, Guyana, Suriname, and Brazil).
M. psyches	Entire country (also in Guyana, Venezuela, and Suriname).
M. surinamensis surinamensis	Entire country (also in other Amazonian countries).

Brazil

Leptomicrurus collaris collaris	Probably western Pará (also in Guyana, Suriname, and French Guiana).
L. narduccii melanotus	Western Brazil (also in Colombia, Ecuador, and Peru).
L. scutiventris	Northwestern Brazil (also in Ecuador, Peru, and Colombia).
Micrurus albicinctus	Rondônia, Brazil.
M. annellatus bolivianus	Probably near Bolivian border (also in Bolivia).
M. averyi	Central Amazon (also in Guyana).
M. corallinus	Southern Brazil (also in Paraguay, Argentina, and Uruguay).
M. decoratus	Eastern and southeastern Brazil.

Distribution by Countries

M. filiformis	Northern Brazil (also in Colombia and Peru).
M. frontalis frontalis	Southeastern Brazil (also in Paraguay and Argentina).
M. frontalis altirostris	Southern tip of Brazil (also in Uruguay and Argentina).
M. frontalis brasiliensis	Eastern Brazil.
M. frontalis multicinctus	Southeastern Brazil.
M. hemprichii hemprichii	Northern Brazil (also in Venezuela and the Guianas).
M. hemprichii ortoni	Western Brazil (also in Colombia, Ecuador, Peru, and Bolivia).
M. hemprichii rondonianus	Rondônia
M. ibiboboca	Eastern Brazil.
M. isozonus	Roraima, northern Brazil (also in Colombia and Venezuela).
M. langsdorffi	Western Brazil (also in Colombia, Peru, and Ecuador).
M. lemniscatus lemniscatus	Northern Brazil (also in the Guianas).
M. lemniscatus carvalhoi	Eastern Brazil (possibly also in Paraguay).
M. lemniscatus diutius	Central Amazon (also in Trinidad, Venezuela, and the Guianas).
M. lemniscatus helleri	Western Brazil (also in Venezuela, Colombia, Ecuador, Peru, and Bolivia).
M. paraensis	Northern and northeastern Brazil and Rondônia.
M. putumayensis	Northwestern Brazil (also in Colombia and Peru).
M. pyrrhocryptus tricolor	Southwestern Brazil (also in Paraguay).
M. remotus	Northwestern Brazil (also in Venezuela and Colombia).
M. spixii spixii	Central Amazon.
M. spixii martiusi	Pará and Mato Grosso (also one record in Paraguay).
M. spixii obscurus	Western Brazil (also in Colombia, Venezuela, Ecuador, and Peru).
M. surinamensis surinamensis	Amazon (also in Colombia, Ecuador, Peru, Bolivia, and the Guianas).
M. surinamensis nattereri	Upper rio Negro (also in Colombia and Venezuela).

Ecuador

Leptomicrurus narducii melanotus	Amazonia and eastern slopes of Andes (Colombia, Peru, and Brazil).
L. scutiventris	Amazonian valleys of eastern slopes of Andes (also in Colombia, Peru, and Brazil).
Micrurus ancoralis ancoralis	Pacific side of the Andes.
M. annellatus annellatus	Upper Amazon and eastern slopes of the Andes (also in Peru and Bolivia).
M. bocourti	Lowland and western slopes of the Andes (also in Peru).
M. catamayensis	Catamayo valley.
M. dumerilii transandinus	Pacific lowlands and northwestern Andes of Ecuador (also in Colombia).
M. hemprichii ortoni	Upper Amazon and eastern slopes of the Andes (also in Colombia, Brazil, Peru, and Bolivia).
M. langsdorffi	Northwestern Amazon (also in Colombia, Peru, and Brazil).
M. lemniscatus helleri	Eastern slopes of the Andes and Amazon (also in Bolivia, Colombia, Peru, Brazil, and Venezuela).
M. mertensi	Southwestern Ecuador (also in Peru).
M. mipartitus decussatus	Pacific lowlands (also in Colombia and possibly Peru).
M. ornatissimus	Amazon and western slopes of Andes (possibly in Peru).
M. petersi	Eastern slopes of the Andes.
M. spixii obscurus	Amazon of eastern Ecuador (also in Colombia, Venezuela, Peru, and Brazil).
M. steindachneri steindachneri	Eastern slopes of the Andes (also in Peru).
M. steindachneri orcesi	Eastern slopes of the Andes.
M. surinamensis surinamensis	Upper Amazon (also in Colombia, Peru, Bolivia, Brazil, Guyana, Suriname, and French Guiana).
M. tschudii olsoni	Pacific side in southern Ecuador.

Peru

Leptomicrurus narducii melanotus	Amazonia side of the Andes (also in Colombia, Ecuador, and Brazil).
L. scutiventris	Upper Amazon (also in Colombia, Ecuador, and Brazil).
M. annellatus annellatus	Amazonian slopes of the Andes (also in Ecuador and Bolivia).
M. annellatus balzani	Probably at frontier with Bolivia (also in Bolivia).
M. bocourti	Northwestern Peru (also in Ecuador).
M. filiformis	Amazonian side (also in Brazil and Colombia).

M. frontifasciatus	Southeastern Peru (also in Bolivia).
M. hemprichii ortoni	Amazonian side (also in Colombia, Ecuador, and Bolivia).
M. langsdorffi	Upper Amazon (also in Colombia, Ecuador, and Brazil).
M. lemniscatus helleri	Amazonian side of the Andes (also in Bolivia, Colombia, Ecuador Brazil, and Venezuela).
M. margaritiferus	Amazonian slopes of the Andes.
M. mertensi	Pacific side (also in Ecuador).
M. mipartitus decussatus	Possibly in the Andes (also in Colombia and Ecuador).
M. ornatissimus	Probably in frontier with Ecuador (also in Ecuador).
M. peruvianus	Northern Peru.
M. putumayensis	Northern Amazonia (also in Colombia and Brazil).
M. spixii obscurus	Amazonia (also in Colombia, Venezuela, Ecuador, and Brazil).
M. steindachneri steindachneri	Eastern slopes of the Andes (also in Ecuador).
M. surinamensis surinamensis	Amazonia (also in other Amazonia countries).
M. tschudii tschudii	Pacific side (also in Ecuador and Bolivia).
M. tschudii olsoni	Northern Peru (also in Ecuador).

Bolivia

Leptomicrurus narduccii narduccii	Santa Cruz region.
M. annellatus annellatus	Northwestern region (also in Ecuador and Peru).
M. annellatus balzani	Yungas region (Probably in Peru).
M. annellatus bolivianus	Eastern Andes of Bolivia (also in Brazil).
M. diana	Prov. Chiquiticos, Santa Cruz.
M. frontifasciatus	Northern Bolivia (also in Peru).
M. hemprichii ortoni	Amazonian region (also in Colombia, Ecuador, and Peru).
M. lemniscatus helleri	Northeastern Bolivia (also in Colombia, Brazil, Ecuador, Peru, and Venezuela).
M. pyrrhocryptus pyrrhocryptus	Southeastern Bolivia (also in Argentina).
M. spixii princeps	Valleys in eastern Andes of Bolivia (also in Brazil).
M. surinamensis surinamensis	Northeastern Bolivia (also in other Amazonian countries).
M. tschudii tschudii	Northwestern Bolivia (also in Peru).

Paraguay

Micrurus corallinus	Southeastern Paraguay (also in Brazil, Uruguay, and Argentina).
M. frontalis frontalis	Central region (also in Brazil).
M. lemnicastus carvalhoi	Possibly northeastern region (also in Brazil).
M. pyrrhocryptus tricolor	Northeastern region (also in Brazil).

Argentina

Micrurus corallinus	Northern region (also in Paraguay, Brazil, and Uruguay).
M. frontalis altirostris	Probably in northeastern region (also in Uruguay).
M. frontalis baliocoryphus	Mesopotamian region of northern Argentina (also in Brazil).
M. pyrrhocryptus pyrrhocryptus	Northern and Central Argentina (also in Bolivia).

Uruguay

Micrurus corallinus	Probably in western Uruguay (also in Brazil, Argentina, and Paraguay).
M. frontalis altirostris	Entire country (also in Brazil, Argentina, and Paraguay).

MAPS

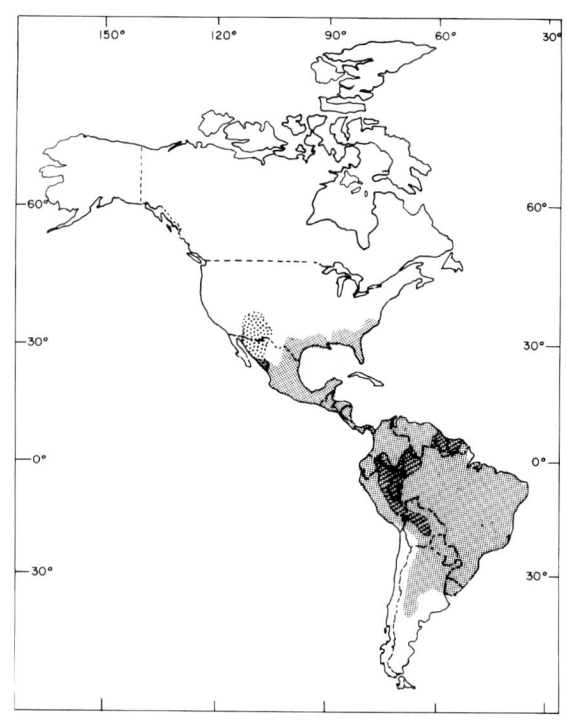

Map 1. Distribution of coral snake genera *Leptomicrurus*, *Micruroides*, and *Micrurus*.

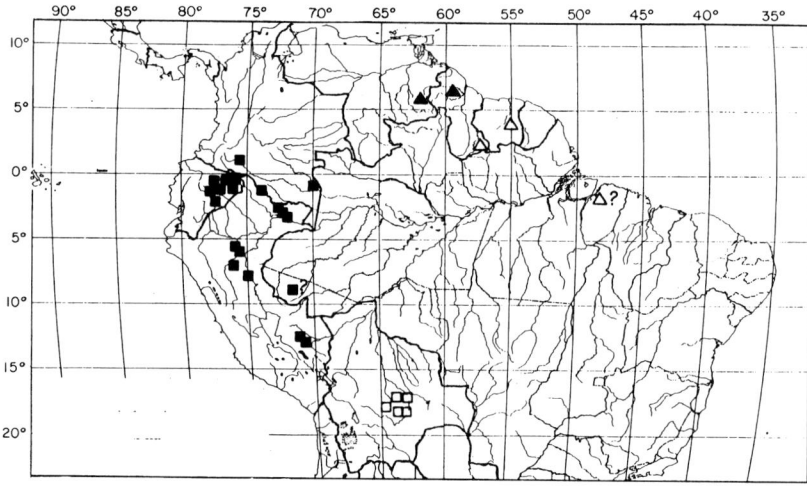

Map 2. Distribution of *Leptomicrurus collaris collaris*, *L. collaris breviventris*, *L. narduccii narduccii*, and *L. narduccii melanotus*.

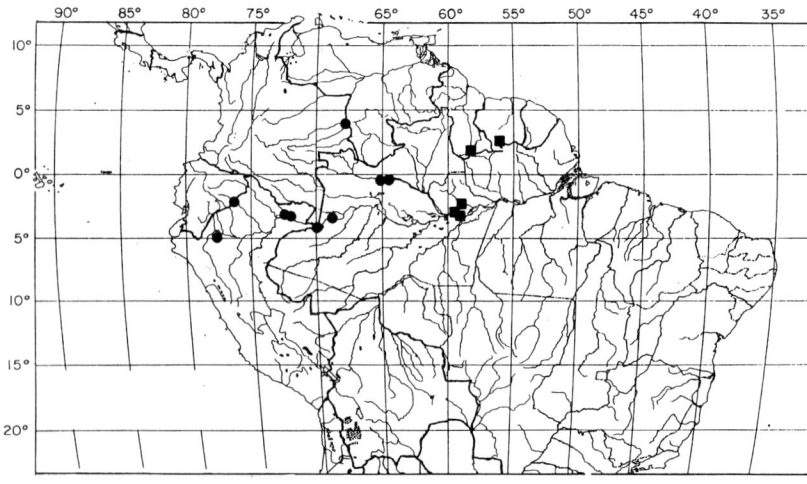

Map 3. Distribution of *Leptomicrurus scutiventris* and *Micrurus averyi*.

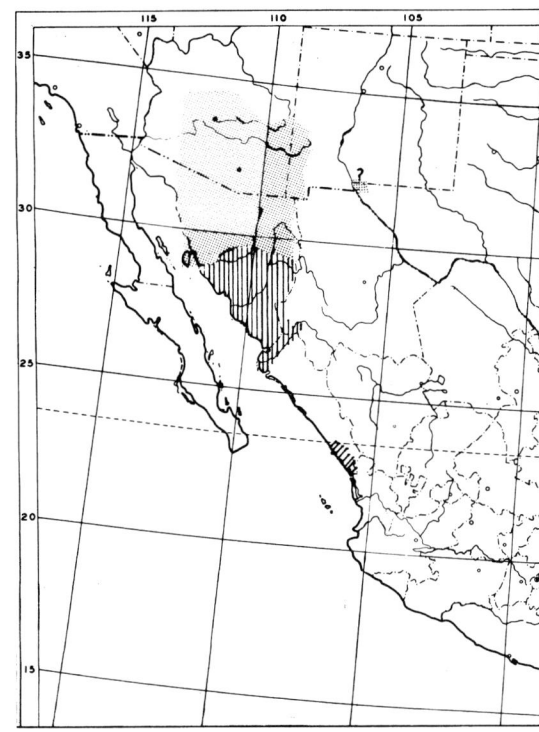

Micruroides euryxanthus euryxanthus
M. euryxanthus australis
M. euryxanthus neglectus

Map 4. Distribution of *Micruroides euryxanthus euryxanthus*, *M. euryxanthus australis*, and *M. euryxanthus neglectus*.

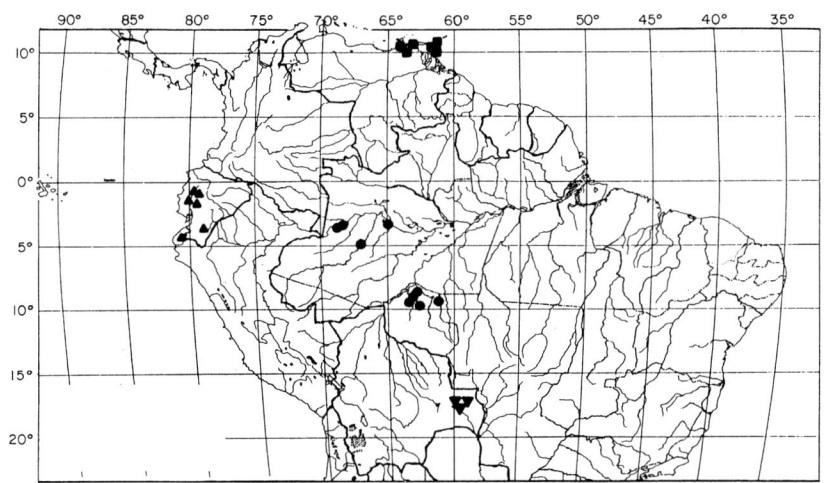

● Micrurus albicinctus
▲ M. bocourti
■ M. circinalis
▼ M. diana

Map 5. Distribution of *Micrurus albicinctus*, *M. bocourti*, *M. circinalis*, and *M. diana*.

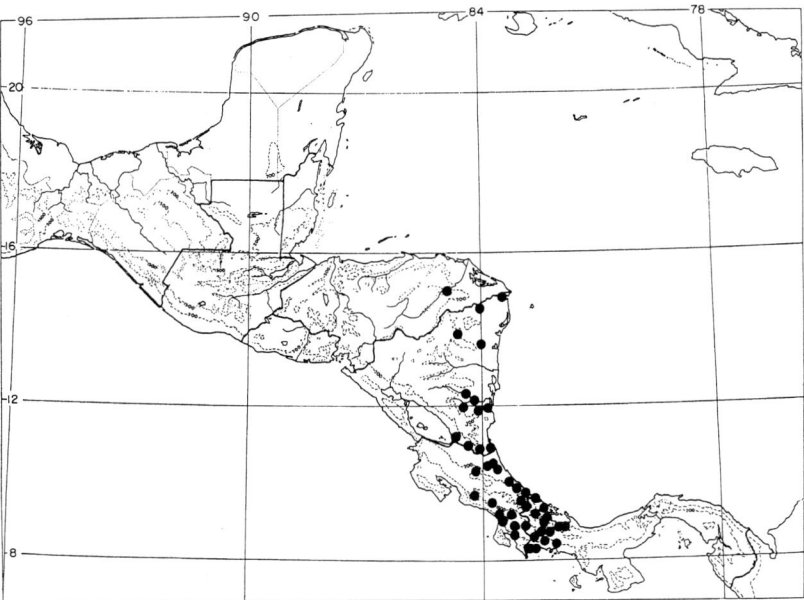

Map 6. Distribution of *Micrurus alleni*.

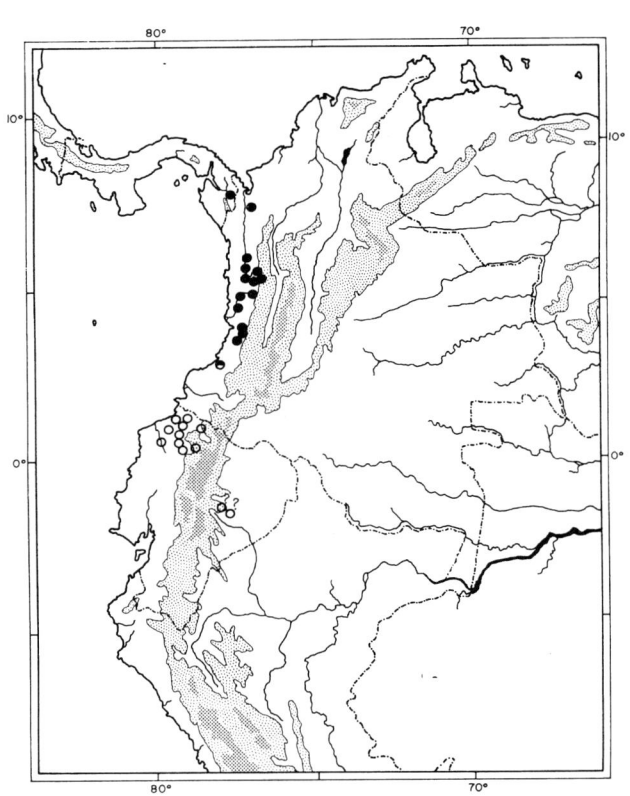

Map 7. Distribution of *Micrurus ancoralis ancoralis*, *M. ancoralis jani*, and intergrades.

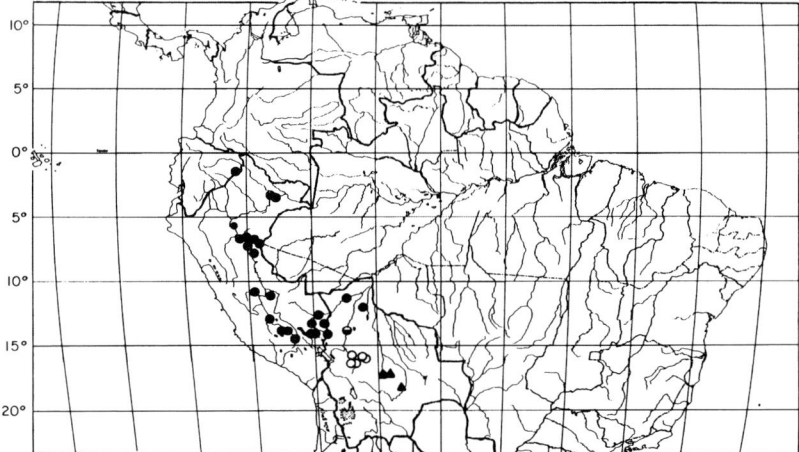

Map 8. Distribution of *Micrurus annellatus annellatus*, *M. annellatus balzani*, *M. annellatus bolivianus*, and intergrades.

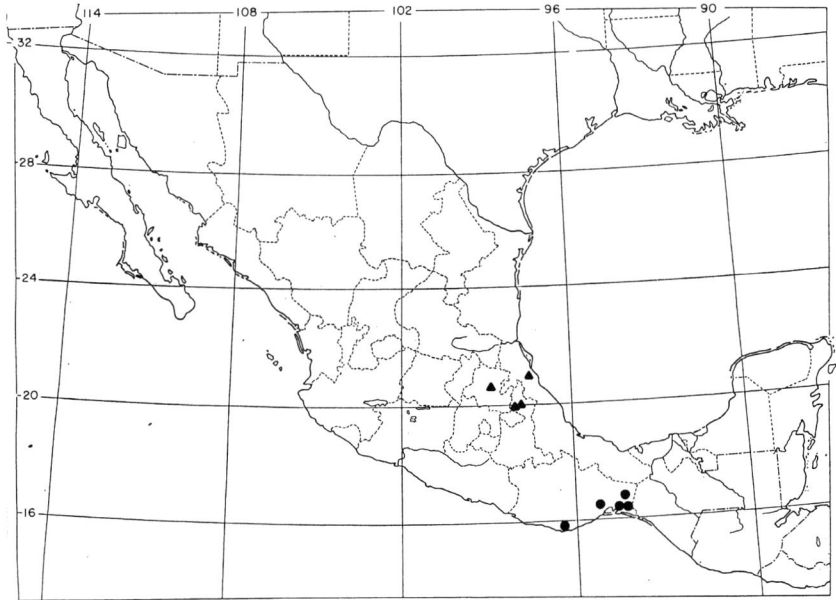

Map 9. Distribution of *Micrurus bernadi* and *M. bogerti*.

- Micrurus browni browni
- M. browni importunus
- M. browni taylori
- M. b. browni × taylori

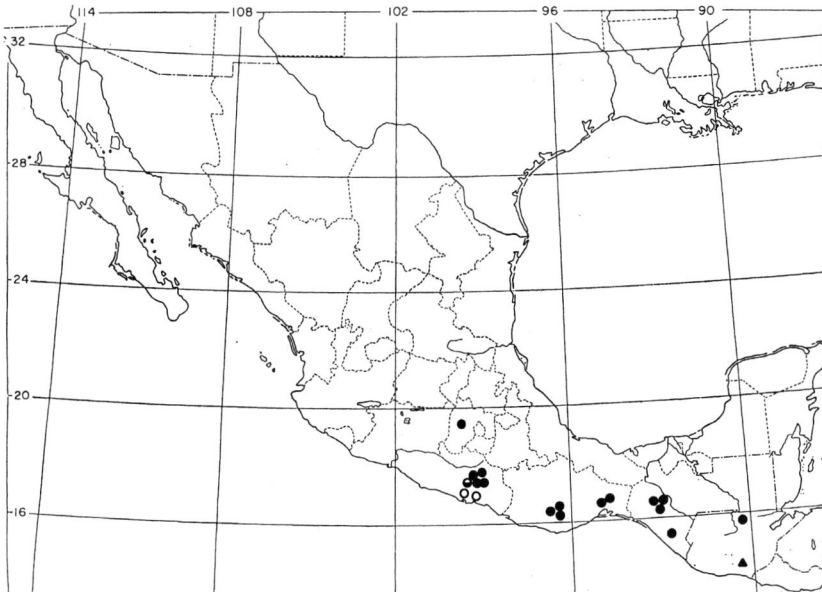

Map 10. Distribution of *Micrurus browni browni*, *M. browni importunus*, *M. browni taylori*, and intergrades.

- Micrurus catamayensis
- M. corallinus
- M. filiformis

Map 11. Distribution of *Micrurus catamayensis*, *M. corallinus*, and *M. filiformis*.

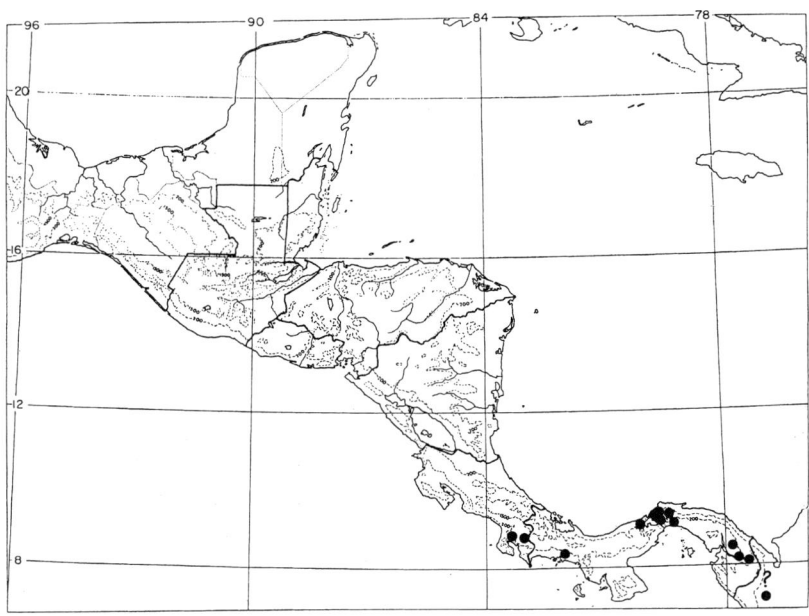

Map 12. Distribution of *Micrurus clarki*.

- ● Micrurus decoratus
- ▲ M. dissoleucus dissoleucus
- ▼ M. dissoleucus dunni
- ■ M. dissoleucus melanogenys
- ☐ M. dissoleucus nigrirostris

Map 13. Distribution of *Micrurus decoratus, M. dissoleucus dissoleucus, M. dissoleucus dunni, M. dissoleucus melanogenys,* and *M. dissoleucus nigrirostris.*

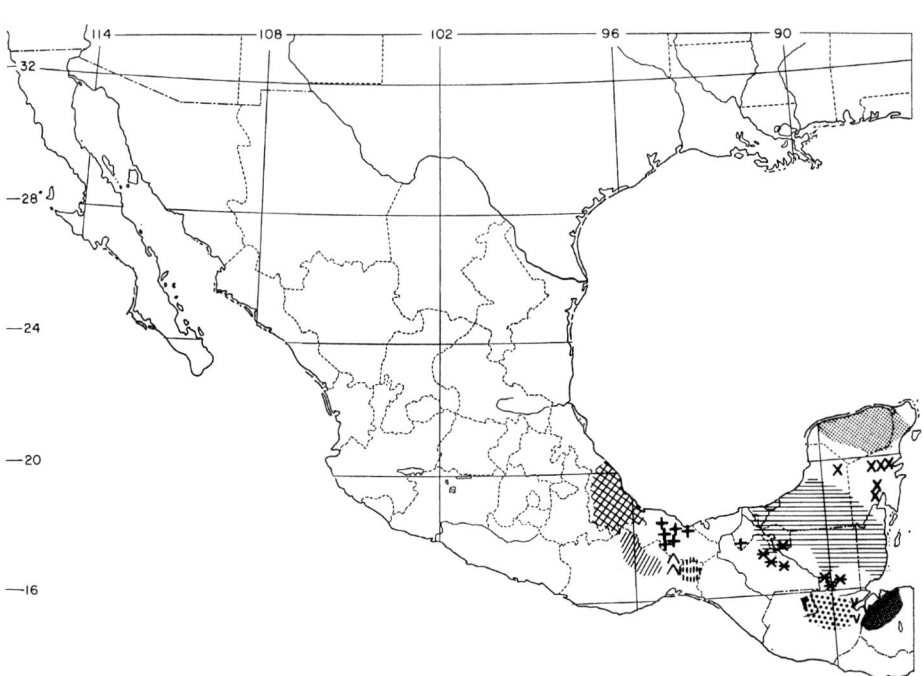

⊠ Micrurus diastema diastema
▨ M. diastema affinis
▰ M. diastema aglaeope
▦ M. diastema alienus
▦ M. diastema apiatus
▦ M. diastema macdougalli
≡ M. diastema sapperi
++ M. d. diastema × sapperi
∧∧ M. d. affinis × macdougalli
VV M. d. aglaeope × apiatus
XX M. d. alienus × sapperi
✻✻ M. d. apiatus × sapperi

Map 14. Distribution of *Micrurus diastema diastema, M. diastema affinis, M. diastema aglaeope, M. diastema alienus, M. diastema apiatus, M. diastema macdougalli, M. diastema sapperi,* and intergrades.

- Micrurus distans distans
- M. distans michoacanensis
- M. distans oliveri
- M. distans zweifeli
- M. d. distans × zweifeli

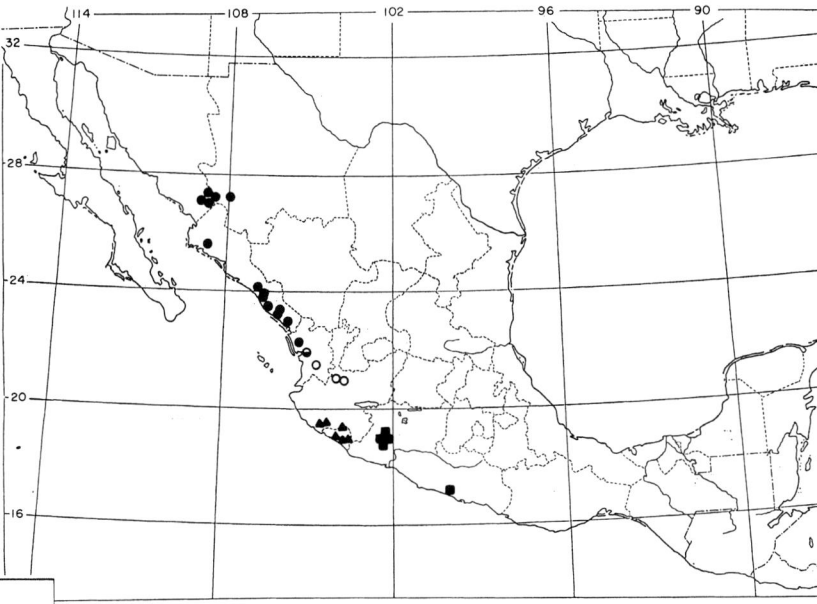

Map 15. Distribution of *Micrurus diastema diastema, M. distans michoacanensis, M. distans oliveri, M. distans zweifeli,* and intergrades.

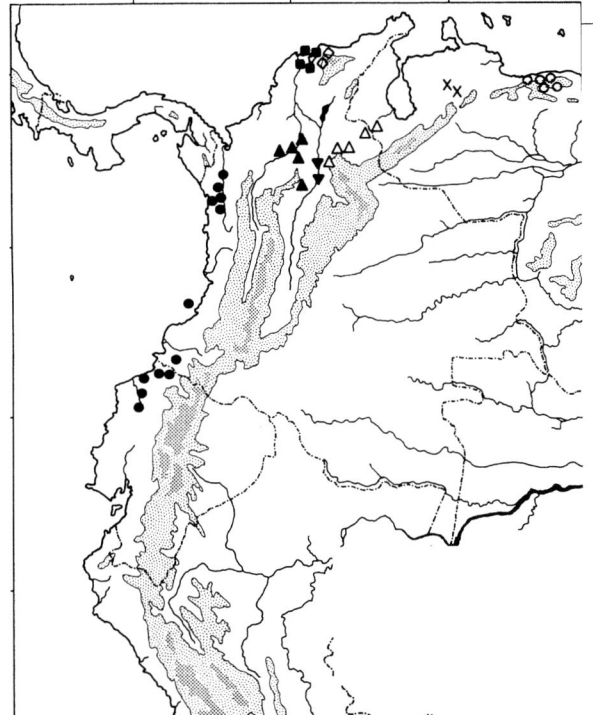

- M. dumerilii dumerilii
- M. dumerilii colombianus
- M. dumerilii antioquiensis
- M. dumerilii carinicauda
- M. dumerilii carinicauda × antioquiensis
- M. dumerilii transandinus
- M. dumerilii venezuelensis
- M. dumerilii carinicauda × venezuelensis

Above 1000 m.

Above 3000 m.

Map 16. Distribution of *Micrurus dumerilii dumerilii, M. dumerilii antioquiensis, M. dumerilii carinicauda, M. dumerilii colombianus, M. dumerilii transandinus, M. dumerilii venezuelensis,* and intergrades.

- Micrurus elegans elegans
- M. elegans veraepacis
- M. ephippifer ephippifer
- M. ephippifer zapotecus
- M. e. ephippifer × zapotecus

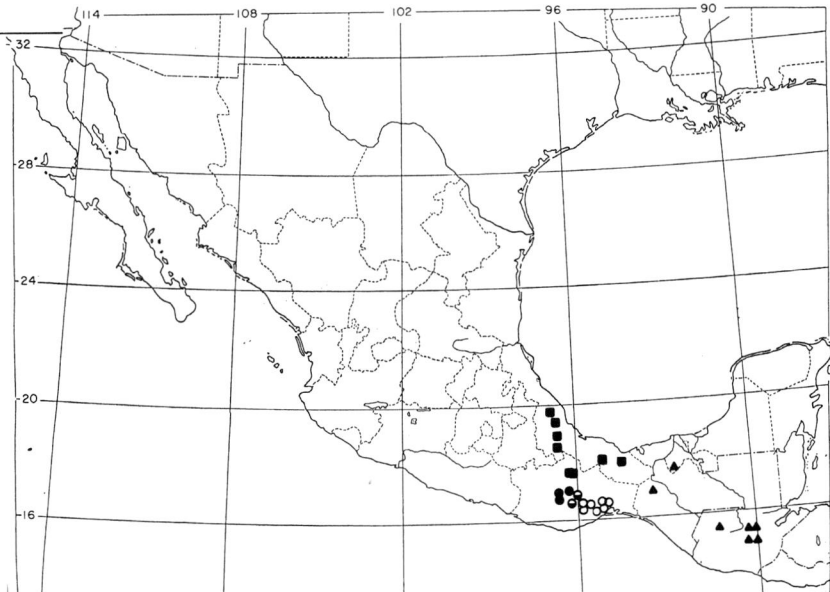

Map 17. Distribution of *Micrurus elegans elegans, M. elegans veraepacis, M. ephippifer ephippifer, M. ephippifer zapotecus,* and intergrades.

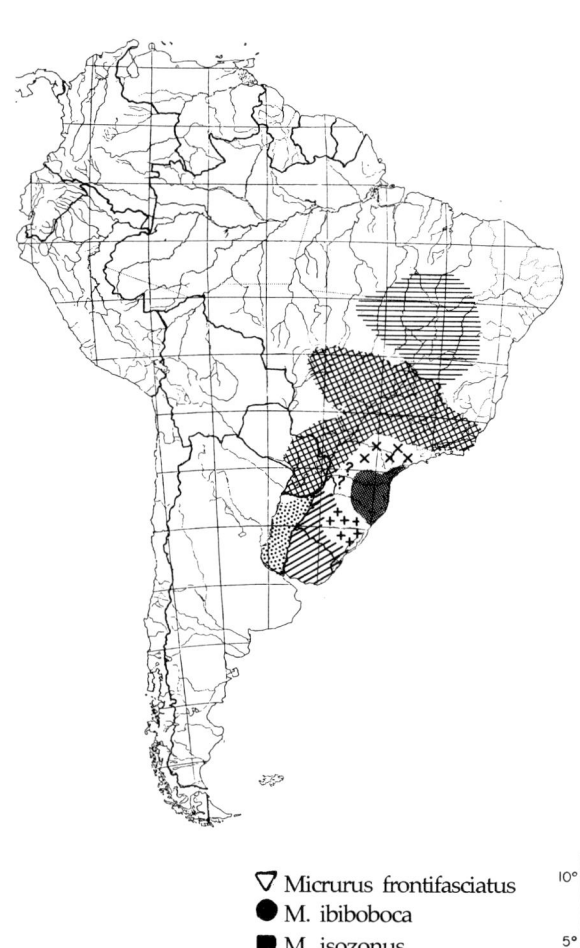

⊠ Micrurus frontalis frontalis
▨ M. frontalis altirostris
▦ M. frontalis baliocoryphus
≡ M. frontalis brasiliensis
▰ M. frontalis multicinctus
× M. f. frontalis × multicinctus
+ M. f. altirostris × multicinctus

Map 18. Distribution of *Micrurus frontalis frontalis, M. frontalis altirostris, M. frontalis baliocoryphus, M. frontalis brasiliensis, M. frontalis multicinctus,* and intergrades.

▽ Micrurus frontifasciatus
● M. ibiboboca
■ M. isozonus
▲ M. langsdorffi

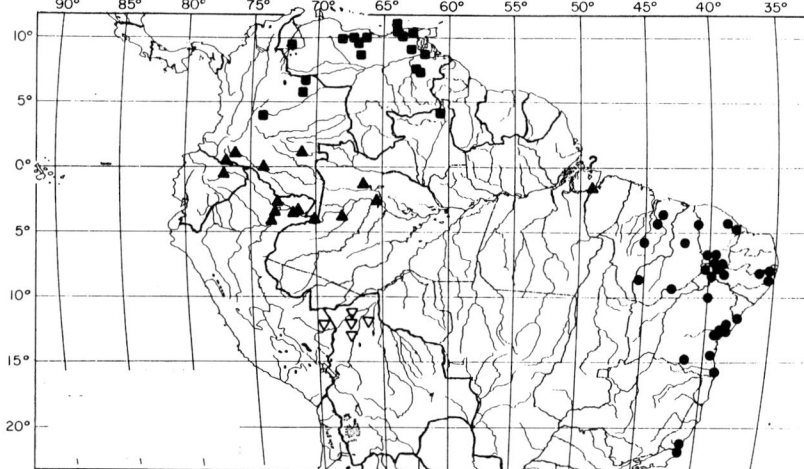

Map 19. Distribution of *Micrurus frontifasciatus, M. ibiboboca, M. isozonus,* and *M. langsdorffi.*

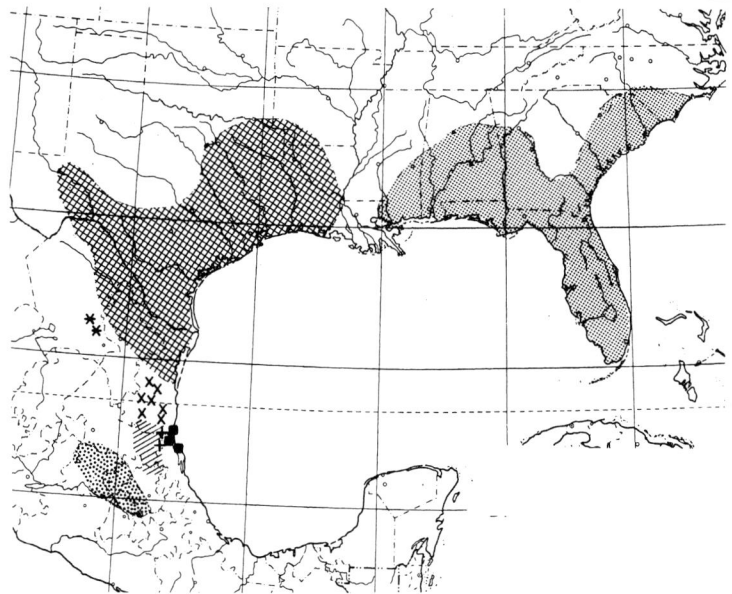

▦ Micrurus fulvius fulvius
▦ M. fulvius fitzingeri
■ M. fulvius maculatus
▨ M. fulvius microgalbineus
⊠ M. fulvius tenere
+ M. f. maculatus × microgalbineus
× M. f. microgalbineus × tenere
✳ [?] M. f. fitzingeri × tenere

Map 20. Distribution of *Micrurus fulvius fulvius, M. fulvius fitzingeri, M. fulvius maculatus, M. fulvius microgalbineus, M. fulvius tenere,* and intergrades.

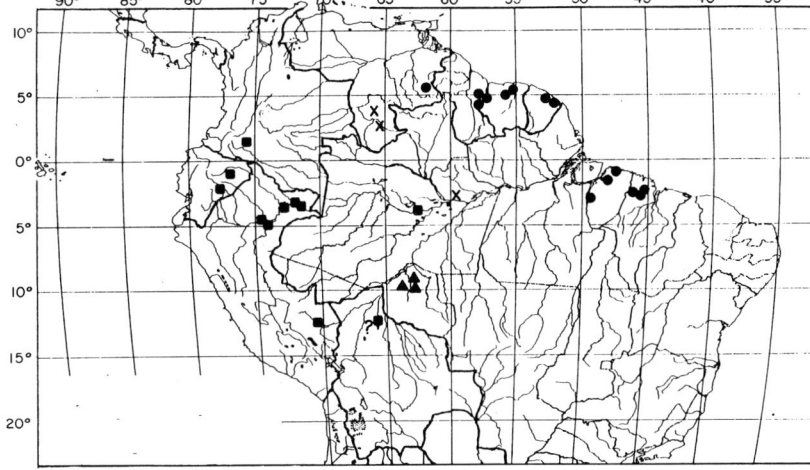

Map 21. Distribution of *Micrurus hemprichii hemprichii*, *M. hemprichii ortoni*, *M. hemprichii rondonianus*, and intergrades.

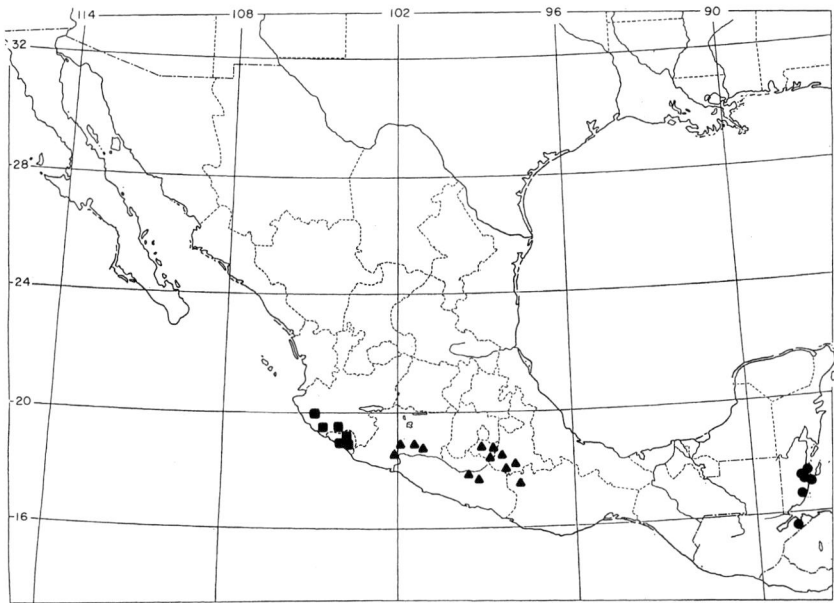

Map 22. Distribution of *Micrurus hippocrepis*, *M. laticollaris laticollaris*, and *M. laticollaris maculirostris*.

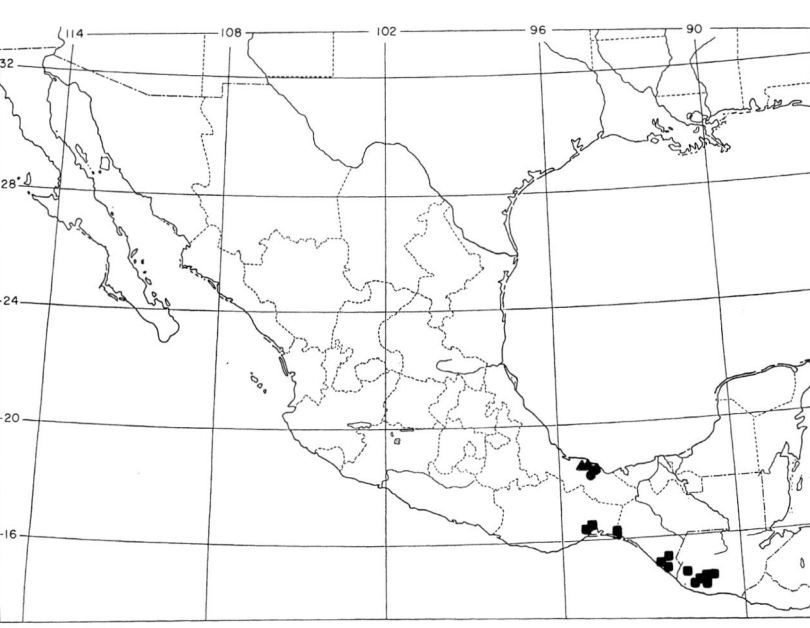

Map 23. Distribution of *Micrurus latifasciatus*, *M. limbatus limbatus*, and *M. limbatus spilosomus*.

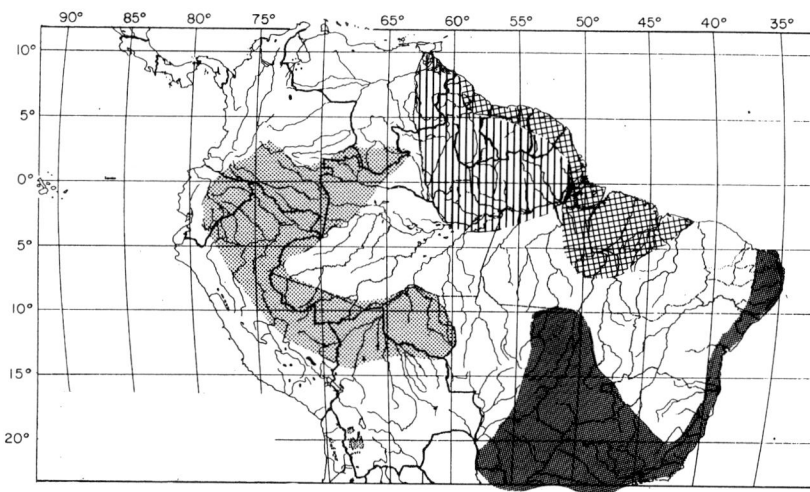

Map 24. Distribution of *Micrurus lemniscatus lemniscatus*, *M. lemniscatus carvalhoi*, *M. lemniscatus diutius*, and *M. lemniscatus helleri*.

- ▩ M. lemniscatus lemniscatus
- ▓ M. lemniscatus carvalhoi
- ⊞ M. lemniscatus diutus
- ░ M. lemniscatus helleri

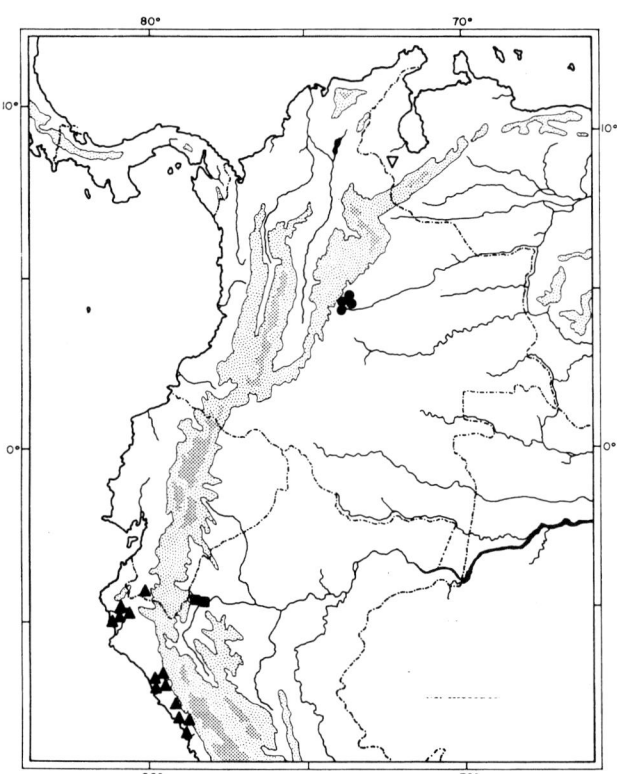

- ■ Micrurus margaritiferus
- ● M. medemi
- ▲ M. mertensi
- ▽ M. meridensis

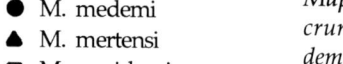

Above 1000 m.

Above 3000 m.

Map 25. Distribution of *Micrurus margaritiferus*, *M. medemi*, *M. mertensi*, and *M. meridensis*.

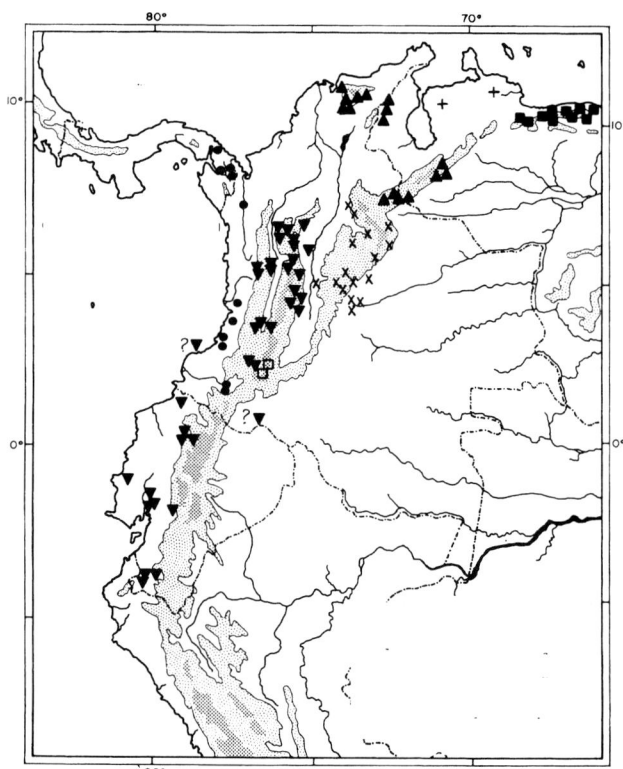

- ● Micrurus mipartitus mipartitus
- ▲ M. mipartitus anomalus
- ▼ M. mipartitus decussatus
- ☐ M. mipartitus popayanensis
- ■ M. mipartitus semipartitus
- X M. m. anomalous × decussatus
- + M. m. anomalous × semipartitus

Above 1000 m.

Above 3000 m.

Map 26. Distribution of *Micrurus mipartitus mipartitus*, *M. mipartitus anomalus*, *M. mipartitus decussatus*, *M. mipartitus popayanensis*, *M. mipartitus semipartitus*, and intergrades.

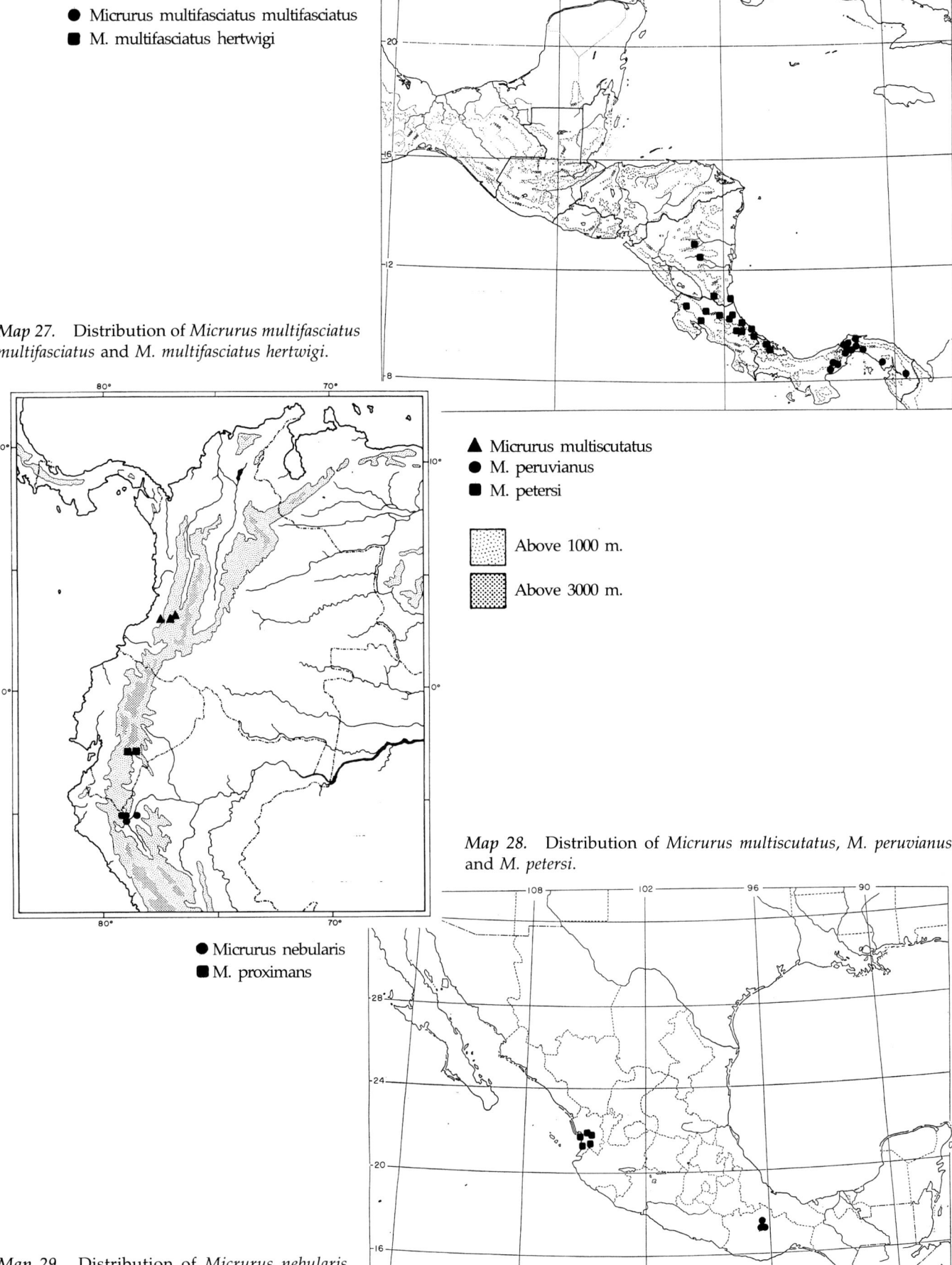

Map 27. Distribution of *Micrurus multifasciatus multifasciatus* and *M. multifasciatus hertwigi*.

Map 28. Distribution of *Micrurus multiscutatus, M. peruvianus,* and *M. petersi*.

Map 29. Distribution of *Micrurus nebularis* and *M. proximans*.

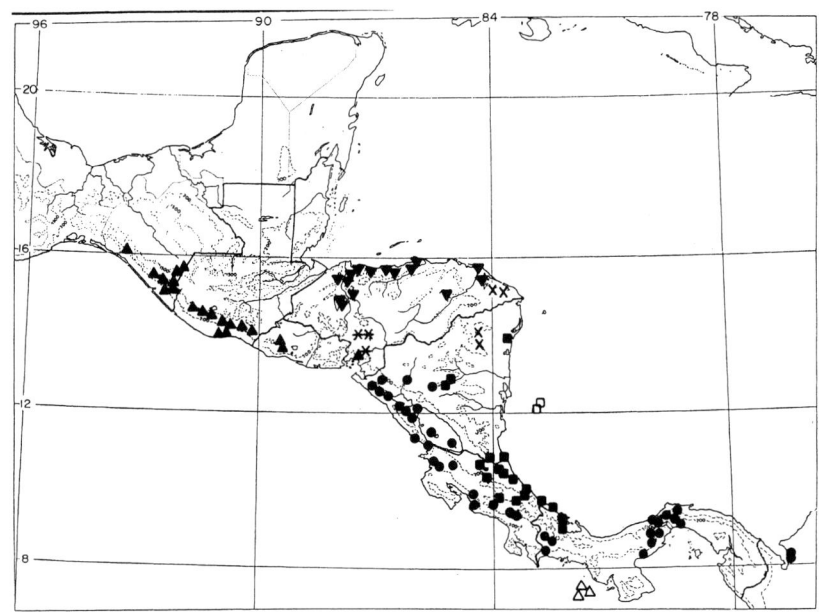

● Micrurus nigrocinctus nigrocinctus
□ M. nigrocinctus babaspul
△ M. nigrocinctus coibensis
▼ M. nigrocinctus divaricatus
■ M. nigrocinctus mosquitensis
▲ M. nigrocinctus zunilensis
X M. n. divaricatus × mosquitensis
✻ M. n. divaricatus × zunilensis

Map 30. Distribution of *Micrurus nigrocinctus nigrocinctus, M. nigrocinctus babaspul, M. nigrocinctus coibensis, M. nigrocinctus divaricatus, M. nigrocinctus mosquitensis, M. nigrocinctus zunilensis,* and intergrades.

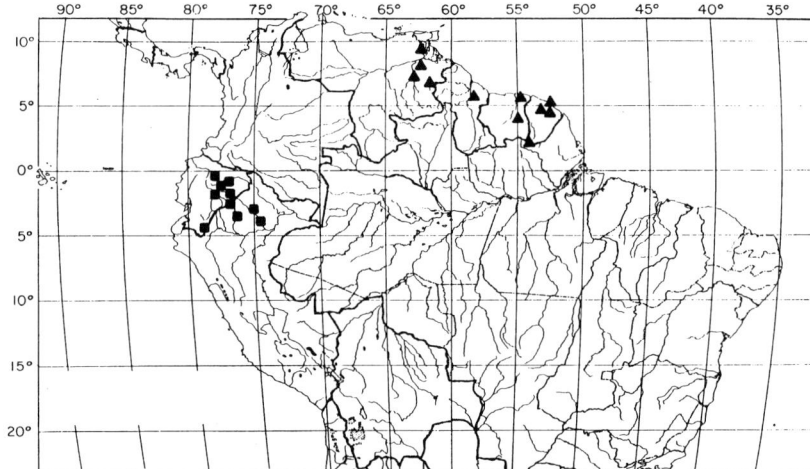

■ Micrurus ornatissimus
● M. psyches

Map 31. Distribution of *Micrurus ornatissimus* and *M. psyches.*

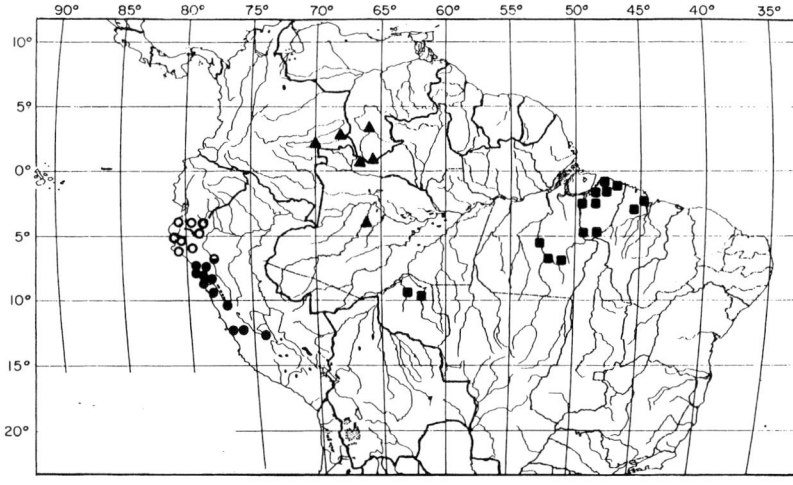

■ Micrurus paraensis
▲ M. remotus
● M. tschudii tschudii
○ M. tschudii olssoni
◓ M. t. tschudii × olssoni

Map 32. Distribution of *Micrurus paraensis, M. remotus, M. tschudii tschudii, M. tschudii olssoni,* and intergrades.

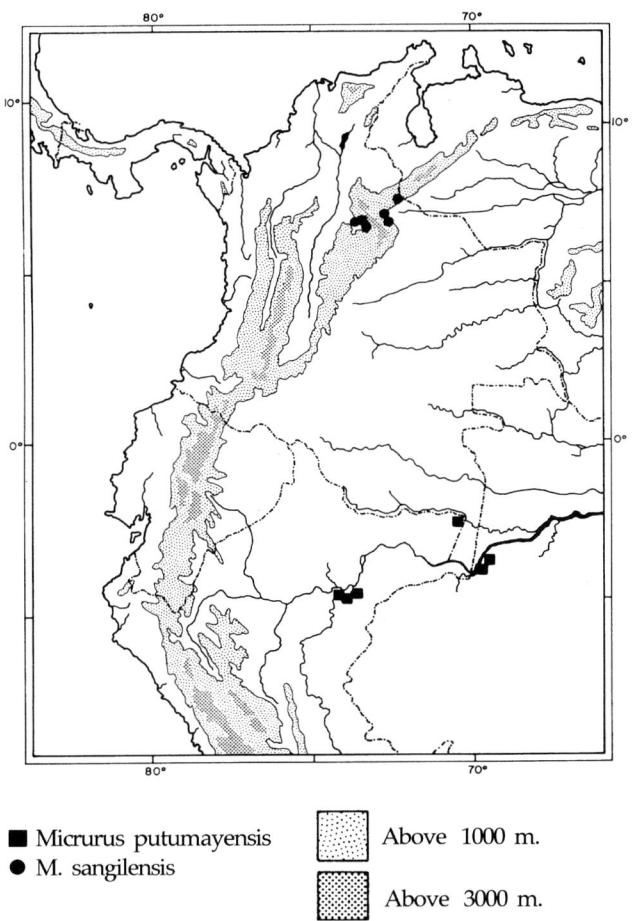

■ Micrurus putumayensis
● M. sangilensis

▓ Above 1000 m.
▓ Above 3000 m.

Map 33. Distribution of *Micrurus putumayensis* and *M. sangilensis*.

● Micrurus pyrrhocryptus pyrrhocryptus
○ M. pyrrhocryptus tricolor

Map 34. Distribution of *Micrurus pyrrhocryptus pyrrhocryptus* and *M. pyrrhocryptus tricolor*.

■ Micrurus ruatanus
▲ M. stewarti
● M. stuarti

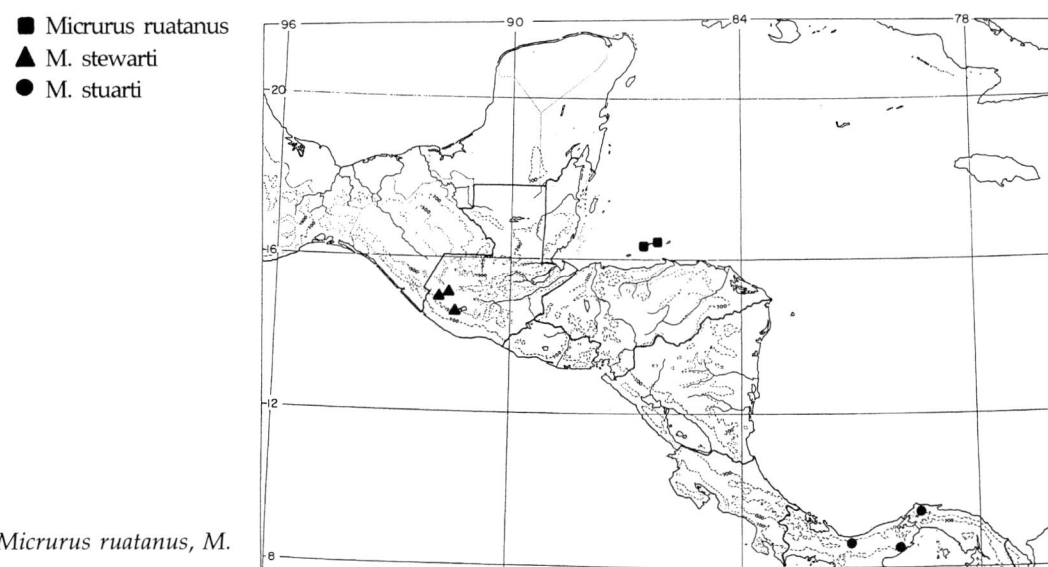

Map 35. Distribution of *Micrurus ruatanus, M. stewarti,* and *M. stuarti*.

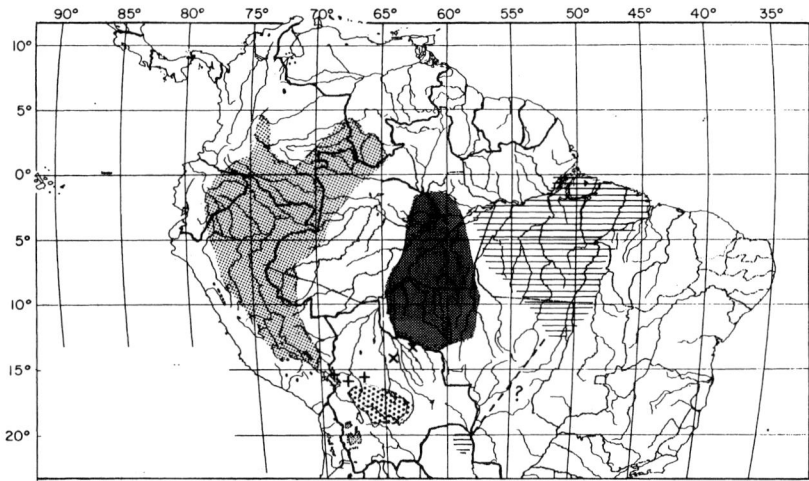

Map 36. Distribution of *Micrurus spixii spixii*, *M. spixii martiusi*, *M. spixii obscurus*, and *M. spixii princeps*.

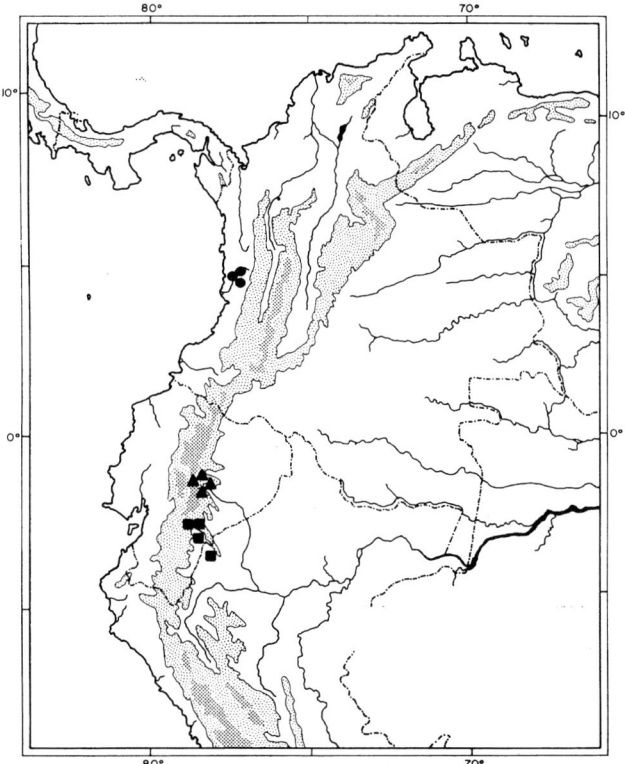

Map 37. Distribution of *Micrurus spurrelli*, *M. steindachneri steindachneri*, and *M. steindachneri orcesi*.

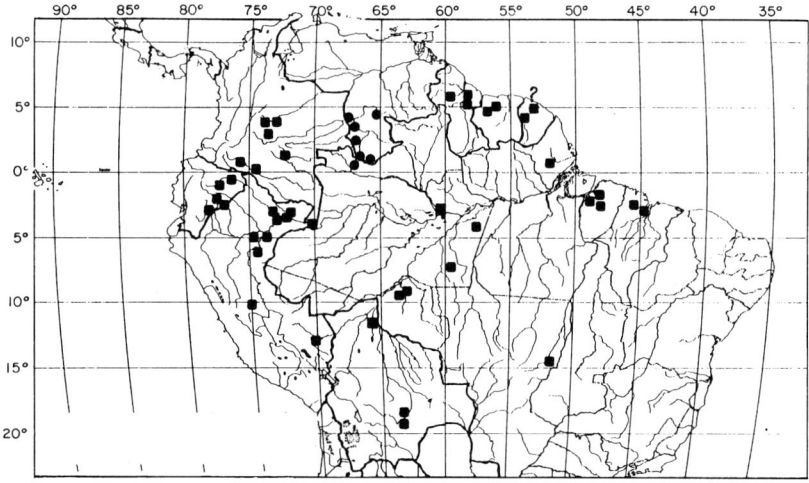

Map 38. Distribution of *Micrurus surinamensis surinamensis* and *M. surinamensis nattereri*.

COLOR SECTION

Color 1. *Leptomicrurus collaris collaris,* dorsal view, from Suriname, Brownsberg. (Photo J. de Bruin.)

Color 3. *Leptomicrurus narduccii melanotus,* from Ecuador, Jatun Sacha, Napo. (Photo J. Caldwell.)

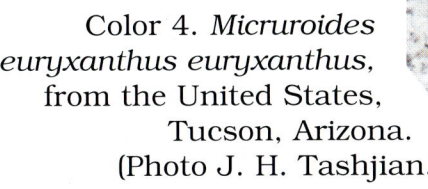

Color 2. *Leptomicrurus collaris collaris,* ventral view, from Suriname, Brownsberg. (Courtesy of M. S. Hoogmoed and Nationaal Naturhistorisch Museum, Leiden.)

Color 4. *Micruroides euryxanthus euryxanthus,* from the United States, Tucson, Arizona. (Photo J. H. Tashjian.)

Color 5. *Micrurus albicinctus*, from Brazil, Usina Hidroeletrica Samuel, Rondônia. (Photo J. Roze.)

Color 6. *Micrurus alleni*, from Costa Rica, San Vito, Cotobrus. (Photo A. Solórzano.)

Color 7. *Micrurus ancoralis jani*, from Colombia. (Photo J. M. Renjifo.)

Color 8. *Micrurus annellatus balzani*, from Peru, Explorer's Inn, Tambopata Reserve, 30 km south of Puerto Maldonado, Madre de Dios. (Photo R. W. McDiarmid.)

Color 9. *Micrurus averyi*, from Brazil, Reserva Ducke, Amazonas. (Courtesy M.S. Hoogmoed and Nationaal Naturhistorisch Museum, Leiden.)

Color 10. *Micrurus bocourti*, from Ecuador, Los Ríos, Cantón Vinces. (Photo U. Kuch.)

Color 11. *Micrurus catamayensis*, from Ecuador, Loja, Loja. (Photo U. Kuch.)

Color 12. *Micrurus clarki*, from Costa Rica, Ponta Gallardo, 7 km west of Golfito, Puntarenas. (Photo M. and P. Fogden; courtesy of A. Solórzano.)

Color 13. *Micrurus corallinus*, from Brazil, Serra de Paranapiacaba, Sete Barras, São Paulo. (Photo I. Sazima.)

Color 14. *Micrurus decoratus*, from Brazil, São João da Boa Vista, São Paulo. (Photo I. Sazima.)

Color 15. *Micrurus diastema aglaeope*, from Honduras. (Photo R. McCranie.)

Color 16. *Micrurus diastema sapperi*, from Belize, Cayo District. (Photo P. Freed.)

Color 17. *Micrurus dissoleucus melanogenys*, from Colombia, Sierra Nevada de Santa Marta. (Photo J. M. Renjifo.)

Color 18. *Micrurus distans distans*, from Mexico. (Photo J. H. Tashjian.)

Color 19. *Micrurus dumerilii transandinus* (above) and *Erythrolamprus mimus micrurus*, a non-venomous mimic (below), both from Colombia, Pto. Merizalde, Valle. (Photo S. Ayerbe.)

Color 20. *Micrurus elegans veraepacis*, from Guatemala, southeast of Puruhá, Verapaz. (Photo W. W. Lamar.)

Color 21. *Micrurus ephippifer zapotecus*, from Mexico, Tejocotes, Oaxaca. (Photo C. M. Bogert.)

Color 22. *Micrurus filiformis*, from Colombia. (Photo J. M. Renjifo.)

Color 23. *Micrurus frontalis frontalis*, upside down, feigning death but with erected tail, from Brazil, Marinqui, São Paulo. (Photo J. Roze.)

Color 24. A false coral snake (mimic), *Oxyrhopus trigeminus*, from Brazil, Alto Araguaio, imitating *M. frontalis* (Color 23 and 27); notice the triad color pattern. (Photo L. J. Vitt.)

Color 25. A false coral snake (mimic), *Simophis rhynostoma*, from Brazil, Fazenda Argentina, Campinas, São Paulo, imitating *M. frontalis* (Color 23 and 27) and *M. lemniscatus* (Color 38); notice the triad color pattern. (Photo I. Sazima.)

Color 26. *Micrurus frontalis altirostris*, from Brazil, Rio Grande do Sul. (Photo T. de Lema.)

Color 27. *Micrurus frontalis brasiliensis*, from Brazil, Goiatuba, Goiás; notice the elevated tail and concealed head. (Photo G. Puorto.)

Color 28. *Micrurus frontifasciatus*, from Bolivia. (Photo N. Kempff.)

Color 29. *Micrurus fulvius fulvius*, from the United States, South Carolina. (Photo L. J. Vitt.)

Color 30. *Micrurus fulvius tenere*, from the United States. (Courtesy of W. E. Duellman and the University of Kansas.)

Color 31. *Micrurus hemprichii hemprichii*, from Brazil, Acampamento Juruá, Rio Xingú, Pará. (Photo L. J. Vitt.)

Color 33. *Micrurus hippocrepis*, from Guatemala, Yzabal. (Courtesy of W. E. Duellman and the University of Kansas.)

Color 32. *Micrurus hemprichii rondonianus*, from Brazil, Usina Hidroeletrica Samuel, Rondônia. (Photo J. Roze.)

Color 34. *Micrurus ibiboboca*, from Brazil, Ilheus, Bahia. (Photo G. Puorto.)

Color 35. *Micrurus isozonus* eating an *Erythrolamprus bizona*, (a non-venomous mimic), from Colombia, Yopal, Casanare. (Photo J. M. Renjifo.)

Color 36. *Micrurus langsdorffi*, from Peru, Estirón, Río Ampi-Yacu, Loreto, dorsal view. (Photo C. W. Myers.)

Color 37. *Micrurus langsdorffi*, ventral view, same specimen as Color 36. (Photo C. W. Myers.)

Color 38. *Micrurus lemniscatus carvalhoi*, from Brazil, Bela Vista, Rio Claro, São Paulo. (Photo G. Puorto.)

Color 39. A false coral snake (mimic), *Erythrolamprus aesculapii*, from Brazil, Vale Verde, Valinhas, São Paulo, imitating *M. lemniscatus* (Color 38); notice the black bands in pairs. (Photo I. Sazima.)

Color 40. *Micrurus lemniscatus helleri*, from Peru, Vic. Huampami, Río Cenepa, Amazonas. (Photo J. E. Cadle.)

Color 41. *Micrurus limbatus spilosomus*, from Mexico, 3 mi SE Tebanca, Sierra de Tuxtla, Veracruz. (Photo H. W. Greene.)

Color 42. *Micrurus mipartitus mipartitus*, a female from Colombia, El Cedral, 24 km on the old road of Cali-Buenaventura, Valle de Cauca, elevation 1800 m. (Photo S. Ayerbe.)

Color 43. *Micrurus mipartitus decussatus*, a female with eggs from Colombia, Yocoto, Valle. (Photo M. A. Tidwell

Color 44. *Micrurus mipartitus semipartitus*, from Venezuela, Guatopo National Park. (Photo L. J. Vitt.)

Color 45. *Micrurus multifasciatus multifasciatus*, possibly from Panama. (Photo E. Seligmann.)

Color 46. *Micrurus multifasciatus hertwigi*, from Costa Rica. (Photo E. Seligmann.)

Color 47. *Micrurus multiscutatus*, from Colombia, Quebrada Guanguí, Río Patía, upper Río Saija, Cauca. (Photo C. W. Myers.)

Color 48. *Micrurus nigrocinctus nigrocinctus*, from Costa Rica. (Photo E. Seligmann.)

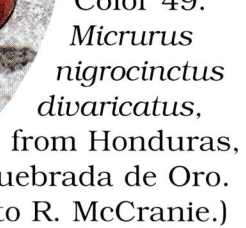

Color 49. *Micrurus nigrocinctus divaricatus*, from Honduras, Quebrada de Oro. (Photo R. McCranie.)

Color 50. *Micrurus nigrocinctus mosquitensis*, from Costa Rica. (Photo E. Seligmann.)

Color 51. *Micrurus paraensis*, from Brazil, Mosqueira, Pará. (Photo G. Puorto.)

Color 52. *Micrurus psyches*, from Suriname, Kamp 8, LBB. (Courtesy of M. S. Hoogmoed, and Nationaal Naturhistorisch Museum, Leiden.)

Color 53. *Micrurus remotus*, from Venezuela, Base Camp, Cerro de la Neblina, Amazonas. (Photo R. McDiarmid.)

Color 54. *Micrurus ruatanus*, from Honduras, Roatán Island, Islas de Bahia. (Courtesy R. McCranie and L. D. Wilson.)

Color 55. *Micrurus spixii martiusi*, from Brazil, Tucurui, Pará. (Photo G. Puorto.)

Color 56. *Micrurus spixii obscurus,* from Peru, Vic. Huampami, Río Cenepa, Amazonas. (Photo J. E. Cadle.)

Color 57. *Micrurus surinamensis surinamensis,* head, from Colombia, Meta. (Photo J. M. Renjifo.)

Color 58. *Micrurus surinamensis surinamensis,* from Brazil, Presidente Figueiredo, Amazonas; notice the flattened body posture (Photo G. Puorto.)

Color 59. *Micrurus tschudii tschudii,* from Peru, Valle de Chillón, north of Lima. (Photo J. Roze.)

Color 60a. Hatching of *Micrurus fulvius tenere*: Emergence from egg.

Color 60b. Hatchling touching the ground.

Color 60c. Half body already emerged.

Color 60d. Hatchling fully emerged; notice the umbilicar cord still connected to egg. (Hatching series photos by W. W. Lamar.)

PATTERN SECTION

Pattern 1. - *Micruroides euryxanthus australis*, from Mexico, Guirococoba, Sonora (MVZ UC 50839, holotype).

Pattern 2. - *Micruroides euryxanthus neglectus*, from Mexico, 26 km NNW Mazatlán, Sinaloa (UMMZ 114637, holotype).

Pattern 3. - *Micrurus ancoralis ancoralis*, from Ecuador (EPQ 4545).

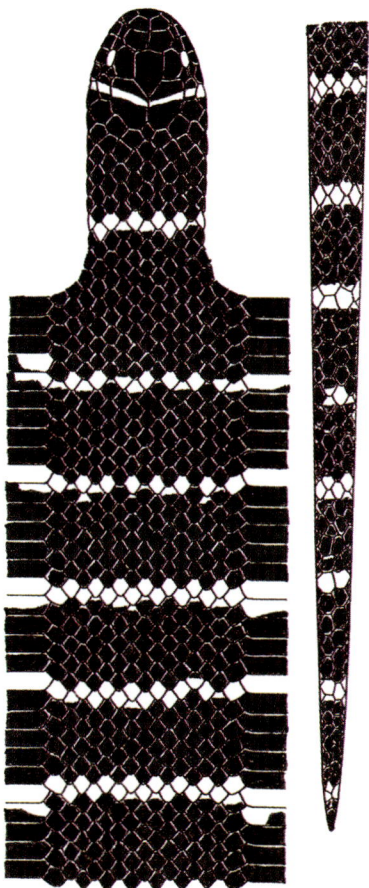

Pattern 4. - *Micrurus annellatus annellatus*, from Bolivia (ZMH 2706).

Pattern 5. - *Micrurus annellatus bolivianus*, from Bolivia, Charobamba River, 50 km NE of Zudañéz, Chuquisaca (ZMH 2706E, holotype).

Pattern 6. - *Micrurus bogerti*, from western coast of Mexico (ZMH 2309).

Pattern 7. - *Micrurus bernadi*, from Mexico, Río Nexaca (AMNH 76432).

Pattern 8. - *Micrurus browni importunus*, from Guatemala, Dueñas, 25 km WSW of Guatemala City in the Antigua Basin, Sacatepequez (BM 64.1.26.41A, holotype).

Pattern 9. - *Micrurus browni browni*, from Mexico, Chilpancingo, Guerrero (FMNH 38494, holotype).

Pattern 10. - *Micrurus browni taylori*, from Mexico, Acapulco, Guerrero (FMNH 10051, holotype).

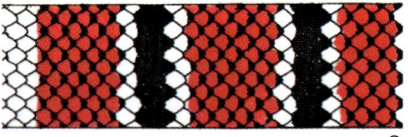

Pattern 11. - *Micrurus circinalis*, variation of middorsal coloration: A) single black bands, from Trinidad (AMNH 64489c), B) accessory black bands, from Trinidad (AMNH 64489g).

Pattern 12. - *Micrurus diana*, from Bolivia, Vicinity of Santiago, prov. Chiquiticos, Santa Cruz (FMNH 195889, holotype).

Pattern 13. - *Micrurus diastema diastema*, from Mexico (MHNP 337/3, type).

Pattern 14. - *Micrurus diastema alienus*, from Mexico, Yucatán (UCM 16086).

Pattern 15. - *Micrurus diastema macdougalli*, middorsal color pattern, from Mexico, El Modelo, Río Calchijapa and Río del Corte, Oaxaca (AMNH 65163, holotype).

Pattern 16. - *Micrurus dissoleucus dunni*, from Panama.

Pattern 17. - *Micrurus dissoleucus dissoleucus*, from Venezuela, Maracaibo, Zulia (MBUCV 8222).

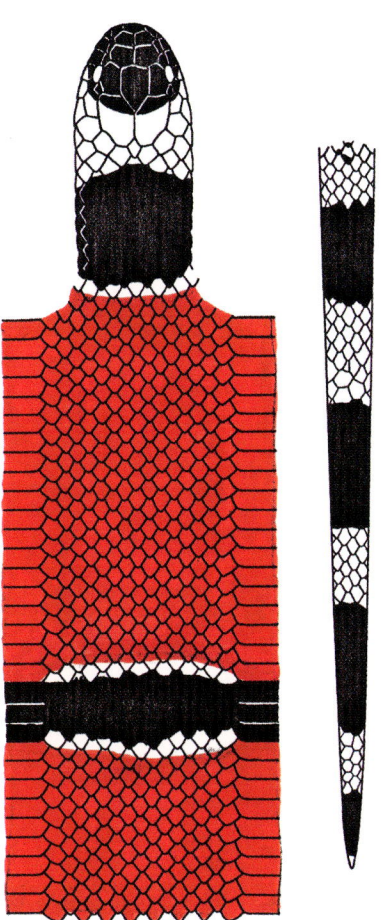

Pattern 18. - *Micrurus distans oliveri*, from Mexico, Periquillo, Colima (AMNH 12780, holotype).

Pattern 19. - *Micrurus distans zweifeli*, from Mexico, Laguna Santa Marta, Nayarit (CAS 95769, holotype).

Pattern 20. - *Micrurus dumerilii antioquiensis*, from Colombia, Santa Rita, north of Medellín, Antioquia (BM 1946.1.17.23, holotype).

Pattern 21. - *Micrurus dumerilii venezuelensis*, from Venezuela, El Valle, Dto. Federal (AMNH 71388, holotype).

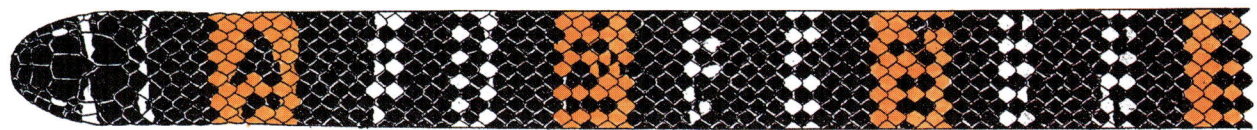

Pattern 22. - *M. elegans elegans,* from Mexico, El Mercadito, Cintalapa, Chiapas (AMNH 45091).

Pattern 23. - Variation of color pattern in *Micrurus fulvius fulvius*: A)AMNH 57520, B)AMNH 77124, C)AMNH 4184, D)AMNH 8000.

Pattern 24. - *Micrurus fulvius fitzingeri*.

Pattern 25. - *Micrurus fulvius maculatus*, middorsal coloration.

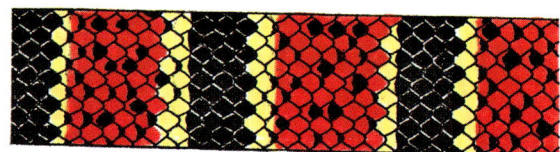

Pattern 26. - *Micrurus fulvius microgalbineus*, middorsal coloration.

Pattern 27. - *Micrurus ephippifer ephippifer*, from Mexico, Tehuantepec, Oaxaca (USNM 111328).

Pattern 28. - *Micrurus frontalis baliocoryphus*, from Argentina, Buenos Aires (ANSP 6840, holotype).

  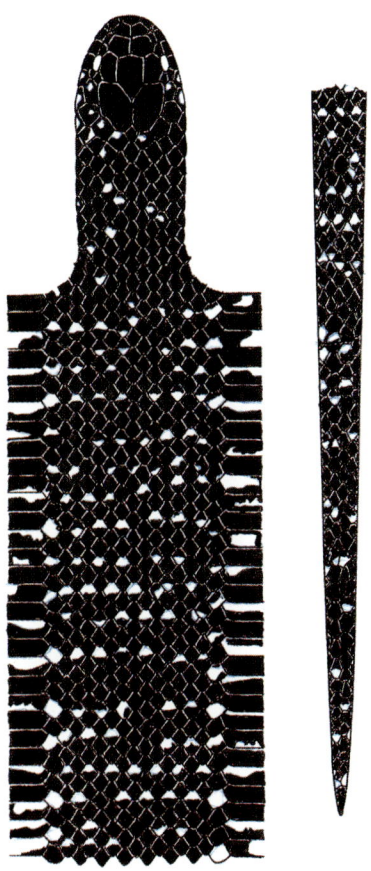

Pattern 29. - *Micrurus laticollaris maculirostris*, from Mexico, Colima, Colima (KU32546 holotype).

Pattern 30. - *Micrurus limbatus limbatus*, from Mexico, southern slope of Volcán Santa Marta, 7 km N of San Andrés Tuxtla, Veracruz (UMMZ 123858, holotype).

Pattern 31. - *Micrurus margaritiferus*, from Peru, Río Santiago at the mouth of Río Marañón (AMNH 53362, holotype).

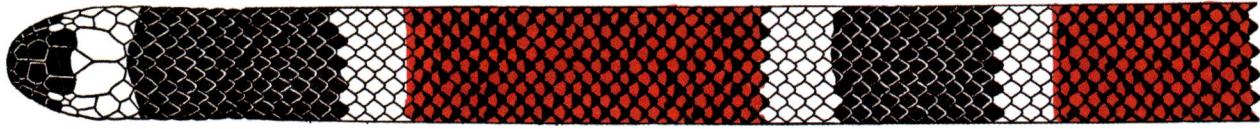

Pattern 32. - *Micrurus latifasciatus*, from Guatemala, Olas de Moca, Solola (AMNH 45091).

Pattern 33. - *Micrurus medemi*, from Colombia, Villavicencio, Meta (1B 7208, paratype).

Pattern 34. - *Micrurus meridensis,* from Venezuela, 1 km NE of Lagunilla, Mérida (USNM 217256, holotype).

Pattern 35. - *Micrurus nebularis*, from Mexico, vivero Rancho Teja, 3 km E of Ixtlán de Juárez, Oaxaca (AMNH 103118, holotype).

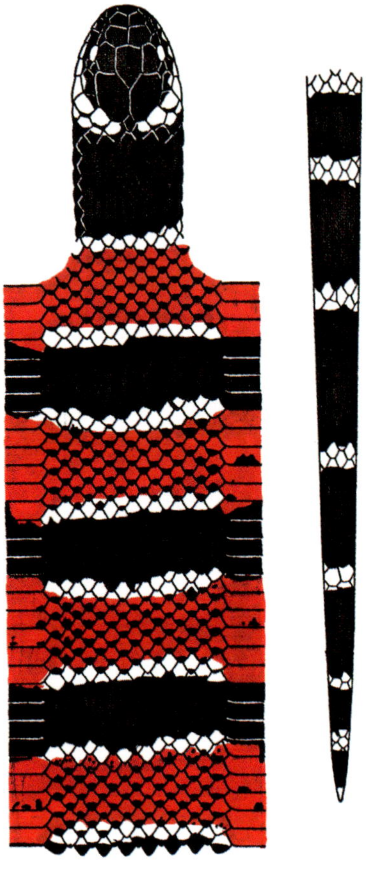

Pattern 36. - *Micrurus mertensi*, from Peru, Valley of Jequetepeque (ANSP 11503).

Pattern 37. - *Micrurus ornatissimus*, from Ecuador, Río Copataza, Pastaza (EPQ 444).

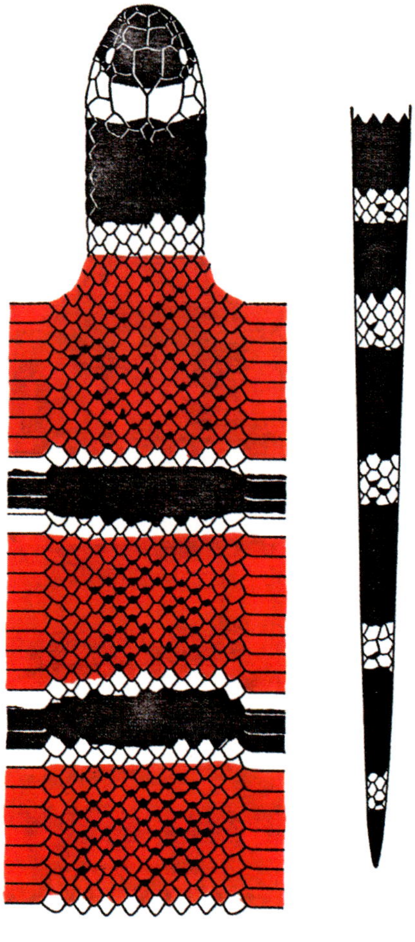

Pattern 38. - *Micrurus proximans*, from Mexico, Nayarit (UNM 10205).

Pattern 39. - *Micrurus nigrocinctus coibensis*, from Panama, Coiba Island (MCZ 37063, paratype).

Pattern 40. - *Micrurus nigrocinctus zunilensis*, from Mexico, San Jerónimo (UIMNH 54908).

Pattern 41. - *Micrurus peruvianus*, from Peru, Perico, Cajamarca (MCZ 17385, holotype).

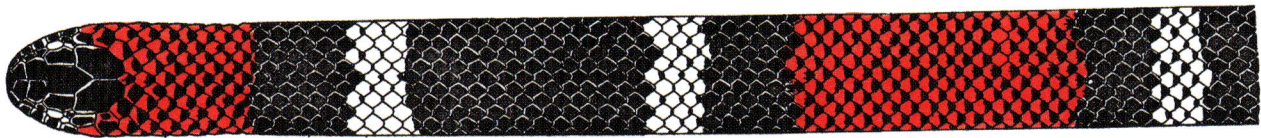

Pattern 42. - *Micrurus pyrrhocryptus phrrhocryptus*, from Argentina, Santiago del Estero.

Pattern 43. - *Micrurus pyrrhocryptus tricolor*, from Brazil, Garandazal, Mato Grosso (1B 16290, holotype).

Pattern 44. - *Micrurus spixii princeps*, from Bolivia, Buena Vista, Santa Cruz (AMNH 35985).

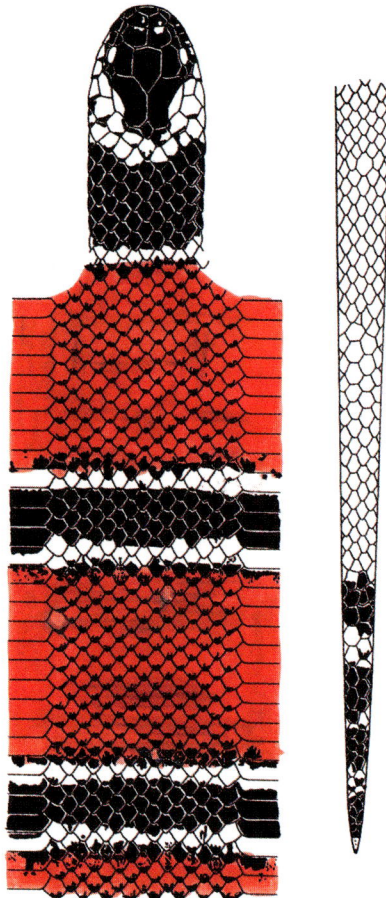

Pattern 45. - *Micrurus sangilensis*, from Colombia, San Gil, Santander (ILS 1503, paratype).

Pattern 46. - *Micrurus steindachneri orcesi*, from Ecuador, Meta trail, Baños (UMMZ 88922, holotype).

Pattern 47. - *Micrurus spurrelli*, from Colombia, Condoto River, Chocó (AMNH 89352).

Pattern 48. - *Micrurus stewarti*, from Panama, Sierra de la Bruja (MCZ 24924, holotype).

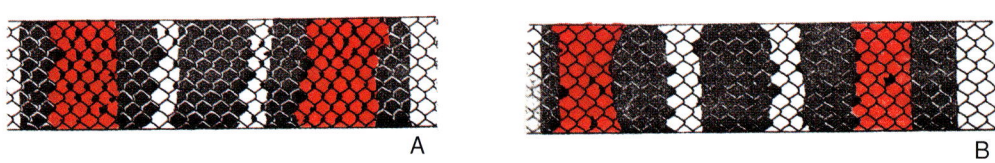

Pattern 49. - *Micrurus tschudii*, dorsal color pattern showing fourth triad: A) *M. t. tschudii*, from Peru, Trujillo (AMNH), B) *M. tschudii olssoni* from Peru (NMB 15637).

Appendix A:
Scientific and Common Names of Coral Snakes

SCIENTIFIC NAME	COMMON NAME
Leptomicrurus	Black-back coral snakes
L. collaris	Guianan black-backed coral snake
L. collaris collaris	Long black-backed coral snake
L. c. breviventris	Short black-backed coral snake
L. narduccii	Andean black-backed coral snake
L. n. narduccii	Bolivian black coral snake
L. n. melanotus	Slender black coral snake
L. scutiventris	Little black coral snake
Micruroides	Western coral snakes
M. euryxanthus	Western coral snake
M. e. euryxanthus	Arizona coral snake
M. e. australis	Sonora coral snake
M. e. neglectus	Sinaloa coral snake
Micrurus	American coral snakes
M. albicinctus	White-banded coral snake
M. alleni	Arrow-headed coral snake
M. ancoralis	Anchor coral snake
M. ancoralis ancoralis	Ecuadorian anchor coral snake
M. a. jani	Choco anchor coral snake
M. annellatus	Annellated coral snake
M. annellatus annellatus	Common annellated coral snake
M. a. balzani	Yungas coral snake
M. a. bolivianus	Bolivian coral snake
M. averyi	Black-headed coral snake
M. bernadi	Saddled coral snake
M. bocourti	False triad coral snake
M. bogerti	Coastal coral snake
M. browni	Sierra Madre coral snake
M. b. browni	Common Sierra Madre coral snake
M. b. importunus	Antigua coral snake
M. b. taylori	Acapulco coral snake
M. catamayensis	Catamayo coral snake
M. circinalis	Trinidad northern coral snake
M. clarki	Clark's coral snake
M. corallinus	Painted coral snake
M. decoratus	Decorated coral snake
M. diana	Diana's coral snake
M. diastema	Diastema coral snake
M. d. diastema	Veracruz coral snake
M. d. affinis	Speckled coral snake
M. d. aglaeope	Splendid coral snake
M. d. alienus	Yucatan coral snake
M. d. apiatus	Spotted nose coral snake

M. d. macdougalli	MacDougall's coral snake
M. d. sapperi	Irregular coral snake
M. dissoleucus	Pygmy coral snake
M. d. dissoleucus	Venezuelan pygmy coral snake
M. d. dunni	Panama pygmy coral snake
M. d. melanogenys	Santa Marta pygmy coral snake
M. d. meridensis	Mérida pygmy coral snake
M. d. nigrirostris	Barranquilla pygmy coral snake
M. distans	Clear-banded coral snake
M. d. distans	Common clear-banded coral snake
M. d. michoacanensis	Michoacan clear-banded coral snake
M. d. oliveri	Colima clear-banded coral snake
M. d. zweifeli	Zweifel's coral snake
M. dumerilii	Capuchin coral snake
M. d. dumerilii	Common capuchin coral snake
M. d. antioquiensis	Antioquian coral snake
M. d. carinicauda	Intermediate capuchin coral snake
M. d. colombianus	Santa Marta capuchin coral snake
M. d. transandinus	Transandean coral snake
M. d. venezuelensis	Venezuelan capuchin coral snake
M. elegans	Elegant coral snake
M. e. elegans	Western elegant coral snake
M. e. veraepacis	Verapaz elegant coral snake
M. ephippifer	Double black coral snake
M. e. ephippifer	Tehuantepec coral snake
M. e. zapotecus	Zapotec coral snake
M. filiformis	Thread coral snake
M. frontalis	Short-tailed coral snake
M. f. frontalis	Brazilian giant coral snake
M. f. altirostris	Uruguayan coral snake
M. f. baliocoryphus	Mesopotamian coral snake
M. f. brasiliensis	Brazilian short-tailed coral snake
M. f. multicinctus	Many-banded coral snake
M. f. tricolor	Pantanal coral snake
M. frontifasciatus	Bolivian triad coral snake
M. fulvius	North American coral snake
M. f. fulvius	Eastern coral snake
M. f. fitzingeri	Guanajuato coral snake
M. f. maculatus	Tampico coral snake
M. f. microgalbineus	Spotted coral snake
M. f. tenere	Texas coral snake
M. hemprichii	Worm-eating coral snake
M. h. hemprichii	Eastern worm-eating coral snake
M. h. ortoni	Western worm-eating coral snake
M. h. rondonianus	Rondonian worm-eating coral snake
M. hippocrepis	Belize coral snake
M. ibiboboca	Ibiboboca
M. isozonus	Equal-banded coral snake
M. langsdorffi	Confused coral snake
M. laticollaris	Double collar coral snake
M. l. laticollaris	Eastern double collar coral snake
M. l. maculirostris	Western double collar coral snake
M. latifasciatus	Long-banded coral snake
M. lemniscatus	Ribbon coral snake
M. l. lemniscatus	Guiana's ribbon coral snake
M. l. carvalhoi	Brazilian ribbon coral snake

M. l. diutius	Trinidad ribbon coral snake
M. l. helleri	Western ribbon coral snake
M. limbatus	Tuxtlan coral snake
M. margaritiferus	Speckled coral snake
M. medemi	Villavicencio coral snake
M. meridensis	Merida coral snake
M. mertensi	Peruvian desert coral snake
M. mipartitus	Red-tailed coral snake
M. m. mipartitus	Pacific Red-tailed coral snake
M. m. anomalus	Santa Marta red-tailed coral snake
M. m. decussatus	Andean red-tailed coral snake
M. m. popayanensis	Popayán coral snake
M. m. semipartitus	Venezuelan red-tailed coral snake
M. multifasciatus	Gargantilla
M. m. multifasciatus	Panama gargantilla
M. m. hertwigi	Costa Rican gargantilla
M. multiscutatus	Cauca coral snake
M. nebularis	Neblina coral snake
M. nigrocinctus	Central American coral snake
M. n. nigrocinctus	Common Central American coral snake
M. n. babaspul	Babaspul
M. n. coibensis	Coiba coral snake
M. n. divaricatus	Honduras coral snake
M. n. mosquitensis	Misquito coral snake
M. n. zunilensis	Zunil coral snake
M. ornatissimus	Ornated coral snake
M. paraensis	Para coral snake
M. peruvianus	Peruvian coral snake
M. petersi	Mountain coral snake
M. proximans	Nayarit coral snake
M. psyches	Northern coral snake
M. putumayensis	Putumayo coral snake
M. pyrrhocryptus	Argentinian coral snake
M. remotus	Remote coral snake
M. ruatanus	Roatán coral snake
M. sangilensis	San Gil coral snake
M. spixii	Amazonian coral snake
M. s. spixii	Central Amazonian coral snake
M. s. martiusi	Black-headed Amazonian coral snake
M. s. obscurus	Black-neck Amazonian coral snake
M. s. princeps	Bolivian Amazonian coral snake
M. spurrelli	Butterfly-head coral snake
M. steindachneri	Piedmont coral snake
M. s. steindachneri	Santiago Piedmont coral snake
M. s. orcesi	Pastaza Piedmont coral snake
M. stewarti	Panamanian coral snake
M. stuarti	Volcano coral snake
M. surinamensis	Aquatic coral snake
M. s. surinamensis	Amazonian aquatic coral snake
M. s. nattereri	Venezuelan aquatic coral snake
M. tschudii	Desert coral snake
M. t. tschudii	Southern desert coral snake
M. t. olsoni	Northern desert coral snake

Appendix B:
Summary of the Composition of Coral Snake Venom

Coral snake venom contains enzymes, nonenzymatic toxins, and miscellaneous nonproteinic substances and metals. The venom can be fractioned and many of the fractions may contain several toxic components.

Enzymes

Phospholipase A2 (PhA2): Present in multiple protein forms; carries out catalysis of the hydrolysis of lipids; also responsible for hemolysis, usually indirect. Molecular weight varies from species to species, between 13,000 and 20,000; molecular weight of PhA2 of *M. fulvius microgalbineus* about 14,000 (Posani et al, 1979). Diverse biochemical properties and pharmacological actions ascribed to PhA2 (Rosenberg, 1979; Russell, 1983), some contradictory; it contributes to facilitating the total impact of the venom; sometimes considered one of the "spreading factors" of venom. Several fractions of venom can contain PhA2.

Hyaluronidase: Found in all coral snake venoms; destroys hyaluronic acid gel barrier between cells and fibers, accelerating the penetration and distribution of venom; known as "spreading factor."

L-amino acid oxidase: Widely distributed enzyme, also in the venom of coral snakes (Jiménez-Porras, 1977); its wide-range catalytic action helps in digestion of the prey. Together with riboflavin it is responsible for the yellow coloration of the venom.

Phosphotases, catalysing the hydrolyses of phosphate bonds in several nucleotids, are:

Phosphodiesterase, found in *M. f. fulvius* venom (Kocholaty et al, 1971), is also considered exonuclease because it catalysis the hydrolysis of polynucleotids, found in almost all snake venoms. It could be involved in the ATPase and DPNase activities as well. Other enzymes of the phosphatase group that act on phosphatase esters are *5'-nucleotidase* or AMPase; *deoxyribonuclease*, also DNAase or endonuclease; *adenosine triphosphatase*, also known as ATPase; and nucleotide *pyrophosphatase*, also NADase or DPNase.

Anticholinesterase, found in the venom of *M. f. fulvius* (Kumar et al, 1973) and also in several Old World elapids, inhibits the action of acetylcholinesterase; this is of importance for transmission of nerve impulses across the synaptic bridge. Venom component responsible for anticholinesterase activity has very high molecular weight, exceeding 100,000, and cannot be dialysed; its action is dependent on the concentration of zinc ions, present naturally in snake venoms.

Nonenzymatic Toxins

A group of nonenzymatic membrane-active polypeptide toxins that act as neurotoxins (CNTX), as cardiotoxins (CTX), and as lytic factors in blood, they probably produce other toxic effects, such as on internal organs and tissues.

Neurotoxins, found in all coral snake venoms, affect neuromuscular junction and are presynaptic or postsynaptic. The more frequent postsynaptic CNTX has curare-like action, found in most coral snakes thus far. It is a basic protein with a low molecular weight, 7,000 to 8,000, and can be dialysed. Presynaptic CNTX, found in *M. corallinus* (Vital Brazil and Fontana, 1984), is basic or moderately acid, with a molecular weight of 12,000 or higher.

Cardiotoxins of low molecular weight, around 7,000, are very basic polypeptides.

Direct lytic factor is a basic protein of molecular weight around 2,000.

Nonprotein Substances and Metals

The nonprotein material is 10% to 20% of dry weight, and includes some lipids, carbohydrates, and riboflavin. Other possible components are nucleosides, nucleotides, and amino acids.

Several metal ions are present including zinc and probably calcium, magnesium, and potassium.

References

Abalos, J. W. 1949. Cuáles son los animales venenosos de la Argentina? Tucumán, 23 pp.

———. 1961. Distribución y densidad de las serpientes venenosas de Santiago del Estero. Acta Krausi Cuad. Inst. Nac. Microbiol. Buenos Aires, 3: 69–70.

———. 1977. Qué sabe usted de víboras? Buenos Aires, Edit. Losada. 175 pp.

———, E. C. Baez, and R. Nader. 1964. Serpientes de Santiago del Estero. Acta Zool. Lilloana, 20: 211–283.

——— and E. Bucher. 1970. Zoo-epidemiología del ofidismo en Santiago del Estero. Bol. Acad. Nac. Cienc. Córdoba, 47: 259–272.

——— and C. C. Mischis. 1975. Elenco sistemático de los ofidios argentinos. Bol. Acad. Nac. Cienc. Córdoba, 51: 55–76.

——— and R. Nader. 1962. La coral *Micrurus lemniscatus frontalis* de Santiago del Estero. An. Inst. Nac. Microb., 1: 84–94.

——— and I. Pirosky. 1963. Venomous Argentine serpents, ophidism and snake antivenin. *In* H. K. L. Keegan and W. V. MacFarlane (eds.). Venomous and poisonous animals and noxious plants of the Pacific region. Oxford, Pergamon Press, pp. 363–371.

Abbott, C. E. 1947. Notes on the behavior of a coral snake in captivity. Proc. Ark. Acad. Sci., 2: 49.

Abuys, A. 1982. Enige korrekties en aanvullende gegevens t.a.v. het boetkje "Surinaamse slangen in kleur" van Joep Moonen e.a., 1979. Litt. Serp., 2: 34–42.

———. 1987a. A new coral snake (genus *Micrurus*) from Surinam. Litt. Serp., 7: 215–220.

———. 1987b. The names of Surinam, part XVIII: family Elapidae, subfamily Micrurinae. Litt. Serp., 7(4): 185–194, 221–242.

———. 1988. Addition to the article "A new coral snake (genus *Micrurus*) from Surinam." Litt. Serp., 8(3): 106.

Achaval, F. 1976. Reptiles. *In* A. Langguth (ed.). Lista de las especies de vertebrados del Uruguay (Reptiles). Mus. Nac. Hist. Nat. Montevideo, pp. 26–29.

———, A. Melgarejo, and M. Meneghel. 1976. Víboras venenosas del Uruguay. Inst. Inv. Cienc. Biol.: 1–6.

———, A. Melgarejo, and M. Meneghel. 1978. Ofidios del area de Salto Grande (Aspectos biológicos y referencias sobre ofidismo). V Reunión sobre aspectos de Desarrollo Ambiental. 31 pp.

Acosta-Solís, M. 1944. Nuevas contribuciones al conocimiento de la provincia de Esmeraldas. Quito, Editorial Ecuador. 606 pp.

Acton, H. W. and Knowles, R. 1921. Snakes and snake-poisoning. In W. Byam & R. G. Archibald (eds.). The practice of the medicine in the tropics, 1: 683–762.

Adler, K. (ed.). 1989. Contributions to the history of herpetology. Soc. Study Amph. Rept., 202 pp.

Ahl, E. 1927. Zwei neue Korallenotter der Gattung Elaps. Zool. Anz., 70(9/10): 251–252.

Aird, S. D. and da Silva, N. J. 1991. Comparative enzymatic composition of Brazilian coral snakes (Micrurus) venoms. Comp. Biochem. Phys., 99(2): 287–294.

Alemán, G. C. 1952. Apuntes sobre reptiles y anfibios de la región Baruta-El Hatillo. Mem. S.C.N. La Salle, Caracas, 12(31): 11–30.

———. 1953. Contribución al estudio de los reptiles y batracios de la Sierra de Perijá. Mem. S.C.N. La Salle, Caracas, 13: 205–225.

Allen, C. E. 1940. Behavior of *Micrurus frontalis frontalis*. Copeia, 1940(1): 51–52.

Allen, E. R. and W. T. Neill. 1950. Coral Snake. Flor. Wild Life, pp. 14–15.

———. 1956. Sports Afield, 135(3): 61–63, 138–141.

Almendariz, A. 1990. Lista de vertebrados del Ecuador. Anfíbios y reptiles. Politécnica, 16(3): 86–165.

Altman, L. K. 1986. New shock therapy for snakebites. N.Y. Times, Science Section, Aug. 5, 1986.

Alvarez del Toro, M. 1960. Reptiles de Chiapas. Gob. Estado Chiapas, Mexico, 204 pp.

———. 1972. Reptiles de Chiapas. 2d. ed. Gob. Estado Chiapas, Mexico, 178 pp.

———. 1983. Los Reptiles de Chiapas. 3d. ed. 1982. Mexico, Publicación del Instituto de Historia Natural. 248 pp.

——— and H. M. Smith. 1956. Notulae herpetologicae Chiapasiae I. Herpetologica, 12: 3–17.

Amaral, A. do. 1921. Contribução para o conhecimento dos ofídios do Brasil. Parte 1. Quatro novas espécies de serpentes brasileiras. Anex. Mem. Inst. Butantan, Secao Ofiologia, 1(1): 1–38.

———. 1922. Contribution toward the knowledge of snakes in Brazil. A. Part I. Four new species of Brazilian snakes. Anex. Mem. Inst. Butantan, 1921, 1: 49–81.

———. 1925a. South American Snakes in the collection of the United States National Museum. Proc. U.S. Natl. Mus., 67(24): 1–30.

———. 1925b. Da invalidez de espécie de Colubrideo Elapineo *Micrurus ibiboboca* (Merrem) e redescripção de *M. lemniscatus* (L.). Rev. Mus. Paulista, 15: 29–40.

———. 1926a. Nota de ophiologia. Sobre a invalidez de um gênero e algumas espécies de ophídios sul-americanos. Rev. Mus. Paulista, 14: 17–33.

———. 1926b. Ophídios de Mato Grosso. Comm. Linh. Telegr. Mato Grosso ao Amazonas, Publ. 84(5): 1–29.

———. 1926c. Studies of Neotropical Ophidia. II. On *Micrurus mipartitus* and allied forms. Proc. New England Zool. Club, 9: 61–66.

———. 1926d. Nomes vulgares de Ophídios do Brasil. Bol. Mus. Nac., Rio de Janeiro, 2: 19–29.

———. 1926e. Notas de ophiologia. la. nota de ophiologia. Sôbre a invalidez de um gênero e algumas espécies de ophídios sul-Americanos. Rev. Mus. Paulista, 14: 17–33.

———. 1927a. Albinismo em "cobra coral." Rev. Mus. Paulista, 15: 53–57.

———. 1927b. The snake-bite problem in the United States and in Central America. Bull. Antivenin Inst. Am., 1: 31–35.

———. 1927c. Studies of Neotropical ophidia. VII. An interesting collection of snakes from west Colombia. Bull. Antivenin Inst. Am., 1: 44–47.

———. 1927d. Tres sub-espécies novas de *Micrurus corallinus*: *Micrurus corallinus riesei*, *Micrurus corallinus corallinus* e *M. corallinus dumerilii*. Rev. Mus. Paulista, 15: 13–25.

———. 1928. Studies of Neotropical ophidia. XI. Snakes from Santa Marta region, Colombia. Bull. Antivenin Inst. Am., 2: 7–8.

———. 1930a. Estudos sôbre ophídios neotrópicos. XVII. Valor sistematico de varias formas de ophídios neotrópicos. Mem. Inst. Butantan, 1929, 4: 3–68.

———. 1930b. Contribuição ao conhecimento dos ophídios do Brasil. IV. Lista remissiva dos ophídios do Brasil. Mem. Inst. Butantan, 1929, 4: 71–125.

———. 1930c. Estudos sôbre ophídios neotrópicos. XVIII. Lista remissiva dos ophídios da região neotrópica. Mem. Inst. Butantan, 1929, 4: 127–272.

———. 1930d. Campanhas antiophídicas. Mem. Inst. Butantan, 5, 193.

———. 1930e. 92. Studies of neotropical ophidia. XV. A rare Brazilian snake. Bull. Antivenin Inst. Am., 4(1): 13–16.

———. 1931a. Studies of neotropical Ophidia. XXIII. Additional note on Colombian snakes. Bull. Antivenin Inst. Am., 4: 85–89.

———. 1931b. Studies of neotropical Ophidia. XXVI. Ophidia of Colombia. Bull. Antivenin Inst. Am., 4: 89–94.

———. 1932a. Notas sôbre chromatismo de ophídios. III. Casos de variação de colorido de sertas serpentes. Mem. Inst. Butantan, 7: 81–87.

———. 1932b. Estudos sôbre ophídios neotrópicos. XXIX. Novas notas sôbre espécies da Colombia. Mem. Inst. Butantan, 7: 103–123.

———. 1933. Mecanismo e genero de alimentação das serpentes do Brasil. Biol. Bol. (São Paulo), N.S. 1: 2–4.

———. 1935. Estudos sôbre ophídos neotrópicos. XXXIII. Novas espécies de ophídios da Colombia. Mem. Inst. Butantan, 9: 219–223.

———. 1937a. New species of ophidians from Colombia. Comptes Rendus. XII Congr. Int. Zool. (Lisbonne, 1935), 3: 1762–1767.

———. 1937b. Remarks on the ophiological fauna of Colombia. Comptes Rendus. XII Congr. Int. Zool. (Lisbone, 1935), 3: 1768–1776.

———. 1944. Notas sôbre a ofiologia neotrópica e brasílica. XI. Subespécies de *Micrurus lemniscatus* (L.) e suas afinidades com *M. frontalis* (Dm. e Bibr.) Pap. Avulsos, Dept. Zool., São Paulo, 5(11): 83–94.

———. 1948a. Ofídios de Mato Grosso (Contribução II para o conhecimento dos ofidios do Brasil). Com. Linh. Telegr. Estrat. Mato Grosso Amazonas. Publicação 84, Anexos 5: Hist. Nat. Zool. 43 pp.

———. 1948b. Ofídios do Pará. Bol. Mus. Paraense E. Goeldi, 10: 149–159.

———. 1974. Ofionimia amerindia na ofiologia Brasiliense. Mem. Inst. Butantan, 37: 1–15.

———. 1978. Serpentes do Brasil: Iconografia colorida. 2d. ed. Ed. da Univ. de São Paulo, 246 pp.

Anchieta, J. de. 1560. loc. cit. in Ordoñez, D. T. L. Joseph de Anchieta: Epistola quadriplurimarum rerum naturalium, etc. Olisipone, 8 p. plus 45 plus 1.

Andersson, L. G. 1899. Catalogue of Linnean type-specimens of snakes in the Royal Museum in Stockholm. Bih. K. Svenska Vetensk. Akad. Handl., 24: 1–35.

Andrews, C. E., J. E. Dees, R. O. Edwards, K. W. Jackson, C. C. Snyder, T. Moseley, J. F. Gennaro, Jr., and G. W. Gehres. 1968. Venomous snakebite in Florida. J. Florida Med. Ass., 55: 308–316.

Andrews, E. H. and C. B. Pollard. 1953. Report of snake bites in Florida and treatment: venoms and antivenoms. J. Florida Med. Assn., 40: 388–437.

Andrews, E. W. 1937. Notes on snakes from the Yucatán Peninsula. Field Mus. Nat. Hist. Publ. Zool. Ser., 20: 355–359.

Angel, M. R. 1983. Serpientes de Colombia. Guía práctica para su clasificación y tratamiento del envenenamiento causado por sus mordeduras. Rev. Fac. Nac. Agron., Medellín, 36: 1–171.

Anthony, J. 1955. Essai sur l'evolution anatomique de l'apareil venimeux des ophidiens. Ann. Sci. Nat. Zool., 11(17): 7–53.

Arnold, R. E. 1984. Treatment of venomous snakebites in the western hemisphere. Mil. Med., 149: 361–365.

Arocha, J. I. 1897. Estadística natural del estado Zulia. Maracaibo, 442 pp.

Araujo, M. L. de. 1978. Notas sobre ovos de serpentes (Boidae, Colubridae, Elapidae e Viperidae). Iheringia, ser. Zool., 51: 9–37.

Ardrey, R. 1970. The social contract. Atheneum Publishers, New York.

Ashley, B. D. and P. M. Burchfield. 1968. Maintenance of a snake colony for the purpose of venom extraction. Toxicon, 5: 267–271.

Ashton, R., S. R. Edwards, and G. R. Pisani. 1976. Endangered and threatened amphibians and reptiles in the United States. Soc. Stud. Amph. Rept., Herp. Circ., 5: 1–65.

Auffenberg, W. 1963. The fossil snakes of Florida. Tulane Stud. Zool., 10(3): 131–216.

Austin, C. R. 1965. Fine structure of the snake sperm tail. J. Ultrastructure Research, 12: 452–462.

Ayerbe, S. 1979. Estudio restrospectivo sobre ofidiotoxicosis en el Departamento del Cauca. Pautas para el manejo de las mordeduras de serpiente. Cuad. Med., Popayán, 4:46–55.

———. 1981. Ofidiotoxicosis micrúrica en el Cauca. Reporte de un caso fatal. Popayán (mimeo), pp. 1–7.

———, L. M. Otero, D. Galves and A. Paredes. 1977. Estudio retrospectivo sobre ofidiotoxicosis en el departmento del Cauca. la. Aspectos herpetológicos, clasificación de las ofidiotoxicosis, aspectos clínicos. Cuad. Med., Popayán, 2(3): 1–7.

———, A. Paredes, and D. A. Galves. 1980. Estudio retrospectivo sobre ofidiotoxicosis en el Departamento del Cauca. Segunda Parte. Aspectos clínicos, epidemiológicos y complicaciones. Cuad. Med., Popayán, 3(1): 33–45.

———, M. A. Tidwell, and M. Tidwell. 1990. Observaciones sobre la biología y comportamiento de la serpiente coral "Rabo de Ají" (*Micrurus mipartitus*). Descripción de una subespecie nueva. Noved. Colombianas, Popayán, 2: 30–41.

Azevedo, A. C. P. 1960. Notes on coral snakes (I–II) (Serpentes - Elapidae). Iheringia, Zool., 14: 1–14.

———. 1961. Notas sobre cobras corais - (Serpentes-Elapidae) III a VII. Iheringia, Zool., 18: 1–23.

———. 1962a. Anomalias observadas em serpentes do gênero *Micrurus* Wagler, 1924 (Serpentes, Elapidae). Iheringia, Zool., 26: 1–6.

———. 1962b. Sôbre uma população de *Micrurus frontalis frontalis* (D. & B., 1854) de Lagoa Santa, Minas Gerais, Brasil (Serpentes, Elapidae). Iheringia, Zool., 27: 1–4.

———. 1964. Variações cromáticas em *Micrurus corallinus* (Wied, 1820). Serpentes, Elapidae. Iheringia, Ser. Zool., 34: 1–15.

Baird, S. F. 1859. Reptiles of the boundary, with notes by the naturalists on the survey. United States and Mexican Boundary Survey under the order of Lieut. Col. W. H. Emory, 3: 1–35.

——— and C. Girard. 1853. Catalogue of North American reptiles in the Museum of the Smithsonian Institution. Part 1. Serpents. Washington, xvi + 172 pp.

Baker, R. H., G. Webb, and E. Stern. 1971. Amphibians, reptiles, and mammals from north-central Chiapas. An. Inst. Biol. Univ. Nac. Auton. Mex., Ser. Zool., 42: 77–86.

Bancroft, E. 1769. An essay of the natural history of Guiana. London, T. Becket and P. A. DeHondt, 402 pp.

Banton, H. J. 1930. A snake doctor of the Mosquito Coast. Mil. Surg., 67: 474–478.

Barbour, T. 1906. Vertebrata from the savanna of Panama. IV. Reptilia and Amphibia. Bull. Mus. Comp. Zool., 46: 224–229.

———. 1923. Notes on the reptiles and amphibians from Panama. Occas. Papers Mus. Zool. Univ. Michigan, 129: 1–16.

———. 1928. Reptiles from Bay Islands. Proc. New England Zool. Club, 10: 55–61.

——— and A. Amaral. 1924. Notes on some Central American snakes. Occas. Pap. Boston Soc. Nat. Hist., 5: 129–132.

——— and A. Amaral. 1928. A new elapid from western Panama. Bull. Antivenin Inst. Am., 1: 100.

——— and A. Loveridge. 1929. Reptiles and Amphibians. Vertebrates from the Corn Islands. Bull. Mus. Comp. Zool., 69: 138–146.

——— and G. K. Noble. 1920. Amphibians and reptiles from southern Peru collected by the Peruvian expedition of 1914–1915 under the auspices of Yale University and the National Geographic Society. Proc. U.S. Natl. Mus., 58: 609–620.

Barrera, A. 1962. La Península de Yucatán como provincia biótica. Rev. Soc. Mex. Hist. Nat., 23: 71–105.

Barrio, A. and M. E. Miranda. 1967. Estudio comparativo morfológico e inmunológico entre las diferentes entidades del género *Micrurus* Wagler (Ophidia, Elapidae) de la Argentina. Mem. Inst. Butantan, 1966, 33(1): 869–880.

Bates, H. W. 1862. Contributions to an insect fauna of the Amazon Valley, Lepidoptera: Heliconidae. Trans. Linn. Soc. London, 23: 495–566.

Bates, L. B. 1928. Snakes and snake-bite accidents of the Panama Canal Zone. Bull. Antivenin Inst. Am., 2: 31–33.

Beçak, W. and M. L. Beçak. 1969. Cytotaxonomy and chromosomal evolution in serpentes. Cytogenetics, 8: 247–348.

Beebe, W. 1919. The higher vertebrates of British Guiana. List of Amphibia and Mammalia. Zoologica, 2(7): 205–216.

———. 1946. Field notes on the snakes of Kartabo, British Guiana and Caripito, Venezuela. Zoologica, 31: 11–52.

———. 1947. Snake skins and color. Copeia, 1947: 205–206.

Behring, E. von and S. Kitasato. 1890. Über das Zustandekommen der Diphtherie-immunität und der Tetanusimmunität bei Tieren. Dtsch. med. Wschr., 16: 1113–1114.

Bellairs, A. 1970. The life of reptiles. 2 vols. Universe Books, New York, 590 pp.

Belluomini, H. E. 1964. Produção de veneno de serpentes em cativeiro. Comparação de resultados entre serpentario exposto e bioterio aquecido. Arq. Inst. Biol., 31(4): 149–154.

Bertoni, A. de W. 1914. Fauna Paraguayana. Catálogos systemáticos de los vertebrados del Paraguay. Peces, batracios, reptiles, aves y mamiferos conocidos hasta 1913. In M. S. Bertoni (ed.). Descripción física y económica del Paraguay. Asunción, Gob. Paraguay, 59: 1–83.

———. 1939. Catálogos sistemáticos de los vertebrados del Paraguay. Rev. Soc. Cientif. Paraguay, 4: 3–59.

Blaney, R. M. and P. K. Blaney. 1978. Notes on three species of *Micrurus* (Serpentes: Elapidae) from Mexico. Herpetol. Rev., 9: 92.

——— and P. K. Blaney. 1979. Variation in the coral snake, *Micrurus diastema* in Quintana Roo, Mexico. Herpetologica, 35(3): 276–278.

Bocourt, M. F. 1870–1909. Etudes sur les reptiles. *In* Duméril, Bocourt, and Mocquard. Mission Scientifique aux Mexique et dans l'Amerique Centrale, recherches zoologiques. Paris, Imprimerie Nationale, sect. 1, pp. i–xiv ("Avant-Propos" by Leon Vaillant) + 1–1012, map, pls. 1–77 in 17 livrs.

Boetger, O. 1886. Aufzählung der von den Philippinen bekannten Reptilien und Batrachier. Ber. Senckenb. Natf. Ges., 1885/1886: 91–134.

Bogert, C. M. 1960. The influence of sound on the behavior of amphibians and reptiles. In animal sounds and communication, AIBS, Publ., 7: 137–320.

——— and J. A. Oliver. 1945. A preliminary analysis of the

herpetofauna of Sonora. Bull. Am. Mus. Nat. Hist., 83: 297–426.

Boie, F. 1827. Bemerkungen über Merrem's Versuch eines Systems der Amphibien. 1ste Lieferung, Ophidier. Isis, (Oken), 20-6: 508–566.

Bolaños, R. 1971. Nuevos recursos contra el ofidismo en Centroamerica. Inst. Clodomiro Picado, 2nd. edit., pp. 1–29.

———. 1972. Toxicity of Costa Rican snake venoms for the white mouse. Am. J. Trop. Med. Hyg., 21: 260–263.

———. 1982. Las serpientes venenosas de Centro América y el problema del ofidismo. Primera Parte. Aspectos zoológicos, epidemiológicos y biomédicos. Rev. Costarric. Cienc. Med., 3: 165–184.

———. 1983. Serpientes venenosas de Centro America: distribución, y patrones cariológicos. Mem. Inst. Butantan, 46: 275–291.

———. 1984. Serpientes, venenos, y ofidismo en Centro América. San José, Costa Rica, Editorial Universidad de Costa Rica, 133 pp.

——— and L. Cerdas. 1980. Producción y control de sueros antiofídicos en Costa Rica. Bol. Ofic. Sanit. Panam., 88: 128–133.

———, L. Cerdas and J. W. Abalos. 1978a. Veneno de *Micrurus* (serpiente de coral). Un antiveneno multivalente de valor panamericano. Bol. Ofic. Sanit. Panam., 84: 128–133.

———, L. Cerdas and J. W. Abalos. 1978b. Venoms of coral snake (*Micrurus ssp.*): report on a multivalent antivenin for the Americas. Bull. Pan Am. Health Org., 12: 23–27.

———, L. Cerdas and R. T. Taylor. 1973. Estudios inmunológicos de los venenos de las principales *Micrurus de Norte América, Centro América, Panamá y Colombia*. (Abstr.), Antioq. Med., 23: 518.

———, L. Cerdas, and R. T. Taylor. 1975. The production and characteristics of a coral snake (*Micrurus mipartitus hertwigi*) antivenin. Toxicon, 13: 139.

———, A. Piva, R. T. Taylor, and A. Flores. 1973. Envenenamiento experimental de bovinos con veneno de *Micrurus nigrocinctus* (coral). Abstracts. IV Congreso de Medicina Veterinaria de Centro América y Panamá. San José, Costa Rica, 10–13 de Octubre de 1973.

———, A. Piva, R. T. Taylor, and A. Flores. 1975. Natural resistance of bovine animals to *Micrurus nigrocinctus* venom. Toxicon, 1975, 13: 369–370.

Boos, H. 1975. Check list of Trinidad snakes. J. Trinidad and Tobago Field Nat. Club, 1975: 22–28.

———. 1984a. A consideration of the terrestrial reptile fauna on some offshore islands north west of Trinidad. Living World Journal. J. Trinidad and Tobago Field Nat. Club, 1983/84: 19–26.

———. 1984b. The status and distribution of important reptiles and amphibians in Trinidad and Tobago. New York, FAO United Nations. 19 pp.

——— and V. Quesnel. 1968. Reptiles of Trinidad and Tobago. Publ. Branch. Minis. Educ. Cult. Trinidad and Tobago. 39 pp.

Booth, E. S. 1959. Amphibians and reptiles collected in Mexico and Central America from 1952 to 1958. Walla Walla Coll. Publ. Dep. Biol. Sci., 24: 1–9.

Boulenger, G. A. 1893–1896. Catalogue of the snakes in British Museum (Natural History). 3 vols. London, Trustees of the British Museum.

———. 1896. Catalogue of the snakes in the British Museum. London, 3: 1–727.

———. 1898a. A list of the reptiles and batrachians collected by the late Prof. L. Balzan in Bolivia. Ann. Mus. Stor. Nat. Genova, 2(19): 128–133.

———. 1898b. An account of the reptiles and batrachians collected by Mr. W. F. H. Rosenberg in western Ecuador. Proc. Zool. Soc. London, 1898: 107–127.

———. 1902a. Descriptions of new batrachians and reptiles from north-western Ecuador. Ann. Mag. Nat. Hist., 7(9): 51–57.

———. 1902b. List of fishes, batrachians, and reptiles collected by the late Mr. P. O. Simons in the provinces of Mendoza and Cordova, Argentina. Ann. Mag. Nat. Hist., 7(9): 336–339.

———. 1902c. Descriptions of new batrachians and reptiles from the Andes of Peru and Bolivia. Ann. Mag. Nat. Hist., 7(10): 394–402.

———. 1905. Descriptions of new snakes in the collection of the British Museum. Ann. Mag. Nat. Hist., 7(15): 453–456.

———. 1913. On a collection of batrachians and reptiles made by Dr. H. G. F. Spurrell, F. Z. S., in the Choco, Colombia. Proc. Zool. Soc. London, 1913: 1019–1038.

———. 1914. On a second collection of batrachians and reptiles made by Dr. H. G. F. Spurrell, F. Z. S., in the Choco, Colombia, Proc. Zool. Soc. London, 1914: 813–817.

———. 1920. Descriptions of four new snakes in the collection of the British Museum. Ann. Mag. Nat. Hist., 9(6): 108–111.

Bourret, R. 1936. Les serpentes de l'Indochine, 2. Catalogue systematique descriptif. Tolousse, H. Basuyau & Cie, (4)+ 505 pp.

Brattstrom, B. H. 1955. The coral snake "mimic" problem and protective coloration. Evolution, 9(2): 217–219.

Breder, C. M., Jr. 1946. Amphibians and reptiles of the rio Chucunaque drainage, Darien, Panama, with notes on their life histories and habits. Bull. Amer. Mus. Nat. Hist., 86: 377–453.

Brongersma, L. D. 1966. Note on *Leptomicrurus collaris* (Schlegel) (Reptilia, Serpentes). Zool. Meded., 41(17): 243–254.

———. 1967. Poisonous snakes of Surinam. Mem. Inst. Butantan, 1966, 33: 73–79.

Brown, B. C. and L. M. Brown. 1967. Notable records of Tamaulipan snakes. Texas J. Sci., 19: 323–326.

——— and H. M. Smith. 1942. A new subspecies of Mexican coral snake. Proc. Biol. Soc. Washington, 55: 63–66.

Brugger, K. 1989. Red-tailed Hawk dies with coral snake in talons. Copeia, 1989(2): 508–510.

Bücherl, W. 1963. Über die Ermittlung von Durchschnitt- und Höchst-Giftmengen bei den haufigsten Giftschlangen Südamerikas, ein Beitrag zur Serumtherapie von Giftschlangenbissen. In Die Giftschangen der Erde. Behringwerk-Mitteil: 67–120.

Buffon, G. L. de. 1769–1770. Histoire naturelle générale et particuliere. Paris: Imprimerie royale.

Burger, W. L. 1955. A new subspecies of the coral snake, *Micrurus lemniscatus*, from Venezuela, British Guiana,

References

and Trinidad; and a key for the identification of associated species of coral snakes. Bol. Mus. Cien. Nat., Caracas, 1(2): 1–19.

Bussing, W. A. 1976. Geographic distribution of the San Juan ichthyofauna of Central America with remarks on its origin and ecology. In T. B. Thorson (eds.). Investigations of the Ichtyofauna of Nicaraguan Lakes. University of Nebraska, pp. 157–175.

———. 1985. Patterns of distribution of the Central American ichthyofauna. In I. G. Stehli and S. D. Webb (eds.) The great American interchange. Plenum Press, New York. pp. 453–473.

Cadle, J. E. 1983. Problems and approaches in the interpretation of the evolutionary history of venomous snakes. Mem. Inst. Butantan, 1982, 46: 255–274.

———. 1984. Molecular systematics of neotropical xenodontine snakes. III. Overview of xenodontine phylogeny and the history of New World snakes. Copeia, 1984(3): 641–652.

———. 1988. Phylogenetic relationships among advanced snakes. A molecular perspective. Univ. Calif. Publ. Zool., 119: 1–77.

——— and G. C. Gorman. 1981. Albumin immunological evidence and the relationships of sea snakes. J. Herpetol., 15(3): 329–334.

——— and Patton. 1988. Distribution patterns of some amphibians, reptiles, and mammals of the eastern Andean slope of southern Peru. In Vanzolini P. E. and Heyer, R. (eds). Proceedings of a workshop on neotropical distribution patterns. January 12–16. 1987. Acad. Brasileira Cienc., Rio de Janeiro, pp. 225–244.

——— and V. M. Sarich. 1981. An immunological assessment of the phylogenetic position of New World coral snakes. J. Zool., London, 195: 157–167.

Calmette A. 1896. Le venin des serpents; physiologie de l'envenimation, traitment des morsures venimeuses par le serum des animaux vaccines. Soc. Ed. Sci., Paris, 72 pp.

Campbell, C. H. 1979. Symptomatology, pathology and treatment of the bites of the Elapid snakes. *In*: Lee, C. Y. (ed). Snake venoms. Handbook Experim. Pharmacology, vol. 52. Berlin, New York: Springer Verlag.

Campbell, J. A. 1973. A captive hatching of *Micrurus fulvius tenere* (Serpentes, Elapidae). J. Herp., 7(3): 312–315.

——— and W. W. Lamar. 1989. The venomous reptiles of Latin America. Ithaca, Comstock Publishing Associates, Cornell University Press, 425 pp.

——— and J. P. Vannini. 1988. Preliminary checklist of the herpetofauna of Finca El Faro, El Palmar, Quetzaltenango, Guatemala. Publ. Ocas. Fundación Intramer. Invest. Trop., 1: 10.

——— and J. P. Vannini. 1989. Distribution of amphibians and reptiles in Guatemala and Belize. Proc. Western Found. Vertebr. Zool., 4(1): 1–21.

Cardoso, J. L. C. 1985. Snakebites at hospital Vital Brazil. A study of 2,908 cases. Abstract. Toxicon, 23: 558.

Carrillo de Espinoza, N. 1977. Arañas y serpientes muy venenosas en el Departamento de Lima. Publ. Mus. Hist. Nat. Javier Pardo, Ser. Divul., 8: 1–8.

———. 1983. Contribución al conocimiento de las serpientes venenosas del Peru de las familias Viperidae, Elapidae e Hydrophiidae. Publ. Mus. Hist. Nat. Javier Prado, Ser. Zool., 30: 1–55.

Cartilha de Ophidismo. 1988. (Cobral). Ministry of Health, Brazil. pp. 1–32.

Casas-Andreu, G. 1981. Lista preliminar de los anfibios y reptiles de la costa de Jalisco. Inst. Biol. Univ. Nat. Auton. Mexico, 5 pp. (Mimeo).

——— and W. López-Forment. 1978. Notas sobre *Micrurus browni taylori* Schmidt and Taylor en Guerrero, Mexico. An. Inst. Biol. Univ. Nal. Auton. Mexico, 49, Ser. Zool., 1: 291–294.

Castro de Elera, F. 1885. Catálogo sistemático de toda la fauna de Filipinas conocida hasta el presente y a la vez de la colección zoológica del museo de PP. Dominicos del Colegio-Universidad de Santo Tomás de Manila escrito con motivo del exposición Regional Filipina Manila, colegio de Santo Tomas, viii, (2): 1–701.

Castro, F. G., Kattan K., and C. Murcia D. 1982. Serpientes corales verdaderas y falsas del Valle del Cauca. COAGRO 4: 15–21.

Cato, D. J. and S. F. Martinez. 1976. Serpientes venenosas de Venezuela. Diagnóstico, pronóstico y tratamiento del accidente ofídico. Caracas, Edit. La Torre.

Cei, J. M. 1979. The Patagonian Herpetofauna. In W. E. Duellman (ed.). The South American herpetofauna: Its origin, evolution, and dispersal. Monogr. Mus. Nat. Hist. Univ. Kansas, 7: 309–339.

———. 1987. Reptiles del centro, centro-oeste y sur de la Argentina. Herpetofauna de las zonas áridas y semiáridas. Mus. Reg. Sci. Nat. Boll. Monogr. 1986. 4: 1–527.

Cendrero, L., F. de Buen, M. A. Freiberg, C. C. Olrog, and J. Yepes. 1972. Zoología Hispanoamericana. Vertebrados. Mexico. Edit. Porrua, 1160 pp.

Cerdas, L. G. 1978. Estudios inmunológicos en venenos de serpientes de coral (Elapidae: Micrurus). Thesis, University of Costa Rica, 35 pp.

———, A. Cornavaca, and R. López. 1986. Ofidismo en la región Atlántica de Costa Rica: Análisis de 164 casos. Acta Med. Costarric. 29: 113–117.

Cervantes, B. Minton de and S. A. Minton. 1975. Geographic distribution: *Micrurus fulvius microgalbineus* (Tamaulipan coral snake). Herpetol. Review, 6(4): 116.

Chance, B. 1970. A note on the feeding habits of *Micrurus f. fulvius* (cannibalism). Bull. Maryland Herpetol. Soc. 6(3): 56.

Chang, C. C. 1979. The action of snake venoms on nerve and muscle. In Lee, C. Y. (ed.) Snake venoms. Handbook Experim. Pharmacology, vol. 52. Berlin, New York, Springer Verlag.

Charas, M. 1685. La Theriaque d'Andromachus. Paris: Laurent d'Houry.

Chippaux, J. P. 1987. Les serpentes de la Guyane Française. Coll. Faune Tropicale 27. Paris. Editions de l'Orstom. 155 pp.

———, J. Galtier, and J. F. Lefait. 1984. Epidemiologie des envenimations en Guyane Française. Bull. Soc. Pathol. Exp. 77: 206–215.

——— and M. Goyffon. 1983. Producers of antivenomous sera. Toxicon, 21(6): 739–752.

Clark, H. C. 1925. Snakes of the Ulua River valley. Annual Report, United Fruit Company Medical Department, 14: 286–297.

———. 1942. Venomous snakes. Some Central American records: Incidence of snake-bite accidents. Am. J. Trop. Med., 22: 37–49.

Clark, R. F. 1949. Snakes of the hill parishes of Louisiana. J. Tennessee Acad. Sci., 24(4): 244–261.

Cliff, F. S. 1954. Snakes of the Islands in the Gulf of California. Mexico. Trans. San Diego Soc. Nat. Hist. 12: 67–98.

Clodomiro Picado Instituto, n.d. Sueros antiofídicos globulinas purificadas de orígen equino. Drug circular. Universidad de Costa Rica.

Cochran, D. M. 1946. Notes on the herpetology of Pearl Islands, Panam. Smithson. Misc. Collect., 106: 1–8.

Coe, C. H. 1891. The poisonous snake of Florida. Sci. Amer., 64: 401.

Cohen, P., W. H. Berkeley, and E. B. Seligmann, Jr. 1971. Coral snake venoms: in vitro relation of neutralizing and precipitating antibodies. Am. J. Trop. Med. Hyg., 20: 646–649.

———, J. H. Dawson and E. B. Seligmann, Jr. 1968. Cross neutralization of *Micrurus fulvius fulvius* (coral snake) venom by anti- *Micrurus carinicauda dumerilii* serum. Am. J. Trop. Med. Hyg. 17: 308–310.

——— and E. B. Seligmann, Jr. 1966. Immunologic studies of coral snake venom. Mem. Inst. Butantan, 33(1): 339–347.

———, E. B. Seligmann, Jr., and W. H. Berkeley. 1967. Coral snake venom: Antibody response in rabbits. Nature, 213: 820–822.

———, W. H. Berkeley, and E. B. Seligmann, Jr. 1971. Coral snakes venoms. In vitro relation of neutralizing and precipitating antibodies. Amer. J. Trop. Med. and Hyg., 20(4): 646–650.

Cole, C. J. and C. R. Leavens. 1971. Chromosome preparations of amphibians and reptiles; improved technique. Herpetol. Rev., 3(6): T-102.

Conant, R. 1975. A field guide to reptiles and amphibians of eastern and central North America. 2d. ed. Boston, Houghton Mifflin, 429 pp.

Coote, J. 1981. The Californian mountain kingsnake (Lampropeltis zonata) and the coralsnake mimic problem. Herptile (6)4: 17–19.

Cope, E. D. 1859. Catalogue of the venomous serpents in the museum of the Academy of Natural Sciences of Philadelphia, with notes on the families, genera and species. Proc. Acad. Nat. Sci. Philadelphia, 11: 332–347.

———. 1860a. Supplement to "A catalogue of the venomous serpents in the Museum of the Academy, etc." Proc. Acad. Nat. Sci. Philadelphia, 12:72–74.

———. 1860b. Catalogue of the Colubrid snakes in the Museum of the Academy of Natural Sciences in Philadelphia, with notes and descriptions of new species. Proc. Acad. Nat. Sci. Philadelphia, 12: 241–266.

———. 1861. Contributions to the ophiology of lower California, Mexico, and Central America. Proc. Acad. Nat. Sci. Philadelphia, 13: 292–306.

———. 1862. Catalogue of the reptiles obtained during the explorations of Parana, Paraguay, Vermejo and Uruguay rivers, by Capt. Thos. J. Page, U.S.N.; and of those procured by Lieut. N. Michler, U.S. Top. Eng., Commander of the expedition conducting the survey of the Atrato river. Proc. Acad. Nat. Sci. Philadelphia, 14: 346–359.

———. 1865. Third contribution to the herpetology of tropical America. Proc. Acad. Nat. Sci. Philadelphia, 17: 185–189.

———. 1868. An examination of the Reptilia and Batrachia obtained by the Orton expedition to Equador and the Upper Amazon, with notes on other species. Proc. Acad. Nat. Sci. Philadelphia, 20: 94–140.

———. 1870. Seventh contribution to the herpetology of tropical America. Proc. Amer. Phil. Soc., 11: 147–169.

———. 1874. Descriptions of some species of reptiles obtained by Dr. John F. Bransford, assistant surgeon, United States Navy, while attached to the Nicaraguan surveying expedition in 1873. Proc. Acad. Nat. Sci. Philadelphia, 26: 64–72.

———. 1875. Checklist of the North American Batrachia and Reptilia, with a systematic list of the higher groups and an essay on geographical distribution. Based on the specimens contained in the U.S. National Museum. Bull. U.S. Natl. Mus., 1: 1–104.

———. 1876a. On the Batrachia and Reptilia of Costa Rica. J. Acad. Nat. Sci. Philadelphia, 2(8): 159–188.

———. 1876b. Report on the reptiles brought by Professor James Orton from the middle and upper Amazon, and western Peru. J. Acad. Nat. Sci. Philadelphia, (2)8: 159–188.

———. 1877. Synopsis of the cold-blooded vertebrata procured by Professor James Orton during his exploration in Peru in 1876–77. Proc. Am. Philos. Soc. 17: 33–49.

———. 1879. Eleventh contribution to herpetology of tropical America. Proc. Am. Philos. Soc., 18: 261–277.

———. 1885. A contribution to the herpetology of Mexico. Proc. Am. Philos. Soc., 22: 379–404.

———. 1886. Thirteenth contribution to the herpetology of tropical America. Proc. Am. Philos. Soc., 23: 271–287.

———. 1887. Catalogue of batrachians and reptiles of Central America and Mexico. Bull. U. S. Natl. Mus., 32: 1–98.

———. 1892. A critical review of the characters and variations of the snakes of North America. Proc. U.S. Natl. Mus., 14: 589–694.

———. 1894. On the lungs of the ophidia. Proc. Amer. Philos. Soc., 33 (145): 217–224.

———. 1895. The classification of the Ophidia. Trans. Amer. Phil. Soc., 18: 186–219.

———. 1896. The geographical distribution of Batrachia and Reptilia in North America. Am. Nat., 30: 886–902, 1003–1026.

———. 1900. The crocodilians, lizards and snakes of North America. Rept. U.S. Natl. Mus for 1898: 155–1270.

Cordeiro, C. L. and A. R. Hoge. 1974. Contribução ao conhecimento das serpentes do estado de Pernambuco. Mem. Inst. Butantan, 1973, 37:261–290.

Coues, E. 1875. Synopsis of the reptiles and batrachians of Arizona; with critical and field notes, and on extensive synonymy. Rep. Geo. Explor. Surv. West 100th Merid. by Geo. M. Wheeler, 5: 585–633.

Cracraft, J. 1985. Historical biogeography and patterns of differentiation within the South American Avifauna: Areas of endemism. In Buckley, P. A., M. Foster, E. S. Morton, R. S. Ridgely, and F. G. Buckley, (eds). Neotropical ornithology. Orn. Monogr. The American Ornithologists' Union, 36: 49–84.

Croulet, C. 1963. A taste of the tropics. Bull. Philadelphia Herpetol. Soc., 11: 1–5.

Cuesta Terrón, C. 1932. Los coralillos mexicanos. An. Inst. Biol. Univ. Mex., 3: 5–14.

Cunha, A. C. M. and A. R. Melgarejo. 1991. Um exemplar de "Cobra coral" *Micrurus corallinus* (Merrem, 1820) com padrão anomalo de coloração (Serpentes: Elapidae). Resumos XVIII Congr. bras. Zool., Univ. Fed. BA Salvador, I–II: 339.

Cunha, O. R. and F. P. Nascimento. 1973. Ofidios da Amazônia. IV. As cobras corais (gênero *Micrurus*) da região leste do Pará. (Ophidia, Elapidae). Nota preliminar. Publ. Avuls. Mus. Goeldi, Sesq. 20: 273–286.

——— and F. P. Nascimento. 1978. Ofídios da Amazônia. X. As cobras da região leste do Pará. Publ. Avuls. Mus. Paraense Emilio Goeldi, 31: 1–218.

——— and F. P. Nascimento. 1982a. Ofidios da Amazônia. XIV. As espécies de *Micrurus*, *Bothrops*, *Lachesis* e *Crotalus* do sul do Pará e oeste do Maranhão, incluindo áreas de cerrado deste estado. (Ophidia: Elapidae e Viperidae). Bol. Mus. Paraense Emilio Goeldi, Nova Ser., Zool., 112: 1–59.

——— and F. P. Nascimento. 1982b. Ofídios da Amazônia. XVII. Revalidação de *Micrurus ornatissimus* (Jan, 1858) diferenciada de *M. langsdorffi* (Wagler, 1824) e distribução geográfica das duas espécies (Ophidia: Elapidae). Bol. Mus. Paraense Emilio Goeldi, Zool., 116: 1–21.

——— and F. P. Nascimento. 1991. Ofídios da Amazônia. XXII. Revalidação e redescrição de *Micrurus albicinctus* Amaral, de Rondônia, e sôbre a validade de *Micrurus waehnerorum* Meise, do Amazonas (Ophidia: Elapidae). Bol. Mus. Paraense Emílio Goeldi, ser. zool., 7(1): 43–52.

———, F. P. Nascimento, and T. C. S. Avila-Pires. 1987. Contribuições do Museu Paraense Emilio Goeldi ao Projeto Carajás. Os répteis da área de Carajás, Pará, Brasil (Testudines e Squamata). Publ. Avuls. Mus. Emilio Goeldi, 40: 9–87.

Curtis, L. 1952. Cannibalism in the Texas coral snake. Herpetologica, 8: 27.

Cuvier, G. L. C. F. D. 1817. Le regne animal. Paris, 8: i–xviii, 1–532.

Daniel, Hno. 1949. Las serpientes en Colombia. Rev. Fac. Nac. Agron. Medellín, 9: 301–333.

Daudin, F. M. 1801–1803. Histoire naturelle et particuliere des reptiles. 8 volumes, Paris.

Davis, W. B. and J. R. Dixon. 1959. Snakes of the Chilpancingo region, Mexico. Proc. Biol. Soc. Washington, 72: 79–92.

——— and H. M. Smith. 1953. Snakes of the Mexican state of Morelos. Herpetologica, 8: 133–143.

De Franco Montalvan, D., I. Alvarez Trejos, and L. A. Mora Watler. 1983a. Mordedura de ofidios venenosos en niños en la región Pacífico Sur. Análisis de ciento sesenta casos. Acta Med. Costarr., 26: 61–70.

———, I. Alvarez Trejos and L. A. Mora Watler. 1983b. Terapia de la mordedura de ofidios venenosos en niños en la región Pacífico Sur. Analisis de ciento sesenta casos. Acta Med. Costarr., 26: 76–80.

Devincenzi, G. J. 1925. Fauna erpetológica del Uruguay. An. Mus. Nac. Hist. Montevideo, 2: 1–65.

D'Empaire, Serrano, Govea, Belloso, Quintero y Rojas. 1921. Geografía Médica del Zulia. Maracaibo, pp. I–VIII, 1–180.

di Tada, I. E., R. A. Martori, M. E. Doucet, and J. W. Abalos. 1978. Venom yield with different milking procedures. In Rosenberg, P. (ed). Toxins, animal plant and Microbiol. Toxicon, Suppl. 1, 1978: 3–7.

Díaz-Gómez, O. 1971. Accidentes por animales ponzoñosos. Trib. Med. (Bogotá) 1971: 6–12.

Ditmars, R. L. 1907. The reptile book. Page and Co., Garden City.

———. 1912. The feeding habits of serpents. Zoologica, 1: 197–238.

———. 1931. Snakes of the World. New York, McMillan Co. 207 pp.

Dix, M. W. 1978. A venom gland in the lower jaw of the coral snake (*Micrurus nigrocinctus mosquitensis* Schmidt). In P. Rosenberg (ed). Toxins, animal, plant and microbial. Oxford: Pergamon Press (Toxicon, Suppl. No. 1): 16–28.

Dixon, J. R. 1979. Origin and distribution of reptiles in lowland tropical rainforests of South America. In W. E. Duellman (ed.). The South American herpetofauna: its origin, evolution, and dispersal. Univ. Kansas Mus. Nat. Hist. Monogr., 7: 217–240.

———, C. A. Ketchersid, and C. S. Lieb. 1971. The herpetofauna of Querétaro, Mexico with remarks on taxonomic problems. Southwest. Nat., 16: 225–237.

——— and P. Soini. 1977. The reptiles of the upper Amazon Basin, Iquitos region, Peru. II. Crocodilians, turtles and snakes. Contrib. Biol. Geol. Milwaukee. Publ. Mus., 12:1–91.

——— and P. Soini. 1986. The reptiles of the upper Amazon Basin, Iquitos region, Peru. 2d. ed. Milwaukee Publ. Mus., 154 pp.

——— and R. G. Webb. 1965. *Micrurus laticollaris* Peters, from Jalisco, Mexico. Southwest. Nat., 10: 77.

Dowling, H. G. 1951. A proposed standard system of counting ventrals in snakes. British J. Herpetol., 1: 97–99.

———. 1975. A provisional classification of snakes. 1974. Yearbook Herpetology. Herpetol. Inform. Search Syst., New York, pp. 167–170.

Duellman, W. E. 1954. The amphibians and reptiles of Jorullo Volcano, Michoacán, Mexico. Occas, Pap. Mus. Zool. Univ. Michigan, 589: 1–22.

———. 1957. Notes on snakes from the Mexican state of Sinaloa. Herpetologica, 13(3): 237–240.

———. 1958. A preliminary analysis of the herpetofauna of Colima, Mexico, Occas. Pap. Mus. Zool. Univ. Michigan, 589: 1–22.

———. 1961. The amphibians and reptiles of Michoacán, Mexico. Univ. Kansas Publ. Mus. Nat. Hist., 15: 1–148.

———. 1965a. Amphibians and reptiles from the Yucatán Peninsula, Mexico. Univ. Kansas Publ. Mus. Nat. Hist., 15: 577–614.

———. 1965b. A biogeographic account of the herpetofauna of Michoacán, Mexico. Univ. Kansas Publ. Mus. Nat. Hist., 15: 627–709.

———. 1966. The Central American Herpetofauna: an ecological perspective. Copeia, 1966(4): 700–719.

———. 1972. South American frogs of the *Hyla rostrata* group. Zool. Mededel. Leiden, 47: 177–192.

———. 1978. The biology of an equatorial herpetofauna in Amazonian Ecuador. Univ. Kansas Mus. Nat. Hist., Misc. Publ., 65: 1–352.

———. 1979a. The South American herpetofauna: A panoramic view. In W. E. Duellman, (ed.) The South American herpetofauna: Its origin, evolution, and dispersal. Monogr. Mus. Nat. Hist. Univ. Kansas, 7: 1–28.

———. 1979b. The herpetofauna of the Andes: Patterns of distribution, origin, differentiation, and present communities. In W. E. Duellman, (ed.) The South American herpetofauna: Its origin, evolution, and dispersal. Monogr. Mus. Nat. Hist. Univ. Kansas, 7: 371–459.

———. 1982a. Quaternary climatic-ecological fluctuations in the lowland tropics: frogs and forests. In G. T. Prance (ed.), Biological diversification in the Tropics. Columbia University Press, New York, pp. 389–402.

———. 1982b. Compresión climática Cuaternaria en los Andes efectos sobre la especiación. In P. J. Salinas (ed.). Zoológica Tropical, Actas VIII Congreso Latinoamericano de Zoología. Mérida, Venezuela, 1982, pp. 177–278.

——— and A. W. Salas. 1991. Annotated checklist of the amphibians and reptiles of Cuzco amazonico, Peru. Occ. Pap. Mus. Nat. Hist. Univ. Kansas, 143: 1–13.

——— and A. Schwartz. 1958. Amphibians and reptiles of southern Florida. Bull. Florida State Mus., 3(5): 181–324.

Dugand, A. 1975. Serpentifauna de la llanura costera del Caribe. Caldasia, 11: 61–62.

Dugès, A. 1885. Notas sobre las coralillas (*Elaps* Schneider). Naturaleza, Mexico, 7: 200–203.

———. 1890. Fauna del estado de Guanajuato, In A. L. Velasco, (ed.) Geografía y estadística del estado de Guanajuato. Vol. 5. Geografía y estadística de la República Mexicana. Mexico, D. F., Secr. Fomento. pp. 287–295.

———. 1891. *Elaps diastema*, var. Michoacanensis. La Naturaleza, Mexico, 1(2): 87.

———. 1896. Reptiles y batracios de los E. U. Mexicanos. Naturaleza, Mexico, 2: 479–485.

Duméril, A. M. C., G. Bibron, and A. H. A. Duméril. 1834–1854. Erpétologie générale ou Historie naturelle complète des reptiles. 9 volumes, atlas. Paris: Librairie Encyclopedique de Roret.

Dundee, H., A. White, and V. Rico-Gray. 1986. Observations on the distribution and biology of some Yucatán Peninsula amphibians and reptiles. Bull. Maryland Herpetol. Soc. 22: 37–50.

Dunham, A. E., D. B. Miles, and D. Reznick. 1988. Life History patterns in squamata reptiles. In Gans, C. and R. B. Huey (eds.) Biology of reptilia. Vol. 16, Ecology B. Defense and Life history. Alan R. Liss, Inc., New York.

Dunn, E. R. 1923. Some snakes from northwestern Peru. Proc. Biol. Soc. Washington, 36: 185–188.

———. 1933. Amphibians and reptiles from El Valle de Antón, Panama. Occas. Pap. Boston Soc. Nat. Hist., 8: 65–79.

———. 1940. New and noteworthy herpetological material from Panama. Proc. Acad. Nat. Sci. Philadelphia, 92: 105–122.

———. 1942. New or noteworthy snakes from Panama. Notulae Nat., Philadelphia, 108: 1–8.

———. 1944a. Los géneros de anfíbios y reptiles de Colombia. III, Tercera parte: Reptiles, orden de las serpientes. Caldasia, 3(12): 155–224.

———. 1944b. Herpetology of the Bogota area. Rev. Acad. Colomb. Cienc. Exactas Fis. Nat. 6: 68–81.

———. 1945. The amphibians and reptiles of the Colombian Caribbean islands San Andrés and Providencia. Caldasia, 4: 121–122.

———. 1946. A small herpetological collection from eastern Peru. Proc. Biol. Soc. Washington, 59: 17–20.

———. 1947. Snakes of the Lerida Farm (Chiriqui Volcano, western Panama). Copeia, 1947: 153–157.

———. 1949. Relative abundance of some Panamian snakes. Ecology, 10: 39–57.

———. 1951. Venomous reptiles of the tropics. In G. C. Shattuck, (ed.) Diseases of the tropics. New York, Appleton-Century Crofts, pp. 741–754.

———. 1954. The coral snake "mimic" problem in Panama. Evolution, 8: 97–102.

——— and J. R. Bailey. 1939. Snakes from the uplands of the Canal Zone and of Darien. Bull. Mus. Comp. Zool. 86: 1–22.

——— and L. C. Stuart. 1951. Comments on some recent restrictions of type localities of certain South and Central American amphibians and reptiles. Copeia, 1951: 55–61.

Echternacht, A. A. 1973. The color pattern of *Sonora michoacanensis* (Duges) (Serpentes Colubridae) and its bearing on the origin of the species. Breviora, 410: 1–18.

Elton, N. W. 1948. The venomous snakes of Panama. Safety Zone Panama. C., pp. 1–7.

Emsley, M. 1977. Snakes, of Trinidad and Tobago. Bull. Maryland Herpet. Soc., 13(4): 201–304.

Engelhardt, G. P. 1932. Notes on poisonous snakes in Texas. Copeia, 1932: 37–38.

Ernst, A. 1877. Idea general de la fauna de Venezuela. Estudios sobre la flora y fauna de Venezuela. Caracas, pp. 280.

Estes, R. and A. Baez. 1985. Herpetofaunas of North and South America during the Late Cretaceous and Cenozoic. Evidence for Interchange? In F. G. Stehli and S. D. Webb (eds.). The Great American Biotic Interchange. Plenum Press, New York, pp. 139–197.

Evans, G. M. 1987. The coral snake question. Herptile, 12(3): 105–107.

Evans, H. E. 1947. Notes on Panamanian reptiles and amphibians. Copeia, 1947: 166–170.

Federsoni Jr., P. A. 1979. Novo artefacto para a extração de venenos de serpentes do gênero *Micrurus* Wagler. Mem. Inst. Butantan, 42: 171–174.

Fernandez Barrán, E. and M. A. Freiberg. 1951. Nombres vulgares de reptiles y batracios de la Argentina. Physis, 20: 303–319.

Ferrari-Pérez, F. 1886. Catalogue of animals collected by the geographical and exploring commission of the Republic of Mexico. Part III: Reptiles and Amphibians. Proc. U.S. Natl. Mus., 9: 182–199.

Fisher, C. B. 1973. Status of the flat-headed snake, *Tantilla gracilis* Baird and Girard, in Lousiana. J. Herp., 7: 136–137.

Fix, J. D. 1980. Venom yield of the North American coral snake and its clinical significance. South Med. J. 73: 737–738.

References

——— and S. A. Minton. 1976. Venom extraction and yields from the North American coral snake, *Micrurus fulvius*. Toxicon, 14: 143–145.

Flores Villela, O., E. Hernandez García and A. Nieto Montes de Oca. 1991. Catálogo de anfibios y reptiles, Ser. Catal. Mus. Zool. "A. Herrera", 3: 1–222.

———, G. Pérez-Higadera [sic], R. C. Vogt, and Palma Muñoz. 1987. Claves para los géneros y las especies de anfibios y reptiles de la región de los Tuxtlas. Mexico, D. F., Univ. Nac. Auton. Mexico, 27 pp.

Flowers, H. H. 1966. A comparison of the neutralization ability of a hererologous coral snake (*Micrurus fulvius*) venom. Amer. J. Trop. Med. Hyg., 15: 1003–1006.

Fonseca, F. da. 1949. Animais peconhentos. Inst. Butantan, São Paulo, 376 pp.

Fowlie, J. A. 1965. The snakes of Arizona. Azul Quinta, Fallbrook, Calif., 164 pp.

Fraser, D. F. 1964. *Micrurus limbatus*, a new coral snake from Veracruz, Mexico. Copeia, 1964(3): 570–573.

———. 1973. Variation in the coral snake, *Micrurus diastema*. Copeia, 1973(1): 1–17.

Freiberg, M. A. 1968. Ofidios ponzoñosos de la Argentina. Cien. Invest. 24(8): 338–353.

———. 1984. El mundo de los ofidios. Buenos Aires. Ed. Albatross, 152 pp.

Frost, D. and S. Aird. 1978. Geographic distribution: *Micrurus laticollaris*. Herpetol. Rev., 9: 62.

——— and J. T. Collins. 1988. Nomenclatorial notes on reptiles of the United States. Herpetol. Rev., 1(4): 73–74.

Fugler, C. M. and A. B. Walls. 1978. Snakes of the Upano Valley of Amazonian Ecuador. J. Tennessee Acad. Sci., 53: 81–87.

Funk, R. 1964. On the reproduction of *Micruroides euryxanthus* (Kennicot). Copeia, 1964(1): 219.

Gadow, H. 1905. The distribution of Mexican amphibians and reptiles. Proc. Zool. Soc. London, 1905: 191–258.

———. 1908. Through southern Mexico. London, Witherly and Co., 527 pp.

———. 1911. Isotely and coralsnakes. Zool. Jahrb., Abt. Syst., 31: 1–24.

Gaige, H. T. 1936. Some reptiles and amphibians from Yucatan and Campeche Mexico. Publ. Carnegie Inst., 457: 289–304.

———, N. Hartweg, and L. C. Stuart. 1937. Notes on a collection of amphibians and reptiles from eastern Nicaragua. Occ. Pap. Mus. Zool. Univ. Michigan, 357: 1–18.

Gallardo, J. M. 1979. Composición, distribución y orígen de la herpetofauna Chaqueña. In W. E. Duellman, (ed.) The South American herpetofauna: Its origin, evolution, and dispersal. Monogr. Mus. Nat. Hist. Univ. Kansas, 7: 299–307.

Gans, C. and W. Elliot. 1968. Snake venoms: Production, injection, action. Adv. in Oral Biol., Academic Press Inc. New York, 3: 45–81.

Gansser, A. 1973. Facts and theories of the Andes. J. Geol. Soc. London., 129: 93–131.

García, E. 1896. Los ofidios venenosos del Cauca. Métodos empíricos y racionales empleados contra los accidentes producidos por la mordedura de esos reptiles. Libreria Colombiana: Cali., 102 pp.

Garman, S. 1877. Reptiles and batrachians collected by Allen Lesley, Esq., on the Isthmus of Panama. Proc. Boston Soc. Nat. Hist., 1876. 18: 402–413.

———. 1884a. The reptiles and batrachians of North America. Mem. Mus. Comp. Zool., 8: 1–185.

———. 1884b. The North American reptiles and batrachians. A list of the species occurring north of the Isthmus of Tehuantepec, with references. Bull. Essex Inst., 16: 1–46.

Gasc, J. P. and M. T. Rodrigues. 1980. Liste préliminaire des serpentes de la Guyane Française. Bull. Mus. Natl. Hist. Nat. Paris, 4(2)A(2): 559–598.

Gates, G. O. 1956. A record length for the Arizona coral snake. Herpetologica, 12: 155.

———. 1957. A study of the herpetofauna in the vicinity of Wickenburg, Maricopa County, Arizona. Trans. Kansas Acad. Sci., 60: 403–418.

Gatti, C. 1955. Las culebras venenosas del Paraguay. Rev. Med. Paraguay, 1(2): 81–100.

Gehlbach, F. R. 1970. Death feigning and erratic behavior in leptotyphlopid, colubrid and elapid snakes. Herpetologica, 26: 24–34.

———. 1972. Coral snake mimicry reconsidered: The strategy of self-mimicry. Forma et Functio, 5: 311–320.

———, J. F. Watkins, and J. C. Kroll. 1971. Pheromone trail-following studies of typhlopid, leptotyphlopid, and colubrid snakes. Behaviour, 40(3–4): 282–294.

Gennaro, J. G. and N. C. McCollough. 1967. Further observations on coral snake bites in the United States: symptoms and therapy. Mem. Inst. Butantan, 1966, 33(3): 855–856.

Gentry, J. and M. H. Smith. 1968. Food habits and burrow associates of *Peromyscus polionotus*. J. Mamm., 49: 562–565.

George, I. 1930. Notes on extraction of venom. Bull. Antivenin Inst. Am., 4(3): 57–61.

Girard, C. 1854. Abstract of a report to Lieut. James M. Gillis, USN., upon the reptiles collected during the USN astronomical expedition to Chile. Proc. Acad. Nat. Sci. Philadelphia, 7: 226–227.

Gittens, T. S. 1935. Snake bite in the United States. Sci. Month., 41: 163–167.

Gliesh, R. 1925. As cobras do Estado do Rio Grande do Sul. Almanak Agric. Brasil, 1925: 97–118.

Gloyd, H. K. 1937. A herpetological consideration of faunal areas in southern Arizona. Bull. Chicago Acad. Sci., 5: 79–136.

———. 1938. A case of poisoning from the bite of a Black Coral Snake. Herpetologica, 1(5): 121–124.

Golay, P. 1985. Checklist and keys to the terrestrial proteroglyphs of the world (Serpentes: Elapidae, Hydrophiidae). Geneva: Elapsoidea, 90 pp.

Gomes, J. F. 1918a. Contribuição para o conhecimento dos ophídios do Brasil. II. Ophídios do Museu Rocha (Ceará). Rev. Mus. Paulista, 10: 503–527.

———. 1918b. Contribuição para o conhecimento dos ophidios do Brasil. III (1) Ophidios do Museu Paraense. Mem. Inst. Butantan, 1: 57–77.

Graham, G. 1977. The karyotype of the Texas coral snake, *Micrurus fulvius tenere*. Herpetologica, 33: 345–348.

Grantsau, R. 1991. As cobras venenosas do Brasil. Bandeirantes, São Bernardo do Campo, S. P., 101 pp.

Gray, J. E. 1829. Synopsis generum reptilium et amphibiorum. Isis von Oken, 22: 187–206.

———. 1845. Catalogue of the specimens of snakes in the collection of the British Museum. London. Trustees of the British Museum, XV + 125 pp.

———. 1849. Catalogue of the specimens of snakes in the collection of the British Museum. London, XV+125 pp.

Greene, H. W. 1972. Mexican reptiles in the Senckenberg Museum. Pittsburgh, Penn., Carnegie Museum, 15 pp.

———. 1973a. The food habits and feeding behavior of New World coral snakes. M.A. Thesis, University of Texas at Arlington, 66 pp.

———. 1973b. Defensive tail display by snakes and amphisbaenians. J. Herpetol., 7: 143–161.

———. 1973c. Comments on aposematism and mimicry among coral snakes. Biologist, 55(4): 144–147.

———. 1976. Scale overlap, a directional sign stimulus for prey ingestion by ophiophagous snakes. 2. Tierpsychol. 41: 113–120.

———. 1984. Feeding behavior and diet of the Eastern coral snake, *Micrurus fulvius*. In R. A. Seigel, L. E. Hunt, J. L. Knight, L. Malert, and N. L. Zuschlag (eds.) Vertebrate ecology and systematics: a tribute to Henry S. Fitch. Univ. Kansas Mus. Nat. Hist., Spec. Publ., 10: 147–162.

———. 1988. Antipredator mechanisms in reptiles. In Gans. C. and R. B. Huey (eds.). Biology of reptilia. Ecology B. Defense and Life history. Alan R. Liss, Inc., New York, 16: 1–152.

——— and R. M. McDiarmid. 1981. Coral snake mimicry: does it occur? Science, 213(4513): 1207–1212.

——— and W. F. Pyburn. 1973. Comments on aposematism and mimicry among coral snakes. Biologist, 55: 144–148.

——— and R. L. Seib. 1983. *Miocrurus nigrocinctus* (coral, coral snake, coralillo). In D. H. Janzen, (ed.). Costa Rican Natural History. Chicago, Univ. of Chicago Press. pp. 406–408.

Gremone, C. and S. Gorzula. 1986. Pt. III. Los reptiles, clase Reptilia. *In* Gremone, C., F. Cervigón, S. Gorzula, G. Medina and D. Novoa (eds.), Fauna de Venezuela. Edit. Biosfera, Caracas, pp. 111–154.

Griffin, L. E. 1916. A catalogue of the ophidia from South America at present (June, 1916) contained in the Carnegie Museum, with descriptions of some new species. Mem. Carnegie Mus., for 1915, 7(3): 163–228.

Grijs, P. 1898. Beobachtungen an Reptilien in der Gefangenschaft. *Elaps fulvius*. Zool. Gart., 39: 276–279.

Grobman, A. B. 1978. An alternative solution to the coral snake mimic problem (Reptilia, Serpentes, Elapidae). J. Herpetol., 12(1): 1–11.

Grocott, R. G. and G. G. Sadler. 1958. The poisionous snakes of Panama. Mt. Hope, Canal Zone, Panama Canal Printing Plant, 38 pp.

Guderian, R. H., Ch. Mackenzie, and J. F. Williams. 1986. High voltage shock treatment for snake bite. The Lancet, Jul 26. 1986: 229.

Gumilla, J. S. J. 1741. El Orinoco illustrado, Historia natural civil y geográfica de este gran río y de sus caudalosos vertientes. Madrid, Manuel Fernández, Tomos I–II: 1–580.

Günther, A. 1858. Catalogue of the colubrine snakes in the collection of the British Museum. London: Trustees of the British Museum. XVI. + 281 pp.

———. 1859: On the genus *Elaps* Wagler. Proc. Zool. Soc. London, 1859: 79–89.

———. 1868. Sixth account of new species of snakes in the collection of the British Museum. Ann. Mag. Nat. Hist., 4(1): 413–429.

———. 1895. Biologia Centrali-Americana. Reptilia and Batrachia. London, xx + 326 pp.

Gutiérrez, J. M. and R. Bolaños. 1979. Cariotipos de las principales serpientes coral (Elapidae: *Micrurus*) de Costa Rica. Rev. Biol. Trop., 27: 57–73.

——— and R. Bolaños. 1981. Polimorfismo cromosómico intraespecífico en la serpiente de coral *Micrurus nigrocinctus* (Ophidia: Elapidae). Rev. Biol. Trop., 29(1): 115–122.

———, B. Lomonte, E. Portilla, L. Cerdas, and E. Rojas. 1983. Local effects induced by coral snake venoms: evidence of myonecrosis after experimental inoculations of venoms from five species. Toxicon, 21(6): 777–783.

———, A. Solórzano, L. Cerdas, and J. P. Vannini. 1988. Karyotypes of five species of coral snakes (Micrurus). J. Herpetol., 22: 109–112.

Haas, G. 1930. Über die Schädelmechanik und die Kiefermuskulatur einiger Proteoglypha. Zool. Jahrb. (Abt. Anat. Ont. Tiere), 52: 95–218.

———. 1952. The head muscles of the genus Causus, Solenoglypha and some remarks on the origin of the Solenoglypha. Proc. Zool. Soc. London, 122: 573–592.

Haffer, J. 1969. Speciation in Amazon forest birds. Science, 165: 131–137.

Hahn, D. E. and C. J. May. 1972. Noteworthy Arizona herpetofaunal records. Herpetol. Rev., 4: 91–92.

Hallowell, E. 1855. Contributions to South American herpetology. Jour. Acad. Nat. Sci. Philadelphia, 2(3): 33–36.

———. 1860. Report of the reptilia of the north Pacific exploring expedition, under command of Capt. John Rogers, USN. Proc. Acad. Nat. Sci. Philadelphia, 12: 480–510.

Halter, C. R. 1923. The venomous coral snake. Copeia, 1923(1): 105–107.

Harding, K. A. and K. R. G. Welch. 1980. Venomous snakes of the world: a checklist. Oxford and New York: Pergamon Press, XII+188 pp.

Hardy, L. D. 1989. Annotated bibliography of snakebite in Latin America. In Campbell J. and W. Lamar (eds.). The venomous reptiles of Latin America. Comstock, Cornell University Press. Ithaca, London, pp. 14–18.

———. 1989. Producers of antivenoms for venomous snakes of Latin America. In Campbell J. and W. Lamar (eds.). The venomous reptiles of Latin America. Comstock, Cornell University Press. Ithaca, London, pp. 18–20.

Hardy, L. M. and R. W. McDiarmid. 1969. The amphibians and reptiles of Sinaloa, Mexico. Univ. Kansas Publ. Mus. Nat. Hist., 18(3): 39–252.

Harnack, M. von. 1953. Die Hautzeichnungen der Schlangen. J. Morph. u. Ökol. Tiere, 41: 513–573.

Harwood, P. O. 1930. A new species of *Oxysomatium* (Nematoda) with some remarks on the genera *Oxysomatium* and *Aplectana*, and observations on life history. J. Parasitol., 17(2): 61–73.

———. 1932. The helminths parasitic in the Amphibia and Reptilia, Texas, and vicinity. Proc. U. S. Natl. Mus., 81(2940):1–71.

References

Hecht, M. K. and D. Marien. 1956. The coral snake mimic problem: A reinterpretation. J. Morphol., 98: 335–364.

Henderson, R. W. 1984. *Scaphiodontophis* (Serpentes: Colubridae): natural history and test of a mimicry-related hypothesis. In Seigel, Hunt, Knight, Malaret, and Zuschlag (eds.). Vertebrate Ecology and Systematics—A Tribute to Henry S. Fitch. Mus. Nat. Hist. Univ. Kansas, Spec. Publ., 10: 185–194.

——— and M. Binder. 1980. The ecology and behaviour of vine snakes (*Ahaetulla, Oxybelis, Thelotornis, Uromacer*): A review. Contr. Biol. Geol. Milwaukee Publ. Mus., 37: 1–38.

——— and L. G. Hoevers. 1975. A checklist and key to the amphibians and reptiles of Belize, Central America. Milwaukee Publ. Mus. Contr. Biol. Geol., 5: 1–63.

———, J. R. Dixon, and P. Soini. 1978. On the seasonal incidence of tropical snakes. Milwaukee Publ. Mus. Contr. Biol. Geol., 17: 1–15.

———, J. R. Dixon, and P. Soini. 1979. Resource partitioning in Amazonian snake communities. Milwaukee Publ. Mus. Contr. Biol. Geol., 22: 1–11.

Hensley, M. M. 1950. Results of a herpetological reconnaissance in extreme southwestern Arizona and adjacent Sonora, with a description of a new subspecies of the Sonoran whipsnake, *Masticophis bilineatus*. Trans. Kansas Acad. Sci., 53: 270–288.

———. 1959. Albinism in North American amphibians and reptiles. Publ. Mus. Mich. State, 1: 135–159.

——— and P. W. Smith. 1962. Noteworthy herpetological records from the Mexican states of Hidalgo and Tabasco. Herpetologica, 18(1): 70–71.

Herzberg, R. 1987. Shocks for Snakebites. Outdoor Life, June, 1987, 5 pp.

Heyer, W. R. 1967. A herpetofaunal study of an ecological transect through Cordillera de Tilaran, Costa Rica. Copeia, 1967: 259–271.

———. 1973. Systematics of the marmoratus group of the frog genus *Leptodactylus* (*Amphibia Leptodactylidae*). Los Angeles Co. Mus. Nat. Hist. Contr. Sci., 251: 1–50.

Hill, W. H. 1971. Pleistocene snakes from a cave in Kendall County, Texas. Texas J. Sci., 22(2): 209–216.

Hoge, A. R. 1952. Notas erpetologicas. 1. Contribuição ao conhecimento dos ofídios do Brasil central. Mem. Inst. Butantan, 24: 179–214.

———. 1956. Uma nova espécie de *Micrurus* (Serp. Elap.) do Brasil. Mem. Inst. Butantan, 27: 67–72.

———. 1958. Tres notas sôbre serpentes brasileiras. I. Sôbre a posição genérica de *Coluber bicintus* Hermann, 1804 e *Xenodon gigas* Dumeril, 1853 (Colubridae). II. Sôbre a posição sistematica de *Enicognathus joberti* Sauvage, 1884 (Colubridae). III. Dimorfismo sexual em *Micrurus s. surinamensis* (Cuvier 1817) (Elapidae). Pap. Avuls. Zool., São Paulo, 13: 221–224.

———. 1965. Preliminary account of Neotropical Crotalinae (Serpentes, Viperidae). Mem. Inst. Butantan, 32: 109–184.

———. 1967. Serpentes do Territorio Federal do Amapá. Atas Simp. Biota Amaz., 5: 217–223.

——— and H. E. Belluomini. 1959. Aberrações cromáticas em sepentes brasileiras. Mem. Inst. Butantan, 1957/1958, 28:95–98.

———, C. L. Cordeiro, and A. R. W. D. L. Romano. 1976. A new subspécies of *Micrurus* from Brazil (Serpentes, Elapidae). Cienc. Cultura, Suppl. 28(7): 417–418.

———, C. L. Cordeiro, and A. R. W. D. L. Romano. 1977. Redescription of *Micrurus donosoi* Hoge, Cordeiro et Romano (Serpentes: Elapinae). Mem. Inst. Butantan, 1976/1977, 40/41: 71–73.

——— and P. A. Federsoni, 1981. Manutenção e crianção de serpentes em cativeiro. Rev. Bioterios, 1: 63–73.

——— and A. R. Lancini. 1960. Nota sôbre *Micrurus surinamensis nattereri* Schmidt e *Micrurus pyrrhocryptus* Cope. Mem. Inst. Butantan, 1959, 29: 9–13.

——— and A. R. Lancini. 1961. Notas sobre la ubicación de la terra typica de varias especies de "serpentes" colectadas por M. Bauperthuis en la "Cote Ferme" y en la "Province de Venezuela". Bol. Mus. Cienc. Nat., 1960: 58–62.

——— and A. R. Lancini. 1962. Sinopsis de las serpientes venenosas de Venezuela. Pub. Ocas. Mus. Cien. Nat. Caracas, Zool., 1: 1–24.

——— and A. R. W. D. L. Romano. 1966. Leptomicrurus in Brasil (*Serpentes-Elapidae*). Mem. Inst. Butantan, 1965, 32: 1–8.

——— and A. R. W. D. L. Romano. 1969. Espécies registradas para o Brasil (Serpentes). Cienc. Cult., Suppl. 21: 454.

——— and A. R. W. D. L. Romano. 1971a. Neotropical pit vipers, sea snakes, and coral snakes. In W. Bucherl and E. Bucheley, (eds.) Venomous animals and their venoms. vol. 2: Venomous vertebrates New York, Academic Press, pp. 211–293.

——— and A. R. W. D. L. Romano. 1971b. *Micrurus hemprichii hemprichii* recorded for Brazil (Serpentes, Elapidae). Mem. Inst. Butantan, 35: 107–109.

——— and A. R. W. D. L. Romano. 1973. Sinopse das serpentes peçonhentas do Brasil. Serpentes, Elapidae, Viperidae. Mem. Inst. Butantan, 1972. 36: 109–207.

——— and A. R. W. D. L. Romano. 1981. Sinopse das serpentes peçonhentas do Brasil, (2da. ed.). Mem. Inst. Butantan, 1978/79, 42/43: 373–496.

———, A. R. W. D. L. Romano, P. A. Federsoni-Junior, and C. L. S. Cordeiro. 1975. Nota previa. Lista das espécies de serpentes coletadas na região da usina hidroelectrica de Ilha Solteira-Brasil. Mem. Inst. Butantan, 1974, 38: 167–178.

———, C. R. Russo, M. C. Santos, and M. F. D. Furtado. 1981. Snakes collected by "Projeto Rondon XXII" to Piaui, Brasil. Mem. Inst. Butantan, 1978/79, 42/43: 87–94.

———, N. P. Santos, C. Heitor, L. A. Lopes, and I. Menezes de Souza. 1973. Serpentes coletadas pelo projeto Rondon VII em Iauarete, Brazil. Mem. Inst. Butantan, 1972, 36: 221–232.

Holbrook, J. E. 1836–1840. *North American Herpetology*. Philadelphia, 4 vols.

———. 1842. *North American Herpetology*. [2nd edition], Philadelphia, 5 vols.

Holman, J. A. 1958. The Pleistocene herpetofauna of Sabertooth Cave, Citrus County, Florida. Copeia, 1958(4): 276–280.

———. 1959a. A Pleistocene herpetofauna near Orange Lake, Florida. Herpetologica, 5(3): 121–125.

———. 1959b. Amphibians and reptiles from the Pleistocene (Illinoian) of Williston, Florida. Copeia, 1959(2): 96–102.

———. 1977. Upper Miocene snakes (Reptilia, Serpentes) from southeastern Nebraska. J. Herpetol., 11(3): 323–335.

———. 1978. The late Pleistocene herpetofauna of Devil's Den Sinkhole, Levy County, Florida. Herpetologica, 34(2): 228–237.

Hoogmoed, M. S. 1979. The herpetofauna of the Guianan Region. In: W. E. Duellman (ed.). The South American Herpetofauna: Its origin, evolution and dispersal. Monogr. Mus. Nat. Hist. Univ. Kansas, 8: 241–279.

———. 1983. Snakes of the Guianian region. Mem. Inst. Butantan, 1982, 46: 219–254.

——— and U. Gruber. 1983. Spix and Wagler type specimens of reptiles and amphibians in the Natural History Museum in Munich (Germany) and Leiden (The Netherlands). Spixiana, Suppl. 9: 319–415.

Howell, T. R. 1957. Birds of a second-growth rain forest area of Nicaragua. Condor, 59(2): 74–111.

Ihering, H. v. 1881. Über den Giftapparat der Korallenschlange. Zool. Anz. 4: 409–412.

———. 1911. As cobras do Brasil. Primeira parte. Rev. Mus. Paulista, São Paulo, 1910. 8: 273–379.

Jackson, D. R. and R. Franz. 1981. Ecology of the Eastern coral snake (*Micrurus fulvius*) in northern peninsular Florida. Herpetologica, 37(4): 213–228.

———, W. F. Ingram III, and W. H. Campbell. 1976 The dorsal pigmentation pattern of snakes as antipredator strategy: A multivariate approach. Am. Nat., 110: 1029–1053.

Jan, G. 1858. Plan d'une iconographie descriptive des ophidiens et description sommaire de nouvelles espèces de serpents. Rev. Mag. Zool., ser. 2, 10: 438–449, 514–527.

———. 1859a. Plan d'une iconographie descriptive des ophidiens et description sommaire de nouvelles espèces de serpents. Rev. Mag. Zool., ser. 2, 10: 122–130, 148–157.

———. 1859b. Additions et rectifications aux Plan et Prodrome de l'iconograpie descriptive des ophidiens. Rev. Mag. Zool. ser. 2: 505–512.

———. 1859c. Spix' Serpentes brasilienses Beurtheilt nach Autopsie der original Exemplare und auf die Nomenclatur von Duméril und Bibron zurückgeführt. Arch. Naturg. 25: 272–275.

———. 1863a. Elenco systematico degli ofidi descritta e designati per l'iconografia generale. Milan, pp. 1–143.

———. 1863b. Enumerazione sistematica degli ofidi appartenenti al gruppo *Coronellidae*. Arch. Zool. Anat. Fisiol., 21(2): 213–330.

———. 1872. In Jan and F. Sordelli. 1860–1881. Iconographie générale des Ophidiens. 3 vols., 50 livr. 300 pls. Milan: chez les auteurs. Londres: Bailliere Tindal and Cox. Paris.

Janzen, D. H. 1980. Two potential coral snake mimics in a tropical deciduous forest. Biotropica, 12: 77–78.

Jiménez-Porras, J. 1963. Comparative biochemical studies on venoms of snakes of Costa Rica. Dissertation Abstracts, XXV(2).

———. 1967. In F. E. Russell and P. R. Saunders (eds.). Animal Toxins, Pergamon Press, Oxford and New York.

———. 1970. Bioquímica, farmacología y fisiopatología de los venenos de serpientes. Rev. Univ. Costa Rica, 28: 43–55.

Johnson, J. D. 1973. New records of reptiles and amphibians from Chiapas, Mexico. Trans. Kansas Acad. Sci., 76: 223–224.

———. 1984. A biogeographic analysis of the herpetofauna of northwestern nuclear Central America. Ph.D. Thesis, Texas A & M University, 127 pp.

Kappler, A. 1881. Holländisch-Guiana. Erlebnisse und Erfahrungen während eines 43 jährigen Aufenthalts in der Kolonie Surinam. Stuttgart, W. Kohlhammer, X+495 pp.

Kardong, K. V. 1980. Evolutionary patterns in advanced snakes. Amer. Zool., 20(1): 269–282.

Kempff, N. M. 1975. Ofidios de Bolivia. Acad. Nac. Cienc. Bolivia, 46 pp.

Kennedy, J. P. 1964. Natural history notes on some snakes of eastern Texas. Texas J. Sci., 16(2): 210–215.

Kennicott, R. 1860. Descriptions of new species of North American serpentes in the museum of the Smithsonian Institution, Washington. Proc. Acad. Nat. Sci. Philadelphia, 12: 328–338.

Kipling, R. 1891. Reingelder and the German flag. In Life's Handicap, being stories of mine one people. McMillan, London, pp. 6–9.

Kitchens, C. S. and L. H. S. van Mierop. 1987. Envenomation by the Eastern Coral snake (*Micrurus fulvius fulvius*). A study of 39 victims. JAMA, 1987, 258(12): 1615–1618. Copyright 1987, American Medical Association.

Klappenbach, M. A. and B. Orejas-Miranda. 1969. Anfíbios y Reptiles. Nuestra Tierra, Montevideo, 11: 68 pp.

Klauber, L. M. 1946. The glossy snake, *Arizona*, with descriptions of new subspecies. Trans. San Diego Soc. Nat. Hist., 10: 311–398.

Klemmer, K. 1963. Liste der rezenten Giftschlangen. In Die Giftschlangen der Erde. Behringw. Mitteil., pp. 255–464.

Knight, R. L. and A. W. Erickson. 1976. High incidence of snakes in the diet of nesting red-tailed hawks. Raptor Res. 10(4): 108–111.

Kocholaty, W. F., B. D. Ashley and T. A. Billings. 1967. An immune serum against the North American coral snake (*Micrurus fulvius fulvius*) venom obtained by photooxidative detoxification. Toxicon, 5: 43–46.

———, T. A. Billings, B. D. Ashley, E. B. Ledford, and G. C. Goetz. 1968. Effect of the route of administration on the neutralizing potency of antivenins. Toxicon, 5: 165–170.

———, E. Boyles-Ledford, J. Daly, and T. A. Billings. 1971a. Preparation of a coral snake antivenin from goat serum. Toxicon, 9: 297–298.

———, E. Boyles-Ledford, J. Daly, and T. A. Billings. 1971b. Toxicity and some enzymatic properties and activities in the venoms of Crotalidae, Elpidae, and Viperidae. Toxicon, 9: 131–138.

Kochva, E. 1978. Oral glands of reptilia. In C. Gans (ed.). Biology of Reptilia. London, Academic Press, 8: 43–61.

Koslowsky, J. 1895. Batracios y reptiles de Rioja y Catamarca (Republica Argentina) recogidos durante los meses de Febrero a Mayo de 1895 (expedición del director del museo). Rev. Mus. La Plata, 6: 357–370.

———. 1898. Ofidios de Mato-Grosso (Brasil). Rev. Mus. La Plata, 8: 3–32.

Kraus, R. and C. R. Botelho. 1923. Sôbre o soro antielapineo. Nova contribuição para o conhecimento de anti-toxinas e co-anti toxinas. Brasil Med., 37: 81.

Kroegel, C. and K. H. Meyer zum Buschenfeld. 1986. Biological basis for high-voltage-shock and treatment for snakebite. The Lancet. 1986. p. 148.

Kumar, V., T. A. Rejent and W. B. Elliott. 1973. Anticholinesterase activity of elapid venoms. Toxicon, 11: 131–138.

Lainson, R., F. P. Nascimento and J. J. Shaw. 1991. Some new species of Caryospora (Apicomplexa: Eimeridae) from Brazilian snakes, and redescription of C. jararacae Carini, 1939. Mem. Inst. Oswaldo Cruz, 86(3): 349–364.

——— and J. J. Shaw. 1973. Coccidia of Brazilian snakes: *Isispora decipiens, Eimeria micruri, E. liophi,* and *E. leimadophi* spp. n., with redescription of *Carysospora brasiliensis* Carini, 1932 and *Eimeria poecilogyri* Carini, 1933. J. Parasitol., 20(3): 358–362.

Lancini, A. R. 1962a. Una nueva especie de serpiente coral (*Serpentes: Elapidae*) del Peru. Publ. Ocas. Mus. Cien. Nat., Caracas, Zool., 2: 1–3.

———. 1962b. Un cambio de nombre para una serpiente coral (*Elapidae: Micrurus*) del Peru. Publ. Ocas. Mus. Cien. Nat., Caracas, Zool., 3: 1.

———. 1962c. Los ofidios de Curupao, Estado Miranda (Venezuela). Acta Biol. Venezuélica, 3(11): 161–172.

———. 1968. Las serpientes del Valle de Caracas. Estudio de Caracas, I. Ecologia Vegetal, Fauna. UCV: 297–325.

———. 1970. Los ofidios. Oficina central de Informacion (Venezuela), 21 pp.

———. 1979. Serpientes de Venezuela. Editorial. Ernesto Armitano, Caracas, 262 pp.

Landy, M. J., D. A. Langebartel, E. O. Moll, and H. M. Smith. 1966. A collection of snakes from Volcán Tacana, Chiapas Mexico. J. Ohio Herpetol. Soc., 5: 93–101.

Lankes, K. 1928. *Micrurus (Elaps) frontalis* D. B. im Terrarium. Bl. Aquar. Terrar. Kunde, 39: 68–72.

———. 1938. *Micrurus (Elaps) lemniscatus* Linne. Bl. Aquar. Terrar. Kunde, 49: 53–54.

Larrick, J. W., J. A. Yost, and J. Kaplan. 1978. Snake bite among the Waorani Indians of eastern Ecuador. Trans. R. Soc. Trop. Med. Hyg., 72: 542–543.

———, J. A. Yost, J. Kaplan, G. King, and J. Mayhall. 1979. Patterns of health and disease among the Waorani Indians of eastern Ecuador. Med. Antropol., 3: 147–189.

Laurent, R. F. and E. M. Terán. 1981. Lista de anfibios y reptiles de la Provincia de Tucumán. Fund. Miguel Lillo, Misc., 71: 1–15.

Lavilla, E. O. and G. J. Scrocchi. 1991. Aportes a la herpetología del Chaco argentino. l. Lista comentada de los taxa colectados por la expedición PRHERP 1985. Acta Zool. Lilloana, 40(1): 21–32.

Lee, J. C. 1980. An ecogeographic analysis of the herpetofauna of the Yucatan Peninsula. Misc. Publ. Univ. Kansas Mus. Nat. Hist., 67: 1–75.

Lema, T. de. 1971a. Analise geografica dos repteis do Rio Grande do Sul. Arq. Mus. Nac., Rio de Janeiro, 54: 61–62.

———. 1971b. Serpentes peçonhentas do Rio Grande do Sul. Iheringia, Divulg. 1: 25–32.

———. 1972. Sobre *Micrurus putumayensis* Lancini, 1962 e sua ocurrencia no Brasil. (Serpentes, Elapidae). Iheringia, Zool., 41: 35–58.

———. 1983. Fauna de serpentes da provincia pampeana e interrelaçoes com as provincias limitrofes. Mem. Inst. Butantan, 1982. 46: 173–182.

——— and A. C. P. Azevedo. 1969. Ocurrencia de *Micrurus decoratus* (Jan) no Rio Grande do Sul, Brasil (Serpentes, Elapidae). Iheringia, Zool., 37: 113–117.

——— and M. E. Fabian-Beurmann. 1977. Levantamento preliminar dos repteis da região da fronteira Brasil-Uruguai. Iheringia. Zool., 50: 61–92.

———, M. E. Fabian-Beurmann, M. Leitao de Araujo, M. L. M. Alves, and M. I. Viera. 1980. Lista de repteis encontrados na regāio da Grande Porto Alegre, Estado do Rio Grande do Sul Brasil. Iheringia, Zool., 55: 27–36.

Lindner, D. 1962. Feeding observations of *Microides*. Bull. Philadelphia Herpetol. Soc., 10(2–3): 31.

Liner, E. A. and A. H. Chaney. 1974. Life history: *Micrurus fulvius tenere*. HISS News J. 1: 186.

Link, G. 1951. Records of the coral snake *Micrurus fulvius* in Indiana and Ohio. Natur. Hist. Misc. 92: 1–5.

Linnaeus, C. 1758. Systema naturae. Editio decima, reformata. Stockholm, vol. 1, 823 pp.

———. 1766–1767. Systema naturae. Editio duodecima. Classis III Amphibia. Stockholm, pp. 347–393.

Loennberg, E. 1894. Notes on Reptiles and Batrachians collected in Florida in 1892 and 1893. Proc. U. S. Natl. Mus., 18: 317–339.

Loewe Jr., C. H. 1948. Effects of venom of Microides upon *Xantusia vigilis*. Herpetologica, 4: 136.

———. 1955. The eastern limit of the Sonoran Desert in the United States with additions to the known herpetofauna of New Mexico. Ecology, 36: 343–345.

———. 1964. The vertebrates of Arizona. Tucson, Univ. Arizona Press, 259 pp.

——— and K. S. Norris. 1955. Analysis of the herpetofauna of Baja California, Mexico. III. New and revived reptilian subspecies of Isla de San Esteban, Gulf of California. Sonora, Mexico, with notes on other satellite islands of Isla Tiburón. Herpetologica, 1: 89–96.

———, C. H., C. R. Schwalbe and T. B. Johnson. 1986. Venomous reptiles of Arizona. Arizona Game and Fish Dept., Arizona. 115 p.

Lomonte, B., M. F. Furtado, M. E. Rovira, E. Carmona, G. Rojas, R. Aymerich and J. M. Gutiérrez. 1990. South American snake venom proteins antigenetically related to Bothrops asper myotoxins. Braz. J. Med. Biol. Res., 23(5): 427–435.

Lopes, R. A., V. Valeri, G. M. Campos, O. V. P. Lopes, and R. M. Faria. 1972. Etude histochimique des mucopolysaccharides des glandes cephaliques de *Micrurus corallinus corallinus* (Wied) (Ophidea, Elapidea). Ann. D'Histochimie, 18(2): 131–139.

Loveridge, A. 1938. Food of *Micrurus fulvius fulvius*. Copeia, 1938(4): 201–202.

———. 1944. Cannibalism in the common coral snake. Copeia, 1944(4): 254.

———, C. R. Schwalbe, and T. B. Johnson. 1986. The venomous reptiles of Arizona. Phoenix, Arizona, Arizona Game and Fish Dept. 115 pp.

Lutz, A. and O. De Mello. 1922. *Elaps ezequieli* e *Rhinostoma bimaculatum*, cobras novas do estado de Minas Gerais. Mem. Inst. Oswaldo Cruz, 15: 138–142 (English), 235–239 (Portuguese).

——— and O. De Mello. 1923. Duas novas especies de colubrideos brasileiros. Folia Med. (Rio de Janeiro) 4: 2–3.

Luykx, P., J. B. Slowinski and J. R. McCranie. 1992. The karyotype of the coral snake *Micrurus ruatanus*. Amph. Reptilia, 13(3): 289–292.

Lynch, J. D. 1979. The amphibians of the lowland tropical forests. In W. E. Duellman (ed.). The South American Herpetofauna: its origin, evolution and dispersal. Monogr. Mus. Nat. Hist. Univ. Kansas, 7: 189–215.

––––– and H. M. Smith. 1965. New or unusual amphibians and reptiles from Oaxaca, Mexico. Herpetologica, 21: 168–177.

––––– and H. M. Smith. 1966. New or unusual amphibians and reptiles from Oaxaca, Mexico. II. Trans. Kansas Acad. Sci., 69: 58–75.

Machado, O. 1945. Estudo comparativo das Elapideas do Brasil. Bol. Inst. Vital Brasil, 5: 37–46.

Machado, J. C. and G. Rosenfeld. 1971. Achados anatomicopatologicos em necroscopia de paciente falecido por envenenamento elapidico. Mem. Inst. Butantan, 35: 41–53.

Magalhães, O. de. 1959. Campanha antiophídica em Minas Gerais. Mem. Inst. Osvaldo Cruz, 56: 291–372.

Malloy, J. F. 1971. Food habits of snakes in an east Texas State Fish Hatchery. Master of Science Thesis, S. F. Austin State University, Nacogdoches.

Mao, S. H., B. Chen, Y. Yin, and Y. W. Guo. 1983. Inmunotaxonomic relationships of sea snakes to terrestrial elapids. Comp. Biochem. Phys., 74A: 869–872.

Marcgravius, G. 1648. *Histoire Rerum Naturalium Brasiliae*. [with an appendix by Joannes de Laet.] Lugduni Batavorum et Amstelodami, vi=293 pp.

Marcuzzi, G. 1950. Ofidios existentes en las colecciones de los museos de Caracas (Venezuela). Noved. Cient. Contrib. Ocas. Mus. Hist. Nat. la Salle, Caracas, Ser. Zool., 3: 1–20.

Marinkelle, C. J. 1966. Accidents by venomous animals in Colombia. Industrial Medicine, 35(7): 587.

Marques, O. A. V. and A. A. Oliveira. 1991. Atividad e habitos alimentares em *Micrurus corallinus* (Serpentes: Elapidae). Resumos XVIII Congr. bras. Zool., Univ. Fed. BA Salvador, i–II: 310.

Martin, P. S. 1958. A biogeography of amphibians and reptiles in the Gomez Farias region, Tamaulipas, Mexico. Misc. Publ. Mus. Zool. Univ. Michigan, 101: 1–102.

Martín del Campo, R. 1935. Nota acerca de la distribución geográfica de los reptiles ponzoñosos en Mexico. An. Inst. Biol., Univ. Mexico, 6: 291–300.

–––––. 1950. Serpientes ponzoñosas de Mexico. Rev. Mex. Cienc. Med. Biol., 8: 103–115.

–––––. 1953. Contribución al conocimiento de la herpetología de Nuevo León. Universidad, Monterrey, 11: 115–152.

–––––. 1955. Productos biológicos del Valle de Mexico. Rev. Mex. Estud. Antrop., 14: 53–77.

–––––. 1984. Herpetología mexicana antigua II. Nomenclatura y taxonomía de las serpientes. Ann. Inst. Biol. Univ. Nac. Auton. Mex., 54 (1983). ser. Zool., (1): 177–198.

Martínez, A. M., R. A. Martínez and S. B. Montanlli. 1992. Actualización de la distribución de los ofidios venenosos (Crotalidae y Elapidae) de la Provincia de Misiones, Argentina, y su relación con la distribución de suero antiofídico. Acta zool. Lilloana, 41: 307–310.

Marx, H. and G. B. Raab. 1973. Major ecological and geographic patterns in the evolution of colubrid snakes. Evolution, 27: 69–83.

Mattes, B. 1860. Abhandlungen über den Zahnbau und die Lebensweise von *Elaps fluvius* Cuv. [sic], *Elaps tenere* B. and G. und *Elaps tristis* B. and G. aus den Vereinigten Staaten von Nord-Amerika und *Elaps corallinus* Pr. Max. aus Brasilien. In Drechsler, A. (ed.), Denkschriften der Naturwissenschaftlichen Gesellschaft Isis zu Dresden, pp. 52–59.

McArthur, R. H. and E. O. Wilson. 1963. An equilibrium theory of insular biogeography. Evol., 17: 373–383.

––––– and E. O. Wilson. 1967. Theory of Island biogeography. Princeton Univ. Press. Princeton, N.J. 203 pp.

McCarthy, C. J. 1985. Monophyly of elapid snakes (Serpentes: Elapidae). An assessment of the evidence. Zool. J. Linn. Soc., 83: 79–93.

McCollough, N. C. and J. F. Gennaro. 1963a. Coral snake bites in the United States. J. Fla. Med. Assn., 49: 968–972.

––––– and J. F. Gennaro. 1963b. Evaluation of the venomous snakebite in the southern United States from parallel clinical and laboratory investigations, J. Florida Med. Ass., 49: 959–967.

––––– and J. F. Gennaro. 1970. Treatment of venomous snakebite in the United States. Clinic. Toxicology, 3(3): 483–500.

McCoy, C. J. 1970. The snake fauna of Middlesex, British Honduras. J. Herpetol., 4: 135–140.

–––––. 1984. Ecological and zoogeographic relationships of amphibians and reptiles of the Cuatro Cienagas Basin. J. Arizona-Nevada Acad. Sci., 19: 49–59.

––––– and N. D. Richmond. 1966. Herpetological type specimens in Carnegie Museum. Ann. Carnegie Mus., 38: 233–264.

McCranie, J. R. 1993. Additions to the herpetofauna of Honduras. Carib. J. Sci., 29(3–4): 254–255.

––––– and L. D. Wilson. 1991. *Geophis fulvoguttatus* Mertens and *Micrurus browni* Schmidt and Smith: additions to the snake fauna of Honduras. Amph.-Retilia, 12(1): 112–114.

McDowell, S. B. 1968. Affinities of the snakes usually called *Elaps lacteus* and *E. dorsalis*. J. Linn. Soc. Zool., 47(313): 561–578.

–––––. 1970. On the status and relationships of the Solomon Island elapid snakes. J. Zool. Lond., 161(2): 145–190.

–––––. 1986. The architecture of the corner of the mouth of Colubroid snakes. J. Herpet., 20(3): 353–407.

Meachem, A. and C. Myers. 1961. An exceptional pattern variant of the coral snake, *Micrurus fulvius* (L.). Quart. J. Fla. Acad. Sci., 21(1): 56–58.

Medem, F. 1965. Bibliografía comentada de reptiles colombianos. Rev. Acad. Colomb. Cienc. Exactas Fis. Nat., 12: 299–346.

–––––. 1969. El desarrollo de la herpetología en Colombia. Rev. Acad. Col. Cien. Exac. Fis. y Nat., 13(50): 149–199.

–––––. 1979. Los anfíbios y reptiles de las Islas Gorgona y Gorgonilla. In H. Prahl, F. Guhl, and M. Grogl (eds.). Gorgona. Bogotá, Univ. de Los Andes, 179 pp.

Meise, W. 1938. Eine neue Korallenschlange aus dem Amazonasgebiet. Zool. Anz., 123 (1/2): 20–22.

Meneses, O. 1974a. Ofidios y ofidismo en el Peru. I. Las serpientes venenosas del Peru. Rev. Inst. Zoonos. Invest. Pecuar., 2: 69–77.

–––––. 1974b. Ofidios y ofidismo en el Peru. II. Aspectos ecológicos de la fauna ofídica ponzoñoza. Rev. Inst. Zoonos. Invest. Pecuar., 2: 79–84.

Merrem, B. 1820. Versuch eines Systems der Amphibien. Marburg, 191 pp.

References

Mertens, R. 1927. Über einige Schlangen in Gefangenschaft: 1 *Micrurus corallinus* Wied. Bl. Aquar. Terr. Kunde, 38: 41.

———. 1941. Eine neue Korallennatter aus Mexiko. Senckenbergiana, 23(4–6): 216–217.

———. 1952. Die Amphibien und Reptilien von El Salvador auf Grund der Reisen von R. Mertens und A. Zilch. Abh. Senckenb. Naturforsch. Ges., 487: 1–83.

———. 1956. Beobachtungen an Korallenschlangen im Terrarium. Aqua. Terr. Zeitschr., 9(3–4): 74–77, 103–106.

———. 1957. Gibt es eine Mimicry bei Korallenschlangen? Nat. und Volk, 87(2): 56–66.

———. 1960. The world of amphibians and reptiles. McGraw Hill Book Co., New York.

———. 1966. Das Problem der Mimikry bei Korallenschlangen. Zool. Jahrb. Syst., 84: 541–576.

Meyer, J. R. 1969. A biogeographic study of the amphibians and reptiles of Honduras. Ph.D. dissertation University of Southern California. 589 pp. Ann. Arbor, Mich. Univ. Microfilms. Diss. Abstr. B Sci. Eng. 70: 5222.

Meylan, P. A. 1982. The squamate reptiles of the Inglis IA fauna (Irvingtonian: Citrus County, Florida). Bull. Fla. State Mus. Biol. Sci., 27(3): 1–85.

Migone, L. E. 1929. Apuntes de climatología y nosografía médica del Paraguay. Rev. Soc. Cient. Parag., 2: 203–222.

Milá de la Roca, F. 1932. Introducción al estudio de los ofidios de Venezuela. Bol. Soc. Venezolana Cienc. Nat., 1: 381–392.

Milstead, W. W. 1960. Relict species of the Chihuahuan Desert. Southwest Nat., 5: 75–88.

———, J. S. Mechan, and H. McClintock. 1950. The amphibian and reptiles of the Stockton Plateau in northern Terrell County, Texas. Texas. J. Sci., 2: 543–562.

Ministry of Health (Brazil). 1988. Cartilha de Ofidismo (Cobral), pp. 1–32.

Minton, J. E. 1949. Coral snake preyed upon by a bullfrog. Copeia, 1949(4): 288.

Minton, S. A. 1967. Paraspecific protection by Elapid and sea snake antivenins. Toxicon, 5: 47–55.

———. 1990. Neurotoxic snake envenomation. Seminars in Neurology, 10(1): 52–61.

——— and B. M. de Cervantes. 1977. Observations on the snakes of Quéretaro, Mexico. Bull. Chicago Herpetol. Soc., 12: 69–74.

———, H. D. Dowling, and F. E. Russell. 1968. Poisonous snakes of the world. A Manual for use by U.S. amphibious forces. Dept. Navy. 212 pp.

——— and M. R. Minton. 1980. Venomous reptiles. Rev. Ed. N.Y., Charles Scribner's Sons. 308 pp.

Minton de Cervantes, B. and S. A. Minton. 1975. Geographic distribution: *Micrurus fulvius microgalbineus*. Herpetol. Rev., 6: 116.

Mitchell, J. D. 1903. The poisonous snakes of Texas with notes on their habits. Trans. Texas Acad. Sci., 5: 19–48.

Mittleman, M. B., 1947. Miscellaneous notes on Indiana amphibians and reptiles. Amer. Midland Natur., 38(2): 466–484.

——— and H. M. Smith. 1949. Remarks on the Mexican subspecies of the coral snake *Micrurus nigrocinctus*. Trans. Kansas Acad. Sci., 52(1): 86–88.

Miyata, K. 1982. A check list of the amphibians and reptiles of Ecuador with a bibliography of Ecuadorian herpetology. Smithsonian Herpet. Info. Ser., 54: 1–70.

Mocquard, F. 1887. Sur une nouvelle espèce d'*Elaps, E. heterochilus*. Bull. Soc. Philom., Paris, 7(11): 39–41.

———. 1899. Reptiles et batraciens recueillis au Mexique par M. Leon Diguet en 1896 et 1897. Bull. Soc. Philom. Paris, 9(4): 154–169.

———. 1908–1909. Etudes sur les reptiles. Mission scientifique au Mexique et dans l'Amérique Centrale. Recherches zoologiques. Part 3. Paris, Imprimerie Impériale. [Livraison 16, 1908, pp. 861–932; Livraison 17, 1909, pp. 933–1012.]

Mole, R. R. 1914. Trinidad snakes. Proc. Agric. Soc. Trinidad Tobago, 14: 363–369.

———. 1924. The Trinidad snakes. Proc. Zool. Soc. London, 1924: 235–278.

——— and F. W. Urich. 1894. Biological notes upon some of the ophidia of Trinidad, B. W. I., with a preliminary list of the species recorded from the island. Proc. Zool. Soc. London, 1894: 499–518.

Moonen, J., W. Eriks, and K. van Deursen. 1978. Surinaamse slangen in kleur. Paramaribo: Kersten & Co., 119 pp.

Moreno, E. and R. Bolaños. 1977. Hemogregarinas en serpientes de Costa Rica. Rev. Biol. Trop., 25(1): 47–57.

Moseley, T. 1966. Coral Snake bite: recovery following respiratory paralysis. Ann. Surg. 163: 943–948.

Mount, R. 1975. The reptiles and amphibians of Alabama. Auburn Univ. Agr. Exp. Sta., Auburn, Alabama. 347 pp.

Moussatche, H. and T. Melendez. 1979. Some pharmacological observations with Elapidae and Crotalidae snake venoms in the Guinea-pig denervated diaphragm. On the specificity of the cholinergic blocade by their venoms. Rev. Bras. Biol., 39(3): 605–610.

———, A. Yates, T. Melendez, and J. Mendoza. 1976. Preliminary report on the fractionation of the venom of *Micrurus nigrocinctus* and the pharmacological properties of the fractions. In Program and Abstracts of the 5th International Symposium on Animal, Plant and Microbiól. Toxins. San José, Costa Rica, p. 60.

Mudde, P. and Van Dijk, M. 1985. Herpetologische waarnemingen in Costa Rica (13). Slangen (Serpentes). Lacerta, 43: 76–180.

Müller, F. 1879. Ituna and Thyridia, a remarkable case of mimicry in butterflies. Proc. Entomol. Soc. London. 1879. xx–xxix.

———. 1878a. Über die Vortheile der Mimikry bei Schmetterlingen. Zool. Anz., 1: 54–55.

———. 1878b. Katalog der im Museum und Universitätskabinet zu Basel aufgestellten Amphibien und Reptilien. Verh. Nat. Ges. Basel, 6: 561–709.

———. 1880. Erster Nachtrag zum Katalog der herpetologischen Sammlung des Basler Museums. Verh. Nat. Ges. Basel, 7: 120–165.

———. 1882. Zweiter Nachtrag zum Katalog der herpetologischen Sammulung des Basler Museums. Verh. Nat. Ges. Basel, 7: 165–175.

———. 1883. Dritter Nachtrag zum Katalog der herpetologischen Sammulung des Basler Museums, Verh. Nat. Ges. Basel, 7: 274–297.

Müller, L. 1926. Neue Reptilien und Batrachier der zoologischen Sammulung des bayerischen Staates. Zool. Anz., 7/8: 192–200.

———. 1927. Amphibien und Reptilien der Ausbeute Prof.

Breslau's in Brasilien 1913–14. Abh. Senckenb. Naturforsch. Ges., 40: 259–304.

Müller, P. 1968. Die Herpetofauna der Insel von São Sebastião (Brasilien). Saarbrücker Zeitung, 68 pp.

———. 1970. Durch den Menschen bedingte Arealveränderungen brasilianischer Wirbeltiere. Natur u. Museum, 100(1): 147–162.

———. 1971. Herpetologische Reiseeindrücke aus Brasilien. Salamandra, 7: 9–30.

———. 1973. The dispersal centres of terrestrial vertebrates in the Neotropical Realm. The Hague: A. Jungk, Biogeografica, 2, 224 pp.

Munjal, D. and W. B. Elliott. 1972. Immunological and histochemical identity of esterases and other antigens in Elapid venoms. Toxicon, 10: 47–54.

Muñoz Alonso, L. A. 1988. Estudio herpetofaunístico del Parque Ecológico Estatal de Omiltemi, Mpio. de Chipalcingo, Guerrero. Thesis Univ. Nac. Aut. Mexico. Ciudad Universitaria. D. F., 111 pp.

Murphy, R. W. 1983. The reptiles. Origin and evolution. In T. J. Case, and M. L. Cody (eds.). Island biogeography in the Sea of Cortez. Berkeley, Univ. of California Press. pp. 130–158 and appendices 6.1 and 6.2.

——— and J. R. Ottley. 1984. Distribution of amphibians and reptiles on islands in the Gulf of California. Ann. Carnegie Mus., 53: 207–230.

Myers, C. W. and A. S. Rand. 1969. Checklist of amphibians and reptiles of Barro Colorado Island, Panama, with comments on faunal change and sampling. Smithson. Contrib. Zool., 19: 1–11.

Nakagawa, M., K. Nakanishi, L. L. Darko, and J. A. Vick. 1982. Structure of cabenergins A-I and A-II, potent anti-snake venoms. Tetrahedron Letters, 23(38): 3855–3858.

Nascimento, F. P., T. C. S. Avila-Pires and O. R. Rodriguez da Cunha. 1987. Os répteis da área de Carajás, Pará, Brasil (Squamata). II. Bol. Mus. Para. Emilio Goeldi, Ser. Zool., 3: 33–65.

———, T. C. S. Avila-Pires, and O. R. Rodriguez da Cunha. 1988. Répteis squamata de Rondônia e Mato Grosso coletados atraves do programa polonoroeste. Bol. Mus. Para. Emilio Goeldi, Ser. Zool., 4(1): 21–66.

Neill, W. T. 1957. Some misconceptions regarding the eastern coral snake *Micrurus fulvius*. Herpetologica, 13: 111–118.

———. 1960. Nature and man in British Honduras. Maryland Natur., 30: 2–14.

———. 1963. Polychromatism in snakes. Quart. Jour. Florida Acad. Sci., 26(2): 194–216.

———. 1965. New and noteworthy amphibians and reptiles from British Honduras. Bull. Florida State Mus., 9(3): 77–130.

———. 1968. Snake eats snake. Florida Wildlife, 21: 22–25.

——— and R. Allen. 1959a. Studies on the amphibians and reptiles of British Honduras. Publ. Res. Div. Ross Allen Rept. Inst., 2(1): 1–76.

——— and E. R. Allen. 1960. Noteworthy snakes from British Honduras. Herpetologica, 16: 145–162.

Nelson, G. 1973. Comments on Leon Croizat's biogeography. Syst. Zool., 22: 312–320.

———. 1975. Historical biogeography: an alternate formalization. Syst. Zool., 23: 555–558.

——— and N. I. Platnick. 1981. Systematics and Biogeography: Cladistics and Vicariance. Columbia University Press, New York.

Nemuras, K. 1967. Notes on the herpetology of Panama. Part 4. Bull. Maryland Herpetol. Soc., 3: 63–71.

Nicéforo María, Hno. 1933. Las serpientes de Villavicencio. In Libro Conmemorativo del segundo centenario de don José Celestino Bruno Mutis y Bosio, 1732–1932. Bogotá, Imprenta Nacional, pp. 199–237.

———. 1942. Los ofidios de Colombia. Rev. Acad. Colombiana Cienc. Exact. Fis. Nat., 5(17): 84–101.

Nickerson, M. A. and C. E. Mays. 1970. A preliminary herpetofaunal analysis of the Graham (Pinaleno) mountain region, Graham Co., Arizona with ecological comments. Trans. Kansas Acad. Sci., 72: 492–505.

Ocaranza, F. 1930. Sistemática de los animales ponzoñosos de la América Latina y acción biológica de sus venenos. Medicina, 10: 357–374.

Oliver, J. A. 1937. Notes on a collection of amphibians and reptiles from the state of Colima, Mexico. Occas. Pap. Mus. Zool. Univ. Michigan, 360: 1–30.

———. 1958. Snakes in fact and fiction. New York, Macmillan, 199 pp.

Orcés, G. 1942. Los ofidios venenosos del Ecuador. Flora, 2 (5–6): 147–155.

———. 1943. Los ofidios venenosos del Ecuador. Flora, 3: 165–170.

———. 1948. Los ofidios venenosos del Ecuador. Rev. Filos. Letr., Quito, 3: 231–250.

Ortenburger, A. I. and R. D. Ortenburger. 1927. Field observations on some amphibians and reptiles of Pima County, Arizona. Proc. Oklahoma Acad. Sci., 6: 101–121.

Orton, J. 1876. The Andes and the Amazon; or, across the continent of South America. 3d ed. New York, Harper and Brothers. 645 pp.

Palmer, B. K. 1986. Geographic distribution. Serpents. *Microides euryxanthus euryxanthus* (Arizona coral snake). Herpetol. Review, 17(1): 27.

Palmer, W. M., A. L. Braswell, and D. L. Stephan. 1974. Noteworthy herpetological records from North Carolina. Bull. Maryland Herpetol. Soc., 10(3): 81–87.

Parker, H. W. 1926. The reptiles and batrachians of Gorgona Island, Colombia, Colombia. Ann. Mag. Nat. Hist., 9(17): 549–554.

———. 1935. The frogs, lizards and snakes of British Guiana. Proc. Zool. Soc. London, 1935: 505–530.

———. 1938. The vertical distribution of some reptiles and amphibians in southern Ecuador. Ann. Mag. Nat. Hist., 11(2): 438–450.

———. 1963. Snakes. W. W. Norton, New York, 191 pp.

Parrish, H. M. 1963. Analysis of 460 fatalities from venomous animals in the United States. Am J. Med. Sci., 245(2): 12–141.

———. 1964a. Snakebite injuries in Louisiana. J. Louisiana St. Med. Soc., 116(7): 249–257.

———. 1964b. Texas snakebite statistics. Texas St. J. Med., 60: 592–598.

——— and L. P. Donovan. 1964. Facts about snakebites in Alabama. 1964. J. Med. Assoc. State Alabama. 33(10): 297–305.

——— and M. S. Khan, 1967a. Bites by coral snakes: report of a case and suggested therapy. J. Am. Med. Ass., 182: 949.

––––––– and M. S. Khan. 1967b. Bites by coral snakes: report of 11 representative cases. Amer. J. Med. Sci., 253: 561–568.

Patton, J. L. 1967. Chromosome studies of certain pocket mice, genus Perognathus (Rodentia; Heteromydae). J. Mamm., 48: 27–37.

Pellegrini Fihlo, A. and O. Vital Brazil, 1976. Origem da paralisia respiratoria causada pela peçonha de *Micrurus frontalis*. Cien. Cultura, 28: 199.

Pérez-Higareda, G. 1978. Reptiles and amphibians from the Estación de Biología Tropical "Los Tuxtlas", Veracruz Mexico. Bull. Maryland Herpetol. Soc. 14: 67–74.

–––––––. 1980. Additions to and notes on the known snake fauna of the Estación de Biología Tropical "Los Tuxtlas", Veracruz, Mexico. Bull. Maryland Herp. Soc., 16(1): 23–25.

––––––– and H. M. Smith, 1986. The status of the Los Tuxtlas (Mexico) false coral snake (Pliocercus). Bull. Maryland Herp. Soc., 22(3): 125–130.

––––––– and H. M. Smith. 1990. The endemic coral snakes of the Los Tuxtlas region, southern Veracruz, Mexico. Bull. Maryland Herp. Soc., 26(1): 5–13.

––––––– and H. M. Smith. 1991. Ofidiofauna de Veracruz. Análisis taxonómico y zoogeográfico. (Ofidiofauna of Veracruz. Taxonomical and zoogeographical analysis). Publ. Especial 7, Univ. Nac. Auton. Mexico, 122 p.

Pérez-Higadera [sic] (=Higareda), G., R. C. Vogt, and O. A. Flores Villela. 1987. Lista anotada de los anfíbios y reptiles de la región de los Tuxtlas, Veracruz. Univ. Nac. Auton. Mexico. 23 pp.

Pérez-Santos, C. 1986a. Las serpientes del Atlántico. Madrid, Mus. Nac. Cienc. Nat., 83 pp.

–––––––. 1986b. Las serpientes del Tolima. Madrid, T. Torreblanca, 96 pp.

––––––– and A. G. Moreno. 1986. Distribución altitudinal de las serpientes de Colombia. Rev. Españ. Herpet., 1: 11–27.

––––––– and A. G. Moreno. 1987. Las serpientes de Cundinamarca (Colombia). Madrid, Graf. Rugarte. 92 pp.

––––––– and A. G. Moreno. 1988. Ofidios de Colombia. Museo Reg. Sci. Nat. (Torino). Monogr. 6, 517 pp.

––––––– and A. G. Moreno. 1991a. Distribución y amplitud altitudinal de las serpientes en Ecuador. Rev. Españ. Herpet., 1990, 5: 125–140.

––––––– and A. G. Moreno. 1991b. Serpientes de Ecuador. Monogr. Mus. Reg. Sci. Nat. (Torino). Monogr. 11, 538 480 pp.

––––––– A. G. Moreno, and A. Garhart. 1993. Checklist of the snakes of Panama. Rev. Esp. Herp., 7: 113–122.

Peters, J. A. 1953. Snakes and lizards from Quintana Roo. Mexico. Lloydia, 16: 227–232.

–––––––. 1955. Herpetological type localities in Ecuador. Rev. Ecuat. Entomol. Parasitol., 2: 335–352.

–––––––. 1960. The snakes of Ecuador. Bull Mus. Comp. Zool., 122(9): 491–541.

––––––– and B. R. Orejas-Miranda. 1970. Catalogue of Neotropical Squamata. Part I. Snakes. Bull. U. S. Natl. Mus., 297: 1–347.

Peters, W. C. 1861. Über eine Sammlung von Schlangen aus Huanusco in Mexico welche das Königl. zoologische Museum kurzlich von Dr. Hille erworden hat. Monatsber. Preuss. Akad. Wiss. Berlin, 1861: 460–462.

–––––––. 1862. Über neue Schlangen des Königl. zoologischen Museums: *Typhlops striolatus*. *Geophidium dubium*, *Streptophorus* (*Ninia*) *maculatus*, *Elaps hippocrepis*. Monatsber. Akad. Wiss., Berlin, for 1861: 922–925.

–––––––. 1869. Über mexicanische Amphibien, welche Hr. Berkenbush in Puebla auf Veranlassung des Hrn. Legationsrath von Scholzer dem zoologischen Museum zugesandt hat. Monatsber. Akad. Wiss., Berlin, 1869: 874–881.

–––––––. 1871. Über eine von Hrn. Robert Abendroth in dem Hochlande von Peru gemachte Sammulung von Amphibien, weche derselbe dem königl. zoologischen Museum geschenkt hat. Monatsber. Akad. Wiss., Berlin, 1871: 397–404.

–––––––. 1881. Über das Vorkommen schildförmiger Verbreiterungen der Dornfortsatze bei Schlangen und über neue oder weniger bekannte Arten dieser Abtheilung der Reptilien. Sitzungsber. Ges. Naturf. Freunde, Berlin, 1881: 49–52.

Pettigrew, L. C. and J. P. Glass. 1984. Neurological complications of coral snake bite. Neurology, 35: 589–592.

Phelps, A. 1989. Poisonous snakes. Blandford Press, London. 237 pp.

Philips, E. 1962. Coral versus false coral . . . no survivors. Bull. Philadelphia Herpetol. Soc., 10(2–3): 31.

Phisalix, C. and G. Bertrand. 1894. Sur la propriete antitoxique du sang des animaux vaccines contre le venin de vipere. C. R. Acad. Sci. 118: 356.

Picado, T. C. 1931. Serpientes venenosas de Costa Rica. Sus venenos. Seroterapia antiofídica. San José, Costa Rica, Alsina, 222 pp.

Pifano, F. 1935. Contribución al estudio de las serpientes ponzoñosas del Estado Yaracuy. Caracas, 16 pp.

–––––––. 1938. Corales ponzoñosas de los valles de Yaracuy. Pesquisas experimentales con la ponzoña del *Micrurus lemniscatus* (Linneo, 1758). Publ. Asoc. Med. Yaracuy, 1: 10–15.

Platnick, N. I. and G. Nelson. 1978. A method of analysis for historical biogeography. Syst. Zool., 17: 1–6.

Pope, C. H. 1937. Snakes alive and how they live. Viking Press, New York, 238 pp.

–––––––. 1955. The reptile world. Alfred A. Knopf, New York, xxv + 325 pp.

Portmann, A. 1964. Colours and patterns in the animal kingdom. CIBA, 163(4): 2–27.

Possani, L. D., A. C. Alagon, P. L. Fletcher, M. J. Varela and J. Z. Juliá. 1979. Purification and characterization of a Phospholipase A2 from the venom of the coral snake, *Micrurus fulvius microgalbineus* (Brown and Smith). Biochem. J., 179: 603–606.

Pough, F. H., Jr., 1964. A Coral snake "mimic" eaten by a bird. Copeia, 1964(4): 223.

–––––––. 1976. Multiple cryptic effects of crossbanded and ringed patterns of snakes. Copeia, 1976: 834–836.

–––––––. 1988. Mimicry and related phenomena. In Gans C. and R. B. Huey (eds.). Biology of reptilia. Vol. 16, Ecology B. Defense and life history. Alan R. Liss, Inc., New York, pp. 153–234.

–––––––. 1991. Recommendations for the care of amphibians and reptiles in academic institutions. Nat. Acad. Press. 33(4): 5–21.

Powers, A. 1974. Description of a female *Micrurus distema macdougalli* Roze from Progreso, Oaxaca, Mexico. Bull. Maryland Herp. Soc., 10(4): 103–104.

Prado, A. 1945. Serpentes do Brasil. São Paulo, Edit. Sitios e Fazendas, Biblioteca Agropecuaria. 134 pp.

——— and A. R. Hoge. 1948. Notas ofiologicas. 21. Obserçoes sobre serpentes do Peru. Mem. Inst. Butantan, 1947, 20: 283–296.

Prance, G. T. 1973. Phytogeographic support for the theory of Pleistocene forest refuges in the Amazon Basin based on evidence from distribution patterns in Caryocaraceae, Chrysobalanaceae and Lecythidaceae. Acta Amaz., 3: 5–28.

Quelch, J. J. 1898. The poisonous snakes of British Guiana. Timehri, 2: 26–36.

Quinn, H. R. 1979. Reproduction and growth of the Texas coral snake *Micrurus fulvius tenere*. Copeia, 1979(3): 453–463.

Rage, J. C. and J. A. Holman. 1984. Des serpents (Reptilia, Squamata) de type nord-americain dans le Miocene Français. Evolution parallele ou dispersion? Geobios, 17(1): 89–104.

Ramírez-Bautista, A., C. Pérez-Higareda and G. Casas-Andreu. 1981. Lista preliminar de los anfíbios y reptiles de la región de los Tuxtlas, Veracruz. Instituto de Biología. Univ. Nat. Auton. Mexico, 6 pp.

Ramsey, G. F. and Klickstein, G. D. 1962. Coral snake bite report of a case and suggested therapy. J. Amer. Med. Assoc., 182: 949–951.

Ramsey, H. W., G. K. Snyder, H. Kitchen and W. J. Taylor. 1972. Fractionation of coral snake venom. Preliminary studies on the separation and characterization of proteins fraction. Toxicon, 10: 67–72.

———, W. J. Taylor, J. W. Borrichow, and G. K. Snyder. 1972. Mechanism of shock produced by an elapid snake (*Micrurus fulvius*) venom in dogs. Am. J. Physiol., 222: 282–286.

Rand, A. S. and C. W. Myers. 1990. The herpetofauna of Barro Colorado Island, Panama: An ecological summary. In A. H. Gentry (ed.). Four neotropical rainforests. New Haven, Yale Univ. Press, pp. 386–409.

Raven, P. H. and D. I. Axelrod. 1974. Angiosperm biogeography and past continental movements. Ann. Missouri Bot. Gard., 61: 539–673.

——— and D. I. Axelrod. 1975. History of the flora and fauna of Latin America. Amer. Sc., 63: 420–429.

Rendahl, H., 1937. Einige reptilien aus Ecuador und Bolivia. Ark. Zool., 29A: 1–19.

——— and G. Vestergren. 1940. Notes on Colombian snakes Arkiv f. Zool., 33A(1): 1–16.

——— and G. Vestergren. 1941. On a small collection of snakes from Ecuador. Ark. Zool. 33A: 1–16.

Rivero-Blanco, C. and J. R. Dixon. 1979. Origin and distribution of the herpetofauna of the dry lowland regions of northern South America. In W. E. Duellman (ed.). The South American Herpetofauna: its origin, evolution and dispersal. Monogr. Mus. Nat. Hist. Univ. Kansas, 7: 281–298.

Robinson, M. 1989. Comentarios sobre una colección de anfibios y reptiles hecha en los alrededores del Río Cunucunuma al norte del Cerro Duida y en la cima del Cerro Marahuaca, Territorio Federal Amazonas. Acta Terramaris, 1: 59–64.

Robison, H. W. 1972. Geographic distribution: *Micrurus fulvius tenere*. Herpetol. Rev. 4(5): 170–171.

Rodríguez, L. B. and J. E. Cadle. 1990. A preliminary overview of the herpetofauna of Cocha Cashu, Manu National Park, Peru. In A. H. Gentry (ed.). Four Neotropical rainforests. New Haven: Yale Univ. Press, pp. 410–425.

Rohl, E. 1949. Fauna descriptiva de Venezuela (vertebrados). 2d. ed. Caracas. Tipografía Americana.

Romano, S. A. R. W. D. L. 1972. Notes of *Leptomicrurus* Schmidt (Serpentes, Elapidae) Mem. Inst. Butantan, 1971. 35: 111–115.

Romer, A. S. 1956. Osteology of the reptiles. Chicago. Univ. Chicago Press.

Rosen, D. 1975. A vicariance model of Caribbean biogeography. Syst. Zool., 24(4): 431–464.

———. 1978. Vicariant patterns and historical explanation of biogeography. Syst. Zool., 27: 159–188.

Rosenberg, H. I. 1967. Histology, histochemistry and emptying mechanism of the venom gland of some Elapid snakes. J. Morph., 123: 133–136.

Rosenberg, P. 1979. Pharmacology of phospholipase A2 from snake venoms. In C. Y. Lee (ed.). Snake venoms. Handbk. Exp. Pharmakol., 52. Berlin: Springer Verlag.

Rosenfeld, G. 1971. Symptomatology, pathology, and treatment of snake bites in South America. In W. Bucherl and E. E. Buckley (eds.). Venomous Animals and their venoms. New York, Academic Press. vol. II: 345–384.

Roux-Estève, R. 1983. Les spécimens-types du genre *Micrurus* (Elapidae) conservés au Muséum National D'Histoire Naturelle de Paris. Mem. Inst. Butantan, 1982. 46: 79–94.

Roze, J. A. 1952. Colección de reptiles del profesor Scorza, de Venezuela. Acta Biol. Venezuélica, 1: 93–114.

———. 1953. Ofidios de Camurí Chicho, Macuto, D. F., Venezuela colectados por el Rvdo. Padre Cornelius Vogl. Bol. Soc. Ven. Cien. Nat. Caracas, 19(79): 200–211.

———. 1954. Nota preliminar sobre los ofidios de la expedición Franco-Venezolana al Alto Orinoco. Arch. Venez. Patol. Trop. Parasitol. Med., 2: 227–234.

———. 1955. Revisión de las corales (Serpentes, Elapidae) de Venezuela. Acta Biol. Venezuélica, 1(17): 453–500.

———. 1957. Ofidios coleccionados por la expedición Franco-Venezolana al Alto Orinoco, 1951 a 1952. Bol. Mus. Cienc. Caracas, 1: 179–195.

———. 1964. La herpetología de la Isla Margarita, Venezuela. Mem. Soc. Cienc. Nat. La Salle, 24: 209–241.

———. 1966a. La taxonomía y zoogeografía de los ofidios de Venezuela. Caracas: Edic. Bibl. Univ. Central Venezuela, 362 pp.

———. 1966b. On the synonymy and type specimens of the coral snakes, *Micrurus corallinus* and *Micrurus ibiboboca* (Marcgravii). Copeia, 1966(4): 369–371.

———. 1967. A check list of the New World venomous coral snakes (Elapidae), with descriptions of new forms. Amer. Mus. Novitates, 2287: 1–60.

———. 1970a. Ciencia y fantasía sobre las serpientes de Venezuela. Caracas, Edit. Fondo de Cultura Cientifica. 162 pp.

———. 1970b. *Micrurus*. In J. A. Peters and B. Orejas-Miranda, Catalogue of Neotropical squamata. Pt. I. Snakes. Bull. U. S. Natl. Mus., 297: 196–220.

———. 1974. *Micruroides. M. euryxanthus*. In Catalogue of American Amphibians and Reptiles. 163: 1–4.

———. 1983. New World coral snakes (Elapidae): A taxonomic and biological summary. Mem. Inst. Butantan, 1982 46: 305–338.

———. 1984. Biopsychosociology of mimicry games and human psychological defenses. New Ideas Psych., 3(1): 14–21.

———. 1987. Summary of coral snakes (Elapidae) from Cerro de la Neblina, Venezuela, with description of a new subspecies. Rev. fr. Aquariol., 14(3): 109–112.

———. 1989. New species and subspecies of coral snakes, genus *Micrurus* (Elapidae), with notes on type specimens of several species. Amer. Mus. Novitates, 2932: 1–15.

———. 1994. Notes on taxonomy of venomous coral snakes (Elapidae) of South America. Bull. Maryland Herp. Soc., 30(4): 177–185.

——— and A. Bernal-Carlo. 1988. Las serpientes corales venenosas del género *Leptomicrurus* (Serpentes, Elapidae) de Suramérica con descripción de una nueva subespecie. Boll. Mus. Turino, 1987, 5(2): 573–608.

——— and N. Jorge da Silva. 1990. Coral snakes (Serpentes, Elapidae) from Hydroelectric Power Plant of Samuel, Rondônia, Brazil, with description of a new species. Bull. Maryland Herp. Soc., 26(4): 169–176.

——— and G. M. Tilger. 1983. *Micrurus fulvius*. In Catalogue of American Amphibians and Reptiles, 316: 1–4.

——— and C. P. Trebbau M. 1958. Un nuevo género de corales venenosas (*Leptomicrurus*) para Venezuela. Acta Cientif. Venezolana, 9(6–7): 128–139.

Ruick, J. D. 1948. Collecting coral snakes *Micrurus fulvius tenere* in Texas. Herpetologica, 4: 215–216.

Russell, F. E. 1963. Venomous animals and their toxins. Time Science Review (London), Autumn, 1963.

———. 1967. Bites by the Sonora coral snake, *Micruroides euryxanthus*. Toxicon, 5: 39–42.

———. 1980. *Snake venom poisoning*. Philadelphia: J. B. Lippincott Co., 562 p.

———. 1983. Snake venom poisoning. Great Neck, New York, Scholium International.

———, R. W. Carlson, W. Wainschel, and J. Osborne. 1975. Snake venom poisoning in the United States: experiences with 550 cases. J. Amer. Med. Ass., 233: 341–344.

——— and L. Lauritzen. 1966. Antivenins. Trans. R. Soc. Trop. Med. Hyg., 60(6): 797–810.

——— and J. Wainschude. 1973. Scorpion stings and spark plug shocks. JAMA, 225(4): 419.

Ruthven, A. G. 1907. A collection of reptiles and amphibians from southern New Mexico and Arizona. Bull. Am. Mus. Nat. Hist., 23: 483–603.

———. 1912. The amphibians and reptiles collected by the University of Michigan-Walker Expedition in southern Veracruz, Mexico, Zool. Jahrb., Abt. Syst., 32: 295–332.

———. 1922. The amphibians and reptiles of the Sierra Nevada de Santa Marta, Colombia. Misc. Publ. Mus. Zool. Univ. Michigan, 8: 1–69.

Sabath, M. and R. Worthington. 1959. Eggs and young of certain Texas reptiles. Herpetologica, 15(1), pp. 31–32.

Sánchez-Herrera, O. and M. Alvarez del Toro. 1980. A range extension for *Thecadactylus rapidcauda* (Gekkonidae) in Mexico, and note on two snakes from Chiapas. Bull. Maryland Herp. Soc., 13(2): 49–51.

Savage, J. M. 1976. A preliminary handlist of the herpetofauna of Costa Rica. Univ. S. Calif., Los Angeles, 2nd. edition, University of Costa Rica, 19 pp.

———. 1980. A handlist with preliminary keys to the herpetofauna of Costa Rica. Allan Hancock Found., Los Angeles, 111 pp.

———. 1982. The enigma of the Central American herpetofauna: dispersal or vicariance? Ann. Missouri Bot. Garden, 69: 464–547.

——— and B. I. Crother. 1989. The status of Pliocercus and Urotheca (Serpentes: Colubridae), with a review of included species of coral snake mimics. Zool. J. Linn. Soc. 95: 335–362.

——— and J. B. Slowinski. 1990. Short note: a simple consistent terminology for the basic colour patterns of the venomous coral snakes and their mimics. Herpet. J., 1: 530–532.

——— and J. L. Vial. 1974. The venomous coral snakes (genus *Micrurus*) of Costa Rica. Rev. Biol. Trop., 21(2), pp. 295–349.

Savitzky, A. H. 1978. The origin of the New World proteroglyphous snakes and its bearing on the venom delivery systems in snakes. Ph.D. Dissertation, University of Kansas, Lawrence, 387 pp.

Sazima, I. and A. S. Abe. 1991. Habits of five Brazilian snakes with coral-snake pattern, including a summary of defensive tactics. Stud. Neotrop. Fl. F. Environ., 26(3): 159–164.

——— and M. Di-Bernardo. 1991. Albinismo em serpentes neotropicais. Mem. Inst. Butantan, 53(2): 167–173.

Schlegel, H. 1837. Essai sur la Physionomie des Serpens. vol. 2, pp. 1–606.

———. 1844. Abbildungen neuer oder unvollständig bekannter Amphibien... I–XVI, Atlas, 50 pls.

Schmidt, K. P. 1928. Notes on American coral snakes. Bull. Antivenin Inst. Amer., 2(3): 63–64.

———. 1932a. Stomach contents of some American coral snakes, with the description of a new species of *Geophis*. Copeia, 1932(1): 6–9.

———. 1932b. A new subspecies of coral snake from Guatemala. Proc. California Acad. Sci. 20(7): 265–267.

———. 1933. Preliminary account of the coral snakes of Central America and Mexico. Field. Mus. Nat. Hist., Zool. ser., 20: 29–40.

———. 1936a. Preliminary account of coral snakes of South America. Ibid., 20(20): 189–203.

———. 1936b. Notes on Central American and Mexican coral snakes. Ibid., 20(20): 205–216.

———. 1937. The history of *Elaps collaris* Schlegel, 1837–1937. Ibid., 20(27): 361–364.

———. 1939. A new Coral Snake from British Guiana. Ibid. 24(6), pp. 45–47.

———. 1952. The Surinam coral snake, *Micrurus surinamensis*. Fieldiana, Zool.; 34(4): 25–34.

———. 1953a. Hemprich's coral snake, *Micrurus hemprichi*. Ibid., 34(13): 165–170.

———. 1953b. The Amazonian coral snake *Micrurus spixi*. Ibid., 34(14): 171–180.

———. 1954. The annellated coral snake *Micrurus annellatus* Peters. Ibid., 34(30): 319–325.

———. 1955. Coral snakes of the genus *Micrurus* in Colombia Ibid., 34(8): 337–359.

———. 1957. The venomous coral snakes of Trinidad. Ibid., 39(8): 55–63.

———. 1958. Some rare or little known Mexican coral snakes. Ibid., 39: 201–212.

—— and F. J. W. Schmidt. 1925. New coral snakes from Peru. Reports on results of the Captain Marshall Field Expeditions. Publ. Field. Mus. Nat. Hist., zool. ser., 12(10): 129–134.

—— and H. M. Smith. 1943. Notes on coral snakes from Mexico. Ibid., 29(2): 25–31.

—— and W. F. Walker. 1943. Peruvian snakes from the University of Arequipa. Ibid., 24(26): 279–296.

Schouten, G. B. 1931. Contribuciones al conocimiento de la fauna herpetológica del Paraguay y de los paises limítrofes. Rev. Soc. Cientif. Paraguaya, 3: 5–32.

Schwartzwelder, J. 1950. Snake-bite accidents in Louisiana: with data on 306 cases. Amer. J. Trop. Med., 30: 575–587.

Scott, N. J. and J. W. Lovett. 1975. A collection of reptiles and amphibians from the Chaco of Paraguay. Occ. Pap. Univ. Conn. Biol. Sci. Ser. 2(16): 257–266.

Scrocchi, G. J. 1990. El género *Micrurus* (Serpentes: Elapidae) en la Argentina. Boll. Mus. reg. Sci. Nat. (Torino), 8(2): 343–368.

——. 1991. Análisis preliminar de la osteología cranial del género *Micrurus* Wagler (Ophidia: Elapidae). Acta Zool. Lilloana, 41: 311–327.

Seba, A. 1734–65. Locupletessimi Rerum Naturalium Thesauri Accurata Descriptio. . . . Amstelaedami, 4 vols.

Selye, C. W., Jr. and G. K. Williamson. 1982. *Micrurus fulvius fulvius*. Herp. Review, 13(2): 48.

Shaw, C. E. and S. Campbell. 1974. Snakes of the American west. New York: A. Knopf, 332 pp.

Shreve, B. 1953. Notes on the races of *Micrurus frontalis* (Dumeril, Dumeril and Bibron). Breviora, 16: 279–296.

Silva da, N. J., Jr., P. R. Griffin, and S. D. Aird. 1991. Comparative chromatography of Brazilian coral snakes (Micrurus) venom. Comp. Biochem. Physiol. B. Comp. Biochem., 100(1): 117–126.

——, S. D. Aird, and J. J. Silva Haad. 1992. Comparative lethality of *Micrurus* venoms. IVth. Pan. Amer. Symposium Anim. Plant Microb. Toxins. Campinas, Brazil. July 27–31, 1992.

Silva Haad J. J. 1994. Los micrurus de la Amazonia colombiana. Biología y toxicología experimental de sus venenos. Colombia Amazónica, 7(1-2): 41–138.

Skutch, A. F. 1960. The laughing reptile hunter of tropical America. Animal Kingdom, 63: 115–119.

Slowinski, J. B. 1991. The phylogenetic relationships of the New World coral snakes (Elapidae: Leptomicrurus, Micruroides and Micrurus) based on biochemical and morphological data. Ph.D. Dissertation, Univ. Microfilms, 152 pp.

——. 1995. A phylogenetic analysis of the New World coral snakes (Elapidae: *Leptomicrurus, Micruroides, Micrurus*) based on allozymic and morphological characters. J. Herpetol., 29(3): xx.

Smith, H. M. 1947. Notas sobre una colección de reptiles y anfíbios de Chiapas. Rev. Soc. Mexicana Hist. Nat., 1946, 7(1/4): 63–74.

—— and P. S. Chrapliwy. 1958. New and noteworthy Mexican herptiles from the Lidicker collection. Herpetologica, 13(4): 267–271.

—— and C. Grant. 1958. New and noteworthy snakes from Panama. Herpetologica, 14: 207–215.

—— and E. H. Taylor. 1945. An annotated checklist and the key to the snakes of Mexico. Bull. U. S. Natl. Mus., 187: i–iv, 1–239.

——. 1950. Type localities of Mexican amphibians and reptiles. Univ. Kansas Sci. Bull., 33(8): 313–380.

——, E. R. Allen, and R. L. Holland. 1970. A new atavistic hyperxanthic chromotype in the coralsnake *Micrurus fulvius* (Linnaeus). J. Herpetol., 4(1/2): 80–83.

Smith, N. G. 1969. Avian predation of coral snakes. Copeia, 1969: 402–404.

Smith, S. M. 1975. Innate recognition of coral snake pattern by a possible avian predator. Science, 187: 759–760.

——. 1976. Predatory behaviour of young Turquise-browed Motmots, *Eumomota superciliosa*. Behaviour, 56(3–4): 309–320.

——. 1977. Coral-snake pattern recognition and stimulus generalization by naive great kiskadees (Aves: Tyrannidae). Nature, 265: 535–536.

Snyder, G. K., H. W. Ramsey, W. J. Taylor, and C. Y. Chiou. 1973. Neuromuscular blockade of chick biventer cervicis nerve-muscle preparations by a fraction from coral snake venom. Toxicon, 11: 505–508.

Soini, P. 1973. Notes on an upper Amazonian coral snake *Micrurus putumayensis* Lancini. J. Herpetol., 7: 306–307.

——. 1974. Polychromatism in a population of *Micrurus langsdorffi*. J. Herpetol., 8(3): 267–269.

Solórzano, A. and L. Cerdas. 1984. Confirmación de la presencia de *Micrurus clarki* Schmidt (Elapidae) en Costa Rica. Rev. Biol. Trop., 32(2): 317–318.

——. 1988a. Ciclos reproductivos de la serpiente coral *Micrurus nigrocinctus* (Serpentes: Elapidae) en Costa Rica. Rev. Biol. Trop., 36(2A): 235–239.

——. 1988b. Incubación de los huevos y nacimiento en la coral gargantilla *Micrurus mipartitus hertwigi* (Serpientes: Elapidae) en Costa Rica. Rev. Biol. Trop., 36(2B): 535–536.

Sosa, B. P., A. C. Alagon, L. D. Possani, and J. Z. Juliá. 1979. Comparison of phospholipase activity with direct and indirect lytic effects of animal venoms upon human red cells. Comp. Biochem. Physiol., 64B: 231–234.

Spix, J. B. von and C. F. P. von Martius. 1823–1831. Reise in Brasilien auf Befehl Sr. Majestät Maximilian Joseph I König von Bayern in den Jahren 1817 bis 1820 gemacht und beschrieben . . . 3 volumes, 1 atlas.

Steindachner, F. 1867. Reise der österreichischen Fregatte Novara um die Erde in den Jahren 1857, 1858, 1859. Zoologischer Theil. Erster Band (Wirbelthiere.) 3. Reptilien. Wien: K-K. Hof- und Staatsdruckerei. 98 pp.

Stejneger, L. 1895. The poisonous snakes of North America. Rep. U. S. Natl. Mus. for 1893, pp. 337–487.

Sternfeld, R. 1913. Die Erscheinungen der Mimikry bei den Schlangen. Sitz. Ber. Ges. Naturf. Berlin, pp. 98–117.

Stevan, L. J. and E. B. Seligmann Jr. 1970. Agar-gel ad acrylamide-disc electrophoresis of coral snake venoms. Toxicon, 8: 11–14.

Stickel, W. H. 1952. Venomous snakes of the United States and treatment of their bites. U.S. Fish & Wildlife Serv., Leaflet, 339, pp. 1–29.

Stoddard, H. L., Sr. 1978. Birds of Grady county, Georgia. Bull. Tall. Timb. Res. Sta., 21: 1–175.

Stuart, L. C. 1950. A geographic study of the herpetofauna of Alta Verapaz, Guatemala. Contr. Vert. Lab. Biol. Univ. Michigan, 45, pp. 1–77.

———. 1963. A checklist of the herpetofauna of Guatemala. Misc. publ. Mus. Zool. Univ. Michigan, No 122, pp. 1–150.
Sutherland, S. K. 1982. Venomous creatures of Australiá: a field guide with notes on first aid. Melbourne: Oxford Univ. Press. 1981. 62 pp.
Taylor, E. H., 1922. The Snakes of the Philippine Islands. Publ. Bur. Sci. Manila, 16: 1–32.
———. 1950. Second contribution to the herpetology of San Luís Potosí. Univ. Kansas Sci. Bull., 33, Pt. 2(11): 441–457.
———. 1951. A brief review of the snakes of Costa Rica. Ibid., 34(1): 3–188.
———. 1954. Further studies of the serpents of Costa Rica. Ibid., 36(11): 673–801.
Taylor, R. T. and R. Bolaños. 1975. Descripción de un método simple y económico para el estudio de cariotipos en serpientes. Rev. Biol. Trop., 23: 177–183.
Taylor, R. T., A. Flores, G. Flores, and R. Bolaños. 1974. Geographical distribution of Viperidae, Elapidae and Hydrophidae in Costa Rica. Rev. Biol. Trop., 21(2): 383–397.
Telford, S. R., Jr. 1955. A description of the eggs of the coral snake *Micrurus f. fulvius*. Copeia, 1955(3): 258.
Test, F. H., O. J. Sexton, and H. Heatwole. 1966. Reptiles of Rancho Grande and vicinity, Estado Aragua, Venezuela. Misc. Publ. Mus. Zool. Univ. Michigan, 128: 1–63.
Theakston, R. D. G., H. A. Reid, J. W. Larrick, J. Kaplan, and J. A. Yost. 1981. Snake venom antibodies in Ecudorian Indians. J. Trop. Med. Hy., 84: 199–202.
Thompson, J. C. 1913. The current status of *Elaps collaris* Schlegel. Notes Leyden Mus. 35: 171–175.
True, F. W. 1883. Bite of the North American coral snakes. Amer. Natur., 17: 26–31.
Tryon, B. W. and H. K. McCrystal. 1982. *Micrurus fulvius tenere* (Texas coral snake) reproduction. Herp. Review, 13(2): 47–48.
Van Denburg, J. 1922. The reptiles of western North America. Vol. 2. Snakes and turtles. Occas. Pap. California Acad. Sci., 10: 615–1029.
Van der Rijst, H. . . . Colourful misuderstanding. Litt. Serpentium, Engl. Ed. 10(5): 206–211.
Van Helmont. 1684. Ortus medicinae. Amsterdam: Elzevier.
Vane-Wright, R. I. 1976. A unified classification of mimetic resemblances. Biol. J. Linn. Soc., 8: 25–56.
Vanzolini, P. E. 1948. Notas sôbre os ofídios e lagartos da Cachoeira de Emas, no município de Pirassununga, Estado de São Paulo. Rev. Bras. Biol. 8(3): 377–400.
———. 1977–1978. An annotated bibliography of the land and fresh-water reptiles of South America (1758–1975). Mus. Zool. Univers. São Paulo, 2 vols.
———. 1985. *Micrurus averyi* Schmidt, 1939, in central Amazonia (Serpentes, Elapidae). Pap. Avuls. Zool. S. Paulo, 36(8): 77–85.
———. 1986. Levantamento herpetológico da área do estado de Rondônia sob a influéncia da rodovia BR 364. Progr. Polonoroeste, Relat. de Pesq., 1: 1–50.
——— and W. R. Heyer. 1985. The American herpetofauna and the interchange. Chapter 18. In F. G. Stehli and S. D. Webb (eds.), The great American biotic interchange. New York and London: Plenum Press, pp. 475–484.
———, P. E. Ramos-Costa, and L. J. Vitt. 1980. Répteis das caatingas. Acad. Bras. Cienc. Rio de Janeiro, 161 pp.
Vaz-Ferreira, R., L. C. de Zolesi, and F. Achaval. 1970. Oviposición y desarrollo de ofídios y lacertilios en hormigueros de *Acromyrmex*. Physis, 29(79): 431–459.
———. 1973. Oviposición y desarrollo de ofidios y lacertilios en hormigueros de *Acromyrmex*. II. Trab. V Congr. Latinoam. Zool., 1: 232–244.
Vick, J. A., H. P. Ciuchta and J. H. Manthei. 1967. Pathophysiological studies of ten snake venoms. In E. E. Russell and P. R. Sanders (eds.), Animal Toxins, New York: Pergamon Press, pp. 269–282.
Villa, J. 1962. Las serpientes venenosas de Nicaragua. Managua: Edit. Novedades, 94 pp.
———. 1972a. Un coral (*Micrurus*) blanco y negro de Costa Rica. Brenesia, 1: 10–13.
———. 1972b. Snakes of the Corn Islands, Caribbean Nicaragua. Ibid., 1: 14–18.
———. 1984. The venomous snakes of Nicaragua: a synopsis. Milwaukee Publ. Mus. Contr. Biol. Geol., 59: 1–41.
———, L. D. Wilson, and J. D. Johnson. 1988. A Middle American herpetology. A bibliographic checklist. Univ. Missouri Press, 132 pp.
Vital Brazil, O. 1980. Venenos ofidicos neurotóxicos. Rev. Ass. Med. Brasil., 26(6): 212–218.
———. 1987. Coral snake venoms: mode of action and pathophysiology of experimental envenomation. Rev. Inst. Med. Trop., São Paulo, 29(3): 119–126.
——— and M. D. Fontana. 1984. Ações préjuncionais e pósjuncionais da peçonha da cobra coral *Micrurus corallinus* na junção neuromuscular. Mem. Inst. Butantan, 1983/84, 47/48: 13–26.
———, M. D. Fontana, and A. Pellegrini Filho. 1977. Physiopathologie et thérapeutique de l'envenomation expérimentale causée par le venin de *Micrurus frontalis*. Ibid., 1976/1977, 40/41: 221–240.
Vitt, L. J. 1992. Lizard mimics millipede. Natl. Geogr. Res. Explor. 8(1): 76–95.
——— and A. C. Hulse. 1973. Observations on feeding habits and tail display of the Sonoran Coral Snake, *Micruroides euryxanthus*. Herpetologica, 29(4): 302–304.
——— and L. D. Vangilder. 1983. Ecology of a snake community in northeastern Brazil. Amph. Rept., 4: 273–296.
Vorhies, C. T. 1929. Feeding of the *Micrurus euryxanthus*, the Sonoran coral snake. Bull. Antivenin Inst. Amer., 2(4): 98.
Vuilleumier, F. 1969. Pleistocene speciation in birds living in high Andes. Nature, 223: 1179–1180.
———. 1970. Biogeography and ecology in South America. F. Hakan, J. Illies, H. Klinge, G. H. Schwalbe and T. Sioli (eds.) (book review). Quart. Review Biol., 45: 105–106.
———. 1977. Qu'est que la biogéographie? C. R. Soc. Biogéogr. (1977) 1978: 41–66.
———. 1980. Ecological aspects of speciation in birds, with special reference to South American birds. In O. A. Reig (ed.) Ecología y Genética de la especiación animal. Equinoccia, Univ. Simón Bolivar, Caracas: 4–66.
Wagler, J. 1824. Serpentum Brasiliensium species novae. In Spix, J. de, Animalia nova sive species novae. Monaco, viii + 75 pp.
———. 1830. Natürliches System der Amphibien, mit vorangehender Klassifikation der Säugthiere und Vögel. München, Stuttgart und Tübingen: J. G. Cotta., vi + 354 pp.
Wehekind, L. 1955. Notes on the foods of the Trinidad snakes. Brit. J. Herp., 2(1): 9–13.

———. 1960. Trinidad snakes. J. Brit. Guiana Mus., 27: 71–76.

Weis, R. and R. J. McIsaac. 1971. Cardiovascular and muscular effects of venom from coral snake, *Micrurus fulvius*. Toxicon, 9: 219–228.

Weldon, P. J., T. S. Walsh and J. S. E. Kleister. 1992. Captive management and sonservation of amphibians and reptiles. In J. B. Murphy, J. T. Collins and K. Adler (eds.). Contributions to herpetology. Soc. for Stud. Amph. Rept.

Werler, J. E. 1951. Miscellaneous notes on the eggs and young of Texan and Mexican reptiles. Zoologica, 36(1): 37–48.

——— and D. M. Darling. 1950. A case of poisoning from the bite of a coral snake, *Micrurus f. tenere* Baird and Girard. Herpetologica, 6(7): 197–199.

Werner, F. 1897. Über einige neue oder seltene Reptilien und Fröshe der zoologischen Sammlung des Staates in München. Sitzber. Akad. Wiss., Munich, 27: 203–220.

———. 1901. Über Reptilien und Batrachier aus Ecuador und Neu-Guinea. Verhandl. Zool. Bot. Gesell., Vienna, 51: 593–614.

———. 1903. Neue Reptilien und Batrachier aus dem naturhistorischen Museum in Brussel. Zool. Anz., 26(693): 246–253.

———. 1904. Über Reptilien und Batrachier aus Guatemala und China in der zoologischen Staats-Sammlung in München, nebst einem Anhang über seltene Formen aus anderen Gegenden. Abhandl. Bayerische Akad. Wiss., 22(2): 343–384.

———. 1927. Neue oder wenig bekannte Schlangen aus dem Weiner naturhistorischen Staatsmuseum. (III Teil). Sitzber. Akad. Wiss., 135: 243–257.

Wickler, W. 1968. Mimicry in plants and animals. New York: McGraw-Hill, 253 pp.

Wied-Neuwied, M. 1820. Über die Cobra Coral oder Cobras Coraes der Brasilianer. Nova Acta Acad. Leop-Carolinae, 10: 105–110.

———. 1824. Abbildungen der Naturgeschichte Brasiliens. Weimar. Lief. 1–15.

———. 1825–33. Beitrage zur Naturgeschichte von Brasilien. Weimar. 4 vols. Weimar: Gr. H. S. priv. Landes—Industrie-Comptoirs.

Williams, J. D. 1988. Las corales. In Cabral, G. B. (ed.). Fauna argentina. Vol. 2. Anfibios y reptiles. Centro Editor de América Latina, Buenos Aires, pp. 1–32.

Willson, P. 1908. Snake poisoning in the United States; A Study based on an analysis of 740 cases. Arch. Intern. Med., pp. 516–570.

Wilson, A. C., S. S. Carlson, and T. J. White. 1977. Biochemical evolution. Ann. Rev. Biochem., 46: 573–639.

Wilson, L. D. 1984. The status of *Micrurus ruatanus* (Günther), a coral snake endemic to the Bay Islands of Honduras. Herpetol. Rev., 15(3): 67.

——— and D. E. Hahn. 1973. The herpetofauna of the Islas de la Bahía, Honduras. Bull. Fl. State Mus. Biol. Sci. 17(2): 93–150.

——— and J. R. Meyer. 1972. The coral snake *Micrurus nigrocinctus* in Honduras. Bull. So. Calif. Acad. Sci., 71: 139–145.

———. 1982. The snakes of Honduras. Milwaukee Publ. Mus. Biol. Geol., 6, 160 pp.

———. 1985. The snakes of Honduras. Milwaukee Public Museum, 2nd ed. 150 pp.

——— and L. Porras. 1983. The ecological impact of man on the south Florida herpetofauna. Univ. Kansas Mus. Nat. Hist. Spec. Publ., 9: 1–89.

World Health Organization. 1981. Progress in the characterization of venoms and standardization of antivenoms. Geneva.

Yanosky, A. A. 1989a. Approche de l'herpétofaune de la Réserve écologique El Bagual (Formosa, Argentine). I. Anoures et Ophidiens, Revue fr. Aquariol., 16(2): 57–62.

———. 1989b. La ofidiofauna de la reserva ecológica El Bagual, Formosa: abundancia, utilización de los habitats y estado de situación. Cuad. Herpet., 4(3): 11–14.

——— and J. M. Chani. 1988. Possible dual mimicry of *Bothrops* and *Micrurus* by the colubrid *Lystrophis dorbignyi*. J. Herpetol., 22(2): 222–224.

Yarrow, P. 1887. Med. News, 50, p. 624.

Zeger, J. C. 1975. Notes on collecting and breeding the eastern coral snake, *Micrurus fulvius fulvius*. Bull. Southeast. Herpetol. Soc., 1(6): 9–10.

Zimmerman, B. L. and M. T. Rodrigues. 1990. Frogs, snakes and lizards of the INPA-WWF Reserves near Manaos, Brazil. In: Gentry (ed.). Four neotropical rainforests. Yale Univ. Press, pp. 426–454.

Zweifel, R. G. 1959. Additions to the herpetofauna of Nayarit, Mexico. Amer. Mus. Novitates, 1953: 1–13.

———. 1966. Guidelines for the care of a herpetological collection. Curator, 9: 24–35.

——— and K. S. Norris. 1955. Contribution to the herpetology of Sonora, Mexico: descriptions of new subspecies of snakes (*Micruroides euryxanthus* and *Lampropeltis getulus*) and miscellaneous collecting notes. Amer. Midland Nat., 54(1): 230–249.

Acknowledgments

Perhaps no herpetologist owes so much to so many colleagues, friends, and associates as I do for advice, help, information, specimens, curious facts, even simple encouragement and, at times, push—all delivered in the friendliest and most collegial way to help me to accomplish the coral snake research that I have been continuing for more than 25 years. The preface partially explains the history.

First, I would like to thank many museums and persons associated with them who generously provided material for my research and received my visits most graciously. In most cases their help was much more than just offering material.

My special thanks to my colleagues and friends at the Department of Herpetology of the American Museum of Natural History, New York, where most of my research was carried out. Not only were they available for professional help and suggestions, but they gently tolerated my sometimes idiosyncratic ways as a part-time herpetologist, part-time Latvian-Latino, and part-time world traveler. They are the late Charles Bogert, curator emeritus; Jay Cole; Darrel Frost; Charles Myers; and Richard Zweifel, my "founding sponsor"; as well as George Foley, Carol Townsend, Margaret Shaw, and Grace Tilger. My across-the-research-desk colleague, Samuel McDowell, shared with me much of his time and knowledge about elapids. Bud Lanyon and Francois Vuilleumier (ornithology); Sydney Anderson, Karl Koopman, and Richard van Gelder (mammalogy); the late Don Rosen (ichthyology); and Max Hecht (paleontology) were available with advice from their disciplines. At the City College of the City University of New York, my base in biology, I received help from Jess Hanks, Linda Mantel, James Organ, Joseph Ossinchak, Alberto Valdéz, and Jack Downey. Invaluable help came from Amanda Bernal-Carlo who shared my calamities and provided daily help in close quarters at the museum, at the university, and at home.

Very special thanks go to my colleague and friend of many years, Herndon Dowling, as well as to Janann Jenner at New York University who helped in preparation of the description of species and by advising on many herpetological problems. Other helpful colleagues at New York University include Carlos Estol, Paul Kelly, and Randy Price. I thank particularly Spence Porter and Janann Jenner for being my language masters.

Considerable help in reading chapters of the manuscript and offering constructive advice and criticism was received from Jay Cole, Harry Greene, Samuel McDowell, Sherman Minton, Charles Myers, Findlay Russell, Richard Zweifel, and particularly from William Lamar who meticulously read every chapter and offered suggestions for improvement.

Many people have helped in advancing my research, but I will mention them later by countries. However, only I am to be blamed for any shortcomings of this book.

In the United States, in addition to the colleagues mentioned above, I would like to specially thank Roger Conant, James Dixon, William Duellman, Carl Gans, Harry Greene, Robert Inger, Alan Leviton, Douglas Rossman, Jay Savage, Hobart Smith, Ernest Williams, the late C. Jay McCoy, James Oliver, James Peters, Lawrence Stuart, Charles Walker and Norman Hartweg; but no less so to also acknowledge the collaboration of Kraig Adler, Bayard Brattstrom, Peter Brazaitis, Jonathan Campbell, Peter Coles, Richard Etheridge, Joseph Gennaro, Itzak Gilboa, Carol Gracie, William Haast, Larry Hardy, Harold Heatwole, David Jameson, Russell Kellogg, Edmund Keyser, Arnold Kluge, James Lazzell, Ernest Liner, Charles Loewe, John Lynch, Hugh McCrystal, Roy McDiarmid, George Rabb, William Riemer, Diana Ronell, Rodolfo Ruibal, Alan Savitzky, Tom Stubbs, Frederic Test, Robert Thomas, Thomas Uzzell, and Larry Wilson; in Puerto Rico, Juan Rivero and Richard Thomas. In the field of venom research, I acknowledge the kind cooperation of my colleague and travel companion, Edward Seligmann, Jr., as well as encouraging support and advice from W. Eliott, Elazar Kochva, Sherman Minton, Herbert Rosenberg, and Findlay Russell, all of whom alleviated my "venom ignorance." John Brown and M. Z. Bierly from Wyeth Laboratories provided information about their antivenin.

In Latin America, in addition to receiving the characteristic warmth of my Latino colleagues and friends, I had the benefit of learning many things about herpetology both in the field and in the halls of the museums and universities. In Mexico, I thank Gustavo Casas-Andreu, William López-Forment, Rafael Martín del Campo, A. Jordán Rodríguez, Josefina Rudich de la Rosa, Miguel Alvarez del Toro, and the late Jordi Juliá Zertuche; in Nicaragua, Jaime Villa, now at the University of Missouri; in Costa Rica, Roger Bolaños, José María Gutiérrez, Douglas Robinson, Alejandro Solórzano, and the late Luís Cerdas; in Colombia, Cristina Ardila, Santiago Ayerbe, Olga Castaño, Vladimir Corredor, Carlos Pérez-Santos (currently in Spain), Jorge Hernández, José Vicente Rodríguez, José Vicente Rueda, Juan Manuel Renjifo, Hermano Roque, Pedro Ruíz, Juan Silva Haad, the late Federico Medem (my ex-compatriot), Armando Dugand, and Hermano Nicéforo María. In Venezuela, my other home country for many years, I thank my colleagues and friends at the Universidad Central de Venezuela and other institutions: Ernesto Foldats, Hermano Ginés, Stephan Gorzula, Abdem Ramón Lancini, Alfredo Paolillo, Santiago Pérez Salas, Félix Pifano, Edgars Rutkis, José Vicente Scorza, Pedro Trebbau, Charles Ventrillon, Alexis Arends, and my late companions, teachers and friends, Francisco Fernández Yépez, Alonso Gamero, and Janis Racenis; in Ecuador, Gustavo Orcés; in Suriname, John de Bruin; in Peru, Nelly Espinoza, Antonio Samanamund Romero, Francisco Cutti Onofre, and the late Oswaldo Meneses; in Bolivia, the late Noel Kempff Mercado; in Uruguay, Federico Achaval, Anibal Melgarejo, Melitta Menehel, and the late Braulio Orejas; in Argentina, Jorge Cranwell, Marcos Freiberg, José Gallardo, José Gassull, Adalberto Ibarra, Virgilio Roig, Jorge Williams, and the late Avelino Barrio.

Brazil, the largest South American country, offered me many opportunities to travel, to study, and to explore coral snakes thanks to a long list of people, most of whom also became my friends in the characteristic Latin American way. My special *estimação brasileira* goes to Pedro Antonio Federsoni, Jr. and his museum team Marcus Buononato, Silvana Calixto, Nayte Vitiello, and Elisabeth Zoksak; to Paulo Vanzolini and Oswaldo Vital Brazil, Jr. for their constant help and availability; and no less to Willy Beçak, Helio Belluomini, Persio De Biasi, Werner Bockermann, Paulo Buhrnheim, João Caballeiro, Joaquin Caballeiro, Henrique Canter, Luiz Cardoso, Carmen Cordeiro, Alma Hoge, Franscisco Nascimento, Teresa Avila Pires, Guiseppe Puorto, Nelson Jorge da Silva, Leandro Silveira, the late Antenor Leitão de Carvalho, Alphonse Hoge, and Bertha Lutz, and many more Brazilian scholars, old and new.

In Europe, in addition to the valuable museum help, I received the cooperation of Ilya Darevski, Alice Grandison, Konrad Klemmer, Benedetto Lanza, Baldur Limburg, Adolf Portmann, Hjalmar Rendahl, Garth Underwood, and many more who extended to me the European collegial hospitality.

The Fundación Mendoza, the Consejo Universitario of the Universidad Central de Venezuela, and the now defunct Fundación Creole in Venezuela, and the Council of Scientific Research of the American Museum of Natural History, the U.S. Public Health Service, the National Science Foundation, Roger Peterson Institute, and the

Acknowledgments

Research Foundation of the City University of New York in the United States, entrusted me with money to carry out research on snakes, particularly coral snakes, for which I thank them all.

Drawings and maps are the contribution in part of Milagros Bernal, Gertrude Fisher, Frances Gibson, Ysabella Hincapié, Frances White, and Frances Zweifel. The generous contributors of photographs are acknowledged under every picture. Marie Bowles, Ethan Russell, and the team at Krieger Publishing Company are to be acknowledged for patiently and professionally working to see the manuscript transformed into a book, while willing proof readers were Narciso Alberti, Yadira Bernal, John Gillen and Orlando Vargas.

The author gratefully acknowledges permission from the Journal of American Medical Association to use a quote from Kitchens and van Mierop, 1987, JAMA, 258(12): 1615–1618; and from Revista de Biología Tropical to use Figs. 46 and 47 from Gutiérrez and Bolaños, 1979, Rev. Biol. Trop., 27:57–73.

List of Museums

The following list of museums includes their abbreviations that appear throughout the text of this book, and the individuals in charge of their collections.

AMNH	American Museum of Natural History, New York (C. M. Bogert, C. J. Cole, D. Frost, C. W. Myers, R. G. Zweifel)
ANSP	Academy of Natural Sciences of Philadelphia (J. Bolhke, E. Malnate)
ASU	Department of Zoology, Arizona State University, Tempe (M. J. Fouquette)
BCB	Bryce C. Brown Collection, Waco, Texas (B. C. Brown)
BM	British Museum (Natural History), London (A. C. Grandison, E. N. Arnold)
CAS	California Academy of Sciences, San Francisco (A. E. Leviton)
CHINM	Colección Herpetólogica, Instituto Nacional de Microbiología, Buenos Aires, Argentina (A. Ibarra)
CLS	Colegio La Salle, León, Nicaragua (Hno. Felipe)
CM	Carnegie Museum, Pittsburgh, Pennsylvania (N. D. Richmond, C. J. McCoy)
CMC	The Charleston Museum, Charleston, South Carolina (A. Sanders)
COM	Centro de Ofidismo, Instituto de Medicina Tropical, Manaos, Brazil (P. Buhrnheim, H. Linhares Lema)
CSJG	Colegio San José de Guaneta, Santander, Colombia
CU	Cornell University, Section of Ecology and Systematics, Ithaca, New York (N. Layne, H. Pough)
DM	Dugès Museum, Guanajuato, Mexico
EAL	Ernest A. Liner Herpetological Collection, Hammond, Louisiana (E. A. Liner)
EPQ	Escuela Politécnica Nacional, Quito, Ecuador (G. Orcés Villagomez)
FAS	Frederick A. Shannon Collection, Wickenberg, Arizona (F. A. Shannon)
FAUCV	Facultad de Agronomía, UCV, Maracay, Venezuela (F. Fernández Yépez)
FMNH	Field Museum of Natural History, Chicago, (R. Inger, H. Marx, G. Mazurek)
GML	Gorgas Memorial Laboratory, Panama (C. Myers)
IB	Instituto Butantan, São Paulo, Brazil (A. Hoge, I. Laporta Ferreira, C. Cordeiro)
IBAM	Instituto de Biología Animal, Facultad de Ciencias Agrarias, Mendoza, Argentina (V. Roig)
ICN	Instituto de Ciencias Naturales, Universidad Nacional de Colombia, Bogotá, Colombia (O. Castaño, P. Ruiz)
ILS	Museo del Instituto La Salle, Bogotá, Colombia (Hno. Nicéforo María, Hno. Roque)
INAS	Instituto Nacional de Salud, Sección Sueros, Bogotá, Colombia (J. M. Renjifo)
INDERENA	Instituto Nacional de los Recursos Naturales Renovables y del Ambiente, Bogotá, Colombia (J. Hernández, J. V. Rodríguez, J. V. Rueda)
INSLP	Institutos Nacionales de Salud, Lima, Peru (O. Meneses García)
IOC	Instituto Oswaldo Cruz, Brazil
IRSNB	Institut Royal des Sciences Naturelles de Belgique, Brussels, Belgium (A. Carpat)
JFC	Joseph F. Copp Collection, La Jolla, California (J. F. Copp)

JV	Jaime Villa Collection, Kansas City (J. Villa)	MZLSU	Museum of Zoology, Louisiana State University, Baton Rouge, Louisiana (D. Rossman)
KU	Museum of Natural History, University of Kansas (W. E. Duellman, J. T. Collins)	MZUSP	Museu de Zoologia da Universidade de São Paulo, Brazil (P. E. Vanzolini)
LACM	Los Angeles County Museum, Los Angeles, California (J. W. Wright, R. L. Bezie)	NCSM	North Carolina State Museum of Natural History, Raleigh (W. Palmer)
LBSC	Long Beach State College (R. Loomis)	NMB	Naturhistorisches Museum, Basel, Switzerland (F. Forcart, C. Unternährer)
MACN	Museo Argentino de Ciencias Naturales, Buenos Aires, Argentina (J. M. Gallardo, J. Cranwell)	NMW	Naturhistorisches Museum, Vienna, Austria (J. Eiselt)
MBUCV	Museo de Biología, Universidad Central de Venezuela, Caracas (J. Racenis, H. Solano)	RAC	Rudy Arndt Collection, Ithaca, New York (R. Arndt)
MCN	Museo de Ciencias Naturales, Caracas, Venezuela (A. R. Lancini)	SA	Collección de Santiago Ayerbe, Popayán, Colombia (S. Ayerbe)
MCZ	Museum of Comparative Zoology, Harvard University, Cambridge, Massachusetts (E. E. Williams, P. Albrecht, J. P. Rosado)	SDMNH	San Diego Society of Natural History of Natural History, San Diego, California (L. M. Klauber)
MD	Dresden Museum, Dresden, Germany	SM	Strecker Museum, Baylor University, Waco, Texas (B. B. Brown)
MHNLP	Museo Nacional de Historia Natural "Javier Prado," Universidad Nacional Mayor de San Marcos, Lima, Peru (N. C. de Espinoza)	SMC	Sherman A. Minton Collection, Indianapolis, Indiana
		SMF	Senckenbergische Naturforschende Gesellschaft, Franfurt-am-Main, Germany (K. Klemmer, R. Mertens)
MHNLS	Museo de La Sociedad de Ciencias Naturales La Salle, Caracas, Venezuela (Hno. Ginés, C. Alemán, J. M. Peláez)	SU	Division of Systematic Biology, Stanford University, Stanford, California (A. Leviton)
ML	Rijksmuseum van Natuurlijke Historie, Leiden, Holland (L. D. Brongersma, M. S. Hoogmoed)	TCWC	Texas Cooperative Wildlife Museum, Texas A. & M. University, College Station (R. J. Baldauf, J. R. Dixon)
		UA	Department of Zoology, University of Arizona, Tucson, Arizona (C. Lowe)
MNHN	Museum National d'Historie Naturelle, Paris (J. Guibè)	UCG	Universidade Católica de Goiás, Goiânia, Goiás, Brazil (N. Jorge da Silva)
MNR	Museu Nacional, Rio de Janeiro, Brazil (A. L. de Carvalho, B. Lutz)	UCM	University of Colorado Museum, Boulder, Colorado (T. P. Maslin, H. M. Smith)
MPEG	Museu Paraense "Emilio Goeldi," Belém, Brazil (O. Cunha, F. Nascimento)	UCMNH	University of Connecticut, Museum of Natural History, Storrs (R. Dubos)
MPM	Milwaukee Public Museum, Milwaukee, Wisconsin (R. W. Henderson, M. Nickerson)	UCR	Departamento de Biología, Universidad de Costa Rica (D. C. Robinson)
MSNM	Museo Civico di Storia Naturale, Milano, Italy (M. Torchio)	UF	Florida State Museum, University of Florida, Gainesville, Florida (W. Auffenberg, P. Meylan)
MVZ	Museum of Vertebrate Zoology, University of California (R. C. Stebbins)		
MZF	Museo Zoologico dell'Universita di Firenze, Florence, Italy (B. Lanza)	UIMNH	University of Illinois, Museum of Natural History, Urbana, Illinois (D. F. Hoffmeister, H. M. Smith)

List of Museums

UMMZ	Museum of Zoology, University of Michigan (C. F. Walker, A. Kluge, R. A. Nussbaum)
UNAM	Laboratorio de Herpetología, Instituto de Biología, Universidad Nacional Autónoma de Mexico (G. Casas-Andreu)
UNM	Collection of Vertebrates, University of New Mexico, Albuquerque (W. G. Degenhardt)
UNT	Facultad de Ciencias Naturales, Universidad Nacional de Trujillo, Peru (A. Samanamud Romero)
UPRM	Departamento de Biología, Universidad de Puerto Rico, Mayaguez, P. R. (J. Rivero)
UPRRP	Universidad de Puerto Rico, Río Piedras (R. Thomas)
USC	University of Southern California, Department of Zoology (J. M. Savage, R. W. McDiarmid)
USL	Department of Biology, University of Southwestern Louisiana, Lafayette (H. D. Wilson)
USNM	National Museum of Natural History, Washington, D.C. (R. Heyer, R. W. McDiarmid, G. Zug, R. I. Crombie)
UTA	University of Texas, Arlington (J. A. Campbell)
ZMB	Museum für Naturkunde, Zoologisches Museum, Humboldt-Universität zu Berlin, Germany (P. Günter, R. Günter)
ZMC	Universitetes Zoologiske Museum, Copenhagen, Denmark (F. W. Braestrup, J. B. Rasmussen)
ZMH	Zoologisches Museum, Hamburg, Germany (W. Ladiges)
ZSBS	Zoologische Sammlung des bayerischen Staates, Munich, Germany

Name Index

Abalos, J. W., 102
Abe, A. S., 71, 73, 79
Achaval, Federico, 70, 302
Adler, Kraig, 5, 302
Ahl, E., 82
Aird, S. D., 105
Alberti, Narciso, 303
Albrecht, P., 306
Alemán, C., 306
Allen, E. R., 33, 64, 113
Alvarez del Toro, Miguel, 8, 302
Amaral, Afranio do, 95, 103
Anchieta, Joseph de, 4
Anderson, Sydney, 301
Andrews, E. H., 113
Angel, Rodrigo, 116
Araujo, M. L. de, 64
Ardila, Cristina, 302
Ardrey, R. 61
Arends, Alexis, 302
Arndt, R., 306
Arnold, E. N., 305
Ashley, B. D., 103, 118
Ashton, R. E. Jr., 9
Auffenberg, W., 306
Ayerbe, Santiago, 64, 66, 72, 116, 199, 251, 302, 306
Azevedo, A. C. P., 64

Baez, A., 89
Baird, S. E., 5
Baldauf, R. J., 306
Barbour, Thomas, 95, 113
Barrio, Avelino, 118, 302
Bates, H. W., 77
Beçak, M. L., 45
Beçak, Willy, 45, 95, 302
Beebe, William, 54, 190
Belluomini, Helio, 29, 101, 302
Berkeley, W. H., 102, 118
Bernal, Milagros, 303
Bernal, Yadira, 303
Bernal-Carlo, Amanda, 41, 301
Bezie, R. L., 306
Bibron, G., 5
Bierley, M. Z., 302
Billings, T. A., 118
Bockermann, Werner, 302
Bocourt, Marie-Firmin, 5
Bogert, Charles M., ix, 54, 252, 301, 305
Bohlke, J., 305
Bolaños, Roger, 45, 46, 47, 96, 102, 118, 302
Botelho, C. R., 118

Boulenger, Geoge A., 5, 15
Bowles, Marie, 303
Braestrup, F. W., 307
Brattsrom, Bayard H., 78, 302
Brazaitis, Peter, 302
Brongersma, L. D., 306
Brown, B. B., 306
Brown, B. C., 305
Brown, John, 302
Brugger, Cristin, 72
Bücherl, Wolfgang, 101
Buffon, 95
Buhrheim, Paulo, 95, 302, 305
Buononato, Marcus, 35, 43, 44
Burchfield, P. M., 103

Caballero, João, 302
Caballero, Joaquin, 75, 302
Cadle, John E., 88, 90, 256, 261
Caldwell, J., Color 3
Calixto, Silvana, 302
Campbell Jonathan, 6, 25, 64, 77, 78, 79, 80, 118, 186, 194, 210, 217, 302, 307
Canter, Henrique Moisés, 112, 302
Cardoso, Jão Luíz, 109, 302
Carpat, A., 305
Carrillo de Espinoza, Nelly, 115, 302, 306
Carvalho, Antenor Leitao de, 302, 306
Casas-Andreu, Gustavo, 72, 302, 307
Castaño, Olga, 302, 305
Cerdas, Luís Gonzalo, 96, 101, 109, 118, 302
Chippaux, J. P., 109
Coe, C. H., 113
Cohen, P., 102, 105, 107, 118
Cole, C. Jay, 301, 305
Collins, J. T., 305
Conant, Roger and Isabelle, 154, 301
Cooper, 94
Cope, Edward D., 5, 23, 77
Copp, J. F., 305
Cordeiro, Carmen, 302, 305
Corredor, Vladimir, 302
Covelo de Zolesi, L., 70
Cranwell, Jorge, 302, 306
Crombie, R. I., 307
Cruz, Oswaldo, 95
Cunha, Oswaldo Rodrigues da, 59, 95, 171, 186, 190, 192, 207, 210, 306
Curtis, L., 62
Cutti Onofre, Francisco, 302
Cuvier, G. L. C. F. D., 4, 221

Darevski, Ilya, 302

Darling, D. M., 113
Darwin, Charles, 78
Daudin, F. M., 4
Dawson, J. H., 118
De Biasi, Persio, 302
De Bruin, John, 247, 302
De Franco Montalvan, D. 109
Degenhardt, W. G., 307
Ditmars, Raymond L., 95
Dix, Michael W., 100
Dixon, James R., 52, 55, 59, 80, 86, 171, 301, 306
Dowling, Herndon, 301
Downey, Jack, 301
Dubos, R., 306
Duellman, William E., 86, 115, 116, 135, 254, 301, 306
Dugand, Armando, 302
Duméril, A., 5
Duméril, A. M. C., 5
Dunn, Emmet R., 25, 78

Edwards, S. R., 9
Eiselt, Josef, 306
Eliott, W. B., 118
Estes, R., 89
Estol, Carlos, 301

Federsoni, Pedro Antonio, Jr., 61, 95, 100, 302
Felipe, Hno., 305
Fernández Yépez, Francisco, 302, 305
Ferreira, Laporta Iara, 95, 305
Fischer, Gertrude, 303
Fix, James, 100, 101
Flowers, H. H., 118
Fogden, M. and P., 249
Foldats, Ernesto, 302
Foley, George, 301
Forcart, F., 306
Fouquette, M. J., 305
Franz, R., 64
Freed, P., 250
Freiberg, Marcos, 302
Frost, Darrel, 301

Gadow, H., 8, 78
Gallardo, José M., 302, 306
Gamero, Alonso, 302
Gans, Carl, 301
García, E., 6, 94
Gassull, José, 302
Gehlbach, Frederick, 58, 73, 77, 78

309

Gennaro, Joseph, 29, 103, 112, 117
Gibson, Frances, 303
Gilboa, Itzak, 302
Gillen, John, 303
Ginés, Hno., 302, 306
Girard, C., 5
Glass, J. P., 113
Gloyd, H. K., 28, 110, 113
Gómez Villegas, César, 118
Gorzula, Stephan, 54, 302
Gracie, Carol, 113, 302
Graham, G., 45, 47
Grandison, Alice C., 302, 305
Grant, C., 62
Gray, J. E., 5
Greene, Harry W., 58, 59, 61, 62, 71, 73, 77, 78, 83, 256, 301
Griffin, P. R., 105
Grijs, P., 74
Grobman, A. B., 78
Guderian, Ronald, 119
Guibè, J., 306
Gumilla, Joseph, Padre, 4
Günter, P., 307
Günter, R., 306
Günther, A., 5
Gutiérrez, José María, 45, 46, 47, 96, 107, 302

Haast, William, 103, 114, 302
Haffer, J., 86
Hallowell, E., 5
Hanks, Jess, 301
Hardy, Larry D., 117, 118
Harnack, Marianne von, 25
Hartweg, Norman, 301
Harwood, P. O., 73
Heatwole, Harold, 54, 55, 302
Hecht, Max K., 78, 88, 301
Henderson, R. W., 52, 55, 80, 306
Hernández, Jorge, 302, 305
Heyer, W. R., 86, 307
Hincapié, Ysabella, 303
Hocking, Pedro, 115
Hoffmeister, D. F., 306
Hoge, Alma, 302
Hoge, Alphonse R., 29, 61, 302, 305
Holbrook, J. E., 5
Holman, J. A., 88
Hoogmoed, M. S., 247, 249, 260, 306
Howell, T. R., 71
Hulse, A. C., 59

Ibarra, Adalberto, 302, 305
Ihering, Hermann von, 95
Inger, Robert F, ix, 301, 305

Jackson, D. R., 64
Jameson, David, 302
Jan, Giorgio, 5, 135
Janzen, D. H., 82
Jenner, Janann, 301
Jiménez-Porras, José, 96, 107
Juliá Zeruche, Jordi, 302

Kahn, M. S., 110, 112, 117
Kellogg, Russell, 302

Kelly, Paul, 301
Kempff Mercado, Noel, 253, 302
Kennicott, R., 5
Keyser, Edmund, 302
Kipling, R., 94
Kitchens, C. S., 110, 112, 113, 115, 117
Klauber, Lawrence M., 95, 306
Klemmer, Konrad, 306
Klickstein, G. D., 112, 117
Kluge, Arnold, 301, 307
Kochalaty, Walter, 118
Kochva, Elazar, 302
Koopman, Karl, 301
Kraus, R., 118
Kuch, U., 249

Lacerda, J. B. de, 95
Ladiges, W., 307
Lamar, William, 6, 25, 55, 77, 78, 79, 80, 115, 118, 171, 186, 194, 210, 217, 251, 262, 301
Lancini, A. Ramón., 302, 306
Lankes, K. 59
Lanyon, Bud, 301
Lanza, Benedetto, 302, 306
Lauritzen, L. 118
Layne, J. N., 71
Lazzell, James, 302
Leavens, Carol, 29
Lema, H. Linhares, 305
Lema, Thales de, 39, 95, 253
Leviton, A., 306
Limburg, Baldur, 302
Liner, Ernest A., 301, 305
Linnaeus, Carolus, 4, 82
Loennenberg, E., 113
Loewe, Charles, 302, 306
Loomis, R., 306
López-Forment, William, 72, 302
Loveridge, A., 62
Lutz, Adolfo, 95
Lutz, Bertha, 302, 306
Luykx, P., 45
Lynch, John D., 86, 302
Lyne, H., 305

Machado, J. C., 106, 107, 109, 113
Malnate, E., 305
Mantel, Linda, 301
Mao, S. H., 88, 89
Marcgavius, Georgius, 4
Marien, D., 78
Marques, Octavio, 79
Martin, Paul, 83
Martin del Campo, Rafael, 8, 302
Martius, C. F. P. von, 4
Marx, Hymen, ix, 305
Maslin, T. P., 306
Maximillian Wied-Neuwied, Prince, 3, 4, 94
Mazurek, G., 305
McCollough, N. C., 29, 112, 117
McCoy, C. Jay, 301, 305
McCranie, R., 49, 54, 250
McCristal, Hugh K., 66, 302
McDiarmid, Roy W., 71, 78, 83, 248, 260, 302, 307

McDowell, Samuel, 16, 21, 22, 25, 35, 38, 40, 41, 42, 87, 301
Medem, Federico, 96, 302
Melgareho, Aníbal, 302
Méndez, Adrián, 113
Meneses García, Oswaldo, 302, 305
Mertens, R., 25, 59, 78, 306
Meylan, P., 306
Minton, J. E., 72
Minton, Madge, 96
Minton, Sherman A., 96, 102, 107, 110, 117, 301, 302, 306
Miranda, M. E., 118
Monehel, Melitta, 302
Moreno, A. G., 142
Moseley, T., 112, 113, 117
Müller, F., 5
Müller, Paul, 53, 86
Munjal, D., 118
Myers, Charles W., ix, 115, 116, 201, 255, 258, 301, 305

Nascimento, Francisco Paiva do, 59, 95, 171, 186, 190, 207, 210, 302, 306
Neill, W. T., 33, 57, 61, 64, 113
Nicéforo María, Hno., 218, 302, 305
Nickerson, M., 306
Nussbaum, R. A., 307

Oliver, James, 116, 301
Orcés Villagómez, G., 207, 302, 305
Orejas, Braulio, 302
Organ, James, 301
Ossinchak, Joseph, 301

Palmer, W., 306
Paolillo, Alfredo, 302
Papenfus, Ted, 115
Parrish, H. M., 110, 112, 117
Peláez, J. M., 306
Pérez-Higareda, 145, 192
Pérez Salas, Santiago, 302
Pérez-Santos, Carlos, 118, 142, 302
Peters, James, 301
Peters, Wilhelm, 5
Pettigrew, L. C., 114
Phillips, Eric, 58
Picado, T. C., 7, 96, 109, 199
Pifano, Félix, 302
Pires, Teresa Avila, 302
Pisani, G. R., 9
Pollard, C. B., 113
Pope, C. H., 110
Porras, Louis, 53
Porter, Spence, 301
Portmann, Adolf, 25, 302
Pough, F. H., Jr., 78, 80, 103, 305
Price, Randy, 301
Puorto, Guiseppe, 79, 253, 255, 256, 259, 260, 261, 302
Pyburn, William, 77, 78

Quinn, Hugh, 64, 65

Rabb, George, 302
Racenis, J., 302, 306
Rage, J. C., 88

Name Index

Ramsey, H. W., 105, 112, 117
Rasmussen, J. B., 307
Reingelder, 94
Rendahl, Hjalmar, 302
Renjifo, Juan Manuel, 25, 118, 248, 250, 252, 255, 257, 261, 302, 305
Richmond, N. D., 305
Riemer, William, 302
Rivero, Juan, 302, 307
Rivero-Blanco, C., 86
Robinson, Douglas C., 302, 306
Rodríguez, A. Jordán, 302
Rodríguez, José Vicente, 302, 305
Roig, Virgilio, 302, 305
Ronell, Diana, 302
Roque, Hno., 302, 305
Rosado, J. P., 306
Rosen, Don, 89, 301
Rosenberg, Herbert, 99, 302
Rosenfeld, G., 106, 109, 112, 115
Rossman, Douglas, 301, 306
Roze, Janis A., 41, 59, 149, 171, 186, 201, 210, 248, 252, 255, 261
Rudich de la Rosa, Josefina, 302
Rueda, José Vicente, 302, 305
Ruibal, Rodolfo, 302
Ruíz, Pedro, 302, 305
Russell, Ethan, 303
Russell, Findlay E., 101, 111, 112, 116, 117, 118, 301, 302
Rutkis, Edgars, 35, 36, 302

Sabath, M., 64
Sanamund Romero, A., 302, 307
Sanders, A., 305
Savage, Jay M., 25, 26, 80, 85, 86, 89, 301, 307
Savitzky, Alan, 35, 90, 302
Sazima, I., 71, 73, 79, 250, 253, 256
Schlegel, H., 5, 132
Schmidt, Karl Paterson, ix, 5, 15, 25, 28, 203
Schwartzwelder, J., 113
Scorza, José Vicente, 302
Scrocchi, G. J., 35, 39
Seba, A., 5, 221

Seib, R. L., 78
Seligmann, Edward, Jr., 9, 96, 102, 103, 105, 107, 118, 164, 258, 259, 302
Sexton, O. J., 54, 55
Shannon, F. A., 116, 305
Shaw, Margaret, 301
Shindler, 112, 113
Silva, Jorge Nelson da, Jr., 95, 100, 105, 139, 302, 306
Silva-Haad, Juan, 102, 116, 118, 221, 302
Silveira, Leandro, 302
Slowinski, J. B., 26, 78, 80, 85
Smith, Hobart M., 25, 62, 145, 192, 301, 306
Smith, Susan, 73
Snyder, G. K., 105
Soini, P., 29, 52, 55, 59, 80, 171
Solano, H., 306
Solórzano, Alejandro, 248, 249, 302
Sordelli, Ferdinand, 5
Spix, J. B. von, 4, 82
Stebbins, R. C., 306
Steinbach, José, 135
Steindachner, F., 5
Stejneger, Leonard, 113
Sternfeld, R., 78
Stevan, L. J., 105
Stickel, W. H., 64, 110
Stuart, Lawrence, 301
Stubbs, Tom, 115, 302

Tashjian, J. H., 247, 251
Taylor, E. D., 25
Taylor, R. T., 118
Telford, S. R., Jr., 64
Test, Frederick H., 54, 55, 302
Theakston, R. D. G., 113
Thomas, A., 307
Thomas, Richard, 302
Thomas, Robert, 302
Tidwell, M. A., 257
Tilger, Grace, 29, 301
Torchio, M., 306
Townsend, Carol, 301
Trebbau, Pedro, 302
True, Frederick, 112, 113
Tyron, B. W., 66

Underwood, Garth, 302
Unternährer, C., 306
Uzzell, Thomas, 302

Valdez, Alberto, 74, 302
Van Gelder, Richard, 301
Van Mierop, L. H. S., 110, 112, 113, 115, 117
Vanzolini, Paulo, 5, 64, 86, 302, 306
Vargas, Oswaldo, 303
Vaz-Ferreira, R., 64, 70
Ventrillon, Charles, 302
Vial, J. L., 25
Villa, Jaime, 9, 53, 67, 203, 302, 307
Vital Brazil, 95, 114
Vital Brazil, Jr., Oswaldo, 106, 112, 114, 302
Vitiello, Nayte, 302
Vitt, L. J., 59, 252, 254, 257
Vuilleumier, Francois, 86, 301
Wagler, J., 4
Wainschude, J., 119
Walker, Charles F., 307
Wall, G. L., 54
Wallace, Alfred R., 77, 82
Weldon, P. J., 103
Werler, John E., 64, 113
Werner, Franz, 5
White, Frances, 303
Wickler, W., 78
Williams, Ernest E., ix, 86, 301, 306
Williams, Jeffrey F., 119
Williams, Jorge, 302
Willson, P., 110, 113
Wilson, H. D., 307
Wilson, Larry, 53, 260, 302
Worthington, R., 64
Wright, J. W., 306

Yarrow, P. 113

Zeger, J. C., 64
Zosak, Elisabeth, 302
Zug, George, 307
Zweifel, Frances, 24, 36, 38, 43, 303
Zweifel, Richard G., ix, x, 9, 301, 305

Subject Index

abnormalities of hemipenis, 24
abundance, 52
Acapulco coral snake, see *Micrurus browni taylori*, 148
activity periods, 54–55
adaptation to urban environment, 53
adrenal gland, 45
Akawai Indians of Guyana, 8
albino coral snakes, 29
albumin immunological distance units, 88
Allen's coral snake, see *Micrurus alleni*, 139
Amazonian aquatic coral snake, see *Micrurus surinamensis surinamensis*, 222
Amazonian coral snake, see *Micrurus spixii*, 215
American coral snakes, see *Micrurus*, 138
American kestrel, 71
anchor coral snake, see *Micrurus ancoralis*, 140
Andean black-backed coral snake, see *Leptomicrurus narduccii*, 134
Andean red-tailed coral snake, see *Micrurus mipartitus decussatus*, 197
Aniliidae as mimics, 78
annellated coral snake, see *Micrurus annellatus*, 142
Antigua coral snake, see *Micrurus browni importunus*, 147
Antioquian coral snake, see *Micrurus dumerilii antioquiensis*, 165
aposematic coloration, 25, 72
aquatic coral snake, see *Micrurus surinamensis*, 221
areas of endemism, 86
Argentinean coral snake, see *Micrurus pyrrhocryptus pyrrhocryptus*, 212
Arizona coral snake, see *Micruroides euryxanthus euryxanthus*, 137
arrow-headed coral snake, see *Micrurus alleni*, 139
Asian elapids, 3, 89
Australian elapids, 3, 89

Babaspul (Creole), see *Micrurus nigrocinctus babaspul*, 203
Balsan coral snake, see *Micrurus laticollaris*, 186
Barranquilla pygmy coral snake, see *Micrurus dissoleucus nigrirostris*, 160
Batesian mimicry, 78
Belize coral snake, see *Micrurus hippocrepis*, 182
Bering land bridge, 87

biogeographical assemblages, 85
biogeotone, 86
biological characteristics of venom, 105–107
bird predators of coral snakes, 71–72
biting in defense, 75
biting mechanism, 99–100
black snake, see *Notechis atra*, 3
black-backed coral snakes, see *Leptomicrurus*, 132
black-headed Amazonian coral snake, see *Micrurus spixii martiusi*, 216
black-headed coral snake, see *Micrurus averyi*, 144
black-neck Amazonian coral snake, see *Micrurus spixii obscurus*, 216
blind snakes, 72
blotched coral snake, see *Micrurus bernadi*, 144
body and tail coloration, 26–29
Bogert's coral snake, see *Micrurus bogerti*, 146
Boicora, 7
Bolivian Amazonian coral snake, see *Micrurus spixii princeps*, 217
Bolivian black coral snake, see *Leptomicrurus narduccii narduccii*, 134
Bolivian coral snake, see *Micrurus annellatus bolivianus*, 143
Bolivian triad coral snake, see *Micrurus frontifasciatus*, 175
Brazilian coral snake, see *Micrurus decoratus*, 151
Brazilian giant coral snake, see *Micrurus frontalis*, 172
Brazilian pit-viper, see *Bothrops jararaca*, 109
Brazilian ribbon coral snake, see *Micrurus lemniscatus carvalhoi*, 190
Brazilian roadside hawk, 71
Brazilian short-tailed coral snake, see *Micrurus frontalis brasiliensis*, 174
Brazilian vine, see *Micania quacho*, 113
broad-banded coral snake, see *Micrurus latifasciatus*, 187
Brown's coral snake, see *Micrurus browni*, 146
bullfrog-eating coral snake, 72
butterfly-head coral snake, see *Micrurus spurrelli*, 218

Cabeza de Chocho (Spanish), see *Micrurus mipartitus decussatus*, 197
Candelilla, 7

Candelilla (Spanish), see *Micrurus dissoleucus*, 158
Candelilla Barranquillera, see *Micrurus dissoleucus nigrirostris*, 150
Candelilla Merideña, see *Micrurus meridensis*, 194
Candelilla Panameña, see *Micrurus dissoleucus dunni*, 159
Candelilla Santamartense, see *Micrurus dissoleucus melanogenys*, 159
Candelilla Venezolana, see *Micrurus dissoleucus dissoleucus*, 158
cannibalism, 61–62, 65, 72, 96
capuchin coral snake, see *Micrurus dumerilii*, 163
Carib coral snake, see *Micrurus psyches*, 210
Catamayo coral snake, see *Micrurus catamayensis*, 148
cats as coral snake predators, 72
Cauca coral snake, see *Micrurus multiscutatus*, 200
Cazadora Anillada, 81
centers of dispersal, 86
centers of endemisms, 86
central Amazon coral snake, see *Micrurus spixii spixii*, 215
Central American coral snake, see *Micrurus nigrocinctus*, 201
Central American coral snakes, 85, 87
chickens, 72
Choco anchor coral snake, see *Micrurus ancoralis jani*, 141
chromosomes, 45, **46**, **47**
chumbé-pé (Guaraní), 3
circulation, 45
Clark census, 78
Clark's coral snake, see *Micrurus clarki*, 149
clear-banded coral snake, see *Micrurus distans*, 161
clines, 90
cloaca, 44, 45
cloacal popping sound, 74
coastal coral snake, see *Micrurus bogerti*, 146
coatis, predators of coral snakes, 72, 73, 83
coátl (Nahuátl), 8
Cobra (Portuguese), 6
Cobra coral (Portuguese), 6
Cobra Coral Amazonica, see *Micrurus spixii*, 215
Cobra Coral Amazonica Boliviana, see *Micrurus spixii princeps*, 217
Cobra Coral Amazonica de Cabeça Preta, 216

313

Cobra Coral Amazonica Pescoço Preto, see *Micrurus spixii obscurus*, 216
Cobra Coral Anelada, see *Micrurus annellatus*, 142
Cobra Coral Aquatica, see *Micrurus surinamensis*, 221
Cobra Coral Aquatica Amazonica, see *Micrurus surinamensis surinamensis*, 222
Cobra Coral Aquatica Venezuelana, see *Micrurus surinamensis nattereri*, 223
Cobra Coral Argentina, see *Micrurus pyrrhocryptus pyrrhocryptus*, 212
Cobra Coral Brasileira Gigante, see *Micrurus frontalis frontalis*, 172
Cobra Coral Cabeça Preta, see *Micrurus averyi*, 144
Cobra Coral Confusa, see *Micrurus langsdorffi*, 185
Cobra Coral Costas Preta, see *Leptomicrurus*, 132
Cobra Coral Costas Preta Andina, see *Leptomicrurus narduccii*, 134
Cobra Coral Costas Preta Curta, see *Leptomicrurus collaris breviventris*, 133
Cobra Coral Costas Preta Guianesa, see *Leptomicrurus collaris*, 132
Cobra Coral da Amazonia Central, see *Micrurus spixii spixii*, 215
Cobra Coral de Cinta Branca, see *Micrurus albicinctus*, 138
Cobra Coral de Faixas, see *Micrurus lemniscatus*, 188
Cobra Coral de Faixas Brasileira, see *Micrurus lemniscatus carvalhoi*, 190
Cobra Coral de Faixas de Guianas, see *Micrurus lemniscatus lemniscatus*, 189
Cobra Coral de Faixas de Trinidad, see *Micrurus lemniscatus diutius*, 190
Cobra Coral de Faixas Iguais, see *Micrurus isozonus*, 184
Cobra Coral de Faixas Occidental, see *Micrurus lemniscatus helleri*, 188
Cobra Coral de Muitos Aneis, see *Micrurus frontalis multicinctus*, 175
Cobra Coral de Rabo Curto, see *Micrurus frontalis*, 171
Cobra Coral de Rondônia, see *Micrurus hemprichii rondonianus*, 182
Cobra Coral de Villavicencio, see *Micrurus medemi*, 194
Cobra Coral Decorada, see *Micrurus decoratus*, 151
Cobra Coral do Pantanal, see *Micrurus pyrrhocryptus tricolor*, 212
Cobra Coral do Pará, see *Micrurus paraensis*, 207
Cobra Coral do Putumayo, see *Micrurus putumayensis*, 210
Cobra Coral Fio, see *Micrurus filiformis*, 170
Cobra Coral Lombrigueira, see *Micrurus hemprichii*, 180
Cobra Coral Lombrigueira Occidental, see *Micrurus hemprichii ortoni*, 181
Cobra Coral Lombrigueira Oriental, see *Micrurus hemprichii hemprichii*, 181
Cobra Coral Meridional, see *Micrurus pyrrhocryptus*, 211
Cobra Coral Mesopotamica, see *Micrurus frontalis baliocoryphus*, 174
Cobra Coral Ornamentada, see *Micrurus ornatissimus*, 206
Cobra Coral Pintada, see *Micrurus corallinus*, 150
Cobra Coral Preta Esbelta, see *Leptomicrurus narduccii melanotus*, 135
Cobra Coral Preta Pequena, see *Leptomicrurus scutiventris*, 135
Cobra Coral Rabo Curto Brasileira, see *Micrurus frontalis brasiliensis*, 174
Cobra Coral Remota, see *Micrurus remotus*, 213
Cobra Coral Septentrional, *Micrurus psyches*, 210
Cobra Coral Septentrional de Trinidad, see *Micrurus circinalis*, 149
Cobra Coral Uruguaia, see *Micrurus frontalis altirostris*, 173
Cobra Coral Verdadeira (Portuguese), 6
cobras, see *Naja*, 3, 4
coffee snakes, 72
Coiba coral snake, see *Micrurus nigrocinctus coibensis*, 204
Colima clear-banded coral snake, see *Micrurus distans oliveri*, 162
Colombian coral snake, see *Micrurus spurrelli*, 218
colonies of coral snakes, 102
color aberrations, 28–29
color pattern as defense mechanism, 73
color pattern for concealment, 25
color patterns, 25–29
coloration, 25–29
Colubridae as mimics, 78
colubrids, 87
common annelated coral snake, see *Micrurus annellatus annellatus*, 142
common capuchin coral snake, see *Micrurus dumerilii dumerilii*, 164
common Central American coral snake, see *Micrurus nigrocinctus nigrocinctus*, 202
common clear-banded coral snake, see *Micrurus distans distans*, 161
common pit viper as predator of coral snakes, 72
common Sierra Madre coral snake, see *Micrurus browni browni*, 147
confused coral snake, see *Micrurus langsdorffi*, 185
conspicuous coloration, 71
convergent evolution, 83
copulation, 20
corail (French), 7
Coral Acintada, see *Micrurus lemniscatus*, 188
Coral Acintada Guayanesa, see *Micrurus lemniscatus lemniscatus*, 189
Coral Acintada Occidental, see *Micrurus lemniscatus helleri*, 191
Coral Acintada Trinitaria, see *Micrurus lemniscatus diutius*, 190
Coral Amazónica, see *Micrurus spixii*, 215
Coral Amazónica Boliviana, see *Micrurus spixii princeps*, 217
Coral Amazónica Cuello Negro, see *Micrurus spixii obscurus*, 216
Coral Amazónica de Cabeza Negra, see *Micrurus spixii martiusi*, 216
Coral Ancla, see *Micrurus ancoralis*, 140
Coral Ancla Chocoana, see *Micrurus ancoralis jani*, 141
Coral Ancla Ecuadoriana, see *Micrurus ancoralis ancoralis*, 140
Coral Anillada, see *Micrurus annellatus*, 142
Coral Anillada Común, see *Micrurus annellatus annelatus*, 142
Coral Antioqueña, see *Micrurus dumerilii antioquiensis*, 165
Coral Argentina, see *Micrurus pyrrhocryptus pyrrhocryptus*, 212
Coral Bandas Claras Colimense, see *Micrurus distans oliveri*, 162
Coral Boliviana, see *Micrurus annellatus bolivianus*, 143
Coral Brasileña Gigante, see *Micrurus frontalis frontalis*, 172
Coral Cabeza de Chocho, 6, see *Micrurus mipartitus decussatus*, 197
Coral Cabeza Flecha, see *Micrurus alleni*, 139
Coral Cabeza Mariposa, see *Micrurus spurrelli*, 218
Coral Cabeza Negra, see *Micrurus averyi*, 144
Coral Capuchina, see *Micrurus dumerilii*, 163
Coral Capuchina Común, see *Micrurus dumerilii dumerilii*, 164
Coral Capuchina Intermedia, see *Micrurus dumerilii carinicauda*, 165
Coral Capuchina Santamartense, see *Micrurus dumerilii colombianus*, 166
Coral Capuchina Transandina, see *Micrurus dumerilii transandinus*, 166
Coral Capuchina Venezolana, see *Micrurus dumerilii venezuelensis*, 167
Coral Catamayense, see *Micrurus catamayensis*, 148
Coral Caucana, see *Micrurus multiscutatus*, 200
Coral Centroamericana, see *Micrurus nigrocinctus*, 201
Coral Centroamericana común, see *Micrurus nigrocinctus nigrocinctus*, 202
Coral Cola Corta, see *Micrurus frontalis*, 171
Coral Cola Corta Brasileña, see *Micrurus frontalis brasiliensis*, 174
Coral Confundida, see *Micrurus langsdorffi*, 185
Coral de Agua, see *Micrurus surinamensis*, 221
Coral de Agua Amazónica, see *Micrurus surinamensis surinamensis*, 222
Coral de Agua Venezolana, see *Micrurus surinamensis nattereri*, 223
Coral de Antigua, see *Micrurus browni importunus*, 147
Coral de Belize, see *Micrurus hippocrepis*, 182
Coral de Clark, see *Micrurus clarki*, 149
Coral de Coiba, see *Micrurus nigrocinctus coibensis*, 204

Subject Index

Coral de Franjas Iguales, see *Micrurus isozonus*, 184
Coral de Laderas, see *Micrurus steindachneri*, 219
Coral de los Volcanes, see *Micrurus stuarti*, 221
Coral de Pantanal, see *Micrurus pyrrhocryptus tricolor*, 212
Coral de Pará, see *Micrurus paraensis*, 207
Coral de Ponzoña (Spanish), 7
Coral de Ponzoña de Mocoa (Spanish), 6
Coral de Tríadas Falsas, see *Micrurus bocourti*, 145
Coral de Villavicencio, see *Micrurus medemi*, 194
Coral de Yungas, see *Micrurus annellatus balzani*, 143
Coral del Desierto, see *Micrurus tschudii*, 223
Coral Diana, see *Micrurus diana*, 152
Coral Diastema, see *Micrurus diastema*, 152
Coral Elegante, see *Micrurus elegans*, 167
Coral Elegante Verapazense, see *Micrurus elegans veraepacis*, 169
Coral Espalda-negra Andina, see *Leptomicrurus narduccii*, 134
Coral Espalda-negra Corta, see *Leptomicrurus collaris breviventris*, 133
Coral Espalda-negra Guayanesa, see *Leptomicrurus collates*, 132
Coral Espalda-negra Larga, see *Leptomicrurus collaris* collaris, 132
Coral Espléndida, see *Micrurus diastema aglaeope*, 155
Coral Gargantilla (Spanish), 6, see *Micrurus multifasciatus* or *Micrurus mipartitus*, 195
Coral Hebra, see *Micrurus filiformis*, 170
Coral Hondureña, see *Micrurus nigrocinctus divaricatus*, 204
Coral Irregular, see *Micrurus diastema sapperi*, 157
Coral Lumbricera, see *Micrurus hemprichii*, 180
Coral Macho, 6
Coral Macho (Spanish), see *Pseudoboa coronata*, 6
Coral Mesopotámica, see *Micrurus frontalis baliocoryphus*, 174
Coral Montañera, see *Micrurus petersi*, 208
Coral Montuna de Pastaza, see *Micrurus steindachneri orcesi*, 219
Coral Morada, 6, see *Micrurus psyches*, 210
Coral Negra Boliviana, see *Leptomicrurus narduccii narduccii*, 134
Coral Negra Esbelta, see *Leptomicrurus narduccii melanotus*, 135
Coral Negra Pequeña, see *Leptomicrurus scutiventris*, 135
Coral Norteña, see *Micrurus psyches*, 210
Coral Norteña, 8
Coral Norteña del Desierto, see *Micrurus tschudi olssoni*, 224
Coral Norteña Trinitaria, see *Micrurus circinalis*, 149
Coral Ornamentada, see *Micrurus ornatissimus*, 206

Coral Panameña, see *Micrurus stewarti*, 220
Coral Peruviana, see *Micrurus peruvianus*, 206
Coral Peruviana del Desierto, see *Micrurus meitensi*, 195
Coral Pintada, see *Micrurus corallinus*, 150
Coral Ponzoñosa (Spanish), 6
Coral Putumayense, see *Micrurus putumayensis*, 210
Coral Remota, see *Micrurus remotus*, 213
Coral Rey (Spanish), 7, see *Micrurus ancoralis jani*, 141
Coral Roatanense, see *Micrurus ruatanus*, 213
Coral Salpicada, see *Micrurus margaritiferus*, 193
Coral Sangilense, see *Micrurus sangilensis*, 214
Coral Santiagueña Montuna, see *Micrurus steindachneri steindachneri*, 219
coral snake, history of studies, 3
coral snake behavior, 8
coral snake beliefs, 5-8
coral snake bite, chewing motion, 100
coral snake bites, 74, 110-111
coral snake concealing coloration, 73
coral snake fossils, 87
coral snake names, 5-8, Appendix A
coral snake parasites, 73
coral snake predators, 71-73
coral snake self-mimicry, 73-75
coral snakes, attacked by army ants, 72
coral snakes, body scales, 13, **15**, **16**
coral snakes, body vertebrae, 15, 16
coral snakes, external features, 13-34
coral snakes, head shields, **13**, **14**, **15**
coral snakes, nematode infections, 73
coral snakes, popular verses, 9
coral snakes, protection in Latin America, 9
coral snakes, protection in the United States, 9
coral snakes, rate of speciation, 90
coral snakes, shedding, 19
coral snakes, skin, 13
coral snakes, supraanal tubercles, **16**
coral snakes, xenodontine origin, 87
coral snakes as endangered animals, 9-10, 53,
coral snakes for research, 102
coral snakes in voodoo ceremonies, 103
Coral Sureña, see *Micrurus pyrrhocryptus*, 211
Coral Sureña del Desierto, see *Micrurus tschudii tschudii*, 224
Coral Tricolor Boliviana, see *Micrurus frontifasciatus*, 175
Coral Uruguaya, see *Micrurus frontalis altirostris*, 173
Coral Venenosa (Spanish), 6
Coral Zunilense, see *Micrurus nigrocinctus zunilensis*, 205
Corales Espalda-negra, see *Leptomicrurus*, 132
Coralilla (Spanish), 6, 7
Coralilla Bandas Claras, see *Micrurus distans*, 161

Coralilla Bandas Claras Común, see *Micrurus distans distans*, 161
Coralilla Bandas Claras Michoacana, see *Micrurus distans michoacanensis*, 162
Coralilla Buena (Spanish), 8
Coralilla de MacDougall, see *Micrurus diastema macdougalli*, 157
Coralilla de Sierra Madre, see *Micrurus browni*, 146
Coralilla de Zweifel, see *Micrurus distans zweifeli*, 163
Coralilla Doble Negra, see *Micrurus ephippifer*, 169
Coralilla Elegante, see *Micrurus elegans*, 167
Coralilla Elegante Occidental, see *Micrurus elegans elegans*, 168
Coralilla Hocico Manchado, see *Micrurus diastema apiatus*, 156
Coralilla Irregular, see *Micrurus diastema sapperi*, 157
Coralilla Mala (Spanish), 8
Coralilla Neblinense, see *Micrurus nebularis*, 201
Coralilla Occidental, see *Micruroides euryxanthus*, 136
Coralilla Salpicada, see *Micrurus diastema affinis*, 154
Coralilla Tehuantepeca, see *Micrurus ephippifer*, 169
Coralilla Veracruzana, see *Micrurus diastema diastema*, 153
Coralilla Yucateca, see *Micrurus diastema alienus*, 155
Coralilla Zapoteca, see *Micrurus ephippifer zapotecus*, 170
Coralillo (Spanish), 6, 8
Coralillo Común de Sierra Madre, see *Micrurus browni browni*, 147
Coralillo Costanero, see *Micrurus bogerti*, 146
Coralillo de Acapulco, see *Micrurus browni taylori*, 148
Coralillo de Arizona, see *Micruroides euryxanthus euryxanthus*, 137
Coralillo de Bandas Largas, see *Micrurus latifasciatus*, 187
Coralillo de Belize, see *Micrurus hippocrepis*, 182
Coralillo de Doble Collar, see *Micrurus laticollaris*, 186
Coralillo de Gunajuato, see *Micrurus fulvius fitzingeri*, 178
Coralillo de Nayarit, see *Micrurus proximans*, 209
Coralillo de Sinaloa, see *Micruroides euryxanthus neglectus*, 138
Coralillo de Sonora, see *Micruroides euryxanthus australis*, 137
Coralillo de Tampico, see *Micrurus fulvius maculatus*, 178
Coralillo de Tuxtla, see *Micrurus limbatus*, 192
Coralillo Ensillado, see *Micrurus bernadi*, 144
Coralillo Manchado, see *Micrurus fulvius microgalbineus*, 179
Coralillo Manchado de Tuxtla, see *Micrurus limbatus spilosomus*, 193

Coralillo Norteamericano, see *Micrurus fulvius*, 176
Coralillo Occidental, see *Micruroides euryxanthus*, 136
Coralillo Occidental de Dobie Collar, see *Micrurus laticollaris maculirostris*, 187
Coralillo Oriental de Doble Collar, see *Micrurus laticollaris laticollaris*, 187
Coralillo Ponzoñoso (Spanish), 8
Coralillo Tejano, see *Micrurus fulvius tenere*, 179
Costa Rica Gargantilla, see *Micrurus multifasciatus hertwigi*, 200
Costa Rican king snake, 81
courtship, 65,
cuicuicoátl (Nehuátl), 8
Cuiva Indians, 8
Culebra Añadida, 80
curandero, 7

death adder, 3
death-feigning, 75
decorated coral snake, see *Micrurus decoratus*, 151
defense against predators, 73
defensive behavior, 71, 73, 74
dentition, **36, 37, 38, 39, 40**, 99
desert coral snake, see *Micrurus tschudii*, 223
destruction of habitat, 10, 53, 54
determination of sex, 19, 20
Diana's coral snake, see *Micrurus diana*, 152
diastema coral snake, see *Micrurus diastema*, 152
digestive tract, 44
dispersal origin, 89
distribution in Amazon, 52, Table 5
diurnal activity, 54, 55, 83
double black coral snake, see *Micrurus ephippifer*, 169
double collar coral snake, see *Micrurus laticollaris*, 186
Duméril's coral snake, see *Micrurus dumerilii*, 163

eastern coral snake, xi, 6, 9, see *Micrurus fulvius fulvius*, 177
eastern diamondback rattlesnake, xi
eastern double collar coral snake, see *Micrurus laticollaris laticollaris*, 187
eastern worm-eating coral snake, see *Micrurus hemprichii hemprichii*, 181
ecological distribution, 51-53
ecological resource partitioning, 55
Ecuadorian anchor coral snake, see *Micrurus ancoralis ancoralis*, 140
Ecuadorian coral snake, see *Micrurus bocourti*, 145
egg incubation in laboratory, 67
egg laying, 65, 66, 70
egg numbers, 67, Table 6
egg quotient, 68, Table 6
egg size, 67, Table 6
egg weight, 66
elapid fossil from Europe, 88
elegant coral snake, see *Micrurus elegans*, 167

embryonic development, 67
emerald tree boa, 3
enemies, 71-73
equal-banded coral snake, see *Micrurus isozonus*, 184
erythrism, 29
esophagus, 44
evolution of coral snakes, 87-90
evolution of island coral snakes, 90
evolution of species, 90

falcons, 72,
false coral snakes, predators of, 71
false coral snakes as predators of coral snakes, 72
fangs, 37, 38, 39
faunal assemblages, 86
feeding, 55, 57-59
feeding excitement, 61, 62
female reproductive cycle, 64
female reproductive system, 64
fight between coral snakes, 96
flattening body in defense, 74
food, 55, 59-61
foraging hunt, 57
fossils of coral snakes, 88, 89

gallbladder, 45
Gargantilla, 6, see *Micrurus multifasciatus*, 199
Gargantilla Costaricense, see *Micrurus multifasciatus hertwigi*, 200
Gargantilla Panameña, see *Micrurus multifasciatus multifasciatus*, 200
Gemela Confundida, 80
genius loci of the Americas, 3, 78
glands, 40, 41, 42, 99
Gondwanaland, 89
great kiskadee, innate avoidance, 82
groove-billed ani, 72
ground snake, 72
growth, 29
Guahibo Indians, 8
Guanajuato coral snake, see *Micrurus fulvius fitzingeri*, 177
Guaraní Indians, 7
Guatemalan false coral snake, 78
Guiana's ribbon coral snake, see *Micrurus lemniscatus lemniscatus*, 189
Guianan black-backed coral snake, see *Leptomicrurus collaris*, 132

habitats, 51-53
Harderian gland, 87
harlequin coral snake, 6, see *Micrurus fulvius*, 176
harlequin snake, see *Micrurus fulvius tenere*, 179
hatching, 69-70,
hatchlings, 69-70
head coloration, 28
head glands, **41, 42**
head muscles, 40, **41, 42**
head shields, **13-15**
heart, 45
heart circulation, 45
hemipenis, 20, **21-24**, 45

hemipenis, defensive protruding of, 74
Hemprich's coral snake, see *Micrurus hemprichii*, 180
high altitude coral snakes, 52
historical source units, 85
homeopathic medicine, 96
Honduras coral snake, see *Micrurus nigrocinctus divaricatus*, 204
huayamacaicha (Guahibo, Acavai and Cuiva Indians), 8
Humahuaca Indians, 4
human influence on distribution, 53-54
Huncabamba Depression, 89
hyoid, 42
hyperxanthism, 28

ibiboboca (Native Brazilian), 3, 7, see *Micrurus ibiboboca*, 183
ibiboca (Native Brazilian), 7
incubation of eggs, 65-66
infralabial glands, **41**, 42
innate avoidance of bright coloration, 72, 77, 82, 83
intermediate capuchin coral snake, see *Micrurus dumerilii carinicauda*, 165
internal anatomy, 44, 45
irregular coral snake, see *Micrurus diastema sapperi*, 157
island coral snakes, 90

jacmars, 71
Jacobson's organ, 57
Jararaca, South American pit viper, 103
javelinas, predators of coral snakes, 73, 83
jaw walking while feeding, 59
jequiriquí (Spanish), see *Abrus precatorius*, 6
juba (Warao Indians), 8

karyotypes, 45, **46, 47**
keels, see supraanal tubercles, **16**
kidneys, 45
king cobra, 3, 4
king snake, see *Lampropeltis*, 74
kiskadees, 72, 73, 83
kraalslang (Dutch), 7
kraits, 3
krarsneke (pidgeon Dutch), 7
kumung (Akawai Indians), 8

Langsdoff's coral snake, see *Micrurus langsdorffi*, 185
laughing falcon, 71
length of coral snakes, 29-34, Table 1
little black coral snake, see *Leptomicrurus scutiventris*, 135
liver, 44
loggerhead shrike, 71
Lombricera Occidental, see *Micrurus hemprichii ortoni*, 181
Lombricera Oriental, see *Micrurus hemprichii hemprichii*, 181
long black-backed coral snake, see *Leptomicrurus collaris collaris*, 132
long-banded coral snake, see *Micrurus latifasciatus*, 187

Subject Index

longest coral snakes, 29–32, Table 1
lung, 45

maccouracourra (Guayan Indians), 8
MacDougall's coral snake, see *Micrurus diastema macdougalli*, 157
Madre de Coral (Spanish), 6
Madreporaria, 5
male reproductive cycle, 64–65
male reproductive system, 64
male sex organs, 20, **21–24**
mambas, 3
mammalian predators of coral snakes, 72
mandibles, 37, 39–40
mandibulary teeth, 39–40, **41**, 100
many-banded coral snake, see *Micrurus frontalis multicinctus*, 175
Matagatos (Spanish), 6
mating, 65, 66
maxillary teeth, 35–40, 99
mbói (Guaraní), 8
mbói-chumbé (Guaraní), 7, 8
mbói-chumbé guasú (Guaraní), 8
mbói-chumbépé (Guaraní), 8
mbói-corá (Guaraní), 8
mbói-yvyvóvó (Guaraní), 8
melanism, 28
melanism, Amazonian phenomenon, 27, 211
melanism of progressive aging, 27
Merida pygmy coral snake, see *Micrurus meridensis*, 194
Merten's coral snake, see *Micrurus mertensi*, 195
Mertensian mimicry, 78,
Mesopotamian coral snake, see *Micrurus frontalis baliocoryphus*, 174
Michoacán clear-banded coral snake, see *Micrurus distans michoacanensis*, 162
microdermatoglyphs, see microornamentation, 16
microornamentation of scales, 16–19
Middle America faunal assemblage, 88
milk snake, 6
mimicry, xii, 29, 71, 73, 77–83
mimicry, alternative explanation, 78, 82
mimicry, answers to objections, 83
mimicry, confirmed by human errors, 82
mimicry, history of, 77–78
mimicry, similarity with catepiller, 82
mimicry, similarity with turtle, 82
mimicry assemblage in Iquitos, 80
mimicry related to growth, 81
mimicry related to size, 81
Misquito Kingdom, 9
molting, 13
motmots, 72, 73, 83
mountain coral snake, see *Micrurus petersi*, 208
mucus secretion, 100
Mullerian mimicry, 78, 81, 83

naca naca (Native Peruvian), 3, 7
Nahuátl, 8
nanim uxirimake (Yanomami Indians), 8
nanim uxirimkyk (Yanomami Indians), 8

Nayarit coral snake, see *Micrurus proximans*, 209
neblina coral snake, see *Micrurus nebularis*, 201
nematodes, as coral snake parasites, 73
neonates, see hatchlings, 69
neotropical rattlesnake, 109
nocturnal activity, 55
North American coral snake, 6, see *Micrurus fulvius*, 176
northern coral snake, see *Micrurus psyches*, 210
northern desert coral snake, see *Micrurus tschudii olssoni*, 224
northern origin of coral snakes, 87
number of teeth, 38, 39, Table 3

Old World elapids, 3, 66, 88, 89
origin of coral snakes, 87–90
ornated coral snake, see *Micrurus ornatissimus*, 206
overpowering the prey, 58
ovulation, 64, 65
Oxacan coral snake, see *Micrurus ephippifer*, 169

Pacific red-tailed coral snake, see *Micrurus mipartitus mipartitus*, 196
painted coral snake, see *Micrurus corallinus*, 150
palatine bone, 35–38, *36*
palatine erector muscle, 38
palatine teeth, 38–39
Panama Gargantilla, see *Micrurus multifasciatus multifasciatus*, 200
Panama pygmy coral snake, see *Micrurus dissoleucus dunni*, 159
Panamanian coral snake, see *Micrurus stewarti*, 220
Panamanian Portal, 89
pancreas, 45
Pantanal coral snake, see *Micrurus pyrrhocryptus tricolor*, 212
Pará coral snake, see *Micrurus paraensis*, 207
parapatric speciation, 86
parasites of coral snakes, 73
Pastaza piedmont coral snake, see *Micrurus steindachneri orcesi*, 219
peafowls, 72
Peruvian coral snake, see *Micrurus peruvianus*, 208
Peruvian desert coral snake, see *Micrurus mertensi*, 195
Peter's coral snake, see *Micrurus petersi*, 208
pheromonal "footprints," 57
physiographical regions, 86
physiographical units of distribution, 87
piedmont coral snake, see *Micrurus steindachneri*, 219
Pinellas County snake bounty, xi, 9
pipe snake, 3, see *Cylindrophis rufus*, 3
polychromatism, 29
polymorphism, 29, 80, 186
Popayán red-tailed coral snake, see *Micrurus mipartitus popayanensis*, 198

predators, innate avoidance of color pattern, 72
predators of coral snakes, 71–72
progressive aging melanism, 27
protean effect in defense, 74
proto-antillean archipelago, 89
pterygoid, 35–38
pterygoid teeth, 38–39
puffbirds, 71
Putumayo coral snake, see *Micrurus putumayensis*, 210
pygmy coral snake, see *Micrurus dissoleucus*, 158

Quetzalcoátl (Nahuátl), 4, 8

Rabo de Ají, 6, see *Micrurus mipartitus anomalus*, 197
Rabo de Ají Andina, see *Micrurus mipartitus decussatus*, 197
Rabo de Ají Payanés, see *Micrurus mipartitus popayanensis*, 198
Rabo de Candela, see *Micrurus mipartitus*, 195
Rabo de Candela (Spanish), 6, see *Micrurus mipartitus*, 195
Rabo de Candela Andina, see *Micrurus mipartitus decussatus*, 197
Rabo de Candela del Pacífico, see *Micrurus mipartitus mipartitus*, 196
Rabo de Candela Santamartense, see *Micrurus mipartitus anomalus*, 197
Rabo de Candela Venezolana, see *Micrurus mipartitus semipartitus*, 199
red ringed snake, 3
red-shouldered hawk, 71
red-tailed coral snake, see *Micrurus mipartitus*, 195
red-tailed hawk, 72, 77
reef-building corals, 5
refugia, 86
refugia model of speciation, 86
regal coral snake, see *Micrurus ancoralis*, 140
remote coral snake, see *Micrurus remotus*, 213
reproduction, 63–67
reproductive cycles, 63–64
reproductive organs, 20, **21–25**
resource partitioning in microhabitats, 55, 56
respiratory system, 45
ribbon coral snake, see *Micrurus lemniscatus*, 188
ribs, 43
Roatán coral snake, see *Micrurus ruatanus*, 213
Rondonian coral snake, see *Micrurus hemprichii rondonianus*, 182

saddle coral snake, see *Micrurus bernadi*, 144
salivary glands, **42**, 44
San Gil coral snake, see *Micrurus sangilensis*, 214
Santa Marta capuchin coral snake, see *Micrurus dumerilii colombianus*, 166

Santa Marta pygmy coral snake, see *Micrurus dissoleucus melanogenys*, 159
Santa Marta red-tailed coral snake, see *Micrurus mipartitus anomalus*, 197
Santiago piedmont coral snake, see *Micrurus steindachneri steindachneri*, 219
scale microornamentation, 16–19
scale organs, 16
scales, 13–16
scales on body and tail, 15–16
scarlet snake, 6
sea snake, 3, 87
searching for prey, 57–58
seasonal cycles, 55
seasonal incidence, 54–55
selbstdarstellung, 25
self-biting of coral snake, 96
self-mimicry, see defensive tail display, 73–75
self-representation, 26
serpent-corail (French), 7
sexual dimorphism, 19–20, 33, 69
shedding, 19
short black-backed coral snake, see *Leptomicrurus collaris breviventris*, 133
short-tailed coral snake, see *Micrurus frontalis*, 171
shortest coral snakes, 32
shovelnose snake, 6
shrikes, 71
Sierra Madre coral snake, see *Micrurus browni*, 146
Sinaloa coral snake, see *Micruroides euryxanthus neglectus*, 138
sit-and-wait hunt, 57
size and growth, 29-33
skeleton, **41**, **43**, **44**
skull bones, **35**, **36**, **37**, **38**
slender black coral snake, see *Leptomicrurus narduccii melanotus*, 135
slender coral snake, see *Micrurus filiformis*, 170
small intestine, 44
smooth-fronted caiman, 72
Sonora coral snake, 6, see *Micruroides euryxanthus australis*, 137
sound production as defense, 45
South American coral snake, see *Micrurus lemniscatus*, 188
South American origin of coral snakes, 87, 88
South American rattlesnake, 103
South American trumpeters, 71
southern coral snake, see *Micrurus pyrrhocryptus*, 211
southern desert coral snake, see *Micrurus tschudii tschudii*, 224
speckled coral snake, see *Micrurus margaritiferus*, 193
spermatozoa, 64, **65**
spleen, 45

splendid coral snake, see *Micrurus diastema aglaeope*, 155
spotted coral snake, see *Micrurus fulvius microgalbineus*, 179
spotted nose coral snake, see *Micrurus diastema apiatus*, 156
Steindachner's coral snake, see *Micrurus steindachneri*, 219
stenophagy, 61
sting of bifurcated tongue, 94
sting with tail spine, 6, 7, 74, 94
stratum corneum, 19
striped Asian red snake, 3
Stuart's coral snake, see *Micrurus stuarti*, 221
sulcus spermaticus, 20, 45
supraanal tubercles, **16**
swallowing the prey, 58–59
sympatric coral snakes of Amazon, 51, 52

tail display, 58, 74–75, 77
tail injuries, 74
tail length, 33
tail length/total length ratio, 33, 34
tail raising as defensive display, 58, 73, 74–75, 77
tail sting, 6, 7, 74, 94
Taiwan coral snake, 3
Tampico coral snake, see *Micrurus fulvius maculatus*, 178
teeth, 35–40
Tehuantepec coral snake, see *Micrurus ephippifer*, 169
Texas coral snake, 6, 9, see *Micrurus fulvius tenere*, 179
thread coral snake, see *Micrurus filiformis*, 170
tlapapalcoátl (Nahuátl), 8
tongue, 44,
tongue flicking, 44, 57, 58, 61, 65
transandean capuchin coral snake, see *Micrurus dumerilii transandinus*, 166
Trinidad northern coral snake, see *Micrurus circinalis*, 149
Trinidad ribbon coral snake, see *Micrurus lemniscatus diutius*, 190
turquoise-browed motmots, innate avoidance, 82
Tuxtlan banded coral snake, see *Micrurus limbatus limbatus*, 192
Tuxtlan coral snake, see *Micrurus limbatus*, 192
Tuxtlan spotted coral snake, see *Micrurus limbatus spilosomus*, 193

umbilical cord, 69
umbilicar scar, 69
Uruguayan coral snake, see *Micrurus frontalis altirostris*, 173

variable coral snake, see *Micrurus diastema*, 152
Venezuelan aquatic coral snake, see *Micrurus surinamensis nattereri*, 223
Venezuelan capuchin coral snake, see *Micrurus dumerilii venezuelensis*, 167
Venezuelan pygmy coral snake, see *Micrurus dissoleucus dissoleucus*, 158
Venezuelan red-tailed coral snake, see *Micrurus mipartitus semipartitus*, 199
venom gland, 40, **41**, **42**
venom gland muscles, 40, **41**, **42**
Veracruz coral snake, see *Micrurus diastema diastema*, 153
Verapaz elegant coral snake, see *Micrurus elegans veraepacis*, 169
vertebrae, 42, **43**, **44**
vertebral column, 42, **43**, **44**, 88
vicariance model, 89
vicariant origin, 89
Villavicencio coral snake, see *Micrurus medemi*, 194
volcano coral snake, see *Micrurus stuarti*, 221
voodoo ceremonies, 103

Warao Indians of Venezuela, 8
warning coloration, 73, 82, 83
west Mexican coral snake, see *Micrurus distans*, 161
western coral snake, 6, see *Micruroides euryxanthus*, 136
western coral snakes, see *Micruroides*, 136
western double collar coral snake, see *Micrurus laticollaris maculirostris*, 187
western elegant coral snake, see *Micrurus elegans elegans*, 168
western ribbon coral snake, see *Micrurus lemniscatus helleri*, 191
western worm-eating coral snake, see *Micrurus hemprichii ortoni*, 181
white-banded coral snake, see *Micrurus albicinctus*, 138
wild turkeys, 72
worm-eating coral snake, see *Micrurus hemprichii*, 180

xenodontine origin of coral snakes, 87, 90

Yanomami Indians, 8
Yucatán coral snake, see *Micrurus diastema alienus*, 155
Yungas coral snake, see *Micrurus annellatus balzani*, 143

Zapotec coral snake, see *Micrurus ephippifer zapotecus*, 170
Zunil coral snake, see *Micrurus nigrocinctus zunilensis*, 205
Zweifel's coral snake, see *Micrurus distans zweifeli*, 163

Scientific Name Index

(Illustrations are marked in italic bold)

Abrus precatorius, 6
Acanthophis antarcticus, 3
Acromyrmex lobicornis, 70
Adelphicos quadrivirgatus, 61, 156, 188
Agkistrodon contortix, 60, 180
Ameiva, 60, 203
Ameiva bifrontata, 159
Ameiva undulata, 156
Amphisbaena, 70, 173, 197, 199
Amphisbaena darwini, 173
Amphisbaena leposternon, 212
Amphisbaena mertensi, 173
Amphisbaena mitchelli, 181
Amphisbaena occidentalis, 60, 224
Amphisbaena roberti, 173, 190
Amphisbaena steindachneri, 173
Amphisbaena vermicularis, 184
Aniliidae, 78, 123
Anilius, 81
Anomalepis mexicanus, 203
Anthurium, 119
Anthurium scandens, 118
Apostolepis, 81, 90
Apostolepis assimilis, 71
Apostolepis quinquelineatus, 216
Aristolochia, 119
Aristolochia Klugii, 118
Atractus, 56, 58, 60, 78, 80, 82, 124, 186, 198, 199
Atractus collaris, 217
Atractus elaps, 80
Atractus sanctaemartae, 197
Atractus trilineatus, 149, 191
Atractus werneri, 55
Aulura anomala, 216

Bachia, 60, 135, 142, 149, 185, 191, 210
Bachia cuvieri, 166
Bachia dorbignyi, 135
Bachia trinasale, 192
Bothrops atrox, 56, 71
Bothrops jararaca, 109
Bothrops pictus, 60, 195
Bucconidae, 71
Bungarus, 3, 66, 74, 88, 99
Buteo jamaicensis, 72
Buteo lineatus, 71
Buteo magnirostris, 71

Caenophidia, 87
Callichthys callichthys, 60, 222
Calliophis, 74, 99
Calliophis macclellandi, 3
Calliophis sauteri, 3
Capsicum annuum, 6, 118
Chilomeniscus, 80
Chilomeniscus cinctus, 60
Clelia, 6, 80
Clostridium, 101
Cnemidophorus, 60, 205
Cnemidophorus deppii deppii, 203
Cnemidophorus gularis, 180
Cnemidophorus lemniscatus ruatanus, 60, 214
Coluber constrictor, 177
Caluber fulvius, see *Micrurus fulvius fulvius*, 177
Coluber lemniscatus, see *Micrurus lemniscatus lemniscatus*, 189
Colubridae, 78, 123, 124
Coniophanes, 203
Coniophanes fissidens punctigularis, 205
Corallia rubra, 5
Corallus caninus, 3
Crotalus, xi
Crotalus adamanteus, xi
Crotalus durissus, 109
Crotalus scutulatus, 102, 116
Crotalus trigris, 102
Crotophaga sulcirostris, 72
Ctenosaurus similis, 203
Cylindrophis rufus, 3, 77

Dendroaspis, 3
Dendrophidion bivittatus, 199
Dermophis mexicanus, 188
Diadophis punctatus, 61, 177, 180
Didelphis, 72
Dipsas, 80, 217
Drepanoides, 81

Elaphe, 80
Elaphe guttata, 177
Elaphe obsoleta, 180
Elaphe phaescens, 156
Elapidae, 3, 87, 88, 123, 124
Elapomorphus, 81, 90
Elaps, 82

Elaps aequicinctus, see *Micrurus mipartitus mipartitus*, 196
Elaps affinis, see *Micrurus diastema affinis*, 154
Elaps aglaeope, see *Micrurus diastema aglaeope*, 155
Elaps alienus, see *Micrurus diastema alienus*, 155
Elaps altirostris, see *Micrurus frontalis altirostris*, 173
Elaps annellatus, see *Micrurus annellatus annellatus*, 142
Elaps anomalus, see *Micrurus mipartitus anomalus*, 197
Elaps apiatus, see *Micrurus diastema apiatus*, 156
Elaps baliocoryphus, see *Micrurus frontalis baliocoryphus*, 174
Elaps balzani, see *Micrurus annellatus balzani*, 143
Elaps batesi, see *Micrurus langsdorffi*, 185
Elaps bernadi, see *Micrurus bernadi*, 144
Elaps bocourti, see *Micrurus bocourti*, 145
Elaps buckleyi, see *Micrurus ornatisimus*, 206
Elaps calamus, see *Micrurs mipartitus decussatus*, 197
Elaps circinalis, see *Micrurus circinalis*, 149
Elaps collaris, see *Leptomicrurus collaris collaris*, 132
Elaps colombianus, see *Micrurus dumerilii colombianus*, 166
Elaps corallinus, see *Micrurus corallinus*, 150
Elaps corallinus obscura, see *Micrurus spixii obscurus*, 216
Elaps corallinus var. crebripunctatus, see *Micrurus diastema diastema*, 154
Elaps decoratus, see *Micurus decoratus*, 151
Elaps decussatus, see *Micrurus mipartitus decussatus*, 197
Elaps diastema, see *Micrurus diastema diastema*, 153
Elaps dissoleucus, see *Micrurus dissoleucus dissoleucus*, 158
Elaps distans, see *Micrurus distans distans*, 161
Elaps distans michoacanensis, see *Micrurus distans michoacanensis*, 162
Elaps divaricatus, see *Micrurus nigrocinctus divaricatus*, 204

Elaps dumerilii, see *Micrurus dumerilii dumerilii*, 164
Elaps ehrhardti, see *Micrurus spixii spixii*, 215
Elaps elegans, see *Micrurus elegans elegans*, 168
Elaps ephippifer, see *Micrurus ephippifer ephippifer*, 169
Elaps epistema, see *Micrurus diastema diastema*, 153
Elaps euryxanthus, see *Micruroides euryxanthus euryxanthus*, 137
Elaps ezequieli, see *Micrurus decoratus*, 151
Elaps fasslii, see *Micrurus steindachneri steindachneri*, 219
Elaps filiformis, see *Micrurus filiformis*, 170
Elaps fischeri, see *Micrurus decoratus*, 151
Elaps fitzingeri, see *Micrurus fulvius fitzingeri*, 178
Elaps fraseri, see *Micrurus mipartitus decussatus*, 197
Elaps frontalis, see *Micrurus frontalis frontalis*, 172
Elaps frontifasciatus, see *Micrurus frontifasciatus*, 175
Elaps fulvius var. sapperi, see *Micrurus distema sapperi*, 157
Elaps gastrodelus, see *Leptomicrurus collaris collaris*, 132
Elaps gravenhorsti, see *Micrurus dissoleucus nigrirostris*, 160
Elaps guatemalensis, see *Micrurus diastema sapperi*, 157
Elaps hemprichii, see *Micrurus hemprichii hemprichii*, 181
Elaps hertae, 82
Elaps hertwigi, see *Micrurus multifasciatus hertwigi*, 200
Elaps heterochilus, see *Micrurus frontalis altirostris*, 173
Elaps hippocrepis, see *Micrurus hippocrepis*, 182
Elaps hollandi, see *Micrurus dissoleucus melanogenys*, 160
Elaps iboboca, see *Micrurus ibiboboca*, 183
Elaps imperator, see *Micrurus langsdorffi*, 185
Elaps isozonus, see *Micrurus isozonus*, 184
Elaps marcgravii, see *Micrurus ibiboboca*, 4, 6, 183
Elaps marcgravii ancoralis, see *Micrurus ancoralis ancoralis*, 140
Elaps marcgravii laticollaris, see *Micrurus laticollaris laticollaris*, 187
Elaps melanocephalus, see *Micrurus nigrocinctus nigrocinctus*, 202
Elaps melanogenys, see *Micrurus dissoleucus melanogenys*, 159
Elaps mentalis, see *Micrurus mipartitus decussatus*, 197
Elaps microps, see *Micrurus mipartitus mipartitus*, 196
Elaps multifasciatus, see *Micrurus multifasciatus multifasciatus*, 200
Elaps narduccii, see *Leptomicrurus narduccii*, 134
Elaps nigrocinctus, see *Micrurus nigrocinctus nigrocinctus*, 202

Elaps omissus, see *Micrurus isozonus*, 184
Elaps ornatisimus, see *Micrurus ornatissimus*, 206
Elaps princeps, see *Micrurus spixii princeps*, 217
Elaps pyrrhocryptus, see *Micrurus pyrrhocryptus pyrrhocryptus*, 212
Elaps regularis, see *Micrurus annellatus balzani*, 143
Elaps riisei, see *Micrurus circinalis*, 149
Elaps rosenbergi, see *Micrurus ancoralis ancoralis*, 141
Elaps ruatanus, see *Micrurus ruatanus*, 213
Elaps scutiventris, see *Leptomicrurus scutiventris*, 135
Elaps semipartitus, see *Micrurus mipartitus semipartitus*, 199
Elaps simonsi, see *Micrurus pyrrhocryptus pyrrhocryptus*, 212
Elaps spurrelli, see *Micrurus spurrelli*, 218
Elaps steindachneri, see *Micrurus steindachneri steindachneri*, 219
Elaps surinamensis, see *Micrurus surinamensis surinamensis*, 222
Elaps tenere, see *Micrurus fulvius tenere*, 179
Elaps tristis, see *Micrurus fulvius tenere*, 179
Elaps tschudii, see *Micrurus tschudii tschudii*, 224
Erythrokompophis, 123
Erythrokompophis mipartitus, 123
Erythrolamprus, 60, 74, 78, 80, 82, 123, 124, 173
Erythrolamprus aesculapii, 54, 58, 71, 72, 78, 79, 82, **256**
Erythrolamprus aesculapii monozona, 79
Erythrolamprus aesculapii venustissimus, 79
Erythrolamprus bizona, **255**
Erythrolamprus guentheri, 80
Erythrolamprus mimus micrurus, **251**
Erythrolamprus venustissimus, 82
Eryx, 74
Eumeces, 60
Eumeces fasciatus, 177, 180
Eumeces tetragrammus brevilineatus, 180

Falco sparverius, 71
Farancia abacura, 177
Ficimia olivaceae, 179
Ficimia publia, 156

Galbulidae, 71
Geophis, 60, 80, 154, 156
Geophis dubius, 207
Geophis dunni, 203
Geophis nasalis, 188, 206
Geophis sallei, 59
Geophis semidoliatus, 168
Gyalopion, 80
Gymnophthalmus, 60
Gymnophthalmus speciosus, 203, 206
Gymnotus, 190
Gymnotus carapo, 59, 60, 222

Helicops, 81, 222
Helmintophis, 203
Herpetotheres chanchinnans, 71
Hydrodynastes, 81, 222

Hydrophiidae, 3
Hydrophiinae, 88
Hydrops, 60, 81, 190, 222
Hydrops triangularis fasciatus, 54
Hydrops triangularis triangularis, 191
Kentropix, 60
Kentropix pelviceps, 217

Lampropeltis, 74, 78, 80, 124
Lampropeltis triangulum, xi
Lampropeltis triangulum blanchardi, 29
Lampropeltis triangulum gaigei, 81
Lanius ludovicianus, 71
Laticauda, 88
Lepidoblepharis sanctaemartae, 197
Lepidophyma flavomaculatum, 156
Leposternon, 190
Leposternon microcephalum, 173
Leposternon polystegum, 58, 184, 191
Leptomicrurus, **14**, 20, 23, 28, 30, 33, 34, 35, 36, 37, 38, 39, 42, 43, 51, 60, 74, 86, 88, 99, 123, 124, 125, 132, 232, 273
Leptomicrurus collaris, **14**, 36, 52, 87, 125, 126, 132, 133, 275
Leptomicrurus collaris breviventris, 30, 33, 39, 132, **133**, 227, 228, 232, 273
Leptomicrurus collaris collaris, 30, 33, 43, 52, 132, 133, 228, 232, **247**, **273**
Leptomicrurus narduccii, 28, 41, 42, 52, 82, 87, 125, 126, 134, 136, 273
Leptomicrurus narduccii melanotus, 16, 18, 30, 33, **38**, 39, 40, **41**, **44**, 52, 63, 73, 85, 135, 227, 228, 229, 232, **247**, 273
Leptomicrurus narduccii narduccii, 19, 30, 33, **134**, 230, 232, 273
Leptomicrurus schmidti, see *Leptomicrurus scutiventris*, 135
Leptomicrurus scutiventris, **17**, 18, 24, **25**, 28, 30, 32, 33, 52, 55, 82, 85, 125, 126, 135, 227, 228, 229, 232, 273
Leptophis ahaetulla, 199
Leptotyphlopidae, 60
Leptotyphlops, 70, 168, 186, 198
Leptotyphlops dulcis, 180
Leptotyphlops goudoti blakewelli, 148
Leptotyphlops humilis, 60, 137
Leptotyphlops humilis dugesi, 209
Leptotyphlops muñoai, 173
Leptotyphlops phenops, 60, 170
Leptotyphlops subcrotillus, 195
Liophis, 60, 80, 190, 191
Liophis breviceps, 54
Liophis chrysostomus, 217
Liophis reginae, 217
Lystrophis, 81

Mabuya, 60, 203
Madreporaria, 5
Malacoptila panamensis, 71
Masticophis flagellum, 180
Mastigodryas boddaerti, 58
Maticora, 74
Micania, 118
Micania quacho, 113, 118
Micruroides, 14, 21, 23, 28, 30, 33, 35, 37, 42, 86, 88, 123, 124, 125, 136, 138, 158, 232, 273

Scientific Name Index

Micruroides euryxanthus, 6, **15**, 23, 51, 60, 74, 87, 99, 128, 136, 273
Micruroides euryxanthus australis, 6, 30, 32, 33, 81, 137, 225, 233, **264**, 273
Micruroides euryxanthus euryxanthus, 6, 9, **24**, 28, 30, 33, **36**, **38**, **43**, 44, 54, 63, 101, 102, 103, 105, 116, 123, 137, 138, 225, 233, **247**, **273**
Micruroides euryxanthus neglectus, 30, 32, 81, 137, 138, 225, 233, **264**, 273
Micrurus, xi, 5, 21, 22, 30, 35, 36, 37, 38, 39, 42, 44, 73, 77, 79, 85, 87, 88, 105, 106, 117, 123, 124, 125, 132, 180, 195, 232, 273
Micrurus affinis mayensis, see *Micrurus diastema alienus*, 155
Micrurus affinis stantoni, see *Micrurus diastema sapperi*, 157
Micrurus albicinctus, 28, 30, 33, 51, 82, 86, 87, 126, 138, 186, 211, 228, 233, **248** 273
Micrurus alleni, 23, 30, 33, 45, 46, **47**, 51, 81, 85, 88, 102, 118, 128, 139, 226, **248**, 273
Micrurus alleni richardi, see *Micrurus alleni*, 139
Micrurus ancoralis, 21, 22, 29, 87, 125, 140, 273
Micrurus ancoralis ancoralis, 22, 29, 30, 33, 140, 141, 229, 230, 234, **264**, 273
Micrurus ancoralis jani, 7, 30, 33, 39, 86, 140, 141, 227, 234, **248**, 273
Micrurus annellatus, 24, 80, 87, 126, 128, 142, 211, 273
Micrurus annellatus annellatus, **25**, 30, 32, 39, 62, 86, 115, 142, 217, 229, 234, **264**, 273
Micrurus annellatus balzani, 14, 30, 33, 142, 143, 229, 230, 234, **248**, 273
Micrurus annellatus bolivianus, 30, 33, 142, 143, 228, 230, 234, **264**, 273
Micrurus annellatus montanus, see *Micrurus annellantus annellatus*, 142
Micrurus antioquiensis, see *Micrurus dumerilii antioquiensis*, 165
Micrurus averyi, 28, 30, 33, 34, 144, 228, 232, **249**, 273
Micrurus bernadi, 23, 27, 28, 30, 33, 39, 41, 79, 87, 126, 144, 193, 225, 234, **265**, 273
Micrurus bocourti, 22, 30, 33, 60, 81, 89, 126, 145, 229, 233, **249**, 273
Micrurus bogerti, 30, 33, 87, 128, 146, 234, **265**, 273
Micrurus browni, 23, 45, 87, 128, 146, 147, 273
Micrurus browni browni, 30, 33, 39, 45, 59, 147, 148, 225, 226, 235, **265**, 273
Micrurus browni importunus, 30, 33, 147, 226, 235, **265**, 273
Micrurus browni taylori, 18, **19**, 30, 33, 63, 65, 72, 146, 147, 148, 225, 235, **265**, 273
Micrurus buckleyi, see *Micrurus ornatissimus*, 206
Micrurus carinicauda, see *Micrurus dumerilii carinicauda*, 165, 167
Micrurus catamayensis, 30, 33, 51, 89, 126, 148, 229, 235, **249**, 273
Micrurus circinalis, 28, 30, 33, 62, 66, 69, 82, 86, 129, 149, 210, 227, 228, 233, **266**, 273
Micrurus clarki, 20, 28, 30, 33, 86, 87, 128, 149, 227, 235, **249**, 273

Micrurus corallinus, 4, 7, 23, 29, 30, 33, 37, 39, 41, 54, 60, 62, 74, 75, 79, 85, 87, 102, 103, 106, 109, 112, 114, 115, 118, 128, 150, 208, 228, 230, 235, **250**, 273
Micrurus decoratus, 21, 30, 33, 39, 85, 87, 126, 151, 228, 236, **250**, 273, 277
Micrurus diana, 30, 33, 85, 126, 152, 211, 230, 233, **266**, 273
Micrurus diastema, 15, 20, 23, 27, 46, 51, 73, 79, 90, 127, 128, 145, 152, 153, 273
Micrurus diastema affinis, 29, 30, 33, 153, 154, 157, 225, 236, 273
Micrurus diastema aglaeope, 28, 30, 33, 153, 155, 156, 157, 226, 236, **250**, 273
Micrurus diastema alienus, 18, 30, 33, 39, 51, 79, 90, 145, 153, 155, 157, 226, 236, **266**, 273
Micrurus diastema apiatus, 28, 30, 33, 45, 46, 79, 90, 153, **156**, 157, 226, 236, 273
Micrurus diastema diastema, 30, 33, 90, 153, **154**, 155, 157, 225, 236, **266**, 273
Micrurus diastema macdougalli, 30, 33, 153, 155, 157, 226, 236, **266**, 274
Micrurus diastema proximans, see *Micrurus proximans*, 209
Micrurus diastema sapperi, 30, 33, 45, 46, 79, 90, 115, 153, 154, 156, 157, 183, 226, 236, **250**, 274
Micrurus dissoleucus, 7, 14, 27, 36, 62, 64, 125, 158, 159, 274
Micrurus dissoleucus dissoleucus, 30, 33, **36**, **38**, 51, 54, 55, 59, 67, 158, 227, 236, **267**, 274
Micrurus dissoleucus dunni, 30, 32, 33, 67, 71, 86, 158, 159, 227, 236, **266**, 274
Micrurus dissoleucus melanogenys, 30, 32, 55, 81, 90, 158, 159, 160, 227, 236, **250**, 274
Micrurus dissoleucus meridensis, see *Micrurus meridensis*, 194
Micrurus dissoleucus nigrirostris, 30, 33, 81, 90, 158, 160, 227, 236, 274
Micrurus distans, 23, 28, 51, 127, 161, 162, 274
Micrurus distans distans, **23**, 30, 33, 81, 85, 161, 163, 226, 237, **251**, 274
Micrurus distans michoacanensis, 30, 33, 55, 161, 226, 237, 274
Micrurus distans oliveri, 30, 33, 161, 162, 226, 237, **267**, 274
Micrurus distans zweifeli, **18**, 30, 33, 161, 162, 163, 226, 237, **267**, 274
Micrurus donosoi, see *Micrurus paraensis*, 207, 210
Micrurus dumerilii, 22, 27, 28, 81, 90, 107, 118, 126, 128, 163, 274
Micrurus dumerilii antioquiensis, 27, 30, 33, 164, 165, 166, 227, 237, **267**, 274
Micrurus dumerilii carinicauda, 27, 30, 33, 164, 165, 167, 228, 237, 274
Micrurus dumerilii colombianus, 27, 30, 33, 55, 81, 90, 163, 165, 166, 227, 237, 274
Micrurus dumerilii dumerilii, 27, 30, 33, 39, 74, 81, 90, 102, 103, 163, **164**, 166, 227, 237, 274
Micrurus dumerilii transandinus, 7, 27, 31, 33, 34, 81, 86, 150, 164, 166, 227, 229, 237, **251**, 274

Micrurus dumerilii venezuelensis, 27, 31, 33, 34, 163, 166, 167, 228, 237, **267**, 274
Micrurus dunni, see *Micrurus dissoleucus dunni*, 159
Micrurus ecuadorianus, see *Micrurus bocourti*, 145, 148
Micrurus ecuadorianus sangilensis, see *Micrurus sangilensis*, 214
Micrurus elegans, 22, 27, 34, 87, 88, 126, 167, **168**, 274
Micrurus elegans elegans, 31, 33, 51, 79, 168, 169, 226, 237, **267**, 274
Micrurus elegans veraepacis, 28, 31, 33, 45, 168, 169, 226, 237, **251**, 274
Micrurus ephippifer, 23, 87, 127, 128, 169, 274
Micrurus ephippifer ephippifer, 27, 31, 33, 39, 51, 169, 170, 226, 237, **269**, 274
Micrurus ephippifer zapotecus, 31, 33, 54, 169, **170**, 226, 237, **252**, 274
Micrurus filiformis, 21, 31, 33, 39, 51, 52, 55, 72, 85, 115, 125, 170, 188, 227, 228, 229, 235, **252**, 274
Micrurus filiformis subtilis, see *Micrurus filiformis*, 171
Micrurus fitzingeri microgalbineus, see *Micrurus fulvius microgalbineus*, 179
Micrurus frontalis, 8, 20, 21, 26, 28, 35, 38, 41, 54, 58, 60, 61, 63, 71, 73, 74, 79, 88, 101, 102, 103, 107, 109, 111, 112, 115, 118, 126, 152, 171, 172, 175, 184, 185, 189, 211, 274
Micrurus frontalis altirostris, 31, 33, 39, 64, 66, 67, 68, 69, 85, 94, 102, 172, 173, 174, 175, 229, 238, **253**, 274
Micrurus frontalis baliocoryphus, 31, 33, 172, 173, 174, 230, 238, **269**, 274
Micrurus frontalis brasiliensis, 20, **22**, 31, 33, 51, 74, 75, 79, 81, 106, 172, 174, 229, 238, **253**, 274
Micrurus frontalis diana, see *Micrurus diana*, 152
Micrurus frontalis frontalis, 31, 33, **35**, **43**, **44**, 58, 59, 64, 75, 79, 102, 152, 172, 229, 230, 238, **252**, 274
Micrurus frontalis mesopotamicus, see *Micrurus frontalis baliocoryphus*, 174
Micrurus frontalis multicinctus, **18**, 31, 33, 102, 172, 173, 175, 229, 238, 274
Micrurus frontalis pyrrhocryptus, see *Micrurus pyrrhocryptus pyrrhocryptus*, 211
Micrurus frontifasciatus, 31, 33, 86, 125, 175, 229, 230, 238, **253**, 274
Micrurus fulvius, 6, 26, 39, 43, 61, 63, 65, 66, 67, 74, 75, 87, **99**, 100, 101, 107, 111, 117, 118, 123, 127, 128, 176, 177, 274
Micrurus fulvius barbouri, see *Micrurus fulvius fulvius*, 177
Micrurus fulvius fitzingeri, 31, 33, 52, 177, 178, 179, 180, 226, 238, **268**, 274
Micrurus fulvius fulvius, xi, 6, 9, 19, 26, 28, 29, 31, 33, 39, **41**, 42, 52, 53, 57, 61, 62, 64, 65, 68, 71, 72, 74, 75, 77, 96, 101, 102, 103, 105, 106, 107, 110, 113, 118, 176, 177, 225, 238, **254**, **268**, 274, 277
Micrurus fulvius maculatus, 31, 33, 177, 178, 179, 226, 238, **268**, 274
Micrurus fulvius microgalbineus, 31, 34, 105, 177, 179, 180, 226, 238, **268**, 274, 277

Micrurus fulvius tenere, 5, 6, 9, **21**, 22, 28, 31, 33, 34, 38, 39, 41, 45, 46, 47, 52, 59, 60, 61, 62, 64, 65, 66, 68, 69, 73, 75, 83, 85, 96, 102, 105, 110, 113, 177, 179, 225, 226, 238, **254**, **262**, 274
Micrurus gallicus, 88
Micrurus helleri, see *Micrurus lemniscatus helleri*, 15, 191
Micrurus hemprichii, 8, 15, 21, 27, 51, 52, 60, 79, 87, 125, 180, 181, 274
Micrurus hemprichii hemprichii, 31, 34, 52, 59, 60, 181, 182, 228, 229, 239, **254**, 274
Micrurus hemprichii ortoni, 6, 7, 31, 34, 52, 55, 60, 181, 182, 228, 229, 239, 274
Micrurus hemprichii rondonianus, 27, 31, 34, 86, 87, 106, 181, 182, 229, 239, **254**, 274
Micrurus hippocrepis, 31, 34, 45, 87, 88, 127, 128, 182, 226, 239, **254**, 274
Micrurus ibiboboca, 4, 21, 22, 31, 34, 39, 41, 51, 62, 87, 125, 183, 228, 229, 238, **255**, 274
Micrurus isozonus, **13**, 19, 20, 21, 31, 34, **35**, 37, **38**, 39, 41, 51, 53, 54, 55, 58, 62, 69, 73, 75, 81, 86, 87, 102, 111, 125, 184, 217, 227, 228, 229, 238, **255**, 274
Micrurus karlschmidti, see *Leptomicrurus scutiventris*, 135
Micrurus langsdorffi, 23, 26, 28, 29, 31, 34, 52, 56, 63, 80, 82, 85, 87, 127, 129, 185, 227, 229, 230, 238, **255**, 274
Micrurus langsdorffi ornatissimus, see *Micrurus ornatissimus*, 186
Micrurus laticollaris, 22, 23, 27, 34, 39, **40**, 87, 88, 114, 126, 186, 211, 274
Micrurus laticollaris laticollaris, 31, 34, 55, 187, 226, 239, 274
Mirurus laticollaris maculirostris, 31, 34, 107, 187, 226, 239, **269**, 274
Micrurus latifasciatus, 23, **24**, 31, 34, 38, 61, 79, 87, 127, 187, 226, 239, **269**, 274
Micrurus lemniscatus, 4, 8, 15, 21, 26, 28, 29, 37, 38, 51, 52, 54, 59, 60, 63, 71, 73, 79, 86, 88, 94, 102, 103, 109, 125, 184, 185, 188, 189, 274
Micrurus lemniscatus carvalhoi, 31, 34, 39, 45, 46, 47, 79, 81, 189, 190, 229, 230, 240, **256**, 274
Micrurus lemniscatus diutius, **21**, 31, 34, 62, 81, 189, 190, **191**, 228, 229, 240, 275
Micrurus lemniscatus helleri, 15, 29, 31, 32, 34, 52, 55, 67, 80, 82, 85, 86, 176, 189, 191, 191, 227, 228, 229, 230, 240, **256**, 275
Micrurus lemniscatus lemniscatus, 31, 34, 52, 54, 189, 228, 229, 240, 275
Micrurus lemniscatus multicinctus, see *Micrurus frontalis multicinctus*, 175
Micrurus limbatus, 23, 51, 74, 79, 87, 126, 275
Micrurus limbatus limbatus, 31, 34, 192, 226, 239, **269**
Micrurus limbatus spilosomus, 28, 31, 34, 192, 193, 222, 239, **256**
Micrurus margaritiferus, 31, 34, 51, 80, 82, 87, 126, 193, 211, 230, 240, **269**, 275
Micrurus medemi, 26, 31, 34, 129, 194, 210, 227, 240, **270**, 275
Micrurus meridensis, 24, **25**, 27, 31, 34, 125, 194, 228, 240, **270**, 275

Micrurus mertensi, 23, 31, 34, 51, 54, 81, 87, 89, 102, 129, 195, 229, 230, 240, **270**, 275
Micrurus mimosus, see *Micrurus langsdorffi*, 185
Micrurus mipartitus, 6, 14, 24, 28, 34, 36, 37, 41, 42, 47, 55, 62, 73, 74, 87, 99, 102, 118, 123, 127, 195, 198, 275
Micrurus mipartitus anomalus, 31, 34, 196, 197, 198, 199, 227, 228, 240, 275
Micrurus mipartitus decussatus, 6, **25**, 31, 34, 39, **41**, 52, 64, 66, 67, 68, 72, 102, 105, 109, 116, 118, 196, 197, 198, 227, 229, 230, 240, **257**, 275
Micrurus mipartitus mipartitus, 31, 34, 60, 64, 86, 107, 115, 116, 196, 227, 240, **257**, 275
Micrurus mipartitus popayanensis, 196, 198, 227, 240, 275
Micrurus mipartitus semipartitus, 18, **19**, 31, 34, **36**, **38**, 52, 53, 54, 57, 72, 75, 81, 196, 197, 199, 228, 240, **257**, 275
Micrurus multifasciatus, 6, 26, 28, 34, 38, 41, 46, 74, 79, 116, 118, 127, 197, 199, 275
Micrurus multifasciatus hertwigi, 31, 34, 45, 46, 47, 51, 67, 71, 85, 96, 102, 107, 199, 200, 226, 227, 241, **258**, 275
Micrurus multifasciatus multifasciatus, 31, 34, 39, 73, 199, 200, 227, 241, 275
Micrurus multiscutatus, 28, 34, 51, 87, 127, 199, 200, 227, 241, **258**, 275
Micrurus nebularis, 31, 34, 51, 87, 127, 201, 226, 241, **270**, 275
Micrurus nicefori, see *Micrurus spurrelli*, 218
Micrurus nigrocinctus, 16, 23, 37, 41, 47, 73, 80, 88, 90, 107, 112, 114, 115, 118, 127, 128, 201, 202, 204, 275
Micrurus nigrocinctus alleni, see *Micrurus alleni*, 139
Micrurus nigrocinctus babaspul, 9, 32, 34, 53, 90, 202, 203, 227, 242, 275
Micrurus nigrocinctus coibensis, 32, 34, 39, 90, 202, 204, 227, 242, **271**, 275
Micrurus nigrocinctus divaricatus, **16**, 23, **24**, 27, 32, 34, 39, 202, 203, 204, 206, 226, 242, **259**, 275
Micrurus nigrocinctus mosquitensis, 23, 32, 34, 45, **46**, 51, 100, 105, 107, 202, 205, 227, 242, **259**, 275
Micrurus nigrocinctus nigrocinctus, 23, **24**, 31, 34, **38**, 39, 46, 54, 62, 71, 75, 81, 85, 90, 96, **100**, 102, 105, 107, 114, 202, 205, 226, 227, 242, **259**, 275
Micrurus nigrocinctus ovandoensis, see *Micrurus nigrocinctus zunilensis*, 205
Micrurus nigrocinctus wagneri, see *Micrurus nigrocinctus zunilensis*, 205
Micrurus nigrocinctus yatesi, see *Micrurus alleni*, 139
Micrurus nigrocinctus zunilensis, 23, 26, 27, 28, 32, 34, **37**, 45, 46, 61, 75, 85, 115, 202, 203, 205, 226, 242, **271**, 275
Micrurus nuchalis, see *Micrurus latifasciatus*, 188
Micrurus nuchalis taylori, see *Micrurus browni taylori*, 148
Micrurus olssoni, see *Micrurus tschudii olssoni*, 224

Micrurus ornatissimus, 32, 34, 80, 82, 206, 229, 230, 242, **270**, 275
Micrurus pachecoi, see *Micrurus nigrocinctus nigrocinctus*, 202
Micrurus paraensis, 32, 34, 51, 52, 129, 207, 210, 229, 242, **259**, 275
Micrurus peruvianus, 23, 32, 34, 39, 86, 87, 208, 230, 241, **271**, 275
Micrurus petersi, 32, 34, 52, 80, 86, 129, **208**, 229, 241, 275
Micrurus proximans, 23, 32, 34, 85, 127, 209, 226, 241, **270**, 275
Micrurus psiches paranesis, see *Micrurus paraensis*, 207
Micrurus psyches, 6, 26, 32, 34, 63, 82, 129, 149, 194, 210, 211, 213, 228, 230, 242, **260**, 275
Micrurus psyches debruini, see *Micrurus paraensis*, 207
Micrurus psyches medemi, see *Micrurus medemi*, 194
Micrurus psyches remotus, see *Micrurus remotus*, 213
Micrurus putumayensis, 23, 32, 34, 39, 52, 55, 56, 82, 85, 87, 210, 211, 227, 229, 230, 243, 275
Micrurus pyrrhocryptus, 26, 102, 107, 109, 126, 211, 275
Micrurus pyrrhocryptus pyrrhocryptus, 32, 34, 39, 62, 85, 101, 102, 103, 212, 213, 230, 243, **271**, 275
Micrurus pyrrhocryptus tricolor, 32, 34, 212, 229, 230, 243, **271**, 275
Micrurus remotus, 32, 34, 129, 210, 213, 227, 228, 229, 242, **260**, 275
Micrurus rondonianus, see *Micrurus hemprichii rondonianus*, 182
Micrurus ruatanus, 32, 34, 45, 60, 90, 127, 213, 226, 243, **260**, 275
Micrurus sangilensis, 22, 26, 32, 34, 126, 214, 227, 243, **272**, 275
Micrurus schmidti, see *Micrurus putumayensis*, 210
Micrurus spixii, 21, 22, 29, 37, 38, **42**, 51, 52, 55, 73, 82, 87, 102, 109, 118, 123, 126, 215, 275
Micrurus spixii martiusi, 29, 32, 34, 52, 215, 216, 229, 244, **260**, 275
Micrurus spixii obscurus, 7, **22**, 26, 27, 32, 34, 39, 43, 52, 55, 62, 63, 79, 85, 96, 101, 102, 215, 216, 218, 227, 228, 229, 230, 244, **261**, 275
Micrurus spixii princeps, 29, 32, 34, 39, 215, 216, 217, 230, 244, **271**, 275
Micrurus spixii spixii, 32, 34, 215, 218, 229, 244, 275
Micrurus spurrelli, 26, 28, 32, 34, 87, 126, 218, 227, 244, **272**, 275
Micrurus steindachneri, 23, 80, 82, 86, 87, 129, 219, 275
Micrurus steindachneri orcesi, 32, 34, 219, 229, 244, **272**, 275
Micrurus steindachneri petersi, see *Micrurus petersi*, 208
Micrurus steindachneri steindachneri, 32, 34, 219, 229, 230, 244, 275
Micrurus stewarti, 27, 32, 34, 79, 87, 220, 224, 243, **272**, 275

Scientific Name Index

Micrurus stuarti, 27, 32, 34, 79, 87, 128, 221, 226, 243, 275
Micrurus surinamensis, xi, **14**, 21, 22, 34, **36**, 37, 38, 39, 41, 42, 44, 46, 51, 52, 55, 60, 73, 74, 82, 87, 101, 102, 105, 107, 109, 116, 118, 125, **221**, 222, 275
Micrurus surinamensis nattereri, 20, 32, 34, 222, 223, 227, 228, 229, 244, 275
Micrurus surinamensis surinamensis, 20, **22**, 32, 34, 39, **42**, 45, 51, 52, 67, 85, 94, 102, 222, 227, 228, 229, 230, 244, **261**, 275
Micrurus transandinus, see *Micrurus dumerilii transandinus*, 166
Micrurus tricolor, see *Micrurus pyrrhocryptus tricolor*, 212
Micrurus tschudii, 21, 22, **37**, 38, 39, **41**, 87, 125, 223, 275
Micrurus tschudii olssoni, 32, 34, 39, **40**, 52, 223, 224, 229, 230, 242, **272**, 275
Micrurus tschudii tschudii, 7, 20, 32, 34, 39, 60, 224, 230, 242, **261**, **272**, 275
Micrurus waehnerorum, see *Micrurus albicinctus*, 138
Monadophis, 123
Monadophis fulvius, 123, see *Micrurus fulvius*, 176

Naja, 3, 6, 46, 66, 88, 99
Nasua, 72, 83
Nerodia taxispilota, 190
Ninia, 60, 80, 154
Ninia atrata, 141, 194
Ninia diademata, 156
Ninia maculata, 205
Ninia sebae, 156, 158, 183, 188, 206
Ninia sebae sebae, 147
Notechis atra, 3

Opheodrys aestivus, 177, 180
Ophioides, 173
Ophiophagus, 66
Ophiophagus hannah, 3
Ophisaurus, 61, 177
Oscaecilia bassleri, 192

Oxyrhopus, 71, 78, 80
Oxyrhopus petola, 54
Oxyrhopus petola petola, 81
Oxyrhopus trigeminus, 79, **252**
Oxyuranus, 21

Paleosuchus trigonotus, 72
Pelamis platurus, 3
Peperomia nummulariefolia, 118
Peripatus, 59, 60, 61, 106
Philodryas patagonensis, 70
Phimophis, 81
Phyllodactylus, 224
Phyllorhynchus, 81
Pliocercus, 60, 74, 78, 79, 80, 81, 82, 83
Pliocercus aequalis, 79
Pliocercus aequalis aequalis, 79
Pliocercus bicolor, 79
Pliocercus elapoides, 78, 79
Pliocercus elapoides diastemus, 79
Pliocercus elapoides salvinii, 79
Pliocercus elapoides schmidti, 79
Pliocercus euryzonus, 71, 79
Pseudoboa, 3, 6, 81
Pseudoboa coronata, 6, 54
Pseudoboa neuwiedii, 6
Pseudosphinx tetrio, 82
Psophia crepitans, 71

Quassia amara, 119

Rana catesbiana, 72
Rhadinaea taeniata aemula, 54, 170
Rhinobothrium, 81
Rhinoclemmys pulcherrima, 82

Salvadora grahamiae, 180
Scaphiodontophis, 60, 80, 81
Scaphiodontophis annulatus annulatus, 80
Scaphiodontophis annulatus dugandi, 80
Scaphiodontophis annulatus venustissimus, 80
Scaphiodontophis annulatus zeteki, 80
Sceloporus undulatus, 180

Scincella, 60
Scincella laterale, 61
Scolecophis, 81
Sibon, 81
Sibon saniola, 156
Sibynomorphus mikanii, 173, 184, 190
Simophis, 74, 81
Simophis rhinostoma, 79, **253**
Siphonops annulatus, 184
Sonora, 81
Sonora episcopa, 180
Sphenomorphus cherriei lampropholis, 205
Stenorrhyna, 81
Stenorrhyna degenhardtii, 156, 169
Stenorrhyna freminvillei, 156
Storeria decayi, 61, 62
Storeria occipitomaculata, 177
Sympholis, 81
Synbranchus marmoratus, 60

Tantilla, 81
Tantilla atriceps, 180
Tantilla canula, 156
Tantilla coronata, 177
Tantilla gracilis, 177, 180
Tantilla melanocephala, 72
Tantilla ruber, 179
Tayassu, 72, 83
Thamnophis marcianus, 180
Tripanurgos, 81
Tropidoclonion lineatum, 180
Tropidodipsas sartorii, 158, 179
Typhlopidae, 60
Typhlops braminus, 147, 148
Typhlops brongersmianus, 192
Typhlops microstomus, 156
Typhlops reticulatus, 186

Urotheca, 79

Vipera psyches, see *Micrurus psyches*, 210
Virginia striatula, 61, 73
Virginia valeriae, 177, 180

Venom and Snakebite Index

Acanthophis antarcticus, 3
accessory venom gland, **99**, 100
acupressure, healing of snakebites, 119
acupuncture, healing of snakebites, 119
ají picante (*Capsicum annuum*), against snakebites, 118
amount of venom, 101
Anthurium, against snakebites in Venezuela, 119
antibodies, against coral snake venom, 114
    against viper antibodies, 114
anticoral polyvalent serum, 118
antiserum, 118
    of Instituto Butantan, 117
    of Instituto Clodomiro Picado, 118
    of Laboratorios Probiol, 118
    of Wyeth Laboratories, 117
antivenin, 117, 118
antivenin against snakebite, 95
Antivenin Institute of America, 95
anturias (*Anthurium scandens*), against snakebites, 118
Aristolochia, against snakebites in Venezuela, 119
Arizona-Sonora Desert Museum, 102
Asiatic elapids, venom gland, 99
autacoids, 107
autopharmacological effect of venom, 107

beliefs, 94
    about protection against snakebites, 4, 7, 8
    about snakebites, 4, 6, 7, 8, 9
biochemical constitution of venom, 107
biological characteristics of venom, 105–107
biological effect of venom, 105
biting mechanism, 99–100
black snake, *Notechis atra*, 3
blood, effects of venom, 107
Bothrops jararaca, snakebite accidents in Brazil, 109
Brazilian pit viper, bites, 109
Brazilian vine (*Micania quacho*), against snakebites, 113, 118
Bungarus, bent venom gland, 99
Bungarus, kraits, 3
bushmaster, venom of, 102

Cabeça de Negro, 118
caiman tooth as protection against snakebite, 4
Calliophis, bent venom gland, 99
Calliophis macclellandi, red ringed snake, 3

Calliophis sauteri, striped Asian red snake, 3
cannibalism, 96
Capsicum annuum, 118
cardiotoxic effect, 106, 107, 111
cardiotoxins, 106, 107
Center for Applied Zoology, Universidad Nacional de Córdoba, 103
Centro de Estudos de Animais Peçonhentos, Goiás, 95
Centro de Ofidismo, Manaos, 95
chemical characteristics of venom, 105–107, 277
Clostridium, venom contaminant, 101
CNTX, 93, 106
cobras, 3, 4, 99
colonies of coral snakes, 102
coral snake anitvenin, 117–118
coral snake, biting mechanism, 99–100
coral snake neurotoxin, 93, 106, 277
coral snake venom antibodies, 114
coral snake venom apparatus 99–100
coral snakebite, 111–116
    chewing motion, 100
    classification of severity, 112
    first aid, 116–117
    nature of, 110–111
    other remedies, 118–119
    professional treatment, 116–117
    statistics, 109–110
coral snakebite accidents, 107, 109–119
coral snakebite envenomation, 112, 113, 114, 115, 116
coral snakebite received by herpetologists, 115, 116
coral snakebite symptoms, 111, 112, 113, 114, 115, 116
coral snakebites, case reports, 94, 113–116
coral snakes,
    fangs, 99
    food in captivity, 103
    for research, 102
    in voodoo ceremonies, 103
    in zoos, 102, 103
coral snakes, effect of its venom to itself, 96
crotalid venoms, 107
Crotalus durissus, snakebite accidents in Brazil, 109
Crotalus scutulatus, fatal snakebite accident, 116
cuararina (*Aristolochia Klugii*), against snakebites, 118

cuartillito (*Peperomia nummulariefolia*), against snakebites, 118
curandero, 7
Cylindrophis rufus, pipe snake, 3, 77

danger of coral snakebites, 110
death adder, *Acanthophis antarcticus*, 3
death rate of coral snakebites, 109, 110
defensive bite, 74, 75
Dendroaspis, mambas, 3
dentition, 99
direct lytic factor, 107
dry venom, 101, 105

eastern coral snake, bite accident, 113
elapid venoms, 107
electric shock,
    for extracting venom, 101
    treatment of snakebites, 119
electrophoresis of venom, 105
electrophoretic venom fingerprints, 105
Especifico Pessoa, 119
evolution of coral snake venom, 93–94
extraction of venom, 96

fangs, replacement, 99
fangs of coral snakes, 37, **38**, 99
fatal coral snakebites, 94, 106, 112, 115, 116
Federsoni method of venom extraction, 100
fight between coral snakes, 96
first aid of coral snakebite, 116
First Internation Symposium of Venomous Animals, 95
freeze–dry of venom, 101

glucoproteins in venom, 105
grooved manibulary teeth, 39, **40**, 42
grooved palatine teeth, 38, 39
grooved pterygoid teeth, 38, 39
guabito amargo (*Quassia amara*), against snakebites in Panama, 119
guaco (*Micania*), against snakebites, 118

head muscles, 40–42
hemolysis, 107
hemolytic action on blood of animals, 107
hemotoxic effect, 111
history of venom research, 94–96
homeopathic healing of snakebites, 119
homeopathic medicine, 96
Hospital of San Pablo, Nicaragua, 109
Hospital San Juan de Dios, Costa Rica, 109
Hospital Vital Brazil, 109

Houston Zoo, 102
human red blood cells, effect of venom on, 107
human snakebite accidents, statistics, 109–110

infralabial venom gland, 42
initial symptoms of snakebite, 112, 113, 114, 116
Institute of Serum-therapy, São Paulo, 95
Instituto Butantan, São Paulo, 95, 101, 103, 109, 112, 117
Instituto Clodomiro Picado, Costa Rica, 95, 100, 102, 109, 112, 117, 118
International Society of Toxinology, 93

Jararaca, bite accidents, 109
Jararacas, South American pit viper, 103
keeping in zoos, 102
king cobra, 102
king cobras, venom of, 102
kraits, 3, 99

Laboratorios Probiol, Colombia, 118
LD50, 101
Leptomicrurus, bent venom gland, 99
Leptomicrurus narduccii melanotus, venom gland and muscles, **41**
lethal dose for adult human, 102
lyophilization of venom, 101, 105

main venom gland, 99, 100
mambas, 3
mandibulary teeth, 100
maxillary teeth, 99
maximum yield of venom, 102
medical treatment of coral snakebite, 117
medicine man, 7
membrane permeability, 111
metallic salt in venom, 105
methods of venom extraction, 100
Miami Serpentarium, 103, 114
Micania quacho, Brazilian vine as snakebite remedy, 113, 118
Micruroides euryxanthus, maxillary teeth, 99
Micruroides euryxanthus euryxanthus,
 characteristics of venom, 105
 in captivity, 103
 in zoo, 102
 lethal dose to humans, 102
 symptoms of envenomation, 116
 venom yield, 101, 102
Micrurus, differences in electrophoretic patterns, 106
Micrurus alleni,
 effective antivenin, 118
 LD50 for mice, 102
 lethal dose to humans, 102
 venom yield, 102
Micrurus annellatus annellatus, report of snakebite, 115
Micrurus corallinus,
 abundance in Brazil, 103
 LD50 for mice, 102
 neurotoxic venom, 106
 report of snakebite, 114, 115

Micrurus corallinus (continued)
 symptoms of snakebite, 112
 venom used for antivenin production, 118
 venom yield, 101, 102
Micrurus diastema sapperi, report of symptomless snakebite, 115
Micrurus dumerilii,
 effective antivenin, 118
 venom effect on muscles, 107
Micrurus dumerilii dumerilii,
 in captivity, 103
 lethal dose to humans, 102
 venom yield, 102
Micrurus filiformis, report of symptomless snakebite, 115
Micrurus frontalis,
 abundance in Brazil, 103
 LD50 for mice, 102
 lethal dose to humans, 102
 local pain from bite, 112
 symptoms of snakebite, 111
 venom effect on muscles, 107
 venom effect on the blood, 107
 venom used in antivenin production, 118
 venom yield, 101, 102
Micrurus frontalis altirostris,
 fatal bite, 94
 lethal dose to humans, 102
Micrurus frontalis brasiliensis, curare-like envenomation, 106
Micrurus frontalis frontalis, lethal dose to humans, 102
Micrurus frontalis multicinctus,
 lethal dose to humans, 102
 venom yield, 102
Micrurus fulvius,
 antivenin, 117
 inducing bite, 100,
 symptoms of snakebite, 111
 venom effect on the blood, 107
 venom gland, **99**
 venom yield, 101, 102
Micrurus fulvius fulvius,
 characteristics of venom, 105
 effective anitvenin, 118
 in captivity, 103
 LD50 for mice, 102
 lethal dose to humans, 102
 price of venom, 96
 report of snakebite, 113
 snakebite accidents, 110
 venom effect on muscles, 107
 venom gland and muscles, **41**
 venom yield, 101, 102
Micrurus fulvius microgalbineus,
 characteristics of venom, 105
Micrurus fulvius tenere,
 characteristics of venom, 105
 lethal dose to humans, 102
 price of venom, 96
 report of snakebite, 114
 snakebite accidents, 110
Micrurus hemprichii, feeding on *Peripatus*, 106
Micrurus hemprichii rondonianus,
 characteristics of venom, 106

Micrurus isozonus,
 killing prey, 111
 lethal dose to humans, 102
 venom yield, 102
Micrurus laticollaris, report of snakebite, 114
Micrurus laticollaris maculirostris, venom effect on the blood, 107
Micrurus lemniscatus,
 abundance in Brazil, 103
 changes in constitution of venom, 94
 LD50 for mice, 102
 lethal dose to humans, 102
 snakebite accidents
Micrurus mertensi,
 lethal dose to humans, 102
 venom yield, 102
Micrurus mipartitus,
 antivenin problems, 118
 bent venom gland, 99
 peculiar venom, 102
Micrurus mipartitus decussatus,
 characteristics of venom, 105
 effective antivenin, 118
 lethal dose to humans, 102
 milking of venom, 101
 report of snakebite, 116
 snakebite accidents, 109
 venom gland and muscles, **41**
 venom yield, 102
Micrurus mipartitus mipartitus,
 report of snakebite, 107, 115–116
 venom effect on tissues, 107
Micrurus mipartitus-multifasciatus group,
 cross immunization, 116
Micrurus multifasciatus,
 antivenin problems, 118
 peculiar venom, 102
Micrurus multifasciatus hertwigi,
 fight, 96
 LD50 for mice, 102
 lethal dose to humans, 102
 local effect of venom, 107
 venom yield, 102
Micrurus nigrocinctus,
 effective antivenin, 118
 local pain from bite, 112
 symptoms of snakebite, 112
 venom effect on the blood, 107
Micrufus nigrocinctus mosquitensis,
 characteristics of venom, 105
 infralabial venom glands, 100
 venom effect on muscles, 107
Micrurus nigrocinctus nigrocinctus,
 characteristics of venom, 105
 LD50 for mice, 102
 lethal dose to humans, 102
 report of snakebite, 114
 snakebite accidents, 109
 venom effect on muscles, 107
 venom extraction, **100**
 venom yield, 102
Micrurus nigrocinctus zunilensis, report of symptomless snakebite, 115
Micrurus pyrrhocryptus, snakebite accidents, 109
Micrurus pyrrhocryptus pyrrhocryptus,
 abundance in Argentina, 103

Venom Index

Micrurus pyrrhocryptus pyrrhocryptus (continued)
  venom yield, 101, 102
Micrurus spixii,
  effective antivenin, 118
  LD50 for mice, 102
  venom gland and muscles, **42**
  snakebite accidents, 109
Micrurus spixii obscurus,
  lethal dose to humans, 102
  self-biting, 96
  venom yield, 101, 102
Micrurus surinamensis,
  characteristics of venom, 105
  effective antivenin, 118
  LD50 for mice, 102
  peculiar venom, 102
  report of snakebite, 116
  snakebite accidents, 109
  venom effect on muscles, 107
Micrurus surinamensis surinamensis,
  lethal dose to humans, 102
  stinging with tail, 94
  venom yield, 101, 102
Micrurus tschudii, venom gland and muscles, **41**
milking venom, 101
Ministry of Health of Brazil, 112
misidentification of a king snake, 114
Mojave desert rattlesnake, venom of, 102
Mojave rattlesnake, fatal bite of, 116
mortality rate of coral snakebite, 109, 116
mucus secretion, 100
Museo Paraense de Ciencias Naturais, Belém, 95
Museum of Comparative Zoology, 95

Naja, cobras, 3, 46, 99
Naja, venom gland, 99
National Communicable Disease Center, Atlanta, 117
National Institutes of Health, Bethesda, 96, 103, 118
National Institute of Health, Bogota, 118
National Museum of Natural History, Washington, 112
natural resistance against venom, 97
neostigmine, 106
neotropical rattlesnake, bite accidents, 109
nerve growth factor, 107
neurotoxic effect, 110
neurotoxins, 93
  effect on chemical messengers, 106
  effect reversed by neostigmine, 106
New York Zoological Park, 95
North American Coral Snake Antivenin, 117

Oklahoma City Poison Control Center, 117
Old World elapids, venoms, 106
Ophiophagus hannah, king cobra, 3, 102
other remedies against snakebite, 118

palatine erector, 38
Panamerican serum, 118
paralysis of snakebite, 112, 113, 114, 115
Pelamis platurus, sea snake, 3

Peripatus, prey of coral snake, 106
pharmacological effect of venom, 106
phospholipase A2, 107
Pinellas County bounty for venomous snakes, xi
plant remedies against snakebites in Colombia, 118–119
plant remedies against snakebites in Venezuela, 119
poison, definition, 93
polypeptides in venom, 105
polyvalent antiserum, 95
preservation of venom, 101
producers of coral snake antivenin,
  Instituto Butantan, Brazil, 112
  Instituto Clodomiro Picado, Costa Rica, 112
  Laboratorios Probiol, Colombia, 118
  Wyeth Laboratories, USA, 112, 117
protein content of venom, 105
proterglyphous elapids, 87

rate of snakebites, 109, 110
replacement fangs, 99
reports of coral snakebite cases, 112, 113, 114, 115
respiratory paralysis, 106, 111

San Diego Society of Natural History, 95
secretory duct of venom gland, 99
self-biting of coral snake, 96
Serpentarium of Santiago de Estero, 103
severity of coral snakebites, 112
skin test for sensitivity to serum, 117
skull and dentition, 35–40
snakebite,
  first aid, 116
  recurrence of pain in bitten area, 113
  medical treatment, 117
snakebite accidents,
  death rate, 109
  in Argentina, 109
  in Brazil, 109
  in Colombia, 109
  in Costa Rica, 109
  in French Guiana, 109
  in United States, 110
  in Venezuela, 109
snakebite case reports, 112–116
snakebite treatment, 110, 116–117
snakebites,
  among Waorani Indians, 11
  danger, 110
  in Alabama, 110
  in Florida, 110
  in Louisiana, 110
  in Texas, 110
soro anti-elapidico, 95
soro anti-elapidico: genus *Micrurus,* 117
South American rattlesnake, 103
statistics of human snakebite accidents, 109–110
sting of bifurcated tongue, 94
suero anti-coral, 109
suero anti-elapídico polivalente anti-micrúrico, 118
suero anti-ofídico anti-coral, 118

symptoms of coral snakebite, 111–116
synergistic action of venom, 106, 110, 111

tail sting, 6, 7, 74, 94
tiger rattlesnake, venom of, 102
Toxicon, 93
toxin, definition, 93
treatment of coral snakebites, 112–113, 114, 115, 116
Universidade Católica de Goiás, 100
University of Costa Rica
University of Kansas Museum of Natural History, 115
University of Louisville School of Medicine, 103
U.S. Army Medical Research Laboratory, Fort Knox, 103

value of coral snake venom, 96
venom,
  action on heart, 106
  action on lungs, 106
  action on kidneys, 106
  action on muscles, 106
  action on nervous system, 106
  action on respiratory system, 106
  autopharmacological effect, 107
  biological characteristics, 105–107
  biological significance, 93
  biochemical constitution, 107
  change of, 94
  cardiotoxic, 94
  chemical characteristics, 105
  curare-type effect, 96, 106
  destruction of muscle tissue, 107
  definition, 93
  effect on brain, 106
  effect on human red blood cells, 107
  effect on membrane permeability, 111
  effect on onychophoran invertebrates, 106
  effect on prey, 96
  electrophoresis, 105
  evolution of, 93
  extraction, 96, **100**, 101
  hemolysis, 107
  hemotoxic, 94
  history of research, 94–96
  its use in medicine, 96
  lethal dose for humans, 102
  maximum yield, 102
  metallic salts, 105
  methods of extraction, 100–101
  neuromuscular blockade, 106
  other remedies, 118
  neurotoxic, 94
  pharmacological effect, 106
  preservation of, 101
  protein content, 105
  synergistic action, 106
  use in homeopathic medicine, 96
  use in medicine, 96
  yellow coloration, 105
venom apparatus, 99–100
venom ducts, 99
venom fingerprints of electrophoresis, 105
venom from mandibulary gland, 100

venom gland, 40, **41**, **42**, 99, 101
venom gland muscles, 40, **41**, **42**
venom gland of Asiatic elapids, 99
venom niche, 94
venom studies, 99
venom toxicity, 101–102, Table 7

venom yield, 100, 101, Table 7
venomous bite, Graeco-Roman world, 94
venomous sea snakes, 3
venoms in biology, 93
venoms of Old World elapids, 106
voodoo ceremonies, 103

Waorani Indians, snakebite incidence, 110, 114
World Health Organization, 118
Wyeth coral snake antivenin, 110, 112, 117
Wyeth Laboratories, 112, 117